Museum Management and Marketing

Museum Management and Marketing reflects upon key trends that have emerged in the application of management and marketing method and theory within the museum and highlights innovative new research and thinking. The Reader considers trends and issues in museum management and marketing from diverse critical perspectives, drawing together a selection of high-quality, intellectually robust and stimulating articles on both theoretical and practice-based learning in the field.

The Reader is divided into three main sections. The first, Museums and Change, addresses the implications of the rapidly shifting contexts within which museums now operate and considers the fundamental reorientation of museum roles and purposes that have occurred in response to rapid and turbulent change. The second section highlights developments in museum management, exploring issues including leadership, strategic planning, performance measurement and workforce development which have emerged as especially critical to contemporary management thinking and practice. The final section, Marketing the Museum, offers wide-ranging perspectives on the increasingly important role of marketing and considers its tremendous potential to shape the relationships which museums have with their audiences and other stakeholders.

Bringing together a collection of key writings concerned with the investigation, study and practice of management and marketing in the museum, this volume will be invaluable to students and museum professionals who wish to develop their knowledge of this ever-changing and challenging field.

Richard Sandell is Deputy Head of the Department of Museum Studies at the University of Leicester. His research interests focus on the evolving social purposes, roles and agency of museums. His recent publications include *Museums, Society, Inequality* (2002) and *Museum, Prejudice and the Reframing of Difference* (2006).

Robert R. Janes is the former President and CEO of the Glenbow Museum in Calgary, Canada. He is Editor-in-Chief of the *Journal of Museum Management and Curatorship* and a museum consultant. His recent books include *Museums and the Paradox of Change* (1997) and *Looking Reality in the Eye: Museums and Social Responsibility* (2005).

Leicester Readers in Museum Studies
Series editor: Professor Simon J. Knell

Museum Management and Marketing
Richard Sandell and Robert R. Janes

Museums in a Material World
Simon J. Knell

Museums and their Communities
Sheila Watson

Museum

Management

and

Marketing

Edited by

Richard Sandell and Robert R. Janes

Routledge
Taylor & Francis Group

LONDON AND NEW YORK

First published 2007
by Routledge
2 Park Square, Milton Park, Abingdon, Oxon OX14 4RN

Simultaneously published in the USA and Canada
by Routledge
711 Third Avenue, New York, NY 10017

Routledge is an imprint of the Taylor & Francis Group, an informa business

© 2007 Department of Museum Studies, University of Leicester for editorial
matter and selection; individual contributions, the contributors

Typeset in 11.5/12.5pt Perpetua by Graphicraft Limited, Hong Kong
Printed and bound in Great Britain by CPI Antony Rowe, Chippenham, Wiltshire

British Library Cataloguing in Publication Data
A catalogue record for this book is available from the British Library

Library of Congress Cataloging in Publication Data
Museum management and marketing / edited by Richard Sandell
and Robert R. Janes.
p. cm.
Simultaneously published in the USA and Canada.
Includes bibliographical references and index.
1. Museums–Management. 2. Museums–Marketing. I. Sandell, Richard,
1967– II. Janes, Robert R.
AM121.M877 2007
069.068–dc22

2006022741

ISBN10: 0–415–39628–X (hbk)
ISBN10: 0–415–39629–8 (pbk)
ISBN10: 0–203–96419–5 (ebk)

ISBN13: 978–0–415–39628–8 (hbk)
ISBN13: 978–0–415–39629–5 (pbk)
ISBN13: 978–0–415–96419–4 (ebk)

Dedication

In memory of Michael M. Ames and Stephen E. Weil – thinkers and practitioners who pointed the way.

Contents

List of Contributors

Morris Abraham is Senior Lecturer in the School of Management at the University of Technology, Sydney.

Victoria D. Alexander is the author of *Museums and Money: The Impact of Funding on Exhibitions, Scholarship and Management* (1997).

Stephen H. Baumann, former Vice-President for Education at the Liberty Science Center in New Jersey, is currently Executive Director of the Kidspace Children's Museum in Pasadena.

Christine Burton is Director of the Postgraduate Program in Arts Management in the Faculty of Business, School of Leisure, Sport and Tourism, University of Technology, Sydney and has extensive experience of cultural planning both in Australia and the UK.

Stuart W. Davies, formerly Director of Strategy and Planning at the Museums, Libraries and Archives Council in the UK, has written extensively on issues of museum management.

Zahava D. Doering is Editor of *Curator: The Museum Journal* and Senior Social Science Analyst, Office of Policy and Analysis, at the Smithsonian Institution.

The late **Peter F. Drucker** is widely regarded as one of the founding fathers of the study of management.

Robert I. Goler is a Professor in the Arts Management Program at the American University (Washington DC).

Des Griffin is former Director and currently Gerard Krefft Memorial Fellow at the Australian Museum, Sydney.

Kirsten Holmes is a Lecturer in Tourism at the University of Surrey with extensive experience of researching volunteers in museums.

Robert R. Janes is former President and CEO of the Glenbow Museum in Calgary, Canada. He is the Editor-in-Chief of the *Journal of Museum Management and Curatorship* and a museum consultant.

Carol M. Komatsuka, is Vice-President of External Affairs at the Japanese American National Museum, Los Angeles.

Emlyn H. Koster is President and CEO at the Liberty Science Center in New Jersey.

Neil Kotler, formerly a Program Specialist at the Smithsonian Institution, is co-author of *Museum Strategy and Marketing: Designing Missions, Building Audiences, Generating Revenue and Resources* (1998).

Philip Kotler is one of the world's leading authorities on marketing and co-author of *Museum Strategy and Marketing: Designing Missions, Building Audiences, Generating Revenue and Resources* (1998).

John P. Kotter is an internationally renowned writer on organizational change and leadership based at the Harvard Business School.

Andy Martin is Head of Leisure Research at MORI (Market and Opinion Research International).

Ruth Rentschler is Executive Director of the Centre for Leisure Management Research and Program Director of the Arts and Entertainment Management Program at Deakin University and has published extensively on museum marketing and related topics.

Eva M. Reussner is a researcher and writer principally concerned with issues of museum management and especially the uses of audience research.

Richard Sandell is Deputy Head of the Department of Museum Studies at the University of Leicester.

Carol Scott is Manager of Evaluation and Audience Research at the Powerhouse Museum in Sydney and past President of Museums Australia.

Alix Slater is Senior Lecturer in Heritage and Museum Management at the University of Greenwich, London.

Sherene Suchy is an experienced researcher and practitioner and is the author of *Leading with Passion: Change Management in the 21st-century Museum* (2004).

Jean-Michel Tobelem has written extensively on museums, management and marketing.

The late **Stephen E. Weil** was Emeritus Scholar at the Smithsonian Center for Education and Museum Studies and an influential thinker and writer whose writings have had a tremendous impact on international thinking and practice in museums.

Series Preface

Leicester Readers in Museum Studies provide students of museums – whether employed in the museum, engaged in a museum studies programme or studying in a cognate area – with a selection of focused readings in core areas of museum thought and practice. Each book has been compiled by a specialist in that field, but all share the Leicester Department's belief that the development and effectiveness of museums relies upon informed and creative practice. The series as a whole reflects the core Leicester curriculum which is now visible in programmes around the world and which grew, forty years ago, from a desire to train working professionals, and students prior to entry into the museum, in the technical aspects of museum practice. In some respects the curriculum taught then looks similar to that which we teach today. The following, for example, was included in the curriculum in 1968: history and development of the museum movement; the purpose of museums; types of museum and their functions; the law as it relates to museums; staff appointments and duties, sources of funding; preparation of estimates; byelaws and regulations; local, regional, etc. bodies; buildings; heating, ventilation and cleaning; lighting; security systems; control of stores and so on. Some of the language and focus here, however, indicates a very different world. A single component of the course, for example, focused on collections and dealt with collection management, conservation and exhibitions. Another component covered 'museum activities' from enquiry services to lectures, films and so on. There was also training in specialist areas, such as local history, and many practical classes which included making plaster casts and models. Many museum workers around the world will recognize these kinds of curriculum topics; they certainly resonate with my early experiences of working in museums.

While the skeleton of that curriculum in some respects remains, there has been a fundamental shift in the flesh we hang upon it. One cannot help but think that the museum world has grown remarkably sophisticated: practices are now regulated by equal opportunities, child protection, cultural property and wildlife conservation laws; collections are now exposed to material culture analysis, contemporary documentation projects, digital capture and so on; communication is now multimedia, inclusive, evaluated and theorized. The museum has over that time become intellectually fashionable, technologically advanced and developed a new social relevance. *Leicester Readers in Museum Studies* address this change. They deal with practice as it is relevant to the museum today, but they are also about expanding horizons beyond one's own experiences. They reflect a more professionalized world and one that has thought very deeply about this wonderfully interesting and significant institution. Museum studies remains a vocational subject but it is now very different. It is, however, sobering to think that the Leicester course was founded in the year Michel Foucault published *The Order of Things* – a book that greatly influenced the way we think about the museum today. The writing was on the wall even then.

Simon Knell   2007
Series Editor

Acknowledgements

The editors are indebted to a number of individuals and organizations for making this book possible. Most importantly, we sincerely thank the following people and organizations for permission to reproduce copyright material. The commitment of these authors to advancing our understanding of museums is a matter of record, and we are grateful for their thoughtful perspectives.

The following were reproduced with kind permission. While every effort has been made to trace copyright holders and obtain permission, this has not been possible in all cases. Any omissions brought to our attention will be remedied in future editions.

Kotter, J.P. (1995) 'Leading change: why transformation efforts fail', *Harvard Business Review*, March–April, 1995: 59–67. Reprinted by permission of *Harvard Business Review*. Excerpt from 'Leading change: why transformation efforts fail' by J.P. Kotter, March–April 1995. Copyright © 1995 by the Harvard Business School Publishing Corporation; all rights reserved.

Weil, S.E. (1999) 'From being *about* something to being *for* somebody: the ongoing transformation of the American Museum' in *Daedalus* 128:3 (summer), pp. 229–258. Copyright © 1999 by the American Academy of Arts and Sciences. Reproduced by permission of MIT Press Journals.

Burton, C. and Scott, C. (2003) 'Museums: challenges for the 21st century', *International Journal of Arts Management*, vol. 5, no. 2. Reproduced by permission of IJAM-HEC Montreal.

Table 4.1 'Mean weekly hours of free time?' From Bittman, 'The Land of the lost weekend? Trends in free time among the working age Australians, 1974–1992?', *Society and Leisure*, 21, vol. 2 1999 published by the European Centre for Education and Leisure Research. Reproduced with permission.

Janes, R.R. (1999) 'Embracing organizational change in museums: a work in progress' in K. Moore (ed.) *Management in Museums*, London and New Jersey, Athlone, 7–27. Reprinted by permission of the Continuum International Publishing Group.

Janes, R.R. (1997) 'Glenbow staff perspectives', in *Museums and the Paradox of Change: A Case Study in Urgent Adaptation*, University of Calgary Press. Rights reverted to the author.

Griffin, D. and Abraham, M. (2000) 'The effective management of museums: cohesive leadership and visitor-focused public programming', reprinted from *Museum Management and Curatorship*, vol. 18, no. 4, pp. 335–368. Copyright © 2000 with permission from Elsevier.

Drucker, P.F. (1977) 'The university art museum: defining purpose and mission', reprinted from *Management Cases*, Drucker, P.F., pp. 28–35. Copyright © 1977 with permission from Elsevier.

Reussner, E. (2003) 'Strategic management for visitor-oriented museums: a change of focus', in *International Journal of Cultural Policy* (http://www.tandf.co.uk/journals/titles/10799893.asp), 9(1): 95–108. Reproduced with permission from Taylor & Francis.

Koster, E.H. and Baumann, S.H. (2005) 'Liberty Science Center in the United States: a mission focused on external relevance' in R.R. Janes and G.T. Conaty (eds) *Looking Reality in the Eye: Museums and Social Responsibility*. Reproduced with permission from University of Calgary Press.

Scott, C. (2002) 'Measuring social value' in R. Sandell (ed.) *Museums, Society, Inequality*, London and New York: Routledge, 41–55. Reproduced with permission of Taylor & Francis.

Table 11.2 'Long term social value of participation in arts projects' from Matarasso, 1997, *Use or Ornament*, Comedia. Reproduced by kind permission of the publisher (http://www.comedia.org.uk).

Weil, S.E. (2003) 'Beyond big and awesome: outcome based evaluation', *Museum News*, vol. 6, no. 3, American Association of Museums. Reproduced with permission.

Sandell, R. (2000) 'The strategic significance of workforce diversity in museums', *International Journal of Heritage Studies* (http://www.tandf.co.uk/journals/titles/10799893.asp), vol. 6, no. 3, pp. 213–230. Reproduced with permission from Taylor & Francis.

Holmes, K. (2003) 'Volunteers in the heritage sector: a neglected audience?', *International Journal of Heritage Studies* (http://www.tandf.co.uk/journals/titles/10799893.asp), vol. 9, no. 4: 341–355. Reproduced with permission from Taylor & Francis and the author.

Suchy, S. 'Emotional intelligence, passion and museum leadership', reprinted from *Museum Management and Curatorship*, vol. 18, no. 1: 57–71. Copyright © 1999 with permission from Elsevier.

Davies, S. (1999) 'Visionary leadership and missionary zeal' in K. Moore (ed.) *Management in Museums*, London and New Jersey: Athlone, 108–132. Reprinted by permission of the Continuum International Publishing Group.

Goler, R.I. 'Interim directorships in museums: their impact on individuals and significance to institutions', from *Journal of Museum Management and Curatorship*, vol. 19, no. 4: 385–402. Copyright © 2004 with permission from Elsevier.

Tobelem, J.M. 'The marketing approach in museums', reprinted from *Museum Management and Curatorship*, vol. 16, no. 4: 337–354. Copyright © 1998 with permission from Elsevier.

Kotler, N. and Kotler, P. 'Can museums be all things to all people?: Mission, goals, and marketing's role', reprinted from *Museum Management and Curatorship*, vol. 18, no. 3: 271–288. Copyright © 2000 with permission from Elsevier.

Doering, Z. (1999) 'Strangers, guests, or clients? Visitor experiences in museums', *Curator*, 42(2): 74–87. Reproduced with permission of AltaMira Press.

Rentschler, R. (2004) 'Museum marketing: understanding different types of audiences', reprinted from F. Kerrigan, P. Fraser and M. Ozbilgin (eds) *Arts Marketing*, 139–158. Copyright © 2004 with permission from Elsevier.

Komatsuka, C. (2005) 'Expanding the museum audience through visitor research' in A. Kikumura-Yano, L. Ryo Hirabayashi and J.A. Hirabayashi (eds) *Common Ground: The Japanese American National Museum and the Culture of Collaboration*. Copyright © 2005 by University Press of Colorado. Reproduced with permission of University Press of Colorado in the format Other Book via Copyright Clearance Center.

Slater, A. (2004) 'Revisiting membership scheme typologies in museums and galleries', *International Journal of Nonprofit and Voluntary Sector Marketing*, vol. 9, no. 3: 238–260. Copyright © 2004. Reproduced by permission of John Wiley & Sons Ltd.

Alexander, Victoria D. (1999) 'A delicate balance: museums and the market-place', *Museum International*, vol. 51, no. 2: 29–34. Reproduced with permission of Blackwell Publishing, the author and journal.

Martin, A. (2002) 'The impact of free entry to museums', *Cultural Trends* (http://www.tandf.co.uk/journals/titles/10799893.asp), vol. 12, no. 47: 3–12. Reproduced with permission from Taylor & Francis and the author.

The editors also wish to thank Simon Knell of the Department of Museum Studies at the University of Leicester and Matthew Gibbons of Routledge, for organizing and facilitating the development of this reader. Additional thanks to Julene Knox for securing permissions for the reproduction of articles we have included and Christine Cheesman for invaluable administrative support. We are very grateful to Yupin Chung, Matthew Hick and Susannah Penn for the highly useful bibliographic research undertaken at the outset of this project. Bill Barkley, Will Philips, the late Michael Ames, Joy Davis and Jane Kelley read an earlier draft of the introductory article and their comments and insights were invaluable. Priscilla Janes provided essential editorial assistance for which we are grateful. We also thank Kersti Krug for providing the reference on self-organization at the Museum of Anthropology in Vancouver, Canada. We continue to benefit immensely from the thoughts and actions of our museum colleagues and, while too numerous to mention by name here, we wish to thank each of them for shaping our thinking and enriching our experience.

Preface

> The great challenge to our times is to harness research, invention and professional practice to deliberately embraced human values – to provide direction for the directed tragedy of technical progress. Stewardship of a heightened order will be essential. Experts . . . perform both center stage and in the wings. And all of us speak from the chorus. The fateful questions are how the specialists will interact with the citizens, and whether the performance can be imbued with wisdom, courage and vision.
>
> W.W. Lowrance, *Modern Science and Human Values*, p. 209

There is no doubt that management, as a body of knowledge and practice, is increasingly instrumental in 'imbuing the performance with wisdom, courage and vision', irrespective of whose performance it happens to be. Sound management and marketing are especially important to museums as social institutions – a perspective that lies at the heart of this book. When the first Leicester Reader on *Museum Management* was published 12 years ago, it was still common for museum management to be a target of disrespect or even scorn by museum workers, either as inappropriate, or as an activity of lesser importance than scholarship, collecting and exhibiting. Although this view may still have currency among disaffected museum workers, the overall museum world has changed with a vengeance in the intervening years. It is surprising, even for veteran practitioners, to contemplate the meteoric entrenchment of management and marketing in museum affairs. Kevin Moore (1994) anticipated this in the first Leicester Reader on *Museum Management*, and he compiled a selection of essential writings that outlined the development of museum management at that time. We note that much has happened since the publication of this seminal collection in 1994. Building on the intellectual foundation of the first Management Reader, our purpose is to introduce the current breadth and depth of museum management and marketing thinking, and we have compiled a diverse selection of some of the best of the research and writing on these subjects with this in mind.

Gone are the days when non-profit management can be called an oxymoron, as it was by a senior Canadian business executive not so long ago. The opposite is true, as evidenced by the quality and range of articles assembled here. All of them demonstrate that management and marketing are not only integral parts of professional museum practice, but have also enabled significant improvements in both the effectiveness and efficiency of museums. These notable improvements range from greater economic self-sufficiency, to a much more sophisticated understanding of the nature and requirements of the visitor experience. Marketing is essential to enhancing our understanding of existing audiences, as well as to increasing our awareness of non-visitors and what museums can do to engage them. The reader will note ample proof of the pervasive role of management and marketing in the articles that follow.

What is not so obvious, although arguably as important, are the various tensions and complexities that have accompanied the adoption and adaptation of mainstream management and marketing techniques. As is the case with all human activity, museum management and marketing are imbued with both strengths and weaknesses, and it is incumbent upon all museum workers, be they professionals or students, to be familiar with the range and meaning of these issues. Our intention in this volume is therefore to deepen the appreciation of the value of thoughtful management and marketing in museums, while at the same time advancing the importance of critical thinking when importing methods and techniques from outside the museum field.

Richard Sandell and Robert R. Janes

Chapter 1

Complexity and Creativity in Contemporary Museum Management

Robert R. Janes and Richard Sandell

The complex world of museums

MUSEUM WORKERS OFTEN JOKE about the public perception of them and their work, noting the widespread belief that museums must be an ideal place to work – peaceful refuges, often elegant, usually clean and definitely not buffeted by the rude demands of a 'real-life' workplace. The non-museum world is continually surprised, however, to learn of the complexities and demands of museum work. Much of this complexity stems from the very nature of the museum enterprise itself, and any discussion of the role of museum management and marketing must begin with an overview of some of these complexities. In short, the range of issues and pressures confronting museums in the twenty-first century is equal to that of any sector of organized life.

Consider that cultural administrators must operate complex organizations with inadequate resources and, unlike administrators in the private sector, are rarely able to accumulate budget deficits to undertake the research and development necessary to improve organizational effectiveness. At the same time, underpaid staff (often unionized) and volunteers must be motivated to perform to high professional standards. Both executives and staff alike must answer to governing bodies consisting of individuals or organizations whose experience and expertise most often lie outside of the visual and heritage arts. This is in contrast to corporate boards, which seldom include anyone other than business people. At the same time, museums and galleries must also provide meaning and enjoyment to a diverse range of publics within the context of changing societal values. Museums, in their role as custodial institutions of the world's material heritage, must also acknowledge and serve two unique communities – our ancestors and those who are not yet born. Neither of these museum constituencies vote nor consume, and thus have no visibility or involvement in the two dominant forces of contemporary society – commerce and politics.

Yet, these silent communities must be served. To add further complexity, most museums must somehow assume all these responsibilities in an era of declining or marginal public funding, while at the same time fostering individual and organizational change to ensure survival and sustainability. Simply making a profit might be seen to be a welcome relief from the potpourri of competing values and interests common to most museums. Museums, however, exist in a world of often baffling complexity and do not have the luxury of a simple profit and loss statement.

Managing these complexities within a rapidly changing world has necessitated substantial changes in mainstream museums, and many of these changes are chronicled in the articles that follow. Embracing both management and marketing responsibilities, however, can still result in polarized thinking among museum professionals, and there is often a tendency to see the adoption of business practices as a cure-all for the non-profit world or, conversely, a scourge to be ignored as fully as possible, although the latter view is far less common than it was a decade ago. It is understandable why polarized thinking emerges in the face of seemingly intractable management complexities, and it is instructive to have a closer look at a sample of these issues and their paradoxical relationships with this in mind. Nonetheless, it will be essential for museums to work through the tension between the dictates of the marketplace and traditional museum values, recognizing that this tension can stimulate creativity and new ways of thinking.

The following collection of management and marketing issues is universally applicable to museums, irrespective of size and history, although larger museums perforce have a greater share. Most, if not all, of these issues are related to an increasing interest in the visitor experience, especially over the past decade. We hesitate to call this a shift from a focus on collections to a focus on visitors, as collections remain a preoccupation for most, if not all, museums. The growing concern with the visitor experience is more accurately seen as an add-on to existing museum responsibilities. This gradual change in perspective has been accompanied by a decline in public funding for museums, notably in North America and Western Europe, coupled with the increasing use of business solutions to address the challenges that beset museums. For example, there has been a decline in museum attendance and the visitor base (Burton and Scott 2003; Martin 2002) that has prompted many museums to increase revenues through high-profile, blockbuster exhibitions and architectural sensationalism. The underlying theme in these initiatives is the conventional wisdom, 'build it and they will come'. Although the long-term success of this approach to business planning remains to be seen, it is generally recognized that these activities are so consumptive of staff time and resources that little of either are left over for other activities. At the same time, despite individual successes in audience development, there has been little change in the traditional visitor profile – those with post-secondary education and relatively high incomes are still the majority of museum goers (Cheney 2002).

These trends, in turn, have resulted in a preoccupation with revenues and attendance as the predominant measures of worth. Not surprisingly, many of the governing authorities responsible for these museums are also beginning to resemble corporate entities, with board members being chosen for their business experience and their fundraising skills. This tendency for business people to select other business people as governing colleagues is a sort of tribalism, and is characteristic of business in general. This tribalism is also embodied in the near absence of any non-profit executives on corporate boards of directors, and this limited perspective has noteworthy implications for both museum governance and operations.

The increasing presence of the business model is also visible in contemporary searches for museum directors, or CEOs, as they are now called in deference to the corporate model. While an advanced degree in a related area or a professional designation may be required, the emphasis in these senior appointments is now clearly on fundraising, financial management, marketing and public relations. Museum critics observe that the pendulum has swung too far, and museums are at risk of eroding their core missions under the leadership of well-intentioned business people whose knowledge and experience are limited to the dictates of the marketplace. This may also partly explain the increasing ennui among various museum executives, weary of the perpetual round of cocktail parties and events required to keep many museums solvent these days. This is not meant to demean the importance of these activities, but rather to highlight the importance of maintaining an intelligent balance between the core mission and economic realities. There is relevant experience to be gleaned from the performing arts in this instance, as dance and theatre companies often have two positions – one for the managing director (read 'business manager') and one for the creative director (read 'scholar' or 'scientist'). A clear protocol is essential in this instance to ensure both adherence to a common vision and effective communication. Museums would be wise to pay attention to the lessons of other sectors, if they are to manage these emerging complexities creatively.

Fortunately, the need for management and leadership training is clearly recognized by the museum sector, and there are a variety of well-established approaches for equipping museum professionals with the knowledge, skills and experience to become leaders and managers. These include the Getty Leadership Institute (USA) and the Clore Leadership Programme (UK), as well as the inclusion of management and marketing training in museum studies programmes around the world. It is important to note that leadership and management potential is not the exclusive domain of those with scholarly, scientific and curatorial credentials. Other museum professionals, whether educators or marketers, also understand the museum context and can make effective leaders and managers. It is clear that contemporary management and marketing issues are broad and deep, difficult to avoid and inextricably interconnected. It is this last characteristic, namely interconnectedness, that may have caught the museum community off guard in its rush to embrace business solutions. It is not necessarily obvious that declining public revenues might ultimately create boards of directors lacking in cultural diversity and community connectedness, and museums are not alone in their confusion. This newfound complexity is reminiscent of the revelations that have emerged in the progression from Newtonian physics to quantum theory. Where scientists once saw the world as a great clock, with independent parts and well-defined edges, they now see a level of connectedness among seemingly discrete parts that are widely separated in time and space (Wheatley 1994: 39). A worldview marked by boundaries and reductionism no longer serves physics or museum management.

Museums are also of this world, and cannot expect to ignore or retreat from this mounting complexity. The challenge is to identify the knowledge and techniques that will best serve the well-being of museums in a manner which befits their particular role, while respecting the attendant ambiguity. It is important to note in this regard that museums are privileged work environments because they, like all non-profits, are organizations whose purpose is their meaning (Handy 1994: 183). This privilege is accompanied by the responsibility to take advantage of one of the most free and creative work environments on the planet through the application of thoughtful management and marketing. For example, an important challenge for museum marketers is to build civic brands around ideas that are less tangible than customer service and efficiency (Demos 2005: 4). Such ideas could include community, shared ownership and collective identity, and could be based on the use of marketing techniques to build brands that produce emotional identification and take credit for the public value that museums create. This is a creative alternative to using the language of the private sector, with its emphasis on individual consumption.

Managing complexity

Surprisingly, and despite the growing body of management and marketing knowledge, a cloud seems to have settled and remained over leadership and management (Greenleaf 1996: 111). A partial answer lies in the observation that management is much more than a bundle of techniques, although many business schools still teach management with this approach. In the words of the late Peter Drucker (1995: 250), 'The essence of management is to make knowledge productive. Management, in other words, is a social function. And in its practice, management is a truly liberal art.' The notion of management as a liberal art is an instructive one, and obligates us to now consider several ideas that encompass this broader view of management, including the need for intelligent change that the twenty-first century demands. The reader will note that some of these ideas are also explored later in this volume, but their potential value in expanding the capacity of museum management justifies some judicious repetition in this introduction.

Self-organization

There is a burgeoning literature, and an enormous management consulting business, devoted to improving organizational efficiency and effectiveness in all sectors of society. A cursory search of the Internet using 'business consulting' revealed 82 pages of text. Whether it is books sold in airport bookshops, or the ever-increasing number of business schools with MBA programmes, the task of helping both profit and non-profit organizations to manage better is a growth industry of extraordinary proportions. The demand is there, at least in the private sector, if a recent survey of UK business consulting fees is any indication. The average salary for a partner or director in a business consulting firm is 109,000 pounds sterling, accompanied by an average bonus of 76,000 pounds sterling, or a total of 375,550 in Canadian dollars (Woodhurst 2005). Yet, despite all the efforts of organizations and their management consultants to understand employees and to manage them more effectively, many employees remain stressed, poorly managed and generally dissatisfied. According to the World Health Organization (Galt 2000: B15; Leka,

Griffiths and Cox 2003), stress, anxiety and depression will become the leading causes of disability in the workplace over the next 20 years.

One way of promoting the growth, development and self-respect of museum workers is to abandon or minimize hierarchical structures – the preferred organizational model for the vast majority of museums. Various museums are learning, however, that creativity can be stimulated by organizing differently (Farson 1996: 102–105), while many small museums have known this all along. A promising development in this regard is the idea of self-organization, a group phenomenon that occurs spontaneously when members of a group produce coherent behaviour in the absence of formal hierarchy within the group, or authority imposed from outside it (Stacey 1992: 6). Decisions are made at the most local level in the organization where they can be made well, and this requires that managers respect and nurture the so-called informal leaders – those individuals who exercise influence and authority by virtue of their competence and commitment, and not because of any formal position in the hierarchy. Informal leaders exist at all levels in all museums and are essential ingredients in effective self-organization by fostering interaction and interdependence. The key point is for management to focus on results, rather than insist upon any particular process or means for achieving the results. David Bohm (quoted in Jaworski 1998: 109), the physicist, writes that human beings have an innate capacity for collective intelligence, based on dialogue. Dialogue does not require that people agree with one another, but rather allows people to participate in a pool of shared meaning that can lead to aligned action. Simply put, hierarchical structures get in the way as staff attempt to navigate across and between organizational boundaries, be they departments, divisions or the manager's office. Responsible autonomy (Fairtlough 2005) is another alternative to hierarchy, and means a group deciding what to do, and being accountable for the outcome. Accountability is what makes responsible autonomy different from hierarchy. Zen Master, Suzuki Roshi, succinctly summarized this new thinking when he said, 'to control your cow, give it a bigger pasture' (quoted in Locke 2000: 28). An instructive example of self-organization is the Museum of Anthropology in Vancouver, Canada (Krug, Fenger and Ames 1999: 254). The boundaries of their position descriptions are flexible, and the museum's informal organizational structure consists of democratic, non-hierarchical committees where the chairs rotate.

Of particular importance to museums is the increasing use of multidisciplinary, multifunctional and cross-departmental teams that may include educators, marketers and security staff, as well as curatorial and exhibition staff. In some instances, these teams also include individuals from outside the museum, who are given both the authority and responsibility for decision making, in partnership with museum staff (Conaty and Carter 2005). Multifunctional teams are essential in cross-fertilizing the rich storehouse of knowledge, skills and experience inherent in museums, not only to develop programmes and exhibitions, but also to enhance the general level of creativity, innovation and problem solving.

Reflexive management

Management is about coping with complexity (Kotter 1990: 103), and a necessary ingredient in effective management is giving up certain unfounded beliefs, such as the belief in managerial control. This is essential because the future is not know-able, as the links between cause and effect in organizations are complex, distant in time and space and very difficult to detect (Stacey 1992: 11). The technical term for this is non-linear feedback, and it means that the links between cause and effect are lost in the detail of what actually happens in between. Because no one can fore-see the future of an organization, managers and staff should not all believe in the same things (Stacey 1992: 4), thereby avoiding the business tribalism mentioned earlier. Museum workers should question everything and generate new perspectives through discussion and dialogue. This approach is much more conducive to cre-ation, invention and discovery, and all these are not only essential in addressing complexity, but they are also prerequisites for innovation and creativity. Typically, most museums continue to build on their strengths, becoming better and better at what they are already doing well. As counterintuitive as it may seem, there are more thoughtful approaches to management.

As the museum world becomes more complex, both managers and staff alike would benefit from greater tolerance of ambiguity, instability and unpredictability, although this is much easier to write about than to do. We are now dealing with what is called open-ended change (Stacey 1992: 150–153), meaning that we do not know with certainty what is causing the changes we are experiencing in our organizations, or what the consequences will be. Old ways of doing things do not necessarily work, and there is abundant confusion and anxiety. Open-ended change is rampant in both our work and personal lives, and it is best addressed by iden-tifying what the problems are, what the opportunities are and then deciding what questions to ask. New mental models have to be developed and shared before the challenges of open-ended change can be addressed (Stacey 1992: 156).

For example, there is a technique used in business to assist with the creation of new mental models, known as scenario thinking or planning (De Geus 1997: 38–54; Schwartz 1996). Scenario planning is about thinking out loud and speculat-ing, not making arguments requiring high burdens of proof (Scearce and Fulton 2004: 23). It is a simple, dynamic and flexible process that results in powerful stories about how the future might unfold in ways relevant to a museum or a par-ticular issue. An even more important result is a greater sense of the context in which an organization operates today, and the contexts in which it may operate in the future. Bearing in mind the growing complexity described in this introduction, museums ignore these reflexive management tools at their own peril.

The second curve

It is common for museum managers to use a variety of change programmes and pro-cesses to cope with this ever-increasing complexity. Many of these programmes are ephemeral, often abandoned and quickly replaced by new and different approaches. Some tough lessons have been learned as a result of the quick fix approach to man-agement; the most important being that change in museums, as in all organizations, must evolve in a way that sustains commitment and individual capacity. This takes time, as change is a long march and needs ongoing leadership (Kanter 2000: 36). Museums may need continuous care, not interventionist cures, and it has been suggested that nursing should be the model for all management (Mintzberg 1996: 66–67). This model implies the importance of steady and consistent caring and nurturing. More ominously, it has been noted (Galt 2000: B15) that it is only a matter of time before employers are held liable for the psychological harm caused to employees by poor management practices.

Whether it is interventionist change or gradual change, the real challenge of intelligent management lies in what is sometimes called second curve thinking. This is in reference to the S-shaped or sigmoid curve, which actually sums up the story of life itself (Handy 1994: 49–63). In effect, people, organizations and civilizations start slowly, grow, prosper and decline. Decline, however, is not inevitable if you adopt second curve thinking. This requires museum staff and leaders to challenge all the assumptions underlying current success, and this must begin with questions. Second curve thinking is admittedly a profound paradox, as it requires change, or scenario planning at least, at a time when all the messages coming through are that everything is fine. This is not as unrealistic as it may sound, if museums are willing to consult people outside of the museum community, as well as hire them, as they will bring in new ideas and fresh perspectives. It is also important to pay particular attention to front line staff, including marketers, as they are in direct contact with visitors and users, and are usually the first to know when something is lacking or not working. In the final analysis, each museum is unique and must find its way in this process. The fundamental requirement of second curve thinking is to be sceptical, curious and inventive before you have to be. If you don't do this before you are forced to, chances are you are already in decline. It requires profound courage to move to the second curve. For many museums, steeped in tradition and relatively privileged as a result of their widely recognized social status within society, second curve thinking may exceed their grasp.

Leadership

Until now, no distinction has been made between management and leadership in this introduction. Although often considered to be one and the same, they are best described as two sides of the same coin. The challenge is to combine them, and use each to balance the other (Kotter 1990: 103). It was noted earlier that management is about coping with complexity. Leadership, on the other hand, is about coping with change (Kotter 1990: 104–107). This can mean a variety of things, but fundamentally it requires keeping people moving ahead, most often in directions they have never taken or are reluctant to consider. This is done, in part, by appealing to people's needs and emotions, including the need for achievement, providing a sense of control over one's life, and fostering the ability to live up to one's ideals. These are powerful considerations, and the study of leadership, like management consulting, is now a huge industry with an enormous literature, as well as an abundance of conferences and experts. This lucrative bandwagon does not diminish the fact that the thinking about leadership has become more intelligent and relevant.

For the longest time, charisma and style were seen to be all-important leadership characteristics. Fortunately, we are now beginning to see how important it is

for leaders to motivate and inspire. This requires that leaders be clear about purpose and direction, be inclusive, model the appropriate behaviours and recognize
and reward success, in addition to the other requirements noted above. Not so
obvious is the need to balance organizational and individual needs, sustain the energy
required to do all of the above and, perhaps most importantly, determine how
deeply to listen to the negative people whose voices are often the loudest. Along
with these requirements is the necessity to acknowledge and support the so-called
informal leaders mentioned earlier – those individuals who have no formal leadership designation, but whose competence and influence are widely recognized and
respected.

Leaders must also not forget the 'Principle of Systematic Neglect' (Greenleaf
1996: 302). For responsible people, there are always more things to be done, or
that ought to be done, and this is especially acute in the world of museums. The
'Principle of Systematic Neglect' requires that effective leaders decide on the important things that need doing, in order of priority, and neglect all the rest. Leaders
are also increasingly required to be psychologically hardy (Kabat-Zinn 1990: 203),
and those who have this hardiness have several things in common. They believe
that they can make things happen; they are fully engaged in giving their best effort
everyday; and, last, they see change as a natural part of life. They see new situations more as opportunities, and less as threats. It is also important for museum
leaders to cultivate awareness, although, surprisingly, such awareness does not
necessarily provide solace. On the contrary, it may disturb and awaken. As one
management writer (Greenleaf 1996: 323) observed, 'the able leaders I know are
all awake and reasonably disturbed'.

What are we learning?

Irrespective of the burgeoning complexities that buffet museums like a strong wind,
it is clear that museum academics, practitioners and educators are paying attention
to these current realities in a variety of ways, as evidenced by the articles in this
volume. It is not sufficient, however, to simply acknowledge management and
leadership complexities without an effort to consider their origin and implications. There are two key protagonists in this rising complexity, the first being the
rapid intervention of marketplace thinking in museum management. Standing
opposite this economic view of the world is the other protagonist – a museum's
capacity for self-reference, meaning the ability to be guided by a clear sense of purpose and values. This concept will be described in more detail shortly. Tempting
as it is simply to create a polemic and dismiss the economic view of the world
as outdated, the situation confronting contemporary museum management is
far denser. It is not an exaggeration to note that creatively managing the tension
between market forces and museum missions may turn out to be the most vital
issue confronting museums in the twenty-first century. At stake might well be the
identity of museums as unique social institutions or, conversely, their destiny as
impresarios in the business of architectural sensationalism and culture as entertainment. This complexity has multiple origins, several threads of which will now
be examined.

The first of these threads is the recognition that museums are complex port-folios. Museums have numerous assets that can be conceived and operated strictly as businesses, including food services, gift shops or facility rentals. Other assets have nothing to do with the marketplace, such as the preservation and care of collec-tions. It is essential for boards and managers to have a clear sense of which is which, and not to confuse the two. Using visitor statistics, for example, to assess the suc-cess of a museum, library or archive is misguided as it ignores the impact of a user who writes a book that is read by thousands of people. It is also not useful to bemoan the abandonment of traditional museum practices in the face of very real economic and social imperatives. To do this is as naïve as insisting that museums must become profit-driven enterprises if they are to survive in the contemporary world. In short, neither the business nor the non-profit sector holds the exclusive keys to a secure future. The world of museums is far too grounded in the uncertainties of everyday life.

Part of this growing confusion, among managers and governing authorities alike, is based on the belief that continuous economic growth is essential to our well-being, and that the consumption of everything is an appropriate means to achieve unlimited growth. There is every reason to believe, however, that limitless economic growth is creating genuine and profound dilemmas, including destruction of the natural environment and serious disillusionment with buying things as a means of personal fulfilment. Much of this looming crisis, along with the attendant pressures on museums, is a result of a widespread misconception in Western society that mar-kets create communities. The opposite is true, as the marketplace and its activities actually deplete trust (Rifkin 1997). It is the organizations of the non-profit sec-tor, not government or business, which build and enrich the trusting, caring and genuine relationships – namely, the social capital – upon which the marketplace is based. These organizations range from political parties, to Girl Scouts, to muse-ums, and there would be no marketplace without this web of human relationships. Social capital is born of long-term associations that are not explicitly self-interested or coerced, and it typically diminishes if it is not regularly renewed or replaced (Bullock and Trombley 1999: 798).

The challenge for museum management is to help governing authorities, staff and society to better understand these complexities and their implications, not the least of which is that the reigning economic growth model is an ideology that has profound implications for museums. This ideology is an integrated set of asser-tions, theories and aims that constitute a socio-political programme. Its primary measure of worth is money, which is at best a crude measure of success when applied to museums. The application of strict economic criteria to museum management is obviously misleading when, for instance, one considers that good collection management is based on a 300- to 500-year business plan, not the quarterly results common to business. In contrast, the average life expectancy of a company is 12.5 years, while the average lifespan of a multinational corporation (Fortune 500 or its equivalent) is between 40 and 50 years (De Geus 1997, 2005). The message is vital – museum managers must be aware and thoughtful as they seek manage-ment solutions to a host of paradoxes and unanswered questions. Bigger is not necessarily better, and millions of dollars or pounds do not guarantee either mar-ket sensitivity or organizational competence. Reputation, name recognition and the trust of visitors are not the property of bigness. These traits are about quality, and worthiness can be achieved by museums of any size. In fact, smallness is often a virtue when you consider the inherent inflexibility of most large museums. Small museums can 'think big' through alliances, cost sharing and creative collaboration, without all the inherent disadvantages of bigness (Ohmae 1998: 20).

A new direction

The other protagonist in the evolving story of management complexity, as mentioned earlier, is the concept of self-reference. This is a fundamental concept that aids in sensible change in a turbulent environment. For all organizations, museums included, self-reference means 'a clear sense of identity – of the values, traditions, aspirations, competencies, and culture that guide the operation' (Wheatley 1994: 94). It can also mean letting go of past practices, and deciding what not to do any longer. Self-reference can be a source of independence from the external environment. As societal forces demand new responses from museums, a strong sense of self-reference provides the foundation for change. This is particularly important in avoiding new ventures and unmindful solutions that underlie the limited lifespans of businesses and corporations noted above. This does not mean, however, that self-reference is a justification to remain beholden to tradition. On the contrary, intelligent self-reference can be a source of strength and stability in a turbulent environment, and allows a reconsideration of the role of museums in contemporary society. Such rethinking is now well underway, and one expression of this is an increasing interest in the social responsibilities of museums (Brown and Peers 2003; Janes and Conaty 2005; Sandell 2002). We will conclude this introduction with a discussion of the meaning and implications of socially responsible museum work.

The idea of a socially responsible museum is grounded in a new sense of accountability, as well as in new approaches to achieving long-term sustainability. This work places a greater emphasis on values, both moral and societal, while also respecting the marketplace. Defining what socially responsible museum work means for museums is neither simple nor formulaic as there are a multitude of possibilities and approaches. It is also important to realize that there are no fixed procedures or rules for engaging in socially responsible museum work, and all museums have the opportunity to explore and discover what is appropriate and useful for them. The underlying premise, however, is the time-honoured assumption that museums exist for the public good. Put another way, social responsibility might be considered the 'will and capacity to solve public problems' (http://www.pew-partnership.org/resources.html). Broadly speaking, being socially responsible can also mean facilitating civic engagement, acting as an agent of social change or moderating sensitive social issues (Smithsonian Institution 2002: 9).

A recent collection of case studies describing socially responsible museums (Janes and Conaty 2005: 8–10; Block 2002: 47–65) revealed that they had at least four values in common, including idealism, intimacy, depth and interconnectedness. Idealism means thinking about the way things could be, and then taking action, rather than simply accepting the way things are. The second value is intimacy, which is about communication and the quality of the contact that is made. Quality communication lies in direct experience and there is no substitute for human relationships, and all the time, energy and attention these relationships require. Depth is about being thorough, complete and building relationships with particular groups of people, as well as about thinking, questioning and reflecting. Finally, there is interconnectedness, reflected in the growing societal awareness of the deep connections between our own well-being and that of our families, organizations, the environment and the whole of humanity. All these values are essential for museums that wish to understand what is important to their communities.

From a practical management perspective, museums also need to ensure that there is a sense of shared purpose, and that a commitment to socially responsible work is enshrined in the museum's mission. In addition, there is an ongoing need for active experimentation and risk taking. Most innovation occurs from hundreds of small changes and ideas which add up to enormous differences. Socially responsible work is also a shared responsibility, and museums must be prepared to reach out to their communities to acquire the expertise and experience they themselves lack. Last, is the vital importance of openness, as boards, staff and volunteers must feel free to discuss their values and beliefs. This makes for a more authentic museum, and is the foundation for socially responsible work.

None of these things will guarantee success in this era of unanswered questions, if one accepts, as the late Peter Drucker noted, that management is a liberal art. Knowledge, flexibility, passion are also essential ingredients in balancing the paradoxes of contemporary museum management. For museums to achieve balance, governing authorities and staff must get much better at defining strategic futures for their museums, while also ensuring that their boards are representative of community diversity and aspirations. One size does not fit all, and the marketplace is but one interpretation of reality. There is also no such thing as a single management approach, or a perfect organizational or leadership model. The key component of management is creativity, including imagination, intelligence, judgement and common sense (Lapierre 2005: 8–9). Gone are the days when one year of experience, repeated 20 times, is acceptable for museum managers and leaders. They must learn continuously, a notable challenge for those who are unwilling or unable to read the museum literature, not to mention the abundant knowledge outside of the museum field. Curators can no longer be content to claim authority on the basis of knowledge that is often exclusively theirs. Knowledge stemming from collections and their stories is a precious resource, and it must be shared in any number of ways. A curator is not only a keeper, but also a messenger of a museum's collective wisdom. Why can a curator not make explicit the successes and failures of our species in a manner that could inform and guide contemporary behaviour, whatever the particular society happens to be? Even as museums seek to include and honour varied perspectives, marketers must come to understand that the customer is not always right, and that all museums have a leadership role in defining the value they add to communities. Together, marketers and curators could begin by simply asking if there are any deficiencies in their community that their museum could help to address. In summary, all these questions reach far beyond education and entertainment as the primary mission.

It is helpful to consider socially responsible museum work as a purpose-filled experiment, whose intention is just as much about learning as it is about achieving (Block 2002: 3). In doing so, the choice of a worthy destination is more important than simply settling for what we know will work. This, in turn, requires a willingness to address issues that have no easy answers, and these are legion, encompassing the need for greater intercultural understanding, our persistent failure to steward the natural environment, the growing plight of the disadvantaged, and the contested ground of consumerism versus the responsibilities of citizenship. As the articles in this volume aptly demonstrate, the challenges of museum management and marketing are many, and much is being done to address these complexities creatively and forthrightly, and in a manner that effects positive change.

The economic necessity of seeing people and communities as museum audiences needs no further explanation, but it is hoped that the exploration of museums as meaningful social institutions will continue to grow to inspire the next generation of museum workers. Understanding does not necessarily mean resolution, however, as it is those problems that we will never resolve that claim the lion's share of our energies (Conroy 1988: 70). What is essential is the need to keep reflection and dialogue alive, and to avoid stagnation, complacency and the tyranny of outmoded tradition. Management and marketing are means to an end, not ends in themselves. They are essential tools with which to address the endless stream of uncertainties, paradoxes and questions that beset any thoughtful museum. The essential task of all sound leadership and management is to ensure both individual and organizational consciousness. Management and marketing, as is true of most of human thought, will continue the ceaseless cycle of new theories, fads and trends. Despite all this activity, there are no silver bullets or panaceas, as this book demonstrates. It is only through heightened self-awareness, both organizational and individual, that museums will be able to fulfil the lofty triad of preservation, truth and access (Weil 2004: 75).

References

Block, P. (2002) *The Answer to How is Yes*, San Francisco: Berrett-Koehler.
Brown, A.K. and Peers, L. (eds) (2003) *Museums and Source Communities: A Routledge Reader*, Oxford: Routledge.
Bullock, A. and Trombley, S. (eds) (1999) *The New Fontana Dictionary of Modern Thought*, London: HarperCollins.
Burton, C. and Scott, C. (2003) 'Museums: challenges for the 21st century', *International Journal of Arts Management*, 5: 56–68.
Cheney, T. (2002) 'The presence of museums in the lives of Canadians, 1971–1998: what might have been and what has been', *Cultural Trends*, 48: 39–72.
Conaty, G.T. and Carter, B. (2005) 'Our story in our words: diversity and equality in the Glenbow Museum', in R.R. Janes and G.T. Conaty (eds) *Looking Reality in the Eye: museums and social responsibility*, 43–58, Calgary, Canada: The University of Calgary Press and the Museums Association of Saskatchewan.
Conroy, F. (1988) 'Think about it – ways we know and don't', *Harper's*, vol. 277, no. 1,662: 70.

De Geus, A. (1997) *The Living Company: habits for survival in a turbulent business environment*, Boston: Harvard Business School Press.

De Geus, A. (2005) *Corporate Longevity*, Leigh Bureau-W. Colston Leigh, Inc. Online. Available http://www.leighbureau.com/keyword.asp?id=2055 (accessed 21 February 2006).

Demos (2005) *Civic Brands: Public Value and Public Services Marketing*. Online. Available http://www.demos.co.uk (accessed 23 February 2006).

Drucker, P. (1995) *Managing in a Time of Great Change*, New York: Truman Talley Books/Plume.

Fairtlough, G. (2005) *The Three Ways of Getting Things Done: hierarchy, heterarchy and responsible autonomy in organisations*, Triarchy Press. Online. Available http://www.triarchypress.co.uk/pages/the_book.htm (accessed 22 February 2006).

Farson, R. (1996) *Management of the Absurd*, New York: Simon and Schuster.

Galt, V. (2000) 'Toxic stress posing major risks: study', *The Globe and Mail*, 25 October: B15.

Greenleaf, R.K. (1996) *On Becoming a Servant-Leader*, D.M. Frick and L.C. Spears (eds), San Francisco: Jossey-Bass Publishers.

Handy, C. (1994) *The Age of Paradox*, Boston: Harvard Business School Press.

Janes, R.R. and Conaty, G.T. (eds) (2005) *Looking Reality in the Eye: museums and social responsibility*, Calgary, Canada: Museums Association of Saskatchewan and the University of Calgary Press.

Jaworski, J. (1998) *Synchronicity*, San Francisco: Berrett-Koehler.

Kabat-Zinn, J. (1990) *Full Catastrophe Living*, New York: Bantam, Doubleday, Dell Publishing Group, Inc.

Kanter, R.M. (2000) 'Leaders with passion, conviction and confidence can use several techniques to take charge of change, rather than react to it', *Ivey Business Journal*, May/June: 32–36.

Kotter, J.P. (1990) 'What leaders really do', *Harvard Business Review*, 68(3): 103–111.

Krug, K., Fenger, A.M. and Ames, M.M. (1999) 'The faces of MOA: a museum out of the ordinary', *Archiv fur Volkerkunde*, 50: 249–263.

Lapierre, L. (2005) 'Managing as creating', *International Journal of Arts Management*, 7: 4–10.

Leka, S., Griffiths, A. and Cox, T. (2003) 'Work organisation and stress: systematic problem approaches for employers, managers and trade union representatives', *Protecting Workers' Health Series No. 3*, World Health Organization: Geneva. Online. Available www.who.int/occupational_health/publications/en/oehstress.pdf (accessed 22 February 2006).

Locke, C. (2000) 'Internet apocalypso', in *The Clue Train Manifesto: The End of Business as Usual*, Chapter one. Online. Available http//www.cluetrain.com/apocalypse, html (accessed 20 January 2002).

Lowrance, W.W. (1986) *Modern Science and Human Values*, London: Oxford University Press.

Martin, A. (2002) 'The impact of free entry to museums', *Cultural Trends*, 47: 3–12.

Mintzberg, H. (1996) 'Musings on management', *Harvard Business Review*, 74: 61–67.

Moore, K. (ed.) (1994) *Museum Management*, London: Routledge.

Ohmae, K. (1998) 'Strategy in a world without borders', *Leader to Leader*, 7: 17–23.

Rifkin, J. (1997) 'The end of work', address on behalf of the Volunteer Centre of Calgary, Palliser Hotel, Calgary, Canada, 13 November.

Sandell, R. (ed.) (2002) *Museums, Society, Inequality*, Oxford: Routledge.

Scearce, D. and Fulton, K. (2004) 'What If?: the art of scenario thinking for non-profits'. Global Business Network. Online. Available http://www.gbn.com/ (accessed 2 January 2006).

Schwartz, P. (1996) *The Art of the Long View: paths to strategic insight for yourself and your company*, New York: Doubleday.

Smithsonian Institution (2002) *21st Century Roles of National Museums: a conversation in progress*, Washington, D.C.: Office of Policy and Analysis.

Stacey, R.D. (1992) *Managing the Unknowable*, San Francisco: Jossey-Bass Publishers.

Weil, S.E. (2004) 'Rethinking the museum: an emerging new paradigm', in Gail Anderson (ed.) *Reinventing the Museum*, 74–79, Walnut Creek, California: AltaMira Press.

Wheatley, M.J. (1994) *Leadership and the New Science*, San Francisco: Berrett-Koehler.

Woodhurst (2005) 'The Woodhurst 2005 Salary Survey'. Online. Available http:// www.woodhurst.com/ (accessed 2 January 2006).

PART ONE

Museums and Change

Introduction to Part One

Richard Sandell and Robert R. Janes

> Management and change are synonymous; it is impossible to under-
> take a journey, for in many respects that is what change is, without
> first addressing the purpose of the trip, the route you wish to travel
> and with whom. Managing change is about handling the complex-
> ities of travel. It is about evaluating, planning and implementing
> operational, tactical and strategic 'journeys' – about always ensur-
> ing that the journey is worthwhile and the destination is relevant.
> R.A. Paton and J. McCalman, *Change Management*, p. 2

MUSEUMS HAVE NOT GENERALLY been renowned for their willingness to
embrace change or, indeed, for their capacity to effectively engage with the
imperatives and opportunities which accompany it (Hushion 1999; Janes 1999;
Lewis 1992). Rather, their reaction has often been characterized by indifference,
caution, scepticism and a desire to retain traditional values and working practices (Middleton 1990; Moore 1994). In recent decades, however, as the pace
of change dramatically increases, resistance and inaction have proved to be
untenable positions to maintain and museums have been forced to confront the
challenges, navigate the obstacles and adapt to the opportunities presented by ever
more complex, unpredictable and highly dynamic operating environments.

Rapid social, economic, political and technological changes have, of course,
been brought to bear not only on museums, but also on organizations of all kinds,
in both the for-profit and not-for-profit sectors. Change has come to be widely viewed
as a ubiquitous, inescapable phenomenon and one which has, as a consequence,
become increasingly central to the discipline of management. Indeed, growing
recognition of the pervasiveness and significance of change is reflected in the
emergence of a large and rapidly expanding body of management literature that
offers an array of models, strategies and tools designed to equip organizations

with the capacity to survive and thrive in turbulent and unpredictable times. Through this literature, 'change management' has emerged as a concept and set of practices concerned not only with strategies for coping with the myriad external forces that can threaten to derail organizations, but also with the strategic advantages to be gained from internal flexibility, organizational agility and the proactive instigation of continuous change from within. The ways in which organizations approach the concept and engage with the realities of change are now viewed by many leading management thinkers as powerful determinants of their future performance – of their ability to succeed or to fail.

The articles we have included in this section shed light on varied aspects of change and approach the topic from very different perspectives. John Kotter, one of the leading thinkers in the field of change management, provides the only contribution to the Reader which is not directly concerned with museums but, instead, draws on experiences and examples from the business sector. While we would argue that management theories developed in the for-profit environment cannot be uncritically and straightforwardly transplanted to the museum context, his accessible and thought-provoking contribution nevertheless offers valuable insights into the process of change and the pitfalls most commonly experienced by organizations attempting to transform and renew themselves. Although first published over a decade ago, Kotter's article also establishes a strong connection between leadership and the process of organizational change, a theme which has, in recent years, received growing attention in the literature on both management and museums and which resurfaces for further consideration in many of the subsequent articles in this volume.

Stephen Weil's seminal article considers how powerful forces of change have radically reshaped the museum from an organization principally focused on collections, preservation and scholarly research to one that must now also be concerned with audiences, education, public service and broader social change. The transformation Weil describes not only illustrates the far-reaching effects of change, but also usefully offers a way to understand the circumstances which have led to the widespread adoption of management and the growing prominence of marketing within museums. His account of change helps to explain the increased interest in, and engagement with, theories and practices stemming from these disciplines which had previously been viewed as irrelevant to, and incompatible with, the world of museums.

Whereas Weil's contribution offers a largely historical account of change, Christine Burton and Carol Scott consider the implications that growing competition, shifting attitudes to leisure time and evolving patterns of leisure consumption might hold for museums today and in the future. Their thought-provoking analysis blends theoretical perspectives from marketing and related disciplines with in-depth empirical investigation of audiences, revealing the value of research (and, in particular, an in-depth understanding of the needs, attitudes, behaviours and expectations of existing and potential audiences) in enabling museums to anticipate and adapt to change.

While the theme of change can be seen to run through many of the articles included in this Reader (and indeed more broadly in the museum studies literature), surprisingly few reflections on the process of organizational change in museums have been published (Gurian 1995). The last two articles in this section offer valuable insights into this topic through the eyes of different individuals involved in a process of renewal at a single institution — the Glenbow Museum in Canada. Robert Janes, the then President and CEO of Glenbow, provides an honest account of the challenges, paradoxes and opportunities presented by organizational change and the impact of these on the institution and its staff. Drawing on concepts from the field of change management, his analysis alerts us to the need for, and the value of, new ways of thinking and new modes of practice to equip museums with the capacity to live with uncertainty. Although the effects on staff are commonly acknowledged in the literature on managing change, they are most frequently viewed from the perspective of senior management in terms of their potential to constrain or to facilitate organizational transformation. The personal experiences of individuals have largely been excluded from accounts of institutional change. The final article helps to address this deficit in understanding by considering the same set of events at Glenbow but, this time, from the perspective of a cross-section of staff occupying different roles within the museum. Their reflections attest to the importance, in any change management process, of understanding, respecting and dealing with an organization's culture — 'the unique configuration of norms, values, beliefs and ways of behaving that characterises the manner in which groups and individuals combine to get things done' (Eldridge and Crombie 1974). As these highly personalized accounts further illustrate, organizational change can be demoralizing, stressful, debilitating and painful and yet, at the same time, exciting, stimulating, energizing and empowering.

References

Anderson, G. (ed.) (2004) *Reinventing the Museum: Historical and Contemporary Perspectives on the Paradigm Shift*, Walnut Creek, California: AltaMira Press.

Eldridge, J.E.T. and Crombie, A.D. (1974) *A Sociology of Organisations*, London: Allen and Unwin.

Gurian, E.H. (1995) *Institutional Trauma: Major Change in Museums and its Effect on Staff*, Washington DC: American Association of Museums.

Hushion, N. (1999) 'Managing change *or* navigating turbulent times', *Museum International*, UNESCO, 51(2): 44–49.

Janes, R.R. (1999) 'Embracing organizational change in museums: a work in progress', in K. Moore (ed.) *Management in Museums*, London and New Jersey: Athlone.

Lewis, P. (1992) 'Museums and marketing', in J.M.A Thompson (ed.) *Manual of Curatorship: A Guide to Museum Practice*, London: Museums Association, Butterworth.

Mason, R. (2006) 'Cultural theory and museum studies', in S. Macdonald (ed.) *A Companion to Museum Studies*, Oxford: Blackwell Publishing.

Middleton, V. (1990) 'Irresistible demand forces', *Museums Journal*, February: 31–34.

Moore, K. (ed.) (1994) *Museum Management*, London and New York: Routledge.

Paton, R.A. and McCalman, J. (2000) *Change Management: A Guide to Effective Implementation*, 2nd edn, London: Sage Publications.

Chapter 2

Leading Change
Why transformation efforts fail

John P. Kotter

O VER THE PAST DECADE, I have watched more than 100 companies try to remake themselves into significantly better competitors. They have included large organizations (Ford) and small ones (Landmark Communications), companies based in the United States (General Motors) and elsewhere (British Airways), corporations that were on their knees (Eastern Airlines), and companies that were earning good money (Bristol-Myers Squibb). These efforts have gone under many banners: total quality management, reengineering, right sizing, restructuring, cultural change, and turnaround. But, in almost every case, the basic goal has been the same: to make fundamental changes in how business is conducted in order to help cope with a new, more challenging market environment.

A few of these corporate change efforts have been very successful. A few have been utter failures. Most fall somewhere in between, with a distinct tilt toward the lower end of the scale. The lessons that can be drawn are interesting and will probably be relevant to even more organizations in the increasingly competitive business environment of the coming decade.

The most general lesson to be learned from the more successful cases is that the change process goes through a series of phases that, in total, usually require a considerable length of time. Skipping steps creates only the illusion of speed and never produces a satisfying result. A second very general lesson is that critical mistakes in any of the phases can have a devastating impact, slowing momentum and negating hard-won gains. Perhaps because we have relatively little experience in renewing organizations, even very capable people often make at least one big error.

Source: *Harvard Business Review*, March–April 1995, vol. 73, no. 2: 59–67.

Error #1: Not establishing a great enough sense of urgency

Most successful change efforts begin when some individuals or some groups start to look hard at a company's competitive situation, market position, technological trends, and financial performance. They focus on the potential revenue drop when an important patent expires, the five-year trend in declining margins in a core business, or an emerging market that everyone seems to be ignoring. They then find ways to communicate this information broadly and dramatically, especially with respect to crises, potential crises, or great opportunities that are very timely. This first step is essential because just getting a transformation program started requires the aggressive cooperation of many individuals. Without motivation, people won't help and the effort goes nowhere.

Compared with other steps in the change process, phase one can sound easy. It is not. Well over 50% of the companies I have watched fail in this first phase. What are the reasons for that failure? Sometimes executives underestimate how hard it can be to drive people out of their comfort zones. Sometimes they grossly overestimate how successful they have already been in increasing urgency. Sometimes they lack patience: 'Enough with the preliminaries; let's get on with it.' In many cases, executives become paralyzed by the downside possibilities. They worry that employees with seniority will become defensive, that morale will drop, that events will spin out of control, that short-term business results will be jeopardized, that the stock will sink, and that they will be blamed for creating a crisis.

A paralyzed senior management often comes from having too many managers and not enough leaders. Management's mandate is to minimize risk and to keep the current system operating. Change, by definition, requires creating a new system, which in turn always demands leadership. Phase one in a renewal process typically goes nowhere until enough real leaders are promoted or hired into senior-level jobs.

Transformations often begin, and begin well, when an organization has a new head who is a good leader and who sees the need for a major change. If the renewal target is the entire company, the CEO is key. If change is needed in a division, the division general manager is key. When these individuals are not new leaders, great leaders, or change champions, phase one can be a huge challenge.

Bad business results are both a blessing and a curse in the first phase. On the positive side, losing money does catch people's attention. But it also gives less maneuvering room. With good business results, the opposite is true: convincing people of the need for change is much harder, but you have more resources to help make changes.

But whether the starting point is good performance or bad, in the more successful cases I have witnessed, an individual or a group always facilitates a frank discussion of potentially unpleasant facts: about new competition, shrinking margins, decreasing market share, flat earnings, a lack of revenue growth, or other relevant indices of a declining competitive position. Because there seems to be an almost universal human tendency to shoot the bearer of bad news, especially if the head of the organization is not a change champion, executives in these companies often rely on outsiders to bring unwanted information. Wall Street analysts, customers, and consultants can all be helpful in this regard. The purpose of all this activity, in

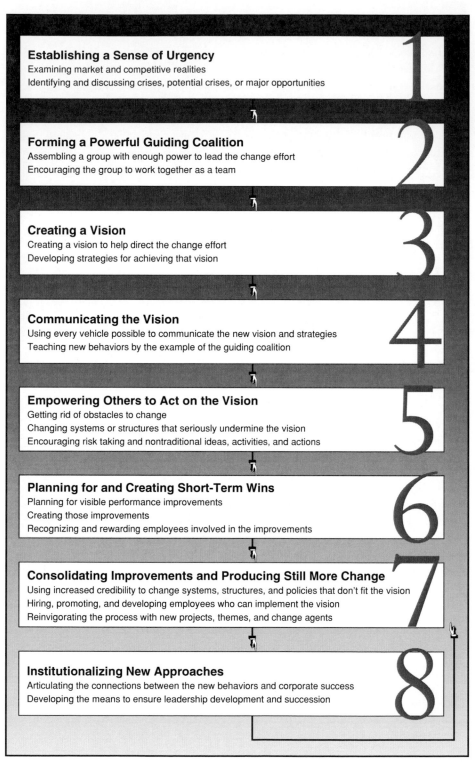

Figure 2.1   Eight Steps to Transforming Your Organization

the words of one former CEO of a large European company, is 'to make the status quo seem more dangerous than launching into the unknown.'

In a few of the most successful cases, a group has manufactured a crisis. One CEO deliberately engineered the largest accounting loss in the company's history, creating huge pressures from Wall Street in the process. One division president commissioned first-ever customer-satisfaction surveys, knowing full well that the results would be terrible. He then made these findings public. On the surface, such moves can look unduly risky. But there is also risk in playing it too safe: when the urgency rate is not pumped up enough, the transformation process cannot succeed and the long-term future of the organization is put in jeopardy.

When is the urgency rate high enough? From what I have seen, the answer is when about 75% of a company's management is honestly convinced that business-as-usual is totally unacceptable. Anything less can produce very serious problems later on in the process.

Error #2: Not creating a powerful enough guiding coalition

Major renewal programs often start with just one or two people. In cases of successful transformation efforts, the leadership coalition grows and grows over time. But whenever some minimum mass is not achieved early in the effort, nothing much worthwhile happens.

It is often said that major change is impossible unless the head of the organization is an active supporter. What I am talking about goes far beyond that. In successful transformations, the chairman or president or division general manager, plus another 5 or 15 or 50 people, come together and develop a shared commitment to excellent performance through renewal. In my experience, this group never includes all of the company's most senior executives because some people just won't buy in, at least not at first. But in the most successful cases, the coalition is always pretty powerful – in terms of titles, information and expertise, reputations and relationships.

In both small and large organizations, a successful guiding team may consist of only three to five people during the first year of a renewal effort. But in big companies, the coalition needs to grow to the 20 to 50 range before much progress can be made in phase three and beyond. Senior managers always form the core of the group. But sometimes you find board members, a representative from a key customer, or even a powerful union leader.

Because the guiding coalition includes members who are not part of senior management, it tends to operate outside of the normal hierarchy by definition. This can be awkward, but it is clearly necessary. If the existing hierarchy were working well, there would be no need for a major transformation. But since the current system is not working, reform generally demands activity outside of formal boundaries, expectations, and protocol.

A high sense of urgency within the managerial ranks helps enormously in putting a guiding coalition together. But more is usually required. Someone needs to get these people together, help them develop a shared assessment of their company's problems and opportunities, and create a minimum level of trust and communication.

Off-site retreats, for two or three days, are one popular vehicle for accomplishing this task. I have seen many groups of 5 to 35 executives attend a series of these retreats over a period of months.

Companies that fail in phase two usually underestimate the difficulties of producing change and thus the importance of a powerful guiding coalition. Sometimes they have no history of teamwork at the top and therefore undervalue the importance of this type of coalition. Sometimes they expect the team to be led by a staff executive from human resources, quality, or strategic planning instead of a key line manager. No matter how capable or dedicated the staff head, groups without strong line leadership never achieve the power that is required.

Efforts that don't have a powerful enough guiding coalition can make apparent progress for a while. But, sooner or later, the opposition gathers itself together and stops the change.

Error #3: Lacking a vision

In every successful transformation effort that I have seen, the guiding coalition develops a picture of the future that is relatively easy to communicate and appeals to customers, stockholders, and employees. A vision always goes beyond the numbers that are typically found in five-year plans. A vision says something that helps clarify the direction in which an organization needs to move. Sometimes the first draft comes mostly from a single individual. It is usually a bit blurry, at least initially. But after the coalition works at it for 3 or 5 or even 12 months, something much better emerges through their tough analytical thinking and a little dreaming. Eventually, a strategy for achieving that vision is also developed.

In one midsize European company, the first pass at a vision contained two-thirds of the basic ideas that were in the final product. The concept of global reach was in the initial version from the beginning. So was the idea of becoming pre-eminent in certain businesses. But one central idea in the final version – getting out of low value-added activities – came only after a series of discussions over a period of several months.

Without a sensible vision, a transformation effort can easily dissolve into a list of confusing and incompatible projects that can take the organization in the wrong direction or nowhere at all. Without a sound vision, the reengineering project in the accounting department, the new 360-degree performance appraisal from the human resources department, the plant's quality program, the cultural change project in the sales force will not add up in a meaningful way.

In failed transformations, you often find plenty of plans and directives and programs, but no vision. In one case, a company gave out four-inch-thick notebooks describing its change effort. In mind-numbing detail, the books spelled out procedures, goals, methods, and deadlines. But nowhere was there a clear and compelling statement of where all this was leading. Not surprisingly, most of the employees with whom I talked were either confused or alienated. The big, thick books did not rally them together or inspire change. In fact, they probably had just the opposite effect.

In a few of the less successful cases that I have seen, management had a sense of direction, but it was too complicated or blurry to be useful. Recently, I asked an executive in a midsize company to describe his vision and received in return a barely comprehensible 30-minute lecture. Buried in his answer were the basic elements of a sound vision. But they were buried – deeply.

A useful rule of thumb: if you can't communicate the vision to someone in five minutes or less and get a reaction that signifies both understanding and interest, you are not yet done with this phase of the transformation process.

Error #4: Undercommunicating the vision by a factor of ten

I've seen three patterns with respect to communication, all very common. In the first, a group actually does develop a pretty good transformation vision and then proceeds to communicate it by holding a single meeting or sending out a single communication. Having used about .0001% of the yearly intracompany communication, the group is startled that few people seem to understand the new approach. In the second pattern, the head of the organization spends a considerable amount of time making speeches to employee groups, but most people still don't get it (not surprising, since vision captures only .0005% of the total yearly communication). In the third pattern, much more effort goes into newsletters and speeches, but some very visible senior executives still behave in ways that are antithetical to the vision. The net result is that cynicism among the troops goes up, while belief in the communication goes down.

Transformation is impossible unless hundreds or thousands of people are willing to help, often to the point of making short-term sacrifices. Employees will not make sacrifices, even if they are unhappy with the status quo, unless they believe that useful change is possible. Without credible communication, and a lot of it, the hearts and minds of the troops are never captured.

This fourth phase is particularly challenging if the short-term sacrifices include job losses. Gaining understanding and support is tough when downsizing is a part of the vision. For this reason, successful visions usually include new growth possibilities and the commitment to treat fairly anyone who is laid off.

Executives who communicate well incorporate messages into their hour-by-hour activities. In a routine discussion about a business problem, they talk about how proposed solutions fit (or don't fit) into the bigger picture. In a regular performance appraisal, they talk about how the employee's behavior helps or undermines the vision. In a review of a division's quarterly performance, they talk not only about the numbers but also about how the division's executives are contributing to the transformation. In a routine Q&A with employees at a company facility, they tie their answers back to renewal goals.

In more successful transformation efforts, executives use all existing communication channels to broadcast the vision. They turn boring and unread company newsletters into lively articles about the vision. They take ritualistic and tedious quarterly management meetings and turn them into exciting discussions of the transformation. They throw out much of the company's generic management education and replace it with courses that focus on business problems and the new vision. The guiding principle is simple: use every possible channel, especially those that are being wasted on nonessential information.

Perhaps even more important, most of the executives I have known in successful cases of major change learn to 'walk the talk.' They consciously attempt to become a living symbol of the new corporate culture. This is often not easy. A 60-year-old plant manager who has spent precious little time over 40 years thinking about customers will not suddenly behave in a customer-oriented way. But I have witnessed just such a person change, and change a great deal. In that case, a high level of urgency helped. The fact that the man was a part of the guiding coalition and the vision-creation team also helped. So did all the communication, which kept reminding him of the desired behavior, and all the feedback from his peers and subordinates, which helped him see when he was not engaging in that behavior.

Communication comes in both words and deeds, and the latter are often the most powerful form. Nothing undermines change more than behavior by important individuals that is inconsistent with their words.

Error #5: Not removing obstacles to the new vision

Successful transformations begin to involve large numbers of people as the process progresses. Employees are emboldened to try new approaches, to develop new ideas, and to provide leadership. The only constraint is that the actions fit within the broad parameters of the overall vision. The more people involved, the better the outcome.

To some degree, a guiding coalition empowers others to take action simply by successfully communicating the new direction. But communication is never sufficient by itself. Renewal also requires the removal of obstacles. Too often, an employee understands the new vision and wants to help make it happen. But an elephant appears to be blocking the path. In some cases, the elephant is in the person's head, and the challenge is to convince the individual that no external obstacle exists. But in most cases, the blockers are very real.

Sometimes the obstacle is the organizational structure: narrow job categories can seriously undermine efforts to increase productivity or make it very difficult even to think about customers. Sometimes compensation or performance-appraisal systems make people choose between the new vision and their own self-interest. Perhaps worst of all are bosses who refuse to change and who make demands that are inconsistent with the overall effort.

One company began its transformation process with much publicity and actually made good progress through the fourth phase. Then the change effort ground to a halt because the officer in charge of the company's largest division was allowed to undermine most of the new initiatives. He paid lip service to the process but did not change his behavior or encourage his managers to change. He did not reward the unconventional ideas called for in the vision. He allowed human resource systems to remain intact even when they were clearly inconsistent with the new ideals. I think the officer's motives were complex. To some degree, he did not believe the company needed major change. To some degree, he felt personally threatened by all the change. To some degree, he was afraid that he could not produce both change and the expected operating profit. But despite the fact that they backed the renewal effort, the other officers did virtually nothing to stop the one blocker. Again, the reasons were complex. The company had no history of confronting problems like this. Some people were afraid of the officer. The CEO was concerned that he might lose a talented executive. The net result was disastrous. Lower-level managers concluded that senior management had lied to them about their commitment to renewal, cynicism grew, and the whole effort collapsed.

In the first half of a transformation, no organization has the momentum, power, or time to get rid of all obstacles. But the big ones must be confronted and removed. If the blocker is a person, it is important that he or she be treated fairly and in a way that is consistent with the new vision. But action is essential, both to empower others and to maintain the credibility of the change effort as a whole.

Error #6: Not systematically planning for and creating short-term wins

Real transformation takes time, and a renewal effort risks losing momentum if there are no short-term goals to meet and celebrate. Most people won't go on the long march unless they see compelling evidence within 12 to 24 months that the journey is producing expected results. Without short-term wins, too many people give up or actively join the ranks of those people who have been resisting change.

One to two years into a successful transformation effort, you find quality beginning to go up on certain indices or the decline in net income stopping. You find some successful new product introductions or an upward shift in market share. You find an impressive productivity improvement or a statistically higher customer-satisfaction rating. But whatever the case, the win is unambiguous. The result is not just a judgment call that can be discounted by those opposing change.

Creating short-term wins is different from hoping for short-term wins. The latter is passive, the former active. In a successful transformation, managers actively look for ways to obtain clear performance improvements, establish goals in the yearly planning system, achieve the objectives, and reward the people involved with recognition, promotions, and even money. For example, the guiding coalition at a U.S. manufacturing company produced a highly visible and successful new product introduction about 20 months after the start of its renewal effort. The new product was selected about six months into the effort because it met multiple criteria: it could be designed and launched in a relatively short period; it could be handled by a small team of people who were devoted to the new vision; it had upside potential; and the new product-development team could operate outside the established departmental structure without practical problems. Little was left to chance, and the win boosted the credibility of the renewal process.

Managers often complain about being forced to produce short-term wins, but I've found that pressure can be a useful element in a change effort. When it becomes clear to people that major change will take a long time, urgency levels can drop. Commitments to produce short-term wins help keep the urgency level up and force detailed analytical thinking that can clarify or revise visions.

Error #7: Declaring victory too soon

After a few years of hard work, managers may be tempted to declare victory with the first clear performance improvement. While celebrating a win is fine, declaring the war won can be catastrophic. Until changes sink deeply into a company's culture, a process that can take five to ten years, new approaches are fragile and subject to regression.

In the recent past, I have watched a dozen change efforts operate under the reengineering theme. In all but two cases, victory was declared and the expensive consultants were paid and thanked when the first major project was completed after two to three years. Within two more years, the useful changes that had been introduced slowly disappeared. In two of the ten cases, it's hard to find any trace of the reengineering work today.

Over the past 20 years, I've seen the same sort of thing happen to huge quality projects, organizational development efforts, and more. Typically, the problems start early in the process: the urgency level is not intense enough, the guiding coalition is not powerful enough, and the vision is not clear enough. But it is the premature victory celebration that kills momentum. And then the powerful forces associated with tradition take over.

Ironically, it is often a combination of change initiators and change resistors that creates the premature victory celebration. In their enthusiasm over a clear sign of progress, the initiators go overboard. They are then joined by resistors, who are quick to spot any opportunity to stop change. After the celebration is over, the resistors point to the victory as a sign that the war has been won and the troops should be sent home. Weary troops allow themselves to be convinced that they won. Once home, the foot soldiers are reluctant to climb back on the ships. Soon thereafter, change comes to a halt, and tradition creeps back in.

Instead of declaring victory, leaders of successful efforts use the credibility afforded by short-term wins to tackle even bigger problems. They go after systems and structures that are not consistent with the transformation vision and have not been confronted before. They pay great attention to who is promoted, who is hired, and how people are developed. They include new reengineering projects that are even bigger in scope than the initial ones. They understand that renewal efforts take not months but years. In fact, in one of the most successful transformations that I have ever seen, we quantified the amount of change that occurred each year over a seven-year period. On a scale of one (low) to ten (high), year one received a two, year two a four, year three a three, year four a seven, year five an eight, year six a four, and year seven a two. The peak came in year five, fully 36 months after the first set of visible wins.

Error #8: Not anchoring changes in the corporation's culture

In the final analysis, change sticks when it becomes 'the way we do things around here,' when it seeps into the bloodstream of the corporate body. Until new behaviors are rooted in social norms and shared values, they are subject to degradation as soon as the pressure for change is removed.

Two factors are particularly important in institutionalizing change in corporate culture. The first is a conscious attempt to show people how the new approaches, behaviors, and attitudes have helped improve performance. When people are left on their own to make the connections, they sometimes create very inaccurate links.

For example, because results improved while charismatic Harry was boss, the troops link his mostly idiosyncratic style with those results instead of seeing how their own improved customer service and productivity were instrumental. Helping people see the right connections requires communication. Indeed, one company was relentless, and it paid off enormously. Time was spent at every major management meeting to discuss why performance was increasing. The company newspaper ran article after article showing how changes had boosted earnings.

The second factor is taking sufficient time to make sure that the next genera-tion of top management really does personify the new approach. If the require-ments for promotion don't change, renewal rarely lasts. One bad succession decision at the top of an organization can undermine a decade of hard work. Poor succession decisions are possible when boards of directors are not an integral part of the renewal effort. In at least three instances I have seen, the champion for change was the retiring executive, and although his successor was not a resistor, he was not a change champion. Because the boards did not understand the transformations in any detail, they could not see that their choices were not good fits. The retir-ing executive in one case tried unsuccessfully to talk his board into a less seasoned candidate who better personified the transformation. In the other two cases, the CEOs did not resist the boards' choices, because they felt the transformation could not be undone by their successors. They were wrong. Within two years, signs of renewal began to disappear at both companies.

There are still more mistakes that people make, but these eight are the big ones. I realize that in a short article everything is made to sound a bit too simplistic. In reality, even successful change efforts are messy and full of surprises. But just as a relatively simple vision is needed to guide people through a major change, so a vision of the change process can reduce the error rate. And fewer errors can spell the difference between success and failure.

Note

John P. Kotter is an internationally renowned writer on organizational change and leadership based at the Harvard Business School. This article was first published in the *Harvard Business Review*, March–April 1995, vol. 73, no. 2, pp. 59–67.

Chapter 3

From Being *about* Something to Being *for* Somebody
The ongoing transformation of the American museum

Stephen E. Weil

A T THE END OF WORLD WAR II, the American museum – notwithstand-ing the ringing educational rhetoric with which it was originally established and occasionally maintained – had become engaged primarily in what my Washington colleague Barbara Franco once called the 'salvage and warehouse business.'[1] It took as its basic tasks to gather, preserve, and study the record of human and natural history. Any further benefit, such as providing the public with physical and intel-lectual access to the collections and information thus accumulated, was simply a plus.

Fifty years later, caught up in the confluence of two powerful currents – one flowing throughout the worldwide museum community, the other specific to the United States – the American museum is being substantially reshaped. In place of an establishment-like institution focused primarily inward on the growth, care, and study of its collection, emerging instead is a more entrepreneurial institution that – if my vision of its ultimate form should prove correct – will have shifted its focus outward to concentrate on providing primarily educational services to the public and will measure its success in that effort by the overarching criterion of whether it is actually able to provide those services in a demonstrably effect-ive way.

This prognostication makes no distinction between museums and museumlike institutions in terms of their funding sources, scale, or discipline. It applies equally to a large statewide historical society, a campus-based natural history museum, and a small, private art gallery. So-called private museums require particular mention. Even the most ostensibly private of American museums – through the combined effects of its own tax exemption and the charitable-contribution deductions claimed

Source: *Daedalus*, vol. 128, no. 3 (summer 1999): 229–258.

by its donors – receives a substantial measure of public support. Given the nature of that support, such private museums are inevitably expected not only to provide a level of public service comparable to that required of so-called public institutions but also to maintain similar standards of accountability and transparency.

Among workers in the field, the response to this ongoing change in the museum's focus has been mixed. Some – a minority, certainly – view it with distress. They argue that the museum – if not at the height of its salvage and warehouse days, then not long thereafter – was already a mature, fully evolved, and inherently good organization in no compelling need of further change. Particularly troublesome, in their view, would be to tamper with the centrality of the collection – even to entertain the notion that the collection might no longer serve as the museum's raison d'être but merely as one of its resources.

A far larger number of museum workers are sympathetic to the museum's evolution from a collection-based organization to a more educationally focused one, but they nevertheless tend to retreat from making institutional effectiveness so exclusive a test of institutional failure or success. Characterizing the museum as analogous in some measure to the university, they argue that the museum's traditional activities of preservation (which may include collecting), interpretation (which may include exhibiting), and scholarly inquiry (above all) are not merely instrumental steps toward an ultimately external outcome but should also be valued in their own right, as ends as well as means. From that moderate position, many still share the vision of an emerging new museum model   a transformed and redirected institution that can, through its public-service orientation, use its very special competencies in dealing with objects to improve the quality of individual human lives and to enhance the well-being of human communities. Vague as those purposes may at first appear, so multifarious are the potential outcomes of which this emerging museum is capable that to use terms any more specific than 'quality of life' or 'communal well-being' would be unnecessarily exclusive.

Finally, at the other extreme are those museum workers who question whether the museum truly is an inherently good organization (or whether it has any inherent qualities at all) and whether the traditional activities of preservation, interpretation, and scholarship have any value in a museum context, apart from their capacity to contribute to an outcome external to the museum itself. Rejecting any analogy with a university, they argue that museum work might better be understood instead as a value-neutral technology and the museum itself as neither more nor less than a highly adaptable instrument that can be employed for a wide range of purposes.

What follows will consider the American museum from this last point of view, examining the currents that now press against it as well as suggesting several possibly unanticipated consequences that may well follow in the wake of those currents. It is based on the twin premises that, first, those pressures now reshaping the museum will continue unabated for the foreseeable future, and second, that in yielding to those pressures nothing innate or vital to the museum will be lost or even compromised. As Adele Z. Silver of the Cleveland Museum of Art wisely observed, 'Museums are inventions of men, not inevitable, eternal, ideal, nor divine. They exist for the things we put in them, and they change as each generation chooses how to see and use those things.'[2]

The museum as public service

In a reflection on the recent history of museums, written for the fiftieth-anniversary issue of the UNESCO magazine *Museum International*, Kenneth Hudson – perhaps the museum community's most astute observer – wrote: 'The most fundamental change that has affected museums during the [past] half century . . . is the now almost universal conviction that they exist in order to serve the public. The old-style museum felt itself under no such obligation. It existed, it had a building, it had collections and a staff to look after them. It was reasonably adequately financed, and its visitors, usually not numerous, came to look, to wonder and to admire what was set before them. They were in no sense partners in the enterprise. The museum's prime responsibility was to its collections, not its visitors.'[3]

Among the several factors to which Hudson points in seeking to account for this change is the enormous increase during the postwar period in both the number and the magnitude of museums. By his count, at least three-quarters of the world's active museums were established after 1945. In no way has the level of direct governmental assistance to these museums kept pace with that growth. In some countries it has remained stagnant; in others – the United States, for one – its vigorous growth in the 1960s and 1970s has been followed by actual decline. The result, almost worldwide, has been the same: to change the mix in the sources of support for museums, with a decrease in the proportion coming directly from governmental sources and a corresponding increase in the proportion that must be found elsewhere.

It seems clear, at the most elementary level, that the greater the degree to which a museum must rely for some portion of its support on 'box-office' income – not merely entrance fees but also the related funds to be derived from shop sales and other auxiliary activities – the greater will be its focus on making itself attractive to visitors. Likewise, the greater the extent to which a museum might seek corporate funding – particularly for its program activities – the more important will be that museum's ability to assure prospective sponsors that its programs will attract a wide audience. Under such circumstances, it should hardly be surprising that museums are increasingly conscious of what might be of interest to the public. The consequence is that museums almost everywhere have, in essence, shifted from a 'selling' mode to a 'marketing' one. In the selling mode, their efforts were concentrated on convincing the public to 'buy' their traditional offerings. In the marketing mode, their starting point instead is the public's own needs and interests, and their efforts are concentrated on first trying to discover and then attempting to satisfy those public needs and interests.

Hudson argues – correctly, I think – that something more profound than mere box-office appeal is involved in this change of focus. He suggests that the museum's growing preoccupation with its audience also may be attributable to the tremendous increase of professionalism within the museum community during the postwar years. The impact of that development – and, as a principal consequence, the equally tremendous growth in the scale, influence, and variety of professional associations – should not be underestimated. The policy positions taken by those professional associations – and the insistent repetition of those policies over time – have played a compelling part in shaping the mind-set and expectations of new practitioners in the field and the larger public as well. As the sociologists Walter W. Powell and

Rebecca Friedkin point out in their analysis of the sources of change in public-service organizations, beyond such changes in focus as may be attributable to changes in the sources of an organization's support – for museums, the box-office factor – institutional change may frequently represent 'a response to shifts in the ideology, professional standards, and cultural norms of the field or sector in which an organization is situated.'[4]

That would appear to be the case for the museum. A broad range of national and local professional organizations have influenced the ideological reshaping of the American museum. Earliest among these was the American Association of Museums (AAM), founded in 1906 as something of a parallel to the United Kingdom's Museums Association, which dates back to 1889. Narrower in focus but also with considerable impact have been the more recently established Association of Science-Technology Centers (ASTC) and the Association of Youth Museums (AYM). Of perhaps lesser consequence for the American museum – but of enormous influence elsewhere – has been the International Council of Museums (ICOM). Descended from the International Museums Office founded under the auspices of the League of Nations in 1927, ICOM was established in 1946 as a UNESCO-affiliated non-governmental organization, head-quartered in Paris.

The publications and program activities of these associations amply document the degree to which they have changed their emphasis over the past several decades, from collections and preservation to public service. Within the AAM, that shift can be attributed directly to the growing influence that museum educators have exercised over the association's public-policy positions. That influence can be traced on an ascending curve, beginning in June 1973 when a group of prominent museum educators threatened to secede from the organization. In June 1976, as a gesture of conciliation, a change in the AAM's constitution granted a committee of educators together with other disciplinary groups a role in the association's governance. With the publication of *Museums for a New Century* in 1984, education was declared to be a 'primary' purpose of museums.[5] This upward curve reached its zenith in May 1991, when the association's governing board adopted the educator-prepared position paper *Excellence and Equity* as an official statement of the association's policy.[6] Woven throughout *Excellence and Equity* are the linked propositions that a commitment to public service is 'central to every museum's activities' and that 'education – in the broadest sense of that word – [is] at the heart of their public service role.'[7]

A similar shift of focus can be traced in the AAM's program of institutional accreditation, first proposed in 1968 and put into operation in 1971. In its earliest phase, accreditation was primarily concerned with how an institution cared for its collection and maintained its facilities. With the passage of time, the scope of accreditation has steadily broadened to consider not only the institutional care of collections but also, as importantly, the programmatic use of those collections. Consider the contrast between the types of concern expressed in the AAM's first accreditation handbook of 1970 and in its most recent one, published in 1997. In the 1970 publication, among the positive traits that might support a museum's accreditation were avoidance of 'crude or amateurish' exhibits, evidence that exhibit cases were dust- and vermin-proof, and a demonstration that the exhibits themselves were 'selected to serve [some] purpose and not just [as] "visible storage."'[8] Regarding special exhibitions, it suggested that the better practice was to offer exhibitions that appealed to the interest of the general public and not simply to that of an 'anti-quarian or dilettante' audience. In the AAM's 1997 publication, the emphasis shifted entirely. Suggested areas of inquiry include whether the 'museum effectively involves its audiences in developing public programs and exhibitions,' whether it 'effect-ively identifies and knows the characteristics of its existing and potential audiences,' and whether it 'effectively evaluates its programs and exhibitions' in terms of their audience impact.[9]

Contrasting quotations from two other AAM publications may suggest how far the rhetoric – if not yet all of the operational practices – of the museum community has evolved during this period. Consider the 1968 *Belmont Report* – a mostly forgotten document that was once thought (wrongly, in the event) to offer an irrefutable argument for the increased federal funding of American museums. Those who produced the report were certainly aware that 'education' would prove the most likely heading under which increased funding could be justified, but they seemed reluctant to relinquish entirely the old-fashioned satis-faction ('pleasure and delight') that museum collections were traditionally thought to provide.[10] 'Art museums,' they explained, 'aim to provide the aesthetic and emotional pleasure which great works of art offer. This is a primary purpose of an art museum. It is assumed that a majority of the people who come regularly to art museums come to be delighted, not to be taught, or preached at, or "improved" except by the works of art themselves. An art museum, especially, is – or ought to be – a place where one goes to get refreshed.'[11] Never adequately explained in the *Belmont Report* was why so much refreshment (particularly in the case of the art museum, where that refreshment was disproportionately consumed by the more affluent members of society) should properly be provided at public rather than private expense.

The escalation in rhetoric is suggestive. Over three decades, what the museum might be envisioned as offering to the public has grown from mere refreshment (the museum as carbonated beverage) to education (the museum as a site for informal learning) to nothing short of communal empowerment (the museum as an instrument for social change). Describing the growth of museums in rural Brazilian communities seeking to discover their roots and preserve a unique history, Maria de Lourdes Horta wrote in a 1997 AAM publication:

> A museum without walls and without objects, a true virtual museum, is being born in some of those communities, which look in wonder to their own process of self-discovery and self-recognition. . . . For the moment, in my country, [museums] are being used in a new way, as tools for self-expression, self-recognition, and representation; as spaces of power negotiation among social forces; and as strategies for empower-ing people so that they are more able to decide their own destiny.[12]

ICOM, like the AAM, has put increasing emphasis on the public-service role of museums. Going still further, it has advanced toward a view – similar to that from Brazil – that museums can play a powerful role in bringing about social change. To some extent, that conviction has grown almost in tandem with the number of developing countries included within its membership base. Given that change in its membership, as well as its ongoing relationship with UNESCO, ICOM's emphasis on social activism must be understood as more than simply a passing phase. It permeates virtually every aspect of ICOM, beginning even with its membership requirements. In contrast to the AAM, which continues to take the more traditional approach of defining museums primarily in terms of their activities – to present essentially educational programs that use and interpret objects for the public – ICOM's statutes were amended in 1974 to redefine 'eligible' museums as those that have among their characteristics the purpose of serving (in an earlier iteration) 'the community' or (in ICOM's current definition) 'society and . . . its development.'[13]

Among the clearest articulations of ICOM's evolving position was a resolution adopted by the membership in 1971 at its ninth general conference. Rejecting as 'questionable' what it called the 'traditional concept of the museum,' with its emphasis 'merely' on the possession of objects of cultural and natural heritage, the conference urged museums to undertake a complete reassessment of the needs of their publics, so that the museums could 'more firmly establish their educational and cultural role in the service of mankind.' Rather than prescribing any monolithic approach to this task, individual museums were urged to develop programs that addressed the 'particular social environment[s] in which they operated.'[14]

At an April 1998 meeting in San José, Costa Rica, 'the first summit of the museums of the Americas,' organized by the AAM in collaboration with some of ICOM's national and other committees, the proposition that museums might play a useful role in social development was taken a step further. In a three-tiered finding that amounted to a syllogism, the 150 delegates representing 33 Western countries took the position that the museum was not merely a potential or desirable instrument for sustainable social advancement but, in effect, an essential one. The logic of that position went as follows: 'First, sustainable development is a process for improving the quality of life in the present and the future, promoting a balance between environment, economic growth, equity and cultural diversity, and requires the participation and empowerment of all individuals; second, culture is the basis of sustainable development; and third (and, in effect, ergo), museums are essential in the protection and diffusion of our cultural and natural heritage.'[15]

This emphasis on social service is the first of the two currents that are pushing the American museum out of the salvage, warehouse, and soda-pop business and toward a new line of work. It is powered both by economic necessity – the box-office factor – and by the museum field's changing ideology as transmitted not only through such major professional associations as the AAM, ASTC, AYM, and ICOM but through countless smaller ones as well. It is coupled with the reality that for many of the more recently founded museums in newly populous parts of this country, it will never be possible – because of scarcity-driven market prices, international treaties and export/import controls, or endangered species and similar legislation – to amass the in-depth and universal collections that were built many years ago by the longer-established institutions. For those older museums, public service may nevertheless be their more viable future. For younger ones, without important collections or any great prospect of ever acquiring them, public service may be their only future.

Evaluating the performance of nonprofits

The second current pushing against American museums is a local one. Its source is in the not-for-profit or 'third' sector of this country's economy, the organizational domain to which the largest segment of those museums belongs and by which all of them are profoundly influenced. Consisting of more than a million organizations – museums accounting for less than 1 percent – and generally estimated to include about 7 percent of the nation's wealth, jobs, and economic activity, the third sector itself is in the midst of profound change as to how it evaluates its constituent organizations as worthy of funding. Increasingly, the principal emphasis of such evaluations is being put on organizational performance – on the results that an organization can actually achieve.

The genesis of this change may be found in the long-simmering sense that the managers of governmental agencies as well as third-sector organizations – both lacking the reality checks of a competitive marketplace as well as the operational discipline required to demonstrate consistent profitability – have rarely been required to apply their resources with the same effectiveness and efficiency that would be demanded of them in a for-profit context.[16] In the case of federal government agencies, Congress's desire to ensure greater effectiveness culminated in the Government Performance and Results Act (GPRA), which was passed with strong bipartisan support in 1993 and which became fully effective in 2000. GPRA requires every federal agency to establish – preferably in objective and measurable terms – specific performance goals for each of its programs and to report annually to Congress on its success in meeting those goals. For the third sector, where nothing so draconian as GPRA has yet to be proposed, this new emphasis on organizational performance nevertheless constitutes a sharp break with past practice.

Two events can be singled out as having accelerated this growing emphasis on performance. One was the 'social-enterprise' model of third-sector organizations developed by Professor J. Gregory Dees at Harvard Business School during the early 1990s.[17] The other was the United Way of America's development and advocacy of outcome-based evaluation as the appropriate means of evaluating the effectiveness of the health and human-service agencies to which it provides funds.[18]

The impact of Dees' social-enterprise model can best be understood by considering some of the ways that third-sector organizations have previously been viewed. As recently as the end of World War II – a time when museums were still in their establishment stage and when survival (as contrasted with accomplishment) was widely accepted as a perfectly reasonable indicator of institutional success – the three adjectives most commonly used to describe such organizations were 'philanthropic,' 'benevolent,' and 'charitable.' Remarkably, none of these referred either to what those organizations actually did or to what impact they might hope or expect to make on some target audience. Their reference instead was to the high-minded motives of the individuals responsible for their establishment and support: philanthropic (from the Greek for a 'lover of humankind'), benevolent (from the Latin for 'somebody wishing to do well'), and charitable (from the Latin also: *caritas*, or 'with loving care'). In the years since, those adjectives have largely been replaced by the terms 'nonprofit' and 'not-for-profit,' notwithstanding the repeated criticism that the third sector is far too large and its work far too important to define it so negatively in terms of what it is not, instead of positively in terms of what it is.[19]

What is particularly striking about Dees' social-enterprise model is its way of cutting through earlier methods of evaluating these third-sector institutions and concentrating instead on 'organizational outcomes,' 'impacts,' or 'results.' In the long run, says Dees, it is those outcomes that matter – not goodwill, not an accumulation of resources, not good process, and not even highly acclaimed programs, but actual outcomes, impacts, and results. In essence, those are the organization's bottom line. Thus envisioned, the social enterprise can be seen as at least partially parallel to the commercial enterprise – similar in having achievement of a bottom line as its ultimate operational objective, yet wholly different because of the way that bottom line is defined. The commercial enterprise pursues a quantifiable economic outcome; the social enterprise pursues a social outcome that may or may not be quantifiable but that, in any event, must certainly be ascertainable.

Dees points to a second important difference between the commercial enterprise and the social enterprise. He calls this the 'social method.' Whereas the commercial enterprise must rely on 'explicit economic exchange relationships, contracts, and arm's-length bargains' to obtain resources and to distribute its product, the social enterprise operates in a different environment. At the input end, it may rely on the voluntary contribution of funds, goods, and/or labor; at the output end, it typically provides its services to the public without charge or at a price below the cost of producing those services. Those differences aside, in the social-enterprise model – just as in the commercial-enterprise one – the ability to achieve an intended bottom line is what distinguishes organizational success from failure.

For the American museum, this is a fresh challenge. To the extent that it has ever accepted that its performance might be legitimately subject to overall and possibly comparative evaluation, its worst-case scenario was that such an evaluation would – like the AAM's accreditation program – be wholly internal. What constitutes a good museum? At one time, it might have been defined in terms of the loyalty and generosity of its benefactors. Later, 'good' might have referred to the magnitude of its resources and the excellence of its staff: a fine collection, a highly regarded and well-credentialed group of curators, an appropriately large endowment, and a substantial building. Among government-related museums, a good museum might be one that adhered to the best practices and highest professional standards in the field, one that did things 'by the book.' Or – as was the case during the heyday of the National Endowments for the Arts and the Humanities, with their emphasis on program funding – it might be a museum at which exhibitions and other programs were considered exemplary by knowledgeable colleagues who worked in peer organizations. What seems so extraordinary, at least in retrospect, is that not one of those approaches took into the slightest account the museum's external impact, on either its visitors or its community.

Curiously, a rigorous bottom-line evaluation, with its primary weight on just such considerations, would not really eliminate any of those other, inner-directed approaches. It would simply incorporate and supersede them. For a museum to achieve a consistently solid bottom-line result, it would still need the ongoing support of generous donors and a spectrum of tangible and intangible resources. It would still need to establish and adhere to sound working practices and to produce

high-quality programing. In the social-enterprise model, all the factors are necessary but not – in themselves or in combination – sufficient. The museum that aspires
to be successful must still manage to combine these elements with whatever else
may be necessary to render the specific public service that it has identified (for itself
and for its supporters) as its own particular bottom line.

And what, for museums, might such a bottom line be? Here, I think, the museum
community can find useful guidance in the evaluation model that the United Way
of America formally adopted in June 1995. Before, the United Way had centered
its evaluation process around the programs of its applicant health and human-
service agencies. In 1995 it determined that it would henceforth concentrate
instead on the results of those programs – on the identifiable outcomes or impacts
that those agencies were able to achieve through those programs.

The key concept in the United Way's newly adopted approach is *difference*.
To qualify for funding, the United Way's applicant agencies are called upon to
demonstrate their ability to make positive differences – differences in knowledge
or attitude or values – in the quality of individual or communal lives.

There are, I think, few people working in the museum field today who doubt
for a moment that museums can meet such a standard. Museums quintessentially
have the potency to change what people may know or think or feel, to affect what
attitudes they may adopt or display, to influence what values they form. As Harold
Skramstad, president emeritus of Henry Ford Museum and Greenfield Village, asked
in 1996 at the Smithsonian's 150th-anniversary symposium in Washington, D.C.,
unless museums can and do play a role relative to the real problems of real people's
lives, then what is their point?

The answer is, with the considerable funding that they receive directly and
indirectly from public sources, American museums must embrace such a role. As
I have written elsewhere,

> If our museums are *not* being operated with the ultimate goal of improv-
> ing the quality of people's lives, on what [other] basis might we pos-
> sibly ask for public support? Not, certainly, on the grounds that we need
> museums in order that museum professionals might have an oppor-
> tunity to develop their skills and advance their careers, or so that those
> of us who enjoy museum work will have a place in which to do it. Not
> certainly on the grounds that they provide elegant venues for openings,
> receptions and other glamorous social events. Nor is it likely that
> we could successfully argue that museums . . . deserve to be supported
> simply as an established tradition, as a kind of ongoing habit, long after
> any good reasons to do so have ceased to be relevant or have long been
> forgotten.[20]

With the ongoing spread of outcome-based evaluation, however, two cautions seem
in order. First, museums need to observe a certain modesty as they identify their
bottom lines, lest they overstate what they can actually accomplish. Grand pro-
clamations, such as those made at the first summit of the museums of America,
may be important in highlighting the museum field's overall capability to contribute meaningfully toward social development. The individual museum that declares

'denting the universe' to be its bottom line may be setting itself up for failure unless and until it can produce a perceptibly dented universe to demonstrate its accomplishment. Museum workers need to remind themselves more forcefully than they generally do that museums can wonderfully enhance and enrich individual lives, even change them, and make communities better places in which to live. But only rarely – and even then, more often than not in synergy with other institutions – do they truly dent the universe.

Second, museums must ensure that the need to assess the effectiveness of their public programs does not distort or dumb down the contents of those programs to the point of including only what may have a verifiable or demonstrable outcome and excluding everything else. The problem is parallel to that faced by the nation's school systems with respect to nationally standardized tests. For all its promise, outcome-based evaluation – like any system – requires a wise and moderate application. Taken to an extreme, it can damage the very institutions that it was designed to benefit.

As part of the worldwide museum community, the American museum is under pressure to make public service its principal concern. Because the museum is also part of the American not-for-profit sector, the nature of the public service it will be expected to provide can be defined in more specific terms: demonstrably effective programs that make a positive difference in the quality of individual and communal lives. Recast in marketing terms, the demand is that the American museum provide some verifiable added value to the lives of those it serves in exchange for their continued support. Recast in blunter terms, the museum is being told that, to earn its keep, it must be something more important than just an orderly warehouse or popular soda fountain.

Ripe for change: exhibiting the living culture

Traditional wisdom holds that an organization can never change just one thing. So finely balanced are most organizations that change to any one element will ultimately require compensating and sometimes wholly unanticipated changes to many others. As the focus of the worldwide museum community continues to shift, from the care and study of collections to the delivery of a public service, I want to examine at least two other aspects of American museums that may be considered ripe for compensating changes. One is the way that they are divided along disciplinary lines by the types of collections they hold – most typically art, history, and science. The other is the way they are staffed and how museum workers are trained. In both respects, the overwhelming majority of American museums and museum-training programs continue to operate as if World War II had only just ended and as if collections were still at the center of the museum's concerns.

With regard to the division of museums by discipline, let me start with an anecdote. During a visit to British Columbia in 1997, I learned of an exhibition mounted earlier that year by the Nanaimo District Museum on Vancouver Island, *Gone to the Dogs*. The exhibition not only traced the history of dogs in the community back to their pre-European roots but also took into account the various ways in which dogs – 'as companions and coworkers' – continued to relate to the community today:

from tracking predators for the Royal Canadian Mounted Police to acting as Seeing Eyes for the visually handicapped to serving as pets. In a Doggy Hall of Fame, local residents were invited to post photographs of favorite dogs as well as brief, typed statements as to why they thought them special. A free film series – *Dog Day Afternoons* – presented feature films about dogs. Supplementary programs addressed local dog-related businesses such as pet grooming and veterinary services and highlighted the work of the SPCA.[21] By all accounts, the exhibition was an enormous success. It brought many first-time visitors to the museum, its popularity required the museum to transfer the exhibition to another local venue and extend the closing date, and, above all, it appeared to have left behind the palpable sense of a public enriched by its recognition of a common bond. In the end, the exhibition proved not to have been so much about dogs as it was about the shared concerns and inter-connectedness of a community.

Almost as striking as the novelty of that exhibition, however, was the recog-nition of how few communities in the United States might ever hope to see a similar exhibition in their own local museums, notwithstanding the ease with which it might be replicated. The mission of the Nanaimo District Museum was defined by geography, not by discipline: It was established to serve the city of Nanaimo and its surrounding district. In seeking to illuminate that region's cultural heritage and link that heritage to its present-day development, no restrictions limited the range of materials that the museum could employ to illustrate such links. In the United States, most museums are confined to specific disciplines. In the 1989 *National Museum Survey* – the most recent broad-based statistical information available – only 8.6 percent of American museums classified themselves as general museums not tied to a particular discipline.[22] If children's museums, generally multidisciplinary, are counted as well, the total is still barely above 15 percent.

For the remaining 85 percent of American museums, to present an exhibition such as *Gone to the Dogs* would generally be considered as beyond their disciplinary boundaries. When collections were at the center of a museum's focus, that discip-linary exclusivity might have made sense. From a managerial perspective, at least, it limited the number of such narrowly trained specialists as discipline-specific curators and conservators who had to be kept on staff. With the refocus of the museum on its public-service function, strong arguments can be advanced for releas-ing the museum from this disciplinary straitjacket – most particularly in commun-ities that have only a single museum or, at best, two. Why should those museums not try to broaden their disciplinary scope? Staffing problems could readily be dealt with through collaboration with local colleges, universities, and research institu-tions, by outsourcing, or through the use of consultants. In the words that James Smithson used to describe his expectations of the institution that was to bear his name – that it be for 'the increase and diffusion of knowledge' – the public-service-oriented museum might well conclude that, rather than pursue both goals with equal vigor, it would make better sense to emphasize 'diffusion,' where the museum's unique competencies lie, and to leave the 'increase' to possibly more competent academic institutions, with which it could closely collaborate.[23]

Easing the disciplinary boundaries of museums would not be as radical a step as it might first appear. A separation into disciplines was never inherent to the museum as an institutional form, even in its origin in those sixteenth- and seventeenth-century cabinets of curiosities. Such a separation was a later development. The Tradescant collection – the founding collection for the Ashmolean Museum at Oxford – comfortably combined natural-history specimens and what its first cata- log of 1656 called 'Artificialls' – objects that ranged from works of art, weapons, and coins to ethnographic materials and Egyptian and Roman antiquities.[24] Many continental European *wunderkammers* were similar. In the United States, the first museums – such as the one Charles Willson Peale opened in Philadelphia in 1786 – held equally eclectic collections. Peale's museum included not only portraits of American Revolutionary War heroes but also fossils, shells, models of machinery, and wax figures of Native North Americans.[25] Throughout the twentieth century, the case for multidisciplinary museums was advanced by museum practitioners as diverse in their views as John Cotton Dana in the first quarter of the century and by the proponents of the ecomuseum in more recent years.[26]

Contemporary museum practice provides ample room to envision museums organized along other than disciplinary lines. One immediate example is the children's museum. In her 1992 survey of children's museums across the United States, Joanne Cleaver credits Michael Spock and his staff – who revived the Boston Children's Museum, starting in 1961 – with having pioneered the idea that 'the museum was for somebody rather than about something.'[27] An alternative institutional form – a museum that is about something but nevertheless is nondisciplinary – is the community or neighborhood museum. One well-established type is the *heimat* ('homeland') museum, an institution that began to appear throughout Germany during the latter part of the nineteenth century and, after some twists and turns, still survives today.[28]

Although *heimat* museums were intended originally to document rural life and popular culture, particularly in their preindustrialized forms, the potential role of these museums in education and community development was recognized by the turn of the century. Under the Nazi regime, it was only a short step from education to propaganda. The *heimat* museums were employed to disseminate a pseudoscientific message of Aryan superiority and to preach a nationalist gospel of blood and soil. Notwithstanding that dark episode, there is something remarkably prescient of current museological thinking in these 1936 observations by a German curator writing about a *heimat*-like museum in Cologne: 'The *heimatmuseum* must not be a kingdom of the dead, a cemetery. It is made for the living; it is to the living that it must belong, and they must feel at ease there. . . . [T]he museum must help them to see the present in the mirror of the past, and the past in the mirror of the present . . . and, if it fails in that task, it becomes no more than a lifeless collection of objects.'[29]

In the contrasting attitudes that German museum workers take toward its post- war continuation, the *heimat* museum can be seen as providing a litmus test by which to separate those who still believe in the primacy of collections from those who now see the museum primarily in terms of public service. Some German colleagues dismiss the contemporary *heimat* museum as beyond the boundaries of the field because, in addition to holding objects, it also serves as an active cultural and social center. For exactly that same reason, other German colleagues consider it to be an especially valuable and viable kind of museum. Outside of Germany, the *heimat* concept has taken on a life of its own. With its emphasis on everyday life and ordinary objects, for example, the Museum of London – which opened in 1976 and which Kenneth Hudson has acknowledged to be 'one of the finest city-biography museums in the world' – might simply be seen as the *heimat* museum writ large.[30]

With regard to neighborhood museums, perhaps the best-known model in the United States is the Anacostia Neighborhood Museum, opened by the Smithsonian Institution in 1967. As an institutional type, the neighborhood museum was described by the late John R. Kinard, Anacostia's founding director: '[It] encompasses the life of the people of the neighborhood – people who are vitally concerned about who they are, where they came from, what they have accomplished, their values and their most pressing needs. Through the various media of its exhibits the museum reflects the priorities already determined by neighborhood people and other community agencies and is, thereby, able to present the issues that demand attention.'[31] Just as few American museums might have had the flexibility to mount the Nanaimo Museum's *Gone to the Dogs*, few might have had the inclination to undertake so bold and neighborhood-specific an exhibition as *The Rat: Man's Invited Affliction*, an early Anacostia project generated by local children and the concern they expressed about the problem of rat infestation in their neighborhood.

Kinard later wrote that it was the *Rat* exhibition that convinced him and his staff that the museum could no longer afford to deal only with life in the past. Its exhibitions, he said, 'must have relevance to present-day problems that affect the quality of life here and now.'[32] That conviction notwithstanding, the museum's focus on its immediate neighborhood was eventually to change. Scarcely more than a decade after the founding of the museum, Anacostia's board of trustees adopted a new mission statement pursuant to which it was to offer a more generalized but still multidisciplinary program dealing with African American history, art, and culture.[33] In essence, it was now to be a community rather than a neighborhood museum, with the understanding that the community it served was to be a national one. In 1987, two years before Kinard's death, the Anacostia Museum officially dropped the description 'neighborhood' from its name and moved from its first site in a converted movie theater to a new, purpose-built facility in a nearby park. In recent years, with additional space at its disposal, its name was changed again to the Anacostia Museum and Center for African American History and Culture.

Neighborhood museums – following the original Anacostia model – have generally been considered in connection with the economically depressed inner city or similar locations, but there appears to be no reason why their use should be so limited. One example of the wider application of the neighborhood museum concept – particularly in its concentration on contemporary issues that affect its constituents – is the remarkable metamorphosis that has occurred at the Strong Museum in Rochester, New York. It was founded as a salvage and warehouse museum almost by default; Margaret Woodbury Strong, its patroness, left it more than three hundred thousand objects after her death in 1969, nearly twenty-seven thousand of them dolls. Several decades into its life and after extensive and even painful consultation with its community, the museum decided to change its original focus and become instead a museum that had special appeal to local families.

From its previous emphasis on life in the Northeast before 1940 – a concentration well supported by Mrs. Strong's collection – it has turned instead to what its director calls 'history that informs civic discourse about contemporary issues.'[34]

Since 1992 the topics examined by its exhibition program have included the cold war, AIDS, bereavement, racism, drug abuse, and health care. It has entered into joint ventures with the Children's Television Workshop for an exhibition built around *Sesame Street* and with the Rochester public library system to integrate a branch library into the museum.

Some observers argue that museums can only achieve this organizational breadth by sacrificing the depth with which they were previously able to address a narrower range of subjects. Others – my Smithsonian colleague Robert D. Sullivan, for one – respond that, whether or not museums are or ever were the most appropriate places for learning in depth, an emerging electronic information environment is rapidly reshaping how information is distributed, and breadth-based learning, typified by the Internet's capacity to provide infinitely branched linkages, will be its hallmark. 'In the same way,' Sullivan says, 'that the printed word as a medium of diffusion encouraged linear, sequential, and vertical ways of thinking, the Internet encourages non-linear, non-sequential, horizontal ways of thinking and connecting knowledge. The instantaneous horizontal connectivity of the Internet collapses time and space and evaporates and/or challenges all efforts by information and knowledge-rich institutions to remain isolated, fragmented, walled chambers.'[35]

For the 'knowledge-rich' American museum to abandon its old scavenger-warehouse business would seem fully synchronous with such a change. All the same, many in the American museum community – and not merely the moderates of whom I spoke earlier – would be reluctant to see museums lose their capacity to deal with knowledge in depth as well as breadth.

New skills for museum management

The second unintended consequence of the American museum's shift in focus away from the care and study of its collections involves the way museums are staffed and how museum workers are trained. Here we enter uncharted territory, but one thing seems clear: Tomorrow's museums cannot be operated with yesterday's skills. Although museums will still require the expertise of the discipline-centered specialists who today hold many of their senior positions, the successful operation of public-service museums will require that those specialists at least share these positions with museum workers of a different orientation and expertise – museum workers who will bring to their institutions a new combination of skills and attitudes.

Along these lines, Leslie Bedford – for many years with the Boston Children's Museum and more recently associated with the Museum Leadership Education Program at the Bank Street School in New York – has proposed the establishment of a training institute that would prepare museum workers for careers in public programing.[36] In her view, a thoroughly trained public programer would be a 'creative generalist' who combines different specialties now scattered both inside and outside the museum. These would include an ability to work directly with community members to assess how the museum might appropriately meet their needs; practical knowledge of how to establish productive collaborations with other community organizations, both for-profit and not-for-profit; understanding of how best to use all the myriad means – exhibitions, lectures, films, concerts, programs of formal education – through which the museum may interact with the community; and knowledge of how to make appropriate use of audience research and various forms of program evaluation.

Going beyond Bedford's proposal, this last skill ought to be in the curriculum of museum-training programs at every level. Its neglect – particularly in management training – may be caused in part by the tangency of such programs with graduate schools of business. In the for-profit sphere, where at least short-term success or failure can be determined from financial and other periodic reports, evaluation simply does not perform the same critical function of measuring effectiveness and distinguishing success from failure that it does among governmental agencies and not-for-profit organizations.

Critical to understand here is the changing standard of not-for-profit accountability. As effectiveness becomes more firmly established throughout the third sector as the overarching criterion of institutional success, accountability will eventually boil down to a single, hard-nosed question: Is this institution demonstrably using the resources entrusted to it to achieve what it said it intended to achieve when it requested and was given those resources? Peter Swords, of the Nonprofit Coordinating Committee of New York, has referred to this enhanced standard as 'positive accountability': being able to show that the resources entrusted to an institution were in demonstrable fact used to accomplish its intended purpose.[37] This positive standard is in contradistinction to what he calls 'negative accountability': being able to show that no financial improprieties have occurred and that all of an institution's funds can properly be accounted for. An organization without the capacity to monitor its outcomes regularly and credibly – unable, that is, to render a positive account of its activities – may no longer be fundable. Nor will meeting such a requirement simply be a matter of appropriate staffing; it will also be a matter of budget. Monitoring program impacts is costly, but it will be no more a dispensable frill tomorrow than filing tax returns or tending to workplace safety are today.

The work that needs to be done is daunting. In many instances it may start with something so basic as getting a museum's leadership to articulate what it hopes or expects its institution to accomplish. That so many museums continue to be so unfocused about their purpose – avoiding any reference to outcomes at all and/or mistakenly defining them in terms of organizationally controllable outputs – is only the beginning of the problem. Compounding it are, first, the extraordinarily wide range of potential museum outcomes – educational, experiential, recreational, and social – and, second, the difficulty in ascertaining the achievement of those outcomes, a difficulty far greater than that in ascertaining the frequently quantifiable results that can be achieved by health and human-service agencies.

Museums may sometimes provide anecdotally recoverable and even life-transforming 'Oh Wow!' experiences.[38] More often, though, the impact of museums on their communities – on their visitors and nonvisitors alike – is subtle, indirect, cumulative, and intertwined with the impact of such other sources of formal and informal educational experiences as schools, religious bodies, and social and affinity groups. Museum management must not only become educated as to how the museum's impact can be captured and described; they must also educate those to whom they are accountable as to what may or may not be possible in rendering their accounts. In no way do these complexities make evaluation any less essential.

On the contrary: Because the value that the museum can add to a community's well-being may not be nearly so self-evident as that provided by an emergency room or a children's shelter, credible evaluation will be all the more critical to the museum's survival.

At the level of institutional leadership, the most important new skill will be the ability to envision how the community's ongoing and/or emerging needs in all their dimensions – physical, psychological, economic, and social – might be served by the museum's particular competencies. The museum has tremendous technical facility in assembling, displaying, and interpreting objects, and a well-interpreted display of those objects may have enormous power to affect what and how people think or know or feel. What then can the museum contribute? Can it be a successful advocate for environmentally sound public policies? In what ways might it help the community to achieve or maintain social stability? Or energize and release the imaginative power of its individual citizens? Can it serve as a site for strengthening family and/or other personal ties? Can it trigger people's desire for further education or training, inspire them toward proficiency in the creative arts or the sciences?

For the newly reshaped American museum to achieve its public-service objectives, even those new skills may not be sufficient. Needed as well may be some attitudinal changes – two in particular. First, museum workers must learn to relax their expectations as to why the public visits their institutions and what it may take away from those visits. Exhibition curators may sometimes imagine a far greater congruence than is really the case between the intensity with which they have prepared an exhibition and the interest that the public may take in the educational content of that exhibition. The public is not a monolith. People come to museums for many different reasons and take many different things out of that experience.

In *Speak to My Heart*, an exhibition opened by the Anacostia Museum and Center for African American History and Culture in 1998, a label text described the community role of the contemporary African American church as 'a safe place to be . . . a haven from the stressful workaday world, a place for personal growth and community nurture, and an outlet for the development and use of natural talents.' How pertinent might such a description be to the museum? Is the museum only important as a place in which to receive the authorized curatorial word, or might it have other legitimate uses as well?[39] That so many different visitors may choose to use the museum in so many different ways should not matter. That it is so open textured as a destination, so adaptable to various public uses should not – at least in the emerging and visitor-centered museum – be regarded as a defect. Rather, it should be understood as one of its greater glories.

The other attitude in need of change involves the museum's relationship to the community. The emerging public-service-oriented museum must see itself not as a cause but as an instrument. Much of the cost of maintaining that instrument is paid by the community: by direct support, by the community's forbearance from collecting real estate, water, sewer, and other local taxes, and by the considerable portion of every private tax-deductible contribution that constitutes an indirect public subsidy from the community. For that reason alone, the community is legitimately entitled to have some choice – not the only choice, but some choice – in determining how that instrument is to be used.

In the emerging museum, responsiveness to the community – not indiscriminate, certainly, but consistent with the museum's public-service obligations and with the professional standards of its field – must be understood not as a surrender but as a fulfillment. The opportunity for museums to be of profound service, to use their competencies in collecting, preserving, studying, and interpreting objects to enrich the quality of individual lives and to enhance their community's well-being, must certainly outdazzle any satisfactions that the old salvage, warehouse, or soda-pop business could ever have possibly offered.

Notes

The late **Stephen E. Weil** was Emeritus Scholar at the Smithsonian Center for Education and Museum Studies and influential museum thinker and writer. The paper was first published in *Daedalus* (summer 1999), vol. 128, no. 3.

1   Notwithstanding that museums throughout all of the Americas might appropriately be so designated, the phrases 'American museum' and 'American museums' are used here to refer solely to museums in the United States. Barbara Franco is director of the Historical Society of Washington, D.C. Her observation was made in conversation with the author, June 1998.

2   Barbara Y. Newsom and Adele Z. Silver, eds., *The Art Museum as Educator: A Collection of Studies as Guides to Practice and Policy* (Berkeley and Los Angeles: University of California Press, 1978), 13.

3   Kenneth Hudson, 'The Museum Refuses to Stand Still,' *Museum International* 197 (1998): 43.

4   Walter W. Powell and Rebecca Friedkin, 'Organizational Change in Nonprofit Organizations,' in *The Nonprofit Sector: A Research Handbook*, ed. Walter W. Powell (New Haven: Yale University Press, 1987), 181.

5   American Association of Museums (AAM), *Museums for a New Century: A Report of the Commission on Museums for a New Century* (Washington, D.C.: American Association of Museums, 1984).

6   AAM, *Excellence and Equity: Education and the Public Dimension of Museums* (Washington, D.C.: AAM, 1992).

7   Ibid., 7.

8   AAM, *Museum Accreditation: A Report to the Profession* (Washington, D.C.: AAM, 1970).

9   AAM, *A Higher Standard: The Museum Accreditation Handbook* (Washington, D.C.: AAM, 1997).

10   AAM, *America's Museums: The Belmont Report* (Washington, D.C.: AAM, 1968).

11   Ibid., 2.

12   From a presentation made during the Smithsonian Institution's 150th-anniversary symposium, Washington, D.C., September 5–7, 1996. The full text appears in *Museums for the New Millenium: A Symposium for the Museum Community* (Washington, D.C.: Center for Museum Studies, Smithsonian Institution, and AAM, 1997); the quoted passage is found on pp. 107–108.

13   ICOM Statutes, sec. 2, art. 3.

14   ICOM *News* 71 (September 1971): 47.

15   Taken from the May 1998 interim report to the AAM board of directors and the
      ICOM executive committee on the summit meeting of the museums of the
      Americas, 'Museums and Sustainable Communities,' San José, Costa Rica, April
      15–18, 1998.

16   See, for example, Judge Richard A. Posner's observation in *United Cancer Council
      v. Commissioner of Internal Revenue*, 165 F3d 1173 (7th Cir 1999): 'Charitable organ-
      izations are plagued by incentive problems. Nobody owns the rights to the profits
      and therefore no one has the spur to efficient performance that the lure of profits
      creates.'

17   J. Gregory Dees' views can be found in two published Harvard Business School
      'notes': *Social Enterprise: Private Initiatives for the Common Good*, N9-395-116
      (November 30, 1994) and *Structuring Social-Purpose Ventures: From Philanthropy to
      Commerce*, N9-396-343 (April 15, 1996).

18   For a basic description of the United Way's approach, see *Measuring Program Outcomes:
      A Practical Approach* (Arlington, Va.: United Way of America, 1996).

19   Nancy R. Axlerod, former president of the National Center for Nonprofit Boards,
      suggested that these negative descriptions of third-sector organizations were no
      less inappropriate than that offered by the father who, on being asked the gen-
      der of his three children, responded that 'two were boys and one was not.'

20   Stephen E. Weil, keynote address to the annual meeting of the Mid-Atlantic
      Association of Museums, Rochester, New York, November 13, 1997.

21   Information about *Gone to the Dogs* and about the Nanaimo District Museum gen-
      erally was kindly supplied by Debra Bodner, the museum's director-curator.

22   All figures are from the data report for the 1989 *National Museum Survey*
      (Washington, D.C.: AAM, 1992).

23   In his 1826 will, through which the Smithsonian Institution was ultimately estab-
      lished, Smithson specifically mandated that it be 'for the increase and diffusion
      of knowledge among men.'

24   Arthur MacGregor, 'The Cabinet of Curiosities in Seventeenth-Century Britain,'
      in *The Origins of Museums: The Cabinet of Curiosities in Sixteenth- and Seventeenth-Century
      Europe*, eds. Oliver Impey and Arthur MacGregor (Oxford: Clarendon Press and
      Oxford University Press, 1985), 147–158.

25   Germain Bazin, *The Museum Age* (New York: Universe Books, 1967), 242.

26   The writings of John Cotton Dana (1856–1929) — beyond question this country's
      most original thinker about museums — were out of print until the publication
      in 1999 of *The New Museum: Selected Writings of John Cotton Dana*, by the Newark
      Museum and the AAM. For an overview of his life, see Edward P. Alexander,
      'John Cotton Dana and the Newark Museum: The Museum of Community
      Service,' in *Museum Masters: Their Museums and Their Influence* (Nashville: American
      Association for State and Local History, 1983). For a selected bibliography of
      Dana's museum-related writings, see *Newark Museum Quarterly* (spring/summer
      1979): 58. For a description of the ecomuseum movement, see Nancy J. Fuller,
      'The Museum as a Vehicle for Community Empowerment: The Ak-Chin Indian
      Community Ecomuseum Project,' in *Museums and Community: The Politics of
      Public Culture*, eds. Ivan Karp, Christine Mullin Kreamer, and Steven D. Lavine
      (Washington, D.C.: Smithsonian Institution Press, 1992), 327–365.

27   Joanne Cleaver, *Doing Children's Museums* (Charlotte, Vt.: Williamson Publishing,
      1992), 9.

28   For a brief history, see Andrea Hauenschild, '"*Heimatmuseen*" and New Museology' (paper delivered at the Third International Workshop on New Museology, Toten, Norway, September 14–19, 1986).

29   Quoted in Alfredo Crus-Ramirez, 'The *Heimat* Museum: A Perverted Forerunner,' *Museum* 48 (1985): 242–244.

30   Kenneth Hudson, *The Good Museums Guide: The Best Museums and Art Galleries in the British Isles* (London: Macmillan, 1980), 102–103.

31   John R. Kinard and Esther Nighbert, 'The Anacostia Neighborhood Museum, Smithsonian Institution, Washington, D.C.,' *Museum* 24, no. 2 (1972): 203.

32   Ibid., 105.

33   Zora Martin-Felton and Gail S. Lowe, *A Different Drummer: John Kinard and the Anacostia Museum 1967–1989* (Washington, D.C.: Anacostia Museum, 1993), 37.

34   Scott G. Eberle and G. Rollie Adams, 'Making Room for Big Bird,' *History News* 51, no. 4 (autumn 1996): 23–26.

35   Robert D. Sullivan is the associate director for public programs at the Smithsonian's National Museum of Natural History. The quoted language comes from 'The Object in Question: Museums Caught in the Net' (unpublished essay presented at the annual meeting of the Visitor Studies Association, Washington, D.C., August 7, 1998).

36   Letter to the author, December 14, 1997.

37   Peter Swords discusses this in 'Form 990 as a Tool for Nonprofit Accountability' (paper delivered at the 'Governance of Nonprofit Organizations: Standards and Enforcement' conference, New York University School of Law, National Center on Philanthropy and the Law, October 30–31, 1997).

38   For a report of one such experience and an argument that such experiences should be given greater weight in visitor studies, see Anna M. Kindler, 'Aesthetic Development and Learning in Art Museums: A Challenge to Enjoy,' *Journal of Museum Education* 22, nos. 2 and 3 (1998): 12–15.

39   I am grateful to Camilla Boodle, a London-based museum consultant, for her suggestion that visitors may find a museum rewarding without necessarily accepting its authority. Conversation with the author, August 1998.

Chapter 4

Museums

Challenges for the 21st century

Christine Burton and Carol Scott

Introduction

SINCE THE 1970S, THE Western industrialized world has witnessed an unprecedented museum 'boom.' This boom is both quantitative in terms of the numbers of new museums established and qualitative in terms of the place that museums now occupy in society. Besides fulfilling the traditional functions of acquiring, conserving and interpreting material culture, contemporary museums are cultural icons in their own right, defining urban landscapes, providing 'symbolic value' for the expression of cultural life and giving incentives to the local economy (Kirchberg 1998: 2).

This boom, though generally perceived positively, may also have adverse consequences as museums compete with one another for a limited market. Kirchberg (1998) notes that in Germany between 1991 and 1996 the number of museums increased by 30% but attendance increased by only 5%. In addition, for the active leisure and cultural participant, the increasing number of leisure options is not confined to museums. New venues and attractions compete for a consumer with less time to spare than ever before.

In spite of the buzz associated with the boom, the demand for museums in terms of attendance does not appear to be keeping pace. The overall trend suggests that the museum sector is struggling to maintain its audiences.

In the United Kingdom, 'Recent statistics show that visitor numbers to museums and galleries appear to be in trouble at a time when a host of new attractions are competing for attention' (Butler 2000: 11). Scottish Tourist Board figures reveal a 15.6% drop in attendance at museums and galleries between May 1999 and May 2000, along with a 30% drop in visitor numbers at heritage sites. This same

Source: *International Journal of Arts Management*, vol. 5, no. 2 (2003): 56–68.

trend has been reported for English museums (Conybeare 1994; Griffiths 1998; Nightingale 1999).

On the Continent, attendance at museums in West Germany declined by 9% between 1991 and 1996 (Kirchberg 1998), while attendance at most culture and history museums in Denmark has dropped by 7% since 1996 (Anderson 2000: 8). Visitor numbers at Italian museums declined markedly between January 1999 and January 2000; attendance was down 23.9% at the Uffizi in Florence, 15.5% at the Palatine Museum in Rome, 20.8% at the Baths of Caracalla and 15–20% at the Palazzo Ducale in Venice (Caton 2000).

In the United States, though a 1997 National Endowment for the Arts survey reported that museum attendance increased from 41% in 1992 to 50% in 1997, there is uncertainty about whether the current boom in American museum attendance can be sustained. Critics point out that the total participation figure masks differences in attendance patterns among different types of museums. Attendance at American social history museums, for example, is not reflective of the overall boom (Lusaka and Strand 1998: 60).

In Australia, the Australian Bureau of Statistics (ABS 1999a) reports that museum attendance declined 12% between 1991 and 1999.

The environment of museum participation

Why is this happening? Why, when more money is being invested in establishing new museums with increasingly high public profiles, is attendance 'flattening' or declining? To address this question, in 1999 the Powerhouse Museum, in conjunction with the School of Leisure, Sport and Tourism at the University of Technology, Sydney, embarked on a study of the nature of leisure in contemporary life and patterns of museum visitation.

This research project was the result of an environmental scan of recent literature, emergent questions and statistical trends. This exercise revealed that there is no simple answer to our question, but that a complex combination of factors are involved, including the profile of museum visitors, the impact of technology, time use, competition and apparently fundamental changes in leisure values and leisure participation.

Who goes to museums?

There is overwhelming evidence, substantiated by research across the globe, that a limited sector of the population regularly choose to visit museums (Bennett 1995; Bourdieu 1991; Hood 1995). Most visitors to museums are well-educated, affluent and versed in deciphering the museum code.

Significantly, however, the increased number and heightened profile of museums over the last 30 years has coincided with the maturation of the post-war 'baby boom' generation. This population phenomenon has witnessed unprecedented numbers of people who are affluent and educated at tertiary levels. The sheer size of this generation, accompanied by the requisite 'cultural capital,' is seen as creating an unprecedented demand for cultural services: 'Part of the middle class, the part created as a consequence of the post-war baby boom, is the real player in this phenomenon. It is this social group, increasingly numerous, affluent, educated and urbanised, that expresses strong cultural demand' (Maggi 1998: 4–5).

The question remains whether this will be a short-lived phenomenon. A combination of a declining birth rate throughout the Western industrialized world and the impact of ageing on the leisure patterns of the current generation is already having an effect on museum attendance. A National Endowment for the Arts report (1996) reveals that the decline in arts participation and museum attendance among the baby boom generation is partly attributable to the increased use of broadcast technology such as television, videocassettes, compact discs and computers.

In terms of museums, the question is the extent to which the combined effects of the ageing of baby boomers and the declining birth rate will affect future attendance.

Enter technology

The impact of broadcast media and home-based entertainment on museum attendance among baby boomers encouraged us to widen the scope of the environmental scan to explore the potential impact of the technological revolution on museum attendance.

Computer ownership, Internet access and the availability of other home-based entertainment systems have grown exponentially over the last 20 years. Two issues interested the research team. The first was the ability of these systems to encourage domestically based leisure with a potential impact on museum attendance. Our scan revealed that more time spent on home computers may indeed result in less 'going out.' Statistics Canada reports that between 1986 and 1992 people spent one extra hour per day at home and that 'the media can lead to reducing the cultural universe of spectators to the dimensions of the household, leading to social isolation and an increasing trend to individualised consumption' (Pronovost 1998: 131).

The scan also raised questions about the impact of technology in terms of the ways in which an emerging generation may be expected to both access information and accord significance to objects.

The hierarchical, linear and narrative structures that characterize the ways in which information is presented in museums differ significantly from the networked information paradigm that computers now make available (Kenderdine 1998). Moreover, as technology enables people to access more and more information across a wide variety of subjects, it is to be anticipated that the subject authority of the museum and its 'transcendent voice' will be challenged (Maggi 1998; Weil 1997).

If the traditional role of the museum is to acquire and preserve objects, the collapse of physical space in this information-based paradigm may require museums to reassess their relationship with objects and collections. In the very near future, the public could demand that museums serve a function that has more to do with interpretation than with the collection and conservation of objects. Information, rather than objects, may be the primary commodity of museums in the future (Anderson 2000; Maggi 1998).

The *virtuality* of experiences offered increasingly through the Internet is blurring the distinctions between what is authentic and what is real. Museums have traditionally been in the 'authenticity' business, but the dichotomy between authenticity and virtuality may not be sustainable. This has important implications for museums that position themselves as offering authenticity through objects alone. 'What it [virtual reality] offers is information, lots and lots of information, and a new, abstract kind of connectedness. What it asks in return is that we shift our allegiance from the physical world to the virtual one' (Hobson and Williams 1997: 40).

The study

The environmental scan had revealed that the areas for investigation were not straightforward. To focus and limit the study, the research partners concentrated on investigating changing leisure patterns within the context of postmodernism and cultural change. This in itself posed a number of challenges, to do not only with definitions but also with aspects of perception and reality of changing work patterns affecting leisure time and choice, new entrant leisure competitors, current consumer behaviour, and the role of the core values of museums within this complex scenario.

Leisure has been defined as 'available' or residual time beyond the obligations of work and family. In the world of the 21st century, the boundaries between work and leisure are becoming diffused. Where leisure was once allocated to evenings, weekends and long annual breaks, the effects of economic globalization and economic rationalization have wrought a change. With globalization comes the demand for business to operate around-the-clock and throughout the year. The result is leisure grasped when available rather than relegated to specific and identifiable times (Caldwell 1998; Gibson 1999).

We wondered if there was evidence for the suggestion that more hours are being spent at work, and, importantly, we wished to explore the possible relationship between increased working hours and leisure choice (Jonson 1998; Pronovost 1998).

We also wanted to examine theoretical positions about postmodern leisure that identify a trend to 'depthless' leisure characterized by fast-paced, ephemeral and entertaining experiences at the expense of intellectual ones (Rojek 1995). The issue for the researchers was to determine whether there was evidence for this theoretical position and, if so, the impact on museum attendance.[1]

Leisure in a changing world

Leisure itself is a multifaceted concept, ever shifting, qualified and dependent on lifestyle, life stages and socio-economic factors. Overlaying this concept are 'leftover' notions of our classic understanding of free time as something that 'should' be used to make us 'better people,' our contemporary lived experience of time stress and overwhelming pressure, and our postmodern consciousness of a fast and fractured existence with multiple leisure choices, from the serious to the superficial.

Museums, once great modernist institutions seen to serve the public well under a model of public good, are now forced to compete in a client-focused environment of leisure consumption. The model of public good is slowly giving way to a model of culture as a commodity and an industry; museums, once the preserve of single narratives, are now being asked to provide – and to market – multiple narratives and multiple experiences for ever hungrier and more fickle leisure consumers.

These two parallel assumptions – changing patterns of leisure and museums unsure and self-reflective of their once secure position – informed the foundation of our research project, Leisure and Change: Implications for Museums in the 21st Century.

Overall, the methodological approach took two distinct but ultimately convergent directions. One concentrated on analysing secondary sources in terms of the emerging theories on postmodern leisure, changes in museum growth and visitor expectations, and the extent to which these assumptions and theories can be substantiated by existing statistical data. The other focused on our own primary qualitative and quantitative research investigating further these theories and assumptions.

Secondary research findings

Chris Rojek (1993, 1995, 2000) is one of the most prolific writers and theorists on the nature of contemporary leisure and cultural consequence.

For Rojek, a postmodern leisure condition is one that is marked by distraction rather than immersion, indifference to the authentic but a curiosity about the simulated or the fake, short-lived intense social interaction, an ever accelerating pace of life, and an ambivalent and contradictory view of risk and contingency in a world that is seen as beyond the control of the individual (1993). Rojek suggests that these patterns of leisure engagement are still speculative and the boundaries of what might be considered modern and what might be considered postmodern are blurred. We are modern and postmodern at the same time, carrying baggage backward and forward and unpacking it as the context demands (1993).

Rojek also maintains that our notion of leisure is caught between two extremes. On the one hand, theorists such as Stebbins suggest that serious leisure – that which can improve the well-being, life chances and social interaction of the individual and community – is still preferable to leisure that is time-wasting, non-productive, anti-social and disengaged (Rojek 2000).

In this paradigm, where might museums position themselves between serious leisure and casual leisure, between the modern and the postmodern?

If these scenarios are not either/or – serious leisure is not always self-actualizing; casual leisure is not always meaningless – the context in which leisure takes place has been influenced by three fundamental conditions: the notion of 'free time,' its perceived oppositional nature to work, and the pace and take-up of technological change.

Our research, informed by different, complex and contradictory theories on the nature of leisure, concentrated on understanding the practice of leisure within the confines of time, work and technology.

We believed that investigating people's practice of leisure and the constraints on leisure would give us some insight into how we might theorize leisure and what impact this would have on one leisure industry – museums.

Time

The Australian Bureau of Statistics defines free time as 'time allocated to social and community interaction and recreation and leisure' (ABS 1998a). This definition implies that there is a rational choice on the part of the individual to 'allocate time' to do something, or even to allocate time to do nothing. It falls outside the notion of casual or anti-social leisure described by Rojek, and consequently could be described as 'acceptable use of time.'

Because of inconsistent data-gathering by the ABS, it is not possible to say that free time has increased or decreased over a period of time or along gender/life cycle lines.

In his comparison of average free time availability, Bittman (1999: 370–371) concludes that there has been an overall increase in free time for both women and men.

It is difficult to draw any conclusions from the data in Table 4.1 alone. In order to state for certain that free time is decreasing for women but increasing for men, we would have to examine other indicators in conjunction with this one. These could include the increase in early retirement for men, increase in paid work (full-time, part-time and casual) for women, restructuring of traditionally male-dominated industries, and increased competition in some industries as a result of globalization and new industry/new economy entrants. Bittman warns that these trends can be cyclical and subject to economic booms and busts, which influence work-time pressure on those in the workforce.

The figures presented in Table 4.1 become more interesting when we overlay them with reports of 'feeling time pressure,' a more subjective measure than the quantitative time diary record. In 1998, the ABS (1998a) recorded for the first time the nature of perceived time pressure on life cycle. The findings were:

—   53% of members of a couple with dependent children always or often felt pressed for time.
—   37% of couples with non-dependent children always or often felt pressed for time.
—   25% of those without children always or often felt pressed for time.
—   41% of lone parents always or often felt pressed for time.

Table 4.1   Mean weekly hours of free time

Year	Men	Women
1974	35.39	32.41
1987	33.04	31.86
1992	35.57	36.58
1997	38.26	35.46

Source: Bittman 1999: 370.

Because there are no earlier statistical data in this area, we are unable to state that these figures reflect perceptions of increasing time deficit or surplus. However, they tend to reinforce Bittman's findings of the extreme time-poor (middle-aged working parents) and the extreme time-rich. Of significance in these figures is the 41% of lone parents feeling pressed for time, compared to 53% of parents with partners.

If this differentiation of free time is all that is available to us, what do people do with their free time?

A comparison of time-use data (ABS 1998a) for the years 1992 and 1997 reveals the following trends:

– decreased time spent on recreational pursuits in general in 1997;
– decreased time spent on sport participation in 1997;
– decreased time spent on audiovisual media in 1997 (although four out of every five minutes of passive recreation was still spent watching TV or listening to CDs/radio);
– decreased time spent talking in 1997 (although women spent more time than men talking and participating in crafts and handiwork activities, while men spent more time than women on computers).

Museum attendance has been steadily decreasing over the past decade. There was a dramatic drop between 1995 (attendance rate: 27.8%) and 1999 (19.9%) (ABS 1999a).

It is interesting to compare these data with those from the national *Recreation Participation Survey* for 1986 and 1991 (the last time recorded) (Department of Sport, Recreation and Tourism 1986; Department of Arts, Sport, the Environment, Tourism and Territories 1991). The figures suggest that visits to museums and galleries were decreasing, while socializing at home, engaging in computer activities and, in particular, shopping were all on the increase – although we should bear in mind the seasonality of some activities and the different methods of gathering data.

Leisure activities that showed increases were shopping (which began to be monitored in 1993), restaurant dining, house maintenance and cinema attendance.

Indeed cinema has been the big winner in attracting audiences. In the past ten years cinema attendance has increased by a staggering 290%. In 1987 it attracted annual admissions of 30.8 million; in 1999 this figure had risen to 88 million (Australian Film Institute [AFI] 2000). Suffering a dramatic decline in attendance primarily as a result of new entrants (videocassette recorders) in the 1980s, cinemas reinvented themselves. The result is that cinema attendance has now become the most popular leisure activity, cutting across socio-economic factors and life cycles, although there is a clear indication that women and young people are the most frequent attendees.

Technology

The newest of new entrants is the Internet and digital technology. It is unclear at this stage what the Internet is replacing as it gathers momentum, taking up residence in more and more homes and becoming indispensable in the work-place. However, a recent study in the United States found that Internet usage is encroaching on social time, replacing old media with new media (60% of respond-ents who were frequent Internet users reported a decrease in television viewing time), encouraging people to spend more time at work and to work longer at home and to spend less time shopping in stores and commuting. Almost half (43%) of US households have Internet access (Nie and Erbring 2000). The most frequent use of the Internet is for e-mail (90%). In Australia the pattern is repeated. Household access to the Internet increased from 14% of all households in May 1998 to 37% of all households in November 2000.

Work

Almost everyone in the workforce believes that they are working more now than in the past, and yet this perception is not borne out by the statistics. What does appear to be happening is a restructuring of a number of key industries, resulting in increasing casualization[2] of the male workforce (although women are more casu-alized than men), a growing perception of job insecurity, and the need to work longer in either a paid or unpaid capacity (ABS 1997, 1998a, 1998b, 1999b).

Even though working hours have decreased over the past century in industri-alized nations, there is some evidence that employees are working more than 45 hours per week, taking fewer holidays and feeling increasingly dissatisfied with the homelife/worklife split (Yann Campbell Hoare Wheeler 1999).

In a survey commissioned by the Australian Council of Trade Unions (ACTU), 55% of respondents worked more than 40 hours per week, with 26% putting in more than 45 hours and 12% more than 50 hours. Only one-third reported overtime payment for additional hours worked. Almost one half felt that health problems had arisen because of the increased working hours. Less than half (44%) indicated that they were happy with the balance between work time and family time.

The results of the ACTU survey reinforce the International Labour Organiza-tion belief, reported by Bittman and Rice, that the new flexibility demanded by industries 'results in a maldistribution of working hours . . . [generating] still more unemployment, increasing precarious employment' (1999: 3). It also reinforces Schor's premise, in *The Overworked American*, that 'the link between economic progress and leisure time in highly industrial societies . . . [has led] to a decline in leisure and that extra productivity has been wasted in an insidious cycle of work-and-spend' (cited in Bittman and Rice 1999: 4).

This overall view of time availability and the choices people make in using that time indicates that, on balance, the less engaged, more simulated and immediately gratifying activities are the winners. There is a perception that some segments of the population are feeling pressed for time and that the pace of work and life is spiralling out of control. This trend has been developing over time and is in keep-ing with the elements that describe a postmodern condition. Yet at this stage it is still only 'facts and figures.' Our primary research attempted to throw more light onto this condition and the free time/leisure choices that people make as a result.

Primary research methodology and findings

When we progressed to the primary research stage, the questions we were interested in exploring were:

- Do people have more or less leisure time now than they did five years ago?
- To what do they attribute this change?
- In terms of leisure activities, what do they do more of now compared with five years ago?
- In terms of home-based leisure activities, what do they do more of now?
- Are there more leisure activities available to them now than there were five years ago?
- Are they spending more on leisure than they did five years ago?
- Do they think of museums as places to go for leisure, and under what circumstances do they visit museums, if at all (holidays, only went at school, only went with parents)?

Environmetrics, a Sydney-based consultancy, worked in collaboration with the research team on administering the qualitative and quantitative aspects of the research, developing guidelines for focus-group discussions and refining our questions for an Australian capital-city Omnibus survey. Both quantitative and qualitative aspects of the research captured attitudes and information from visitors and non-visitors to museums.

Four focus groups were formed: two groups of young people (aged 20–24), one 'museum active' and one 'museum non-active'; and two groups of older/middle-aged people (35–45), one 'museum active' and one 'museum non-active.'

On the basis of the results of these focus-group discussions, a series of questions was developed and administered to 1,100 adults as part of an Omnibus survey in five Australian cities: Sydney, Melbourne, Brisbane, Adelaide and Perth.

Patterns emerging from the qualitative data

Although we expected leisure patterns and time availability to be influenced by life-cycle stages, there were surprising elements, reinforcing many of the assumptions about the contemporary postmodern/modern split. The most striking were:

- A perception that more leisure activities are available to people now than previously and that this change has increased the pace of life. Areas of increased activity cited by participants were restaurants, performing arts productions and venues, festivals and other events, and movies. In addition, participants felt that they had increased their leisure spending and that leisure had become more commodified.
- While some people embraced this range of choice, indeed doubling up on a number of leisure activities to fit them in, others felt overwhelmed and longed for the days of less choice – they were 'lost in leisure.'

- Notions that leisure has to be earned and that time has to be filled: *[If] I have a day off, I can't waste that day – I plan a number of activities* (female youth); *We are addicted to being busy* (female non-museum visitor); *I can't go to the beach if I know there is a chore to do – sometimes I feel I have to set myself a chore . . . I feel guilty if I don't do something* (female youth).
- A blurring of leisure, work and obligation time. Many felt that work encroached on weekends and they doubled up on activities, with entertaining clients as both a work and a leisure activity. Some felt that they were investing in work now to collect leisure later in life.
- Use of the Internet was increasing but there was no perception that it was a substitute for an activity; rather, it was seen as a tool for communicating with friends and family. Of those who spent considerable time on the Internet, there was a perception that this time replaced that spent sleeping, using the telephone, watching television, reading and doing household chores.
- Most participants felt they were working longer hours now than five years ago, although some men had made a deliberate choice to downscale work in order to spend more time with family. In most instances, participants were positive about their work, describing it as *challenging, productive, stimulating, fun, rewarding* and *people interactive*. Negative associations included *necessity, stressful, enjoy it but wish it would slow down, draining, repetitive* and *out of control*.
- Young non-museumgoers felt that going to a museum was something you did at school or over the age of 40. *Once you've been to a museum, you've seen it* (young male). Older non-museumgoers liked the idea of museums but did not think there was anything there for them. Still others indicated that their children were not interested in going and that they perceived museumgoing as expensive. They did not want to take a risk with their leisure time doing something that they would not like or that would be too expensive.
- Young museumgoers perceived museums as one activity among many they were involved with. They felt that they would remain loyal to museum visiting but that this pursuit required effort. Those with children were likely to take them to museum exhibitions for fun as well as out of duty and felt that over the past ten years museums have become better designed and more *user friendly*.

Patterns emerging from the quantitative data

The most popular activity among the surveyed population was cinema attendance, with 79% attending in the last 12 months. This is a higher attendance rate than the national average of just over 62% (ABS 1997). Attendance at a sporting event came in at 51% (national average: 44%). Museum attendance rated 33% (28% in 1997 and 19% in 1999).

In relation to leisure time, the findings were:

- Compared to five years ago, 51% had less time, 31% had more time and 11% had about the same amount of time.
- Younger people were inclined to report that they had less time, those over 50 to have the same amount of time.

–   Changes in availability of time were primarily to do with changes in work-
     ing hours, followed by family obligations, rather than increases in leisure
     choice.
–   The leisure activity reported as increasing most compared to five years ago
     was eating out (56%), followed by movies (43%), pub/clubs (35%), sport-
     ing events (27%), live theatre (21%), theme parks (16%), art galleries (16%)
     and museums (13%). The vast majority of respondents believed they did more
     of at least one activity now than five years ago (80%).
–   The home-based leisure activity reported as increasing most was reading (60%),
     followed by gardening (55%), entertaining (46%), watching free-to-air TV
     (39%), watching videos (37%), using computers (36%), doing nothing
     (22%) and watching pay TV (21%).
–   Respondents who increased their museumgoing also increased their pub/
     clubgoing and home-based leisure.
–   Respondents who reported more leisure time were more engaged with cul-
     tural activities when going out and more likely to switch off or do nothing
     when at home.
–   Respondents who reported less leisure time added only theme park visitation
     to their repertoire and increased their home activity in the areas of enter-
     tainment, computers and pay TV.
–   73% of respondents felt that there were more leisure activities available now
     than five years ago; just under 40% felt that their spending on leisure had
     increased over the five-year period.
–   34% of respondents did not include museumgoing on their list of possible
     leisure activities, while 31% went to museums only when at school. Fifty-
     two percent reported that they usually visited museums while on holiday and
     reported an increase in this activity over the five year period. Those who as
     children had been taken to museums and galleries by their parents were more
     likely to visit as adults and had increased their visitation over the five-year
     period.

Outcomes

In the light of the findings from this study, museums face both long-term and short-
term challenges. In the longer term, museums will be compelled to consider their
role in a postmodern society and key issues, including:

–   How do museums define their core business at the beginning of the 21st
     century?
–   Is this core business of museums sustainable within the context of the
     changing values of the 21st century?
–   How will the changing values of society impact on the core business of
     museums?
     In the short term, museums face immediate concerns related to positioning
     museums in the context of competition and changing leisure patterns, and
     capitalizing on motivation to visit.

The remainder of this paper addresses both the long-term role of the museum within postmodern society and the immediate issues facing museums – strategic positioning and survival in the competitive leisure industry.

Museums in the 21st century

Museums are products of modernity and their development is deeply implicated in the formation of the nation state. But modernism is ending with the new millennium, and with it go many of modernism's key values of stability and permanence, authenticity, grand narratives and even history itself. In a postmodern world, what are museums and what should their role be?

In many ways, the position of museums today is contradictory and ambivalent. On the one hand, they retain many of their traditional distinctive features – their authoritative and legitimizing status, their role as symbol of community, their 'sitedness,' the centrality that they give to material culture, the durability and solidity of objects, the non-verbal nature of many of their messages, and the fact that audiences enter and move within them (MacDonald 1996). On the other hand, they are challenged by new information technologies, increasingly mobile and heterogeneous communities, and the demand for contemporary programs that demonstrate usefulness and 'relevance.'

Within this volatile and changing environment, the final quarter of the 20th century witnessed a dramatic alteration in the relationship of the museum with its public. From a position of unquestioned subject authority and moral superiority in which the museum's role was to variously raise the level of and morally elevate public understanding and refine taste and sensibility, the museum of the late 20th century began to redefine its relationship with its public within principles of increasing equality and democratization.

Critical to the redefining of this relationship were several factors: the emergence of a highly discerning and educated public contiguous with the baby boom generation; the development of a consumer- and customer-oriented society, and the integration of principles of customer service into the public sector beginning in the early 1990s; the conceptualization of a 'new' museology in which the visitor is recognized as bringing a living reality to the museum experience rather than the morally and intellectually blank slate assumed by museums in the late 19th and early 20th centuries; the establishment of principles of institutional accountability for public spending; and the general decline in respect for institutions of authority, public office and professional expertise (Bennett 1995; Weil 1997).

All of these factors in combination have required the museum to reflect upon and reconsider the terms under which it relates to its public.

It is this redefining of relationship that is at the core of what the museum in a postmodern world may become. In this respect, there is some convergence in thinking. Elaine Henmann Gurian (1996) envisages that museums will increasingly have a role as sites of 'safe congregant behaviour' where communities can confront, debate and exchange ideas in one of the few remaining secure public forums, and Weil (1997: 260) sees the museum reinventing itself to become a centre 'available to its supporting community to be used in pursuit of its communal goals.' This reinvention will further alter the power relationship between the authority of the museum and the public. In the near future, he predicts, 'it will primarily be the public' who will make the decisions.

The increasing focus on the public also impacts on the ways in which museums are using audience research to inform marketing and positioning. The museum of the 21st century will be taking account of the changing patterns of leisure participation and behaviour evident in the outcomes of this study.

Consumer patterns

Respondents in all of the focus groups spoke of an increased pace of life in general: *I can't relax like I used to; there is no down time; [I feel pressure to] do more.* This increased pace of life, combined with a perception of less time in which to undertake an increasing array of leisure options, is creating new consumer patterns. In many ways these new consumer patterns are a response to coping with the phenomenon of *more* to do and *less* time in which to do it.

Six consumer patterns were identified from the qualitative research, reflecting the range of individual responses to the phenomenon of doing more at a faster pace and in less time.

Leisure **achievers** cope with the situation through careful planning and good organization of the time available. They are thus able to experience a wide range of activities across the leisure spectrum and are willing to undertake activities alone in order to fit in as much as possible.

Others **double up** by choosing activities that address several experiences in one. These are people who listen to a band at a pub while having a drink with friends or who combine attendance at a concert with proximity to a new and untried restaurant.

While the achievers and the doublers are both characterized by an element of planning, **spontaneous** consumers do not plan at all. These people, identified as an emerging consumer phenomenon (Caldwell 1998), respond to the moment and will choose to do what is on hand when time becomes available. They are generally people in demanding professional jobs that leave them 'time-poor' and prone to making immediate decisions about where they will go that day and what they will do.

There are two other groups that are dependent on external structure and therefore behave more reactively in their patterns of leisure choice. These are the **peer driven**, whose leisure choices are determined by the decisions of others, and the **frustrated**, who find it difficult to cope with the multitude of choices available and who seek situations where the decisions are made for them. These are the people who will respond favourably to a leisure experience that is packaged.

Finally, families have their own distinct reactions to the current leisure situation. Though parents sacrifice their own leisure time to facilitate the leisure needs of their children (driving them to sporting activities, dropping them off at parties, arranging for them to go to holiday camps, etc.), this same emphasis on generation-specific leisure activities results in **fractured family** leisure patterns. Parents experience difficulty organizing whole-family leisure activities.

An additional factor is the ingredient of money. Both the qualitative and the quantitative stages of the study revealed that people are spending more money on leisure activities than they did five years ago. Families, in particular, cite the increased cost of new forms of leisure such as home computers and pay TV, and the difficulty of interesting children in less expensive leisure pursuits such as going to the beach, having family picnics, going for a walk and visiting museums.

The study suggests that museums need to take the following into account in their marketing plans:

–   Museums offer value for money at a time when leisure is perceived to be increasingly expensive.
–   For families, museums offer value for money and a location for needed family time.
–   Promotions need to be customized to take account of different leisure consumption patterns.
–   In a fast-paced world, people are seeking leisure packages that enable them to undertake several activities within a short space of time.

Leisure positioning

It is evident that perceptual factors may create barriers to museum participation. The attributes associated with museums differ from those related to the ideal leisure attraction. Museums are perceived to be in a different field of activity to leisure. The fact that this museum 'field' is an intellectual and educational experience, requiring some of the mental engagement and commitment that is becoming less attractive in today's world, may be a further deterrent.

Moreover, the attributes associated with museums explain to some extent the reason why museums consistently appeal to a subset of the population rather than the population at large. Overall, museumgoers represent a highly educated sector of the population. Familiarity with the museum code is intrinsically linked with class and educational structures (Bennett 1995; Bourdieu 1991). Those who have been socialized into museumgoing at an early age tend to seek an educative element in many of their other leisure experiences as well (Hood 1995).

Interestingly, many museums could legitimately argue that they are offering what the general leisure consumer is seeking. Museums are *fun*, they are *exciting*, they are *good places to take the family* and they offer *great value for money*. However, it appears that museums are failing to capitalize on and claim these attributes to demonstrate the valid synergy between what consumers want and what museums have to offer. Museums have the opportunity to include in their branding not only the attributes that they meaningfully own, but also the attributes associated with an ideal leisure experience.

In positioning, therefore, there appear to be two issues to consider. If museums are to increase attendance, they need to position themselves as attractions with many of the attributes associated with the 'ideal' leisure activity. And museums need to promote themselves as the owners of another set of attributes that are unique to museums.

What makes a museum special?

Museums are what is known in marketing terms as *values* brands. Corporate brands and product brands are familiar. A values brand has an enduring core purpose, which creates a long-term bond with those sectors of the population that share the same values (Kiely and Halliday 1999). Moreover, there is a desire for a lasting future of the brand because of customer allegiance to the brand's underlying values.

Importantly, museums offer more than the short-term experience of a visit. They are valued because they are institutions that contribute to social value. The museum 'incorporates not only objects but, more importantly, the intellectual heritage, the history, values and traditions of society; it also emphasises continuity by suggesting the requirements to preserve what is valued from previous generations so that this may be inherited by the descendants of present members of society' (Department of Finance 1989: 24).

What museums offer differentiates and distinguishes them from the ephemeral, the transient and the depthless. What museums need to celebrate, advocate and promote is their role as catalyst for building social value.

Authenticity

A further distinguishing characteristic of the museum experience is authenticity. We were interested in whether the increasing penetration of simulated experiences and information technology into people's daily lives is compromising notions of what is 'real' to the extent of devaluing the authentic experience of the museum.

The results of the present study are somewhat hopeful in this regard. Though penetration of computer use was high and use of the Internet was increasing, the qualitative research indicated that virtual experiences were not yet perceived to be an acceptable substitute for the authentic experience that museums offer.

However, simulation and virtual reality may emerge as potent competitors, affecting museums' relationship to their publics in fundamental ways. The potential impact of virtual versus real remains an unknown but vexing question. It may be that, in a postmodern world, 'Authentic and unauthentic experiences are no longer placed in contradiction to each other. Indeed the search for the authentic has, in the late twentieth century, become increasingly irrelevant if not abandoned. The authentic has disappeared' (Jonson 1998: 4).

Conclusion

In the emerging leisure environment of the 21st century, museums face a challenge. Less time and more to do serve to put pressure on consumers. New leisure activities that offer novelty and difference test loyalty to the established and the known. A trend to ephemeral and depthless pastimes is juxtaposed with choices that require intellectual engagement. What can museums do to ensure a place in this new, postmodern world?

In our research, visitors and non-visitors may have all agreed that museums were in general a 'good thing' – who would necessarily be against museums or motherhood? When it comes to acting on those beliefs, however, a different picture emerges. They do not really believe that museums are places where they will find fun, excitement or even necessarily emotional or spiritual fulfilment. Many people now believe that other parts of the environment fulfil that aspect of their being. When they search for meaning, they commune with nature as an antidote to the highly consumerist fast-paced lifestyle most embrace.

Our further research is leading us into an exploration of the mind of the consumer: how consumers make choices about leisure and where (even if) museums surface on the landscape of leisure choice. It is our belief that we can begin to reposition museums more meaningfully if we understand in more depth the factors involved in making decisions about leisure. This is not to place in jeopardy the core values of museums in research, scholarship and education, but rather to better understand what value the consumer gives to the sharp end of these core functions: the exhibitions, experiences and environments that are the public face of the museum industry.

Notes

Christine Burton is Director of the Postgraduate Program in Arts Management in the Faculty of Business, School of Leisure Sport and Tourism, University of Technology, Sydney and has extensive experience of cultural planning both in Australia and the UK. **Carol Scott** is Manager of Evaluation and Audience Research at the Powerhouse Museum in Sydney and past President of Museums Australia. This paper was first published in the *International Journal of Arts Management*, 2003, vol. 5, no. 2.

1   That there was some initial evidence for this trend came from a separate research study undertaken at the Powerhouse Museum in Sydney (Boomerang! 1998).
2   Casualization is defined as work that is characterized as non-permanent, contract, temporary or part-time.

References

Anderson, H.C. 2000. 'Entrance Fees Simply Aren't a Major Factor.' *Museums Journal*, October, pp. 8–9.
Australian Bureau of Statistics. 1997. *Cultural Trends in Australia: A Statistical Overview.* Cat. #4172.0. Canberra: Author.
—— 1998a. *How Australians Spend Their Time: 1997.* Cat. #4153.0. Canberra: Author.
—— 1998b. *Part-time, Casual and Temporary Employment: October 1997.* Cat. #6247.1. Canberra: Author.
—— 1999a. *Attendance at Selected Cultural Venues: 1999.* Cat. #4114.0. Canberra: Author.
—— 1999b. *Wage and Salary Earners: September Quarter 1998.* Cat. #6248.0. Canberra: Author.
Australian Film Institute. 2000. *Cinema Industry Data.* Research & Information, AFC, as a supplement to *Get the Picture.* Sydney: Author.
Bennett, T. 1995. 'That Those Who Run May Read: Museums and Barriers to Access,' in *Towards 2000.* Sydney: Powerhouse Publishing.

Bittman, M. 1999. 'The Land of the Lost Weekend? Trends in Free Time Among Working Age Australians, 1974–1992.' *Society and Leisure*, Vol. 21, no. 2, pp. 353–378.

Bittman, M., and J. Rice. 1999. 'Are Working Hours Becoming More Unsociable?' *SPRC Newsletter*, no. 74 (August), pp. 3–5.

Boomerang! Integrated Marketing and Advertising Pty. Ltd. 1998. *Powerhouse Museum Brand Audit and Positioning Options* (in-house report prepared for Powerhouse Museum). Sydney: Powerhouse Museum.

Bourdieu, P. 1991. *The Love of Art: European Art Museums and Their Public*. Cambridge: Polity Press.

Butler, T. 2000. 'Help! People Needed to Fill Huge New Spaces.' *Museums Journal*, August, p. 11.

Caldwell, M. 1998. 'The Spontaneous Consumer.' *Australian Leisure Management*, no. 11 (October/November), pp. 12–13.

Caton, J. 2000. 'Italy's Ghost Museums.' *Museums Journal*, August, p. 26.

Conybeare, C. 1994. 'Visitor Levels Drop Over Poor Summer.' *Museums Journal*, November, p. 9.

Department of Arts, Sport, the Environment, Tourism and Territories. 1991. *Recreation Participation Survey*. Canberra: Author.

Department of Finance. 1989. *What Price Heritage?* Canberra: Author.

Department of Sport, Recreation and Tourism. 1986. *Recreation Participation Survey*. Canberra: Author.

Gibson, R. 1999. 'We're Not Going on a Summer Holiday.' *The Age*, 21 January, p. 3.

Griffiths, J. 1998. 'BM Still on Top But New Growth Elusive.' *Museums Journal*, July, p. 7.

Heumann Gurian, E. 1996. 'A Savings Bank for the Soul.' Paper presented at the 1996 Museums Australia Conference, Sydney.

Hobson, J.S., and P. Williams. 1997. 'Virtual Reality: The Future of Leisure and Tourism?' *World Leisure and Recreation*, Vol. 39, no. 3, pp. 34–40.

Hood, M. 1995. 'Audience Research Tells Us Why Visitors Come to Museums and Why They Don't,' in *Towards 2000*. Sydney: Powerhouse Publishing.

Jonson, P. 1998. 'Leisure in the 21st Century.' Paper presented at the Evaluation and Visitor Research in Museums Conference: Visitor Centre Stage – Action for the Future, Canberra, 4–6 August.

Kenderdine, S. 1998. *Inside the Meta-Centre: A Cabinet of Wonder*. Available: amol.org.au/about_amol/part1/asp (accessed 2 June 1999).

Kiely, M., and M. Halliday. 1999. 'Values: New Brand for the Millennium.' *Executive Excellence* (Australian Edition), Vol. 16, no. 3 (March).

Kirchberg, V. 1998. *The Changing Face of Arts Audiences: The Kenneth Myer Lecture*. Arts and Entertainment Management Program, Deakin University.

Lusaka, J., and J. Strand. 1998. 'The Boom – And What to Do About It.' *Museum News*, November/December, pp. 54–60.

MacDonald, S.G. 1996. 'Theorising Museums: An Introduction,' in *Theorizing Museums*, S. MacDonald and G. Fyfe, eds. Oxford: Blackwell/Sociological Review.

Maggi, M. 1998. *Advanced Museums/Innovation on Museums*. Italy: Fondazione Rosselli.

National Endowment for the Arts. 1996. *Age and Arts Participation: With a Focus on the For the Arts Baby Boom Cohort*. Available: arts.endow.gov/pub/Researcharts/Summary34.html (accessed 6 July 1999).

—— 1997. *Survey of Public Participation in the Arts*: *Summary Report Executive Summary*. Available: arts.endow.gov/pub/Researcharts/Summary39.html (accessed 6 July 1999).

Nie, N.H., and L. Erbring. 2000. *Internet and Society: A Preliminary Report*. Stanford, CA: Stanford Institute for the Quantitative Study of Society.

Nightingale, J. 1999. 'Cultural Therapy for Sale.' *Museums Journal*, May, pp. 39–42.

Pronovost, G. 1998. *Trend Report: The Sociology of Leisure*. Thousand Oaks, CA: Sage.

Rojek, C. 1993. *Ways of Escape*. Lanham, MD: Rowland & Littlefield.

—— 1995. *Decentring Leisure*. London: Sage.

—— 2000. *Leisure and Culture*. Basingstoke: Macmillan.

Sydney Venue Monitor 1999. Sydney: Environmetrics.

Weil, S.E. 1997. 'The Museum and the Public.' Museum Management and Curatorship, Vol. 16, no. 3, pp. 257–271.

Yann Campbell Hoare Wheeler. 1999. *Employment Security and Working Hours: A National Survey of Current Workplace Issues*, ACTU, July 1999. Available: actu.asn.au/campaign/wt/survey/sld001.htm

Chapter 5

Embracing Organizational Change in Museums
A work in progress

Robert R. Janes

Introduction

IN ADDRESSING THE SUBJECT of organizational change in museums, I can-not avoid the topic of management – a topic which is increasingly under fire from both staff and management pundits alike. A cloud has apparently settled over all leadership and management in any form (Greenleaf 1996: 111).

Please consider this description of current management practices (Norfolk Group 1995). A Japanese company and an American company had a boat race, and the Japanese won by a mile. The Americans hired analysts to figure out what went wrong. They reported that the Japanese had one person managing and seven row-ing, while the Americans had seven managing and only one rowing. The American company immediately restructured the team. Now they had one senior manager, six management consultants and one rower. In the rematch, the Japanese won by *two* miles. So the American company fired the rower, who was later rehired on contract for twice the pay. I should add that the Canadian boat in this apocryphal race never left the starting line, because no agreement could be reached on which of the country's two official languages, French or English, should be used in the race.

It has also been observed (Farson 1996: 117) that too many senior managers who may have been at the job 30 years don't necessarily have 30 years of experience – they have more like one year of experience, 30 times.

Seriously, a new and valuable message is emerging, which is that management is a curious phenomenon. It is generously paid, enormously influential and often significantly devoid of common sense (Mintzberg 1996: 61). Although management, especially change management, can be at once impossible and absurd, it is not a lost cause. Lasting change comes only from the adoption of sound management

Source: pp. 71–127 in K. Moore (ed.) (1999) *Management in Museums*, London and New Jersey: Athlone.

principles that are practised on a continuing basis (Farson 1996: 121). There are no quick fixes, no matter how big or small the organization is, or what the particular work happens to be.

In this era of management hype and flavour-of-the-month techniques, one thing cannot be overstated. That is – outside experts do not necessarily know the answers that an organization needs to solve its problems or improve itself (Keating, Robinson and Clemson 1996: 34). In fact, an organization's members are often the real experts on the organization's problems, and on what is needed to improve it. Most museum workers already know the answers to many of their current organizational problems – the only difficulty being that much of this knowledge is tacit, or remains untested. The purpose of this paper is to provide a summary case study of our efforts at change at Glenbow, along with some reflections on what we have learned, all in an effort to make some of the tacit knowledge about change in museums more explicit.

All of us know that change and adaptation occur with great difficulty in museums. My most vivid testimony to this is the death threat I received during the most painful of our organizational initiatives – the reduction of 25 per cent of our staff (Janes 1995). There could hardly be a more stark reminder of the impact of these events on individual human beings than such a threat. Nor is there a more cogent reminder of the responsibilities we have for the decisions we make and the actions we take to ensure the survival and prosperity of our museums.

Significant change requires a form of dying (De Pree 1992: 35), and it is foolish to expect that organizational change will not anger, frustrate and disappoint people. This is especially true when the changes go far beyond cosmetic tinkering. At Glenbow, we are insisting upon new ways of thinking and acting which will make us more responsive to the communities we serve. Change in museums does not have to be a zero-sum game, where progress can come only at the cost of dearly held values (Traub 1995: 60). The key to pushing, without the organization pushing back, is balanced inquiry and action. The indiscriminate use of trendy solutions is as destructive as a stubborn reverence for tradition. Because organizational change is chaotic, uncertain and often mysterious, we have no choice but to try to be as intelligent and caring as we can. In a 1995 survey of 29 North American museums, conducted by Martha Morris (1995) of the National Museum of American History, fully 83 per cent of the respondents said they had recently undergone some degree of organizational change. We should not be surprised by this, nor disturbed, as it is in the nature of complex adaptive systems to change. This is also true of our families, our relationships and our lives (Flower 1995: 1).

Please note that I do not question why museums exist or whether they should be replaced by something else. My main interest is in museums as organizations, a subject which has received remarkably little attention in the museum literature (Griffin 1987: 389). These concerns should not be dismissed as mere process, however, for the manner in which a museum does its work will either permit or preclude innovation, inclusive thinking and the persistent questioning of the status quo, all of which are fundamental aspects of a museum's role. It is undoubtedly easier, and more useful, to try to fix situations, rather than people, by making structural changes in the organization. Circumstances are powerful determinants of behaviour. As someone once observed, nobody smokes in church (Farson 1996: 130).

Most of the issues addressed in this paper are not particularly new or original. Despite this, it is best to view Glenbow's change process as a summary of an experimental work-in-progress, which may be useful in navigating the stormy seas between organizational realities and societal needs. We shall undoubtedly find it easier to change museums than to change the world (Phillips 1995: 3).

A brief introduction to Glenbow

Glenbow's uniqueness lies in the sum of its four parts – a museum, art gallery, library and archives – all under one roof and under one administration. Glenbow's western Canadian research library is the largest of its kind in Canada. The Glenbow Archives is the largest non-government archive in Canada, with 2 million photographs and manuscript collections occupying two shelf miles. Our art gallery, with a permanent collection of over 28,000 works, attracts almost one third of our annual visitors. Our museum includes the disciplines of ethnology, military history, cultural history and mineralogy, for a total permanent collection of 2.3 million objects.

Glenbow does not restrict its work to the city of Calgary. We also operate a rural and special loans program which makes objects available to non-museum environments, including the Calgary International Airport. These programs served nearly 900,000 Albertans last year, as well as visitors from all parts of the globe. To fulfill these responsibilities, we currently employ 86 full-time staff and 33 part-time. We are also deeply indebted to 300 active volunteers.

Continuous change

When I arrived as the new Executive Director in 1989, it was clear that major changes were in the offing. Although Glenbow is remarkably self-sufficient for a Canadian museum, we still require a major contribution annually from the provincial government of Alberta. An agreement to provide this funding had come to an end coincidental with my arrival, and we developed a corporate and strategic plan in 1990 as the basis for securing multiyear funding from the province. All of us were weary of the one-year-at-a-time, crisis management approach common to the funding of public agencies in Canada. Thus began our six years of continuous change, which is still unfolding.

Although financial concerns were a major stimulus for this initiative, there were other reasons which contributed to a perceptible, albeit largely unspoken, desire for change among Glenbow staff. To begin with, Glenbow had been without an Executive Director for a lengthy period prior to my arrival, and the institution was drifting. There was also a widespread belief among staff in 1989 that Glenbow's management was simply top-heavy. All these factors had created dissatisfaction with the status quo, so that even if stable funding from the province had been available, Glenbow was in need of a thoughtful overhaul.

Our corporate and strategic plan was a first for Glenbow, in that it enabled all staff to become involved. This plan was also a first for Canadian museums, in incorporating explicit performance measures and standards, as well as a set of principles outlining how we would treat each other as individuals and as staff (Janes 1995: 18–28). Unfortunately, the provincial government rejected both our plan and our request for multiyear funding out of hand, presumably because multiyear funding was not only a foreign concept to them, but would also mean a loss of provincial control over Glenbow. One cautionary note on planning. At its best, planning can be a synonym for collective learning. At its worst, it becomes a sterile preoccupation. Planning is a tool – no more and no less.

As infuriating as this was, in retrospect there was a hidden benefit to this impasse. It forced Glenbow's executive staff to confront the future with a vengeance, in the face of declining government support. We did some financial projections five years out, and glimpsed a huge deficit and eventual bankruptcy for Glenbow by 1998. A 20 per cent reduction in operating expenses was required. With this kind of massive budgetary reduction, it is impossible simply to tinker with the organization chart. In short, we were confronted with the responsibility and opportunity to renew Glenbow by increasing our capacity for change.

The six strategies

This realization spawned another staff and Board exercise, based on the assumption that people will become committed to that which they help create (Beer 1988: 4). There is no doubt that openness to good ideas is the best assurance of organizational vigour (Boyd 1995: 175). This work resulted in six strategies which are designed to improve our overall effectiveness, increase revenues and decrease expenditures. They continue to guide all our efforts at change. These strategies have been discussed elsewhere (Janes 1995: 29–38), so they will only be summarized here. These strategies include:

1   Developing non-commercial partnership with other non-profit organizations – For example, our Library and Archives have developed an electronic database in partnership with nearly a dozen other archives in the province. This has greatly enhanced public access to our collections, in a cost effective manner.

2   A new form of organization – We recognize that organizational structure must embrace change, not just accommodate it. We also accept the need to reposition ourselves continuously, and that this requires unprecedented organizational flexibility. I realize that this is a far cry from current museum practice based on boundaries and control, but consider the paradox that 'the more freedom in self-organization, the more order' (Jantsch 1980: 40). Two attributes of our new organization are useful examples. We collapsed 22 functional departments into five multidisciplinary work units, and one of these units, the Library/Archives, chose to work as a self-managed team. The director of this unit is elected by his or her peers for a two year term, and staff observe that rotating their director keeps staff fresh, reduces the sense of hierarchy and promotes team work.

We are becoming increasingly comfortable with the idea of organizational asymmetry at Glenbow. An organization will include a variety of coherent groups within it, each of which is a unique entity with different requirements for learning and growing (Keating, Robinson and Clemson 1996: 42). It seems sensible to recognize this.

3   Public service – The main purpose of this strategy is to develop new and creative ways of serving the public, and this has become our most challenging task. We need to become more market-sensitive, not necessarily market-driven.

4   Business processes and cost reductions – The purpose here is to continually examine how Glenbow can simplify and improve its work in order to reduce operating costs, bureaucracy and the weight of tradition. This work is never-ending and requires constant vigilance, whatever the size of the organization.

5   Deaccessioning – Or the removal of objects from our collections. We openly designed and implemented a multi-year deaccessioning plan to sell millions of dollars of high-value objects which are irrelevant to our mandate (Ainslie 1996), in order to create a restricted trust fund which would generate income to be used exclusively for the care of collections. Needless to say, this initiative has been controversial. It has also been successful.

6   Commercial activities – The focus of this strategy is developing business ventures to generate additional revenue, and we started a new business unit called Glenbow Enterprises, which exists solely for this purpose.

None of these strategies is sufficient by itself. Their strength lies in their interaction, and in the balance they bring to our work.

Lay-offs

In addition to adopting these strategies as our blueprint for change, we laid off 25 per cent of our core staff (or 31 people) as part of our plan to become sustainable, with all of the attendant individual and organizational injury. Despite the corporate celebration of legendary lay-off greats like 'Chainsaw Al' Dunlop of Scott Paper and 'Neutron Jack' Welch of General Electric, laying off people is a traumatic and hurtful undertaking. It has taken Glenbow staff well over two years to reconcile the pain, and even so the experience has left an almost gun-shy quality in some otherwise healthy, competent staff.

Repeated lay-offs are not a long-term solution to the difficulties which currently bedevil our organizations, and recent news from the corporate world bears this out. Although lay-offs have apparently become a strategic business manoeuvre to be used in both good times and bad (Tough 1996: 37), recent research in the United States (*The Economist* 1996: 51) reveals that nine out of ten firms which outperformed their industries over a ten year period had stable structures, with no more than one reorganization and no change (or an orderly change) in the chief executive.

There are some lessons in these revelations for museums. To begin with, while downsizing may necessarily be thrust upon us, it must be part of a broader plan. Cuts must be made in the right places, so that the organization reinforces its most promising activities. In doing this, one must ask and answer the two most salient questions – what is the central purpose of the museum and what resources are required to achieve it?

The critically important resources, of course, are people and their knowledge. Once again, there are lessons to be learned from the private sector, where middle managers have endured a highly disproportionate share of the lay-offs. It is important to realize, however, that middle managers often serve as the synapses and memory within an organization's brain (*The Economist* 1996: 51). We took a different approach and asked at the outset of our reorganization – who are the people who own the knowledge which makes Glenbow unique? It turned out that most of these individuals were our department heads – the museum world's middle managers. I cannot imagine where Glenbow would be today without them.

It is imperative to pay particularly close attention to who the knowledge-owners are in a museum, especially if staff reductions are being contemplated as part of a reorganization. Avoid dumbsizing at all costs. This is a recently identified phenomenon wherein management does not realize a given job is necessary until it has been eliminated (Jackson 1996: 87). Posterity will undoubtedly judge the value of corporate restructuring in the late twentieth century. As John Kenneth Galbraith (1994) observed in this regard, 'generally, people have been very resistant to attributing a causal role in history to stupidity'.

Morale and discontent

The individual and organizational injuries which accompany major change necessitate some comment on staff morale, an increasingly complex topic, fraught with both assumptions and paradoxes. Most managers and executives associate 'morale' with a happy and satisfied work force (Farson 1996: 141). In fact, the Webster's Collegiate Dictionary (Mish 1986: 771) says nothing about happiness and satisfaction. Rather, it talks about 'a sense of common purpose with respect to a group', or 'a sense of purpose and confidence in the future'. This indicates that measuring staff satisfaction, something we have done for several years at Glenbow, may not be all that useful. In fact, there is reason to believe that such surveys may foster staff dependence on Glenbow, as satisfaction surveys do not necessarily encourage staff to assume ownership of their problems and to take personal responsibility for effecting change (Janes 1995: 71). It is too easy to answer the survey questions and then sit back and say that 'I've done my part. Now it's up to them.'

Even if this were not the case, one must question whether happiness or satisfaction are necessary to the task at hand. Research has revealed that remarkable and effective people are not necessarily comfortable or happy. They can be ruthless, boring, stuffy, irritating and humourless, and museums, as are all organizations, are dependent upon such people (Farson 1996: 142). Our challenge as museum workers is to allow effective people to prosper in our organizations.

These thoughts lead to yet another remarkable phenomenon – the paradox of discontent. The paradox is that improvement in human affairs leads not to satisfaction, but to discontent, albeit a higher order of discontent than existed before. The psychologist, Abraham Maslow (Farson 1996: 93), advises managers to listen not for the presence or absence of complaints, but rather to what people are complaining about. In very healthy organizations, there would be complaints having to do with needs for self-actualization – such as 'I don't feel my talents are being fully utilized', or 'I'm not in on enough things around here'. These are high-order complaints, compared to complaints about such things as working conditions. This is the paradox. Only in an organization where people are involved, and their talents are being used, would it occur to someone to complain about these issues. Do I dare suggest that museum managers should judge their effectiveness by assessing the quality of discontent they engender? It is something we might well think about, if we recognize that improvement does not necessarily bring contentment, but often its opposite (Farson 1996: 94).

Where have six years of continuous change at Glenbow left us? At first glance, the scorecard is not encouraging. For example, the provincial contribution to our operating budget has now decreased by 39 per cent since 1989/90. In addition, Glenbow's full-time, core staff has decreased from 137 in 1989/90 to 86 today, for a decline of nearly 40 per cent. There is no doubt that we have suffered some major setbacks.

It is also true that many museum employees throughout North America are feeling exhausted, and rightfully so. Six years ago, Glenbow staff and volunteers were thrust into what we believed was a temporary state of budgetary madness, from which we would emerge ready to return to business as usual. We have emerged – stronger, smarter and much leaner – but now there appears to be no rest for the weary.

There is some instruction in this seeming disillusionment, however, which might help us to approach the twenty-first century more calmly and more productively. First, no matter how hard we might will it so, there will be no return to 'normal', whatever that might be. To idealize the past is all too human, even when that 'past' is largely responsible for the discontent which led to change in the first place (Janes 1995: 153). Second, we must learn to live with the notion that we will never find that mythical plateau where we can pause and say 'we have made it'. There will never be a final, desirable state when the change is over.

There may be some comfort, or at least understanding, in the idea that museums need continuous care, not interventionist cures. Henry Mintzberg (1996: 66–7), Canada's maverick management professor, suggests that nursing should be the model for management. This model implies the importance of steady and consistent nurturing and caring. These in turn must be rooted in mutual respect, common experience and deep understanding – not in quick fixes or off-the-shelf management solutions.

The future: opportunities and hazards

Setbacks and fatigue aside, the future is upon us and what follows is a sample of the opportunities awaiting any museum which is poised to seize them. Predictably, these opportunities exist in a world of chaos and ambiguity, alongside a variety of hazards, each with sufficient potential to damage, if not derail, the museum enterprise. These, too, will be identified, along with some brief reflections on what can be learned from all of this.

Creating meaning

Opportunities abound for all museums to fulfill their purpose. That is, to provide some answers to the fundamental question – what does it mean to be a human being (Postman 1990: 55–8)? Our visitors, indeed North American society, are searching for answers. Museums can help; perhaps even show the way. For example:

- A local child attended Glenbow's new and innovative Museum School, the first of its kind in Canada. In an unsolicited letter from this child's parent, we learned that this family's dinner conversation had changed because of their daughter's new-found awe and excitement. The emotion is so palatable in this letter that I get a lump in my throat every time I read it.

Another example:

- At the conclusion of an exhibition commemorating the fiftieth anniversary of the Second World War, our exhibition team hosted a reception for the war veterans who had served as interpreters throughout the show. Unscheduled and unannounced, a frail, 80 year old survivor of a Japanese prisoner-of-war camp rose and spoke. He said that, as a result of Glenbow's exhibition, he now felt recognized and valued as a citizen and a soldier for the first time in his life.

All museums must continually embrace the responsibility of providing meaning to people, and nothing is meaningful until it is related to one's own experience. Meaning, which is really a growth in one's experience (Greenleaf 1996: 304), requires a leap of imagination from the individual's fund of experience to whatever is being communicated. Museums must tempt the listener to make that leap of imagination.

Growing people

The second and third examples are best described as opportunities which have yet to be fully realized, and they have more to do with museums as organizations and how we do our work. The first of these opportunities requires that we promote the growth and development of our intellectual resources more effectively. Most people would agree that museums are knowledge-based organizations, and that the knowledge of our staff, along with our collections, are the most important assets. Although collections management has evolved its own body of method and theory, surprisingly little attention has been given to nurturing professional intellect (Quinn et al. 1996: 71).

It may be that this current period of institutional struggle could result in greater concern for the development of this human potential (Greenleaf 1996: 215). One aspect of this new ethic must be a greater concern for how staff think, feel, act and grow, because growing self-reliant and competent staff is the responsibility of all museums. This must begin with hiring the best people available, and then encouraging their development through repeated exposure to complex, real problems. Perhaps most importantly, leading organizations in various sectors are maximizing their intellectual capital by abandoning hierarchical structures (Quinn et al. 1996: 76), such as the departmental/divisional hierarchy, which is still the hallmark of so many museums. Many organizations are learning that scale can be the enemy of creativity (Farson 1996: 104–5), and that creativity can be stimulated by organizing differently.

One alternative to hierarchy is in the project-based organization, where professionals use self-organizing networks to do projects and solve problems, and then disband when the job is done. This is the true meaning of interdisciplinary work, where the organization's capabilities exceed the sum of its parts. In an ideal world, the most effective organization would be one in which structure develops and changes as a natural expression of purpose (Owen 1992: 138). We are not there, yet, but some Glenbow staff say that we are close at times. In any event, this is the thinking behind our multidisciplinary work units. These work units are actually flexible pools of knowledge and experience, whose members work individually, collectively and across the organization, depending upon the work to be done. There is a refreshing informality to all of this, and our challenge now is to develop a performance management and development system based on both collective and individual work.

The scope for creativity and initiative should be just about limitless in a well-run museum. There are very few other workplaces which offer more opportunities for thinking, choosing and acting in ways that can blend personal satisfaction and growth with organizational goals. These opportunities constitute the true privilege of museum work, and it is up to all of us to seize them. As Charles Handy (1994: 77) writes, 'if we wait around for someone to tell us what to do, we shall wait a long time'.

Collective leadership

The third and last opportunity has to do with the nature of executive leadership in museums. My interest is in the idea of collective leadership, and I wonder if the time has come to experiment with this approach? There are basically two organizational traditions (Greenleaf 1977). In the hierarchical tradition, one person is the lone chief at the top of a pyramidal structure. We apparently see no other course, be it a museum, corporation or university, than to hold one person responsible. All of us know, at least privately, that the 'great man' model of leadership increasingly resembles the emperor with no clothes.

There are many museums where something different is actually happening. A group of people at the top of the organization, with shared responsibilities and clear accountabilities, are developing strategies together, and reaching decisions by consensus. Put another way, leadership is less the property of a person than the property of a group (Farson 1996: 144). This is collective leadership and most closely resembles the second organizational tradition, primus inter pares, or first among equals. This tradition apparently goes back to Roman times, although there is little mention of it in the voluminous leadership literature, nor virtually any references to its use in modern-day society.

The principle is simple: there is still a 'first', a leader, but that leader is not the chief executive officer. The difference may appear to be subtle, but it is important that the primus constantly test and prove leadership among a group of able peers (Greenleaf 1977: 61). Leadership is distributed among the members of a group, with each member playing a vital role, such as taskmaster, counsellor, joker and so on. If one concedes that senior managers often act like self-interested feudal barons (Hout and Carter 1995: 135), and, further, that the chief responsibility of an effective CEO is to foster interaction and interdependence within the senior group, it may be that the primus model could move us one step closer to effective, collective leadership. Why not extend this opportunity and responsibility for collective leadership to all staff, or at least senior staff, to give them the opportunity to provide fresh perspectives and to learn more about the overall operation?

It might be difficult to identify the leader in a group that is working well. In fact, one writer (Mintzberg 1996: 64) suggests that great organizations do not need great leaders – just competent, devoted and generous leaders, who know what is going on. He cites Switzerland as an organization that really works. Yet, hardly anyone ever knows who is in charge, because seven people rotate in and out of the job of head-of-state on an annual basis.

Hazards

In addition to these and countless other opportunities yet to be realized, there are also numerous hazards for museums as the century comes to a close. The term hazard, in this regard, denotes risks and dangers, not insurmountable obstacles or lethal threats. Nonetheless, the hazards discussed are real enough, and they have already demonstrated their capacity to demoralize, demean and otherwise divert museum workers from the task at hand.

Paradoxes

The first of these hazards is the prevalence of paradox in contemporary museum work. Paradoxes are things which are simultaneously contradictory, unbelievable and true or false. The problem is that they can wear us out, or at best, leave us discouraged and frustrated. Consider the following paradoxes:

- at a time of diminishing resources, museums must provide new and creative ways of serving a growing and diverse public, or;
- at a time when a concerted effort must be made to identify new ways of enhancing the sustainability of museums, it is all most can do to keep the wolf from the door. Designing and testing new ideas cost time, energy and often money.

Some of the most useful thinking that deals with paradoxes is that of Charles Handy (1994: 12–13), who notes that paradoxes are like the weather – 'something to be lived with, not solved, the worst aspects mitigated, the best enjoyed and used as clues to the way forward'. He also observes that 'the secret of balance in a time of paradox is to allow the past and the future to co-exist in the present' (1994: 63). Museums can provide this unique perspective on behalf of society, but we are going to have to do a much better job of integrating the past, present and future in our programs and services.

Self-reference

Avoiding the second hazard requires that all museums cultivate their capacity for self-reference (Wheatley 1992: 95, 146–7). This is our ability to be guided by a strong sense of our own competencies as an organization, so that as the organization changes, it does so by referring to itself – meaning the skills, traditions and values which have guided its operations. People in the business world call this 'sticking to the knitting'.

This idea of self-reference is an important one, especially when considering our current financial pressures. There is a growing belief among governments and the public that museums must become more commercial, and embrace the notion that the customer is always right. Although we at Glenbow are adamant about an absolute commitment to public service and maximum self-sufficiency, we must do this in a thoughtful and balanced way, as knowledge-based institutions, not commercial enterprises.

For example, Glenbow happens to host weddings to enhance revenues. However, if hosting profitable weddings means closing public galleries in order to do so, then we are losing sight of our purpose and are no longer engaging in self-reference. We do this at our own peril. The hazard here is a fuzzy sense of self-reference, which can destroy a museum just as surely as it has destroyed those many corporations which have strayed too far from their core business.

Marketplace ideology

The importance of organizational self-reference leads to the third hazard, which Canadian author John Ralston Saul (1995: 2) has dubbed the 'crisis of conformity', or more colourfully, 'the great leap backwards'. He is referring to North America's slavish adherence to the ideologies of corporatism and the marketplace, and to putting self-interest over public good.

The assumption that either business or the non-profit sector holds the exclusive keys to the future must be avoided. As we all know, business has never had a monopoly on virtue, effectiveness or accountability. Business has everything to say about value in the marketplace, but often has less to say on the subject of responsibility, except perhaps to shareholders. At the same time, business is rich in experience when it comes to organizing work, marketing and adding value. Why would we ignore these lessons, especially when we can choose what is most germane to our particular needs?

Having said this, we must not ignore our responsibility to make known the inherent limitations of marketplace ideology for long-term heritage preservation. All custodial institutions have enduring obligations to the dead and to the unborn, as well as to the live customer. Yet the dead and the unborn neither vote nor buy; they have no voice in the dynamics of the marketplace. We must make it known that museum collections are similar to other fundamental resources like the natural environment, in that they are collective property, essential to our identity and well-being, and unable to speak for themselves. There will always be a public responsibility for their care – a responsibility which has nothing to do with the marketplace. Collections are really about our humanistic consciousness (Saul 1995).

Unfortunately, these complexities of time and collective memory seem to have escaped the imagination of many politicians and officials, who are increasingly judging museums by the sole criterion of the number of people through the door. High attendance induced by blockbusters, like profits, are momentary. Both can quickly disappear. It is things like reputation, name recognition and the trust of visitors and supporters which will allow museums to stand the test of time (Flower 1995: 6). In the idiom of the marketplace, this means quality and market share. Museums are, in fact, diversified portfolios. Some of their work can be subjected to market forces, such as restaurants and product development. Other activities, such as collections care and knowledge generation, bear no relation to the market economy, and probably never will. As one famous entertainer observed (Livesey 1996: 25), 'the point of life is not to sell things to make the most amount of money. It's to find your true calling and work that is purposeful.'

Stress

The fourth and final hazard concerns all museum staff, as it has to do with the cumulative stresses and strains of continuous change in our work. We must be aware of the inherent dangers and develop our own stress management programs. Emotions run extremely high when we talk about change in museums, and dealing with emotions, one's own and those of colleagues, is perhaps the most difficult part of the change process. We should always be alert to ideas and concepts that provide some comfort and hope amid all the stress, and several of them will be mentioned here. First of all, it is okay to make up solutions as you go along, because there is no 'right way' waiting to reveal itself or be discovered. This cannot be overstated, as it is fundamental to the creative process. I suggest, however, that it is useful to pay attention to other people's experiences.

Second, do not fear ambiguity. In the museum world, which has raised the practice of 'no surprises' to a high art, few things make us more frantic than increasing complexity (Wheatley 1992: 109). We also have a hard time with questions that have no readily available answers. It is not necessary to fear ambiguity or complexity, however, if we can just give up our preoccupation with details and refocus our attention on the bigger picture. Organizations need order, but they also need its opposite – spontaneity, some chaos and even messiness.

A third source of comfort may be the realization that it is okay to stir things up. It may even be our responsibility. We must do this in order to provoke questions and create challenges. One writer (Wheatley 1992: 116) observes that when things finally become so thoroughly jumbled, we will reorganize our work at a new level of effectiveness. I do not know if this is true, but I am willing to accept it as a possibility. My challenges as President and CEO continue to be balancing the needs of the organization with those of the staff, and determining how deeply I should listen to the negative people whose voices I tend to hear the loudest. Perhaps the biggest challenge is to remain mindful of what we really need to do, rather than relying solely on the things that we are already doing well (Farson 1996: 108).

Finally, it is okay to admit the discomfort one feels as a result of organizational change. I see in retrospect how silly I was about this during the low points of Glenbow's change process. I was too embarrassed to tell my colleagues that I was going to see a counsellor to deal with the distress I was feeling. Stress becomes a hazard when you do not deal with it openly and constructively.

Afterthoughts

Whether it is continuous change, opportunities or hazards, the most important constant for all of us is our attitude towards learning. In the final analysis, all our efforts at change are about learning. This means learning from experience, learning from people, and learning from successes and failures. Learning organizations, as is true of individuals, are those which are skilled at creating, acquiring and sharing knowledge, and then using this knowledge to modify their behaviour (Garvin 1993). Learning really means collectively increasing your capacity to do something that you could not do before (Walmsley 1993: 40). We must consider the very real possibility that we, as individuals, are the predominant creative forces in our own lives, as well as in the lives of the organizations within which we work.

Yet, despite all our efforts at learning, museums are many things at once and none of us will ever know them completely (Morgan 1986: 340–1). Irrespective of the details in this paper, I can claim only a partial understanding of Glenbow. We can only know organizations through our experience with them, which means there can be a huge difference between the rich reality of an organization, and the knowledge we are able to gain about that organization. This continuous learning may help to explain the roller coaster ride which best describes museum life in the 1990s.

At the risk of oversimplifying, three necessities which may help to distill all our efforts at change and growth at Glenbow are worthy of note:

- The first is the need for shared purpose. Every employee must have an understanding of the museum's purpose, and how he or she contributes to it.
- Second, is the need for active experimentation. Most innovation occurs from hundreds of small changes and ideas which add up to enormous differences, and we must encourage such thinking in all that we do.
- Last, is the vital importance of openness. We recognize that there will always be tension between the individual and the organization, but that we must deal with this conflict openly, creatively and in non-manipulative ways. There is no doubt that candid communication requires a balance of power.

These three imperatives are really the test of authenticity in our work.

It might be useful to think of your museum as a Gothic mansion of sorts (Emberley 1996: 278). It is filled with secret rooms and hidden staircases, as well as surprises, some horrors and many unanticipated discoveries. It is full of clutter, sometimes verging on the intolerable, along with a certain amount of rot and decay. At the same time, it is replete with hopes of renovation and renewal. It is both a safe haven and a landmark, and beckons people to come inside – not knowing what they may find. They may even be offended, but surely this is a good thing – is not being offended part of learning how to think (Emberley 1996: 240)? The message is clear – our work in museums is full of possibilities and pitfalls, most of which can be used, adapted or confronted.

So, if reality is the pawn of ideas, and there are few, if any, assurances about the outcome of our efforts at change, where does that leave us? Personally, I take heart in the words of Charlotte, the gray spider, in E.B. White's wonderful book, *Charlotte's Web* (1952: 64). Charlotte said:

Never hurry,
Never worry,
Keep fit
And don't lose your nerve.

We at Glenbow can only aspire to Charlotte's advice, because we hurry all the time, we worry a lot and I have no idea how fit each of us is. But, we have not lost our nerve, and we have no intention of doing so.

Note

Robert R. Janes is former President and CEO of the Glenbow Museum in Calgary, Canada. He is the Editor-in-Chief of the *Journal of Museum Management and Curatorship* and a museum consultant. This paper was first published in Kevin Moore's edited volume, *Management in Museums* (1999).

References

Ainslie, Patricia (1996) 'The Deaccessioning Strategy at Glenbow, 1992–97', *Museum Management and Curatorship* (Elsevier Science Ltd.), 15 (1): 21–35.
Beer, Michael A. (1988) 'Leading Change', *Harvard Business School*, Note 9-488-037 (Cambridge MA).
Boyd, Willard L. (1995) 'Wanted: An Effective Director', *Curator*, 38 (3): 171–84.
De Pree, Max (1992) *Leadership Jazz* (New York: Bantum Doubleday Dell Publishing Group, Inc.).
Emberley, Peter C. (1996) *Zero Tolerance: Hot Button Politics in Canada's Universities* (Toronto: Penguin Books Canada Ltd.).
Farson, Richard (1996) *Management of the Absurd* (New York: Simon and Schuster).
Flower, Joe (1995) 'The Change Codes'. Internet address: http://www.well.com/ user/bbear/change_codes.html.
Galbraith, John K. (1994) Interview, *The Financial Post*, Toronto, 2 July 1994.
Garvin, David A. (1993) 'Building a Learning Organization', *Harvard Business Review*, July–August: 16–31.

Greenleaf, Robert K. (1977) *Servant Leadership* (Mahwah, NJ: Paulist Press).

—— (1996) *On Becoming a Servant–Leader: The Private Writings of Robert K. Greenleaf* (D.M. Frick and L.C. Spears – editors) (San Francisco: Jossey-Bass Inc.).

Griffin, D.J.G. (1987) 'Managing in the Museum Organization I. Leadership and Communication', *The International Journal of Museum Management and Curatorship*, 6 (4): 387–98.

Handy, Charles (1994) *The Age of Paradox* (Boston, MA: Harvard Business School Press).

Hout, T.M. and Carter, J.C. (1995) 'Getting it Done: New Roles for Senior Executives', *Harvard Business Review*, November–December: 113–45.

Jackson, Tony (1996) 'Corporate America is Dumbsizing', *The Financial Post*, 25 May, p. 87.

Janes, Robert (1995) *Museums and the Paradox of Change* (Calgary: Glenbow).

Jantsch, Erich (1980) *The Self-Organizing Universe* (Oxford: Pergamon Press).

Keating, C., Robinson, Thomas and Clemson, Barry (1996) 'Reflective Inquiry: A Method for Organizational Learning', *The Learning Organization*, 3 (4): 35–43.

Livesey, Bruce (1996) 'Gimme, Gimme', Financial Post Review, *The Financial Post*, 28 September, pp. 24–5.

Mintzberg, Henry (1996) 'Musings on Management', *Harvard Business Review*, 74 (4) July–August: 61–7.

Mish, F.C. (Editor-in-Chief) (1986) *Webster's Ninth New Collegiate Dictionary* (Springfield, MA: Merriam-Webster, Inc.).

Morgan, Gareth (1986) *Images of Organization* (Newbury Park, CA: SAGE Publications, Inc.).

Morris, Martha (1995) 'Survey on Strategic Planning, Organizational Change and Quality Management', Unpublished report available from the Deputy Director's Office, National Museum of American History, Smithsonian Institution, Washington, DC.

Norfolk Group (1995) *Norfolk News*, Fall/Winter, Calgary, Canada.

Owen, Harrison (1992) *Riding the Tiger: Doing Business in a Transforming World* (Potomac, MD: Abbott Publishing).

Phillips, Will (1995) 'Red Alert For Museums: A Crisis in Response Ability'. Part I, Extended Version. Unpublished paper available from the author.

Postman, Neil (1990) 'Museum as Dialogue', *Museum News*, 69 (5): 55–8.

Quinn, J.B., Anderson, P. and Finkelstein, S. (1996) 'Managing Professional Intellect: Making the Most of the Best', *Harvard Business Review*, March–April: 71–80.

Saul, John Ralston (1995) *The Unconscious Civilization* (Concord, Ontario: House of Anansi Press Limited).

The Economist (1996) 'Fire and Forget?' *The Economist*, 20–26 April, pp. 51–2.

Tough, Paul (1996) 'Does America Still Work?' in Forum, *Harper's Magazine* (May), 292 (1752): 35–47.

Traub, James (1995) 'Shake Them Bones', *The New Yorker*, 13 March, pp. 48–62.

Walmsley, Ann (1993) 'The Brain Game', *The Globe and Mail Report on Business Magazine*, April, pp. 36–45.

Wheatley, Margaret J. (1992) *Leadership and the New Science* (San Francisco: Berrett-Koehler Publishers, Inc.).

White, E.B. (1952) *Charlotte's Web* (New York: Scholastic Book Services).

Chapter 6

Museum Staff Perspectives on Organizational Change

Glenbow Museum Staff

Susan Kooyman

SUSAN KOOYMAN IS AN ARCHIVIST with Glenbow's Library and Archives. She spearheaded a two-year project which developed a computerized finding guide to the manuscript collections. During the reorganization, the Library and Archives lost both a head librarian and a chief archivist. Instead, this area now operates as a self-managed team, and elects its own director for a two-year term.

'I love the challenge of change – the idea that you can just jump in and do the work. The stress comes with the idea that you're never going to be a master in your field. We are now being told that that is not going to happen. It's something you see throughout society. It means that you can never relax and look around you and enjoy the fruits of your labour. You can't be old and venerated for a lifetime of knowledge. It's frustrating. You have to develop the stamina to be constantly relearning, re-inventing, the rest of your life. Similarly with automation, the work is never done; a database is a living, evolving thing. At no point is a project ever done, you're constantly revising and adding to it; and the technology is constantly changing, being upgraded, becoming obsolete.

'Archives stood still for 50 years, but in the last 20 years, radical changes have been introduced. We used to set our own standards and each archive had its own peculiarities. We now have professional standards and suddenly there's a set of rules: what to acquire, how to appraise, how to describe things.

'The expectations of the public have changed and sped up with automation. For example, the fax machine has made a big difference. You can see it in the types of requests. The researcher who writes a letter, for example, is usually older. They

Source: Robert R. Janes (1997) *Museums and the Paradox or Change*, Calgary: Glenbow.

write in a rather formal style, giving details of what they need. They don't expect a reply to their enquiry for a couple of weeks or even a month.

'The people who fax want something and they want it right now. They fax in the morning, and usually it's in a casual style, no salutation – the request is sometimes more like a demand – and they want the information by noon. They're on the phone in the afternoon asking where the information is.

'It's often easier to deal with phone enquiries. It gives us a chance to explain that we have limited staff and to clarify what they need and when we can deliver it. But then with voice-mail, people leave long messages and they expect timely responses. You can come in in the morning and have seven voice-mail messages waiting and as you try to deal with one, two more come in. Voice-mail artificially leads people to believe we can get back to them right away.

'In terms of doing less with less, we made a conscious decision to dedicate more time to work on the arrangement and description of our collections. We had completely neglected that part of our work in order to deal with researchers. Now we have two archivists on the reference desk and the rest work on the collections. The public may have to wait a minute or two; in that sense, we made a conscious decision to decrease public service, but not to a level that will affect their needs.

'We have introduced fees for service. There's a philosophical struggle. Archives have always been free. With the Provincial Archives, for example, there's a belief that the taxpayers pay to have these records available. It's a little different at Glenbow. We've started to send out bills to researchers. Ten dollars minimum for minor photocopying and mailing, more for research time. We send the information with a form that says, nicely, why we are charging and please send us the money, with 7% GST, in the enclosed envelope.

'It's surprised us. In the records storage area, we asked for voluntary donations from donor organizations for the costs of caring for collections, $35 a metre. Forty percent of the organizations have voluntarily paid us, half came with letters of thanks for the service, and saying, bill us every year. We never even considered charging before the fees for service came up. But it's no problem, and we've brought in over $5,000.

'When we received a Canada Council grant to do a description of the holdings as a repository guide, we switched over from our old manual system. It helped the Archives get used to the whole idea of change because when the reorganization came, the computer had enabled us to link our holdings intellectually – the photos, manuscripts and other media. This enabled us to combine the reference desks. We used to have separate photo archives and manuscript archives. We changed that to one central reference desk, one spot for reference services. The Library and Archives share the same software; the public can go to any computer in the room and find everything we have.

'We've stopped being specialists, we're now generalists with specialities. Ultimately, we're all trying to make our records available to our users. You never hear anyone here say, "it's not in my job description." We all serve our users. It's amazing how we've streamlined procedures. We are really working together as a team in the Library and Archives.

'We are a self-managed team and we take it quite seriously. We don't have to ask permission on issues like whether we should open on Saturday afternoons.

We have frequent, spontaneous brainstorming sessions, and experiment. In the old system, you had department heads talking to assistant directors, then reporting back "no." It was very frustrating. I love this whole self-management thing.

'It's challenging for the elected director. I think they feel like an MLA (Member of the Legislative Assembly), answerable to their constituents (us!). The director of Library and Archives represents our needs to Strategy Group and communicates back from them to us. The director position is really a communication device, *not* a boss. They are elected and when their term is finished they go back to where they were before. None of us have ever been management before, so it's easy to fit back into the team structure.

'Every single day of our life, we understand our purpose. But I can never stop and put my feet up. That worries me more than anything. It's burning us out. There's no slow period.'

Joe Konrad

The late Joe Konrad started at Glenbow in October 1980 as comptroller. After a week, he became assistant director, administration, then chief financial officer, Board secretary and now chief financial officer and director, Central Services. 'This is a place of a thousand titles,' he laughs.

'There's been a radical change in the management at Glenbow. It used to be top-down management. You saw that in the budget process. It used to be me sitting down at my kitchen table over the weekend and saying to everyone on Monday, here's your budget. Now the process is the other way. We go around and ask people what they need, then we do a "reality check" together and adjust the budget needs to the revenues. We're asking people to be responsible and by and large they have been. But that's a break in tradition.

'I prefer this management style – it's the way I prefer to operate – mentoring, providing advice, making suggestions. It's results-oriented and you leave people to decide how they can best achieve those results. That's not appropriate in a top-down structure, and I've been criticized in the past for taking that approach. In the old days, you'd let everyone know what results you expected, but it's different now, people are more involved. I think it's the only way people can grow and I think it works. Ninety-eight percent of the time people appreciate being treated that way. I think there's still some confusion about who's responsible for what. Not everyone on staff can step in and get something done. It takes longer this way. Our security department, for example, was a very top-down operation, but that's changed a lot. People like it if you involve then in coming up with new ways of doing things.

'We still have a few hold-outs, but I think they're trying. We've reached a stage when we have to start producing results. Personally, I think we've done enough orientation, talking about public service, strategic planning – we have to produce some products. Now's the time to do it. I'm not sure we've proven we have the capability to do that right yet.

'The whole relationship between union and management has changed. It began to change during the layoffs. We were open, and involved the union in financial matters. Everyone used to play the game, you don't play all your cards. You always have to behave that way, it's set up by legislation but it's just not necessary. There's no reason to hide. We tried to move negotiations in that direction. We can negotiate, but we're not protecting shareholders; we're not generating profits here. Yet we were locked into this goofy procedure of confrontational negotiation. Now it's issues-based. We don't take a position on issues. We both look at the contract and decide how we can resolve issues so both sides win. It's quite different. We have a joint management/union committee that is trying to create working conditions that work for employees and for Glenbow. I much prefer this.

'I work closely with our Board and there's been changes there as well. We very much have a working board right now. They seem to require more information, more timely information. Knowledge is power and they need information to make decisions.

'We also have a union person sitting in on the Board meetings, as an observer but they also contribute to the discussion. That's relatively new. The union wanted a full representative on the Board, but our Board is very small and we need everyone on it to raise money or contribute specific expertise.

'I think we had to change. It was clear that we couldn't continue to sustain ourselves at the levels we were spending. We were effective, but not necessarily efficient. We had to find a better way.

'In the reorganization we avoided some of the mistakes corporations made. They eliminated middle management, but we felt that's where our depth of knowledge was and we tried to keep the people. Saving that knowledge base was kind of unique and maybe that's what carries us through. We didn't extend a blanket offer of early retirement, like corporations do. In that way, they often lose their most marketable people who go out and start their own businesses. I was really hopeful that in keeping this knowledge-base and expertise, we would move ahead. I think it's taking a little longer than a lot of us had expected.

'People in this business are not entrepreneurial; that isn't what makes them good at their job. They're academically trained, they use established research methods. It's more difficult for them to think in terms of cost-recovery: What's most efficient? What don't I have to do? We haven't formally gone through in a systematic way, and identified low-value work and chucked it.

'But it has to change. Our photography area is a good example. We've always provided publication-quality photographs, but now we're asking what the customer really needs. They may only need a reference print. It doesn't always have to be a Cadillac; people sometimes just want Chevys. And it works. It's market-driven. I'm not sure we're very good yet at finding out what the market wants. We're still learning. But I'm optimistic.'

Kirstin Evenden

Kirstin Evenden is a recent graduate from the University of British Columbia. She came to Glenbow in October 1993 as an independent intern, working with senior curator of cultural history, Sandra Morton Weizman, on research for an exhibition on growing up in western Canada. She continued with Glenbow on a contract to coordinate the Youth Curator Project, a regional initiative sponsored by the Alberta Museums Association to involve Alberta youth in museums.

'I came because of Sandra Morton Weizman. I'd heard about her approach in making museums relevant to communities. I'd heard about the institution, that it was well-respected, and willing to take risks, to try interdisciplinary things. I was an independent intern. I'd finished school, so I didn't have the backing with the university. Glenbow was one of the few institutions that was willing to be flexible. I don't think a lot of people in the museum community take professional development of young people seriously. It's a lot of work; I understand that.

'Specifically I worked with the childhood project. I shared similar interests in feminist social history and the social history of childbirth. The project gave me an exposure to a whole variety of things. I was an *ad hoc* member of the exhibit team and I learned about the politics of team projects, about curatorial and programming roles. I had a lot of freedom and I was given a lot of challenges. I wrote labels, an article for the magazine and did a lot of research.

'I had a six-month internship which was very good. Most are for four months over the summer. That extra two months gives you time to figure out what's going on and to develop your skills.

'Glenbow was in a state of flux when I got there. Everyone was really busy with the new fourth floor exhibits, but they were focused and that gives a sense of purpose and unity. But I'd hear little comments all the time, and I'm certain being an intern created some worry that I was doing the work that other people should have had.

'The state of flux continued after completion of the fourth floor. Morale worsened; a lot of people finished their contracts and left.

'There's the old-fashioned idea of curators as keepers of the knowledge. People my age know there are no permanent jobs. Contracting is the next best thing we can do. It also means you can do really fun stuff. I like working in a team, but I'm also very self-directed. As a contractor, if you find someone who can take up your idea and run with it, it's great. But there's also risk-taking, and you wonder where your next meal is going to come from. I tell the teenagers that jobs don't exist, work exists. It's good to be multi-skilled. That way you have lots of different people circulating and that means the product is different, but also the process is different too.

'The thing that I've noticed about Glenbow is that it is much more bureaucratic than, say, the community museums I've worked on with the Youth Curator Project. At Glenbow, it's like you have to go through five people to get one decision, whereas in smaller institutions, five decisions will be made by one person.

'Working with adolescents on the youth project, I've noticed that people at Glenbow find it out of the ordinary to have teens around. There wasn't a lot of comfort with that age group. There's all this talk about having a noisy vibrant place, but it actually gives some people conniptions. I really realized how quiet a place this is.

'There's a difference of attitudes between baby boomers and Generation X, my generation. We don't have delusions about having permanent places of work. We know we'll probably have five or six jobs, totally unrelated, probably more project-oriented. We have to be flexible. My training is issues-driven, not object-driven. That's not necessarily a generation shift, but a shift in academic training.

I'm interested in community outreach. I am interested in working outside of these four walls, but *for* these four walls.

'I spoke with one guidance counsellor at the high school who was late for a meeting because she was dealing with a suicide attempt by one of the students. Another teacher gives out gift certificates for food because some of his students don't have enough to eat. And then you come back to Glenbow and find people sitting around talking about how to improve public service. It's so arrogant. Most people don't have that luxury.

'High schools are noisy, crowded, smelly, hip, alive, vibrant, totally exhausting. I think all museum people should do a little secondment in schools so they can learn about audiences. There's diversity in our society; schools are full of them.

'The change in structure at Glenbow meant that doing something like the Youth Curator Project was feasible. I don't think every museum would be able to do it. Glenbow should be proud for taking it on.

'One of the problems of museums is the high culture/local culture division. I see high culture as paintings on the wall, objects behind the glass, not necessarily interpreted very well. Generation X – my friends, are very cultured but they don't necessarily visit the museum. They like interesting films, interesting television, books, pop culture. They are into seeing new and different things.

'Some people my age had a bad experience with history in high school. It's like pulling teeth to get us to think about history. But I tell the students on the Youth Curator Project that history is a tool. It's a means of getting your point across for contemporary issues. That's why history is important; it informs the way I behave every day as a woman in this culture. They sort of get it. It's a hard link – making history relevant as a way of connecting with local, community and personal identity.'

Dennis Slater

Dennis Slater is a curator/writer at Glenbow who also takes on programming responsibilities for Glenbow's international collections. A typical day may include working with an enthusiastic group of high school student writers, planning a tattooing workshop, interviewing a First Nations veteran from the Second World War and teaching an evening class in African art. Change for him has meant being laid off from his position as assistant curator in Glenbow's ethnology department where he had worked for 15 years and transferring to a permanent half-time position as curator/writer with a new work unit, Publications and Research. He is physically separated from the ethnology collection and has had to shift his focus and his professional priorities.

'The layoff was hard. At that point, I had worked here for 15 years. I'd gone through the ranks, and knew the collection intimately. Being laid off told me that that didn't matter. Separating me from the collection added insult to injury. I felt disoriented, betrayed, unacknowledged and unrecognized.

'Certain people still haunt the social structure of the building. I don't think the contribution they made to the social structure was recognized. Reluctance, social rapport, guilt, fear – that doesn't show up on organization charts. When you've worked with someone closely, bounced ideas off them, got creative sparks and then suddenly one of you is gone, there's a lot of grief, coping. It's hard to talk about it.

'Eventually I embraced the chaos. I said if this place is different, I'll be different too. I can build a different place for me here. I had to sit down and ask myself questions about my profession – what is a curator now? Professionally, I'm not a curator in the traditional sense – I see myself as a writer with collection interests. But it took a year to get that in my head. I now see the collections and their potential very differently. I no longer inhabit that definition.

'Right now Glenbow is like one of those snowflake balls. Everything has been turned upside down. It's in confusion, no one knows how to get anything done.

'We're in a period of transition. We say that the new structure is flatter, meaner, but it's all rhetoric until we act upon it. There's a great deal of residue from the old hierarchical structure.

'This place has tremendous potential. Two years later, I can say that this change was a tremendous idea but to develop it into what's intended is going to take time. A learning organization is as close a definition of chaos than anything else. Before, the organizational way you got things done was you were on a ladder and if you were in most favoured status and more aggressive in meetings, you got things done. Hierarchy strangled a good deal of creativity.

'Now if you have an idea, you can go to people and make it fly. I take a free-wheeling Cossack approach. Let's take a look and see if we can make it work. There's more problem-solving now. Before the change, decisions were solved at the top of the structure. Now it's been turned upside down, and anyone has the right to ask questions.

'Before, there was a good deal of myth-making – the staff wasn't allowed to talk to the Board – the model was that those at the top have the wisdom to make good decisions. We realize more now that these are just humans and they make mistakes, but some people are still allowed to make more mistakes than others. The forgiveness and encouragement level varies from unit to unit. There are pockets of belief. This polarity makes things unbalanced. There is insecurity in a climate of creativity.

'The responsibility quotient is so high, people knock themselves out. Juggling 20 things at a time is certainly stressful, but it's exciting.

'The greatest possibilities lie in putting people with the greatest differences together. I like it if people see different things. A climate of respect is crucial. There's an energy when you put like and unlike together and some surprising creativity. The work units allow us to interact. We're creating a climate of teams. Socially, teams teach you. Teams can be dynamic, respectful. There's a good potential to adapt, to be flexible, creative, think differently.'

Lisa Christensen

Lisa Christensen's recent life with Glenbow has been marked by almost constant upheaval. She was laid off as curatorial assistant of art in Glenbow's art department during the reorganization, then hired back as the new volunteer manager. After a year in the position, she applied for and was accepted into the position of associate curator of art with Glenbow's Collections Management unit. During the strategic planning process, she worked on the team investigating new forms of organization for Glenbow.

'It's tougher to do things now. Change has been going on so long, it takes so much time to make decisions. There's so much policy and process. The apathy of people gets you down. People are not in the jobs they want to be in. One colleague refers to part of her "new" job as degrading and humiliating. People are quick to use change as an excuse, even three years later. When you say, let's redo the new acquisitions case, for example, you hear, no we can't do it. The reaction to change makes it very easy to say we don't have enough staff. Everyone respects that and they back off.

'I fear for my profession within the scope of Canadian institutions. We have designers curating shows. It is more important to be pals on a team than to ask who has training and sound knowledge of the collections.

'I really believe in the theory of Bob's change. I don't believe we've evolved enough as a human race to pull it off. It would be great if all of us were nice and helpful and accommodating to other people but people have their jobs to do and sometimes you have to put your foot down. Too much time is spent weighing opinions and everyone's contribution and trying to do this team thing gets in the way of being able to weigh the decisions based on your knowledge of an area. Specialities exist for a reason.

'The work ethic has not really changed – people still work hard, tasks get done, the in-boxes are emptied, but there's no greater respect for each other's contribution than before. Public service hasn't become automatic, and no one takes action because they are too busy, not their area, etc. By not taking action, all the internal stuff continues. Human nature is simply not there yet.

'In retrospect, we had this big wheel of Glenbow to turn but instead of fixing the bumps, adjusting the air and straightening the alignment, we just went out and got a different wheel. We still have a big wheel that's just as tough to turn. We are evolving back to where we were.

'Personally, I'd probably be a lot further ahead in the old system even in my old "lower status" job. Now, I have this title but I am still a glorified curatorial assistant according to my job description. All of the other things, I do outside of my actual job, just like before!

'But many good things have happened. Ethnology, cultural history and military history collections are being shown more – there's a real push to display them. I mourn the art collection, there's been no art program. The community gallery is great until just recently and it is still very tenuous with no clear focus. I admit that to my delight I have more time to research the collections, doing label copy and processing loans, so my knowledge of what we have is getting better all the time.

'I've learned a lot about myself and how much my ego was caught up in my (curatorial) title. I was devastated when I was laid off, even though I knew it was coming. I sort of had to take a breather and get myself together again.

'Most of all I miss the peer support, the casual discussions of ideas and possible programs, the personal development. Within the old art department, if something was put forward and found to be a sound idea, you could proceed – that was fabulous, and when it would happen – everyone knew their role in it. It's not so easy anymore. A lot of people aren't too enthusiastic. Roles have changed so much, some key roles don't exist anymore.

'Teamwork allows too much room for discussion. Members of the team drag out discussion over the design instead of relying on the designer's specialized knowledge. The curators have to compromise standards to keep the group happy. Keeping our staff happy shouldn't be what Glenbow's about.

'The new form of organization I hoped for wasn't based on what's on the organizational chart. It was a workplace with a very clear and very obvious work ethic. I thought we would all grow into this ethic and it would become the core of everything we do. This ethic was characterized by people who wanted to work hard, who were mature, who were sure of their roles and empowered to achieve the goals set out personally and institutionally.'

Valerie Cooper

Valerie Cooper joined Glenbow in March 1994 as manager of volunteer resources. She was hired three weeks before Glenbow's major fourth floor gallery redevelopment opened to the public and an important volunteer recognition event. Some of the volunteers she met with had been with Glenbow for years and were confused and distrustful of the change situation. They felt alienated and left out of the picture. Valerie's natural enthusiasm was put to the test immediately.

'I was so excited. I didn't have any baggage about Glenbow. As soon as I walked in, I thought, this is a new position, created after restructuring, I'll have an opportunity to develop a volunteer program which benefits the whole organization.

'I've been through downsizing before. It's really quite political. People who have been left behind are grieving for lost friendships and working relationships. I felt that some Glenbow employees thought they could do my job and were angry that they hired outside instead of recruiting internally.

'I enjoy strategic planning and visionary work. When there's low morale it takes a lot of energy to reroute people. The volunteer program needed structure. The volunteers still wanted independence, but we gave them structure, and they could articulate roles so they feel some comfort in the direction Glenbow's heading. We have volunteers sign partnership agreements between themselves and Glenbow now. We record hours, we are seeing healthier, more productive work from our volunteers and increases in the requests for volunteers from staff.

'I started feeling comfortable about last November, seven months after I started. That's a reflection of the volunteers having an extra year to adapt to change. But comments like "this was the best Christmas party we've had in years" indicate that people are starting to thaw. Once the social side of things opens up, there's good discussion at other levels.

'This is a new, different, exciting way of working. There's an opportunity to try what you think, to be innovative, both professionally and in the industry. There's a big sense of accomplishment in making it work. People respect your expertise, and there's new collegial alliances between lateral staff members and management.

'Change is positive, maturing, challenging, and it doesn't happen at the same time in a large organization. It's a way of life in the 90s, the only way to survive is to learn to deal with stress, learn how you want to position yourself in your organization, in business and in the community.

'Volunteers are professional and well educated. They have limited time, and they have a need to touch base with their inner calling whether that's family or the community. Volunteer participation in the last ten years has taken off like crazy. It's part of the business plan of most non-profit organizations and many for-profit businesses.

'There's a strong future for volunteers at Glenbow. We offer many volunteer opportunities and require increased volunteer involvement which enables staff to carry out their work. The bottom line is that staff numbers should remain low and we should increase our volunteer involvement in fundraising and other areas of Glenbow. We are continuing to build a diversified volunteer skill base. Volunteers are more actively out in the public. Glenbow volunteers have a more concentrated exposure in our community.

'Volunteer resources is increasing its accountability in terms of what exactly our volunteers are doing and why. We have 300 volunteers and we recently did an interest inventory. The volunteers really appreciated the phone call. They really liked the idea that they could work in other areas of the museum. Others just liked what they are doing and wanted to stay there, which is great too!

'I have a lot of sympathy for what's gone on but I'm looking ahead. What's that saying – "lead, follow or get out of the way." It gets to that point after time has passed and people are eager to move on.'

Wendy Smith

During the reorganization, Wendy Smith moved around the building. A secretary in the production department, she was moved to secretary for the newly formed Glenbow Enterprises work unit where she worked for both the shop staff and the fundraising area. She waited several months for a director to be appointed to her work unit and several months until Enterprises staff worked out a strong working relationship. As a result of mutual decision and shared responsibilities among colleagues, Wendy became functions coordinator responsible for renting Glenbow galleries and theatre out for private functions, coordinating catering and even assisting with wedding arrangements.

'I really feel like I'm able to accomplish things here. In other areas of the museum, people are overloaded and their area might not exactly be their speciality. We're brand-new – Enterprises didn't exist. We're a revenue unit, and it's all up to us as to how it would work out. I haven't had any special training as functions coordinator. I'd done rentals before and loved it, but never expected to draw on those skills at Glenbow.'

Wendy has been with Glenbow six-and-a-half years, a length of time which surprises her. It's gone quickly and for the most part, she enjoyed the variety of jobs. Being in limbo, not knowing her role in the newly formed work unit was difficult.

'Being in limbo, it's a problem with self-image. You can't slot yourself. I wanted sometimes to leave, to go somewhere where there was structure. I'm not afraid of losing my job – there's no such thing as job security – I really believe that. In this job I'm really independent and there's an outside focus. Constantly dealing with the public brings you back to what it's all about really quick. I'm out there in the "real world" every day.

'We've come a long way and we all make mistakes,' she laughs. 'I'm always coming across things I've never done before. But we're not put down for trying. It's our own fault if we get overstressed. I like to be exposed to different things, to maybe do it once and try something new to see what it's like, but then sometimes I forget to stop doing it and end up with all this work.'

Wendy enjoys the independence of her position which encourages and depends on her taking the initiative. 'I have to make my own decisions. My director can't walk me through this.

'I'm a people person and I knew that given the right choice and chance I could be a good connection to the public. This job focused and channelled that and developed that within. In turn, it's given me more confidence. Failures are successful stepping stones. I see a new attitude coming around in Glenbow. Now it's more "help me with this, I'll help you, we'll all benefit."

'I didn't realize how long change was going to take at Glenbow. It's like gaining weight, it takes a long time to put it on and you can't take it off in two weeks.

'To **do** new is different than to **think** new – some people still can't adapt. Maybe they feel their job is at stake. I must say, I'm happy to have a new attitude. I don't like to stay stagnant. I like new things, to see progress and to be part of progress. When stagnant it becomes a vicious circle, no confidence, in limbo. I never used to think about things like this, but the restructuring made me look into myself. Where do I want to go? What can Glenbow do for me? What can I do for Glenbow – do I stay or do I go? Once you figure that out, what's right for you, it's right for Glenbow. It's a win-win situation, and I'm really glad it happened to me.'

Jim Shipley

Jim Shipley is a professional photographer and works with a Calgary photo lab. It is only recently that he has been able to come into Glenbow comfortably to visit friends and make professional calls. For more than eight years he was a photographer and darkroom technician at Glenbow, an active member of the union and enthusiastic instigator of staff social events. He was laid off on February 22, 1993.

'It's taken until January this year to be able to look at Glenbow and not feel hurt.

'I thought I was going to survive the layoffs. It was only about a week beforehand that I started hearing rumours that my happy little picture might not work out. I'm an eternal optimist and I suppose I did say what if that happens, well we'll deal with it when it happens.

'The counselling wasn't useful for me. It wasn't very organized; they didn't seem prepared and weren't able to give really good advice. Most of it was common sense, positive reinforcement. I didn't take any of the courses – I had a pretty strong idea of what I was going to do.

'I had my business already set up as an independent photographer. But with leaving Glenbow and the pressure, and the baby (Jim became a parent subsequent to the layoffs) – the time you thought you could do things in was cut in half. Also, I didn't have the portfolio to support the commercial end. I'd done museum-style photography and black and white work, but Glenbow doesn't have a colour lab and I didn't have that experience.'

Jim kept his studio and photography work, but took on a full-time job as a sales rep with a photo lab, a job where he draws on his photography knowledge with his outgoing, persuasive, conversational style.

'My learning curve has just skyrocketed. That part of "Life after Glenbow" has come true. The money is nowhere as good, and I'm working twice as hard. I really miss my third Fridays! Looking back, people in the photo lab at Glenbow have a very easy job.

'I've learned what's required to take a business and run with it. People who run their own businesses are workaholics. You have to be. I realize that I'm not. I work hard, but I know what to do with my free time. Getting laid off put a crimp on me financially, but I didn't have to sell my house.

'Professionally I found I was quite well regarded. I was a photographer, I had run a lab. Glenbow has a good reputation, it never hurts you to be from Glenbow. But I know a lot more professionally now. The politics of Glenbow get in the way sometimes, the in-house meetings and politics. Also Glenbow doesn't have a colour lab and there wasn't really any talk about digital photography. Well I have to sell it now, so I have to know it. I'm taking some courses. You have to get up to date. Everyone's working that way now. Photo labs and presses, and pre-presses and graphic houses, all the services are overlapping.

'I have a sense of confidence. It took a bit of a beating, the four months between February and August when I left Glenbow, I just had to hang around – it was a sad time. I felt like I was being ignored and was only getting vague answers. That's the kiss of death for some people. When you're laid off and you come back on term or contract, and you truly love this place, you feel like a fifth wheel.

'It did hurt – why me? That's just the way it is. I would have bumped, I had more seniority, but I figured, no. But then when I was hurting financially, I started thinking, what if I'd fought and stayed. That was the source of my angst.

'When you're laid off, you're still an employee of the company. You feel dumped off. Time heals everything – that's an old saying, but some sayings are old because they're true.

'We have 12 people where I work now, the boss is the owner and when he wants something done, he pitches in and does it too. At Glenbow there was a lot of meetings, and things had to be passed on for union and management approval.

'I feel better now. If I got canned tomorrow, I'd still feel bad, but I know a lot of people now – business is who you know. So I know I could survive.'

Gerry Conaty

Gerry Conaty, senior curator of ethnology, was hired as head of Glenbow's ethnology depart-ment, but within two years of his hiring, he was moved to a new work unit, separated from his collections, and became part of a team fast tracking a multidisciplinary exhibition on warriors around the world. He now works in the Program and Exhibit Development work unit, and has developed significant relationships between Glenbow and the First Nations.

'I was hired in October 1990 as head of ethnology. Bob had come here as director the year before and that was a big drawing card, I was really interested in being
somewhere where there was a possibility of making the First Nations an integral
part of the institution without the bureaucratic politics. Bob had a reputation
for being in the fore in terms of developing community and native relations with
museums in the North. I was interested in the collections but more for the kind
of relationships they could create with the First Nations. Museums need native
people to be a more visible part of what we do and sometimes that can happen
through the collections. It's the kind of basic research that curators should be doing
all the time – continually talking to the people from whence the objects came; every
time you talk to someone, you learn a little bit. You can stare at an artifact for
years, but when you are in a context where that object is being used, suddenly you
can see it in an entirely different way.

'The restructuring in February 1993 perhaps wasn't as big a change for me as
it was for many long-time employees. My adaptation started in October 1990 when
I joined Glenbow. The strategic plan was in place and I was trying to figure it out
and find my way around Glenbow. That takes a while. Then the renovations and
development of the new fourth floor galleries happened. It was pretty difficult to
create a department "feel" or "thrust" while the fourth floor was the priority. There
wasn't time for me or other staff to relearn and rethink how to do exhibits. We
just had to do it. There was a two-year deadline. It took the entire time just to do
the nitty gritty work for an exhibition without being innovative. I was still learning Glenbow politics, the relationships with the Board. Bob was learning at the same
time. We began lending sacred objects to communities and looking at cultural artifacts differently. So for me the change really started on October 1, 1990.

'I didn't find the strategic plan all that new – I had been used to yearly planning and evaluation in my previous job. Also, I think graduate school can really
teach you how to plan long-term research projects.'

In February 1993, 18 of Glenbow's departments disappeared and staff were
reallocated into six multidisciplinary work units. Gerry was assigned to Program
and Exhibit Development, which didn't have a director at the time. His ethnology
colleagues were now working on projects in different work units. He, along with
other department heads, felt alienated, lost, devastated.

'After the layoffs it took a little while to notice the change. I really noticed it
when the Collections Management unit started to form as a group. Beth and Seema
(ethnology colleagues) were in Collections Management and that unit was up and
running. They were going ahead without consulting me as their department head
which they would have done before the changes. I was away from my collections.
I moved into the conservator's office for a while, and then moved down to a small
office on the fifth floor, so I was physically separated from the collections.'

Gerry was no longer a department head and there was no director for his new
work unit. His role at Glenbow seemed ambiguous. Several Glenbow curators have
seen their role change from research and care of the collections to facilitators, reflecting the new shift towards public service and teamwork.

'I am concerned about the standards of the research we undertake. The museum
ethnologist's role has changed immensely over the past decade as First Nations have
demanded (rightly, I think) a greater say in how they are portrayed in exhibits and

programs. But to really understand what the First Nations are saying about their own cultures, it is important for curators to spend a great deal of time with native people and to experience, as much as possible, First Nations cultures. Then we can begin to use our curatorial knowledge and skill to create exhibits which are meaningful to First Nations and which give non-natives a glimpse into native cultures. But these exhibits and programs must be the product of cooperation and consultation between curators and natives.

'I worry that, in the absence of discipline-based departments, there will be a diminished impetus for curators to maintain a high level of community-based research. In the face of shrinking budgets and increased demand for more exhibits and more programs there will be growing pressure from senior management to abandon time-consuming consultation. As curators, we may end up developing exhibits with only minimal and uncritical research. Or, we may hire academic experts from outside of the institution and serve only as facilitators, enabling them to develop exhibits. In either case, Glenbow may well lose an important knowledge-base — a base which is vital if we are to continue as an important cultural centre and educational institution.'

Much of Glenbow's exhibition and programming work is done through multidisciplinary teams where curators, designers and programmers, sometimes with outside advisors, develop themes and storylines for exhibitions. Gerry Conaty worked on the *Warriors* team, developing an exhibition gallery discussing warriors through the centuries and around the world.

'Teams can be very good. I see a difference between interdisciplinary and multidisciplinary teams. Interdisciplinary are when curators of different disciplines – ethnology, art, military history, cultural history – and programmers or designers bring their own perspectives of their discipline and work out a theme. *Warriors* worked like that. It started with the curators of military history and ethnology looking at our collections and talking about the similarities and differences. That was the fun part. Then we needed a programmer to contribute the perspective of "how do you want people to feel when they look at things." In a multidisciplinary approach, a theme is developed and you bring in objects from different cultures to illustrate it.

'Would I apply for my job today? My feelings on this are ambiguous. Bob no longer fills a mentorship role for me, partly because we don't meet that often to discuss issues of mutual concern, and partly because I sense his focus has shifted from native studies to management studies. I also feel that after five years of developing good relationships with the First Nations and setting some precedents in this area, there remains great confusion at Glenbow about our role and relationship with First Nations. I'm not sure how the Strategy Group perceives this relationship or how they would support further developments.'

Donna Livingstone

Donna Livingstone is director of Publications and Research, and has been with Glenbow for eight years, first as editor/assistant manager, marketing and public relations and then as head of publications. Prior to the reorganization at Glenbow, she had not held a management position. As director of Publications and Research, she is responsible for a work unit of eight people and for developing Glenbow's long-term publishing program.

'Several things have saved me. First, the fact that I didn't have any managerial experience has been a blessing in some ways. I didn't have a history in running a department in a certain way or old managerial practices to retool for the new flattened organization. Everything was new, including the work unit, so that has made it easier for me. I could start from scratch.

'Second, our work unit is the smallest and most easily focused, and the people in it are highly articulate, outspoken, creative and supportive. I think working with this particular group of people has made my learning curve as a manager much easier. It's also been humbling. I thought that I had all the publishing answers and that I would just chart the path and everyone would follow. Well, working in a team situation has meant that the path becomes much more interesting, there's a lot of bends and curves and sometimes I'm the one who follows. It makes me laugh; it makes me crazy, but I always look forward to our next meeting. There's a great comfort in working with a good team.

'Also, my history with Glenbow has helped me. I've been here during severe cutbacks and during glorious blockbusters and have come to realize how amazingly resilient we are. Museums and museum people are survivors. The funny thing is, we don't really believe we are. At least once a month in the last eight years, someone will come up to me, shake their head and say, "It's never been this bad, people are stretched to the limit, we're not going to survive." It reminds me of Scotty on the *Enterprise* telling Captain Kirk "The engines will never hold, sir. She's going to blow."

'The engine that holds Glenbow together is the people who work here. It's a terrifically creative, critical and cranky bunch. Everyone works far too hard for far too little money, and they do it because they care about what they're doing more than any business I know.

'The reorganization has been the biggest thing we've ever gone through as an organization, and I think we're surviving even this. We're not on steady legs yet, but we're surviving. It has been a long, exhausting, searching kind of experience that has made us all question our values, our professionalism, our futures. When you dig that deep, you have to come up with a different way of doing business. And a greater honesty I hope. We're too thin on resources to play games any more. There's no time.

'All this strategic planning makes my palms itch sometimes. I get impatient. I want to *do* things, show some results. It's taken three years, but it's finally starting to sink in that the new organization, the new way of thinking, is a result. It's ongoing, but it's a tool to do the things we do better. We needed to go into that kind of detail, to ask those painful questions in order to change. My epiphany may have come earlier than others' because I'm involved directly in the strategic planning and heard the language sooner. But we're starting to see the tools of change in action.

'The biggest change I've noticed is that we're starting to listen. Museums have been so big on communicating, so eager to tell all our stories that we forget to listen. Well we're starting to listen – to teenagers, to visitors, to corporations, to researchers, to community groups. It's starting to sink in that we don't have all the answers and that the knowledge we have has a lot of dimensions. On the other hand, it doesn't mean that all we do is listen or that we pander to the lowest common denominator. I believe that we can do sparkling, creative, exciting, intelligent things with the extraordinary resources we have here. I know that sounds like Pollyanna, but so what. People remember her because she wanted to do things. How many cynics' names do you remember?

'The one thing that worries me is that we haven't figured out how to say no. It's like smoking, I guess: you can only quit if you want to. I don't believe we want to give anything up. It gets back to caring so much about what we do. We can't comprehend that any of the work we do is of low value. Yet we all want to take on new projects. What we have to figure out is how to do the important core work, but in a different way, that allows us room for new ideas, new projects. That's the next challenge.

'I once told a colleague that there isn't a week that goes by at Glenbow that I don't come in to work convinced that this is the day they're going to find out that I really don't know what I'm doing. She pointed out that we're trying to break new ground all the time, so maybe I really don't know what I'm doing. That was rather unsettling, but comforting too. It means it's okay to experiment, take a few risks. They don't always work, but you always end up a little bit ahead, a little more limber. To go back to the Star Trek analysis, we're not on the old *Enterprise* anymore. Maybe it's more appropriate now to follow Captain Picard's directive and "Engage."''

Note

Various staff at the Glenbow Museum contributed to this chapter which was first published in Robert R. Janes' book *Museums and the Paradox of Change: A Case Study in Urgent Adaptation* (1997).

Museum Management

Introduction to Part Two

Richard Sandell and Robert R. Janes

. . . organizations end up being what they think and say, as their ideas
and visions realize themselves.

G. Morgan, *Images of Organization*, p. 133

I N RECENT DECADES, THERE has been growing recognition among museum
professionals of the potential that management theories and practices hold
to enable their institutions to clarify purposes and goals, to organize their wide-
ranging resources in more efficient and effective ways to meet stated objectives,
and to respond proactively to the challenges and opportunities presented by
change (Fopp 1997; Janes 1997; Moore 1994). The growing significance of management in museums can be attributed to a range of factors, including declining
public funding, the shifting expectations of audiences and other stakeholders,
new forms of competition, increased pressures for accountability, and the
emergence of new roles and priorities. Although once widely viewed as unnecessary and irrelevant, inappropriate and undesirable, management has become an
increasingly integral part of museum practice and consequently mission statements,
strategic plans, staff development initiatives and performance measurement systems are now familiar aspects of everyday working life for most practitioners.

Although museum management has undoubtedly achieved growing prominence, it has remained a neglected field of research until relatively recently
(Moore 1998). Early writing on the topic was framed by a degree of uncertainty
about the role, potential dangers and future significance of management in
museums but, today, a much broader consensus about its value is reflected in
a burgeoning and increasingly sophisticated body of literature. The selection of
articles in this section of the Reader reflects this development in thinking and
attitudes. Both academic researchers and museum practitioners provide a variety
of critical perspectives on wide-ranging aspects of museum management and

present the findings of empirical investigations that have pursued more specialized lines of enquiry, very often fuelled by emerging practice-driven imperatives.

In the for-profit sector, a considerable number of studies have been directed towards identifying the attributes and approaches to management that are shared by the most highly performing business corporations, in an attempt to distil lessons from which other companies might usefully learn. The best-known of these is perhaps Peters and Waterman's (1982) landmark study, *In Search of Excellence*. Adopting a broadly similar approach, Des Griffin and Morris Abraham present the findings of an in-depth study of the effectiveness of museums that draws on quantitative and qualitative data from over 30 museums in five different countries. Their comprehensive and detailed analysis highlights the management characteristics shared by effective museums including, among others, cohesive leadership, a strong sense of shared values, good communication, concern for staff training and development, the strategic use of resources and a focus on achieving positive outcomes for audiences. This opening contribution usefully highlights many key themes which are pursued in greater depth by subsequent contributors.

The articles by Peter Drucker, Eva Reussner, and Emlyn Koster and Stephen Baumann are concerned, in different ways, with the purpose, priorities and strategic direction of museums and science centres. The late Peter Drucker, an influential and renowned writer in the field, offers a provocative account of board–management conflict in a fictional university art museum that, although first published nearly 30 years ago, nevertheless resonates with contemporary debates surrounding the evolving roles and priorities of museums. Reussner brings marketing thinking to bear on the subject of strategic management and proposes a conceptual model with which, she argues, museums can achieve their audience-focused missions while simultaneously reconciling the demands of other constituencies. Koster and Baumann place the mission and programmes of the Liberty Science Center in New Jersey in the context of growing international interest in the potential for museums to operate as agents of social change. Their thoughtful account of the reorientation of the institution highlights the benefits and challenges in the adoption of a socially relevant and responsible mission.

Museums are increasingly called upon not only to have a clear sense of purpose and direction, but also to devise ways of assessing and evidencing the achievement of their goals. Carol Scott discusses the difficulties bound up in attempts to measure the social value of museums and she highlights the need for approaches that can capture their complex, long-term and unique outcomes. The late Stephen Weil similarly argues that museums must develop methods and techniques that will enable them to capture the differences that they make to the lives of the individuals and communities they serve, while he also cautions of the dangers inherent in adopting inappropriate measures.

The articles by Richard Sandell and Kirsten Holmes shed light on different aspects of human resource management in museums. Reflecting broader concerns in management thinking and drawing on concepts and approaches developed in the business environment, Sandell explores the controversial issue of workforce diversity. Reviewing approaches that have been deployed to redress the skewed nature of the workforce with which museums have tended to operate, he argues for the adoption of an integrated, museum-specific approach to diversity management. Museums are somewhat unusual in their reliance on voluntary workers and yet, as Holmes points out, relatively little in-depth research into the motivations and experiences of the latter has been carried out. Her revealing study suggests new ways of thinking about this important resource and challenges many of the assumptions on which approaches to volunteer management are based.

The remaining three articles in this section reflect the growing international interest in the issue of leadership in cultural organizations. What constitutes effective leadership, what qualities do successful leaders possess and what part do they play in shaping organizational performance? Sherene Suchy blends approaches from management, psychology and the business world to examine the characteristics of directors in major art museums and highlights the organizational conditions that can facilitate strong leadership. Stuart Davies explores leadership in relation to questions of organizational purpose and direction as embodied in mission statements. His analysis of the functions that leaders perform, and the qualifications and qualities they possess, helps to challenge the widely held assumption that leadership is necessarily confined to the activities of a single individual at the head of the institution. Finally, Robert Goler's empirical investigation into the topic of interim directorships focuses on the period of transition associated with a change in organizational leadership and explores the impacts of different management solutions on both individuals and institutional culture and performance. The specialized nature of this perceptive investigation reflects the increasing maturity of the field of museum management research.

References

Fopp, M. (1997) *Managing Museums and Galleries*, London and New York: Routledge.

Janes, R.R. (1997) *Museums and the Paradox of Change*, Calgary: Glenbow Museum and the University of Calgary Press.

Moore, K. (ed.) (1994) *Museum Management*, London and New York: Routledge.

Moore, K. (1998) *Management in Museums*, London and New Brunswick: Athlone.

Morgan, G. (1986) *Images of Organization*, Newbury Park, California: Sage Publications.

Peters, T.J. and Waterman, R.H. (1982) *In Search of Excellence: lessons from America's best-run companies*, New York: Harper and Row.

Chapter 7

The Effective Management of Museums

Cohesive leadership and visitor-focused public programming

Des Griffin and Morris Abraham

Introduction

THIS IS THE FINAL PAPER of a project commenced in 1995 which has explored
what constitutes effectiveness in museums. From experts we sought *assessments*
of effectiveness for a range of museums (and an indication of the extent to which
research, collections, public programs and marketing contributed to those assessments) and from staff of those museums we sought responses to a *questionnaire*
on management practices (see Methods below; the questionnaire is printed as
Appendix A): the assessments and questionnaire responses were compared. We
accept Kahn's definition of effectiveness (in Goodman *et al.* 1981: 240), 'meeting
the constraints and meeting or exceeding the goals specified by the dominant coalition [of constituencies]'. Further, outcomes should be related to the policy framework in which the organisation works and to the objectives the organisation seeks
to achieve (Osborne *et al.* 1995). We recognise that what constitutes effectiveness often depends on who one asks – different constituencies have different views
deriving from the nature of their exchange with the organisation – and that effectiveness is a construct both value-based and time-specific, a political rather than
scientific concept (Kanter and Brinkerhoff 1981). We have used approaches to the
assessment of effectiveness which attempt to mirror the perceptions of significant
constituencies, rather than ones which those who manage and work in museums
think are appropriate.[1]

So far this project has identified a suite of some 28 items as characterising those
museums rated by experts as most effective – by reputation (Griffin *et al.* 1999).
These include a concern for quality, shared goals, good communication, attention
to training and strategic allocation of resources. Cohesion – working collaboratively

Source: *Museum Management and Curatorship*, vol. 18, no. 4 (2000): 335–368.

towards common goals in the context of shared values – is a common feature: this includes senior managers working together as a team, goals of the museum supported by staff, goals of departments cohesive and well integrated, staff encouraged to respect the skills and contribution of others, a high degree of commitment by staff along with a high sense of involvement, and so on. Whilst the responses to all these items from more effective museums differ significantly from those for less effective museums, the correlations between the questionnaire responses for those items and the assessments are not always statistically significant.

In the more effective museums, public programming emphasises strategic approaches to achieving positive outcomes for visitors including provision of a variety of learning strategies, ensuring that exhibits are in working order and attending to problems 'on the floor'. The first of these strategies represents a recognition of constructivist approaches to learning, of the visiting experience as being much more than just inspection of the exhibits but rather an opportunity for a further elaboration of one's understandings. It is important to note that the significant relationships between the assessments of effectiveness by experts is with marketing and public programming and not with research and collections. Not surprisingly, positive scores in assessments in the former two areas are correlated with better scores in the public program items in the questionnaire. Those museums that demonstrate leadership and cohesion also are those judged by both experts and staff to have effective public programs.

The effective management of change in museums is characterised by patient and considered leadership (Abraham et al. 1999). In those which have managed change effectively – performance of the museum was judged by staff to have improved as a result of the change – leadership was able to translate external needs to internal vision and then to employee action, integrate tasks, structures, processes and systems at the technical, political and cultural levels, and integrate management practices to build internal and external unity. Time and resources were allocated to the change process. The change was clearly linked to the strategic issues facing the organisation, the nature of the future organisation and the advantages of the proposed changes were carefully communicated to key internal groups of staff. Museums associated closely with government are generally, but not uniformly, significantly less effective across many items from leadership to public programming: this we have ascribed to close and centralised control exerted by government, an emphasis on compliance and a focus on the financial bottom line (Griffin and Abraham 1999). The processes adopted by government do not consitute best business practice. This project is the first to identify, by means of quantitative survey, the key characteristics which contribute to effectiveness of a group of like organisations in the nonprofit sector. Broadly there is agreement between the characteristics of effectiveness in museums and the features of effective commercial or forprofit organisations.

In this paper we consider the results of factor analysis of questionnaire responses – a method of reducing sets of interrelated variables (items) to a few key factors – as well as qualitative data from questionnaire respondents and interviews with museum directors and other senior managers. Differences between museums in different countries, museums of different kinds and differences in the perceptions of museum staff in different disciplines are also explored. We relate the results to those previously reported, especially so far as they concern the roles of leaders and managers, governments and boards, and the importance of public programs, particularly learning. We conclude with some commentary on broader implications for museum futures.

Background

Museums as organisations

Museums and the behaviour of their staff and boards have been examined by a number of authors (Griffin 1987, 1988; Griffin, 1991a,b; Gurian 1995, 1999; Janes 1997, 1999; Moore 1999; Newlands 1983; Strong 1998; Weil 1994a,b, 1995). Many accounts of leadership and management in museums are anecdotal, but a few are analytical. Recent developments in museums in the United States of America have been considered by a number of commentators (in Graubard 1999). Much media commentary on museums has focused on change and funding problems as well as new approaches to public programming, but very little commentary attempts to analyse museums as organisations or deal seriously with issues of leadership and management. The role of managers and leaders is seldom examined in this context of change of funding, change of focus from collection and scholarship (internal or input oriented) to visitor, visitor experience and learning (external or output oriented).

Organisational effectiveness

Museums, like other effective organisations, should make a difference to the constituencies they serve and/or operate in. Such an approach to nonprofit organisational effectiveness is credited (by Weil 1999) to J. Gregory Dees' 'social enterprise' model of the 1990s and to the outcome-based evaluation developed and advocated by the United Way of America in its funding of health and human services agencies. Weil says:

> [museums must] through demonstrable effective programs . . . make a positive difference in the quality of individual and communal lives. Recast in marketing terms, the demand is that the American museum provide some verifiable added value to the lives of those it serves in exchange for their continued support.

Although commercial organisations can use some financial measure of effectiveness – Collins and Porras (1994), in their study which showed the important contribution that shared values make to success, used change in stock price over 50 to 150 years – there is still a question of the relationship between many of the financial measure(s) selected and the longer term performance of the firm.

Four features typify effective forprofit enterprises. First, they focus on vision and core values and build a culture to support these (Collins and Porras 1994, 1996). They are able to envision the future through knowledge of industry trends and relate the organisation's work to them (Hamel and Prahalad 1994: 27). Second, they focus on people: recruiting new staff, career development, promotion from within and work force satisfaction (Fisher and Kahn 1997; Pfeffer 1994). High performance work practices also include contingent compensation, employee participation, higher wages and reduction of status differences (Pfeffer 1996). Third, they focus on teamwork (Dunphy and Bryant 1996; Guzzo and Dickerson 1996) and fourth, they build a learning orientation (Kofman and Senge 1995). Organisational culture is no less important to the effectiveness of nonprofits than it is in commercial organisations (Carl and Stokes 1991 *et seq*; Krug 1992; Herman *et al.* 1994).

Leadership and governance

Despite some claims to the contrary, leadership significantly influences organisational performance. Leader differences account for performance variation *within* firms to a substantial degree (Thomas 1988; Bass 1990; Finkelstein and Hambrick 1996). Effective leaders build 'organisational capability':

> a shared mindset concentrating on creating a capacity for change through understanding and managing organisation systems and empowering employees to think and act as leaders. (Ulrich and Lake 1991)

Transformational leadership influences followers by getting them to transcend their self-interests for the good of the group (Bass *et al.* 1996: 10). Above all, leaders trust others (Kouzes and Posner 1990). The principal effect of leaders is their influence on the 'organisational climate' through the leadership styles they deploy: these styles derive from mature emotional intelligence (Goleman 2000). Climate influences, significantly and positively, outcomes including financial performance. An authoritative style is especially positive but affiliative, coaching and democratic styles are also effective; coercive and pace-setting styles have a negative effect. More effective leaders deploy several different styles. A leader's expectations are the key to a subordinate's performance and development (Livingston 1969). Prominent leaders of business have been quoted by some authors as focusing on developing people first. Bob Galvin of Motorola (in Hinterhuber 1996) asserts:

> We measure the effectiveness of the true leader, not in terms of the leadership he exercises, but in terms of the leadership he evokes . . . but in terms of growth in competence, sense of responsibility, and in personal satisfactions among many participants. Under this kind of leadership it may not always be clear at any given moment just who is leading. Nor is this important. What is important is that others are learning to lead well.

Goran Lindahl, of Asea Brown Boveri (in Bartlett and Ghoshal 1994), sees his most important role as coach and developer of his management team on which he spends 50% to 60% of his time: the empowerment of a manager is a gradual delegation process that requires substantial top-management involvement.

Museums, especially those part of government (in Australia, Canada and the United Kingdom), have been pressured to adopt those aspects of commercial practice (and labelled as 'business practices') which are claimed to lead to more efficient use of public funds. Working smarter has come to be no more than costing less, and in other words, more efficient! Effectiveness has thus been conflated with – subsumed by – efficiency. In any event, these are the views of boards and governments (Griffin 1991a; Griffin and Abraham 1999). Directors are as likely to be chosen for their fundraising skills – their diplomacy in courting benefactors – as for their prominence as scholars (Boyd 1995; Nowlen 1994); emphasis on the role of the director or CEO as coach and vision developer, as someone skilled in leadership and management, seems to be seldom favoured. The parody of the advertisement for the director of an art museum given by Goldberger (1994), at a time when there were many vacancies in American art museums, is surely well known:

> Wanted: charming erudite executive with the diplomatic skills of a foreign service officer, the financial skills of an investment banker and the social skills of a 1950s wife. Position requires the academic background of a serious scholar, with the willingness to allow most of this to go unused in favour of poring over budgets and staffing issues. Long hours, low pay and the chance to see your name in the papers everytime you make even the slightest wrong move . . .

What is needed – it is said – is results, results in the moneyraising and cost cutting departments.

Boards are part of leadership and management notwithstanding their principal role in governance. Effective boards, according to Carver (1990) see that:

> good governance calls for the board's role in long-range planning to consist chiefly in establishing the reason for planning [that] planning is done to increase the probability of getting somewhere from here [and recognise that] enunciation of that 'somewhere' is the board's highest contribution. 'In a manner of speaking, boards participate most effectively in the planning process by standing just outside it . . . a model of governance is a framework within which to organize the thoughts, activities, structure, and relationships of governing boards.'

Effective boards recognise that both board and executive are essential to the proper functioning of an organisation, that they are equal and need to cooperate rather than waste time arguing about who is superior or who is responsible for policy (Drucker 1990).

Museums and public programs: education and learning

Museums are considered by many to be principally educational institutions as well as, or rather than, collecting institutions. If so, the nature of learning in such institutions must be understood. Roberts (1997: 132) says:

the essence of the education enterprise [in a museum] is the making of
meaning. Whether it involves visitors interpreting their experience or
museum personnel interpreting collections, meaning making is at the
heart of the endeavours of both.

Hein and Alexander's (1998) review stresses that visitors' previous knowledge,
attitudes and interests greatly influence their meaning making. Learning is an active
process of experiences being incorporated into already held understandings. The
1990s saw a considerable increase in the debate about museums as places of learning (Durbin 1996; Pitman 1999; Roberts 1997; Hein 1998); many museums have
deliberately devoted greater resources to visitor and audience research, especially
in the USA and Australia.

Notwithstanding over 75 years of research undertaken on learning in museums (let alone the centuries of research on learning generally), there is still not in
the wider community a clear shared view as to how people learn and consequently
of how exhibits should be presented and interpreted. Often attempts by museums
to appeal to a broader public are branded as 'dumbing down' or Disneyfication.
Because attempts by museums to emphasise education in their interpretation and
presentation of collections and exhibits seem not to have been as successful as hoped,
there has been a tendency to emphasise entertainment as the experience which
the visitor seeks and should get: the term edutainment has thus been coined. On
the other hand, research on art displays and their interpretation at the Cleveland
Art Institute (Schloder et al. 1994) and at the Denver Art Museum (Grinstead
and Ritchie 1990), for instance, revealed, amongst other things, that visitors both
want their learning experiences to be directly related to the objects they see and
have diverse learning styles, so a variety of interpretive strategies should be provided. Successful interpretation for the primary audience – the general public
– means 'accepting where they [the visitors] are' – keeping their backgrounds,
preconceptions and values in mind and that, for instance, labels should be written
for them.

Griffin and Symington (1997) and others have compared family and school group
visits to museums. Jeffery-Clay (1998) points out:

museums are ideal constructivist learning environments. They allow
visitors to move and explore freely, working at their own pace. They
encourage group interaction and sharing. They allow personal experience with real objects. They provide a place for visitors to examine and
expand their own understanding. As museum professionals it is our job
to build and enhance these environments to pull the visitors into the
experience, allowing them to explore in ways that pique their curiosity and encourage them to investigate and make comparisons to their
own lives and experiences. Programs and exhibits must be carefully crafted
and tested to assure that they enhance visitor knowledge and/or feelings
without encouraging misconceptions.

Such a view sees the museum as a place of learning facilitation rather than expert
knowledge.

Methods

As previously explained (Griffin *et al.* 1999), a total of 33 museums, selected to include art museums, science centres and aquaria, located in five countries were assessed through two independent instruments, the expert *assessment* and the *questionnaire*. 'Experts' in each of those countries were asked to assess the participating museums on a five point scale from 1 (=excellent in all respects) through 5 (=poor in most respects) with 3 (=good in many respects) and 6 (=don't know or insufficient information available to make an assessment). Assessors were also asked to indicate which of four aspects of performance – (a) public programs including exhibitions and educational services/programs, (b) breadth and depth of collections, (c) quality of research and scholarship, and (d) marketing and promotion – contributed positively to their assessment of each museum. A museum was not to be considered as excellent just because it was large, old or a 'National' institution. A total of 66 assessors provided 241 individual assessments. Most museums were assessed by more than six experts and many by more than ten.

A questionnaire (Appendix A) sought information from each respondent on six of their own demographics and on perceptions of the performance of eight areas of the respondent's museum: leadership, governance, purpose, structure, training, communication (common to most organisations) and information technology and public programs (as they are particular to museums). There was a summary section at the end. Each respondent was asked to indicate their level of agreement with the statements in the questionnaire again using a five point scale from 1 (=strongly agree) through 5 (=strongly disagree) with 3 (=neither agree nor disagree), and 6 (=don't know or sufficient information not available). The questionnaire was filled out by museum staff. The CEO of each museum was asked to distribute 25 questionnaires on a random basis in the ratio of one senior manager (CEO or person reporting directly to the CEO) to two middle managers (others with line responsibilities) to two operations staff. Confidentiality was guaranteed. A total of 594 responses to the questionnaire were received from the 33 museums.

Previous papers have reported the results of analyses of relationships between expert assessments and scores for questionnaire items and differences between the averaged responses for the better (=higher rated or reputationally more effective) museums and the worse (lower rated or less effective) museums. In this paper the results of factor analysis of the questionnaire responses are reported; the analysis was carried out with the factors extracted by Principal Component analysis and using Oblomin rotation with Kaiser normalisation, which reduce the interrelated variables to a smaller number of underlying *factors*. Analysis of the data was principally at the organisational level, individual responses from each museum being averaged. To improve the robustness (reliability) of the data, a limited sample of 23 museums was selected by eliminating all those with less than three assessments and less than 12 responses to the questionnaire.

Qualitative analysis involved four questions in the questionnaire which asked for narrative comments. These questions were:

> [Additional comments]: elaborate on [your answer to] any question
> Major issues for the next three years: list three issues which you believe

will face the organisation in the next three years: they may be the same
issues addressed in the questionnaire or similar to them
The future: list three areas in which you feel the organisation lacks sufficient
knowledge and/or skills at present to deal effectively with future opportunities and problems
[Other issues]: comment on any issues whatsoever not raised

Responses were grouped into seven categories: change, cohesion, resources,
sponsorship/fundraising, external factors (government, competition), local issues
(the museum itself) and marketing. Qualitative analysis also involved interviews
with directors and senior staff of the museums which participated in the project, whilst the quantitative information from the questionnaire responses has also
allowed exploration of differences between countries, various types of museums
and the discipline of the respondent: averaged responses at the institution level were
compared in respect of the first two aspects and individual responses were averaged and compared in respect of the last.

Results

General comments

We have arranged the results in relation to the two principal issues addressed by
this paper: leadership and public programming. The results from factor analysis and
qualitative considerations are placed within those main topics. Differences in respect
of country, museum and discipline of respondent are then dealt with.
   Factor analysis of the 23 selected museums for which there is robust data (three
or more assessments and 12 or more responses) led to settling on a five factor solution: whilst total variance is explained by 22 factors, five factors together explain
71% of the variation and beyond that the nature of the factors becomes increasingly incoherent (Appendix B, Tables 7.1–7.6). Three of the five factors are significant: factor 1 concerning leadership, factor 2 concerning public programming and
factor 5 concerning governance (a leadership activity). The better 11 and worse 12
museums differ significantly from each other in respect of factors 1, 2 and 5 but
not factors 3 or 4 (Table 7.5). The correlation coefficients between each of the five
factors emerging from analysis of the 23 museums (Table 7.6) are not significant
beyond the 0.05 level (although factors 1 and 4 and 5 are correlated with each
other at the 0.1 level).
   The third factor concerns Information Technology items only and accounts
for slightly more than 7.1 of the variation. The fourth factor, which accounts for
just less than 6.1 of the variation, concerns public programming but emphasises
participation: in the contribution of ideas for programs (item 58), in an understanding of the criteria for program choice (59) and in teamwork (items 31 and 57),
whilst evaluation is an important positive element (item 56). Neither of these
two factors correlates with expert assessments and neither distinguishes the better
(those rated as more effective) from the worse museums. Accordingly they are not
dealt with further here.

The contribution of collection strength (breadth/depth/age of collections) to the assessment is negatively correlated with factor 1 and with factor 5. The contribution of research and scholarship to the assessment is negatively correlated with factor 5. In other words, those museums and similar institutions with the better scores tend to be valued by assessors for their marketing and public programming strengths. Indeed traditional museums with substantial resources devoted to collections and scholarship tend to have poor factor scores. Charting the scores for factors 1 and 2 from the five factor solution for each museum reveals no coherent or distinct groupings; the same is true of attempts to group them by aggregated scores for the questionnaire items. Clearly features such as type of museum, country, size of museum and so on are not attributes shared by museums grouped by their effectiveness. (The issue of country and type of museum is dealt with below.) Factor analyses using the data from *all* museums produce factors similar to those for the 23 selected museums – leadership and public programming being the first two – although the relative prominence of items concerning leadership and cohesion changes and the individual items included vary somewhat. Analyses of individual responses (as opposed to averaged responses from each museum) produce similar factors also, again with variations in the individual items contributing to the factors.

In summary, the factor scales resulting from these analyses emphasise leadership, cohesion and public programming as characterising effectiveness, as do the analyses based on the items themselves reported earlier. Only the emphasis on cohesion and leadership is stronger: it is cohesive leadership which is important, leadership which encourages development of shared values, a commitment to agreed standards of quality and to effective communication, leadership which provides opportunities for training and rewards superior performance in terms of agreed and understood standards.

The results from *qualitative data* strongly support the conclusions that leadership and cohesion are the important elements of effective museums. The data is of two sorts (as explained above): narrative responses to the open-ended questions in the questionnaire and interviews with senior managers at many of the museums in the study. (It should be recalled that the study of the management of change also strongly supported the critical role of leadership and cohesion.) Respondents from lower rated museums generally have more comments than respondents from the higher rated museums, especially concerning leadership and change and the effects of downsizing on services to the public. This is particularly so for general comments on any issue not raised in the questionnaire. When asked to consider major issues for the next three years, issues of change and cohesion emerged strongly. Marketing skills and knowledge (understanding and ability to reach diverse audiences, knowledge of visitors, ability to develop 'product', merchandising and fundraising/development) were highlighted as areas of knowledge and skills particularly important to the museum's future but often were ones in which the museum was noticeably deficient.

There are differences concerning country, museum-type and discipline of respondent.

Cohesive leadership

Factor analysis

The first factor (Table 7.1), which we term *cohesive leadership*, explains just over 44% of the total variation: the leadership items included emphasise the long-term and vision (items 66 and 9) as well as supportive change management and modelling of appropriate behaviour (items 12 and 13). Quality issues (from the 'Purposes' section of the questionnaire) are important (items 19, 24, 25, 26), as are integration of objectives (20 and 68) and understanding of and support for the goals of the museum (22 and 23). Training and development as well as attributes of the learning organisation are also evident (items 35, 36). Cohesion, including staff participation in decisions affecting them, is clearly an underlying theme of the factor evident in up to ten items. Factor 5 (Table 7.3) consists of Board items only and accounts for just over 5.1. of the variation: involvement in fundraising (item 18) is the most prominent. Examination of correlations between each factor and demographic attributes of the museums (Table 7.6) shows significance for factor 1 with government connections – those with better scores are *not* associated with government – and age of respondent – the museums with better scores have *younger* staff. Not surprisingly, higher factor 1 scores are strongly correlated with positive scores for the individual items in the leadership section of the questionnaire. However, scores for factor 5 are not correlated with the average of items in the Board section of the questionnaire! (Good scores for the average of Board items correlate with good scores for factors 2 and 4.)

Qualitative evidence

Narrative responses to the questionnaire

Responses to the narrative sections of the questionnaire overwhelmingly concerned leadership and training; purpose, structure and communication also received much comment. Two issues, change and cohesion, stand out. Comments elaborating responses to the questionnaire addressed leadership and Board issues as well as communication. In responding to 'issues not raised in the questionnaire', over 25% of responses dealt with change and cohesion. Change dominated the response to major issues for the next three years, 40% of responses concerning change, twice as many as dealt with resources including financial resources (for which one-fifth came from three of the 30 museums). When respondents were asked to identify areas in which sufficient knowledge and/or skills to deal effectively with future opportunities was lacking, over 25% addressed the ability to deal effectively with change and advancing of cohesion.

Overall, responses mentioned downsizing, the lack of a clear communication of vision and the holding of different perceptions of the vision by senior managers, and the lack of expertise in management as opposed to expertise in technical skills amongst senior managers. There was a range of other matters, including clinging to old hierarchies, managing in crisis mode, an emphasis on reactive rather than proactive practices, making decisions on limited information, lack of communication, people given little opportunity for creativity and responsibility, gruelling schedules and a lack of personnel resources, and domination by an accounting agenda. Attention was drawn to downsizing by attrition and a consequent lack of planning so as to control the outcomes of it such that the museum benefitted, the negative effect of downsizing on services to the public, on standards and on staff morale and the lack of adequate recompense for the additional demands placed on staff and on management to rebuild staff esteem and worth.

Examples of positive comments from the museums judged as more effective follow:

> We have huge and difficult challenges in the next few years as we approach opening day. I feel like we are well supported by senior staff during this.

> I don't think we are leaving any important area untouched . . . I understand though that in Human Resources, we will be working on developing an efficient and effective tracking program over the next couple of years to accommodate the increased staffing levels due to our planned expansion.

> This organisation has just undergone a focused attempt to identify strategic issues and opportunities. As a result, its vision, sense of direction and team spirit has improved and sharpened. In addition, recognition by management that some changes were needed in the decision-making process has led to some easing of bureaucratic restrictions and expectations of further improvements.

However, there are some negative comments from the more effective museums:

> Senior managers need to release more responsibility to middle managers. Micro management does not work; numerous meetings take place in order to have 'team' involvement . . . people [become] frustrated. Skills can be learned with experience. Too many team meetings leave too little time to do the necessary work.

> Our organisation has always been committed to new technology and educating the public. However, in meeting and exceeding the usual goals of opening and operating the [museum we] have missed great opportunities to be a ground beating organisation from within the institution. Issues such as employee provided day-case, sick leave time banks and job sharing have been overlooked . . . Many have told us the [museum] is 'the best in the world' . . . we have not used our vast financial and supportive resources to be the 'best' organisation 'to work for' in the world!

> Our Board is comprised of many members, most of which the typical [museum's] team members are never informed of. Outcomes of Board

meetings are not common knowledge. The interaction between the Board and senior management is not readily shared. Individuals are hired on their strengths regarding a certain position and then feel inadequate when expected to take on additional roles to be a part of the 'team' giving individuals the opportunity to expand their knowledge in a more comfortable way would produce better overall results.

Comments by staff in the less effective museums provide a contrast with these:

Current vision document is being interpreted by individuals, department and division [in] totally different [ways] . . . the institution still lacks a clear vision and a clear set of priorities . . . we manage in a crisis mode and make too many decisions that are short term or avoid making those tough calls . . .

Scheduling is so gruelling, personnel resources are so modest, and funds are so tight that it is difficult to carve out 'reflective' time to effectively work on critical documents, such as long-range strategic planning; staff 'retreats', for all their shortcomings, have not been utilised enough or effectively to gain true consensus on long-range institutional goals. From a management standpoint, I think the museum's greatest challenge over the next few years will be to increase the active participation of the board.

One of the difficulties will be trying to serve the needs for many different client groups both internal and external . . . [this aim is] being challenged by our many different users (cultural groups, donors, sponsors, researchers, general public, etc.), while our resources are shrinking.

I feel that the institution has great difficulty in trying to get the staff to work towards a shared vision and purpose. The communication is very poor . . . It is also very formal. Most (not all) senior managers are never seen by most staff. When communication does happen, it is usually top down . . . Management [is]more comfortable with command and control model than one more adapted to teamwork.

We do not have any proper staff training or staff development. We are lacking a staff orientation program, computer skills are all over the place, no customer service training for internal or external customers, training is also required for working within a team environment. Managers need proper training. We also need to develop standards.

We really need a commitment to the staff. So that they are also treated as a resource not a liability.

Interviews
One of the comments made to one of us (DJGG) on the first visit to the Monterey Bay Aquarium, south of San Francisco, was that when staff make a mistake, they aren't criticised, they are asked what they have learned from the event: this was

confirmed on a subsequent visit. When the Aquarium was being planned the staff were sent to other aquaria to find out what they were like so as to help them plan their own. (This contrasts with some museums undergoing building development where Board members are sent to visit other museums: they return to give their views seemingly knowing more than the staff who are expected to plan and run the new museum.)

At COSI, a science centre in Columbus, Ohio (with branches elsewhere in that State), a wide variety of approaches were used by former President Roy Shafer to achieve a common vision. All staff wore the same T-shirt when in the building, an event – 'First Thursday' – was held each month after work at which staff of the host department explained their functions and activities and role-played various activities. Senior management referred to themselves as the 'support team' and attended project teams as a 'coach'. Shafer explains:

> The question is how do we get individuals across an organisation to make the same kind of decision when faced with the same dilemma? How do we assure that hundreds of people faced with thousands of transactions every day, will all make the same decision, on behalf of the organisation? Because that is what we are asking them to do. We can't give them a book to find out the information.

Referring to Collins and Porras's study, Shafer continued:

> The only answer they would contend, and I would agree, is values. We have to help them learn how to decide, not what to decide. We spent probably a third of our time reinforcing core values. Through every mechanism we could dream of. From performance bonuses to performance planning to first Thursdays . . . The organisation in essence that sets the standards . . . But if the organisation doesn't adopt those standards, as a basis for performance, the CEO can't make those stick. What the CEO does today has no impact on people's experience today. It has impact on their experience six months from now, or six years from now, but not today . . . We were organised in floor teams with direct delivery across divisions . . . The leadership team is called the support team, not the management team. Everybody is a manager. My job in a leadership role is to support the good work of the team members.

> Typically what we would do is try to give an opportunity for change to meet the standard, over a reasonable period of time. When the change didn't occur then we would change players. People should never, unless they have worked effectively to avoid feedback, they should never be surprised at their performance review. That should never be a moment of surprise. They can deny it, but it shouldn't be a moment of surprise. We had to apply an enormous amount of energy every day. You could never let up, not for a moment. In fact, I don't think that I've really understood just how draining that was and the energy volume it required until I stopped doing it.

Responses in discussions with senior managers from COSI and the Monterey Bay Aquarium were remarkably similar: in both senior managers irrespective of their area of responsibility were able to talk authoritatively on program issues and spoke very positively about their colleagues and about training and development matters. At COSI senior managers frequently talked of the positive contribution of staff on the various project teams.

The Royal British Columbia Museum in Victoria, British Columbia (Canada), a mixed museum comprised of natural history, history and anthropology collections and exhibits, is funded principally by the provincial government. In 1992 it commenced a series of important changes following dramatic reorganisation in 1985–86 which had involved declaring all positions vacant and rehiring staff, a 'scaring' process (Barkley in Janes 1997). The 1992 changes focused on what the museum was doing and for whom, what the public thought of the museum's activities; it did not focus on restructuring or downsizing! Extensive consultation with staff and volunteers was followed by consultations with community groups, special interest groups and the general public. Staff groups were established to deal with functional areas from research and collections to public programs and operations. Barkley reports:

> Museums must be seen by the public to add value to their lives and to the life of the community . . . We are storehouses of information, not just curious objects . . . We can help build bridges of understanding between people of various races, religions, interests and backgrounds . . .

As changes developed and new ways of operating were put in place, the opportunity was frequently taken to celebrate success; but the opportunity to celebrate failure was also taken (Barkley, pers. comm. 1999).

Teamwork, the training of staff to work in teams and induction of new staff are significant features of the best organisations. At The Natural History Museum (London) a new induction program was introduced by Director Neil Chalmers soon after his arrival in 1989. Chalmers explains:

> we now have a two day induction course which we manage very carefully and it is mostly for the new recruits and this is followed by a four and a half day back up course and . . . we hope to give them that within the first four months after they have arrived.

Science North, a science centre in Sudbury, Ontario, Canada, recognised for innovation in its public programming, when faced with likely reductions in funding around the time of its move to greater involvement with government in the early 1990s, sought the views of staff on ways in which funds might be reduced. The result was savings in several areas and a small salary rise for staff. (The staff of Provincial government organisations concurrently received no salary rises and in addition were required to pay a social dividend – work for a short time without pay.)

The way the Board works with senior management also distinguishes the best museums, according to the questionnaire responses. The interviews and narrative responses to the questionnaires again support this. The chair of the Board at one of the best museums asserted that there should be no more than six meetings a year:

> if there are any more, staff get involved in demonstrations of their work; that's what happens over at [another place].

At one of the lower rated museums the Board (in the mid-1990s) had developed no shared view of the museum's purpose. This was not surprising considering that it comprised members from two different authorities and none of the Board took any part in fundraising or generating support from government agencies. In another museum, the Board took over development of the mission and vision statement, completed the process behind closed doors and delivered the statements to senior management. The result was a staff united as never before, against the Board. In many museums, boards can nevertheless be involved in similar activities, in focusing their efforts on aspects of the financial situation in which they believe they are expert, such as merchandising, or on marketing because they believe they know about it.

Visitor-focused public programming

Factor analysis

Factor 2 (Table 7.2) explains 8% of variation and is comprised of items relating to concern for the visitor, ensuring that exhibits work (items 52 and 51), awareness of differing learning styles of visitors – providing a variety of interpretive strategies (53) and attention to the resources allocated to advertising (60). Three items from outside the Public Program section are included: they concern rewards (item 40), communication (item 43) and induction of new staff (38). Factor 2 is significantly correlated with overall expert assessment and with the positive contribution of public programming and of marketing to the assessment. As with factor 1, those museums with better factor 2 scores tend to be not associated with government and have younger staff. There are suggestions in the data that greater rates of change have reduced the level of teamwork and participation in public program development and that recent physical development – e.g. a new building – stimulates public programming. Positive scores for the individual items in the public program section of the questionnaire are correlated with higher factor 2 scores (and with factor 4 scores also).

Qualitative results

Narrative responses to the questionnaire
Few of the responses dealt with public programming, but a positive comment from one of the more effective museums may be quoted:

I do not feel the organisation lacks sufficient knowledge. I do feel we need to provide our visitors with an exclusive experience. Our centres must provide many positive and fun learning experiences of families and our overall audience will find other avenues for learning/entertainment.

Interviews

At Monterey Bay Aquarium, Executive Director Julie Packard concerns herself with 'image': image includes even the text interpretation for exhibits (which are widely regarded as amongst the best in the world). Her involvement with the budget process, on the other hand, is confined to discussing the gap between revenue and expenditure, before senior managers consider the details, and discussing the outcome of those discussions. The significance is that at Monterey Bay Aquarium, it is the visitor who is receiving the principal focus of the CEO, not the money. Furthermore, one of the things that newly appointed Director Neil Chalmers did at The Natural History Museum (London) shortly after he started was to take all senior managers to Disneyland to learn the essence of customer service. Customer service training is now given to all staff as part of their induction program. (The Disneyland visit led some academic critics to fear that the Museum's exhibitions were going to take on the features of Disneyland exhibitions, though Disneyland happens to be known worldwide for the excellence of its concern for its 'guests'!)

In the less effective museums, conflicts are not uncommon, frequently over the relative authority of staff members in project teams concerned with exhibitions. In one, various approaches to exhibition development – seen as advances by some – have been discarded eventually following opposition by one of the more powerful groups. Other groups sought to exercise power through the way they requested information and set standards. One commentator explained.

> [as] the new exhibit professionals became more and more professionalised they took on another museum culture where their goals became not to serve the public but to arrange matters for their own convenience, their own way of life and to serve certain professional goals as opposed to public goals. My favourite example is exhibit labels. The designers didn't like the look of them so they make them as small as possible. And another thing is reduce the contrast: black on white is ugly so they want to have a tone on top, then . . . cutting the label size so that you can hardly read it. If you walk through this place you will see loads of exhibit labels that you cannot read.

The influence of country, museum-type and discipline

When museums of different kinds and in different countries are compared some important differences emerge, particularly distinguishing science museums and science centres, natural history museums and art museums, whilst there also seem to be differences in the perceptions of different groups of staff (Appendix C). There are numerous significant differences between the museums of different countries. In particular, US museums score more positively in areas of leadership, governance and public programming. Overall distinctions between the museums of different countries concern appropriate modelling behaviour by senior managers, regular performance assessment and information transfer. However, country is not a principal explanation for the major distinctions of the more effective museums. Although many of the museums in this study are mixed, it would appear that science museums and science centres have more effective governance than other types of museum, and art museums less effective governance. Science museum staff give more positive responses to questions concerning public programming than do staff from other areas; this is particularly so in relation to a focus on the visitor. Finally, there are a number of significant differences in the responses of people from different discipline areas/job classifications which are evident when individual responses are analysed. These especially concern four groups: curatorial/conservation, education and exhibitions, finance and human resources (HR) and public relations respondents. Curatorial and collection management staff are less positive about the museum than are other staff; the same is true of education/exhibitions staff.

Discussion and conclusions from this study

Every approach to analysis of the results of this study, whether quantitative or qualitative, shows that leadership and cohesion are the critical factors for the successful museum. The characteristics of effective museums are those which align with the features of discipline (alignment of initiatives with the organisation's overall direction), stretch (stimulation of people to achieve of their best), trust and support (including openness of managers to questioning) which have been identified by the work of Bartlett and Ghoshal (1994; Ghoshal and Bartlett 1997). More than that, the factor analysis reported here emphasises that it is not simply leadership which is important, it is also cohesive leadership which gives support to, and encourages involvement of, staff in matters which directly affect them including training and development. This is important, as well as a focus on quality and on organisational learning. On the other hand, in the less effective museums there is profound concern over the way in which those with the responsibility to make decisions about the organisation behave, alarm about future resources and uncertainty about the future in general; conflict is evident. The deep feelings voiced about ineffective management of change in some museums clearly illustrates this. The cluster of features characterising cohesive leadership resembles the leadership styles which contribute to an effective organisational climate (Goleman 2000). These include setting a clear long-term vision for the organisation, modelling of appropriate behaviours and giving support to staff. Unfortunately though, much of the managerialist approach adopted by some governments and boards of museums in pursuit of 'results' has led to the deployment of coercive and pace-setting styles which leave little room for individual initiative and increase stress levels amongst staff.

Leadership, training and communication are issues of importance in distinguishing the museums of different countries: it would be appropriate for those responsible for museums in Australia, Canada and the United Kingdom to carefully note the performance of US museums in these important areas. Organisational reform emphasises leadership as building shared values: that is one of the conclusions of this project. Cohesion is advanced when the values of the organisation match the values of the people in it (Newlands 1983); the matching of staff to structure, goals and organisational climate is more important than formal management systems such as written goals, objectives, policies and procedures. A convergence of people, power and structure to focus on specific task objectives giving play to sensitivity, creativity and independence of thought and relying on expert power rather than personal power or authority is the climate Newlands considers to be the desirable one for museums. In many museums, especially traditional ones, it is difficult to develop such an approach because the values of certain professional groups are not shared by other groups. They are a professional bureaucracy (Griffin 1987; Mintzberg 1983), having considerable control over their own work, seeking control over the work of others and thus difficult for management to control. In Mant's (1994) terms the professionals are often more binary – competitive – whilst others are ternary, relationships being seen in a context of co-operation to achieve shared goals. This is particularly so in respect of public programs, especially exhibitions. Research/ curatorial staff may believe that truth exists and only has to be discovered, whilst public program staff may believe knowledge exists in the individual and varies from person to person (Hein 1998).

Ames (2000) observes:

> Museums are complex social organisations composed of intertwined layers of routines, obligations, schedules and competing interests that frequently inhibit prompt or consistent responses to new initiatives. In addition, archaeologists, anthropologists and art historians working in museums maintain allegiances to the traditions of their own professions, sometimes even at the expense of the interests of the institutions which employ them.

The conflict and disagreements about public programs have been dealt with by McLean (1999: 89):

> Traditionally, most museum exhibitions have been a one-way conversation . . . Curators assembled the objects, established the conceptual framework, and wrote the exhibition 'statement' and labels. Designers then packaged the curatorial material . . . Afterwards educators prepared interpretive materials . . . While this process ensured that the depth of curator's passion and knowledge made it out into the galleries, it was fraught with problems, particularly when the curator's true affections were aimed at other scholars, leaving a majority of visitors in the dark.

The results of the analysis of perceptions of staff from different disciplines lends quantitative support to these assertions: differences most frequently concern public programs. These same issues are those which appear to distinguish museums of different kinds. It would appear that in science centres and science museums there are fewer differences between staff in their perceptions so making for greater levels of cohesion. (There are also strong suggestions in the data that science centres/museums receive more positive assessments; and thus greater cohesion does indeed lead to greater effectiveness.) Clearly also the effective museum pays strategic attention to visitors and doing so is significant in the minds of assessors. The same three items of the Public Program section of the questionnaire which are included amongst the 28 items distinguishing the most effective museums are also included in factor 2 in the five factor solution. Those three items are also in fact reported as being amongst the ten best (i.e. lowest scoring) items in museums generally (Griffin *et al.* 1999: 49); item 54 indicating that 'educational offerings attempt to address the full range of knowledge, attitudes and understandings that visitors bring with them' is also amongst the ten best items.

In museums generally, we can conclude, the increasing understanding of the nature of learning and meaning making has placed the visitor at the centre of the visiting experience: the museum provides many opportunities to arrive at inter-pretations of their world without compromising integrity (Jeffery-Clay 1998). Such approaches recognise that learning is an experience which is more effective if it is enjoyable. Griffin and Symington (1997) point out, as have others, that whilst families visiting museums characteristically determine for themselves which exhibits they visit, how long they spend looking at them and talking amongst themselves, many school group visits lack those features. If school groups were to be allowed to plan their visit and control it they would then assert they were both enjoying themselves and learning. These attributes accord with the important recent find-ings about learning in informal settings (Durbin 1996; Falk and Dierking 1992, 2000; Hein 1998; Hein and Alexander 1998; Roberts 1997; and Pitman 1999).

Consequences for museum futures

A museum is an organisation of people, not primarily an entity concerned with caring for and displaying collections, notwithstanding the importance of those func-tions (Griffin 1987, 1988, 1991b).

Better museums give attention to values and to the development of a shared culture including views about why the particular museum exists and where it is going. Successful organisational reform generally emphasises transformational lead-ership, attention to communication about the nature of the changed organisation, and the shaping of its culture and climate, *not* to cost cutting, downsizing or restruc-turing. Our study demonstrates the truth of this in museums and like organisations. Effective boards contribute to the goals rather than intervene in executive man-agement issues. In particular they see that change is managed so as to enhance the organisation's effectiveness rather than strengthen the power of certain managers. These issues are far more important than matters such as structure – organisational design – which receives such a lot of attention in some places.

Measuring or assessing a museum's merits must focus on how to develop the critical values which distinguish museums from other public institutions and con-stitute the basis of the very way in which they contribute to the community and to society, even to the uplifting of the human spirit. It is these very things which too many governments and boards have forgotten in the rush for financial resources which no longer seem to be coming from an increasingly affluent society in the free markets of the 'globalized' world.

New thinking is required of many governments and boards in respect of how their museums, like other organisations, are to work effectively and exploit the opportunities of the future. A greater focus is needed on what actually leads to effectiveness in the long term. Establishing agreed statements of vision, mission and assessment of performance, seeing that strategic thinking as well as planning takes place, and genuinely encouraging creativity and risk taking are positive. Individual and short-term contracts, a focus on the financial bottom line, restructuring and downsizing, however, make no contribution to success. Neither does frequent intervention in process by board or government.

Much more care is needed in choosing people for leadership positions (Fernandez-Araoz 1999; Bennis and O'Toole 2000): because leadership is as important in museums as in all other organisations. Boards and others need to agree on what leadership is and how to recognise and support it. For their part, staffs of museums can come to realise that museums can be managed as are other organisations but that this does not mean the adoption of managerialist practices and its negative effects in all domains. Genuine leadership and management can be a contribution to achieving everyone's goals for the museum. Equitable employment means people at all levels being able to pursue the tasks and objectives for which they were hired and developing and expanding those. It also means the right to be respected for genuine contribution rather than being discriminated against on the basis of one's role. In short, good museums, like good arts organisations, have lessons for commercial organisations, just as the latter have lessons for others.

Most particularly, the future of museums must be pursued in the context of making a difference to people's lives, not merely for the purposes of ensuring the survival of the museum with its traditional activities and behaviours (Weil 1994a,b, 1999). The indicators and markers used to assess success must reflect that. Appointing directors principally for their fundraising and public relations skills ignores the fundamental role of cohesive leadership which only the chief executive can play. Boards and governments alike must be as prepared to undergo assessment of their performance and their contribution as much as they expect the management and staffs of the museums for which they are responsible.

The items and factors which emerge from this study as characterising effectiveness are practices and processes. Like leading indicators in economic forecasting they are not aims in themselves! But if museums are positive in these attributes it is highly likely that they will succeed over the long term because of their ability to learn from the past and the 'industry', foster and exploit creativity whilst always co-operatively focusing on why the organisation is there and what it is supposed to be doing for whom. Encouraging such practices and processes is the principal role of leaders and senior managers as Collins and Porras (1994, 1996), Hamel and Prahalad (1994), Bartlett and Ghoshal (1994) and Ghoshal and Bartlett (1997) have shown. It is a matter of how people work together and how decisions are reached (Hout and Carter 1995). Boards and governments have a responsibility to recognise that and media commentators would do well to do so as well. So would all working in and associated with museums.

Acknowledgements

Funding for travel and other costs in the early years of this study were provided by the Australian Museum Trust. The early stages of this project were partly supported by the Canadian Museum of Nature, Ottawa (CMN) which assisted travel to all Canadian organisations included in this project (by DG in 1995). We are especially grateful to Dr Alan Emery, former President of CMN, for his encouragement. We also wish to thank the numerous Chief Executives, Directors and staff members at the 33 museums, science centres and aquaria who agreed to complete questionnaires and participate in interviews and the expert assessors who provided assessments of the museums.

Discussions with Dr Roy Shafer (former President of COSI, Columbus, Ohio) especially focused on what emerged as critical aspects of this study. Discussions with Drs Emery, Neil Chalmers (The Natural History Museum, London), Bill Barkley (Royal British Columbia Museum, Victoria) and Donald Duckworth (Bishop Museum, Honolulu) were also very helpful, as was the advice of the late Professor Michael Ames (former Department of Anthropology and Sociology, University of British Columbia, Vancouver) and Dr Paulette McManus (London).

Ms Gail McCarthy (Australian Museum) prepared, distributed and collated the assessments and questionnaires. We are grateful to Elise Kelly of the Australian Museum for her considerable assistance with the factor analyses. We also want to thank Lynda Kelly of the Australian Museum for assistance with analysis of the narrative responses to the questionnaire. The ongoing discussions with Tim Sullivan (then of the Australian Museum) were invaluable in clarifying the meaning of this study and the role of museums and how they might succeed; his comments on earlier drafts of the paper were invaluable.

Appendix A List of statements in 75-item questionnaire

Questions 1 through 7 sought demographic information which is not dealt with further here.

LEADERSHIP

8   Senior managers have championed a vision for the organisation
9   Senior managers are concerned mainly with long-term, strategic issues
10   The CEO spends substantial time seeking support from outside the organisation in order to improve this organisation's standing
11   Senior managers work together effectively as a team to achieve the goals of the organisation
12   Senior managers give time and support to those staff who have trouble adapting to the new ways of doing things
13   Senior managers model appropriate behaviour for the rest of the organisation

BOARD

14　New members of the governing Board are chosen in consultation with the Chair of the Board and the CEO

15　Knowledge and skills in industry practice and standards are important criteria for choosing members of the Board

16　The Board concerns itself mainly with the long-term vision of the organisation

17　There is substantial and visible trust between the Board and the CEO

18　Members of the Board contribute actively to fundraising

PURPOSE

19　Goals and objectives are devised to ensure that those who should benefit from the organisation's activities are satisfied with what we produce

20　Objectives for divisions/departments/sections clearly integrate with those for the organisation as a whole

21　Allocation of resources to projects is based on a careful assessment of the value of the outcomes to the future of the organisation

22　Goals and objectives for the organisation are understood by staff

23　The organisation's goals and objectives are supported by staff

24　Staff are expected to understand/recognise the appropriate quality standards to be achieved in their work

25　There is encouragement in goal setting to pay attention to the quality of the process as well as to quantifiable outcomes

26　We aim to ensure that completed projects meet the required standards first time

STRUCTURE

27　Some of the tasks now undertaken by the organisation should be outsourced to some other agency or company

28　People at all levels are encouraged to take responsibility for the decisions they make

29　Senior managers refrain from making decisions which should and can be made at lower administrative levels

30　Staff are able to go to people in other sections to get help in fixing problems affecting their work without having to go first to a supervisor or manager for permission

31　Many of the activities and projects in the organisation are carried out by teams

32　Staff are encouraged to develop respect for the skills and contribution of others in the organisation

33　There are well developed opportunities for management and staff to work in a variety of different jobs

34   Decisions that affect me and my work are discussed fully with me by my supervisor

TRAINING

35   There are genuine opportunities for staff to improve their skills and knowledge
36   Staff to receive training/development are involved in formulating the nature of the training/development program/priorities
37   There are adequate and clear procedures in place for hiring appropriately qualified/skilled new staff
38   There is an established system for induction of all new employees
39   Performance of staff is assessed at regular intervals
40   Rewards are based on contribution to pre-established and known standards rather than vague opinions on the worth of individual effort
41   Staff have been trained to operate effectively in teams

COMMUNICATION

42   Information is transferred quickly and efficiently through the organisation to all those who need to know
43   Staff take an active interest in the information that is communicated to them
44   We have learned a great deal from past experiences and practices in this organisation
45   We are very interested in learning from what other organisations do well
46   Senior managers are interested in new ideas and are keen on trying them out in this organisation
47   Problems are carefully explored and their nature agreed on before solutions are developed and applied
48   Most people in different sections try to work on new ways of doing things rather than being stuck in fixed patterns
49   We systematically review projects, programs and practices in this organisation

PUBLIC PROGRAMS

50   Senior managers show their active interest in visitors and public programs by their frequent presence on the floor of public galleries
51   Problems experienced by visitors with public programs are speedily and appropriately attended to by staff of the relevant section
52   There is a clear commitment by relevant staff to ensuring that exhibits are in working order at all times
53   Visitors are provided with a variety of ways (interpretive strategies) in which to understand the meaning of the exhibits/programs
54   Educational offerings attempt to address the full range of knowledge, attitudes and understandings which visitors bring with them

55   Marketing staff use the results of market research to help program staff develop effective programs
56   The staff/consultants who undertake evaluation of public programs co-operate to improve program effectiveness by contributing the results of their work to decisions about programs
57   Exhibits and other public programs are developed by education, exhibition and other staff as well as research and curatorial staff working together
58   Ideas for public programs are contributed by staff from throughout the organisation
59   All those involved in public programs clearly understand the criteria for program choice
60   The amount of money allocated to advertising and promoting public programs is based on knowledge of what expenditure is required to reach the desired proportion of the target market
61   Staff responsible for conservation of collections work to ensure that wherever possible the objects will be available for use in public programs and scholarship
62   Public program staff are accepted by others including research and curatorial staff as important contributors to the future of the organisation

INFORMATION TECHNOLOGY

63   Appropriate resources are allocated to the continual improvement of information technology
64   Management of the collections makes maximum use of information technology to improve access by the public and other interested parties to knowledge of the collections
65   The development of the use of information technology is being done in the context of an overall policy which focuses on how the organisation may benefit in meeting its service to the public

SUMMARY

66   The CEO and senior management group set a clear vision with long planning horizons (LEADERSHIP)
67   Board members actively use their knowledge, skills and commitment to further the organisation's mission (BOARD)
68   The goals and objectives of various departments/sections are cohesive and well integrated with those of the organisation as a whole (PURPOSE)
69   Structure is flexible, responsive and shows co-operation between its parts (STRUCTURE)
70   High degree of commitment, resources and planning (TRAINING)
71   Good work is recognised and equitably rewarded (TRAINING)
72   High sense of awareness, involvement and feeling part of the team (COMMUNICATION)

73   A learning orientation is encouraged (COMMUNICATION)
74   Public program development and marketing are clearly focused on visitors as important stakeholders (PUBLIC PROGRAMS)
75   Technology is up to date with market development and usage is widespread (INFORMATION TECHNOLOGY)

Appendix B Factor scales

Table 7.1   Five factor solution for 23 selected museums, all items included. Factor 1, Cohesive Leadership. Composition of the factor together with factor loading. Items in **bold** are amongst those signficantly distinguishing the better (higher rated) museums at the 0.1 level or above

QN	SECTION	DETAIL	LOADING
66	**LEADERSHIP**	**The CEO and senior management group set a clear vision with long planning horizons**	0.865
26	PURPOSES	We aim to ensure that completed projects meet the required standards first time	0.847
9	**LEADERSHIP**	**Senior managers are concerned mainly with long-term, strategic issues**	0.836
70	**TRAINING**	**High degree of commitment, resources and planning**	0.826
25	**PURPOSES**	**There is encouragement in goal setting to pay attention to the quality of the process as well as to quantifiable outcomes**	0.816
35	TRAINING	There are genuine opportunities for staff to improve their skills and knowledge	0.816
32	**STRUCTURE**	**Staff are encouraged to develop respect for the skills and contribution of others in the organisation**	0.802
20	**PURPOSES**	**Objectives for divisions/ departments/sections clearly integrate with those for the organisation as a whole**	0.767
28	STRUCTURE	People at all levels are encouraged to take responsibility for the decisions they make	0.748
8	**LEADERSHIP**	**Senior managers have championed a vision for the organisation**	0.744
68	**PURPOSE**	**The goals and objectives of various departments/sections are cohesive and well integrated with those of the organisation as a whole**	0.741

Table 7.1   (*continued*)

QN	SECTION	DETAIL	LOADING
36	TRAINING	Staff to receive training/development are involved in formulating the nature of the training/development program/priorities	0.707
13	**LEADERSHIP**	**Senior managers model appropriate behaviour for the rest of the organisation**	0.707
22	**PURPOSES**	**Goals and objectives for the organisation are understood by staff**	0.695
12	LEADERSHIP	Senior managers give time and support to those staff who have trouble adapting to the new ways of doing things	0.693
19	**PURPOSES**	**Goals and objectives are devised to ensure that those who should benefit from the organisation's activities are satisfied with what we produce**	0.691
10	**LEADERSHIP**	**The CEO spends substantial time seeking support from outside the organisation in order to improve this organisation's standing**	0.686
24	PURPOSES	Staff are expected to understand/recognise the appropriate quality standards to be achieved in their work	0.678
23	**PURPOSES**	**The organisation's goals and objectives are supported by staff**	0.662
44	**COMMUNICATION**	**We have learned a great deal from past experiences and practices in this organisation**	0.660
72	**COMMUNICATION**	**High sense of awareness, involvement and feeling part of the team**	0.659
69	**STRUCTURE**	**Structure is flexible, responsive and shows co-operation between its parts**	0.644

Table 7.2   Five factor solution for 23 selected museums, all items included. Factor 2, Visitor-focused Public Programming. Composition of the factor together with factor loadings. All the items are amongst those signficantly distinguishing the better (higher rated) museums at the 0.1 level or above

QN	SECTION	DETAIL	FACTOR LOADING
52	PUBLIC PROGRAMS	There is a clear commitment by relevant staff to ensuring that exhibits are in working order at all times	0.795
51	PUBLIC PROGRAMS	Problems experienced by visitors with public programs are speedily and appropriately attended to by staff of the relevant section	0.772
53	PUBLIC PROGRAMS	Visitors are provided with a variety of ways (interpretive strategies) in which to understand the meaning of the exhibits/ programs	0.740
40	TRAINING	Rewards are based on contribution to pre-established and known standards rather than vague opinions on the worth of individual effort	0.739
43	COMMUNICATION	Staff take an active interest in the information that is communicated to them	0.646
38	TRAINING	There is an established system for induction of all new employees	0.601
60	PUBLIC PROGRAMS	The amount of money allocated to advertising and promoting public programs is based on knowledge of what expenditure is required to reach the desired proportion of the target market	0.550

Table 7.3   Five factor solution for 23 selected museums, all items included. Factor 5, Supportive Board. Composition of the factor together with factor loadings. Items in **bold** are amongst those signficantly distinguishing the better (higher rated) museums at the 0.1 level or above

QN	SECTION	DETAIL	FACTOR LOADING
18	**THE BOARD**	**Members of the Board contribute actively to fundraising**	−0.861
14	THE BOARD	New members of the governing Board are chosen in consultation with the Chair of the Board and the CEO	−0.859
15	**THE BOARD**	**Knowledge and skills in industry practice and standards are important criteria for choosing members of the Board**	−0.724
67	**THE BOARD**	**Board members actively use their knowledge, skills and commitment to further the organisation's mission**	−0.684
27	**STRUCTURE**	**Some of the tasks now undertaken by the organisation should be outsourced to some other agency or company**	0.571

Table 7.4   Total variance explained by factors in the factor analysis for 23 selected museums. Five factors explain 71% of the variation

FACTOR	TOTAL CONTRIB	PERCENT OF VARIANCE	CUMULATIVE PERCENT	ROTATION TOTAL
1	29.930	44.014	44.014	25.476
2	5.543	8.019	52.033	8.868
3	5.067	7.451	59.484	7.193
4	3.960	5.824	65.308	12.668
5	3.588	5.276	70.584	10.898

Table 7.5 Factor analysis – means (AVGE) and standard errors (ST ERR) – for better 11 and 12 worse museums together with correlation coefficients (r) with expert assessment for three factors emerging from the five factor solution for the 23 selcted museums. P(t) is the probability of the two means (AVGE) being the same. The direction of the correlation between assessment and factor score has been varied so that positive score means positive correlation[a]

FACTOR	DESCRIPTOR	BEST AVGE	ST-ERR	WORST AVGE	ST-ERR	P(t)	ASSESS
1	Cohesive Leadership	0.4247	0.2788	−0.3893	0.2704	0.0484	0.1477
2	Public Programming	0.5181	0.1883	−0.4749	0.3070	0.0130	0.4636*
5	Active Board	−0.4878	0.2713	0.4471	0.2595	0.0212	0.3734*

Note: [a]* significant at the 0.05 level.

Table 7.6 Correlations between factors for the five factor solution for 23 selected museums and expert assessments of the museums. Factor 2 is signficantly correlated with expert assessment and with the influence of public programs (PUB PROG) and marketing (MARK) on the assessment score (ASSES) but not research (RES) or collections (COLL). The direction of the correlation between assessment and factor score has been varied so that positive score means positive correlation[a]

FCTR	FAC 2	FAC 3	FAC 4	FAC 5	ASSES	PUB PROG	COLL	RES	MARK
1	0.186	0.191	−0.337	−0.335	0.148	0.041	−0.504*	−0.254	0.146
2	1	0.083	−0.142	−0.112	0.464*	0.460*	−0.225	−0.247	0.571**
3		1	−0.130	−0.042	−0.173	−0.048	0.010	−0.329	−0.054
4			1	0.135	0.005	0.109	0.207	0.216	−0.085
5				1	−0.373*	−0.034	0.377*	0.435*	−0.232

Note: [a]* significant at the 0.05 level; **significant at the 0.01 level.

Table 7.7   Correlations between factors for the five factor solution for 23 selected museums and demographic attributes of the museums. Government (GOVT) has a negative impact on factors 1 and 2. Museums with high scores in factor 1 have younger staff. (Change is a rough aggregate of incidents (high score denotes greater change), 'LastDev' is a score for the time of last major physical development of the museum (low score is most recent), 'Res' is a score for the relative importance of research in the museum's activities (high score means more), 'Size' is a numerical representation of the number of staff in the museum (high score means more staff), 'Perm' is the indicator of the number of respondents permanently employed (high score is higher number), 'Age' is age of respondent (low score denotes youth). The direction of the correlations between demographic attributes and the scores for factors 4 and 5 have been varied so that positive score means positive correlation[a]

FACTOR	GOVT	Change	LastDev	Res	Size	Perm	Age
1	−0.394*	0.293	0.060	−0.264	−0.368	−0.267	−0.482**
2	−0.306	0.185	0.522**	−0.325	0.418*	−0.186	−0.295
3	0.087	0.183	0.048	−0.060	−0.280	−0.510**	−0.120
4	−0.221	0.409*	0.232	−0.140	0.002	−0.157	−0.328
5	−0.659**	−0.243	−0.106	−0.458*	0.001	−0.266	−0.226

Notes: [a]* significant at the 0.05 level; ** significant at the 0.01 level.

Appendix C   The influence of country, museum-type and discipline

Country differences

There are more differences between museums from the USA and those of other countries in questionnaire scores – and the scores of US museums are on average better than others. Of the 28 significant items distinguishing the better museums, 16 are involved in distinctions between countries. The US museums differ significantly from those in *all* other countries in ten items but from each of the other countries in up to 17 items. In all 30 items are involved in these distinctions between US museums and those in other countries. The US museums are better in all cases where there is a difference with the exception of item 36, involvement of staff in formulating their training program, where UK museums score better than those from the USA. Canadian museums are better than UK museums in all of the items which distinguish museums in the two countries.

By and large the same items distinguish the museums of the different countries from each other. Four items most frequently figure in the distinctions: modelling by senior managers of appropriate behaviour (13), regular assessment of performance (39), efficient information transfer (42) and an active interest by staff in the information communicated to them (43). Leadership and Board items are more important issues in comparisons of museums in the USA with those in other countries. Public programs are a significant issue in comparisons of the USA with all others and with US–Australia and Canada–Australia comparisons. Training, communication and information technology are also areas of difference.

Differences between types of museums

The data concerning museums of different types (Table 7.8) is not really robust enough to draw firm conclusions. However, some general features seem to emerge. Where there are differences, they mainly concern the Board and Public Programs. The staff of science centres and museums generally have more positive perceptions than do those of other museums; art museum staff are less positive. Public program items distinguish almost all kinds of museums. In most cases these differences are more apparent when individual responses are analysed, especially where issues concerning the Board are concerned; this would be due to the larger number of cases in the samples.

Differences between discipline areas

The greatest differences between the staff of different discipline areas are between curatorial/research respondents on the one hand and finance/HR on the other (Tables 7.9 and 7.10). Generally, curatorial respondents are less positive – or perhaps more sceptical, than most others including information management/library respondents. Finance/HR respondents are generally more positive; so are public relations staff. Education/exhibitions respondents are generally less positive than most other staff.

The items which are principally involved in discriminating between staff of different discipline areas particularly concern public programs. There are differences also in respect of some demographic items such as administrative level and length of service: staff in finance, HR and public relations areas are generally employed at lower levels and have been employed for less time in the museum than staff in curatorial and most other areas.

Table 7.8   Possible differences between 'museums' of different kinds: NATH=natural history museum; SCI-C=science centre or science museum; HIST=history museum; ART=art museum. The symbol + indicates that the first of the pairs has a significantly better score than the second. For example, natural history museums are less likely to speedily attend to problems with public programs than are science centres whilst science centres are more likely to provide a variety of ways in which to understand the meanings of exhibits

QN	SECTION	DETAIL	NATH vs SCI-C	SCI-C vs HIST	SCI+C vs ART	NATH vs ART	HIST vs ART
26	PURPOSES	We aim to ensure that completed projects meet the required standards first time		−	−		
51	PUBLIC PROGRAMS	Problems experienced by visitors with public programs are speedily and appropriately attended to by staff of the relevant section	−	+			

Table 7.8   (*continued*)

QN	SECTION	DETAIL	NATH vs SCI-C	SCI-C vs HIST	SCI+C vs ART	NATH vs ART	HIST vs ART
53	PUBLIC PROGRAMS	Visitors are provided with a variety of ways (interpretive strategies) in which to understand the meaning of the exhibits/programs	−	+	+		+
54	PUBLIC PROGRAMS	Educational offerings attempt to address the full range of knowledge, attitudes and understandings which visitors bring with them			+		+
57	PUBLIC PROGRAMS	Exhibits and other public programs are developed by education, exhibition and other staff as well as research and curatorial staff working together			+	+	+
59	PUBLIC PROGRAMS	All those involved in public programs clearly understand the criteria for program choice	−		+		
60	PUBLIC PROGRAMS	The amount of money allocated to advertising and promoting public programs is based on knowledge of what expenditure is required to reach the desired proportion of the target market	−	+			
62	PUBLIC PROGRAMS	Public program staff are accepted by others including research and curatorial staff as important contributors to the future of the organisation	−		+		

Table 7.9   Comparison of perceptions of Curatorial and Conservation (Curat), Finance and Human Resource (FinHR) and Education and Exhibitions (Educ) staff with the perceptions of all other staff; + indicates that the first of the pairs has a significantly better score than the second, e.g. curatorial/conservation staff are less likely than other staff to consider that objectives for departments integrate with those for the organisation as a whole, whilst staff in finance and human resource areas are more likely to consider that objectives are integrated across departments than are staff from other disciplines/departments

QN	SECTION	DETAIL	Curat vs all others	FinHR vs all others	PR vs all others	Educ vs all others
2	ADMINLEV	Administrative level	−	+	+	
5	LENSERV	Length of service	−	+	+	
20	PURPOSES	Objectives for divisions/departments/sections clearly integrate with those for the organisation as a whole	−	+		−
51	PUBLIC PROGRAMS	Problems experienced by visitors with public programs are speedily and appropriately attended to by staff of the relevant section	−	+		+
56	PUBLIC PROGRAMS	The staff/consultants who undertake evaluation of public programs co-operate to improve program effectiveness by contributing the results of their work to decisions about programs	−	+		−
59	PUBLIC PROGRAMS	All those involved in public programs clearly understand the criteria for program choice	−			−
60	PUBLIC PROGRAMS	The amount of money allocated to advertising and promoting public programs is based on knowledge of what expenditure is required to reach the desired proportion of the target market		+	−	−
61	PUBLIC PROGRAMS	Staff responsible for conservation of collections work to ensure that wherever possible the objects will be available for use in public programs and scholarship	+	−		
62	PUBLIC PROGRAMS	Public program staff are accepted by others including research and curatorial staff as important contributors to the future of the organisation	+			−

Table 7.10   Comparison of perceptions of staff from various disciplines – Curatorial and Conservation (Curat), Finance and Human Resource (FinHR), Public relations (PR) and Education and Exhibitions (Educ); + indicates that the first of the pairs has a significantly better score than the second, e.g. Curatorial/Conservation staff are more likely than Education/Exhibitions staff to consider that problems with public programs are speedily attended to but less likely than staff from Finance and Human resources areas

QN	SECTION	DETAIL	Curat vs Educ	Curat vs FinHR	Educ vs FinHR	PR vs Curat	PR vs FinHR	PR vs Educ
2	ADMINLEV	Administrative level	−	−		+	−	
5	LENSERV	Length of service	−	−		+	−	
20	PURPOSES	Objectives for divisions/departments/ sections clearly integrate with those for the organisation as a whole	−	−		+		+
51	PUBLIC PROGRAMS	Problems experienced by visitors with public programs are speedily and appropriately attended to by staff of the relevant section	+	−		+	−	−
56	PUBLIC PROGRAMS	The staff/consultants who undertake evaluation of public programs co-operate to improve program effectiveness by contributing the results of their work to decisions about programs	+	−	−	+	−	+
59	PUBLIC PROGRAMS	All those involved in public programs clearly understand the criteria for program choice	+		−	+		+
60	PUBLIC PROGRAMS	The amount of money allocated to advertising and promoting public programs is based on knowledge of what expenditure is required to reach the desired proportion of the target market	+	−			−	+

Table 7.10   *(continued)*

QN	SECTION	DETAIL	Curat vs Educ	Curat vs FinHR	Educ vs FinHR	PR vs Curat	PR vs FinHR	PR vs Educ
61	PUBLIC PROGRAMS	Staff responsible for conservation of collections work to ensure that wherever possible the objects will be available for use in public programs and scholarship	+	+		−	+	
62	PUBLIC PROGRAMS	Public program staff are accepted by others including research and curatorial staff as important contributors to the future of the organisation		+		−		+

Notes

Des Griffin is former Director and currently Gerard Krefft Memorial Fellow at the Australian Museum, Sydney. **Morris Abraham** is Senior Lecturer in the School of Management at the University of Technology, Sydney. This paper was first published in 2000 in *Museum Management and Curatorship*, vol. 18, no. 4.

1   The work of Herman Heimovics (1994) and Herman *et al.* (1994) are examples of the use of performance indicators identified as appropriate by those working in the sector, an approach termed relativist (or social constructivist), the view that each approach to the evaluation of effectiveness is equally valid and that there is no real organisational effectiveness, only judgements of effectiveness. We do agree that evaluation should not be done by anyone from any of the constituencies involved in transactions with the organisation. Zammuto (1984: 612) observes, 'Much of the historical confusion surrounding the definition and criteria of organisational effectiveness has been caused by the process of societal evolution' and much of it 'parallels dilemmas found in management practice'.

References

Abraham, M., Griffin, D.J.G. and Crawford, J. (1999) Organisation change and management decision in museums. *Management Decision*, 37(10), 736–751.
Ames, M.M. (2000) Are Changing Representations of First Peoples in Canadian Museums and Galleries Challenging the Curatorial Prerogative? In (pp. 73–89) *The Changing Presentation of the American Indian*. National Museum of the American

Indian, Smithsonian Institution, Washington, DC in association with University of Washington Press (Seattle).

Bartlett, C.A. and Ghoshal, S. (1994) Changing the role of top management: beyond strategy to purpose. *Harvard Business Review*, Nov/Dec, 79–88.

Bass, B.M. (1990) *Stogdill and Bass's Handbook of Leadership*. Free Press, New York.

Bass, B.M., Avolio, B.J. and Atwater, L. (1996) The transformational and transactional leadership of men and women. *Applied Psychology: An International Review*, 45(1), 5–34.

Bennis, W. and O'Toole, J. (2000) Don't hire the wrong CEO. *Harvard Business Review*, May/June, 170–176.

Boyd, W.L. (1995) Wanted: an effective director. *Curator*, 38(3), 171–184.

Carl, J. and Stokes, G. (1991) Ordinary people, extraordinary organizations. *Nonprofit World*, 9(4), 8–12; 9(5), 18–26; 9(6), 21–26.

Carver, J. (1990) *Boards that Make a Difference*. Jossey Bass, San Francisco.

Collins, J.C. and Porras, J.I. (1994) *Built to Last. Successful Habits of Visionary Companies*. Century, London.

—— (1996) Building your company's vision. *Harvard Business Review*, Sept/Oct, 65–78.

Drucker, P. (1990) Lessons for successful nonprofit governance. *Nonprofit Management and Leadership*, 1(1), 7–14.

Dunphy, D. and Bryant, B. (1996) Teams: panaceas or prescriptions for improved performance? *Human Relations*, 49(5), 677–699.

Durbin, G. (ed.) (1996) *Developing Museum Exhibitions for Lifelong Learning*. The Stationery Office, London.

Falk, J.H. and Dierking, L. (1992) *The Museum Experience*. Whalesback Books, Washington, DC.

—— (2000) *Learning from Museums. Visitor Experiences and the Making of Meaning*. Altamira Press, Walnut Ck, CA.

Fernandez-Araoz, C. (1999) Hiring without firing. *Harvard Business Review*, July/Aug, 108–120.

Finkelstein, S. and Hambrick, D.C. (1996) *Strategic Leadership. Top Executives and their Effects on Organisations*. West Publishing, St Paul, MN.

Fisher, A. and Kahn, J. (1997) The world's most admired companies. *Fortune*, October 27, 48–49, 51–54, 56, 60, 62, 64, 66.

Ghoshal, S. and Bartlett, C.A. (1997) *The Individualized Corporation*. HarperBusiness, New York.

Goldberger, P. (1994) Doesn't Anybody Want this Job? *The New York Times*, 26 April, Section 2.

Goleman, D. (2000) Leadership that gets results. *Harvard Business Review*, March–April, 78.

Goodman, P.S. and Pennings, J.M. *et al.* (1981) *New Perspectives on Organizational Effectiveness*. Jossey Bass, San Francisco.

Graubard, S.R. (ed.) (1999) America's museums. *Daedalus*, 128(3), 1–337.

Griffin, D.J.G. (1987) Managing in the museum organisation I. Leadership and communication. *International Journal of Museum Management and Curatorship*, 6, 387–398.

—— (1988) Managing in the museum organisation II. Conflict, tasks, responsibilities. *International Journal of Museum Management and Curatorship*, 7, 11–23.

—— (1991a) Museums – Governance, Management and Government, or why are so many of the apples on the ground so far from the tree? *Museum Management and Curatorship*, 10(3), 293–304.

—— (1991b) Management and leadership in museums. *Australian Library Journal*, 40(2), 125–151.

Griffin, D.J.G. and Abraham, M. (1999) Management of Museums in the 1990s: Governments and Organisational Reform. In (pp. 45–92) K. Moore, *Management in Museums. New Research in Museum Studies*, vol. 7. The Athlone Press, London and New Brunswick, NJ.

Griffin, D.J.G., Abraham, M. and Crawford, J. (1999) Effective management of museums in the 1990s. *Curator*, 42(1), 37–53.

Griffin, J.M. and Symington, D.J. (1997) Moving from task-oriented to learning-oriented strategies on school excursions to museums. *Science Education*, 81(6), 763–779.

Grinstead, S. and Ritchie, M. (eds) (1990) *The Denver Art Museum Interpretive Project*. Denver Art Museum, Denver, CO.

Gurian, E.H. (1995) *Institutional Trauma. Major Change in Museums and its Effect on Staff*. American Association of Museums, Washington, DC.

—— (1999) What is the object of this exercise? A meandering exploration of the many meanings of objects in museums. *Daedalus*, 128(3), 163–184.

Guzzo, R.A. and Dickerson, M.W. (1996) Teams in organisations: recent research on performance and effectiveness. *Annual Review of Psychology*, 47, 307–338.

Hamel, G. and Prahalad, C.K. (1994) *Competing for the Future*. HBR Press, Cambridge, MA.

Hein, G.E. (1998) *Learning in the Museum*. Routledge, London.

Hein, G.E. and Alexander, M. (1998) *Museums: Places of Learning*. American Association of Museums, Washington, DC.

Herman, R.D. and Heimovics, R.D. (1994) A cross-national study of a method for researching non-profit organisational effectiveness. *Voluntas*, 5(1), 86–100.

Herman, R.D. *et al.* (1994) *The Jossey-Bass Handbook of Nonprofit Leadership and Management*. Jossey Bass, San Francisco.

Hinterhuber, H.H. (1996) Oriental wisdom and western leadership. *The International Executive*, 38(3), 287–302.

Hout, T.M. and Carter, J.C. (1995) Getting it done: new roles for senior executives. *Harvard Business Review*, Nov/Dec, 133–146.

Janes, R.R. (1997) *Museums and the Paradox of Change. A case study in urgent adaptation*. Glenbow Museum, Calgary (second edition).

—— (1999) Embracing Organizational Change in Museums: A Work in Progress. In (pp. 7–27) K. Moore, *Management in Museums. New Research in Museum Studies*, vol. 7. The Athlone Press, London and New Brunswick.

Jeffery-Clay, K.R. (1998) Constructivism in museums: how museums create meaningful learning environments. *Journal of Museum Education*, 23(1), 3–7.

Kanter, R.M. and Brinkerhoff, D. (1981) Organizational performance: recent developments in measurement. *Annual Review of Sociology*, 7, 321–349.

Kofman, F. and Senge, P.M. (1995) Communities of Commitment: The Heart of Learning Organizations. In (pp. 14–43) S. Chawla and J. Renesch (eds), *Learning Organizations: Developing Cultures for Tomorrow's Workplace*. Productivity Press, Portland, Oregon.

Kouzes, J.M. and Posner, B.Z. (1990) The credibility factor: what followers expect from their leaders. *Business Credit*, 92(5), 24–28.

Krug, K. (1992) Excellence in arts management: in search of characteristics common to well-run arts organisations. *Muse*, spring X(1), 48–53.

Livingston, J.S. (1969) Pygmalion in management. *Harvard Business Review*, Jul/Aug, 81–89.

McLean, K. (1999) Museum exhibitions and the dynamics of dialogue. *Daedalus*, 128(3), 83–107.

Mant, A. (1994) *Leaders We Deserve*. Currency Press, North Melbourne.

Mintzberg, H. (1983) The Professional Bureaucracy. In *Structure in Fives*. Prentice Hall, New York.

Moore, K. (ed.) (1999) *Management in Museums. New Research in Museum Studies*, vol. 7. The Athlone Press, London and New Brunswick.

Newlands, D.L. (1983) Stress and distress in museum work. *Muse*, summer 1(2), 18–33.

Nowlen, P. (1994) 'Museums in Troubled Times.' Keynote Address, British Museums Association 100th Anniversary Meeting, ms.

Osborne, S.P., Bovaird, T., Martin, S., Tricker, M. and Waterston, P. (1995) Performance management and accountability in complex public programs. *Financial Accountability and Management*, 11(1), 19–37.

Pfeffer, J. (1994) Competitive advantage through people. *California Management Review*, 36(2), 9.

—— (1996) When it comes to 'best practices' – why do smart organisations occasionally do dumb things? *Organisational Dynamics*, 25(1), 33–44.

Pitman, B. (ed.) (1999) *Presence of Mind. Museums and the Spirit of Learning*. The American Association of Museums, Washington, DC.

Roberts, L. (1997) *From Knowledge to Narrative. Educators and the Changing Museum*. Smithsonian Institution Press, Washington, DC and London.

Schloder, J.E. *et al.* (1994) *The Visitors Voice*. The Cleveland Museum of Art, Cleveland, OH.

Strong, R. (1998) *The Roy Strong Diaries 1967–1987*. Phoenix, London.

Thomas, A.B. (1988) Does leadership make a difference to organisational performance? *Administrative Science Quarterly*, 33, 388–400.

Ulrich, D. and Lake, D. (1991) Organisational capability: creating competitive advantage. *Academy of Management Executive*, 5(1), 77–92.

Weil, S.E. (1994a) Creampuffs and hardball. *Museum News*, September–October 1994, 42–43.

—— (1994b) 'Organization-wide Assessment of Museums: An Immodest Proposal.' Paper presented at the International Council of Museum's International Committee on Management (September 9–10, 1994), ms.

—— (1995) Progress Report from the Field. In (pp. 19–31) *A Cabinet of Curiosities: Inquiries into Museums and their Prospects*. Smithsonian Institution, Washington, DC.

—— (1999) From being *about* something to being *for* somebody: the ongoing transformation of the American museum. *Daedalus*, 128(3), 229–258.

Zammuto, R.F. (1984) A comparison of multiple constituency models of organisational effectiveness. *Academy of Management Journal*, 9(4), 606–616.

Chapter 8

The University Art Museum
Defining purpose and mission

Peter F. Drucker

V ISITORS TO THE CAMPUS were always shown the University Art
Museum, of which the large and distinguished university was very proud. A
photograph of the handsome neoclassical building that housed the museum had long
been used by the university for the cover of its brochures and catalogues.

The building, together with a substantial endowment, was given to the university around 1912 by an alumnus, the son of the university's first president, who
had become very wealthy as an investment banker. He also gave the university his
own small, but high quality, collections – one of Etruscan figurines, and one, unique
in America, of English Pre-Raphaelite paintings. He then served as the museum's
unpaid director until his death. During his tenure he brought a few additional
collections to the museum, largely from other alumni of the university. Only rarely
did the museum purchase anything. As a result, the museum housed several small
collections of uneven quality. As long as the founder ran the museum, none of the
collections was ever shown to anybody except a few members of the university's
art history faculty, who were admitted as the founder's private guests.

After the founder's death, in the late 1920s, the university intended to bring
in a professional museum director. Indeed, this had been part of the agreement
under which the founder had given the museum. A search committee was to be
appointed, but in the meantime a graduate student in art history who had shown
interest in the museum, and who had spent a good many hours in it, took over
temporarily. At first, she did not even have a title, let alone a salary. But she stayed
on acting as the museum's director and over the next thirty years was promoted
in stages to that title. But from the first day, whatever her title, she was in charge.
She immediately set about changing the museum altogether. She catalogued the
collections. She pursued new gifts, again primarily small collections from alumni

Source: pp. 28–35 in P.F. Drucker (1977) *Management Cases*, London: Heinemann.

and other friends of the university. She organized fund raising for the museum. But, above all, she began to integrate the museum into the work of the university. When a space problem arose in the years immediately following the Second World War, Miss Kirkhoff offered the third floor of the museum to the art history faculty, which moved its offices there. She remodelled the building to include classrooms and a modern and well-appointed auditorium. She raised funds to build one of the best research and reference libraries in art history in the country. She also began to organize a series of special exhibitions built around one of the museum's own collections, complemented by loans from outside collections. For each of these exhibitions she had a distinguished member of the university's art faculty write a catalogue. These catalogues speedily became the leading scholarly texts in the fields.

Miss Kirkhoff ran the University Art Museum for almost half a century. But old age ultimately defeated her. At the age of 68 after suffering a severe stroke, she had to retire. In her letter of resignation she proudly pointed to the museum's growth and accomplishment under her stewardship. 'Our endowment', she wrote, 'now compares favourably with museums several times our size. We never have had to ask the university for any money other than for our share of the university's insurance policies. Our collections in the areas of our strength, while small, are of first-rate quality and importance. Above all, we are being used by more people than any museum of our size. Our lecture series, in which members of the university's art history faculty present a major subject to a university audience of students and faculty, attract regularly three to five hundred people; and if we had the seating capacity, we could easily have a larger audience. Our exhibitions are seen and studied by more visitors, most of them members of the university community, than all but the most highly publicized exhibitions in the very big museums ever draw. Above all, the courses and seminars offered in the museum have become one of the most popular and most rapidly growing educational features of the university. No other museum in this country or anywhere else', concluded Miss Kirkhoff, 'has so successfully integrated art into the life of a major university and a major university into the work of a museum.'

Miss Kirkhoff strongly recommended that the university bring in a professional museum director as her successor. 'The museum is much too big and much too important to be entrusted to another amateur such as I was forty-five years ago,' she wrote. 'And it needs careful thinking regarding its direction, its basis of support and its future relationship with the university.'

The university took Miss Kirkhoff's advice. A search committee was duly appointed and, after one year's work, it produced a candidate whom everybody approved. The candidate was himself a graduate of the university who had then obtained his Ph.D. in art history and in museum work from the university. Both his teaching and administrative record were sound, leading to his present museum directorship in a medium-sized city. There he converted an old, well-known, but rather sleepy museum to a lively, community-orientated museum whose exhibitions were well publicized and attracted large crowds.

The new museum director took over with great fanfare in September, 1971. Less than three years later he left — with less fanfare, but still with considerable noise. Whether he resigned or was fired was not quite clear. But that there was bitterness on both sides was only too obvious.

The new director, upon his arrival, had announced that he looked upon the museum as a 'major community resource' and intended to 'make the tremendous artistic and scholarly resources of the Museum fully available to the academic community as well as to the public'. When he said these things in an interview with the college newspaper, everybody nodded in approval. It soon became clear that what he meant by 'community resource' and what the faculty and students understood by these words were not the same. The museum had always been 'open to the public' but, in practice, it was members of the college community who used the museum and attended its lectures, its exhibitions and its frequent seminars.

The first thing the new director did, however, was to promote visits from the public schools in the area. He soon began to change the exhibition policy. Instead of organizing small shows, focused on a major collection of the museum and built around a scholarly catalogue, he began to organize 'popular exhibitions' around 'topics of general interest' such as 'Women Artists through the Ages'. He promoted these exhibitions vigorously in the newspapers, in radio and television interviews and, above all, in the local schools. As a result, what had been a busy but quiet place was soon knee-deep in schoolchildren, taken to the museum in special buses which cluttered the access roads around the museum and throughout the campus. The faculty, which was not particularly happy with the resulting noise and confusion, became thoroughly upset when the scholarly old chairman of the art history department was mobbed by fourth-graders who sprayed him with their water pistols as he tried to push his way through the main hall to his office.

Increasingly the new director did not design his own shows, but brought in travelling exhibitions from major museums, importing their catalogue as well, rather than have his own faculty produce one.

The students too were apparently unenthusiastic after the first six or eight months, during which the new director had been somewhat of a campus hero. Attendance at the classes and seminars held in the art museum fell off sharply, as did attendance at the evening lectures. When the editor of the campus newspaper interviewed students for a story on the museum, he was told again and again that the museum had become too noisy and too 'sensational' for students to enjoy the classes and to have a chance to learn.

What brought all this to a head was an Islamic art exhibit in late 1973. Since the museum had little Islamic art, nobody criticized the showing of a travelling exhibit, offered on very advantageous terms with generous financial assistance from some of the Arab governments. But then, instead of inviting one of the university's own faculty members to deliver the customary talk at the opening of the exhibit, the director brought in a cultural attaché of one of the Arab embassies in Washington. The speaker, it was reported, used the occasion to deliver a violent attack on Israel and on the American policy of supporting Israel against the Arabs. A week later, the university senate decided to appoint an advisory committee, drawn mostly from members of the art history faculty, which, in the future, would have to approve all plans for exhibits and lectures. The director thereupon, in an interview with the campus newspaper, sharply attacked the faculty as 'elitist' and 'snobbish' and as believing that 'art belongs to the rich'. Six months later, in June, 1974, his resignation was announced.

Under the by-laws of the university, the academic senate appoints a search committee. Normally, this is pure formality. The chairman of the appropriate department submits the department's nominees for the committee who are approved and
appointed, usually without debate. But when the academic senate early the following
semester was asked to appoint the search committee, things were far from 'normal'.
The Dean who presided, sensing the tempers in the room, tried to smooth over
things by saying, 'Clearly, we picked the wrong person the last time. We will have
to try very hard to find the right one this time.'

He was immediately interrupted by an economist, known for his populism,
who broke in and said, 'I admit that the late director was probably not the right
personality. But I strongly believe that his personality was not at the root of the
problem. He tried to do what needs doing and this got him in trouble with the
faculty. He tried to make our museum a community resource, to bring in the
community and to make art accessible to broad masses of people, to the blacks and
the Puerto Ricans, to the kids from the ghetto schools and to a lay public. And
this is what we really resented. Maybe his methods were not the most tactful
ones – I admit I could have done without those interviews he gave. But what
he tried to do was right. We had better commit ourselves to the policy he wanted
to put into effect, or else we will have deserved his attacks on us as "elitist" and
"Snobbish".'

'This is nonsense,' cut in the usually silent and polite senate member from the
art history faculty. 'It makes absolutely no sense for our museum to try to become
the kind of community resource our late director and my distinguished colleague
want it to be. First, there is no need. The city has one of the world's finest and
biggest museums and it does exactly that and does it very well. Second, we here
have neither the artistic resources nor the financial resources to serve the community
at large. We can do something different but equally important and indeed unique.
Ours is the only museum in the country, and perhaps in the world, that is fully
integrated with an academic community and truly a teaching institution. We are
using it, or at least we used to until the last few unfortunate years, as a major educational resource for all our students. No other museum in the country, and as far
as I know in the world, is bringing undergraduates into art the way we do. All of
us, in addition to our scholarly and graduate work, teach undergraduate courses
for people who are not going to be art majors or art historians. We work with the
engineering students and show them what we do in our conservation and restoration work. We work with architecture students and show them the development
of architecture through the ages. Above all, we work with liberal arts students,
who often have had no exposure to art before they came here and who enjoy our
courses all the more because they are scholarly and not just "art appreciation". This
is unique and this is what our museum can do and should do.'

'I doubt that this is really what we should be doing,' commented the chairman
of the mathematics department. 'The museum, as far as I know, is part of the graduate faculty. It should concentrate on training art historians in its Ph.D. programme,
on its scholarly work and on its research. I would strongly urge that the museum
be considered an adjunct to graduate and especially to Ph.D. education, confine
itself to this work, and stay out of all attempts to be "popular", both on campus
and outside of it. The glory of the museum is the scholarly catalogues produced

by our faculty, and our Ph.D. graduates who are sought after by art history faculties throughout the country. This is the museum's mission, which can only be impaired by the attempt to be "popular", whether with students or with the public.'

'These are very interesting and important comments,' said the Dean, still trying to pacify. 'But I think this can wait until we know who the new director is going to be. Then we should raise these questions with him.'

'I beg to differ, Mr. Dean,' said one of the elder statesmen of the faculty. 'During the summer months, I discussed this question with an old friend and neighbour of mine in the country, the director of one of the nation's great museums. He said to me: "You do not have a personality problem, you have a *management* problem. You have not, as a university, taken responsibility for the mission, the direction, and the objectives of your museum. Until you do this, no director can succeed. And this is *your* decision. In fact, you cannot hope to get a good man until you can tell him what your basic objectives are. If your late director is to blame – I know him and I know that he is abrasive – it is for being willing to take on a job when you, the university, had not faced up to the basic management decisions. There is no point talking about *who* should manage until it is clear *what* it is that has to be managed and for what."'

At this point the dean realized that he had to adjourn the discussion unless he wanted the meeting to degenerate into a brawl. But he also realized that he had to identify the issues and possible decisions before the next faculty meeting a month later. Here is the list of questions he put down on paper later that evening:

1   What are the possible purposes of the University Museum:

   (a)   To serve as a laboratory for the graduate art history faculty and the doctoral students in the field?
   (b)   To serve as major 'enrichment' for the undergraduate who is not an art history student but wants both a 'liberal education' and a counter-weight to the highly bookish diet fed to him in most of our courses?
   (c)   To serve the metropolitan community – and especially its schools – outside the campus gates?

2   Who are or should be its customers?

   (a)   The graduate students in professional training to be teachers of art history?
   (b)   The undergraduate community – or rather, the entire college community?
   (c)   The metropolitan community and especially the teachers and youngsters in the public schools?
   (d)   Any others?

3   Which of these purposes are compatible and could be served simultaneously? Which are mutually exclusive or at the very least are likely to get into each other's way?

4   What implications for the structure of the museum, the qualifications of its director and its relationship to the university follow from each of the above purposes?

5   Do we need to find out more about the needs and wants of our various potential customers to make an intelligent policy decision? How could we go about it?

The dean distributed these questions to the members of the faculty with the request that they think them through and discuss them before the next meeting of the academic senate.

How would you tackle these questions? And are they the right questions?

Note

The late **Peter F. Drucker** is widely regarded as one of the founding fathers of the study of management. This paper was first published in 1977 in Drucker's book, *Management Cases*.

Chapter 9
_____

Strategic Management for Visitor-oriented Museums
A change of focus

Eva M. Reussner

Introduction

A S PUBLIC INSTITUTIONS, NON-PROFIT museums need to act in line with
cultural policy guidelines. There are a number of museum-related cultural policy guidelines that can be considered as general principles applicable to museums
in the Western world. For example, enabling access for and use by broad and diverse
audiences as well as the facilitation of learning are generally acknowledged as two
important museum functions (cf. Hooper-Greenhill 1994; Falk and Dierking
1995; Weil 1997; Sandell 1998; Hooper-Greenhill 1999; Falk and Dierking 2000;
Bradburne 2001). Beyond their common ground, cultural policies certainly have a
history and characteristics specific to their country. In Germany, for example, museum
policies are influenced by the democratic demand 'Kultur für alle!' – 'Culture for
Everyone!' – that, in the seventies, promoted the idea of a broad cultural participation to overcome limitations that are based on class differences (DFG 1974). Linked
to this idea of enabling access for a representative part of society is the concept of
cultural education that regards museums as places of informal learning (Nuissl 1987).
Today, the demand to be responsive to the public is still the imperative. In 1995,
the German assembly of the federal ministers of culture and education emphasised
that museums need to further open up to the public (KMK 1996). In the same
document, the educational purpose of museums that first came up in 1969 is underlined as being still an important museum function in the nineties (KMK 1996).

Extending the perspective on museum policies to the international context
inevitably highlights issues related to the interlinked processes of globalisation and
fragmentation. In this context, showcasing cultural diversity, providing spaces for

Source: *International Journal of Cultural Policy*, vol. 9, no. 1 (2003): 95–108.

cultural expression and for experiencing identity as well as gaining knowledge and understanding of other cultures are increasingly relevant (UNESCO 1998). The expected humanistic benefits of cultural participation and expression are underlined in particular in relation to minorities and indigenous peoples (Kahn 1997; UNESCO 1998). Australia and New Zealand are excellent examples in recognition of these principles: The Council of the Australian Museums Association developed special policies in relation to Australian museums and their indigenous peoples (1993), and the broad space dedicated to Maori culture at the National Museum of New Zealand Te Papa Tongarewa is a clear political demonstration of the recognition of New Zealand's 'first peoples'.

Cultural policy influences the ways in which museums shape society and community relationships. However, these guidelines are not easy to implement in an age of economic restraint and growing competition in the leisure sector (Ambrose and Runyard 1991; Kotler and Andreasen 1996; Landschaftsverband Rheinland 1997; Klein 2001). Museums are being challenged to attract visitors together with maintaining their financial viability, without compromising their obligations to society. Not least, fulfilling their duties as public institutions is vital for museums in order to legitimate public finding. As a consequence, museums experience a tension between the strategic demand to develop visitor-oriented museum services and the political demand to fulfil their social mandate as public institutions.

As a possible approach to deal with these challenges, museums have welcomed the concept of strategic management, derived from the for-profit sector. In general, strategic management is concerned with ensuring success in the long term, dealing with changing contextual conditions and competition (Thompson and Strickland 1993; Hill and Jones 1995). Since the nineties, there have been efforts to transfer this concept of strategic management to museums of all kinds (cf. Kovach 1989). Strategic management is expected to support museums in bringing their mission into action, and thus proving that museums make a difference. But the ways in which strategic management has been translated to the museum sector appear inappropriate for the visitor-oriented museum.

Related work

A review of publications shows three kinds of approaches to strategic management for museums and non profit organisations in general. First, some authors focus on business aspects that are without doubt highly relevant for museums (Kovach 1989; Oster 1995). But a business-focused approach makes it difficult to incorporate the humanistic duties of museums. Second, some publications are characterised by an emphasis on strategic *planning* (Ambrose and Runyard 1991; Denis, Langley and Lozeau 1993; Moulton 1997; Kawashima 1998). Notwithstanding the central role of strategic planning, this approach lacks a comprehensive view of strategic management, that is, giving attention to the functions vital for an effective preparation and implementation of strategies. The third group of publications promotes a focus on external marketing (Kotler and Andreasen 1996; Kotler and Kotler 1998, 2000). As it emphasises the external relations of museums, this approach is very close to a visitor-related concept of strategic museum management. Nevertheless, it needs to be recognised that the demand for broad cultural participation not only requires an increase in visitor numbers, but also an increased *variety* of museum audiences. At the same time, the educational mission of museums and the commitment to visitor-orientation require an internal focus on the visitor and the visiting experience itself.

An alternative approach

By focusing on business aspects, strategic planning or external marketing, publications on strategic management for non-profit organisations, cultural institutions or museums lack a comprehensive concept of strategic management suitable for visitor-oriented museums. Considering these shortcomings, this paper recommends a change in focus in strategic museum management.

A strategic concept for visitor-oriented museums needs to be more *comprehensive* in three respects: First, a comprehensive strategic concept for museums needs to be in line with the guidelines of cultural policy and the duties of museums as public institutions. Strategic management can only be appropriate and valuable for visitor-oriented museums on condition that it pays tribute to the educational purpose and social mandate of museums: that is, providing access, enabling social inclusion and promoting cultural diversity. Second, the principles of visitor-orientation need to be considered to make a museum visit attractive and worthwhile. And finally, it is questioned whether strategic considerations, if they are solely relevant in planning and marketing, have the impact on overall museum work that they could and should have. Museum work as a whole has to be committed to the overall strategic direction.

The contribution of this paper is two-fold. First, it extends strategic management into the context of non-profit museums, incorporating the basic museum guidelines found in Western cultural policy. Second, it presents a model for a more comprehensive strategic museum management process. In particular, the paper takes a closer look at the ways in which strategic management can be valuable for visitor-oriented museums.

This paper is organised as follows: First, a model of the strategic management process for non-profit museums is described. To interpret this model for visitor-oriented museums, the strategic implications of visitor-orientation are outlined before describing strategic museum management in this special context. Within that frame, audience research and evaluation are assessed as tools for strategic museum management.

Strategic management for non-profit museums

From strategic planning to strategic management

As a first step towards comprehensive strategic museum management, this paper advocates a shift similar to that which took place in private business during the seventies: from strategic *planning* to strategic *management*. With this move, the focus changed from an emphasis on long-term planning to goal-oriented, but flexible and comprehensive strategic management. The concept of *strategic planning* originally emerged in the sixties in the for-profit sector (Staehle 1999). Strategic planning is concerned with long-term planning of the organisation's development, based on information on the organisation's contextual conditions and relevant trends and developments. Driven by the insight in the seventies that strategic orientation should not be narrowed to the single planning function, a change of focus occurred. Now, the concept of a *strategic management* encompasses all functions and levels of management-broadened perspectives (Kreilkamp 1987; Johnson and Scholes 1997; Staehle 1999). This shift needs to be followed by museums in order to ensure a comprehensive strategic perspective on museum work: strategic issues have to become relevant in all organisational levels of a museum.

Comprehensive strategic museum management

The principles and common tools of for-profit strategic management need to be interpreted according to the specific conditions of non-profit museums. As a second step towards a more comprehensive strategic management concept, it is suggested to consider the duties of museums as public institutions, related to the guidelines of cultural policy, and combine them with the basic principles of strategic management, as found in strategic management publications (Kreilkamp 1987; Thompson and Strickland 1993; Harrison and St. John 1994; Hill and Jones 1995; Johnson and Scholes 1997; Mintzberg, Quinn and Ghoshal 1999). Thus, strategic museum management consists of organising, planning, leading and monitoring all areas of museum work, such as collections, research, exhibitions, public programs, administration and marketing, in view of the museum's primary goals. The museum's goals are argued as being defined by cultural policy and the challenges represented by competition and changing contextual conditions. In order for museums to cope with the challenges they face, strategic museum management requires self-assessment, competitor analysis and monitoring of strategically relevant developments in the museum's context. On that basis, strategic museum management provides goal-directed, value-guided and future-oriented thinking.

These principles form the basic elements of a comprehensive model of the strategic museum management process proposed as follows.

The model shown in Fig. 9.1 represents a synthesis derived from publications on strategic management, with particular references to Kreilkamp (1987: 61), Kotler and Andreasen (1996: 65) and Steinmann and Schreyögg (1997: 155). While it is acknowledged that a model necessarily is an abstraction from reality, showing an ideal process rarely found in practice, it nevertheless emphasises the basic principles that are considered as most important. The strategic management process model presented here aims to serve this purpose. It shows the museum in its context, which includes the museum field, the cultural and leisure sector, the community context and the national and legislative framework. The model emphasises the relations between the different stages of the strategic management process. Strategic management implies an iterative process with a number of feedback cycles. Next, a short description of the different stages and their interrelations is given,

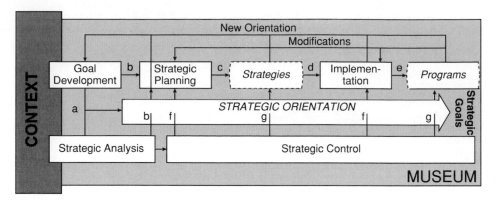

Figure 9.1   Basic elements of the strategic museum management process

incorporating the specific conditions of non-profit museums (cf. Kreilkamp 1987; Thompson and Strickland 1993; Harrison and John 1994; Hill and Jones 1995; Johnson and Scholes 1997 and Steinmann and Schreyögg 1997). In discussing the model and its application, the interrelations between each stage are identified by lower case letters.

Goal-development

Usually, the starting point of the strategic management process is *goal-development* and goal-definition. It serves to clarify and determine the major goals that are to become the focus of the overall strategic direction. Through goal-development, preliminary goals are laid down and formulated in a more concrete way.

In determining their central goals, museums are bound to prescribed functions and guidelines. The museums' purposes are to collect, preserve and investigate objects that are of cultural relevance, to provide access to their collections in a way that enables the cultural participation of a wide and diverse section of the population, including the provision of access and representation for minorities, and to facilitate informal education. The determination of goals is also influenced by values and standards such as professionalism, the wish to contribute to a better understanding of culture and society, a commitment to lifelong learning and respect of the visitors' needs and interests. Additionally, museums need to take into consideration the interests of stakeholders and the services of competitors within the leisure and cultural industry in general and the museum field in particular. Because museums are not independent in defining their aims and purposes, in the model, a reference to the museum's context is shown. Within the frame of given purposes and guidelines, museums translate these general goals into concrete, more operational objectives for the specific museum and have to decide on strategic priorities that will form the major focus of the museum's effort. During goal-development, contextual information is required. *Strategic analysis* provides this information.

Strategic analysis

Strategic analysis helps museums clarify their strategic goals and provides information for planning. Apart from analysing the museum context, strategic analysis represents a reflective step on the current status of the museum and its position within this context. Therefore, strategic analysis consists of an *organisational analysis* to identify strengths and weaknesses of the museum, and an *environmental analysis* to learn about the threats and opportunities in the museum context.

The internal analysis shows which factors a museum can rely on to achieve its strategic goals: for example, certain knowledge of its staff, certain qualities of its collection or its public image. But it is equally important to find out weaknesses threatening or at least diminishing the success of museum work. Examples for areas of external analysis are: the competitive situation within the museum field, demographic trends and leisure preferences. The focus of strategic analysis is defined by the strategic goals. At the same time, strategic analysis helps to clarify these strategic goals in showing which ones are recommendable, achievable and appropriate to the museum (a). Strategic analysis helps museums set priorities in relation to perceived gaps or positions of strength. Furthermore, the data gained through strategic analysis informs the planning of strategic programs.

Strategic orientation

Refined goals and the findings of the strategic analysis determine the strategic orientation, which serves as a guideline for museum work. Strategic orientation represents the guiding principle that supports museums in achieving previously defined goals. As value-guided, goal-referenced and future-oriented thinking, strategic orientation gives museum work a direction. To enable successful museum work and a shared strategic orientation, attention should be given to the development of consensus on and support for major goals, values and guiding principles, expounded in the museum's mission statement.

Strategic planning

Strategic planning is considered as the core stage of strategic management (cf. Kreilkamp 1987: 25). Strategic planning produces *strategies* that are designed to achieve the previously defined major goals. It distinguishes between overall corporate strategy and the number of substrategies that translate the general strategy into more concrete activities that complement each other, while being adjusted to the different operational areas of museum work. If, for example, it is a major goal to open the museum for senior audiences, this is reflected in the goals set for exhibition development, public programming and marketing activities. Strategic planning focuses on the strategic goals, while at the same time building on the findings of strategic analysis (b) and, if necessary, demanding additional information from strategic control, as plans progress (f). As strategic plans generally are designed for longer periods, it is important to leave room for flexibility in order to react on unforeseen events and developments that make a modification of strategies necessary.

Implementation

After formulation (c), the strategies need to be implemented in museum practice (d). Through *implementation* of the strategies, the *programs* designed to achieve the major goals of the museum are brought into action (e). Extending the previous example, now, the new marketing campaign focusing on seniors is launched, guided exhibition tours designed for seniors are offered and special offers at the museum shop are introduced. It is the purpose of strategic management to ensure that the originally intended strategy is brought into action. To this end, *strategic control* fulfils an important task.

Strategic control

Contrary to publications locating strategic control at the final stage of the strategic management process, *strategic control* here is conceived as a process accompanying and supporting the other stages of strategic management (f) (cf. Steinmann and Schreyögg 1997: 157). On the one hand, the function of strategic control is to provide further information, if needed, in order to support strategic planning. On the other hand, it has to review designed strategies, to supervise their implementation and to initiate modifications in programs in order to ensure the achievement of strategic goals. Finally, in a more narrow sense, strategic control is understood as the final judgement of the measures' progress and success in the light of major goals (g). This can be done either for a single activity or for a whole set of programs. As a consequence, those findings indicate the need for a reorientation of goals as well as for modifications in strategies.

General management functions such as leadership and communication are important to coordinate and align the different stages of the strategic management process and, above all, to develop a widespread acceptance of strategic thinking throughout museum work. The basic principles of strategic management can be applied to diverse museum priorities, such as visitor-orientation. Before the strategic management model is translated to visitor-oriented museums, the strategic implications of visitor-orientation are examined.

Strategic implications of visitor-orientation

Nowadays, many museums consider visitor-orientation as the central principle of their work (cf. KGSt 1989; Hooper-Greenhill 1994; Landschaftsverband Rheinland 1997; Weil 1997; Günter 1998; Graf 1999; Klein 2001). This development shows both a change in the understanding of the role of museums and a change in attitude of museums towards their users. Since the 19th century, museums have undergone an evolution from the private 'Wunderkammer' (cabinet of curiosities), only open to a tiny and chosen audience, to institutions open to the public. Weil predicts that the relation between museums and the public will reach a state in which 'it will be the public, not the museum, that occupies the superior position. The museum's role will have been transformed from one of mastery to one of service' (Weil 1997: 257).

Visitor-oriented museums acknowledge that paying attention to preconditions, needs and interests of visitors is important for the success of museum work. Only by considering their audiences' point of view, can museums gain the interest of a variety of visitors and offer them a valuable, enjoyable and at the same time educational experience.

Museums that aim to fulfil their mandate and at the same time wish to be attractive need to bring together the museum perspective on visitors with the visitor perspective on museums. The museum perspective on visitors is influenced by cultural policy in terms of cultural participation, social inclusion and informal education, notwithstanding the commercial aspects. The visitor perspective on museums is shaped by having multiple choices of leisure and cultural attractions and the expectation of an enjoyable, satisfying and valuable museum experience (cf. Doering 1999). Whereas the museum perspective determines the criteria for effectiveness and success of museum work in the long term, the visitor perspective shows that museums operate in a competitive context. Museums need to demonstrate value in relation to the needs and expectations of their audiences and services provided by other cultural or leisure attractions. This means that even visitor-orientation is an area where strategic thinking is necessary.

To achieve visitor-related goals in a competitive environment, museums need to pay attention to two dimensions of visitor-orientation:

(a) from an external perspective, museums need to develop attracting power, in order to enable access and cultural participation and to cope with competition;
(b) from an internal perspective, museums need to ensure that their services are appropriate to visitors, in order to enable an enjoyable and educational museum experience.

Being attractive and at the same time appropriate to their audiences are vital factors for long-term museum success. Because of their central role, these goals can be considered strategic goals of visitor-oriented museums. The following section discusses how strategic management can support museums in a visitor-focused approach to museum work.

Strategic management for visitor-oriented museums

In the last section it was argued that, in order to remain or become relevant to a broad public, museums need to focus strategically on the needs, interests and preconditions of their audiences. In visitor-oriented museums, strategic museum management is concerned with audience development in an external perspective and, in an internal perspective, with visitor-focused product development, ranging from exhibitions to visitor programs and service quality.

External visitor focus

A strategic focus on visitors puts audience development among the primary aims of museums. Audience development implies maintaining the core audience, building a broader audience base, attracting diverse audiences and building relationships with the community. But the limits of audience development need to be acknowledged. Treinen (1996) has found that the group of potential visitors that can be motivated to visit a museum is rather small: between 15 and 20% of the adult urban population. Museums should be clear about their real visitor potential and try to build on relationships with actual visitors who can be encouraged to make multiple visits.

Having determined the two major goals of audience development – broadening the audience base and encouraging repeat visitation – strategic planning then allows the design of effective audience development strategies. In order to develop marketing activities, information is needed from strategic analysis on the actual and the potential audiences, their preferences and characteristics, and on the audiences and services of competing museums. This enables museums to determine their potential audiences and gives indications for strategies to reach out to certain target groups and how to gain distinctiveness in comparison to competing attractions.

Actual visitors are the most powerful means of advertising as they promote the museum by word-of-mouth (Kotler and Andreasen 1996: 43). But repeat visitation and recommendations depend on the perceived value of the museum experience (cf. Thompson and Strickland 1993: 109). In order to retain and enlarge their attracting power, museums not only rely on an effective marketing campaign, but they also need to offer a high-quality museum experience. A good marketing campaign is of no use if the museum experience does not meet the visitor's expectations. Hence, the internal focus on visitors plays an essential role for the success of museum work.

Internal visitor focus

Paying attention to the museum audience is a precondition for an enjoyable museum experience as well as for the fulfilment of the museum's educational purpose. On the one hand, one has to acknowledge that a museum visit is a leisure experience and a social experience (Falk and Dierking 1992). This means, museums need to develop strategies that create interest in their subjects and services, enable recreation and social interaction. In addition, the contribution of quality service, good orientation and a welcoming atmosphere to a satisfying visit should not be neglected. To initiate engagement with exhibits and occupation with certain subjects, museums need to take into consideration the conditions under which informal learning is possible and encouraged and examine the effectiveness of exhibits. The internal visitor focus demands museum services appropriate to visitors by acknowledging their motives, interests and needs in visitor-related strategies of museum work.

Being appropriate to a diverse museum audience is not easy; and it cannot be fulfilled completely. But instead of designing museum services for a stereotyped audience, museums need to create a broad range of programs aimed at specific subgroups of visitors, e.g. children, or subaudiences defined through sophisticated attitudinal and lifestyle segmentation methods, such as Schulze's (1992). These differentiation strategies support museums in becoming attractive to a variety of visitors.

Visitor-orientation as strategic orientation

As visitor-orientation is considered strategically important for museum work, it has to be conceived as the orientation that gives museum work a focus and provides guidance. Visitor-orientation is not an *end* in itself, but a *means* to achieve the major goals of museums. It is the leading principle that should be followed throughout museum work.

The central idea of visitor-orientation shapes the attitudes of museum staff throughout the organisation, allowing audiences' needs, interests and preconditions to influence the direction of museum work.

The role of audience research and evaluation

In order to find out what makes museums attractive and in which form museum work is appropriate to their visitors, museums need information concerning their audiences, such as which groups of the population currently are brought into the museum, what are the conditions under which learning in an informal setting is possible and what are the visitors' attitudes towards the museum's programs and services. *Visitor studies* and *evaluations* are useful tools to gather reliable information about museum visitors in a systematic way (cf. Loomis 1987; Screven 1990). In addition, *non-visitor research* can also provide useful information (cf. Kirchberg 1996; Schäfer 1996). Audience research here is conceived as consisting of both visitor and non-visitor research as well as evaluation. The methods of audience research that many museums already use can be interpreted from a strategic perspective and used accordingly.[1]

Whereas visitor studies provide information on a more general level, such as the audience profile and levels of satisfaction, evaluations assess museum services in more detail. The classical objects of museum evaluation are the exhibitions, but the principles of evaluation can be applied to the whole range of the museum's services. Evaluations can provide detailed assessments of exhibitions, programs, visitor services, commercial outlets and other museum services. The function of evaluations is not a mere critique of museum work, but to initiate a constructive learning process. Audience research and evaluation can help a museum on its way towards a strategic orientation by supporting goal-defining, strategic planning and the implementation of measures. Used in this way, audience research and evaluation can be considered as means of strategic analysis and strategic control.

Audience research and evaluation as strategic analysis

For visitor-oriented museums, information about their visitors and the potential visitors in their environment is relevant to assess their internal situation as well as their position in the museum's environment. Through visitor surveys and status-quo evaluation, audience research contributes to the *organisational analysis*.

A *visitor profile* survey paints a picture of the parts of the population the museum has reached. It can describe the demographic and psychographic characteristics of its audiences, which at the same time allow drawing conclusions on the target groups still underrepresented. Additionally, this information can help to customise the museum's services for different audiences. A *visitor experience* survey adds useful information in assessing the qualities and weaknesses of the visiting experience, including all aspects of museum services, from the exhibitions and educational programs to the opening hours, the assortment of the museum shop and the service quality in the museum café. If this information is related to visitor characteristics, museums can draw useful conclusions differentiated for diverse audiences.

In the frame of strategic analysis, a so-called *status-quo evaluation* is suitable to assess the current status of museum work. Existing services are reviewed concerning their strengths and weaknesses to find out where changes are necessary. In this assessment, visitor-responsiveness is an important criterion to judge the exhibition, the educational program or special events.

To complement the internal analysis of a museum, *non-visitor research* and *comparative studies* support the *environmental analysis*. To help museums develop attracting power, the environmental analysis collects information about the popularity and the public image of a museum, but also on socio-economic trends, leisure preferences, cultural attitudes and patterns of media consumption.

Non-visitor research does not use museum visitors as primary sources of information, but focuses on those that never or seldom find their way to the museum (cf. Kirchberg 1996; Schäfer 1996). On the one hand, it helps to identify target groups that could be reached by the museum, and, on the other hand, non-visitor research provides insight in motives and particularly in barriers for a museum visit that need to be overcome to really open the museum to a broad public.

Concerning visitor-orientation, *comparative studies* focus on the services of other museums, cultural and leisure institutions (cf. Oster 1995: 144f.). For example, subjects of comparison can be the attendance figures of other museums or cultural and leisure institutions, their visitor programs and exhibitions, as well as service quality and marketing activities. While, on the one hand, this comparison provides an overview concerning the services of competitors, on the other hand, it allows to identify which factors contribute to the success of other museums. The museum then has to assess whether it could also utilise those factors or find a niche to distinguish its services from its competitors and develop a unique profile.

Audience research and evaluation as strategic control

Evaluations can also be considered as parts of *strategic control* as they aim to accompany the development and implementation of programs in a critical way. *Front-end evaluation* provides information at the initial stage of planning, i.e. it takes place before a project is concretely planned and brought into action. The intention is to get an idea of the perceptions of the visitors to avoid the implementation of expensive, but ineffective measures. *Formative evaluation* takes place during the planning stage and helps to find out the best ways to design exhibits, programs, marketing campaigns or other activities. Formative evaluation aims to optimise measures before their final implementation. As it initiates corrections and modifications if the achievement of the goals is endangered, it fulfils the tasks of strategic control. Even with a very careful preparation, problems can appear after implementation. *Remedial evaluation* helps to identify and remove such problems so that museum staff can put the finishing touches to their exhibitions and programs. Finally, the exhibition, respectively the programs are judged in terms of success in view of the strategic goals through *summative evaluation*. The function of summative evaluation is to assess the effectiveness and efficiency of the programs, i.e. if the exhibition, the visitor program, a new marketing campaign or an event achieved their goals and if the investment was worth its effect. Summative evaluation does not necessarily relate to a single program, but can as well assess a set of different activities. Whatever task is concerned, visitor-orientation is the primary benchmark to judge the success of museum work.

Conclusions

This article has described a new, comprehensive approach to strategic management for visitor-oriented museums, overturning the focus on business, formal planning and external marketing. This paper proposed a change of focus in strategic museum management towards including cultural policy guidelines and the principles of visitor-orientation, in order to overcome the tension between the strategic demand to develop visitor-oriented museum services and the duties of museums as public institutions.

A comprehensive model of the strategic management process has been proposed. Due to limited space, the implications of strategic management for visitor-oriented museums have been described briefly. While focusing on visitor-orientation, the strategic museum management model proposed in this paper could be applied to other aspects of museum work, for example, research excellence or optimising the museum's financial performance.

Proposing a model for the strategic management of visitor-oriented museums, this paper is conceptual in nature. The practical implementation of this model goes beyond the scope of this paper. However, there are some issues that should be kept in mind when implementing the concept of strategic management. Taking the audiences' perspectives seriously is a prerequisite for strategically successful visitor-oriented museum work. The concept of strategic management is not applicable from one day to the other, but requires first of all developing strategic thinking and raising awareness of the basic strategic principles throughout the institution. The application of this model at particular museums certainly needs to be elaborated and adapted to the individual museum conditions. To avoid translation problems, museums do not need to adopt all the methods and tools of strategic management derived from private business, but procedures they use can be reinterpreted with a strategic focus, as, for example, audience research.

The ways in which museums can benefit from audience research, as suggested in this paper, go far beyond current common uses of audience research and evaluation. Audience research and evaluation can be considered as instruments for strategic analysis and control and used to review the whole range of museum functions. Certainly this is subject to the availability of resources – not only in financial terms, but also of expertise in order to obtain reliable and useable results. Nevertheless, also low-effort methods like a heightened interest in the activities of competitors, learning from studies conducted by other institutions and simple procedures like the collection of museum visitor postcodes may turn out to be very useful to strategically position the museum vis-à-vis its competitors *and* its audience.

Notes

Eva M. Reussner is a researcher and writer principally concerned with the issues of museum management and especially the uses of audience research. This paper was first published in 2003 in the *International Journal of Cultural Policy*, vol. 9, no. 1.

1   The link between strategic museum management and audience research is hardly covered in publications, except for two conference presentations, one by Tim Sullivan on the 1998 Conference 'Visitors Centre Stage: Action for the Future' in Canberra, demonstrating how audience research and evaluation have influenced the development of a corporate strategy at the Australian Museum, Sydney. The second contribution is made by his colleague Lynda Kelly, listing a strategic use among the important functions of audience research in museums in her opening address at the Evaluation and Visitor Research Special Interest Group Day of the 2001 Museums Australia Conference. This paper complements their view with the theoretical incorporation of audience research into the model of the strategic museum management process and a detailed description of its role within that process.

References

Ambrose, T. and Runyard, S., eds (1991) *Forward Planning. A Handbook of Business, Corporate and Development Planning for Museums and Galleries* (London; New York).

Bradburne, J.M. (2001) 'A new strategic approach to the museum and its relationship to society', *Museum Management and Curatorship* 19, 75–84.

Council of Australian Museums Association Inc. (1993). *Previous Possessions, New Obligations: Policies for Museums in Australia and Aboriginal and Torres Strait Islander People.*

Denis, J.L., Langley, A. and Lozean, D. (1993) 'The paradoxes of strategic planning in the public sector', *Optimum. The Journal of Public Sector Management* 24, 31–41.

Deutsche Forschungsgemeinschaft (DFG) (1974) *Denkschrift Museen. Zur Lage der Museen in der Bundesrepublik Deutschland und Berlin (West)* (Boppard).

Doering, Z.D. (1999) 'Strangers, guests, or clients? Visitor experiences in museums', *Curator* 42, 74–87.

Falk, J.H. and Dierking, L.D. (1992) *The Museum Experience* (Washington, DC).

—— eds (1995) *Public Institutions for Personal Learning: Establishing a Research Agenda* (Washington, DC).

—— (2000) *Learning from Museums: Visitor Experiences and the Making of Meaning* (Walnut Creek, CA).

Graf, B. (1999) 'Besucherorientierung als Leitziel der Museumsarbeit in der Bundesrepublik Deutschland', in *Geöffnet! das Museum für den Besucher. Proceedings of the 10th Bavarian Museum Day*, Landshut, 7–9 July 1999, Munich, 21–29.

Günter, B. (1998) 'Besucherorientierung: eine Herausforderung für Museen und Ausstellungen', in Scher, Marita Anna, eds *(Umwelt-) Ausstellungen und ihre Wirkung* (Oldenburg), pp. 51–55.

Harrison, J.S. and St. John, C.H. (1994) *Strategic Management of Organizations and Stakeholders. Theory and Cases* (St. Paul, MN).

Hill, C.W.L. and Jones, G.R. (1995) *Strategic Management – An Integrated Approach*, 3rd Edn (Boston, MA).

Hooper-Greenhill, E. (1994) *Museums and Their Visitors* (London).

—— ed. (1999) *The Educational Role of the Museum*, 2nd Edn (London; New York).

Johnson, G. and Scholes, K. (1997) *Exploring Corporate Strategy*, 4th Edn (Hertfordshire).

Kahn, D.M. (1997) 'Community-bezogene Ausstellungen', *Museumskunde* 62, 48–53.

Kawashima, N. (1998) 'Planning ahead', *Museums Journal* 3/1998, 34f.

Kirchberg, V. (1996) 'Museum visitors and non-visitors in Germany: A representative survey', *Poetics* 24, 239–258.

Klein, H.-J. (2001) 'Let's do it! Ein Plädoyer für Besucherorientierung, Besucheranalyse und Evaluation', *Museum Aktuell* 65, 2639–2643.

Kommunale Gemeinschaftsstelle für Verwaltungsvereinfachung (KGSt) (1989) *Die Museen. Besucherorientierung und Wirtschaftlichkeit* (Cologne).

Kotler, N. and Kotler, P. (1998) *Museum Strategy and Marketing. Designing Missions, Building Audiences, Generating Revenue and Resources* (San Francisco).

—— (2000) 'Can Museums be All Things to All People?: Missions, Goals, and Marketing's Role', *Museum Management and Curatorship* 18, 271–287.

Kotler, P. and Andreasen, A.R. (1996) *Strategic Marketing for Non profit Organizations*, 5th Edn (Upper Saddle River, NJ).

Kovach, C. (1989) 'Strategic management for museums', *The International Journal of Museum Management and Curatorship* 8, 137–148.

Kreilkamp, E. (1987) *Strategisches Management und Marketing* (Berlin).

Kulturausschuß der Kultusministerkonferenz (KMK) (1996) 'Handreichung des Kulturausschusses der Kultusministerkonferenz zu den Aufgaben der Museen', *Museumskunde* 61, 104–106.

Landschaftsverband Rheinland, eds (1997) *Das besucherorientierte Museum* (Cologne).

Loomis, R.J. (1987) *Museum Visitor Evaluation: New Tool for Management* (Nashville, TN).

Mintzberg, H., Quinn, J.B. and Ghoshal, S. (1999) *The Strategy Process* (London; New York).

Moulton, J. (1997) *The Art of Strategic Planning: Visions And Strategies For Cultural Organisations* (Melbourne).

Nuissl, E. (1987) *Bildung im Museum: zur Realisierung des Bildungsauftrages in Museen und Kunstvereinen* (Heidelberg).

Oster, S.M. (1995) *Strategic Management for Nonprofit Organizations: Theory and Cases* (New York; Oxford).

Sandell, R. (1998) 'Museums as agents of social inclusion'. *Museum Management and Curatorship* 17, 401–418.

Schäfer, H. (1996) 'Non-visitor research: an important addition to the unknown', in Visitor Studies Association (Ed.) *Visitor Studies: Theory, Research and Practice*,

Vol. 9, Selected Papers from the 1996 Visitor Studies Conference, Jacksonville, Alabama, 195–205.

Schulze, G. (1992) *Die Erlebnis-Gesellschaft. Kultursoziologie der Gegenwart* (Frankfurt; New York).

Screven, C. (1990) 'Uses of evaluation before, during and after exhibit design', *ILVS Review: A Journal of Visitor Behavior* 1, 36–66.

Staehle, W.H. (1999) *Management: eine verhaltenswissenschaftliche Perspektive*, 8th Edn (Munich).

Steinmann, H. and Schreyögg, G. (1997) *Management: Grundlagen der Unternehmensführung. Konzepte–Funktionen–Fallstudien*, 4th Edn (Wiesbaden).

Thompson, Jr., A.A. and Strickland, A.J. (1993) *Strategic Management. Concepts and Cases*, 7th Edn (Boston, MA).

Treinen, H. (1996) 'Das Museum als kultureller Vermitdungsort in der Erlebnisgesellschaft', *Vom Elfenbeinturm zur Fußgängerzone: Drei Jahrzehnte deutsche Museumsentwicklung. Versuch einer Bilanz und Standortbestimmung* (Landschaftsverband Rheinland, Opladen), pp. 111–121.

UNESCO (1998) *World Culture Report. Culture, Creativity and Markets* (Paris).

Weil, S.E. (1997) 'The museum and the public', *Museum Management and Curatorship* 16, 257–271.

Chapter 10

Liberty Science Center in the United States

A mission focused on external relevance

Emlyn H. Koster and Stephen H. Baumann

Introduction

A PRODUCTIVE NEW CONSCIOUSNESS seems to have at last gained a foot-
hold in the museum field – one that, simply put, calls upon museums to be
focused as much on their usefulness as on their popularity. But this is not a new
calling. In his concept of the 'new museum' that accompanied the founding of The
Newark Museum in New Jersey in 1909, John Cotton Dana (1856–1929) advocated: 'learn what aid the community needs and fit the museum to those needs' (Dana
1999). Museums might arguably have taken this step sooner, and with less anguish,
had Dana's writings been more available in the years after his death (Weil 1999).

The American Association of Museums (AAM) was founded in 1906. Three-
quarters of a century would pass before the profound intent of Dana's philosophy
began to resurface (American Association of Museums 1984, 1992), leading to
a national initiative in 1998 to examine and encourage the civic engagement of
museums (American Association of Museums 2002). A scholarly assessment of trends
in the U.S. museum field over the late twentieth century has concluded: 'The field
shifted from internally focused and collection-driven organizations to externally focused
and market driven organizations with greatly broadened stakeholders' (Harvard
University, John F. Kennedy School of Government 2001).

The Canadian Museums Association (CMA) was founded in 1947. In 1995,
its joint conference in Montreal with the Société des Musées Québécois had the
theme *Museums: Where Knowledge is Shared*. Its publication recalled the 1972 and
1989 declarations of the International Council of Museums (ICOM) in Chile and The
Netherlands that museums are a powerful force for human development and places

Source: pp. 85–111 in R.R. Janes and G.T. Conaty (eds) (2005) *Looking Reality in the Eye*:
museums and social responsibility, Calgary: University of Calgary Press.

where the public can look for the meaning of the world around them. However, in the same paper (Koster 1995), it was concluded that the missions and perceptions of most museums are, in fact, rarely reflective of such declarations. In 1996, at the symposium marking the 150th anniversary of the Smithsonian Institution, Harold Skramstad challenged museums to adopt mission statements that go beyond what the museum collects, preserves and interprets to explicitly state what the museum's beneficial outcomes are intended to be in community terms (Smithsonian Institution 1997). The president of the Canadian Museums Association has recently wondered: 'Are we really interacting with our society or are we just pretending to do so in order to soothe our conscience?' (Brousseau 2003).

The term 'social responsibility' is now entrenched as a summary descriptor of concerted efforts by for-profit and non-profit organizations to improve society and undo harm where harm has been done. Taking a broader perspective, we need to remind ourselves that efforts to improve the human condition must be combined with efforts to improve the condition of Planet Earth in environmental terms (Leahy 2003) for its urban, rural and wilderness areas. In the new calling, therefore, it is incumbent upon all types of museums – natural history, human history, art, science and technology – to become reflective about their external relevance to pressing human and environmental contexts.

The dictionary defines relevance as relating to the matter(s) at hand. Synonyms are meaningful, pertinent and symbiotic: antonyms are self-absorbed, detached and elitist. In the museum context, being truly relevant demands identification of external challenges to which the museum's expertise can be directed and make a positive difference. It is not simply a matter of trying to engage the community in what the museum wants to do (Carbonne 2003). Rather, it needs to be about a wholehearted externalization of purpose.

The following recent developments beyond the non-profit field help us to understand the profound implications of the relevance concept. In corporations, there is a spectrum of consciousness from self-interest to the common good (Barrett 1998). Barrett points out that movement across this spectrum is preferably driven by the organization's internal desire to be beneficial to the world as well as to be profitable, but organizations are commonly obliged to adopt this philosophy because of financial difficulty or external pressure. Leaders of organizations are being called upon to be social activists, establishing and clarifying the social agenda for their organizations (Parston 1997). The alignment of these lines to philosophy and practice in the museum field is explored elsewhere (Koster 1999). Richard Barker (Barker 2002) has delved into the point of leadership and, referring back to Aristotle's philosophy, develops the fundamental premise that it is, at the core, about harmonious pursuit of positive consequences in the world. This is similar to the Japanese ethical principle of 'kyosei' which encourages individuals and organizations to live and work together for the common good (Barrett 1998). And further in this regard, Stephen Covey (Covey 1990) usefully distinguishes the meaning of efficiency and effectiveness; he considers efficiency to be about doing things right and effectiveness to be about doing the right thing. In a graphic metaphor, Covey talks about efficiency in terms of how well you climb a ladder, whereas effectiveness is about in which direction you first decide to lean the ladder. In the increasingly popular field of performance metrics (U.S. National Center for Nonprofit Boards 2001b), it is much easier to quantify efficiency than effectiveness. For museums, while it may be tempting to compare visitors per square foot per year among museums as an efficiency indicator, if the visitor's learning experience is peripheral to the challenges and opportunities facing that community, then this metric says nothing about the museum's effectiveness. *In Search of Excellence* was a best-selling business book first published in 1982 (Peters and Waterman 1982). In hindsight, it was focused on efficiency aimed at maximum corporate profits. Today's definition of organizational excellence revolves around the common good, about doing the right thing, about effectiveness.

Certainly, museum expertise is well suited to help educate the public on the daunting array of challenges facing the world today (Worldwatch Institute 2003). These include: inter-cultural friction; the need to lift the horizons of disadvantaged communities in meaningful and sustainable ways; environmental stewardship and slowing the decline in biodiversity, as well as the depletion of natural resources; coping with constant societal evolution because of technological advance; thinking long term and in the big picture about our past and present actions; and educational reform that harnesses the value of all community resources. Increasingly, museum professionals are airing their thoughts about the greater usefulness of their institutions in society (e.g., Koster 1995; Casey 2001; Weil 2002; Brousseau 2003; Worts in press).

As importantly, museums should also be places where humanity's positive activities inspire us. These include: reduction in the rate of our population growth; enhanced disease prevention and other medical advances; the development of technologies that help to overcome disabilities; the greater availability of communication technologies; the progress toward universal gender equality and civil rights; the commitment to foreign aid; the rise of environmentalism and increased research into renewable energy sources; increased availability of learning resources; and the value we place in conserving historically valuable structures. With the word 'museum' having its roots in Greek 'as the place of the Muses,' we should remind ourselves that the institution of the museum is a unique and enduring one that is fundamentally for reflection and insight.

Science-technology centres have in many ways accelerated the relevancy movement in museums (Koster 1999). The reasons include increased flexibility in the absence of a defining collection, the need to devise exhibitions and programs explicitly for a public education purpose, the application of new technologies that extend the reach of the museum, the fact that their core subject matter is a primary driver in the progression of society, and an increasing reflection on the optimal niche of this type of museum in the infrastructure of how people acquire their knowledge about science and technology.

Introduction to Liberty Science Center

North America's first major science museums were the Franklin Institute in Philadelphia and Museum of Science and Industry in Chicago, opening in 1824 and 1933, respectively. The Museum of Science in Boston and the California Museum of Science and Industry in Los Angeles, now the California Science Center, both opened in 1951. The first institutions devoted exclusively to interactive learning experiences were the Exploratorium in San Francisco and the Ontario Science Centre in Toronto, both opening in 1969. Reflecting a rapid increase in popularity of this new kind of museum, the Association of Science-Technology Centers (ASTC), based in Washington, D.C., was founded in 1973. The Canadian Association of Science Centres (CASC) is a strengthening, newer entity for national advocacy and collaboration. Today, virtually every American state and Canadian province is well served by ASTC or CASC member institutions.

New Jersey's Liberty Science Center is situated in a state park on the Hudson River shore in Jersey City, opposite lower Manhattan and next to Ellis Island and the Statue of Liberty. This 170,000 sq. ft., non-profit institution was conceived in 1980 as a helping hand to the region's education and workforce development. It opened in January 1993, following a US$68 million collaborative, private- and public-sector campaign.

Lying between New York City and Philadelphia and rising westwards toward the Appalachians, New Jersey is America's most densely populated state and culturally one of its most diverse states. Although New Jersey has the highest percentage of postgraduate degrees in science and technology, the nation's top high-school graduation rate and highest average household income, almost one in ten of its citizens live below the poverty line. Liberty Science Center is New Jersey's most popular museum, and the only New Jersey destination listed in New York City tourist guides and authorized for field-trip use by New York public schools. Our host community of Jersey City is a fast-growing part of the New York metropolitan region, and is well served by light-rail, ferry and subway mass transit systems. Its Hudson shorefront is a glistening, new, high-rise cluster of businesses and residences with new hotels. Behind this skyline are revitalized residential streetscapes, but inland many of its low-rise neighbourhoods are in an economically depressed, and still only slowly improving, condition.

Mindful of this regional socio-demographic picture, Liberty Science Center's mission is to be *an innovative learning resource for lifelong exploration of nature, humanity and technology, supporting the growth of our diverse region and promoting informed stewardship of the world.* Multimedia learning environments consist of themed floors on the environment, health and invention, the largest IMAX® dome theatre in the United States and one of its few 3D laser theatres.

Although its early years were financially unstable, the Center's proactive role in the community and region became a solid foundation for strong recovery and enduring growth, thereby enabling its tenth anniversary in January 2003 to be a time for much celebration. Today, it is known for an unusually varied suite of onsite, offsite and online educational programs that are intertwined with exhibitions and aligned with state and national curriculum standards at each grade, its great diversity of audience, the frequency of its voice in both conferences and in the literature on the trend of science centres to be more useful institutions (e.g., Schiele and Koster 2000), and its community services in the aftermath of the terrorist attacks on the World Trade Center (Koster 2002).

This article profiles three of Liberty Science Center's mission-driven learning experiences, each unique in the museum field, and each with a strong flavour of social responsibility. Each follows the same format, first framing the matter at hand, then describing the program in response to it. All three also incorporate educational technologies to a degree not typical in the museum field. At Liberty Science Center, we strive to use the resources and collaborations that result from value-added application of networked communication technologies that invigorate the learning of science. We subscribe to the view that technologies connecting home, school, the workplace and institutions of learning offer unparalleled opportunities to provide access to science education, strengthen learning and teaching, and sustain lifetime learning, no matter where and no matter when.

Following these illustrative program profiles, the article concludes by reflecting on the recent trend of social entrepreneurship in non-profit organizations, and on how a museum's sustainability is strengthened by active adoption of a socially responsible mission.

Examples of a socially responsible mission in action

Reaching underserved audiences: Abbott Partnership Program

Science centres, many of which are located in urban settings and dedicate themselves to science learning opportunities for all, face no greater challenge than the attraction, involvement and retention of underserved audiences (Falk 1998). In its early period, Liberty Science struggled to find ways to serve the school and family audiences from its most challenged communities, including its host community of Jersey City. With a public school enrolment of thirty-two thousand, fewer than a thousand were using Liberty Science Center each school year. The surrounding districts of Newark, Hoboken and Elizabeth, each less than ten miles away, were equally detached from the learning opportunities that we offered.

Liberty Science Center started to develop its Abbott Partnership Program in 1997 for the state's most educationally at-risk districts. A New Jersey Supreme Court ruling in the Abbott vs. Burke case addressed inequities in educational funding by establishing a new and permanent extra funding stream intended to improve academic performance in these schools.

We were challenged to find a partner with significant financial resources and unquestioned commitment to science learning for underserved audiences. The obvious collaborator was the New Jersey Department of Education. It manages the educational reform efforts in place in the thirty Abbott districts. We convinced both education officials and policy advisors to the state governor that our programming would add value to their science improvement initiatives. We were not in search of a handout, but instead stressed our desire to earn their financial support through collaborative involvement with science education reform. We demonstrated how our field-trip, travelling science and videoconferencing curriculum materials were all aligned with, and supportive of, New Jersey's core curriculum content standards. We demonstrated how our teacher professional development workshops, institutes and professional days were attuned to the emerging state certification requirements. We suggested the inclusion of a third emphasis on the family, to extend school and science centre learning into the home. We offered to provide families with a free family pass for use at Liberty Science Center, a quarterly newsletter and monthly community evenings as part of an inclusive package of science education services. The state legislature welcomed this comprehensive program as a novel approach that matched the strengths of the science centre with the needs of their constituents.

This education initiative has been recognized for its innovation in the museum field, winning the social responsibility award for the year 2000 from the New York Society of Association Executives. Through a yearly grant-in-aid from the state government, Liberty Science Center has been enabled to provide students, teachers and families from these districts with a menu of onsite, offsite and online experiences that address the science education needs of these underserved communities. During the 2001–02 school year, 159,711 Abbott district students (91,316 through onsite programming, 62,800 through offsite, school-based programming and 5,595 through online videoconferencing) benefited from our programs. Also, 1,063 Abbott district teachers participated in school day, weekend and summer professional development workshops. Over twenty-five thousand family members from Abbott communities used their free family pass to enjoy the excitement of a Liberty Science Center visit. Annual program funding has increased from us$1.7 million in 1997–98 for the three largest districts under direct state government control, to us$6.0 million for the total of twenty-eight Abbott districts in 1998–2000, to us$6.6 million since the start of the 2000–01 school year, when twenty-eight grew to thirty eligible districts. Even in the toughest of times for the economy of New Jersey in 2003, support for the Liberty Science Center's Abbot Partnership Program was sustained at us$6.1 million. This also comes at a time when it seems almost universal, at least across the United States, that governments are cutting back on their funding of cultural institutions quite significantly.

Key to the management and delivery of these programs is the articulation of a yearly service agreement between Liberty Science Center and each district. Ahead of each school year, our staff travel to each district where they meet with district leaders, curriculum specialists and principals to construct a menu of interactions that use science centre resources to support school and district science learning objectives. This mutually generated contract identifies which students, teachers, schools, grade levels or classrooms will benefit from the state-sponsored interactions. In these discussions, we fashion many distinctive strategies focussed on grade levels across a district, individual schools, teams of teachers, exceptional students or special projects. Key to these conversations and the agreements that result is the recognition that customization of our science learning offerings is an innovation that brings the greatest value to our school partners.

Teachers from Abbott district schools are now active participants in our ongoing professional development activities. Implementation of the Abbott teacher ambassador program is a chief reason for the increase in their participation. There are 423 schools in the thirty Abbott districts. In each school, we have identified an ambassador who acts as our liaison for all student and teacher interactions. Armed with an electronic mailing list, website resources and an ambassador tool kit containing detailed support materials and scheduled events at Liberty Science Center, these ambassadors are establishing strong, year-round bonds for us in each Abbott school. Their presence and the ongoing interactions that take place directly between us and schools are responsible for an important shift in perception which has moved our offerings from traditional supplementary resources to an integral resource that contributes to the school science program.

Liberty Science Center's commitment to the provision of outstanding science education experiences for New Jersey's Abbott district students, teachers and families has helped redefine our educational and institutional programs. We are energized by the learning opportunities that arise when we collaborate directly with teachers, principals and district leaders. We are elated to see the joy and enthusiasm when Abbott families from many different cultures experience their first onsite visit. We are ecstatic to see students engaged in a curriculum-aligned discovery challenge, an electronic field-trip or a cow's eye dissection, and know that we are making a positive impact on science learning. While the Abbott Partnership Program has enabled us to bring much value to the science education needs of our community, we are most proud of the changes we have undergone as a result of the value the community has brought to us.

Prior to the establishment of the Abbott Partnership Program, Liberty Science Center was essentially serving only the more affluent parts of the surrounding region. Now, our reach is broad and our ability to make a difference in the science learning of all of our constituents is greatly enhanced.

Also critical to our success was the identification of a new place for Liberty Science Center in the too-often distinct worlds of informal and formal science education. Tradition identifies the science centre as the domain of informal learning, while schools occupy the domain of formal learning. The New Jersey Department of Education oversees the world of formal K–12 education, and to become a serious partner with them we had to demonstrate that we understood, and could operate within, this domain. Demonstrations of our expertise in inquiry-based learning and science content were not enough to win them over. Presentation of Liberty Science Center as a dynamic learning environment was impressive, but did not speak to our ability to work in schools with students, teachers and principals to support their science learning objectives. We had to demonstrate our expertise on issues related to core-curriculum standards, learning frameworks, school-reform models, teacher professional development requirements and student achievement. We had to rethink and articulate the role for a science centre in the world of formal science education. We were successful in reshaping all that we had to offer so that the decision-makers in formal education were confident in our ability to add value within their system. Many science centres are also capable of finding this place for themselves.

Like most science centres, Liberty Science Center is perceived as an interactive and engaging learning destination for schools and families. To succeed with the state-wide Abbott Partnership Program, we had to enhance this perception so that our audience saw us as an interactive and engaging learning resource. Significant aspects of our work with the Abbott districts could not take place onsite. Bus transportation is problematic, and teachers will only travel so far and so often for professional-development opportunities. To make an impact across all thirty Abbott school districts, it was necessary to fully engage in technology and travel to make our educational resources totally accessible. This commitment to a portfolio of onsite, offsite and online science learning experiences sets the stage for students, teachers and families to interact with the science centre every day, instead of once or twice a year. This new self-image prepares science centres to compete and thrive in a new, wired and more competitive science learning infrastructure.

Tackling youth smoking: the unfiltered truth

The statistics are stark, yet stupefying. With so much science generating so much data, how is it possible that the use of tobacco continues to be the number-one adolescent public health problem in the United States? Well over a quarter of all high-school students in grades 9 to 12 are smokers, along with almost 15 per cent of all eighth graders (U.S. Center for Disease Control 2001). Each day, more than five thousand additional young people try smoking for the first time, and another more than two thousand become daily smokers (U.S. Department of Health and Human Services 2001).

In 2000, the tobacco companies spent us\$59.6 million in advertising expenditures for the most popular youth brands in youth-oriented magazines. Spending from the recent master settlement between the federal government and major tobacco companies has not reduced youth exposure to advertisements for these brands. Magazine advertisements for the brands reached more than 80 per cent of young people in the United States an average of seventeen times each during the year 2000 (King and Siegel 2001).

Spurred by the urgency to decrease the diseases and deaths that result from smoking, and supported by funds made available through the above-mentioned national master settlement agreement, the New Jersey Department of Health and Senior Services sought innovators to join their comprehensive tobacco-control program. Liberty Science Center jumped at the opportunity to become a partner in the effort to reach fourth to twelfth graders with a message about the realities of youth smoking.

An initial visit to see firsthand Liberty Science Center's diverse youth audience and innovative educational programs in May 2000 convinced the Commissioner of Health and Senior Services that we were right for the task at hand. The Commissioner saw the science centre teeming with eager learners, while live videoconferencing connections brought science educators on the exhibit floors to remote New Jersey classrooms. We also explained that travelling science educators were in schools doing assembly programs, classroom workshops and dance performances to illustrate the science of muscles and bones. With a yearly youth audience exceeding 450,000, one-third of which represents the most underserved communities in New Jersey, Liberty Science Center was viewed as a unique resource whose contribution to the battle against tobacco would complement already established community partnerships, cessation programs and media campaigns.

During the summer of 2000, program developers and science educators began to pinpoint the concepts and goals that would form the foundation for our program. Research, focus groups and brainstorming scrutinized existing tobacco-education programs and helped to identify a distinct niche for us that would build on our strengths and not replicate existing endeavours. Four key goals became the basis for the development of the content and delivery of our program: 1) decrease the acceptability and initiation of tobacco use among those aged 9–17; 2) increase youths' understanding of the harmful effects of tobacco use and the creation of tobacco products; 3) increase awareness of the negative effects of smoking in community and personal settings; and 4) increase the awareness and knowledge of how the tobacco industry uses strategic marketing to mask the negative aspects of tobacco use and tobacco products.

During this development process, it seemed to us that one initiative or experience would not suffice. We wanted to create a set of integrated experiences, each able to stand on its own, so that our youth audience was presented with multiple opportunities, in a variety of media, to interact with our anti-tobacco messages.

In October 2000, we submitted a request for funding to the Department of Health and Senior Services for our tobacco-education program entitled *The Unfiltered Truth*. A us$783,000 grant was approved for development and implementation, with funding beginning on January 1, 2001. Our program has three components and all were actively underway during the 2001–02 school year.

Extreme Choices is an onsite, 3D laser show written by playwright Michael Hollinger and co-produced by Lightspeed Design Group and Liberty Science Center. Fifteen minutes long, the show presents an adolescent in an arcade playing a new, high-tech game called *Extreme Choices*. Urged on by his peers and intrigued by the promise of a prize when he successfully finishes the challenge, the young player and the audience face a dwindling set of choices as the game progresses. The game takes command, much like a burgeoning nicotine addiction, until fantasy becomes a bit too close to reality and all involved are uncomfortably engulfed in the strong anti-smoking message. While *Extreme Choices* is the name of the game, it is about simple choices of when and how much to smoke that lead to extreme consequences down the road. Crafted to send home only one or two important ideas, the show uses the power of the visual and aural environment to first engage the audience in the game before switching to become a tool to drive home the show's climax. Over two hundred thousand youth guests have seen *Extreme Choices*.

Hot Air is a forty-five-minute dramatic production, also written by Michael Hollinger, that is performed in middle schools throughout New Jersey. Co-produced by Playwright's Theater of New Jersey and Liberty Science Center, the play features six professional actors who portray three middle-school students and six adults in a story that meshes smoking, athletics, advertising and family relationships. Jessica is a budding track star who cannot seem to quit smoking. Her father is in advertising and has a new cigarette company account that wants to promote smoking among teens. Numerous conflicts start to emerge, and with humour layered throughout the story, the audience is entertained and informed about the evils of both smoking and the corporate deceit behind tobacco sales and marketing. In this play, the audience sees character development and understands more intricate storylines; things that are not possible in an experience like *Extreme Choices*. In *Hot Air*, the dramatic medium allows multiple messages about issues related to smoking to be explored and resolved. After each show, the cast takes questions from the audience, and whether performed in a gym, cafeteria or auditorium, it is clear that the key messages in the show are coming across loud and clear. *Hot Air* was performed over 190 times during the 2001–02 school year, and will be seen at 235 shows during the 2002–03 school year. Over eighty thousand students will see *Hot Air* during its two-year run.

The Science Behind Tobacco is an extensive website (Liberty Science Center 2001) providing information, images, links and interactives about the cultivation of tobacco, the manufacturing of cigarettes and the health effects of tobacco use. Intended for both youth and adult viewers, the website provides classroom guides for both *Extreme Choices* and *Hot Air*, while presenting science background information that elucidates the relationship between the tobacco plant, the cigarette maker and the nicotine addiction that leads to serious health consequences. Unlike the more temporal and location-specific constraints inherent in a play and a 3D laser show, *The Science Behind Tobacco* website is a readily available resource able to be explored and visited at the user's discretion. The website first appeared in November 2001 and in the first year there have been 180,000 unique visits.

A critical component of *The Unfiltered Truth*, the entire program was an extensive evaluation effort conducted by The Conservation Company from Philadelphia, Pennsylvania. We worked with them to develop a variety of survey instruments that enabled us to collect both quantitative and qualitative data from surveys, interviews and focus groups to measure the impact of this tobacco education program. The evaluation effort collected data at the science centre, in schools and through an online instrument on the website. Data collection and analysis were completed in June 2002. The evaluation indicated that each component was successful in delivering a strong anti-tobacco message. Students understood that *Hot Air* and *Extreme Choices* were about choices, and that the choices characters made were similar to the choices children believe they have to make in their lives. Students reported that both the play and the 3D laser show demonstrated how poor choices lead to bad health consequences. Most importantly, the data indicated that the greatest impact of *Hot Air* and *Extreme Choices* was to help students understand the negative impacts of smoking on health and well-being. *The Science Behind Tobacco* was rated highly as an interesting, easy-to-understand, well-produced website for research and learning about tobacco and the health effects of smoking (Conservation Company 2002).

Liberty Science Center's tobacco-education program received high marks from the Department of Health and Senior Services and our viewing audience. Additional funding was received to extend the run of *Hot Air* through the 2002–03 school year, and to develop three new multimedia interactives for *The Science Behind Tobacco* website. Many schools that booked *Hot Air* during its initial run have rebooked for the 2002–03 school year, and have also visited and seen *Extreme Choices*. Indications are that the website is serving as a valuable adjunct in support of the two other initiatives, and providing important content for both student and teacher learning. The presentation of a comprehensive program about tobacco use through initiatives that hit hard and true has offered a unique opportunity for conversations that are relevant and socially responsible. For us, commitment to telling the straight story in innovative and thought-provoking ways about the nation's number-one public health issue is the essence of our mission.

Learning from a hospital operating room: Live from . . . Cardiac Classroom

Liberty Science Center provides experiences that seek to make a difference in young lives by making science and technology understandable. Whether crawling in the pitch-black tunnel to come to terms with sensory deprivation, holding a hissing cockroach to get close to nature, constructing something from parts in our invention area or exercising in our bodies-in-motion area, our young guests are immersed in audio, visual and kinaesthetic experiences that are unique and memorable.

For all science centres, and for museums generally, building on such successes with young learners to make an impact on high-school students is an ongoing challenge. Mere multi-sensory interactions with the rudiments and objects of science and technology are not the experiences most likely to inspire the next generation of science thinkers and doers. For older students, it is critical that the presentation of science is seen as a human endeavour of mind, spirit and activity that is integrally linked to addressing individual and societal challenges. Creating ways to incorporate real things, real processes and real demonstrations of science that present the most current science thinking, research and practice provides the most certainty that high-school students will become engaged with the world of science and technology.

Liberty Science Center's *Live from . . . Cardiac Classroom* is an innovation that succeeds in meeting this challenge. Through the weekly presentation of live, open-heart coronary-bypass surgery, students from rural, suburban and urban schools come onsite to interact with science and technology as it happens. The patient, the surgical team and the students are immersed in a real life-and-death drama. Whether because of genetics or a combination of lifestyle choices, the patient's future is inter-twined with multiple aspects of science and technology. For most, the excitement and relevance of science learning has never been so real. Whether contemplating the patient and issues related to illness and recovery, or the surgical team and issues of knowledge, skill and preparation, students are moved by the experience. Inclusive of the learning strengths we attribute to exhibition, mediated programming and the appropriate use of technology, *Live from . . . Cardiac Classroom* provides high-school students with an extraordinary and compelling experience that they will never forget.

Live from . . . Cardiac Classroom is a program that uses two way videoconferencing technology to connect seventy-five middle- or high-school students at the science centre to a cardiac surgical suite at Morristown Memorial Hospital, twenty-five miles away in mid-northern New Jersey. For two hours while open-heart coronary-bypass surgery is in progress, students are immersed in a unique learning experience that extends their knowledge and understanding of anatomy and physiology, lifestyle choices that determine health consequences, the diversity of careers in the medical field and how research and new technology are changing the health and medical professions. Well prepared through access to web-based, standards-aligned curriculum materials, students interact directly with all members of the surgical team to better understand the teamwork, experience and differentiated skills required to mend a malfunctioning heart. Our educators, audiovisual staff and volunteers facilitate the audio and video interactions while surgical instruments, materials and devices circulate around the room and questions come in a steady stream from the engaged audience.

Begun in 1998 as a result of the imagination of Liberty Science Center trustee and practising cardiologist William A. Tansey III, MD, *Live from . . . Cardiac Classroom* is a regular feature of our weekly school-year programming. As of January 2003, we have presented 210 surgeries, usually five or six per month, reaching eleven thousand students and other guests. An annual allocation of us$50,000 for technology upgrades, materials and supplies, plus in-kind investment on the part of the hospital, now support an initial equipment and set-up investment of us$350,000. Two-thirds of our student participants pay us$15 to attend, and one-third particip- ate free of charge as part of our service to underserved school districts.

It often begins in the same way. *Live from . . . Cardiac Classroom* uses two-way videoconferencing technology to connect middle- and high-school students to a cardiac surgical suite. The multiple plasma screens and the audio feed go live and the students are greeted with an operating room scene not unlike *ER* or from the Learning Channel on cable television. Blue-green gowns, high-intensity lights and a flurry of activity may make you think that you are watching television or a pre- recorded video. Then, in a split second, it changes. 'Good morning, Liberty Science Center. Today, we have a 47-year-old female, overweight, a lifetime smoker, with no history of heart disease in her family. We anticipate doing four grafts today, but we won't know for sure until we see the heart. . . . I can see we have a full room today: tell me a little about your class and your school.'

Even with a visit to the website and classroom lessons in preparation for the surgery, students now understand that they are participating in something remark- able and unique. This is not a simulation or an edited-for-television medical pro- cedure. *Live from . . . Cardiac Classroom* is the real thing, and for the next two hours the sights, sounds, knowledge, interactions and feelings that accompany authentic experiential learning will be elevated as each student becomes a participant in the drama. Our work to engage guests in impactful, experiential learning uses many modalities. Exhibition offers information, objects and interactives in support of free-choice exploration and discovery. Mediated programming adds the human ele- ment, to facilitate and guide learning and investigation. Technology breaks through the boundaries of time and space to enhance the breadth and depth of what we offer. *Live from . . . Cardiac Classroom* creatively combines the strengths of each of these modalities to present a learning opportunity like few others.

A unique collaboration is required to present and sustain *Live from . . . Cardiac Classroom*. Three partners – Atlantic Health System, Mid-Atlantic Surgical Associ- ates and Johnson & Johnson – work with us to maintain the educational excellence and programmatic distinctiveness of what we offer. Atlantic Health System is our hospital partner that supports the technology infrastructure in the operating room, the dedicated T1 videoconferencing connection to the science centre, and all the members of the medical team except the surgeons. Mid-Atlantic Surgical Associates is the surgical practice whose four doctors donate their time and expertise to make their surgical suite and our videoconferencing theatre a dynamic learning envir- onment. Johnson & Johnson is our corporate sponsor, whose annual funding and counsel enables the sustenance and growth of the innovation. The American Heart Association is a new contributor of program enhancements.

Partnerships are key to the success and excellence of so much that we strive to accomplish as institutions of learning. For five years now, science educators, doctor/scientists, hospital administrators and corporate professionals have pooled their resources and found the common ground and mutual commitment to learn- ing. The whole is now literally much greater than the sum of the parts. Partnerships of this degree and longevity are rare, but when they do occur, significant endeav- ours result from the collaboration.

Science centres, museums and all institutions of learning are facing change and stress as they try to come to grips with the proper role for emerging, networked communications technologies as a learning tool for the future. Over the past decade, as we have experimented with websites, webcasts, satellite links, remote cameras and videoconferencing, we have struggled to find meaningful and cost-effective applications. Prototypes and temporarily funded experiments have come and gone, with few meeting the tests of fiscal and programmatic sustainability. *Live from . . . Cardiac Classroom* has not only survived, but continues to prosper and evolve as it matures. Why this application of videoconferencing succeeds while so many others fail is simple and significant. *Live from . . . Cardiac Classroom* is fundamentally about an extraordinary learning experience: it is not about the capabilities and coolness of videoconferencing technology. Its instruments, environment, content, messages and people are the primary and special elements of the learning experience. The technology that enables the opportunity is less important. All along, the contributions from each partner in the collaboration have focussed on the learning goals as paramount, and the intricacies of the technology as secondary.

Liberty Science Center strives to be an innovative resource for the lifelong exploration of nature, humanity and technology. *Live from . . . Cardiac Classroom* is a signature embodiment of the integrated learning experiences that we develop to ensure that we achieve our mission. Engagement with this program provides a window into our commitment to relevance, social responsibility and the growth of our diverse region. Establishing connections for learners that make an impact and promote further thought and investigation is the benchmark for relevance. This program connects with students, and provides images and ideas that connect what they have been told with how they live their lives. They see for themselves how choices to smoke, eat poorly or ignore physical fitness will lead to potential health consequences. Vivid images and answers to their own questions help make this link. *Live from . . . Cardiac Classroom* provides the opportunity to make these messages real for a teenage audience that is seldom moved or affected by words, books or the advice of teachers or parents.

New Jersey is often referred to as the 'medicine cabinet to the world.' Many major pharmaceutical and medical technology companies are headquartered in our state. Liberty Science Center was formed through efforts of corporations and research institutions to help stimulate the growth of science and technology professions that are so critical to the economy of New Jersey. *Live from . . . Cardiac Classroom* provides a consummate and unmatched opportunity for career education. From the first moment to the closing suture, students see a real view of the world of work and the teamwork that is required to achieve excellence. Each professional on the surgical team takes a turn with the microphone to share with students the education, professional training and responsibilities required by each job. These conversations have stimulated students to now see the roles of surgeon, physician assistant, perfusionist, medical technician, researcher, instrument designer and science educator as equally interesting and viable career options.

Learning that inspires young adults to examine their lifestyle choices and think ahead to entertain professions in science and technology exemplifies how this program advances our institutional mission. Too often innovations like *Live from . . .*

Cardiac Classroom find their implementation and impact with those who have the resources to invest. Many underserved students and schools miss the opportunity to be part of these initiatives. We are proud that this program provides us with another opportunity to promote the growth of our region for all of its citizens, not just those who have the resources.

In 2002, *Live from . . . Cardiac Classroom* garnered the prestigious single annual Award for Innovation from the worldwide Association of Science-Technology Centers (ASTC), a program co-sponsored by U.S.-based BBH Exhibits/Clear Channel Entertainment. In addition, an adjacent mini-theatre presentation of the operating room experience in its four main aspects – i.e., surgical procedure, tools and equipment, anatomy and career paths – for all other visitors has garnered five awards, including one from the American Association of Museums.

Reflections for the museum field

Although one may be convinced that the search for relevance is a prudent one (Covey 1990; Koster 1999), the question arises: Does the pursuit of relevance also lead to growth in a museum's operating resources?

We submit that the foregoing program examples of Liberty Science Center solidly indicate that this is indeed the case. That is, if a museum positions itself so as to attract sustainable external resources on the basis of its declared and clear added value to the outside world, then the museum clearly develops a more secure financial footing. The opposite is clearly also true – who wishes to fund irrelevant activities? It is, however, the case that there continue to exist museums, and to a lesser extent science centres, where earned and contributed funds support missions that are oriented more to internal interests than the common good. If a museum is generously supported by endowment revenue and/or by grants from philanthropists whose interest lies in a more classical museum mission, then it is entirely possible for that museum to continue to live in an internally focussed mode, oblivious to any external accountabilities.

Other types of informal learning institutions have shown the trend toward heightened external consciousness more graphically, often as a result of public pressure. For example, it is no longer acceptable for zoos to have a single representative of an animal species in a barred cage or, more recently, for an aquarium to train killer whales to perform circus-like acts in a pool. Less dramatically in the museum context, amassing a collection simply for the sake of amassing a collection is an indicator of institutional self-absorption. A human history museum can use its collection simply to display and identify the material output of a chapter in history, or it can endeavour to interpret that chapter in its prevailing social context. A natural history museum can display the fossil record of ancient life with or without mention of rapid, human-caused rates of declining biodiversity and increasing extinction. A science centre may not be presenting to its visitors any of the major science and technology issues that are pertinent to its region. A museum can simply open its doors to its traditional audience, or it can actively try to engage a broader audience with its resources. Museums of all kinds have choices, choices that characterize them as being negative, neutral or positive influences with respect to the needs of humanity and this planet.

A strong adjunct to the rise in social responsibility has been the recently advancing notion of social entrepreneurship. In 1995, Harvard University's Kennedy School of Government published a synthesis of its two decades of research and reflection on creating public value in government (Moore 1998). One of the next major contributions to the field was the notion that socially responsible non-profits could 'profit' by partnering with like-minded commercial corporations (Steckel, Simons, Simons and Tanen 1999).

Next came a new series of publications in the field of social entrepreneurship. In 1998, the National Center for Nonprofit Boards in the United States issued an informative pamphlet about merging mission and money (Boschee 1998), followed by a special issue of its periodical on the topic (U.S. National Center for Nonprofit Boards 2001a). Then in 2001, a team at Stanford University published a benchmark synthesis on its three years of work about social entrepreneurship (Dees, Emerson and Economy 2001). Placing a greater emphasis on creating social value than on how much profit is made, this team proposed that social entrepreneurs act as agents of change in the following five sequential ways: 1) adopting a mission to create and sustain social value; 2) recognizing and relentlessly pursuing new opportunities to serve that mission; 3) engaging in a process of continuous innovation, adaptation and learning; 4) acting boldly without being limited to resources in hand; and 5) exhibiting a heightened sense of accountability to the constituencies served and for the outcomes created.

There are close parallels between this course of action and what has transpired at Liberty Science Center. Specifically, our mission statement has a clear statement of 'so what?' Faced with financial difficulties in our early years, then with new leadership who had been advocating John Cotton Dana's type of philosophy (Dana 1999) since the mid-'90s (Koster 1995), Liberty Science Center's mission was restated to be clearly oriented to the common good in human and environmental terms. We then had the conviction that we could significantly add, in a sustainable way, to Liberty Science Center's operating resources by contracting out with the state government for the innovative application of our educational programs to those who needed our resources most. In turn, this program has most definitely heightened our sense of accountability to the large underserved audience with whom we are now a major, interdependent partner.

We believe that there are, in turn, parallels of this situation to be found in all types of museum (Gurian 2002), especially those dedicated to finding new revenues from discerning sources. In terms of earned revenue, it is an axiom that the public votes with its feet. Following the trend in tourism, the world's largest industry, in which cultural and ecological reasons for travel now outweigh strictly recreational reasons, we think that the changing state of the world will increasingly make people seek more meaningful experiences about what is useful to know about the world. Although museums often regard attendance as a major performance parameter, with admission revenue among the main earned-revenue sources, it is unwise to equate popularity with external usefulness (Koster 1999) or individual enlightenment (Kimmelman 2001). In terms of contributed revenues, a pronounced trend is already clear. Driven by the movement toward social responsibility and a clear interest in tangible and useful outcomes, an increasing number of corporations, and already most foundations, are at a point of demanding that what they support has demonstrable benefits to society and/or the environment.

For museums, the optimal philosophy and practice therefore seem clear. For reasons of both usefulness and revenue, museums should indeed pursue a course of increased external consciousness. John Cotton Dana had an appropriate and beneficial vision for museums whose time seems to be now finally arriving: learn what the community needs, he advocated, and fit the museum to those needs. As earlier noted, for natural history museums – and here we would add zoos, aquariums and botanical gardens – it is also recognized nowadays that such institutions need to learn what the environment needs and fit the institution to those needs. If a museum still has the luxury of a more classical course of self-interest, its lifetime may well be finite, as public and contributor tastes change with the evolving atmosphere of the world in which we live.

Note

Emlyn H. Koster is President and CEO and **Stephen H. Baumann** is former Vice-President for Education at the Liberty Science Center in New Jersey and currently Executive Director of the Kidspace Children's Museum in Pasadena. This chapter first appeared in *Looking Reality in the Eye: Museums and Social Responsibility* edited by R.R. Janes and G.T. Conaty (2005).

References

American Association of Museums (1984) *Museums for a new century: A report of the Commission on Museum for a New Century*. Washington, D.C.: American Association of Museums.
—— (1992) *Excellence and equity – Education and the public dimension of museums*. Washington, D.C.: American Association of Museums.
—— (2002) *Mastering civic engagement: A challenge to museums*. Washington, D.C.: American Association of Museums.
Barker, Richard (2002) *On the nature of leadership*. Lanham, Maryland: University of America Press.
Barrett, Richard (1998) *Liberating the corporate soul*. Boston: Butterworth-Heinemann.
Boschee, Jerr (1998) *Merging mission with money*. Washington, D.C.: U.S. National Center for Nonprofit Boards.
Brousseau, Francine (2003) True or false? *Muse*, 21, 23.
Carbonne, Stan (2003) The dialogic museum. *Muse*, 21, 36–39.
Casey, Dawn (2001) Museums as agents of social and political change. *Curator*, 44(3), 230–36.
Conservation Company (2002) Evaluation of the Liberty Science Center tobacco education program, June 2002. Available from Liberty Science Center.
Covey, Stephen (1990) *The seven habits of highly effective people: Powerful lessons in personal change*. New York: Simon & Schuster.
Dana, John Cotton (1999) *The new museum: Selected writings by John Cotton Dana*. Edited by William A. Peniston. Newark, N.J.: Newark Museum Association; Washington, D.C.: American Association of Museums.
Dees, Gregory, Emerson, Jed and Economy, Peter (2001) *Enterprising nonprofits: A toolkit for social entrepreneurs*. New York: John Wiley & Sons.

Falk, John (1998) Visitors – who does, who doesn't, and why? *American Association of Museums Museum News* (March/April), 38–43.

Gurian, Elaine (2002) Choosing among the options: an opinion about museum definitions. *Curator*, 45(2), 75–88.

Harvard University, John F. Kennedy School of Government (2001) *Museums in the United States at the turn of the millennium: An industry note*. Conference of the U.S. Museums Trustee Association, Museum Governance in a New Age, October 4–7, 2001.

Kimmelman, Michael (2001) Museums in a quandary: Where are the ideals? *The New York Times* (August 26).

King, Charles and Siegel, Michael (2001) The master settlement agreement with the tobacco industry and cigarette advertising in magazines. *New England Journal of Medicine*, 345(7), 504–11.

Koster, Emlyn (1995) The human journey and the evolving museum. In Michel Côté and Annette Viel (Eds.), *Museums: Where knowledge is shared* (pp. 81–98). Quebec City: Société des musées québécois and Musée de la civilisation.

—— (1999) In search of relevance – science centers as innovators in the evolution of museums. *Daedalus, Journal of the American Academy of Arts and Sciences*, 128, 277–96. (Issue devoted to *America's Museums*, Stephen Graubard, Ed.)

—— (2002) A tragedy revisited. *Muse*, 20, 26–27.

Leahy, Stephen (2003) Greening stewardship. *Muse*, 21, 22–26.

Liberty Science Center (2001) *The science behind tobacco*. www.lsc.org/tobacco.

Moore, Mark (1998) *Creating public value: Strategic management in government*. Cambridge, Massachusetts: Harvard University Press.

Parston, Greg (1997) Producing social results. In Frances Hesselbein *et al.* (Eds.), *The Organization of the Future* (pp. 341–48). San Francisco: Jossey-Bass.

Peters, Tom and Waterman, Robert (1982) *In search of excellence: Lessons from America's best-run companies*. New York: Harper & Row.

Schiele, Bernard and Koster, Emlyn (2000) *Science centers in this century*. Sainte-Foy, Quebec: MultiMondes.

Smithsonian Institution (1997) *Museums for the new millennium: A symposium for the museum community*. Proceedings of a conference commemorating the 150th anniversary of the Smithsonian Institution, September, 5–7 1996, Washington, D.C.: Center for Museum Studies/American Association of Museums.

Steckel, Richard, Simons, Robin, Simons, Jeffrey and Tanen, Norman (1999) *Making money while making a difference*. Homewood, Illinois: High Tide Press.

U.S. Center for Disease Control (2001) Monitoring the future study. University of Michigan, November 2, 2001.

U.S. Department of Health and Human Services (2001) Substance abuse and mental health services administration. Summary findings from the 2000 National Household Survey on Drug Abuse.

U.S. National Center for Nonprofit Boards (2001a) Profit potential: advancing your mission through social entrepreneurship. *Board Member*, 10(5), 1–15.

—— (2001b) Mission accomplished: The board's role in outcome measurement. *Board Member*, 10(8), 1–15. U.S. National Center for Nonprofit Boards.

Weil, Stephen E. (1999) Introduction. In Dana, John Cotton, *The new museum: Selected writings by John Cotton Dana*. Edited by William A. Peniston. Newark, N.J.: Newark Museum Association; Washington, D.C.: American Association of Museums.

—— (2002) *Making museums matter*. Washington, D.C.: Smithsonian Institution Press.

Worldwatch Institute (2003) *State of the world 2003 — Special 20th anniversary edition.* New York: W.W. Norton and Company.

Worts, D. (2003) 'On the brink of irrelevance? Art museums in contemporary society' in M. Xanthodaki, L. Tickle, V. Sekules (eds), *Researching visual arts education in museums and galleries: an international reader.* Dordrecht, Boston: Kluwer Academic Publishers, 215–233.

Chapter 11

Measuring Social Value

Carol Scott

A MAJOR OUTCOME OF THE POLICIES of microeconomic reform that have swept Western industrialised countries since the mid-1980s has been the introduction of increased accountability for the expenditure of public monies. Generally, the model that has been adopted to account for the use of resources in the public sector is one in which performance is measured against quantitative indicators. The application of this model to the museum sector has generated considerable debate and discussion regarding the limited ability of short-term, quantitative indicators to adequately reflect both the complexity of the role that museums play in society and the long-term contribution that they make to social value.

This chapter is in three parts. First, it will give a brief synopsis of the issues generated by the introduction of the performance measurement model to assess the work of museums. Second, it will describe two models that have been developed to assess the long-term social value of participation in the community arts sector with relation to the vexed question of assessing the long-term impacts of museums. Finally, it will explore some indicators on which the long-term benefits and contributions of museums might be assessed.

Introduction

Following World War II, governments of Western industrialised countries embarked upon a period of economic expansion that was to last for a quarter of a century (Redfern 1986). Large investment in public spending was one of the characteristics of this time and governments had sufficient resources to respond to the changing demands of the community. Initially concerned with basic needs, government

Source: pp. 41–55 in R. Sandell (ed.) (2002) *Museums, Society, Inequality*, London: Routledge.

responsibility expanded into increased welfare and social services, subsidies for all branches of the arts, consumer protection and protection for the environment. The level of expenditure could be sustained during the post-war period of rapid economic growth but, with the economic downturn of the 1970s, governments were faced with the necessity of reducing spending (Douglas 1991: 1). Significant changes introduced in the 1980s and 1990s saw governments reverse the expansionist trend through policies of economic reform that sought 'economies' in public spending. In Australia, the intent of a 'Review of Commonwealth Development in Museums and Similar Collecting and Exhibiting Institutions' was indicative of this trend:

> To review the Commonwealth's involvement in the development of museums, collecting and exhibiting institutions and other collections owned by the Commonwealth, with a view to identifications of any duplication and scope for economies amongst museums, existing and proposed, and to examine other ways to limit the call on the Commonwealth to meet the recurrent funding needs of existing and proposed museums and institutions. (Department of Finance 1989: 1)

These changes have had a major impact on museums. Of necessity, museums have had to diversify their funding base, often through the combination of admission charges and increased external sponsorship. In addition, the introduction of fiscal accountability and performance evaluation has ensured that museums and other public agencies account for the public monies they receive (Cossons 1988).

Performance evaluation as an accountability system fits comfortably within the corporate 'management for results' approach that has enjoyed currency since the introduction of economic reform (Redfern 1986; Douglas 1991). A key ingredient of 'management for results' is ongoing evaluation to provide a mechanism for assessing the progress of programmes and determining whether intended outcomes have been achieved. In addition, *performance evaluation*, as the name implies, requires demonstrable and tangible outcomes for assessment. These tangible results are measured against numerical targets to identify increased efficiency in the use of resources. As the model has been more associated with quantitative indicators, it has also become more commonly referred to as *performance measurement*.

Not surprisingly, indicators of successful museum performance arising from this model are predominantly quantifiable and include items such as the number of visitors to the museum, the numbers of users of facilities such as websites, the number of new exhibitions presented and travelled, the number of publications produced, educational programmes offered, objects conserved and registered, etc. (Scott 1991; Office of Arts and Libraries 1991; Ames 1991; COCOG 1997). Moreover, these indicators are most often compared with either a previous year's performance or with the performance of other museums in order to ascertain trends and patterns of resource usage.

A new vocabulary has accompanied the introduction of performance evaluation/ measurement and 'management for results'. It is argued that sound management is based on an efficient use of resources (*inputs*) as well as concern for the results (*outputs*). Therefore, governments provide funds to museums (*inputs*) and museums use these funds for programmes, facilities and services (*outputs*). The *efficient* use of resources is the main criterion on which performance is based. Efficiency is determined by whether the result of a programme justifies the amount of effort invested and whether the same result could have been achieved by another programme undertaken for less cost.

It can be argued that the introduction of performance measurement has had some positive effects:

- the information about resource usage within a given period can be used to effect economies or apply for increased resources on the basis of programme needs;
- the quantitative data produced can be used to identify emergent trends across museums;
- the process of developing indicators to assess performance can achieve clarity of mission and purpose through collective objectives setting (Ames 1992);
- the necessity of providing data for accountability and reporting can result in improved management information systems;
- performance measurement is a management tool that provides information for decision makers; and
- goal setting for performance targets can give museums a clear and corporate direction at which to aim.

Nevertheless, the introduction of performance measurement has generated considerable discussion and debate. In general terms, critics have questioned the appropriateness of applying a system to the public sector that was originally based in the commercial sector where a profit-making bottom line lends itself more comfortably to quantitative measurement. Specifically, they argue that the multidimensional briefs and wide range of stakeholders characteristic of public sector institutions make meaningful performance assessment a much more complex issue. Specifically, the difficulties of quantifying the long-term, intangible outcomes of museum performance have been highlighted (Ames 1992; Bud *et al.* 1991; Walden 1991).

However, the adaptation of performance measurement to the public sector has not been a static process. The model has evolved over the last decade and it is now recognised that inputs and outputs should result in *outcomes*. The *impact* and *effectiveness* of performance are, therefore, important additional criteria for assessment (Weil 1994).

At first glance, the inclusion of *outcomes* as a key component of the performance evaluation model would seem to set the stage for a more reliable and comprehensive assessment of public sector institutions. However, the prevalent performance evaluation model has been constructed to *measure* rather than to *assess* performance, continuing to limit it to quantifiable, tangible and numerical data. Moreover, it stops short of assessing long-term benefits because it is generally tied to the short-term inputs of the government of the day and, as such, is as much about government performance as institutional performance.

A decade after the introduction of performance measurement, the debate continues. Moreover, it does so within a climate of accelerated social change in which the relationship between the museum and its public is being renegotiated (Ellis 1995; Weil 1997). 'Accountability' has moved from fiscal accountability to encompass accountability to the public. Increasingly, the tax-paying public are exerting their right to ask whether the considerable expenditure allocated to museums is justified.

> As crunch time approaches, however, and as the demands that are made on the public and private resources available to the non-profit sector continue to grow at a faster rate than those resources themselves, virtually every museum may find itself faced with several much tougher questions – not creampuffs this time but hardball.
>
> Without disputing the museum's claim to worthiness, what these questions will address instead is its *relative* worthiness. Is what the museum contributes to society commensurate with the annual cost of its operation? Could some other organization (not necessarily a museum) make a similar or greater contribution at lesser cost? (Weil 1994: 42)

The pressure on museums to demonstrate public accountability has forced important questions to the fore. Specifically, it has focused attention on perceived value for money in terms of whether museums actually provide benefits to the public and what kind of changes museums effect in the world beyond their doors. The notion, prevalent during the post-war years, that museums provide a 'public good' and are, therefore, deserving of funding is now under question. Museums find themselves in the situation of having to *prove* that they are providing outcomes that have long-term social benefit.

In this situation, museums face a clear challenge to 'work together to clarify and better articulate the long term impact and importance of the different outcomes museums produce' (Weil 1996: 65).

Assessing long-term social value

If museums are increasingly required to demonstrate that they provide long-term benefits to the community, how are they going to do this? The limitations of evaluation methods based on the numerical measurement of short-term, demonstrable outcomes have been discussed. What then are the alternatives? If we move into assessing long-term social value, we are in the realm of the qualitative. What models exist that assess qualitative outcomes?

Recent studies from the community arts field indicate that viable models to assess long-term, qualitative outcomes exist. Both Williams (1997) and Matarasso (1997) developed studies that set out to assess whether participation in arts programmes resulted in long-term social value for both individual participants and communities.

Williams's study, *Creating Social Capital*, was commissioned by the Community Cultural Development Board of the Australia Council. The study sought to assess whether or not there were long-term social, educational, artistic and economic outcomes as the result of participation in community arts projects. Draft indicators for each of these four generic outcomes were abstracted from grant application acquittals. These indicators were then tested by survey on a select sample of 232 people who represented a range of paid organisers, community volunteers and observers associated with community arts projects throughout the country. The respondents were asked to rate the degree to which any of the outcomes, outlined in Table 11.1, had occurred as the result of participation in a community arts pro- ject occurring two years previously. An analysis of nine case studies provided additional context for the findings.

A similar study, undertaken in the United Kingdom between 1995 and 1997, was reported by Matarasso (1997). This project sought to identify the social impact of participation in arts projects through selecting eight case studies and conducting depth interviews and discussion groups with participants. A questionnaire was also completed by over 500 people involved in the projects. Six broad categories of outcomes were identified to provide a framework within which to categorise the data from the case studies. These six categories were: personal development, social cohesion, community empowerment and self-determination, local image and iden- tity, imagination and vision, and health and well-being. While the Australian study was constructed to *test* a list of potential long-term outcomes arising from com- munity arts participation, the British study sought to *elicit* these indicators in the process of the research. In both studies, a combination of qualitative methods (depth interviews, focus groups and/or case study analyses) and quantitative methods (sur- veys) were used. In addition, both studies shared the common aim of seeking to determine whether participation in the arts resulted in long-term social value to individuals and communities and to further clarify what the range of those outcomes might be. As Table 11.2 demonstrates, the studies shared similar outcomes and both concluded that participation has multiple, long-term benefits for both indi- viduals and communities.

These studies have important relevance for similar issues facing the museum field. First, in both studies the overwhelming response was that long-term social value occurred as the result of cultural participation:

> over 90% of respondents reported that projects delivered ongoing com- munity development outcomes. These included the establishment of valuable networks, the development of community pride and the rais- ing of public awareness of a community issue. Over 80% of respondents also reported a decrease in social isolation in the community as a result- ing benefit. Improved understanding of different cultures or lifestyle was reported by more than two thirds of respondents. (Williams 1997: 2)

As importantly, these studies demonstrate that models exist to validly assess qualitative outcomes.

Museums and long-term social value

So, what unique, long-term benefits do museums contribute to society? In differen- tiating museums from other organisations, emphasis must be given to the experience that museums provide for people to engage with *objects* (Weil 1994: 43).

Table 11.1 Long-term value of participation in community arts projects

Social benefits	Educational benefits	Artistic benefits	Economic benefits
Established networks of ongoing value	Communicating ideas and information	Further work of artistic merit	Developed local enterprise
Developed community identity	Planning and organising activities	Further training or education in the arts	Led to employment
Raised public awareness of an issue	Collecting, analysing and organising information	Developed groups or arts activities	Improved productivity in business/public community
Lessened social isolation	Solving problems	Developed creative talents	Enhanced or developed tourism
Improved understanding of different cultures and lifestyles	Using technology	Improved access to arts education or training	Attracted new resources to the community
Improved recreational options	Using mathematical ideas and techniques	Increased sales for artworks or developed audiences	Improved or developed public facilities
Inspired action on a social justice issue			Improved planning and design of public spaces
Increased appreciation of the value of community arts projects			Improved consultation between government and community
			Created cost savings in public expenditure
			Improved crime prevention

Source: Williams 1997

Table 11.2 Long-term social value of participation in arts projects

Personal development	Social cohesion	Community empowerment	Local image and identity	Imagination and vision	Health and well-being
Increased personal confidence and self-worth	Reduced social isolation	Built community organisational capacity	Developed pride in local traditions and cultures	Helped people develop creativity	Had a positive impact on how people feel
Extended involvement in social activity	Developed community networks	Encouraged local self-reliance	Contributed to a sense of belonging and involvement	Eroded the distinction between creator and consumer	Provided an effective means of health education
Gave people an active voice to express themselves	Promoted tolerance and conflict resolution	Helped people extend control over their lives	Created community traditions	Allowed exploration of values, meanings and dreams	Contributed to a more relaxed atmosphere in health centres
Stimulated interest and confidence in the arts	Provided a forum for multicultural understanding	Provided insight into political and social ideas	Involved residents in environmental improvement	Enriched the practice of professionals	Provided enjoyment
Provided forums to explore personal rights	Helped validate the contribution of a whole community	Facilitated effective public consultation	Provided a basis for developing community activities	Encouraged risk taking	Improved quality of life of people with poor health
Contributed to educational development of children	Promoted cross-cultural contact and co-operation	Involved local people in community regeneration	Improved perceptions of marginalised groups	Helped communities raise vision beyond the immediate	
Encouraged adults to take up education and training opportunities	Promoted contact across generations	Facilitated the development of partnerships	Helped transform the image of public bodies	Challenged conventional service delivery	
Helped build new skills and provided work experience	Helped address issues of crime	Built support for community projects	Made people feel better about where they live	Raised expectations about what is possible	
Contributed to people's employability	Provided offender rehabilitation routes	Strengthened community co-operation			

Source: Matarasso 1997

The role that objects can play in personal and collective memory, identity and meaning has been discussed by Silverman (1995, 1997), Kirschenblatt-Gimblett (1999) and Burnett (1999):

> [memory] links us to a past, a generational history and a wider, shared cultural memory. The point at which one's personal memories intersect with and are shared with others – family, friends, grandparents, a community, a nation – is a critical factor in the formation of both personal identity and a sense of cultural belonging. On the one hand, memory binds and connects us to a sense of place and historical lineage. At the same time it threatens to disintegrate under the weight of time and somehow 'fail' us. This is where – at a personal level – stories, photographs, lockets, trinkets, films and videos are used and collected by many to recall people, events and places. Somehow, we believe that our pasts are contained or made more permanent by these mementos. (Burnett 1999: 45)

Through objects, museums can provide unique experiences associated with the collective meaning, sharing, discussion and debate that are the foundation of good citizenry. Through objects, museums can reinforce personal identity and belonging. Objects convey a sense of place and can, therefore, introduce outsiders to the significance of a culture through its material heritage. Research on objects can reveal new knowledge. The stories told through objects in a museum setting have educative value. All of these outcomes are features of social value, that 'attachment of meaning to the things which are fundamental to personal and collective identity' (Johnston 1992: 10).

There is evidence in the literature that museums contribute in all these ways. Perhaps three categories will help to simplify the impact that museums have on long-term social value. Museums can be shown to contribute to collective and personal development, economic value and educational value.

Collective and personal development

How do museums facilitate collective and personal development? From even a cursory glance at the literature, there is evidence to support five areas:

- providing a forum for the discussion and debate of emergent social issues;
- affirming personal identity;
- fostering tolerance and understanding;
- providing reverential and commemorative experiences; and
- creating a collective identity through a shared history and a sense of place.

Discussion and debate

Heumann Gurian refers to museums as sites for 'peaceful congregant behaviour' (1996) in which issues of community concern can be discussed in one of the few safe forums left available for public debate. This theme is echoed eloquently by both Weil (1997) and Maggi (2000), who envision a museum of the future that will be a centre for community confrontation, exchange and debate; what Maggi describes as a 'forum museum',

> where not only the objects of the past are shown, but the culture for the future is built, a forum that must help the community to grow . . . it is a dynamic museum, serving above all as a cultural animator in trying to interpret community changes. (2000: 51–52)

Personal identity

If social inclusion is to be realised, then the ability of the museum to allow a variety of stories to be told is critical. Weil suggests that this is exactly what a museum in a postmodern world can do, when every text is allowed to:

> have as many versions – all equally correct – as it has readers. Translated into museum terms, that would suggest that the objects displayed in the museum do not have any fixed or inherent meaning but that 'meaning making' or the process by which these objects acquire meaning for individual members of the public, will in each case involve specific memories, expertise, viewpoint, assumptions and connections that the particular individual brings. (1997: 269)

Lois Silverman has identified the special contribution that museums make to confirming this sense of special personal identity. Through remembering and connecting, visitors can affirm an individual sense of self.

> For one visitor, an important component of self-identity could be that of the knowledgeable expert, influencing her to draw upon and share her special knowledge and competencies. For another, a sense of himself as 'family historian' might activate 'relevant family stories', leading to a more subjective experience of an exhibit. (1995: 162)

Self-identity is not confined to personal selection, engagement and perspective. It can also be reflected in a sense of belonging, affiliation and identity as part of a collective whole; what Silverman describes as 'who am I as a group member?' (1995: 163).

Increased understanding and tolerance

A further dimension of social inclusion is the need for a corporate citizenry that fosters tolerance for difference and cross-cultural understanding. Museums have great potential to transcend differences as well as to communicate about them (Silverman 1993: 10).

Fred Wilson's moving description of 'Mining the Museum' (1996) to reveal hitherto invisible experiences of African-Americans is an example. In the course of his exploration of the African-American cultural reality, he invites us to ask questions of the objects in ways that touch our collective humanity and compassion. Highlighting black children relegated to the shadows of a painting, he poses questions for these children that reveal their loneliness and marginal place in the society of pre-Civil War America: 'Who calms me when I am afraid?', 'Am I your friend? Am I your brother? Am I your pet?'

Half a world away, at the Powerhouse Museum in Sydney, an exhibition titled *Precious Legacy: treasures from the Jewish Museum in Prague* was presented in 1999. The objects were part of a collection that had been rescued from the Holocaust by the Jewish community. The comment forms completed by visitors reveal the power of an exhibition to develop cross-cultural understanding (Scott 1999: 10):

> For me an excellent insight into Jewish life and religion. I now better understand a Jewish friend of mine who said that 'Judaism is not a religion, it is a way of life'.

> A very touching and informative exhibition. Gave me an insight into Jewish life and suffering.

Reverential and commemorative experiences

War museums and memorials all over the world provide a focus to remember and honour the war dead and the sacrifices made in the names of freedom, cultural preservation and democracy. In many instances, these museums have moved beyond the celebratory focus of the past to embrace and recognise the victims of war as well as its heroes. They are 'places for inward and sober reflection' (Weil 1997: 261). The commemoration of critical events enables a culture to develop a shared history, which is 'the crucial element in the construction of an "imagined community" through which disparate individuals and groups envision themselves as members of a collective with a common present and future' (Anderson in Glassberg 1996: 11–12).

Collective identity through a shared history and sense of place

This 'imagined community' is composed of the myths and symbols that hold together diverse groups in a society. Through objects, the symbolic construction of a common history around which a national or local sense of identity can be forged is played out in museums. Linked to this is a sense of place formed through the layering of social, cultural, historical, economic, natural and personal associations that together give a locale its special character and meaning (Johnston 1992; Glassberg 1996). Many local museums and historical societies reflect a powerful sense of place through the collection of artefacts that represent the social, cultural, historical, economic, natural and personal associations that people have forged within a locale.

Economic value

The 'sense of place' that museums confirm has implications for economic value. As economic rationalism continues to dominate public sector institutions, museums are finding that they are required to 'perform a broader range of economic functions, often as part of complex urban re-development strategies' (Tufts and Milne 1999: 614). This 'economisation of culture' (Sayer in Tufts and Milne 1999) is evident in the role that museums are increasingly playing in popular leisure and urban tourism. Related to the 'sense of place' discussed above, museums are used as key attractors to define the overall tourism experience through their ability to 'reflect an essential sense of a particular time and place unavailable elsewhere' (Tufts and Milne 1999: 616). Museums enable cities to market themselves as cultural centres that appeal to residents, tourists, professionals and investors.

In addition, the synergy between cultural and consumption experiences has resulted in a trend to capitalise on the combination. A visit to a museum can involve an economic spend including admission fees, the purchase of food and drink and buying souvenir products imbued with the meaning of the exhibitions seen. Increasingly, heritage precincts are being constructed that offer both cultural attractions and the opportunity to purchase high-quality consumer goods. As urban redevelopment initiatives and tourist attractions, these precincts are part of carefully constructed urban revitalisation schemes.

Educational value

A recent study undertaken at the Powerhouse Museum in Sydney revealed that museums continue to be associated with learning and education. Museums were defined as places where one could have an *educational, intellectual* and *absorbing* experience (Boomerang! 1998).

The fact that the learning acquired in museums can be recalled long after the museum visit has been documented by Falk and Dierking (1995) and McManus (1993). Analysing these studies and a study undertaken by Bitgood and Cleghorn (1994), Ferguson (1997) suggests that the unique type of learning experience offered by museums, one which is mediated through objects, is particularly effective in stimulating visual memory. The visual memory of the object serves as a trigger to stimulate associated learning to a degree that purely semantic memory (knowledge-based concepts and facts) cannot. Interestingly, across the three studies that Ferguson analysed, visual memory accounted for approximately 55 per cent of responses while semantic memory was less than half of that. In addition, museums are predominantly a social experience and there is abundant evidence that learning mediated through social interaction has longer-term 'holding power' (Falk and Dierking 1992).

Conclusion

Ensuring that the long-term contribution of museums to social value is assessed may be a matter for survival. Though the 1970s and 1980s saw an unprecedented boom in the establishment of museums throughout the industrialised world with attendance numbers attaining new highs, the 1990s began to witness evidence of declining attendances (Kirchberg 1998; Australian Bureau of Statistics 1999).

More leisure options, less time (Australian Bureau of Statistics 1998), more individualised and home-based leisure (Pronovost 1998), the ageing of the 'baby boomers' and the impact of technology (Maggi 1998) are all cited as contributors to dwindling attendances. However, recent leisure theory also suggests that the pace of leisure is speeding up and, as an antidote to increasing pressure in the workplace, people are seeking depthless, less committed forms of leisure that promise fun, entertainment and time out at the expense of education, learning and intellectual experiences (Rojek 1995; Jonson 1998).

If this is the case, then museums need to promote themselves as being agents capable of offering a value experience that has a social impact beyond the ephemeral and the transitory. They are perfectly positioned to be able to do so, thus demonstrating, to themselves and to the public to whom they are accountable, that the museum experience is unique, authentic and long term.

Note

Carol Scott is Manager of Evaluation and Audience Research at the Powerhouse Museum in Sydney and past President of Museums Australia. This paper was first published in *Museums, Society, Inequality* (2002) edited by Richard Sandell.

References

Ames, P. (1991) 'Measures of merit?', *Museum News*, Sept./Oct.: 55–56.
—— (1992) 'Breaking new ground: measuring museums' merits', *MUSE*, spring: 15–16.
Australian Bureau of Statistics (1998) *How Australians Spend Their Time: 1997* (Cat. of Statistics No. 4153.0), Canberra: ABS.
—— (1999) *Attendance at Selected Cultural Venues: 1999* (Cat. of Statistics No. 4114.0), Canberra: ABS.
Bitgood, S. and Cleghorn, A. (1994) 'Memory of objects, labels and other sensory impressions from a museum visit', *Visitor Behaviour* ix(2): 11–12.
Boomerang! Marketing and Advertising Pty Ltd (1998) *Powerhouse Museum Brand Audit and Positioning Options: In-house Report Prepared for the Powerhouse Museum*, Sydney: Powerhouse Museum.
Bud, R., Cave, M. and Haney, S. (1991) 'Measuring a museum's output', *Museums Journal*, January: 29–31.
Burnett, D. (1999) 'Whenever I hear the word memory, I reach for my laptop' in *Exploring Culture and Community for the 21st Century: A New Model for Public Arts Museums*, Ipswich, Qld: Global Arts Link.
Cossons, N. (1988) 'Performance indicators in museums', paper delivered at The Development of Performance Indicators seminar, organised by the Museums Association of Australia, Canberra, November 1988.
Council on the Cost of Government (1997) *Arts and Culture: Service Effort and Accomplishments*, Sydney: NSW Council on the Cost of Government.

Dept of Finance (1989) *What Price Heritage? The Museums Review and the Measurement of Museum Performance: Issues for Discussion*, Canberra: Dept of Finance.

Douglas, L. (1991) 'The politics of performance: measuring the value of museums', unpublished paper submitted for the Graduate Diploma in Arts Management, University of Technology, Sydney.

Ellis, R. (1995) 'Museums as change agents', *Journal of Museum Education*, spring/ summer: 14–17.

Falk, J. and Dierking, L. (1992) *The Museum Experience*, Washington, DC: Whalesback.

—— (1995) 'Recalling the museum experience', *Journal of Museum Education* 20(2): 10–13.

Ferguson, L. (1997) 'Evaluating learning', *Museums National* 5(4), May: 15–16.

Glassberg, D. (1996) 'Public history and the study of memory', *Public Historian* 18(2): 7–23.

Heumann Gurian, E. (1996) 'A savings bank for the soul', paper presented at the Museums Australia Conference 1996, Sydney.

Johnston, C. (1992) *What Is Social Value? A Discussion Paper*, Canberra: Australian Government Publishing Service.

Jonson, P. (1998) 'Leisure in the 21st century', paper presented to the Evaluation and Visitor Research in Museums Conference: Visitor Centre Stage – Action for the Future, Canberra, 4–6 August.

Kirchberg, V. (1998) 'The changing face of arts audiences. The Kenneth Myer Lecture', Deakin University: Arts and Entertainment Management Program.

Kirschenblatt-Gimblett, B. (1999) 'Objects of memory' in *Exploring Culture and Community for the 21st Century: A New Model for Public Arts Museums*, Ipswich, Qld: Global Arts Link.

Maggi, M. (1998) *a.muse: Advanced Museums*, Italy: Fondazione Rosselli.

—— (2000) 'Innovation in Italy: the a.muse project', *Museum International* 52(2): 50–53.

Matarasso, F. (1997) *Use or Ornament? The Social Impact of Participation in the Arts*, Stroud, Glos.: Comedia.

McManus, P. (1993) 'Memories as indicators of the impact of museum visits', *Museum Management and Curatorship* 12: 367–380.

Office of Arts and Libraries (1991) *Report on the Development of Performance Indicators for the National Museums and Galleries*, London: Office of Arts and Libraries.

Pronovost, G. (1998) *Trend Report: The Sociology of Leisure*, Thousand Oaks: Sage.

Redfern, M. (1986) *Performance Measures in the Public Sector: A Digest*, London: British Library (British Library R & D Report 5905).

Rojek, C. (1995) *Decentring Leisure*, London: Sage.

Scott, C. (1991) 'Report on the outcomes of a consultancy to develop performance indicators for national collecting institutions', prepared for the Cultural Heritage Branch of the Department of the Arts, Sports, the Environment, Tourism and Territories, April.

—— (1999) *Precious Legacy: Report on Visitor Feedback for the Powerhouse Museum*, Sydney: Evaluation and Audience Research Department, Powerhouse Museum.

Silverman, L. (1993) 'Making meaning together', *Journal of Museum Education* 18(3): 7–11.

—— (1995) 'Visitor meaning-making in museums for a new age', *Curator* 38(3): 161–170.

—— (1997) 'Personalising the past: a review of literature with implications for historical interpretation', *Journal of Interpretation Research* 2(1): 2–3.

Tufts, S. and Milne, S. (1999) 'Museums: a supply side perspective', *Annals of Tourism Research* 26(3): 613–631.

Walden, I. (1991) 'Qualities and quantities', *Museums Journal*, January: 27–28.

Weil, S.E. (1994) 'Creampuffs and hardball: are you really worth what you cost?', *Museum News* (US), 73(5), Sept./Oct.: 42–43, 60, 62–63.

—— (1996) 'The distinctive numerator', *Museum News*, Mar./Apr.: 64–65.

—— (1997) 'The museum and the public', *Museum Management and Curatorship* 16(3): 257–271.

Williams, D. (1997) *Creating Social Capital*, Adelaide: Community Arts Network of South Australia.

Wilson, F. (1996) 'The silent message of the museum', paper presented at the Museums Australia Conference: Power and Empowerment, Sydney.

Chapter 12

Beyond Big and Awesome
Outcome-based evaluation

Stephen E. Weil

W HEN STEPHEN JAY GOULD, the great science writer and evolutionary
theorist, passed away in May 2002, the obituaries in both the *New York Times*
and the *Washington Post* noted that his interest in what would become his life's work
had been kindled by a visit with his father to the American Museum of Natural
History when he was 5 years old. 'I dreamed of becoming a scientist, in general,
and a paleontologist, in particular,' he subsequently wrote, 'ever since the
Tyrannosaurus skeleton [both] awed and scared me.'

Four things seem worth noting here. First, if the museum is a 'learning' experience, what was it that Gould learned as a 5-year-old museum visitor? Was it only
something the curator hoped to communicate about dinosaurs (they're big, they're
awesome)? Or did he also learn something about himself, about what genuinely
caught his interest and stirred his imagination?

Second, it seems striking that neither of the newspapers reported this anecdote
as something bizarre or exceptional. While museums struggle over how intended
learning might compare with actual learning, the outside world seems perfectly
relaxed with the notion that there might be some connection between an early museum
experience and a later life or career choice.

Third, assume that the museum had done an exit interview or some other form
of visitor research on the day young Gould made his first visit. Would the full impact
of that visit have been recognized?

Fourth, how could you adequately describe the outcome of that visit? Was it
simply the impact on Gould himself that mattered, or did the visit ultimately have
important consequences for his students at Harvard or his hundreds of thousands
of readers throughout the world? Is Gould's case unique, or can we generalize that
the impact of a museum may frequently extend well beyond those who enter its

Source: *Museum News*, vol. 6, no. 3 (2003): 40–53.

doors and ripple throughout the community or even the world in ever-widening circles?

In other words, what can a museum learn from its visitors' experiences – both inside and outside its walls? In evaluating a museum's worthiness, the starting point must be the positive and intended differences that it makes in the lives of the individuals and communities that constitute its target audience. The critical issue is not how those differences are measured but that such differences must become and remain an institution's central focus.

As a prelude to a discussion of outcome-based evaluation, consider the following overarching and relatively theoretical propositions about museums in general and about learning in museums.

First, today there is widespread agreement, at least in the United States, that the measure of a museum's worthiness is no longer an *internal* assessment of what it might possess – a superior collection, a talented staff, splendid facilities, a hefty endowment – but an *external* consideration of the benefits it provides to the individuals and communities it seeks to serve.

Second, to echo the maxim that was so forcefully set out in AAM's 1991 publication *Excellence and Equity: Education and the Public Dimension of Museums*, it is 'education – in the broadest sense of that word – [that lies] at the heart of [every museum's] public service role.'

Third, donors and grant-makers are decreasingly willing to accept simply as a matter of faith that recipient museums have achieved their educational or other intended outcomes. More and more, they are asking for some proof of performance. Daunting as the prospect may be, it will be essential for this country's museums to develop credible systems of feedback that will allow them to monitor the impact of their efforts and make adjustments when necessary.

The bottom line

Let us start with the first proposition, that in determining the worthiness of a museum, the primary measure is the extent to which it can produce positive outcomes for the individuals and communities it seeks to serve. Two questions arise immediately: What do we mean by 'outcomes'? And how do these 'outcomes' fit into the overall conception of what a museum is and does? Concerning the first question, the best answer to my mind was offered in the mid-1990s by the United Way of America, a pioneer in the use of outcome-based evaluation to determine the allocation of its grant funds. To be successful, a United Way applicant must be able to demonstrate its ability to bring about some beneficial changes for individuals and/or populations that participate in its programs. The areas in which such changes may occur, though, are remarkably broad. They may '. . . relate to behavior, skills, knowledge, attitudes, values, condition, status, or other attributes. They are what participants know, think, or can do; or how they behave; or what their condition is, that is different following the program.'

These are almost precisely the kind of differences – most particularly, differences in skills, knowledge, attitudes, and values – that museums aspire to make through their educational activities. How, though, do these outcomes fit into an overall conception of the museum?

To answer that question, I'll refer to the 'social enterprise model' that J. Gregory Dees, a professor at Stanford's Graduate School of Business, first proposed some years ago when he was teaching at the Harvard Business School. Let's begin by envisioning a large box; that's the button factory. To get it started, investors will pour money in through the top; the factory then purchases the equipment and raw materials it needs to make buttons. It also hires mechanics, designers, machine operators, and clerks to design, produce, and keep track of the buttons. Now, from the bottom of the box, we can see the factory's output: millions and millions of buttons. Do those buttons constitute the factory's real bottom line? Are they the outcome that the investors were hoping for when they made their investments? Of course not. One more thing has to happen. Somebody has to sell those buttons and convert them into money.

That money – that's the bottom line, the outcome everyone wanted, the reason the whole enterprise was constructed in the first place. The buttons were only an output, an internal manifestation, something wholly within the factory's capacity to produce. To produce the outcome – the money – one more critical ingredient was required: what economists call 'demand.' A market had to want the buttons, to think they had value. Assuming the factory finds such a market and is able to sell enough buttons to be successful, some of that bottom-line button money can go back to the investors in the form of dividends. Most of it, however, will recirculate back to the top so the factory can purchase more materials, upgrade its equipment, retain its workers, and start a new cycle of button-making. In the best of all scenarios, it may even become a perpetual motion button factory, able to continue these cycles indefinitely with no further infusion of capital.

Let us now envision a second box; this one is a museum. Again, money will pour in through the top, this time as contributions, grants, and other public and private support. Some of that money will be used to acquire raw materials: objects, library books, information technology. The rest may be spent to hire workers – in this case, such specialists as curators, conservators, exhibit designers, and educators – to process the raw materials into such valued products as exhibitions, public lectures, catalogues, gallery guides, and specialized tours.

These valued products eventually will emerge from the second box as publicly accessible programs. But are these programs, these outputs, the museum's bottom line? Are they the outcomes that its donors and grant-makers sought when they gave money to the institution? Again, the answer is 'of course not.' Something more has to happen. The programs need to reach and have a positive impact on an audience. Unless they make some kind of a difference to that audience, they might just as well never have happened.

For the museum, that *difference* is the bottom line, the desired outcome, the reason the whole enterprise was constructed in the first place. Just as the button factory could only convert its output (buttons) into its desired bottom-line outcome (money) through a market that values those buttons, the museum can only convert its output (programs) into its desired bottom-line outcome (a beneficial impact) if a potential audience thinks its offerings have value.

That museums and other social enterprises have so much in common with business enterprises does not mean that the business model is now dominant and other kinds of organizations are under pressure to follow its example. In fact, in recent years we have come to recognize that business, social, and governmental organizations have long been structured and operate in startlingly similar ways. Common to all of them is the degree to which they commandeer and exercise dominion over the scarce resources the larger society has available. Common as well is the growing expectation that these organizations, in exchange for their temporary appropriation of those scarce resources, must return a commensurate quantum of value back to that larger society. Commenting on the case of the business enterprise, management expert Peter Drucker has observed: 'A business that does not show a profit at least equal to its cost of capital is socially irresponsible. It wastes society's resources. Economic performance is the basis; without it a business cannot discharge any other responsibilities, cannot be a good employer, a good citizen, a good neighbor.'

As profits are to a business, so outcomes are to a museum. The museum that does not provide an outcome to its community is as socially irresponsible as the business that fails to show a profit. It wastes society's resources.

An opportunity to learn

How, then, is the museum to justify itself? With that question, we come to the second of our three propositions, i.e., that the museum justifies itself through the educational activities that lie at the very heart of its public service role. 'Education,' though, is a remarkably spacious concept. It includes both the notion of teaching or imparting knowledge (as in 'to educate') and the not always reciprocal notion of receiving or acquiring knowledge (as in 'to be educated'). In seeking to understand itself (or explain itself to others), a museum must think about how it intends to be educational – like the police academy or a vocational/career school, like a liberal arts college or a great research university, or like a public library?

A museum also must think about where it positions itself on the continuum that runs from providing formal instruction at one end to serving as a site for self-directed learning at the other end. In a recent draft of a strategic plan for learning in museums, the United Kingdom's Council for Museums, Archives and Libraries seems distinctly inclined toward the self-directed learning end of this continuum: 'Definitions of and approaches to learning have changed considerably. . . . Learning is no longer seen simply as being at the receiving end of the transmission of knowledge and information: rather, it is a process which requires the participation of the learner, which people approach in a variety of different ways, and which is linked to improving the quality of people's lives.'

That the public itself may be increasingly sensitive to this distinction is suggested by some focus group research conducted in 2001 by students at the Winterthur Program in Early American Culture. In their study, focus group members reacted in sharply different ways to the notion that either a 'teaching' or a 'learning' component might be included as an integral part of a hypothetical museum visit.

The prospect of being taught elicited an almost wholly negative response. But the prospect that visitors might be given an opportunity to learn was considered highly positive.

In that same Winterthur study, a second pair of words – 'entertainment' and 'recreation' – provoked a similar set of conflicting responses. 'Entertainment' was viewed in negative terms; 'recreation' was seen as correspondingly positive. Common to both sets of words was the difference between being a passive museum visitor to whom something is done – you are taught, you are entertained – and being an active one who takes the opportunity to learn for herself and/or pursue her own recreation.

Whether a museum should primarily be a place for teaching or one for learning is something about which even its own staff may disagree. In my own experience, curators, particularly those with the heaviest academic credentials, incline toward what my Smithsonian colleague Zahava Doering has called the 'baby-bird' theory of museum education. That's an approach in which the museum, as an all-knowing mother bird, carefully chews up appropriate helpings of fact and opinion and then, beakful by beakful, doles them out to the fledgling visitor. Educators occupy a middle ground; for them, the museum is a place where a variety of teaching methodologies and free-choice learning opportunities can be fruitfully combined. At the other end of the continuum, the manager of visitor services cares only that some aspect of a visit – whether the shop, restaurant, parking, rest rooms, or even the objects on exhibit – makes a visitor happy and eager to return.

Let's imagine three groups of visitors to an exhibition of Greek and Roman pottery. Members of the first group, though they found their museum visit generally pleasurable, had little or no interest in this particular exhibition. They walked through it quickly and paid scant attention. In consolation, think about what Indiana University's Lois Silverman and three of her research colleagues wrote some years ago in the fall 1996 *Journal of Museum Education*: 'Although visitors say they come to museums to learn things, more often than not the social agenda takes precedence. Quality family time, a date, something to do with out-of-town guests, a place to hang out with friends: those are some of the primary reasons people choose to go to museums.'

Our second group of visitors is prepared to invest time looking carefully at the objects and reading the labels. They may wait for a docent's tour, pick up and study the gallery handouts, and have animated discussions with each other. Given the nice symmetrical fit between their interests and those of the curator, we can expect that they'll enjoy their visits. In carrying out its educational role, the museum clearly will have served these visitors as a teacher.

My central concern, however, is with the third group, who include:

- an elderly immigrant from Greece for whom the exhibition triggers an enormous outpouring of pride in her ancestors' achievements;
- two brothers whose younger sister has recently died and who find a degree of solace in the notion that, the potential brevity of life notwithstanding, art and beauty can somehow endure;
- an amateur potter who regularly scavenges through ceramics exhibitions in search of forms that she might adapt to her own use;

- a tourist for whom the exhibition evokes pleasurable memories of his recent trip to Rome;
- and a pair of young lovers who amuse themselves by concocting improbable mythologies to explain the amorous and other activities depicted on the pottery.

Let's hypothesize further that this third group did not do particularly well at learning to tell the difference between a Greek pot and a Roman one. But just because their agendas are not congruent with the curator's, should we classify their visits as failures? Or should we be open to the possibility that the museum is a place in which some visitors may learn little or nothing and still find pleasure, others will learn more or less what the museum is trying to teach, and still others may experience something of value, even if it isn't what the museum intended? In a great research university or even a police academy, this casual hodgepodge of the intentional and the accidental might not be tolerable. Daydreaming at police academy might even be dangerous. In the museum, though, we must remain sensitive to those peculiarly unstructured and frequently unexpected aspects of the visit that can make it such a different and idiosyncratic experience.

For example, Mike Wallace, a professor at the City University of New York, has suggested that the most important outcome for history museums might be in 'helping visitors [to] develop their historical sensibilities, strengthening their ability to locate themselves in time, and enhancing their capacity as citizens to be historically informed makers of history.' The underlying notion is that one genuinely important outcome of a history museum's exhibition program might be to enhance the capacity of citizens to govern themselves in a better informed way.

That notion could certainly be extended to other types of museums as well. Consider the Hall of Biodiversity at the American Museum of Natural History, which reflects the museum's efforts – and these are the staff's own words – 'to alert the public to the critical roles biodiversity plays in sustaining life as we know it and to the ecological crisis we now face.' This is not just about contemplation or passive understanding but, rather, is a call to social and political action.

An art museum might help its visitors to hone still other skills. In a memorable address delivered at AAM's 1980 annual meeting in Boston, the late Harvard philosopher Nelson Goodman argued that rather than simply cultivate an appreciation for art or engender an interest in art history, an art museum should function as an 'institution for the prevention and cure of blindness.' The works of art displayed in such a museum contribute to that function, he said, when '. . . by stimulating inquisitive looking, sharpening perceptions, raising visual intelligence, widening perspectives, bringing out new connections and contrasts, and marking off neglected significant kinds, they participate in the organization and reorganization of experience, and thus in the making and remaking of our worlds.'

It takes more than good intentions

Let us move on to the third proposition: that museums, faced with ever-more explicit demands for accountability, must develop credible systems of feedback that will allow them to monitor and report on the impact of their educational efforts. As they develop these systems, it seems to me that they must take into account the widest range of educational experiences possible in a museum.

In the case of our second hypothetical group, most of whom did learn how to distinguish a Greek pot from a Roman one, that should be relatively easy. Far tougher to deal with are the cases in which the museum's intentions and its visitors' experiences do not overlap quite so neatly. Like those wayward daydreamers in our hypothetical third group. Like the young Stephen Jay Gould whose life work was rooted in a childhood museum visit. In fact, most of us can remember a visit that indelibly marked the museum as the kind of place where we might some day like to work.

One caution should be noted: a museum might be better off with no system in place for gauging its impact than with a bad one that uses an inappropriate set of measures. This point was forcefully made in a May 30, 2002, *Chronicle of Philanthropy* article by Peter Frumkin, assistant professor of public policy at the John F. Kennedy School of Government. Writing about nonprofit organizations' widespread and continuing failure to develop more meaningful measures for documenting the effectiveness of their 'programmatic bottom line,' Frumkin warns that there may be a growing tendency to substitute financial measures instead. The great advantage of financial measures is that they can readily be connected to such familiar quantitative benchmarks as return on endowment, year-to-year fluctuations in membership dues, or the relationship of annual revenue to annual expense. 'The problem that this creates in the nonprofit world is clear,' Frumkin writes:

> From foundations and universities to hospitals and museums, nonprofit groups of all kinds, but particularly large institutions, are understandably led to focus on financial measures of performance because they are so much more concrete and robust than programmatic ones. They are also what outsiders can observe easily and compare quickly in sizing up one organization's management compared with another.

Consider just how preposterous such financial measures would be if they were used to evaluate the Armenian Genocide Museum and Memorial, a new museum scheduled to open in downtown Washington, D.C., between 2007 and 2010. Today, historians (Turkish ones aside) accept that more than 1 million Armenians were killed by the Ottoman Empire during a 1915–16 campaign to uproot them from the territory that would ultimately become Turkey. Tens of thousands more were forced into exile, many coming to the United States. Descendants of this latter group have been primarily responsible for organizing the Genocide Museum and raising its estimated $100-million cost. Among the museum's goals will be to make a historical record of the 1915–16 massacre, to develop a genocide-prevention component, to tell the story of the Armenian diaspora, and to celebrate the rebirth of the Armenian community in the United States and elsewhere. Its future location, a former bank building located two blocks from the White House, makes it clear that the audience for that story is intended to be far larger than the anticipated annual attendance of 250,000.

On what basis will supporters of the Genocide Museum measure its success or failure? Certainly by whether its programs make their intended educational impact on the public, and not by whether its revenues consistently exceed its expenses. Of course, a museum, like any organization, must be attentive to its revenues and expenses. What makes the museum so different from the button factory, though, is the inadequacy of those terms to define its success or failure. For the museum, the bottom line must be a programmatic outcome, not a fiscal one.

The case of the Armenian Genocide Museum also suggests that it may be simpler to establish a credible approach to evaluation when an institution's goals are clearly defined and it can articulate with some precision what sort of an educational impact it hopes to make. Such clearly defined goals are by no means universal in the field. For older museums that trace their roots back to that time when a museum might, indeed, have been its own excuse for being – institutions established decades before the phrase 'mission statement' had even been coined – the first steps in constructing a system of program evaluation may well involve the clarification of its institutional purpose. If evaluation is nothing more than a means to determine whether an organization is achieving its desired outcomes, a first step must be to ensure that all the important players – trustees, staff, and volunteers inside the museum; donors and visitors outside the museum – share some basic understanding of what those outcomes are.

One financial aspect must, however, be addressed in even the most program-based system of evaluation. That's the question of cost effectiveness. Suppose a regional museum in rural Texas proposes to do an exhibition about tornadoes. Its educational objectives are clear. It wants visitors to learn how to anticipate a tornado and prepare their homes and look after their family's safety in the event one occurs. In seeking support, though, the museum may be asked not only about its intended educational impact, but also whether an exhibition is the most cost-effective way to impart that knowledge. What if, at a fraction of the exhibition's cost, somebody else could teach as much to as many people, in as memorable a way, through an illustrated publication, a videotape, or a television special?

In the past, when museums and other nonprofits were focused on outputs rather than outcomes, that was less of a problem. Museums could point to a unique output – the exhibition – that nobody else could match. Today, however, organizations with the most varied of outputs might pursue a common outcome. The downside for museums is that they may face competition from less costly providers. But the upside, which to my mind is far more than compensatory, is that a focus on outcomes may open the door for collaboration. If several community groups have a common and concurrent interest in tornado awareness, for example, perhaps their collaborative impact will far exceed the sum of their separate achievements. In the magical world of collaboration, two plus two can frequently make five.

Concerning Frumkin's observation that not-for-profit organizations have failed to develop meaningful measures to document the impact of their programs, that certainly has not been due, at least among museums, to any lack of serious effort. For a variety of reasons, though, museums have turned out to be difficult cases when it comes to evaluation. One problem was pointed out by Jay Rounds of the University of Missouri-St. Louis in the July/August 2001 issue of *Museum News*. There is, he noted, an almost complete disjunction between evaluation techniques that are essentially verbal and numerical and museum-going experiences that may be primarily visual.

Another problem relates to timing. The impact of museums on their visitors tends to be cumulative over time, subtle rather than obvious, indirect rather than direct, and more often than not deeply entangled with the impact made by a myriad of other community organizations. The most apt analogy might be to a liberal arts college. Determining the ultimate impact of a museum visit through an exit interview is like determining on a student's graduation day what her liberal arts education might contribute to society. It may take, in fact, the better part of a lifetime for that contribution to become evident. Think again about the 5-year-old Stephen Jay Gould. Think about your own experiences.

To add to this complexity, the variety of objectives that are pursued by museums today is astonishingly diverse, not only between museums of different disciplines but even between museums within a single discipline. One art museum may aspire to induce in its visitors a purely aesthetic response; another might envision itself as a teaching institution. A third art museum might center itself around creativity; a fourth might seek to interest visitors in the interplay of such aesthetic concepts as complexity, unity, and intensity. And a fifth might aspire to Nelson Goodman's ideal: to be an institution 'for the prevention and cure of blindness.' Add to these the equally diverse agendas of history and natural history museums, science centers and children's museums, and you will begin to grasp part of this complexity.

To grasp the full complexity of museum evaluation, though, requires multiplying those institutional agendas by the equally diverse personal agendas of museum visitors. Some come to browse pleasurably, to be with friends or family, or to enjoy one of the few community spaces where they can safely share the company of strangers. Some come specifically to be taught. And some come because the museum offers them a particularly stimulating environment that invites them to learn about life, about stuff, about themselves.

What this complexity suggests is that, over time, the museum field will need to develop a vast arsenal of richer and more persuasive ways to document and/or demonstrate the myriad and beneficial outcomes that may occur for their individual visitors and have impact on the community beyond. Some of these ways may be quantitative but, to the horror of some social scientists, a great many may be anecdotal or qualitative. What is critical is that these evaluation techniques fit the real complexity of what museums actually do. It would be a calamity beyond telling – the equivalent of the 'teaching to the test' phenomenon in our public schools – if museums were to dumb down their work to squeeze into the strait-jacket of whatever assessment tools happen to be available.

Where does that leave us? Hopefully, with this understanding: that outcome-based evaluation, at least at this stage, is not about the use of any specific technique, or metric, or the imposition of any particular management style. It is, rather, a way of thinking, what Institute for Learning Innovation Director John Falk referred to as 'state of mind' at the 2002 AAM Annual Meeting in Dallas. From this point of view, the primary measure used to evaluate a museum's worthiness is the positive and intended differences that it makes in the lives of the individuals and communities that constitute its target audiences. That is the outcome, the achievement, toward which every activity undertaken in the museum should be aligned.

The critical point is not how this achievement should be measured but, rather, that striving after such an achievement becomes and remains the museum's central focus. A museum may have a championship-caliber staff, a splendid building, superb collections, great management, great programs, great everything. But if it makes no difference to anybody, if it has no impact, if no good outcomes follow from what it does, then all it can be is a great so *what?*: a gorgeous and resplendent wheel spinning prettily in the air.

As recently as two generations ago, organizations like museums were primarily about good intentions. The vocabulary used to describe them centered on such words as philanthropic or charitable or benevolent. *Bene volent* — to wish somebody good! Those days are gone. Museums are no longer their own excuse for being. As the resources they require have become greater and greater, so, too, have the expectations of those called upon to provide those resources. What is demanded today is that organizations perform, deliver, and demonstrate their effectiveness. Good intentions may still be where museums begin but, today, positive impact is where they have to finish.

Note

The late **Stephen E. Weil** was Emeritus Scholar at the Smithsonian Center for Education and Museum Studies and influential museum thinker and writer. This article was first published in 2003 in *Museum News*, vol. 6, no. 3.

Chapter 13

The Strategic Significance of Workforce Diversity in Museums

Richard Sandell

. . . if your inclination, disposition, education, training and experience impel you to enter the museum world, you will understand us museum-minded people when we say: museums are looking for people with the educational and emotional background to carry on the 'museum idea'. We who have spent our lives in museums want our work continued and improved upon, so that the mighty impact of museums on their communities continues to give perspective, understanding, pleasure, and recreation to all those who take advantage of their many offerings.[1]

DESPITE THE SOCIAL NATURE of museum goals, with which one might reasonably associate an environment in which workforce diversity exists and is respected, valued and encouraged, the profession is, at least in terms of ethnicity, relatively homogeneous. This paper argues that the paucity of ethnic minorities in museum employment in the UK, particularly at middle and senior levels, is a product of, and is perpetuated by, outdated workplace cultures and structures. Structural causes of inequality are shown to be manifest within museums' service delivery, as well as recruitment and selection practices that together account for the under-representation of ethnic minorities within the workforce. Of course, this is not solely an issue for UK museums. Indeed, the experiences of museum sectors in, for example, the USA have identified similar reasons for minority under-representation.[2]

Museums have long engaged with issues of diversity. Debate around the elitist nature of museum audiences pervades international academic discourse and, in recent years, has fuelled increasing professional interest in approaches that can diversify and broaden audience profiles to more accurately mirror the plurality of society. However, in the UK, despite explicit recognition in the early 1980s that

Source: *International Journal of Heritage Studies*, vol. 6, no. 3 (2000): 213–230.

the profession itself was insufficiently diverse, there has been relatively little discussion or action taken to redress this imbalance. Further, there has been little empirical research into either the reasons behind the imbalance in the workforce or the implications this holds for museums and the achievement of their objectives.

In contrast, there has been increasing interest, particularly within the private sector in the UK, USA, South Africa and Australia, around the strategic significance of a diverse workforce. The term 'diversity management' has rapidly gained currency and widespread acceptance within the human resource management field, generating a wealth of research, and associated rhetoric, around the economic, as well as social, political and moral implications of nurturing and valuing diversity within the workforce. Similarly, whilst the museum sectors and individual museums in, for example, the USA, South Africa and Australia have taken action to increase representation of ethnic minorities within their workforce profile, the UK has lagged behind.

This paper seeks to explore the context within which recent initiatives to enhance career opportunities for ethnic minorities in the UK, through an approach characterised by positive action, have emerged and considers their potential efficacy.[3] This paper contends that diversity in the museum workforce will increasingly become a strategic imperative for museums if they are successfully to become more reflective of diverse societal concerns and meet the contemporary challenges presented by a political agenda that is dominated by issues of social inclusion and access. Furthermore, it is proposed that the concept of 'diversity management', as understood within the field of human resources management, whilst having much to offer the sector, can be usefully broadened to take account of the uniqueness of museum goals and practices. The paper concludes by positing the view that diversity within the museum context must be understood in terms of dynamic interrelationships between the organisation's workforce, its approach to service delivery and its audience. A tentative conceptual framework is proposed within which initiatives to enhance diversity throughout the museum can be considered.

The extent of, and reasons for, ethnic minority under-representation

The first comprehensive analysis of the UK museum sector workforce in 1993 confirmed what many in the profession already knew. The survey found that 'ethnic minorities are under-represented with 2.2% of the total museums' workforce nationally, most of whom are concentrated in security and support roles. This compares with 3.9% from the ethnic minorities in the UK workforce as a whole.'[4]

The report suggested that this under-representation might be linked to the attitudes that ethnic minorities hold towards museums and museum visiting in general, and highlighted the need for further research in this area.[5] Six years later, in 1999, a further workforce survey for the Cultural Heritage National Training Organisation (CHNTO), formerly the Museum Training Institute (MTI), found that whilst limited improvement had occurred, ethnic minorities were still significantly under-represented, accounting for just 4% of the workforce compared with over 7% in the labour force of the UK as a whole.[6] Perhaps unsurprisingly, these findings are not dissimilar to those that emerged from a nation-wide survey in the USA in 1984 which found 'the number of minorities on staff to be less than five percent and, of them, most were in maintenance and security jobs'.[7]

In the UK, museums have traditionally adopted a passive response to the problem. Under-representation may be commonly attributed to the demographic profile of the region and a lack of applications from ethnic minority candidates.[8] Implicit in this response is the notion that museums do not operate discriminatory practices and that responsibility for change lies, therefore, not with the museum, but with people from ethnic minority communities, their attitudes and aspirations. In fact, research shows that there are many graduates and qualified people from ethnic minorities within the labour market,[9] suggesting a need to consider more closely the reasons for their persistent under-representation within the profession. Though there exists little museum-specific empirical research to explain the statistics, findings from other sectors provide some illumination and begin to suggest the interrelated sociocultural and structural reasons for this imbalance.

Perceptions of employer commitment to equality of opportunity

In a recent survey of ethnic minority graduates, occupational psychologist Pearn Kandola found that 'The way an organisation is perceived in terms of its approach to equal opportunities will greatly influence the volume of applications it attracts from the ethnic minority student population.'[10] Such findings have been influential in encouraging particularly large private sector employers to re-examine the images they project to potential ethnic minority employees.[11] However, what implications do these findings hold for an examination of ethnic minority under-representation within the museum sector?

Recent research into the attitudes of ethnic minorities towards museums and galleries (commissioned by the Museums and Galleries Commission to explore barriers to visiting rather than impediments to employment) reveals a predominant feeling of exclusion. Several participants in the research refer to museums and galleries as a 'white space' or 'white people's territory'.[12] The report identifies a number of key factors contributing to these perceptions including a lack of relevant exhibits, negative and even offensive images and representation of the histories of ethnic minority people within a dominant colonial paradigm. Such attitudes towards museums as places to visit begin to suggest reasons for ethnic minority under-representation in the workforce.

The culture of 'homosocial reproduction'

Research into racial discrimination within specific professions also suggests that employers' perceptions of the suitability of candidates are equally important.[13] Some organisations, which may not necessarily operate direct racial discrimination, nevertheless may develop corporate cultures that reflect the norms, attitudes and values of the dominant majority and can serve indirectly to exclude ethnic minorities.[14] Within such organisations can exist a tendency to recruit to an implicit model, one

Table 13.1 Inclusive and exclusive approaches to recruitment and selection

Exclusive	Inclusive
A narrow and fixed view of the criteria and how they manifest themselves	An objective set of criteria, open to the various ways in which they manifest themselves
A focus on the 'type' of person who will be acceptable to the organisations and where they are likely to come from	Open to people of various types and backgrounds
Merit is insufficient	Merit alone is sufficient

that reflects the existing demographics of the profession. This process has been termed 'homosocial reproduction'.[15] Where these exclusionary cultures exist, discriminatory practices are commonly manifest within the recruitment and selection procedures of an organisation.

Kandola and Fullerton apply Jenkins's research into racism and discrimination in the labour market to the recruitment and selection processes that can operate within an organisation (see Table 13.1). This model contrasts the approach of the 'exclusive' organisation that may indirectly discriminate against people from ethnic minorities with that of the 'inclusive' organisation.[16]

This model provides a useful starting point for considering the extent to which museums might operate as exclusive organisations. Indeed, if we apply this model to the museum-specific situation we might add:

Offers programmes and contains collections which reflect Euro-centric and similarly biased histories	Holds collections and presents programmes which reflect the needs, interests and concerns of diverse communities
Pursues a passive, 'open-door' approach to both audiences and employee recruitment	Proactively targets under-represented audiences and employees

To what extent can the exclusive approach presented by Kandola and Fullerton be found within traditional recruitment and selection practices predominant in the museum sector? More specifically, do museums have a tendency to recruit to an implicit model that perpetuates homogeneity within the workforce?

Within an environment where competition for jobs is high it has become widely acknowledged that a significant period of unpaid work experience combined with a postgraduate qualification in museum or heritage studies may be the minimum requirement for entry into the profession. Even then, entry-level positions may often be at a relatively junior level with the expectation that individuals will advance to more senior positions on gaining further experience. To what extent might these requirements, whilst not directly discriminating against ethnic minorities, indirectly serve to inhibit their entry to the profession?

Useful parallels can be drawn with explanations for the under-representation of ethnic minorities within the British political system. Geddes explores this issue through a consideration of the selection procedures for party political candidacy in relation to the availability of potential candidates in the marketplace. As Geddes states, active participation in politics can be costly in both time and money, thus, 'If an individual is in low-paid employment or unemployed, then the potential costs of political activity may be prohibitive.'[17] Geddes suggests that the economic inequality experienced by ethnic minorities in the labour market might therefore influence their career choices and account, at least in part, for their under-representation in British politics.[18] The socioeconomic constraints identified by Geddes might similarly help to account for ethnic minority under-representation in the museum profession, which often demands a period of unpaid work experience and a postgraduate qualification, both of which have significant cost implications.

Geddes also suggests that the limited availability of seats and low level of incumbency turnover further inhibits ethnic minority representation within the political system.[19] It might be argued that those professions, within which employers experience labour shortages and difficulties in recruiting, may be pressurised into exploring diversity initiatives to broaden the pool of potential applicants.[20] In contrast, such pressures are, for the most part, absent from the museum sector that is characterised by high competition for a limited number of opportunities.[21]

A further way in which the exclusive approach can be detected within museums' recruitment practices is the methods that are most commonly employed to advertise middle- and senior-level museum positions. With often limited resources for the recruitment process, advertisement of opportunities may be focused within museum-specific media whose readership is largely confined to existing museum workers and those actively seeking to enter the profession. Such practices, focused internally within existing professional circles, inevitably restrict wider awareness of employment opportunities.

Many museums are, one might argue, characterised by the exclusive approach, outlined above, reinforcing perceptions amongst ethnic minority communities of the museum as a predominantly white organisation in terms of its status as an employer and also in the services it provides. Similar accusations of exclusive recruitment practices might also be levelled at universities offering pre-entry museum studies training. With often intensive competition for places, the model candidate emerges as a person with a good first degree, often in a traditional discipline, a commitment to a museum career demonstrated through often extensive voluntary work and, with limited and diminishing funding opportunities, the ability to pay for course fees and subsistence for a year.

The emergence of imperatives for workforce diversity

Why, until recently, has little action been taken to address the issue of ethnic minority under-representation in the museum workforce, confirmed by the (then) MTI as long ago as 1983? It is possible to identify a number of factors that have contributed towards this inaction.

In the USA, issues of diversity in the labour market and workforce have been debated in political and organisational arenas for several decades. Ginsberg cites the reasons that resulted in increasing US labour market diversity in terms of both gender and ethnicity. These include the impact of the Second World War on the labour force when unemployment dropped to below 2% (resulting in new and increased opportunities for employment for both women and ethnic minorities); the civil rights movements of the 1960s and associated sociopolitical pressures resulting in legal actions over discrimination; major immigration acts in the mid-1960s and mid-1980s; and increased access to, and funding for, higher education and its effects on life choices affecting women.[22]

During the 1970s and 1980s, alongside this growing diversity in the labour market there emerged greater recognition of the structural causes of gender and racial inequality. This recognition led to growing pressures to develop policies based on 'remedial action'; initiatives motivated by the view that 'policies are needed to counteract the effects of past discrimination'.[23] Within this highly politicised environment, the USA witnessed the rapid growth of equal opportunity and affirmative action initiatives in both public and private sector institutions. In contrast, affirmative action (or positive action as it is referred to in the UK) has, historically, had much less influence on recruitment policy and practice in Britain.

The Conservative administration from 1979 to 1987 proved less than conducive to the development of equality and diversity initiatives. The Race Relations Act 1976, which permitted employers to introduce positive action programmes, and the publication of the Scarman report following the riots of 1981, which presented a case for positive action, led some local authorities to introduce such programmes. However, these initiatives found little political favour under the administration of the Conservative central government. Instead, the central government response to increasing racial tensions in the early 1980s focused on increased powers for the police, concerns about immigration and initiatives to encourage privately funded regeneration of deprived areas. Most notably, the Greater London Council (GLC) adopted aggressive positive action initiatives on gender, race and sexuality and was criticised by some sections of the national media which labelled the authority as 'loony left'. Mrs Thatcher's abolition of the GLC in 1985 also served to inhibit the adoption and development of positive action programmes by other local authorities that became cautious about giving race equality programmes a high profile.[24]

More recently, the political environment since the election of New Labour in 1997 has created a climate in which diversity issues have found explicit central government support. Indeed, the government itself has called for all organisations to consider issues of racial equality within the workplace.[25] The Commission for Racial Equality has further raised the profile of these issues with the launch, in 1997, of the Leadership Challenge, 'to encourage those people at the helm of our organisations to take personal action to end racial discrimination'.[26] With government backing the campaign has secured the support of leaders in a range of private and public sector organisations. Furthermore, the sensitive and emotive issues raised by the Stephen Lawrence Inquiry report have given urgency to equality and diversity imperatives and raised the question of institutional racism, not only for the police service but for all public sector organisations.[27]

The strategic significance of workforce diversity

Alongside increased political support there has been increasing academic and business interest in the role of diversity in improving the effectiveness of organisations. A growing body of research within the field of human resource management has fuelled interest within the private sector into what has become widely known as the 'business case' for diversity. The emergent rhetoric has claimed that businesses can gain competitive advantage from the development of a diverse workforce, an argument that has proved to be an effective catalyst for diversity initiatives. Despite limited empirical evidence, 'An increasingly popular hypothesis is that diversity can give you a "richness" that cannot be provided by the homogenous workforce . . . [and] . . . some managers believe that a diverse workforce can outperform a homogenous one of comparable talent'.[28] The business case for diversity is an argument that focuses primarily on the *pragmatic* and *economic* rather than the *moral* or *social* imperatives for diversity. As a result, the preponderance of literature exploring the business case for diversity focuses on private sector organisations, although there are interesting examples from the not-for-profit sector.[29]

The Industrial Relations Service cites diversity initiatives in the UK implemented by supermarket chain, Asda, the bank, Lloyds TSB, and local government authority, Manchester City Council, each of which has been motivated to tackle diversity primarily by a pragmatic, business-based rationale. For these organisations, the business case for diversity is comprised of 'demographic arguments relating to labour force supply; access to a more diverse range of skills and talent, as well as more effective use of those already in existence; retention; and improving customer satisfaction and market penetration'.[30]

The business case suggests that organisations operating within a marketplace that is diverse will be better equipped to meet its objectives if that diversity is reflected in its own workforce. Unsurprisingly, this argument has exerted a powerful pressure on private sector organisations exposed to the competitive forces of the market, but to what extent can the business case motivate change within the museum sector?

It is helpful here to consider research within the private sector in the USA, which found that organisations that were insulated from change were less likely to explore diversity issues. In particular, those organisations that experienced little difficulty in recruiting to positions were less likely to have been proactive in developing diversity initiatives. Similarly, little action was taken where managers did not perceive diversity as strategically important.[31] These findings might suggest that the UK museum sector's apathy may be in part attributable to the intense competition that exists for positions. Further, the limited awareness amongst museum managers of the importance of equal opportunity practices within the workplace, evidenced by the findings of the Museums Association's Equal Opportunities Awareness Study in 1993, might suggest a denial of the systems and structures inherent in the sector which serve to exclude ethnic minorities and indicate that many have not perceived the strategic significance of workforce diversity.[32]

More recently, that significance is becoming increasingly difficult for the sector to ignore. Since the election of New Labour, the combating of social exclusion has become central to government policy initiatives and museums have faced mounting pressures to demonstrate their relevance to the widest possible audiences.[33] The strategic importance of working to diversify audiences has been underlined with the creation of new funding streams designed specifically to encourage access initiatives.[34] The political prominence of issues of social inclusion has therefore presented museums with a strategic imperative to consider diversity issues and, whilst pressure has been focused on the need for museums to attain diversity in their audiences, there is increasing interest in workforce diversity and its role in enabling organisations successfully to achieve their objectives.

Recent developments

Within this context, recent initiatives in the UK have emerged. At its annual conference in September 1998, the Museums Association presented the ambitions of a national project that would increase the accessibility of museum careers to people from ethnic minorities and called for responses from museums and other related bodies with which a range of pilot projects could be developed. In recognition of the complexity of sociocultural reasons for the under-representation of ethnic minorities in museums, a number of complementary strands have emerged which together seek to enable proportional ethnic minority representation at all levels within the sector. These include discussions with central government's Department for Culture, Media and Sport to secure support for the appointment of more ethnic minority trustees and commissioners within public museum organisations, projects to introduce the possibility of museum careers to school age children through work experience, and a bursary scheme for ethnic minority graduates, offered in partnership with higher education institutions, to undertake postgraduate museum studies training.[35] The preponderance of initiatives implemented to date have been characterised by the use of positive action or preferential treatment (more commonly known as 'affirmative action' in the USA).

Focusing on the positive action training initiatives, through the establishment of a bursary scheme for postgraduate museum studies courses,[36] this section explores the rationale behind, and potential efficacy of, this approach within the museum sector, one that has been increasingly questioned within the field of human resource management and which, in the USA, has been the subject of contentious political and legal dispute. Indeed, the USA has witnessed a growing backlash against affirmative action resulting in the dismantling of programmes, and in some areas, prohibition of this approach to recruitment.[37]

The Museums Association established two pilot positive action training opportunities for the academic year beginning autumn 1999.[38] The aim of the initiatives is to create a pool of well-qualified ethnic minority candidates who would be well positioned to secure employment within the UK museum profession at middle or senior levels. This is to be achieved through attracting and training suitably qualified applicants from UK ethnic minorities and, through this process, to begin to convey to ethnic minority communities the growing commitment to issues of diversity within the sector as a whole. Two positive action training opportunities have now been established. One offers a funded place on a one year postgraduate Museum Studies course. The second is the creation of a positive action traineeship in partnership with Nottingham City Museums. The traineeship, within the museum's

Access Team, provides museum experience and training on a part-time basis over two years through the same postgraduate course. Both the full-time and part-time training opportunities offer a contribution towards books, Museums Association membership and the opportunity to take advantage of free attendance at the Association's annual conference and other training seminars. Both opportunities are based on positive action being reserved for applicants from ethnic minority groups under-represented in museum employment.[39]

The development of approaches to diversity

At this point the paradigmatic shift needs to be considered, which has taken place within diversity thinking evidenced in increased questioning of the efficacy and morality of positive action and its focus on discrimination against, and under-representation of, minorities.

Roosevelt Thomas Jr identifies three approaches to diversity: 'affirmative action', 'understanding diversity' and 'managing diversity'. Positive or affirmative action initiatives are defined as 'artificial efforts to assure that selected elements of the societal and organizational diversity mixture receive equal opportunity as participants in a given organizational setting'.[40] Such approaches, which grew to be commonplace in the USA in the 1970s and 1980s were designed to *create* diversity in the workforce. As a more diverse workforce was achieved as a result of such initiatives, organisations began to explore ways in which the diverse workforce could be encouraged to work together productively and harmoniously based on the tolerance, understanding and valuing of differences between individuals. This approach, which Roosevelt Thomas Jr labels 'understanding diversity', included, for example, 'special days highlighting the culture of a particular racial or ethnic group'. In the last decade the term 'managing diversity' (also commonly referred to as 'diversity management') has emerged. For Roosevelt Thomas Jr, 'Managing diversity initiatives are efforts to create an environment that works naturally for the total diversity mixture. Here the focus is on the mixture, and managing is defined as empowering or enabling all employees.'[41]

These differing approaches to diversity in the workplace have evolved in response to changing political, social and economic pressures. Affirmative or positive action grew in the 1960s and 1970s based in large part on the concept of 'remedial action' – the 'view that such policies are needed to counteract the effects of past discrimination'.[42] Since the mid-1980s, however, there has been increasing questioning of this approach on both moral and pragmatic grounds. Though there is not the scope within this paper to do justice to this debate, some of the key reasons that have contributed towards a backlash against positive action need to be addressed, in order to consider the efficacy of the training initiatives recently introduced through the UK's higher education sector.[43]

The role and implications of positive action

Where aggressive affirmative action programmes have been linked to inflexible quotas for the recruitment of minorities, affirmative action has come to be associated with the lowering of standards and perceived as an attack on meritocratic principles of selection. In order to fulfil quota requirements, unqualified or less qualified applicants have been recruited on the basis of their membership of preferred minority groups rather than on merit. Such actions have resulted in a 'stigma of incompetence'.[44] Heilman's research identified the unintended, psychological consequences of affirmative action programmes whereby recipients of preferential treatment may experience feelings of inadequacy and, similarly, colleagues outside of the programme may be more likely to view their success unfavourably. This 'stigma of incompetence' presents a particular dilemma for the positive action programmes recently introduced through the UK's higher education sector. Normal course-entry requirements include a commitment to a career in museums most often demonstrated through a significant period of (often unpaid) work experience in a museum environment. Since, as has already been discussed at the beginning of this paper, people from ethnic minorities are less likely to have gained such experiences, it is impractical to demand such a requirement. Rather, evidence of skills and experience has been sought that will be *equally* valuable to the sector but which might have been secured by the applicant through different means.

Critics of affirmative action in the workplace also highlight the potential of such programmes to polarise different groups and engender resentment and cynicism amongst non-preferred groups.[45] Such potential pitfalls highlighted the importance of making clear the philosophy and rationale behind the current positive action programmes. Importantly, the positive action training initiatives do not guarantee participants museum employment but rather seek to create a pool of appropriately trained, experienced, qualified and diverse candidates that will, in time, help museums to achieve their overall objectives and, indeed, benefit all those employed in the sector.

Advocates of diversity management argue that one of the most significant weaknesses in the affirmative action approach is that it promotes assimilation rather than pluralism. Affirmative action has been seen as 'a one way process that [requires] minorities to adopt the norms and practices of the majority',[46] placing the responsibility for adaptation and change on the individual rather than the organisation. Such criticisms have served to move diversity practice away from those based on the assimilation models of the 1960s and 1970s towards a pluralistic model of diversity management – an approach that acknowledges and accepts differences and values them within the organisation. Within the diversity management approach, the individual is not required to adapt to the organisation, rather the employer 'will be open to the possibility of changing organizational culture and systems'.[47] Such concerns might appear to have a particular resonance for the museum sector. To what extent will the current approach to diversity, characterised by positive action, produce a pool of qualified and experienced minority candidates who will face pressures to assimilate or conform on entering the profession? Certainly those existing minority employees interviewed as part of the Museums Association's 1993 report into awareness of equal opportunities issues cited 'personal isolation and frustrated attempts to create change' within their organisations.[48] Such findings might suggest that, alongside positive action initiatives, the sector as a whole must move towards greater understanding of the significance and value of diversity in the workforce and seek to adopt the approach presented by advocates of diversity management.

For some, affirmative action and diversity management are mutually exclusive approaches that cannot work effectively alongside each other.[49] For others, though affirmative action is in itself inadequate, artificial and symptomatic of wider organisational structures and systems that discriminate, it can usefully co-exist alongside diversity management in certain situations. Roosevelt Thomas Jr contends that 'in the short term, Managing Diversity will not make affirmative action and Understanding Diversity unnecessary, but all these can function as a parallel set of efforts. In the long run however, effective implementation of Managing Diversity will make the other two unnecessary.'[50]

How might the UK's positive action initiatives be viewed in the light of contemporary disfavour with preferential treatment? What implications does the wider shift from positive action to diversity management hold for the museum sector and the potential long-term impact of the postgraduate training initiatives? It might be argued that the current approach will address the supply problems cited by many museum managers (that they do not get the applications from appropriately qualified minorities), but what of the demand side impediments discussed earlier? Museums must still address the issues of assimilation and monolithic and exclusionary workplace cultures to ensure that they encourage, welcome and embrace diversity if the initiatives are to be effective in the long term.

The need for such cultural change within employing museums as a prerequisite for the long-term success of affirmative action initiatives has been clearly identified within South Africa. In a 1997 report to the South African Museums Association, Keene highlights the need for a 'mind-set change' within all South African museums if the process of transforming the sector is to be successful. 'It is important for museums to accept that cultural diversity is very positive and will enable them to achieve their organisational goals in serving the community . . . A museum corporate culture which values diversity must be encouraged and used in a positive way . . . An enabling environment has to be created as a first priority.'[51]

I would further like to contend that the museums sector *needs* positive action to reach a position from which it can effectively manage diversity. As Sessa states, 'To manage diversity effectively, a corporation must value diversity; it must have diversity, and it must change the organization to accommodate diversity and make it an integral part of the organization.'[52] At present, the sector lacks cultural diversity and can perhaps only learn to attract and nurture it as positive action begins to bring about a change in the workforce profile.

Towards a museum-specific model of diversity management

Current positive action initiatives to diversify the workforce might, therefore, be seen as the start of a continuum along which the sector must advance. As the effects of positive action increase diversity within the sector's workforce, organisations will be required to adopt the more holistic approach advocated by diversity management if the resultant heterogeneity is to be maintained and utilised to achieve organisational goals.

However, it might also be argued that the uniqueness of museum goals and practices requires a more holistic view of diversity, one that extends beyond the

Figure 13.1   Diversity management in the museum – a conceptual framework

internal staff management issues that are the focus of the concept of 'diversity management'. The dynamic interrelationships that might exist between the museum's workforce, its collections and programmes and its audiences should be considered in order to posit a museum-specific view of diversity management. Figure 13.1 offers a tentative conceptual framework within which diversity management and the role of positive action, and other diversity initiatives can be understood within the museum context. The model suggests a way in which diversity in museum programmes, audiences and workforce are interconnected. The model suggests that the three elements are interrelated so, for example, increasing diversity in the museum workforce might enable that organisation to increase diversity in both service delivery and audience profile.

There has been little direct research to support the claim that museums *require* diversity in their workforce if they are to successfully meet their objectives of engaging with diverse audiences. However, the data that are emerging from research into the business benefits experienced by companies that have enhanced workforce diversity begin to establish such a link.[53] Furthermore, the recent research exploring attitudes to museums amongst ethnic minorities suggests that a significant barrier to visiting is the perception of the organisation as a 'white space'. Indeed, one Indian participant in the research explicitly identifies the changed perceptions brought about through the employment of non-white staff.

> Museums over the years have started being more user friendly. Ten years
> ago it was a white regime, the exhibits they have were very much geared

to the white community. It was only when they realised they have an ethnic community, one of the first things they did was employ some-one from an ethnic minority, a well qualified person, and I think this is something which should be done more widely. And that gave a lot of impetus, we are very lucky here.[54]

The report goes on to make a number of recommendations including increased consultation with communities and the development of ongoing relationships, reassess-ment of collecting policies, the promotion of positive images and highlighting the contribution of ethnic minorities in collections. The researchers suggest that their findings indicate that 'dynamic and committed museum officers, often from ethnic minority communities, play an important role in the development of such initiatives'.[55]

Effective diversity management would recognise that opportunities for ethnic minority professionals should not be confined solely to positions that exploit their cultural background to create links with minority communities (e.g. outreach). However, it might also be argued that whatever their position in an organisation, an individual's personal experiences and cultural background may influence the internal agenda and, in doing so, encourage a greater diversity in its service delivery, thereby enhancing its ability to engage with diverse audiences.

Within this model, the circle of diversity that links workforce, programmes and audiences can be enhanced through museum intervention at different points. Positive action within training, recruitment and selection practices seeks to enhance diversity in the workforce. Similarly, museums can achieve greater diver-sity within their service delivery by adopting participatory approaches to the devel-opment of exhibitions, collecting projects and events, whilst marketing and audience development initiatives can enhance diversity in audiences. The model sug gests that for a museum to effectively manage and sustain diversity in all areas it must understand the dynamic interrelationships that exist between each element of the organisation.

Evidence of a commitment to this holistic approach to diversity can be iden-tified within Australian initiatives. The publication in 1993 of *Previous possessions, new obligations* provided principles and policies to guide Australian museums in their relationships with Aboriginal and Torres Strait Islander peoples. The policy document, which includes guidance on the employment and training of indigenous peoples, also makes recommendations in relation to such issues as acquisition, storage, access and display, acknowledging the interrelationships between differ-ent aspects of museum activity.

The responsibilities of museums range from the return of human remains and the involvement of indigenous people in collection man-agement and cultural presentations through to employment and gover-nance . . . This fundamentally important and broad scope of the policy is intended to recognise the fact that Aboriginal and Torres Strait Islander peoples have a right to be involved in all aspects of care, management and presentation of their culture.[56,57]

Conclusion

This museum-specific model of diversity management is intended to highlight the significance of workforce diversity and its relationship to the museum's ability to achieve its objectives. It would suggest that workforce diversity could play a key role in enhancing the museum's performance but that such initiatives cannot be conceived in isolation. This model further highlights the need for research that can establish the nature of the processes by which the museum can effectively manage diversity in all its activities.

With limited empirical data in this area, the role and significance of workforce diversity can only be tentatively suggested at present, though it is likely that this issue will receive further interest and generate further action as awareness of the strategic significance of diversity in all aspects of the museum increases within the sector.

Notes

Richard Sandell is Deputy Head of the Department of Museum Studies at the University of Leicester. This paper was first published in 2000 in the *International Journal of Heritage Studies*, vol. 6, no. 3.

1   W.A. Burns, *Your future in museums*, New York: Richards Rosen Press, 1967, p. 129.
2   See, for example, J.R. Glaser and N.J. Fuller, 'Growing our own: a model training program for diversifying the labor force', in *Museum training and cultural diversity*, International Committee for the Training of Personnel, ICOM 18th General Conference and 19th General Assembly, 1998, p. 51.
3   Though the examples given focus on ethnic minority representation and the experiences of the UK, USA, Australia and South Africa, it is useful to recognise that many of the issues that emerge have a relevance to both museums internationally and to issues of diversity in terms of gender, age and so forth.
4   Museum Training Institute, *Museum sector workforce survey: an analysis of the workforce in the museum, gallery and heritage sector in the United Kingdom, Report prepared for the by the Management Centre, Bradford University*, April 1983, p. 5.
5   The report also tentatively suggested a growing imperative for museums to address the issues it highlighted. 'Demographic trends in the population in general show that ethnic minorities will make up an increasingly large proportion of the population by the end of the century. This being so, museums might be well advised to redouble their efforts to increase the numbers of visitors from outside their traditional clientele', p. 154.
6   D. Berry-Lound and D. Parsons, *The cultural heritage labour market – a statistical report for the Cultural Heritage National Training Organisation*, May 1999, p. 20.
7   J.R. Glaser and N.J. Fuller, op. cit., note 2.
8   MTI, op. cit., note 4; S. Ollerearnshaw, 'Colour conscious', *Museums Journal*, November 1990, p. 31.
9   S. Ollerearnshaw, op. cit., note 8.
10 M. Whitehead. 'Ethnic minority graduates lured by equality policies', *People Management*, 29 July 1999, p. 17.

11   In focus group research to identify why ethnic minorities might not identify the
     bank as an attractive employer, Lloyds TSB found that their image was one of
     the most significant factors. In particular the images contained within a pro-
     motional literature featured a predominantly white staff. Similarly, in the same
     article, Marie Gill, group employee relations manager at retailer, Asda, stated:
     'If the workforce is all white then we are seen as a white employer and ethnic
     minorities won't apply because we have the wrong image.' Industrial Relations
     Service, 'Improving recruitment and promotion opportunities for ethnic minor-
     ities', *Equal Opportunities Review*, No. 85, May/June 1999, p. 16.

12   BMRB International, *Cultural diversity: attitudes of ethnic minority populations
     towards museums and galleries*, London: Museums and Galleries Commission,
     1998, pp. 21, 53.

13   S. Ollerearnshaw, op. cit.

14   In their research into access to chartered accountancy, the Commission for Racial
     Equality found that firms 'tended to recruit to an implicit "model" of a well-rounded,
     able candidate who had to show intellectual ability, social and leadership skills
     and high motivation. They looked at evidence, such as academic attainments and
     positions of responsibility at school, holding office in societies and choice of vaca-
     tion jobs. These indicators may be less appropriate for applicants from minority
     racial groups.' S. Ollerearnshaw, op. cit., p. 32.

15   R.M. Kanter, 1977, cited in J.A. Gilbert, B.A. Stead and J.M. Ivancevich, 'Diversity
     management: a new organizational paradigm', *Journal of Business Ethics*, No. 21,
     1999, p. 71.

16   R. Kandola and J. Fullerton, *Managing the mosaic: diversity in action*, London: Institute
     of Personnel Development, 1994, p. 129.

17   A. Geddes, 'The "logic" of positive action?: ethnic minority representation in Britain
     after the 1992 General Election', *Party Politics*, Vol. 1, No. 2, 1995, p. 280.

18   There is evidence that such economic disadvantage persists. A report by the
     Policy Studies Institute in 1996 found that whilst some ethnic minority groups
     had improved their position within the labour market, 'The African-Caribbeans
     and particularly the Pakistanis and Bangladeshis are consistently in lower level
     jobs and suffer from higher unemployment rates than the white population.'
     T. Jones, *Britain's ethnic minorities*, London: Policy Studies Institute, 1996, p. 156.

19   A. Geddes, op. cit., note 17.

20   Jackson cites research amongst human resources managers in the USA which found
     that one of the reasons why some organisations had been slow to respond to issues
     of diversity was the ease with which they were able to recruit high calibre can-
     didates. S.E. Jackson and Associates, *Diversity in the workplace: human resources
     initiatives*, New York: Guilford Press, 1992.

21   R. Friedman, 'Museum people. The special problems of personnel management
     in museums and historical agencies', in K. Moore (ed.) *Museum management*, London:
     Routledge, 1994.

22   E. Ginzberg, Foreword in S.E. Jackson and Associates, *Diversity in the workplace:
     human resources initiatives*, New York: Guilford Press, 1992, p. xiv.

23   P. Burstein, 1992, cited in R. Kandola and J. Fullerton, op. cit., note 16.

24   S.M. Teles, 'Why is there no affirmative action in Britain?', *American Behavioral
     Scientist*, Vol. 41, No. 7, 1998, p. 1,019.

25   The imperatives to address such issues are couched not only in moral terms but
     also supported by business arguments – Gordon Brown, Chancellor of the

Exchequer, supporting the CRE's Leadership Challenge, a campaign to end racial discrimination in the workplace stated, 'I want to see racial equality on the agenda of every boardroom in this country, not only because it is morally right, but because it is good for business and good for Britain.' M. Whitehead, op. cit., note 10.

26   Commission for Racial Equality, *The Leadership Challenge: Progress Report 1999*, London: Commission for Racial Equality, 1999.

27   Commission for Racial Equality, op. cit., note 26, p. 54.

28   R. Roosevelt Thomas Jr, 'Managing diversity: a conceptual framework', in S.E. Jackson and Associates, op. cit., note 20, p. 310. Researchers have subsequently sought to give weight to these rhetorical claims and to develop models that can inform business diversity practice. See, for example, R. Kandola and J. Fullerton, op. cit.

29   See, for example, M.K. Gowing and S.S. Payne, 'Assessing the quality of the federal workforce: a program to meet diverse needs', in S.E. Jackson and Associates, op. cit.

30   The article offers evidence that to meet the needs of a culturally diverse customer base, the organisation must reflect that diversity in its workforce. 'At one branch of Lloyds TSB, based in a large Bangladeshi community, the recruitment of more staff from the local ethnic minority population increased the bank's branch sales of pensions, life insurance and other financial products by 30–40% over a six month period.' This was attributed to the establishment of a link with the local community and the widening of their available pool of talent enabling them to recruit top quality staff. Industrial Relations Services, op. cit., note 11.

31   S.E. Jackson, op. cit., pp. 5–6.

32   Certainly research conducted by McCann Matthews Millman for the Museums Association in 1993 found that equal opportunities policies had had little impact on organisational practices. Overall they found that 'Museums need to be persuaded of the necessity, usefulness and benefits of having an EO policy.' McCann Matthews Millman, *Museums Association: Equal Opportunities Awareness Study; conclusions and recommendations*, London: McCann Matthews Millman Limited, 1993, p. 13.

33   The museums' potential to promote social inclusion has become an increasingly important topic within professional debates. In broad terms, museums have responded to these issues in two main ways. For many their contribution to social inclusion has been to demonstrate their success in broadening audiences, whilst a minority have sought to explore their potential to contribute towards tackling the social problems experienced by those identified as socially excluded. For a full discussion of these issues see R. Sandell, 'Museums as agents of social inclusion', *Journal of Museum Management and Curatorship*, Vol. 17, No. 4, 2000.

34   For example, the creation of the Heritage Lottery Fund's Museums and Galleries Access Fund in 1998.

35   Museums Association, *1998/9 Annual Report*, London: Museums Association, 1999.

36   The Museums Association and the Department of Museum Studies, University of Leicester have jointly created a pilot bursary scheme.

37   For a full discussion of the assault on affirmative action within the USA and the wider implications of the controversy see R. Post and M. Rogin (eds), *Race and representation: affirmative action*, New York: Zone Books, 1998.

38   These have been developed in partnership with the University of Leicester which had, for some time, recognised that it received very few applications from UK

ethnic minorities despite attracting a culturally diverse student body drawn from overseas. In recognition of its role as provider of pre-entry professional training the University responded to the Museums Association's call for partners to explore possible ways forward.

39   Subsequently, funding has been secured to create two Paul Hamlyn Foundation/ Museums Association Bursaries for each of the two academic years, beginning 2000 and 2001, linked to the one year postgraduate Museum Studies course at the University of Leicester.

40   R. Roosevelt Thomas Jr, op. cit., note 28, pp. 307–308.

41   R. Roosevelt Thomas Jr, op. cit.

42   P. Burstein, op. cit., note 23.

43   See J.A. Gilbert, B.A. Stead and J.M. Ivancevich, op. cit., note 15, for a useful summary of these debates.

44   M.E. Heilman, quoted in R. Kandola and J. Fullerton, op. cit., p. 135.

45   S.E. Jackson and E.B. Alvarez, 'Working through diversity as a strategic imperative', in S.E. Jackson & Associates, op. cit.

46   S.M. Nkomo cited in R. Kandola and J. Fullerton, op. cit., p. 8.

47   R. Roosevelt Thomas Jr, op. cit., p. 312.

48   McCann Matthews Millman, op. cit., note 32, p. 4.

49   See, for example, R. Kandola and J. Fullerton, op. cit., p. 5.

50   R. Roosevelt Thomas Jr, op. cit., p. 311.

51   R. Keene, *Towards an affirmative action policy for South African museums*, Eastern Cape: South African Museums Association, 1997, pp. 2–3.

52   V.I. Sessa, 'Managing diversity at the Xerox Corporation: balanced workforce goals and caucus groups', in S.E. Jackson, op. cit., p. 37.

53   See note 30.

54   BMRB, op. cit., note 12, p. 42.

55   BMRB, op. cit., p. 5.

56   Museums Australia Inc., *Previous possessions, new obligations: a plain English summary of policies for museums in Australia and Aboriginal and Torres Strait Islander peoples*, Melbourne: Museums Australia, 1993, p. 2.

57   The Australian Museum, Sydney, has been notably proactive in implementing these policies with the creation of its own Aboriginal Heritage Unit, employing Aboriginal staff, and the Aboriginal Museums' Outreach Program, 'designed to provide Aboriginal communities within [New South Wales] access to professional museum training and advice in the planning and running of their own cultural centres and Keeping Places'. Museums Australia Inc., op. cit., note 56.

Chapter 14

Volunteers in the Heritage Sector
A neglected audience?

Kirsten Holmes

MUSEUMS AND HERITAGE ATTRACTIONS worldwide involve a large number of volunteers. Indeed, *ICOM News*, the newsletter of the International
Council of Museums, recently dedicated an issue to volunteers and friends of
museums across the world, including Norway, Singapore, Romania and Canada.[1]
According to Canadian Heritage, volunteers constitute 65% of the workforce in
museums,[2] and museum volunteers and their own association, the American Association of Museum Volunteers, represents volunteer managers in the USA. Many
museums in Australia and New Zealand are also dependent on volunteers. In the
USA and Canada, volunteering has become very professional, with the role of the
volunteer teacher and interpreter (or docent) often requiring a college-level
course,[3] and these professional procedures have begun to influence volunteering in
other countries, including the UK[4] and Australia,[5] over the past decade.

Volunteering in museums and heritage visitor attractions has a long history
within the UK, with many museums founded entirely by volunteers. In 1998, it
was estimated that the 1,188 registered museums and galleries, which responded
to the Museums & Galleries Commission's DOMUS survey, involved 25,206
volunteers. Compared with their 12,590 permanent staff and 2,775 part-time staff,
this meant that volunteers outnumbered full-time equivalent staff by nearly two to
one.[6] Most recently, Resource: the Council for Museums, Archives and Libraries
found that 92% of museums involved volunteers.[7]

While much previous research has focused specifically on registered museums,
volunteers undertake very similar roles across the heritage sector, as found by the
British Association of Friends of Museums (BAFM) study, which included
members of the Historic Houses Association (an association for private owners of
historic houses), the Pilgrim's Trust (which represents churches and cathedrals)

Source: *International Journal of Heritage Studies*, vol. 9, no. 4 (2003): 341–355.

and the National Trust for England and Wales (an independent charity founded for the preservation of natural and cultural heritage and the largest single involver of volunteers in the UK). The volunteers included in this study were all active volunteers in that they actively came in and helped rather than taking the more supportive role of a Friend. Volunteers in the UK can also be involved in the management of the museum or attraction, as a trustee.[8] However, little is talked about of the role of volunteers as advocates for the organisation, as is the case in museums in the USA and Canada, where it is understood that, to the visitor, the volunteer *is* the museum. As well as behind-the-scenes work, including documentation, conservation and research, volunteers are highly involved in front-of-house activities, and in the UK this is the growing area.[9] Both within museums and heritage attractions, volunteers are engaged as room stewards, that is having a fixed station in an enclosed building and as guides, whether outside or within an enclosed building. In addition they may also help out at reception, in the shop and the café and with education work.

Previous research has found that subject matter, rather than the physical characteristics of the museum or heritage attraction, has the most significant impact on the types of people who are likely to volunteer. For example, industrial museums, whether enclosed or open air, are more likely to attract male rather than female volunteers.[10] The choice of case studies in the methodology reflects the diversity of volunteer roles and volunteer-involving organisations.

Two models of volunteering

The literature on volunteering has grown over the past decade and has developed along two philosophical paradigms for viewing volunteers: the economic model and the leisure model. The economic model analyses volunteers as filling the gaps in provision between the private and public sectors.[11] The policy importance of volunteers is their contribution to the economy. This means that it is justifiable to measure the 'work' of volunteers and compare it to the economic contribution of workers in other sectors of the economy. Thus the economic model considers volunteers as unpaid workers and this model has dominated in museums and heritage attractions in the UK, USA, Canada and Australia.

The dominance of the economic model within the museums sector is likely to be for two main reasons: the perceptions of paid museum workers and the volunteer experiences of paid museum workers. First, volunteers, as unpaid workers unbound by contracts of employment, have traditionally been considered as unreliable and unprofessional.[12] These concerns have led to efforts to ensure that volunteers are trained, have clear descriptions of their roles within the organisation and their commitment to fulfilling their shifts, usually in the form of a volunteer agreement. Secondly, paid museum workers' typical experiences of volunteering themselves have been as aspiring professionals, seeking work experience for entry into the profession. Thus, their motivations have differed considerably from the significant proportion of older volunteers, who have other motives.

Over the past decade the voluntary sector in the UK has begun to adopt a professional approach to volunteer management.[13] Traditionally, volunteer management in the UK has taken an *ad hoc* approach, as detailed in Mattingly's 1984 study of volunteering in museums and art galleries in the UK.[14] Features of the *ad hoc* approach include having no individual with responsibility for the volunteers; no induction or training programme, including basic health and safety training (rather, training is on the job); no repayment of volunteers' out-of-pocket expenses; and no standard. Since Mattingly's study, museums and heritage attractions in the UK have faced a number of influences, both external and internal, which have promoted a more structured approach to volunteer management, termed 'professional volunteer management'. This consists of managing volunteers as unpaid staff. Indeed, professional volunteer management seeks largely to replicate personnel practices with a volunteer workforce[15] and is characterised by a top-down approach to management.

These influences have included the availability of guides on volunteer management from the USA and Canada,[16] where volunteers have long undertaken a very formal role as docents. In addition, increasing competition for both funding and visitors in the UK, coupled with the requirements of funding bodies (such as the Heritage Lottery Fund) for museums and heritage organisations to demonstrate competent management practice, has had its impact on volunteer management. The move to a more professional approach to volunteer management mirrors moves towards professionalisation within the UK museums profession. These moves are illustrated by the Museums Association's change to an associateship based on continuous professional development rather than examination. The assimilation of good practice procedures within UK museums and heritage attractions also owes much to the introduction of Museum Registration, which sets standards for museums to achieve before they can be eligible for certain funds.

Various writers have endorsed this professional approach across the heritage sector and notably this is replicated in the BAFM guide to managing heritage volunteers. However, research examining volunteers' motives has found that while the professional approach may have advantages for both managers and volunteers, this may not be appropriate for leisure-seeking volunteers. In addition, the proportion of respondents to the National Trust and BAFM studies stating that their primary motivation was to gain work experience leading to paid work was small, with 21% and 5%, respectively.

In contrast to the economic model, the leisure model considers the act of volunteering to constitute a leisure experience. This approach finds its origins in the UK with Bishop and Hoggett's study of voluntary leisure groups,[17] but this premise has been developed further.[18] Leisure researchers divide all the time available in the day into four categories: paid work; work-related time, such as travel; obligatory time, such as sleeping and washing; and unobligated free time. Since volunteering is not paid work, they argue that it takes place within the last category of unobligated free time, the same categorisation for leisure.

Is volunteering, then, a leisure activity? Previous research on the motivations of volunteers within the UK has found that managers cite interest in subject as the primary reason for volunteering,[19] while volunteers cite *doing something enjoyable*. Indeed, volunteer respondents to a survey conducted by the National Trust for England and Wales listed the following benefits as derived from their activities:[20]

- I really enjoy it (98%);
- I meet people and make friends through it (85%);
- It gives me a sense of personal achievement (78%);
- It gives me a chance to do things I am good at (74%);
- It broadens my experience of life (73%).

While working as a volunteer coordinator at the National Museum of Science and Industry, McIvor investigated the motivations of the volunteers there and found that they were highly motivated because they were both learning themselves and helping others to learn, they gained immediate feedback from both visitors and staff and had a high degree of autonomy in that they could just leave. These volunteers were trained and deployed as staff, but their motivations to work and perceived benefits were found to be more akin to those of visitors. She concluded that volunteers are 'effectively visitors who participate actively'.[21]

Could volunteering, then, be a form of visiting? If so, what benefits do visitors gain from their (leisure) experiences? Hood devised six attributes that make up an enjoyable leisure activity based on a study of visitors at Toledo Art Museum. These are the attributes visitors look for in a leisure experience. If they expect to find these at a museum they will visit a museum, rather than another leisure venue. Since volunteers may be active visitors, will they look for these attributes in their own leisure experiences, such as their volunteering? These attributes are listed in Table 14.1.[22]

Hood's six characteristics of an enjoyable leisure experience bear a close resemblance to the benefits given by respondents to the National Trust survey, discussed above. In particular, volunteers stated that they meet people, make friends and that they gain a sense of personal achievement from their activities. This suggests that volunteers do derive some similar benefits from their activities as visitors derive from their visit, supporting McIvor's assertion that volunteers are active visitors.

Hood's enjoyable leisure experience proposes that key motivators are 'doing something worthwhile', 'opportunity to learn' and 'social interaction'. Given the correlation between volunteers' responses to the National Trust survey and leisure theory, the leisure paradigm offers a compelling model for considering volunteering.

So, if volunteering is leisure for these older, socially motivated volunteers then where do they fit in the organisation? Are they 'active visitors', as McIvor contends, or are they unpaid employees?

Table 14.1   Six attributes of an enjoyable leisure experience

- Challenge of new experiences
- Doing something worthwhile
- Feeling comfortable in one's surroundings
- Opportunity to learn
- Participating actively
- Social interaction

Method

In order to investigate further the meaning of volunteering for museum and heritage volunteers, eighty-three volunteers at ten case studies in England and Wales were interviewed to gain views on their motivation. Since volunteers give their time freely, interviews took place during or immediately after their volunteering to ensure no extra burden was placed on them. However, this meant that only a limited number could be interviewed, as volunteers tend to help out at most once or twice a week. Thus, the interviews were supplemented with a postal questionnaire which included a further 139 volunteers, giving a total sample of 222. Volunteers were sampled randomly, both for interviews and the postal questionnaire, thus ensuring that all volunteers had an equal chance of being included in the study.

The ten case studies included a national museum (a museum funded directly from the UK government through the Department of Culture, Media and Sport); a preserved steam railway, owned and managed by a charitable trust; three properties varying in size owned by the National Trust for England and Wales, described above as an independent charity, involving more than 30,000 volunteers each year; a property owned by English Heritage (the UK government's official advisory body for the historic environment, which also owns and manages historic properties, open to visitors); three open-air museums, varying in size and subject matter (from industrial heritage to sculpture park – a series of exhibits located within an outdoor, rather than enclosed, environment, although this may include some enclosed spaces); and an historic ship, also owned and managed by a charitable trust. The aim was to gain a wide cross-section of museums and heritage visitor attractions that commonly involve volunteers. In particular, the National Trust, open-air museums and transport heritage museums were identified as involving the largest numbers of volunteers in the UK.[23] Moreover, by including traditional, enclosed museums, historic properties and open-air sites, it was hoped to capture among the respondents the full range of roles in which volunteers are engaged. The response rates from both the interviews and the survey are presented in Table 14.2.

While no attempt was made to limit this study to any particular age group, the respondents' characteristics corresponded with the National Trust and BAFM studies. Those aged over sixty years represented 63%, and only 8% of respondents were aged less than forty-four years. In addition, 75% of respondents stated that they were retired. The gender breakdown of the sample – 60% male, 40% female – reflects gender imbalance at transport heritage museums and attractions. Respondents demonstrated a full range of length of service, from less than six months (9%) to more than ten years (19%).

The volunteers were questioned about their initial motivation and why they continue to volunteer, in order to ascertain their different motivations fully. The responses were analysed using a combination of content and template analysis.[24] That is, while some categories were derived from past research and theory, as detailed above, others were allowed to emerge from the responses, so that the categories would not be unduly prescriptive. Respondents could, and often did, cite more than one motive, and therefore the number of citations does not correspond to the number of respondents.

Table 14.2   Volunteer response rate by case study

Case	Interviews (No.)	Postal survey (No.)
National Trust property (> 200 volunteers)	12	12
National Trust property (100–120 volunteers)	3	12
National Trust property (< 30 volunteers)	10	23
English Heritage property	13	17
Open-air museum (industrial heritage)	10	[a]
Open-air museum (vernacular)	11	10
Open-air museum (sculpture)	3	6
Historic ship	6	10
National museum	11	16
Steam railway	6	13
Total (all cases)	85	119

Note: [a] Amberley Museum undertook a volunteer research and development project prior to the fieldwork period for this study, which involved a postal survey to the volunteers. The data from this study were used to support the interviews, as a further survey was thought likely to generate a low response rate from over-surveyed volunteers.

Results and discussion

Tables 14.3 and 14.4 report on volunteers' motives, as derived from the content analysis. Table 14.3 presents volunteers' initial reasons for volunteering, while Table 14.4 presents their motives for continuing to volunteer. The number of citations for each motive is shown in parentheses. Within the content analysis, work-related motives include not only references to work experience but also any comment where the activity was described or compared to work.

In Table 14.3, it is clear that the primary reason for volunteers' offering their services is in order to pursue an interest. While *pursue interest* was cited eighty-nine times, *volunteering as work* was mentioned by only six respondents, and only eight respondents stated that they were seeking work experience. These findings add weight to those of the BAFM and National Trust surveys, demonstrating that

Table 14.3   Volunteers' initial motives

- Pursue interest (89)
- Keep active in retirement (28)
- Social opportunities (17)
- Help/do something worthwhile (16)
- Work experience (8)
- Enjoyment/recreation (7)
- Work-like motives (6)
- Feel comfortable in the surroundings (2)
- Challenge (2)
- Learn new skills (1)

Table 14.4   Volunteers' reasons for continuing to offer their services

- Social opportunities (59)
- Enjoyment/recreation (51)
- Colleagues (30)
- Learning/new skills (23)
- Help/do something worthwhile (23)
- Satisfaction/sense of achievement (21)
- Work-related motives (15)
- Pursue interest (14)
- Feeling comfortable in surroundings (14)
- Keep active in retirement (11)
- A sense of belonging (11)
- Challenge (7)
- Commitment (6)
- Self-development (5)

while work experience is a motive for volunteering, only a small proportion of the total number of museum and heritage volunteers seeks work experience. However, the high number of *pursue interest* citations suggests that managers do have a good idea as to what motivates their volunteers, as subject interest was cited by manager respondents as the primary motivation for their volunteers in Mattingly's study, at least initially, to offer their services.

The importance of subject interest is further illustrated in volunteers' actual responses:

> I wanted to learn about art and the history and be with people. I'm even learning French as there's quite a few French people. (Volunteer, historic house)

> I've always had a love of history and the year before I retired they were advertising for volunteers. I thought it would be nice. (Volunteer, historic house)

> A lifelong love of all things railway and a wish to get more involved. (Volunteer, national museum)

> Interest in railways, best steam railway in the country and company. (Volunteer, steam railway)

The responses in Table 14.3 also correlate with the benefits gained by visitors, listed in Table 14.1, specifically 'doing something worthwhile', 'opportunity to learn' and 'social interaction'. *Keeping active in retirement* can be compared to Hood's 'participating actively' or the 'challenge of new experiences'.

Table 14.4 shows that the volunteers' initial reasons for volunteering may not be the same as those that lead them to continue to offer their services. Indeed *pursue interest* has decreased in importance, while *enjoyment or recreation* and *social opportunities* stand out as the most important motives. In addition, the categorisation of *colleagues* makes social opportunities even more significant as a motive. It needs to be noted that *helping the organisation* does feature as a motive, but there were only fifteen citations of work-related motives, where volunteers considered volunteering to be similar to work, rather than leisure.

The content analysis presented in Table 14.4, further illustrated by volunteers' actual responses, highlights the importance of opportunities for social interaction:

> I enjoy meeting the different people. It's something different, I can't put my finger on it. (Volunteer, historic house)

> [It's a] social occasion with other blokes. (Volunteer, historic ship)

> The friendly atmosphere; nearly all the volunteers are regular Thursday volunteers. The more you learn the more you enjoy. (Volunteer, historic house)

However, *enjoyment and recreation* are also frequently cited:

> I enjoy it. It's a big boys' playground, a hobby like golf. (Volunteer, open-air museum)

> I don't come here for what I can get out. I expect personal satisfaction. It's a worthwhile organisation, I enjoy visiting it anyway and I can help to keep it open. (Volunteer, open-air museum)

Learning and developing skills were both listed twenty-three times, along with *helping the organisation* and *doing something worthwhile*:

> I'm getting to know the permanent staff. We're one big happy family and I'm acquiring knowledge. (Volunteer, national museum)

Both general social opportunities, such as meeting people and specifically meeting friends, were by far the most cited reasons for volunteering, overtaking subject interest and helping the organisation. Since enjoyment was rated as the most important motivator in the BAFM and National Trust surveys, as reported above, it is no surprise that this features so highly as a motivator among the respondents from the case studies. Indeed, *enjoyment* was cited several times by respondents in all ten case studies. Again, the correlation between the motives cited in Table 14.4 and Hood's attributes of an enjoyable leisure experience, is significant. *Social opportunities, learning new skills* and *doing something worthwhile* were three of the most cited motives and are closely related to Hood's 'doing something worthwhile', 'opportunity to learn' and 'social interaction'. In addition, two of Hood's other attributes – 'feeling comfortable in one's surroundings' and 'challenge of new experiences' – are also represented in Table 14.4 by a number of citations. This is particularly the case with the eleven citations of *sense of belonging* which, when added to the thirty citations of *colleagues*, suggests that volunteers view themselves as more than simply active visitors, and that they consider themselves a part of the organisation.

Table 14.5   Number of work citations compared with leisure citations

	Work-related citations	Enjoyable leisure-related citations
Initial motivation (Table 14.3)	14	29
Continuing to volunteer (Table 14.4)	15	154
Total	29	183

However, their leisure-seeking motives show that they clearly have a different psychological contract with the museum or heritage visitor attraction than paid staff.

As discussed above, the content analysis presented in Tables 14.3 and 14.4 is designed to note motives that are indicative of an enjoyable leisure experience as shown in Table 14.1. The low incidence of work-related citations has already been noted. Table 14.5 compares the number of work-related citations with the number of enjoyable leisure-related citations. In Table 14.3, eight respondents cited *work experience*, while six others cited work-related motives. In contrast, two volunteers cited *challenge*, two noted *comfortable in surroundings*, seven cited *enjoyment*, and one respondent cited *learning* and seventeen noted *social opportunities*. So, added together, there were fourteen work-related citations and twenty-nine leisure-related citations. *Doing something worthwhile* was excluded from Table 14.5 as it was classed as both a characteristic of enjoyable leisure and a work-related motive. This exercise is carried out for both tables and the results are given in Table 14.5.

Leisure-related comments clearly outweigh the number of work-related citations and the following volunteers' comments show that they do not view their activities as work:

> As a volunteer you can't expect benefits. If you want benefits you get a job. You do what you want to do and try not to let people down. (Volunteer, historic monument)

> It's nice to come back here as the duties are infrequent . . . to do something totally different from work. (Volunteer, national museum)

> The beauty of being a volunteer is that you carry on until you don't enjoy it. (Volunteer, steam railway)

The comments of those younger volunteers, who are still working full-time, provide additional support for this premise:

> It provides me with an opportunity to follow an interest. Also it is a major factor in relaxing me from my full-time work. (Volunteer, national museum)

> it's different from [meeting] the public where I work at the Abbey National, you just get them arguing, but here people take an interest, that's why they come. (Volunteer, historic house)

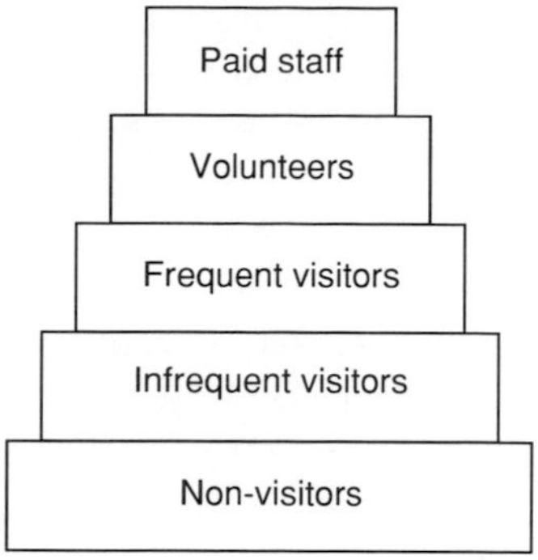

Figure 14.1   A hierarchy of visiting

It appears that the majority of volunteers are seeking leisure and the similarity between volunteers' motives and visitors' motives is significant. While museums have typically viewed volunteers as unpaid staff, it would be more appropriate to see them as a particular segment of the museum's audience. This premise is supported by the significant proportion of older, retired volunteers and the relative decrease in work experience as a motive. However, volunteers should not simply be equated with visitors; rather, they form a distinct group of a museum's audience, as insiders rather than the outsiders that most visitors would be. These are individuals who have developed a strong attachment and commitment towards one particular museum or heritage attraction. They have chosen to 'visit' one place at an in-depth level, rather than many more at the relatively superficial level of the average visitor. It would seem logical, given that visitors are often segmented as non-visitors, infrequent and frequent visiting,[25] that volunteering forms the next level of visiting in a hierarchy of visiting. In addition, as volunteers see themselves as belonging to the organisation, they also form a bridge between visitors and paid staff, thus taking on a dual role as both part of the museum but also part of its audience. This theorisation is presented in Figure 14.1, where the ultimate visitor is a member of the paid staff, since this is the goal of a significant minority of volunteers.

Researchers have noted that there is a decline in visiting among older people. Marker and Opinion Research International (MORI) found that while individuals aged sixty-five and over constitute 19% of the population, they account for only 15% of visitors to museums and galleries, although this group was noted for visiting more frequently than other age groups. This supposed decline corresponds with the take-up in volunteering. Unfortunately, there are no longitudinal data to show whether there is a relationship between taking up volunteering and reducing visiting, as it may be that volunteers are also the people who continue to visit when they are older. If volunteering is an extension of visiting, as proposed in Figure 14.1, then it is time for a rethink of the role that volunteers play within the museums and heritage community.

Implications for managing volunteers

It should not be surprising that the economic model of volunteering and a top-down approach to volunteer management has predominated within museums and heritage visitor attractions within the UK, as paid staff involved with volunteer management and supervision are likely to have experienced volunteering as part of their own professional development. Indeed, as the BAFM and National Trust surveys show, work-experience-seeking volunteers are clearly still a significant segment of volunteers in museums, albeit a smaller segment than they may have been in the past.

While this source of volunteers may constitute a decreasing proportion of volunteers, museums need to consider how they can best target the pool of potential older, retired individuals. Since subject interest is the most common draw for new volunteers, it would seem practical to target individuals who have already shown an interest. Moreover, given that social opportunities motivate volunteers to continue to help at an organisation, it is clear why word-of-mouth recommendation is a popular means of recruitment. As retirement appears to have such a significant role in individuals' decision to volunteer (as shown in Tables 14.3 and 14.4), the most effective way of recruiting new volunteers would seem to be targeting individuals who are either newly retired or are about to retire and who have shown an interest in the organisation, or similar organisations.

Obviously this recommendation will only serve to recruit similar volunteers to those already involved and contradicts more frequently made recommendations to try and increase the diversity of museums and heritage volunteers. However, the significant role played by social interaction in maintaining and developing a committed, long-serving group of volunteer supporters may be why museum volunteers are not typically a diverse group of individuals. Indeed, museums and heritage attractions may have to choose between a committed, socially cohesive group of volunteers and a diverse group of volunteers, that is one carefully constructed as an artificial group by the museum.

The recommendation regarding recruitment links with the finding that museum and heritage volunteers also feel part of the organisation. As well as helping the organisation through recruitment of new volunteers, museums might consider ways in which their active volunteers could be involved in advocacy for the museum, as in the USA and Canada. While this is a more typical role in the UK for Friends' organisations, active volunteers might also be engaged as spokespeople for the museum or heritage visitor attraction as well as advocates for the visitors. Indeed, museums and heritage visitor attractions would do well to consult their volunteers regarding programming and the production of materials, such as guidebooks and information panels, for their visitors. This would also appeal to their need to learn and give them new challenges, as required by an enjoyable leisure experience.

Managers must also consider the importance of social opportunities in the continuing motivation of volunteers. For example, in a country house, if volunteer room-stewards are dispersed in different rooms they are likely to become bored and frustrated on a quiet day, with few visitors. Therefore, it is important to consider ways in which the volunteers' needs may be met, without compromising their important role for the museum. This may be through the provision of breaks for lunch and tea in a communal room, as was the case in some of the case studies included in this research, but it may also be through the deployment of volunteers. For example, one case study scheduled two volunteers per shift at a remote part of the site for safety reasons. However, this could as easily be for social reasons and both volunteers stated that they preferred to share their shift with another person.

The concept of leisure-seeking, retired volunteers might be a cause for concern for managers, since leisure-seeking suggests unreliability. However, the length of service given by the respondents, with nearly one-fifth of respondents having helped at their organisation for ten years or longer, suggests that this is not necessarily the case. Volunteers clearly feel a part of the organisation they are helping, even though they have a different psychological contract compared with paid staff.

Conclusions

Research on volunteers has developed along two models: the economic model, which views volunteers as unpaid workers, and the leisure model, which considers volunteering to be a leisure activity. Within museums and heritage visitor attractions, the economic model has predominated both within the UK and elsewhere. However, this may ignore the largely retired volunteers' motives and thus may affect recruitment and retention of these volunteers, on whom so many organisations depend.

The volunteer respondents in this study reported largely leisure motives as their reasons for both initially volunteering and continuing to offer their services. These findings support those of previous studies, which suggested that a significant proportion of volunteers are leisure-seeking rather than seeking work experience. Indeed, leisure-seeking volunteers dominate numerically, with only 5% of respondents to the BAFM survey pursuing work experience. In particular, the motives and benefits reported by volunteers in this study bear a strong correlation between the benefits gained from visiting in Hood's model of an enjoyable leisure experience. Thus, it seems that volunteering for the majority is an extension of visiting. However, these findings do not simply suggest that volunteers are the same as visitors; rather, they are a unique segment of the museum's audience, which must be considered appropriately. After all, they have chosen to dedicate a considerable amount of time in specifically getting to know one museum or heritage attraction and demonstrate a significant commitment towards that organisation above that of a visitor. Indeed, the benefits reported by volunteers show that they consider themselves a part of the organisation they are helping. The relationship between volunteering and visiting is presented in Figure 14.1 as an extension of visiting and a bridge between visitors and paid staff.

These findings suggest that museums should question the advice they receive on volunteer management and reconsider how the volunteers fit within the organisation, not only as advocates for visitors but also considering their role as a bridge between paid staff and visitors. This clearly has implications for both volunteer recruitment and retention and recommends giving volunteers a more active role in the planning and delivery of material for visitors. Paradoxically, in the case of front-of-house volunteers, they may be both visitors and yet form part of the visitor experience for other visitors. The implications of this dual role demand further investigation.

This research has focused on the UK experience, which in recent years has been highly influenced by US and Canadian models of volunteering, as have volunteer programmes in Australia. However, there has been little written on the involvement of volunteers in different cultures, and this is an area open to further research.

Notes

Kirsten Holmes is a Lecturer in Tourism at the University of Surrey with extensive experience of researching volunteers in museums. This paper was first published in 2003 in the *International Journal of Heritage Studies*, vol. 9, no. 4.

1   ICOM, *ICOM News: friends of museums*, Vol. 55, No. 4, Paris: International Council of Museums, 2002.

2   Canadian Museums Association, 'The role and impact of voluntarism at museums', Canadian Museums Association, 2001, <www.museums.ca/volunteers/voluntarismdiscussion.htm>, accessed 20 August 2003.

3   S. McIvor and S. Goodlad, *Museum volunteers: good practice in the management of volunteers*, London: Routledge, 1998.

4   British Association of Friends of Museums, *The handbook for heritage volunteer managers and administrators*, Glastonbury: BAFM, 1999.

5   R. Van Tienen, 'Museums and volunteers: the volunteer manager', paper presented to the Museums Australia annual conference, Canberra, 2001.

6   A. Creigh-Tyte and B. Thomas, 'Employment', in S. Selwood (ed.) *The UK cultural sector: profile and policy issues*, London: Policy Studies Institute, 2001.

7   Resource, *Volunteers in the cultural sector*, London: Institute for Volunteering Research & Resource, 2002.

8   S. Millar, *Volunteers in museums and heritage organisations: policy, planning and management*, London: HMSO, 1991.

9   British Association of Friends of Museums, *Heritage volunteer training project stage one report – draft*, Camberley: BAFM, 1998.

10   K. Holmes, 'Changing times: volunteering in the heritage sector 1984–1998', *Voluntary Action*, Vol. 1, No. 2, 1999, pp. 21–35.

11   C. Gratton, G. Nichols, S. Shibli and P. Taylor, 'Local authority support to volunteers in sports clubs', *Managing Leisure*, Vol. 3, No. 3, 1998, pp. 119–127.

12   E. Hooper-Greenhill and A. Chadwick, 'Volunteers in museums and galleries: a discussion of some of the issues', *Museums Journal*, Vol. 84, No. 4, 1985, pp. 177–178.

13   Institute of Volunteering Research, *Issues in volunteer management: a report of a survey*, London: Institute of Volunteering Research, 1998.

14   J. Mattingly, *Volunteers in museums and galleries: the report of a survey into the work of volunteers in museums and galleries in the United Kingdom*, Berkhamsted: The Volunteer Centre UK, 1984.

15   I. Cunningham, 'Human resource management in the voluntary sector: challenges and opportunities', *Public Money and Management*, April–June 1999, pp. 19–25.

16   See, for example, J. Kuyper, *Volunteer programme administration: a handbook for museums and other cultural institutions*, Washington, DC: American Council for the Arts, 1993; V. Cooper, *Laying the foundation: policies and procedures for volunteer programs*, Calgary: Glenbow Museum, Art Gallery, Library and Archives, 1996.

17   J. Bishop and P. Hoggett, *Organising around enthusiasms: mutual aid in leisure*, London: Comedia, 1986.

18   K. Henderson, 'Volunteerism as leisure', *Journal of Voluntary Action Research*, Vol. 13, No. 1, 1984, pp. 55–63.

19   Holmes, op. cit. (note 10).

20   The National Trust, *Volunteering with the National Trust: summary of the findings of the 1997 survey*, Cirencester: The National Trust, 1998.

21   McIvor and Goodlad, op. cit. (note 3).

22   M.G. Hood, 'Staying away: why people choose not to visit museums', *Museum News*, Vol. 61, No. 4, 1983, pp. 50–57.

23   M. Hanna, *Sightseeing in the UK 1997*, London: BTA/ETB Research Services, 1998.

24   N. King, 'Template analysis', in C. Cassell and G. Symon (eds) *Qualitative methods and analysis in organizational research: a practical guide*, London: Sage, 1998.

25   Hood, op. cit. (note 22).

Chapter 15

Emotional Intelligence, Passion and Museum Leadership

Sherene Suchy

Introduction

T HE DIRECTOR OF THE Metropolitan Museum of Art in New York has stated, 'Passion is what sells the museum. The Development Office paves the way and the Director's charisma and passion makes the difference' (de Montebello 1996). This assertion was one of the starting points for research into the complexity of museum leadership which brought together three domains of expertise: museum management, psychology and business (Suchy 1998). In response to numerous enquiries following two papers on museum leadership presented at the 1998 ICOM Triennial congress in Melbourne, Australia, this article has been written to describe the starting points for the original research on change, challenges and complexity surrounding museum leadership. The international research on the director's role in art museum leadership has revealed, first and foremost, the critical importance of passion. A deep feeling in the heart for the work in hand sustains art museum directors on a daily basis, as well as contributing to the vision of the organisation. Passion, energy and creativity are baseline competences for leadership roles.

Charisma, that elusive characteristic which defines leaders with panache, may actually be a set of learnable skills called emotional intelligence. And passion, that sense of being deeply connected with work which is highly meaningful, is essential for all directors wishing to create a presence for their museums. The directors of over forty-five major art museums in Australia, Canada, the United States of America and the United Kingdom who participated in personal interviews for an international research project between 1995 and 1998 all shared a common strategy as they managed major change processes in the 1990s (Suchy 1998). They

Source: *Museum Management and Curatorship*, vol. 18, no. 1 (1999): 57–71.

all spoke of the need to keep passion alive by remaining connected with some part of the job which had 'heart' in it. According to the Director of the Isabella Stewart Gardner Museum in Boston, this meant staying connected with one's own source of creativity.

> To keep passion alive in trying times, you have to think, read, write, and see contemporary work. Practice your own area of creative talent. Feed yourself, as only then can you feed the organisation. Do not lose your own sense of creativity. Maintain relationships with people who may be friends and colleagues who continue to inspire you. (Hawley 1996)

This observation is relevant for directors of any organisation. Although the art museum was case studied for particular reasons, outcomes from the research are applicable across a broader range of organisations. Remaining connected with some part of the job which has 'heart' in it requires two things. First, increasing awareness of ways to maintain pleasure and challenge in life depends on how often we experience a phenomenon referred to as flow. Second, we need to learn how to make the connection between flow and the core competencies of emotional intelligence for leadership effectiveness. The core competencies include intentionality, creativity, resilience, interpersonal connections and managing constructive discontent (Q-metrics 1996).

Flow theory and executive decision making

Mihaly Csikszentmihalyi (1990: xi, 1993; Csikszentmihalyi and Hermanson 1995; 1999), a psychologist at the University of Chicago, has been working since 1975 with flow theory. Flow theory provides a framework and words for an experience many people have described as a 'rush', 'being totally in tune' or 'decision making high'. There are several characteristics or evidence of an individual in flow. The person is usually totally involved in the current experience and fully concentrating on the task at hand. They are enjoying themselves. They exhibit high self esteem because their skills are well paced with the task at hand. And, they have a sense that the activities in which they are engaged are important to future goals. Writers on emotional intelligence such as Goleman (1996: 90–93) have referred to flow as a state of 'self-forgetfulness' where individuals 'exhibit a masterly control of what they are doing, their responses perfectly attuned to the changing demands of the task'.

The research undertaken by the present author on art museum leadership used an executive interview technique to map levels of challenge and the directors' experience of flow (Stamp 1993; Jaque and Clement 1994; Suchy 1998). When art museum directors appeared to be in flow with the challenges of leadership, they appeared energised and spoke passionately about their work. It also became clear that one of the keys to flow was skilled practice. This allowed the individuals to get into flow more often because they had mastered the moves of the task at hand and so there was less effort required. Mastering art museum leadership, according to the Director of the National Gallery of Canada in Ottawa, requires a 'willingness to change, to grieve, learn, live and learn. It is a process of growth, making mistakes and living through them' (Thompson 1996). Certainly the director's role in any type of museum leadership is a complex job, but staying connected to some part of the job which has 'heart' in it keeps passion alive. Keeping passion alive, or staying in flow, depends on five conditions. Csikszentmihalyi (1990) maintained that the five conditions are necessary for any activity in which the emotion of pleasure, a sense of achievement, and effective decision making are desired outcomes. The first condition depends on clarity around expectations, goals and interactions. In other words, the release of leadership energy involves creating and negotiating clear goals, expectations and interactions regarding tasks.

The second condition involves the perception that someone is attending to and taking a positive interest in what the director is doing. This means material resources and positive forms of moral support from trustees, staff and other stakeholders in the organisation. Leadership can be an isolating job. As the Director of the Tate Gallery in London observed: 'I do realise that often I am very alone. It is frightening that there are only one or two people around the world one can share one's ideas and thoughts with' (Serota 1996). This is why it is important for all museum directors to have access to and participate in professional networks where they can exchange ideas in an environment dedicated to creative leadership development. The role of the trustees or other senior management is of particular importance in maintaining the perception of support. When this support is perceived negatively, the conditions for flow are reduced. Lack of support and conflict undermines leadership confidence. According to some directors, they have often felt caught and unsupported between conflicting stakeholders such as unions, staff and trustees (Sano 1995; Parker 1995).

While the third condition involves a sense of choice and discretion in decision making, it also includes full responsibility for the outcomes. Provided that the level of organisational challenge is commensurate with the level of skill available, museum directors need to be able to exercise their judgement fully to maximise a sense of flow. This may not always be possible in an organisation where leadership roles are shared between the museum director and the board of trustees. Difficulties in this area are to be expected and require higher than average levels of skill in 'emotional intelligence', e.g. constructive discontent and interpersonal connections. For example, the Director of the Isabella Stewart Gardner Museum in Boston has noted that, 'Trustees can enable a museum and they are also capable of arresting action through the demise of public and foundation funding' (Hawley 1996). The Director of the Yale Center for British Art in New Haven has described situations where lack of trustee support could lead to 'decision making paralysis' and dysfunctional leadership (McCaughy 1996).

The fourth condition for flow involves a sense of trust which allows total involvement with the task or activity without concern for well-being. In other words, museum directors will be most in flow when their positions are not under threat. The perception of threat can be interpreted in several ways. For some museum directors this may mean threatened loss of job or funding cuts to the organisation as a whole. Others may feel that they cannot immerse themselves in the job because of conflicts with senior management/boards, staff or industrial relation problems. Conditions which bar total involvement in the job undermine the museum director's judgement and ability to create a positive presence for the museum. For example, the Director of The Fine Arts Museums of San Francisco confessed that, 'I continually have to suppress my creative judgement to deal with power struggles which is frustrating and results in great anger' (Parker 1995). Finally, the fifth condition involves the need for increasingly complex challenges over time. Museum directors continue to experience pleasure in their work when the job continues to stretch their skills or capability. Too much or too little stretch or disruptions to the other four conditions reduces the sense of pleasure. For example, the Director of the National Gallery of Art in Washington, D.C. observed that, 'It would be nice to have a little fun again' (Powell 1996). As he reflected on changes impacting museums in the 1990s (funding cuts), it became increasingly apparent that the expectations around museum leadership had changed dramatically. Maintaining a sense of flow and a 'heart' for the work in such an environment was undoubtedly presenting major challenges.

Passion, flow and emotional intelligence

When conditions for flow are present and challenges are well balanced with skills, museum directors should experience a sense of well-being as well as effective decision making. In the museum context, the outcome of being in flow is a feeling of passion and meaningful work. As indicated earlier by the Director of the Metropolitan Museum of Art in New York, 'Passion is what sells the museum'. Directors who have learned how to manage increasingly complex challenges with increasing levels of leadership skill, for example, emotional intelligence, create a strong presence for their museums internally and externally.

Researchers and writers on emotional intelligence (Gardner 1983: 237–276; 1995; Goleman 1996: xii–xiii; Cooper and Sawaf 1996; Glynn 1996; Pennar 1996) have described EQ as a combination of self-control, zeal, persistence, the ability to motivate oneself, a basic flair for living, the ability to read another's innermost feelings and handling relationships smoothly. Research suggests that IQ contributes to 20% of life success and EQ makes up the rest or 80%. First, there are emotions, then there is thought. We cannot choose the emotions we have. There is immediate perception, then reflective thought, if we have emotional intelligence. The relationship between emotional intelligence and leadership was highlighted by Gardner (1983: xxiv) over a decade ago as 'capacities that cut across intelligences and affect other people in ways that may be as emotional and social as they are cognitive'. Gardner's (1995) research on leadership markers provided a very valuable framework for the research on the director's role in art museum leadership (Suchy 1998). The best leaders were those individuals who were able to express unspoken collective sentiments to guide their organisation toward its goals in a way that was emotionally nourishing and a pleasure to be around. Consequently, the original doctoral research undertaken by the present author on the director's role in art museum leadership has been developed into a six-week leadership program based in Australia with an emphasis on what Cooper and Sawaf (1996) defined as optimal leadership performance. Optimal leadership performance uses twenty well-defined emotional intelligence skills to increase resilience under pressure, develop trusting relationships and create the future or, what one art museum director has called 'that vision thing' (Kolb 1996). The program focuses on seven emotional intelligence competences which are directly related to leadership effectiveness: trust, compassion, intuition, constructive discontent, interpersonal connections, resilience and creativity. The program enables participants to use EQ to embody their leadership story in optimal leadership performance.

Creating optimal leadership performance as an art museum director while sustaining a sense of flow is a delicate balancing act. It is a subtle inner process which is not given to scientific measurement. It involves harmonising an emotional and intuitive sense of the world in creative collaboration with the rational or linear mind. The Director of the National Gallery of Victoria in Melbourne described this experience as taking 'pleasure in drawing together diverse experience and doing lots of things at once. To be creative is emotionally satisfying. To set frameworks is analytically satisfying' (Potts 1995). This collaboration is not always a controllable process, nor does it create a life without tension. The Director of The Art Gallery of New South Wales in Sydney described it as a process of 'keeping things slightly on edge . . . a slight tension keeps things creative . . . one must keep imbalances to maintain energy' (Capon 1995). The search for ways to stay in flow, as well as remaining passionate about one's work can be a potentially volatile process. This was described by the Director of the Yale Center for British Art in New Haven.

> Museums tend to fragment without good direction as they are volatile organisations. You have to have people with imagination in an art museum and that has volatility. People with imagination believe in the rightness of their intuition. But passion does not equal the rational! Feelings are volatile and unstable. A successful museum depends on the interaction of the many e.g. community, audience, staff. It is about relationships and how they are managed. (McCaughy 1996)

One of the richest outcomes from the research on the director's role in art museum leadership was the exciting connection between individual flow and cultural development. Csikszentmihalyi referred to the need for increasingly refined skills to maintain pleasure in activity or flow as a key contributor to the development of culture overall. The connection between individual flow and cultural development is found in the ways people seek to extend their skills and what they use to provide meaning in their lives. There is a strategy shared between people who are most successful at creating meaning in their lives. That strategy involves connecting with creativity and the arts in some way. This strategy underscores the critical role which museums and other types of cultural institutions play as potential sites for meaning making.

> The necessity to develop increasingly refined skills to sustain enjoyment is what lies behind the evolution of culture. It is what motivates individuals and cultures to change to more complex entities. The rewards of creating order in experience provide the energy that propels

evolution. . . . To create harmony in whatever one does is the last task that the flow theory presents to those who wish to attain optimal experience. It is a task that involves transforming the entirety of life into a single flow activity, with unified goals that provide constant purpose. There is much knowledge, or well-ordered information, accumulated in culture, ready for this use. Great music, architecture, art, poetry, drama, dance, philosophy, and religion are there for anyone to see as examples of how harmony can be imposed on chaos. Yet so many people ignore them, expecting to create meaning in their lives by their own devices. (Csikszentmihalyi 1990: 213 and 235)

The way directors represent the art museum as a site for 'meaning making' depends on how they have mastered a range of leadership skills. When directors have mastered their emotions in a way to convey effectively their passion, the art museum's potential as a site for 'meaning making' becomes readily apparent. For example, the Director of The Art Gallery of New South Wales in Sydney addressed a public forum on collection development with a very emotional interpretation about art's ability to reflect values that 'touch deep places in the heart' (Capon 1996), while Goleman (1996: 8) described, 'knowing something is right in your heart [as] a different order of conviction or truth'. Since 1996, Capon's expression of private passion in public places has engaged the hearts of others with significant increases in individual and corporate support during a decade of declining Australian government dollars. The Director of the National Gallery of Canada in Ottawa described the leadership role as utterly dependent on having an emotional conviction or passion about the unique value of the arts in our personal and business lives.

> Leadership depends on the willingness to change and knowing your subject well. To see that means developing a passion for some part of the arts so that it becomes an anchor in yourself. Having that anchor in what is important means you can feed and sustain yourself. Looking at art is developing non-linear thinking. That is art's greatness. Business and medicine are only just now looking at the concept of non-linear thinking. (Thompson 1996)

The forty-five plus directors and assistant directors of art museums who were interviewed during the international research project on art museum leadership shared a range of personal passions and strategies to sustain their sense of flow. Out of their shared experiences, five key themes emerged. The five themes included: a passion for the primary product; a commitment to social principles or romanticism; building trusting relationships through education; entrepreneurism and innovation; and constructive discontent as a way of creating the future. These five themes were viewed as a significant insight into the challenges which art museum directors face. They have been subsequently developed and are used as case studies in the Australian-based six-week leadership development program for leaders in a broad range of organisations noted above. The case studies are used to illustrate the importance of emotional intelligence skills and the need to create conditions for flow so that art museum directors are not swept away by the everyday demands of their jobs. Extracts from the case studies have been included in this article so as to share the art museum directors' rich insights and illustrate the relationship between passion, flow and optimal leadership performance.

A passion for the primary product

A passion for the primary product, in the art museum context, has been described as love for the visual arts. The Director of the Victoria and Albert Museum in London described this as a 'love of objects, design, and aesthetics' (Borg 1996), while the Director of the Yale Center for British Art in New Haven emphasised how important it was for the art museum director to have this 'love of objects', as well as a belief in the institution or people would not support it financially.

> To do the director's job well, you have to have the desire to communicate the beauty and power of art. To communicate about context and people in different ways. To be passionate about this form of human greed which has no social drawbacks! And you have to have pleasure in what you are doing. To be a director, you have to look at lots of works of art. To love things and objects far from your own taste. You have to want to communicate about objects. You have to have ideas about objects and how they relate to one another. It is a unique area. It provides the opportunity to combine thought and action in a way like no other job. (McCaughy 1996)

According to the Director of The Art Gallery of Ontario in Toronto, acting as the caretaker and interpreter for the visual artist and their creations was a 'great privilege and pleasure'.

> My passion? The visible pleasure of people in front of a painting. I am steward of thousands of artists, alive and dead. I feel an obligation to make their vision understood by our visitors. There are thousands of voices and visions in this gallery . . . (Anderson 1996)

The Director of the Art Gallery of Western Australia in Perth demonstrated a deep commitment to the museum as a site for spiritual renewal. Renewal involved time for 'drifting' in a venue which offers new ideas and the experience of visual art as a catalyst for personal change. The Director described furthermore the importance of gallery guides who shared the same passion and who could act as visual translators, creating meaningful museum experiences for the public.

> My passion is about bringing great experiences to people through great art. Bringing people in touch with the real thing. In a world without enough time for 'drift', full of simulation and laminex . . . we need to see a labor of love, great beauty, evidence of great ages. This is what it's all about and it needs to be supported by an intelligent way of helping people to 'see it'. (Latos-Valier 1996)

The Director for The Art Institute of Chicago (Wood 1996) also expressed passion and pleasure in how 'art looks'. He too was aware that his leadership role demanded a balance between the passionate and the rational, and he used the museum's mission statement as a way of balancing potential chaos in decision making processes.

A passion for social vision or romanticism

Leadership seems to need a sense of romanticism or social vision which motivates people to extend themselves and to reach for higher level goals. Romanticism, by definition, has an increased focus on the individual, man's fundamental irrationality and a sense of mystery. According to Spate (1980: 17), romanticism has an 'emphasis on truth to individual experience' which often places the artist – whether writer, painter or social revolutionary – at a distance from others because they have a 'prophetic insight into things that ordinary mortals' may not understand. Mimi Gaudieri (1996), the coordinator for the American Association of Art Museum Directors, described several directors in the United States of America and Canada as 'shapers' of ideas in museum leadership based on their keen sense of social vision. Indeed, the Director of the Cleveland Museum of Art described the impact of 'romantic notions from the '60s' as a major influence on his approach to leadership. The 1960s in the United States was an era of social revolution and experimentation: the civil rights movement, challenges to authorities and control, a search for ways to expand consciousness, and an exploration of new forms of personal relationships.

> After fifteen years, I know organisations and communities have *genius loci*. The director's job is to recognize the inherent structure of these entities, including the museum. My job is to coax and coach genius to the surface. The first dawn of realization is my passion. My democratic spirit is based on a 1960s spirit. That spirit was based on a passion embedded in works of art that are messages about humanity over time. My passion is to reveal those messages . . . to express a democratic spirit by sharing widely. First of all, it is a difficult job and without passion, you just cannot do the director's work. You come to work for the heart of it. Like a musical conductor, to create harmony. I am a mediator, a builder of bridges, a coordinator of x and y who then get sent on their way. (Bergman 1996)

The passion for people demonstrated by the Director of the Museum of Fine Arts in Houston was based on a very personal commitment to art museums as a source of social capital for the development of community life.

> The connection between my role and the mission for the museum is easy to answer. To make the art museum an institution of everyday life. To evolve into a broad based cultural center rather than a place where beautiful art is kept secure. Everyone can then think art museums are

part of the environment. This can be done in a number of ways. This museum sponsors an annual run with 5,000 runners over a five-mile course. It starts and finishes in our sculpture garden. It is a big success. We also stage a singles night that attracts 5,000 people each year. We sponsor clay pigeon shoots. Other museum colleagues laugh at some of the things we do. I love the idea that people can come here for all sorts of things. (Marzio 1996)

Directors with a passion for romanticism are evidently shaping the art museum as a place which carries messages about humanity over time and offers life enrichment. In a leadership role, a passion for romanticism is a commitment to creating a context for personal insight based on a belief in *genius loci*. How a director creates this context depends on a range of skills, most significantly language skills. The way words and language are used is a form of leadership marker, according to Gardner (1995). They are essential tools for museum directors to translate their personal passion into leadership stories which engage the hearts of others.

A passion for education

Directors who are excited about interacting with people through education and discovery are building trusting relationships. Trusting relationships are evidence of essential emotional intelligence skills. Several art museum directors described their passion for enabling insight in others through education strategies. They had a clear sense of the relationship between creativity, imagination and education as a process of discovery. In this sense, a passion for education has involved a love of 'drawing forth', 'bringing out', 'eliciting', 'leading' and 'developing' others. The Director of the Dennos Museum Center in Traverse City Michigan used his enthusiasm for discovery as a major shaper for the museum's mission through the mission statement, *Come Alive Inside*:

> My passion is prompting people to question, how does this relate to me? It is about the act of discovery! Pure visual art has a limited appeal in the community due to the art world's focus on contemporary art and a lack of audience access to this form. The community in general does not have the visual language to understand art, particularly contemporary art. Combining a visual arts program focused on state-based artists with an international music program has been hugely successful. The center continues to offer 'discovery' themes of interest to the community based on active research. For example, environmental awareness was imaginatively explored through literature, visual arts, and chamber music specifically composed for a series of performances at the center. (Jenneman 1996)

The Director of the J. Paul Getty Museum in California described his representational role for the museum as a process of connections and relationships. He stressed the relationship between his role and the vision for the museum, focusing on 'dreams'. One of the main drivers behind the dreams was the art museum director's pleasure in teaching and an ongoing search for ways to unleash ideas in others. He described his role: 'As a leader, my job is about setting goals which connect our dreams about this museum. These dreams are looked at annually and transformed into objectives and tasks' (Walsh 1995). On the other hand, the Director of the Freer Gallery of Art/Arthur M. Sackler Gallery in Washington, D.C., described providing an external presence for the museum as one of the biggest recent changes around the director's role. Extending the art museum's influence depended upon the director's passionate commitment to what he saw as 'the intrinsic beauty and richness of artistic and cultural expression in all its forms in the hope of transcending race, representative, interpretative, and audience barriers' (Beech 1996).

> As a college student, I never thought I would like to work in or lead a museum. I liked to teach. The opportunity to be a director, though, was ideal. Our duty here is to make the museum interesting for the family groups who come. The Freer Gallery was opened in 1923 as a walled garden for Asian art. We now have to open to the public as we have no right to be a walled garden. We need to serve well, to be accessible. Having taught for fifteen years enables me to excite others about Asia through Asian art. (Beech 1996)

According to the Director of the neighbouring Hirshhorn Museum, the Smithsonian Institution's overall vision is played out through its various component parts (Demetrian 1996). The Smithsonian's vision is to achieve the greatest diffusion of knowledge possible (Bello 1993: 9). This over-arching vision provided an ideal opportunity for the Hirshhorn Museum Director to focus on education as a specific aspect of the Museum's mission. The value and emphasis placed on education grew from its Director's early experience in art education in secondary schools. He had a passion for expanding what he saw as a 'narrow view of art'.

> This job is basically fun! Some parts are more enjoyable than others. If I don't have certain kinds of information, it presents a challenge to find the what, why, and how to operate. Works of art are all different. When different pieces can be put together to create a dialogue, the art museum is then a place of ideas. (Demetrian 1996)

In this vein, the Director of the National Gallery of Canada, in Ottawa, described her passion for people as a key source of leadership energy. Creative thinking, adaptability and the pleasure of working with people were fundamental aspects of the art museum director's representational role.

> A good director has to like people and the process of bringing them in touch with art. You have to like even the pompous people. You have to be excited about the work with the public. This can only be based on understanding the greatness of the art objects being worked with. (Thompson 1996)

Furthermore, the Director of the Please Touch Museum in Philadelphia described her passion for children as her commitment to that Museum. In this museum director's view, her passion for children and their journey of discovery had to be lived out in such a way that people around her would support her commitment through their loyalty to her and the Museum. She explained how important it was to have an outlet for passion outside of the museum also in order to sustain the energy required for the leadership role. This was particularly critical because leadership involved challenges totally unrelated to the original domain of expertise.

> The director is the leader. You just can't order other people to do things. As a leader, you have to have a deep commitment to what you are doing so the staff will do what you ask them to do. They need to see your commitment. My passion is kids! But it isn't just my passion that sustains my spirit . . . I am sustained by a gifted, talented group of people dedicated to the museum and loyal to me. This means all of my director challenges are reduced. . . . Directors who are discipline trained may sometimes find it hard to keep up confidence as so little of a director's role has to do with the training of their particular discipline. It is important to have another outlet for energy. Although my passion is kids, my outlet is actually gardening and golf. (Kolb 1996)

Art museum directors with a passion for education and the public are shaping museums based on a love of and ability to 'generate ideas' in others. They use the art museum's collection both as a way of transforming what people see through the education process, and as a basis to create relationships between people both within and external to it. As a place for 'discovery' and 'ideas', these directors described the art museum as a social or cultural 'center' rather than a site for beautiful objects. They were acutely aware that they needed to embody their commitment actively in ways which enabled others to recognise their leadership vision.

Passion for entrepreneurship and innovation

Entrepreneurship is one of the characteristics necessary for art museum leadership in and beyond the 1990s due to radical cuts in government funding for cultural institutions internationally. Directors who share this passion have been actively shaping and reinventing themselves as leaders of business enterprises, rather than museums. A working definition for an entrepreneur is an 'individual who seizes an opportunity, takes a risk, and makes it financially successful' (Ottley 1995). Another definition concerns a state of mind in which a cause is identified and an opportunity cultivated or created which can be turned into a profit (Aberdene and Naisbitt 1994: 319–334). Typically, entrepreneurship has focused on an individual's response to an opportunity and the ability to adapt readily to change. Entrepreneurship and innovation in the museum context may be defined as 'non-routine, significant, and discontinuous change' (Mezias and Glynn 1993: 78) which embodies a new idea that may not be consistent with the current concept of the organisation's business. When Senge (1990) researched learning organisations, he found leaders with a passion for innovation. For museum directors to manage change successfully, innovation is critical in areas such as marketing, merchandising and customer service delivery. These were the key focal areas occupying the Director of the National Gallery of Victoria in Melbourne who was creating a new presence for his museum.

> My job as director is to balance a belief in the institution and the reality of marketing. I am not reluctant to enter commercial activity but we cannot wear the museum's mission on our sleeve in the process e.g. to promote and understand the visual arts. We are not exactly about 'entertainment and access' but about creating greater understanding so people will want to know more about the visual arts. (Potts 1995)

The Director of the Isabella Stewart Gardner Museum in Boston had been recruited to lead that Museum at a time when the focus was clearly on financial issues. Her sense of 'entrepreneurial risk taking' was expressed as a commitment to contemporary artists and a search for profitable ways in which to engage the local community.

> My passion was to work with artists and contemporary work that drives. I used that passion to look at how we were part of a neighborhood where people could walk to this museum from three neighborhood schools. We decided to work on this advantage. To do this, we engaged research through Harvard University regarding learning theory to push the museum's envelope. I got hit over the head by the Trustees for this! This introduced a whole new issue for my role as a director. (Hawley 1996)

Furthermore, the Director of The Museum of Contemporary Art in Los Angeles stressed that he did not want the external presence of the Museum to be based on the ideas of any one person alone, director or curator. The art museum director's passion was based on the desire to 'work with artists and to be in the contemporary world where all things are open to question. To look at the fact that there is more than one way to get on a horse' (Koshalek 1996). As a result of this philosophy, The Museum of Contemporary Art creates a range of entrepreneurial activities providing an avenue for many people with a passion for the arts.

> Ideas and energy are the most important characteristics a director of an art museum can have. The director has to be capable of saying 'What's Next' in terms of the goals, strengths, and a concept for the museum to make it unique. This means bringing things to life constantly with artists. That is how we keep this place alive. This can be expressed in many ways. (Koshalek 1996)

In addition, the Director of the Queensland Art Gallery in Brisbane had shaped the vision for museums based on a keen interest in political entrepreneurism to ensure that museum's continued success as a public institution.

> You can't take yourself too seriously, you have to stay dynamic or it becomes boring. My own personal interest in politics helped me a lot. . . . As a director, you look for what can be done, not what can't. This requires skills and talent in advocacy and maintaining a position of high credibility with the mainstream of the Queensland Public Service. . . . Every institution needs to be a shaper of change. (Hall 1995)

Museum directors with a passion for entrepreneurism and innovation have used their leadership roles to focus on marketing, merchandising and investments which have 'had a return on the dollar'. Their passion has reflected a complex form of individual creativity as they have actively embraced 'risks' and a search for 'new possibilities' to enable profitable museum enterprises to be undertaken. This included a willingness to explore opportunities and learn from a range of non-traditional entrepreneurial enterprises in a museum context. Vecchio *et al.* (1995) identified this willingness to experiment with entrepreneurship as a prerequisite for successful leadership in the 1990s and beyond, and they have described the characteristics of entrepreneurism as the ability to adapt to, shape and create new environments.

A passion for constructive discontent

A passion for constructive discontent has been described as an appreciation of diversity and difference, investigation, examination and the use of the organisation as a 'site for debate' for future development. The Director for the Whitney Museum of American Art in New York explained his passion for the museum as a place for 'personal and community discovery':

> I learned how a museum is a social instrument for use by self and others. I saw museums as part of a community's health both socially and mentally. I learned how a museum plays a role in the lives of people from different social levels, not just the rich people which is what I originally thought. I learned that a contemporary art museum is about collecting, recording, reporting, mirroring, and is a site for delight. I fell in love with art, its power and its liability. I was prompted to live an examined life and saw the art museum as a mirror to that examination of life. It is a place for the contest of values and ideas. My job is to present the menu and if the audience likes it, they are the ones who then find their way. I learned all about passion through a project in California. I learned about people who really do 'good deeds'. I learned what was real, respected, and dangerous, I learned about survival [through a series of potentially life threatening accidents]. I learned that museums need people with passion, not functionaries. (Ross 1996)

The Director of the Museum of Contemporary Art in Chicago described a relationship between how the leader creates an external presence to the museum and constructive discontent. His vision for the museum had been carefully constructed from the value the director placed on 'contemporary culture' and the interface with the public. He was excited about exploring all the known and unknown forces which make up the concept of culture, as well as ways to re-create culture for new foundations for the future.

> Sometimes, what we do is closer to journalism than history. We are investigating rather than reporting on contemporary culture. The world is one with few compass points. It is about managing ambiguity and uncertainty. (Consey 1995)

Focusing on change and change management as an ongoing interface between people creating contemporary culture, the Director of The Museum of Modern Art in New York saw his leadership role in the museum as a 'change agent'. Change, exploration and evolution were key themes in his commitment to enabling the museum as a site for 'active community engagement'.

> We need to ask what to create for tomorrow. We need to use our minds and act as think tanks to think abstractly. . . . MoMA was founded with a missionary spirit and propelled over the last 65 years with that spirit. We work in a world context, forging common ground between ambitious visions of the staff and the trustees. I, as Director, am the mediator of this process. . . . Managing change is an apt description of what I do. I am part of a larger pattern of relationships. . . . My focus is on how to take the status quo toward an evolution, balancing roots and history at the same time. This involves creating team leadership with a shared goal and a common vision. (Lowry 1996)

Another leader who has thrived on change, diversity and difference is the Director of The Saint Louis Art Museum and his pleasure and experience in change management has enabled him continually to reposition or reinvent his Museum within a contemporary context.

> I enjoy the interface between individuals, collections, and the role of museums in the community intersect. I enjoy the link to plural or diverse audiences. I hugely enjoy difference. I thrive on difference. The translation of this passion into the vision for The Saint Louis Art Museum has been a sixteen-year commitment to a publicly owned museum which has a global agenda like the Victoria and Albert [in London]. The founder of this museum in 1879 put no boundaries on what constituted art. He started this museum with an open-ended agenda. This came into play and got lost between 1940–60. It needed to be refound. It made a difference to re-vision the organisation with a big, open agenda. If we are able to continue to grasp the excitement of that, then we will continue to be successful. (Burke 1996)

Directors with a passion for constructive discontent have viewed their leadership roles slightly differently from other art museum directors. They have seen themselves more as 'change agents', at ease with the 'ambiguity' and 'uncertainty' integral to contemporary culture. Their passion for 'change', 'diversity' and 'examination' has shaped their representation of the art museum as a 'social instrument'. Their passion for investigation and a fascination for 'the edge', or 'faultlines', in cultural development has suggested that the art museum should be represented as a site for ideas rather than objects, for social debate rather than passive celebration.

Conclusion

Art museum directors who are leading with passion constitute individuals in flow and they are totally engaged with the challenges at hand. Flow theory suggests that it is possible to develop an approach which enables the experience of flow more often and more easily when the five conditions for flow are met. These conditions include clear goals, support, discretionary decision making, a sense of trust which allows total involvement in the task, and increasingly complex challenges over time. These conditions need to be present organisationally in order to create a context for current and potential leaders to demonstrate masterly control and pleasure in the job. In executive decision making, the match between level of challenge and leadership skill is essential for evidence of flow in effective decision making.

Pleasure in the job has been described in terms of a personal anchor or source of creativity which sustained art museum directors on a very personal level. When an art museum director was in flow and working from the 'heart', it was most evident as contagious emotional energy. Creating and sustaining this energy is an ongoing challenge for anyone in such a leadership role. This energy was actually described by one New York based executive search consultant as 'the bottom line for "new breed" museum directors' (Nichols 1996). Translating energy into optimal performance appears to rely increasingly on what has become known as emotional intelligence skills. With increased mastery of these skills, art museum directors can increase effectiveness under pressure, develop trusting relationships and create the museum's future or 'that vision thing'. In conclusion, what matters in effective art museum leadership is a passion for life, creativity and imagination. When this passionate energy is expressed through a range of executive level skills, including emotional intelligence, people respond in positive emotional and social ways.

Note

Sherene Suchy is an experienced researcher, and practitioner and author of *Leading with Passion: Change Management in the 21st-century Museum* (2004). This article was first published in 1999 in *Museum Management and Curatorship*, vol. 18, no. 1.

References

Aberdene, P. and Naisbitt, J. (1994) *Mega trends for women*. Arrow. London.
Anderson, M. (1996) Interview with Max Anderson, Director of The Art Gallery of Ontario, in Toronto, 25 June 1996.
Beech, M. (1996) Interview with Milo Beech, Director of the Arthur M. Sackler Gallery and the Freer Gallery of Art, in Washington, D.C., 18 April 1996.

Bello, M. (1993) *The Smithsonian Institution, A World of Discovery: an exploration of behind-the-scenes research in the arts, sciences, and humanities.* Washington, D.C.: Smithsonian Institution.

Bergman, R. (1996) Interview with Robert Bergman, Director of the Cleveland Museum of Art, in Cleveland, 23 June 1996.

Borg, A. (1996) Interview with Alan Borg, Director of the Victoria and Albert Museum, in London, 2 May 1996.

Burke, J. (1996) Interview with James Burke, Director of The Saint Louis Art Museum, in Saint Louis, 7 June 1996.

Capon, E. (1995) Interview with Edmund Capon, Director of The Art Gallery of New South Wales, in Sydney, 13 April 1995.

—— (1996) Public presentation on fund-raising given by Edmund Capon, Director of The Art Gallery of New South Wales, in Sydney.

Consey, K. (1995) Interview with Kevin Consey, Director of the Museum of Contemporary Art, in Chicago, 12 June 1995.

Cooper, R. and Sawaf, A. (1996) *Executive EQ: emotional intelligence in leadership and organizations.* Grossett/Putnam. New York.

Csikszentmihalyi, M. (1990) *Flow: the psychology of optimal experience.* Harper and Row. New York.

—— (1993) *The evolving self: a psychology for the third millennium.* Harper Perennial. New York.

Csikszentmihalyi, M. and Hermanson, K. (1995) Intrinsic motivation in museums: what makes visitors want to learn? *Museum News*, 74, 34–62.

—— (1999) *Flow in the applied environment.* Seminar held 18 March 1999, School of Leisure and Tourism, University of Technology Sydney, Australia.

de Montebello, P. (1996) Interview with Philippe de Montebello, Director of The Metropolitan Museum of Art, in New York, 11 April 1996.

Demetrian, J. (1996) Interview with James Demetrian director of the Hirshhorn Museum and Sculpture Garden, in Washington, D.C., 16 April 1996.

Gardner, H. (1983) *Frames of mind: the theory of multiple intelligences.* Basic Books. New York.

—— (1995) *Leading minds: an anatomy of leadership.* Basic Books. New York.

Gaudieri, M. (1996) Telephone interview with Mimi Gaudieri, Coordinator for the Association of Art Museum Directors, in New York, 4 June 1996.

Glynn, M. (1996) Innovative genius: a framework for relating individual and organizational intelligences to innovation. *Academy of Management Review*, 21, 1,081–1,111.

Goleman, D. (1996) *Emotional intelligence: why it can matter more than IQ.* Bloomsbury. London.

Hall, D. (1995) Interview with Doug Hall, Director of the Queensland Art Gallery, in Brisbane, 20 February 1995.

Hawley, A. (1996) Telephone interview with Anne Hawley, Director of the Isabella Stewart Gardner Museum, in Boston, 4 April 1996.

Jaque, E. and Clement, S. (1994) *Executive leadership: a practical guide to managing complexity.* Blackwell. Cambridge, Massachusetts.

Jenneman, E. (1996) Interview with Eugene Jenneman, Director of the Dennos Museum Center, in Traverse, 13 May 1996.

Kolb, N. (1996) Telephone interview with Nancy Kolb, Director of the Please Touch Museum, in Philadelphia, 21 June 1996.

Koshalek, R. (1996) Interview with Richard Koshalek, Director of the Museum of Contemporary Art, in Los Angeles, 2 April 1996.

Latos-Valier, P. (1996) Telephone interview with Paula Latos-Valier, Director of the Art Gallery of Western Australia, in Perth, 2 September 1996.

Lowry, G. (1996) Interview with Glen Lowry, Director of The Museum of Modern Art, in New York, 12 April 1996.

McCaughy, P. (1996) Interview with Patrick McCaughy, Director of the Yale Center for British Art, in New Haven, 15 April 1996.

Marzio, P. (1996) Telephone interview with Peter Marzio, Director of the Museum of Fine Arts, in Houston, Texas, 27 June 1996.

Mezias, S. and Glynn, M. (1993) The three faces of corporate renewal: institution, revolution and evolution. *Strategic Management Journal*, 31, 235–256.

Nichols, N. (1996) Telephone interview with Nancy Nichols, Executive Recruitment Consultant with Heidrick and Struggles, in New York, 13 June 1996.

Ottley, D. (1995) Telephone interview with Dr Dennis Ottley, senior lecturer in marketing and entrepreneurship in the Faculty of Management at the University of Western Sydney, Hawkesbury, 15 August 1995.

Parker, H. (1995) Interview with Harry Parker, Director of The Fine Arts Museums of San Francisco, in San Francisco, 14 June 1995.

Pennar, K. (1996) How many smarts do you have? *Business Week*, September, 16, 52–55.

Potts, T. (1995) Interview with Tim Potts, Director of the National Gallery of Victoria, in Melbourne, 11 August 1995.

Powell, E. (1996) Interview with Earl Powell, Director of the National Gallery of Art, in Washington, D.C., 17 April 1996.

Q-metrics (1996) *EQ Map*. Trade marked product of Essi Systems and AIT in San Francisco, California.

Ross, D. (1996) Interview with David Ross, Director of the Whitney Museum of American Art, in New York, 11 April 1996.

Sano, E. (1995) Interview with Emily Sano, Director of the Asian Art Museum of San Francisco, 15 June 1995.

Senge, P. (1990) *The fifth discipline: the art and practice of the learning organization*. Doubleday. New York.

Serota, N. (1996) Interview with Nicholas Serota, Director of The Tate Gallery, in London, 30 April 1996.

Spate, V. (ed.) (1980) *French painting: the revolutionary decades 1760–1830*. Australian Gallery Directors Council Ltd. Sydney.

Stamp, G. (1993) Well-being at work: aligning purposes, people, strategies, and structures. *The International Journal of Career Management*, 5, 1–36.

Suchy, S. (1998) *An international study on the director's role in art museum leadership*. Doctoral thesis available through the library at the University of Western Sydney Nepean. Sydney, Australia.

Thompson, S. (1996) Interview with Shirley Thompson, Director of the National Gallery of Canada, in Ottawa, 25 June 1996.

Vecchio, R., Hearn, G. and Southey, G. (1995) *Organisational behavior: life at work in Australia*. Harcourt Brace. Sydney.

Walsh, J. (1995) Interview with John Walsh, Director of the J. Paul Getty Museum, in Santa Monica, 7 June 1995.

Wood, J. (1996) Interview with James Wood, Director of The Art Institute of Chicago, in Chicago, 26 June 1996.

Chapter 16

Visionary Leadership and Missionary Zeal

Stuart W. Davies

Introduction

IT IS NECESSARILY CONVENIENT that complex issue areas be divided up into management units for the purposes of teaching, training and personal development. Each then proceeds to grow specialists and develop its separate literatures, its separate conferences and even its separate journals. But one significant problem in doing this is that important linkages between the units may be obscured or lost. Business management studies are no exception. In this paper two usually quite distinct 'topics' are covered – leadership and museum statements. Leadership is often seen as the domain of organizational behaviour or human resource management. All organizations need good leaders and academic enquiry has focused on 'what makes a good leader' and how good leadership relates to good organizational performance. On the other hand, mission statements belong to the domain of strategic management (although they may be sometimes hijacked by marketing academics desperate to poach all the best ideas). Mission statements are placed at the pinnacle of a process designed to produce good strategies and, if not to guarantee business success, at least manage or reduce the consequences of uncertainty in the environment.

This paper looks at both these topic areas in the context of museum and gallery management. It reviews the literatures, presents research findings and discusses the implications for the museum manager. The evidence for museums is drawn from four principal sources: interviews with managers; focus group discussions with managers; a questionnaire survey; and a contents analysis of mission statements. For the gathering and analysis of data the author would especially like to thank Nichola

Source: pp. 108–132 in K. Moore (ed.) (1999) *Management in Museums*, London and New Jersey: Athlone.

Johnson and participants on the annual UEA Museum Leadership Programme, all
the managers who have generously cooperated with the project and Helen Watts
for assisting with the analysis of data.

Leadership: finding a definition

Studying leadership is difficult because of the vast amount of literature and the lack
of generally accepted principles or undisputed models. This was recognized as a
problem over ten years ago.

> Decades of academic analysis have given us more than 350 definitions
> of leadership. Literally thousands of empirical investigations of leaders
> have been conducted in the last seventy-five years alone, but no clear
> and certain unequivocal understanding exists as to what distinguishes
> leaders from non-leaders, and perhaps more important, what distinguishes
> effective from ineffective leaders and effective organisation from ineffect-
> ive organisations. Never have so many labored so long to say so little.
> (Bennis and Nanus 1985)

This rather pessimistic view can now be credibly challenged, but it remains true
that leadership consistently denies the simple categorizations or models so beloved
of business management academics and MBA teachers.

The first point to make is that leadership is recognized as being very important in an organization. Its importance can be overemphasized to the point of being
romanticized and the link between leadership and organizational performance is difficult to demonstrate, but the importance attached to leadership by all stakeholders
(as well as leaders themselves) is a clear indication that we are dealing with a critical factor in organizational management and success.

Defining leadership, we have already been told, is difficult. This paper will adopt
one of the simpler but effective definitions on offer (Shackleton 1995).

> Leadership is the process in which an individual influences other group
> members towards the attainment of group or organisational goals.

It is an attractive definition because it places emphasis on the leader as an influ-
encer, the relationship between him or her and the group (or 'followers' as they
are sometimes called) and the need to keep the attainment of goals clearly in focus.
Much of this paper's discussion of leadership draws on Shackleton's excellent
assessment of the issues.

Other definitions put emphasis on power, style, charisma, follower compliance,
empowerment and transformation. The variations on the leadership theme are almost
endless. Bennis and Nanus (1985), for example, considered that leadership was about
path finding and 'about doing the right things'. The leader provides the vision and
strategic thinking for an organization while the manager is much more of a 'doer',
the one who implements the vision. Kotter (1990) suggested four key roles of a
leader (as opposed to a manager):

1. Establishing direction
2. Aligning people
3. Motivating and inspiring
4. Changing outcomes

The leader, in this view, has considerable responsibility for challenging the order and stability apparently craved for by managers, and driving change in the organization. Shackleton (1995) emphasizes the influencing role of a leader, as seen in his definition which this paper adopts. This view is a useful reminder that leaders may not necessarily be linked to a particular function in the organization but may earn their spurs through the impact they have on others' actions rather than by their own. This may of course be particularly pertinent in organizations where stakeholder management is important, which will often include museums and galleries.

Leadership theories: traits, style, contingency and attributes

A number of theoretical frameworks or approaches to explain leadership have been developed, none of which has proved to be entirely satisfactory when empirically tested. The main four have been traits, style, contingency and attribute theories. Each has something to offer towards our understanding of leadership in the context of museums and galleries.

Early research assumed that it would be possible to identify traits or characteristics which are shared by good leaders and therefore, of course, to identify future leaders. A considerable amount of research by psychologists and others has succeeded in identifying a few traits which generally distinguish leaders from non-leaders.

- Drive
- Leadership motivation
- Honesty and integrity
- Self-confidence
- Cognitive ability
- Knowledge of the business

However, attempts to identify a simple formula for leadership effectiveness foundered because so much depends on the situation, the nature of the organizational goals and who the 'followers' are.

Disillusionment with the traits approach led to researchers looking at leadership style, and seeking to establish which style was the most effective. Scales of style – typically ranging from authoritarian to democratic and consultative – were created and techniques developed to assess where leaders should be placed along it. Some scales were linear while others tried to balance two or more factors (such as being goal-orientated or people-orientated) in a grid arrangement. Unfortunately, all the models turned out to be flawed by the fact that leaders often act differently depending on the situation they find themselves in. Good leaders have no one style; they are often style chameleons.

The response to this has been to develop contingency theories. These recognize that leadership style and behaviour is dependent (contingent) upon the context. Contingency theorists have explored the relationship between situation (context) and behaviour. Unfortunately, it is difficult to agree on which of the many contextual variables or factors are most important and what impact they have on leadership anyway. What has emerged is that context must be important but, so too, is the relationship between leader and follower. This has been the major concern of attribution theorists.

Attribution theory suggests that any event can have a variety of causes, and is concerned with how people react to events and each other. We should be able to observe the behaviour of leaders and followers and then attribute causes to that behaviour. However, 'cause and effect' may not be simple or clear cut and attribution theories fall down when the boundaries between perception and reality are blurred or not understood. 'Effective leadership lies just as much in recognizing the perceptions of the parties involved, as it does in the reality of what actually takes place' (Shackleton 1995: 57).

If none of these four theoretical approaches has provided 'the answer', the research associated with them has helped to clarify the general nature of leadership. Most importantly leadership is now understood not to be a single entity applicable on all occasions, but rather to have a number of variations which may be more applicable or appropriate depending on circumstances. In other words, the research suggests that we should move from focusing solely on the qualities and skills we expect leaders to display towards a more rounded view which includes the environmental factors influencing leadership.

It does, however, appear to be possible to identify seven groups of factors which make significant contributions to the existence of effective leadership in an organization. Not all organizations (or leaders) will display all of these at once but together they seem to offer a tenable framework. These seven may be described thus:

1. *Self-awareness leadership*
    To be effective, leaders must want to be leaders. They must want the power, influence and status it brings, even if their reasons for wanting it may vary enormously. They must also have the energy, drive and self-confidence that is necessary both to achieve leadership and to be effective leaders. Self-awareness of their own ambition encourages – it is contended – the development of self-awareness in others.

2. *Strategic leadership*
    Leaders have cognitive ability and can use their intelligence in a practical way to observe, understand and assess what is happening around them. Above all else, this enables them to develop a vision for the organization which many researchers have recognized as a significant part of leadership.

3. *Charismatic leadership*
    In Greek, the word 'charisma' means 'divinely inspired gift'. However, research suggests that charismatic leaders are those who have developed the ability to motivate and inspire followers, although they are often helped if the values of leader and followers are similar.

4. *Relationship leadership*

    The relationship between leaders and followers is clearly important. Crucial to this may be the leader's use of power. Is he or she sensitive to the needs and feelings of others? Is power used appropriately and sparingly while influence is the main tool of leadership? Effective leaders will probably possess 'referent power' – they will possess qualities admired by their followers.

5. *Professional leadership*

    Effective leaders 'know their business' and are professionally respected by their followers. They influence their followers through their possession of 'expert power'.

6. *Situational leadership*

    The ability of the leader to 'read', understand and adapt to the situation he or she is operating in at any one time may be crucial to effective leadership. The leader needs to react and adapt intelligently to the situation, being flexible in style and approach.

7. *Transformational leadership*

    An effective leader will recognize the need for change and make it happen. The vision will be set and communicated to the whole of the organization. The leader will set the agenda, monitor the change process and set a good example, ensuring constancy between the vision (and its underlying values) and the leader's own actions. A review of the evidence suggests that 'most researchers agree that transformational leadership involves creating a new vision which points the way to a new state of affairs for a desirable future' (Shackleton 1995: 129).

Linking theory to practice

So what does all this management theory tell us that might be helpful in understanding leadership in a practical museum management context? The answer is partly dependent on what question you ask. If we wanted to know what makes a good leader we might get the answer that it all depends on what you want!

We have seen that leaders usually have certain traits or characteristics, such as drive, motivation (the desire to be leaders), self-confidence, cognitive ability and knowledge of the business. But they will also be aware of the advantages and disadvantages of the type of style they adopt, whether it be autocratic, consultative, people-orientated or goal-orientated. The intelligent leader will also understand that the same style is not appropriate at all times for all occasions and with all people. Flexibility of style would seem to be important. That flexibility would also be a recognition that the qualities required of a leader may vary according to the context in which he or she is operating and the same leader may need to change his or her approach as the situation changes. And in all this the leader will be aware that his or her effectiveness depends upon his or her relationship with the 'followers' and his or her ability to 'read and understand' their needs and expectations. This necessary skill is not made any easier to acquire by the fact that perception may be more important than reality. What people believe to be so may matter more than what is actually so and therefore a 'good' leader may have to understand those perceptions in order to effectively lead the organization. In short, leadership is complicated.

Much of the academic management research has started from the 'what makes a good leader' viewpoint because it is assumed that good leaders are important in business, capable of making the difference between success and failure. Further-more, despite the emphasis laid on 'knowledge of the business' and 'situational context' in the academic literature, many practitioners retain the assumption that leadership consists of a bundle of skills which can be readily transferred. By implica-tion, therefore, the results of many decades of leadership research in a business context, ought to enlighten issues surrounding museum leadership. Is this actually so?

Museum leadership research

What should be the agenda for research in this area? It would certainly be pos-sible to add to the existing literature by examining any of the theories or testing any of the models in a museum context. This would make a useful contribution to the leadership literature. However, it would imply that the most appropriate research should focus on 'the leader' as an individual and accept the agenda already developed in business and psychological research. It would also imply an assump-tion that leadership in public or not-for-profit organizations is similar to that of organizations in the for-profit sector.

Recent research focused on the University of East Anglia's annual Museum Leadership Programme (for senior museum managers) has taken a different approach. It has asked the question 'what do museums need in leadership' and attempted to create a 'photofit' of a good museum leader from an organizational needs perspective rather than identify effective leaders and analyse them. In this the research has been influenced by Meindl who has called for the 'reinvention of leadership', changing research from being 'leader-centred' to being follower-centred. The principle here is that we should try and determine what the followers (or the organization) need and leadership should fulfil this only to the extent that it is necessary. In other words, organizations and followers only subscribe to the leadership that they need rather than being driven or dragged along by a leader acting out established perceptions of what role he or she should be fulfilling.

The first research exercise was a focus group of 12 senior managers from a variety of museum organizations (including National, local authority and inde-pendent museums). None of the managers was the head of his or her organization. The objective of the exercise was to explore whether or not there were any 'special' features of leadership in museums and galleries which could be identified and subsequently used as a 'blueprint' for 'good' leadership. No knowledge of the academic literature was assumed or offered, reducing the likelihood that this approach would be challenged at the outset.

The group began by identifying a list of current issues facing museums and galleries in the UK. It was assumed that these issues would probably form the key agenda of most museum leaders – thus also assuming the leader's strategic role. The issues identified were:

- Declining public funding
- Constant change
- Demand for accountability
- National Lottery
- Increasing expectations
- Market forces
- Costs
- Productivity/VFM
- Politics

There was general agreement that change was endemic in museums and that good leadership was needed to deal with it. Discussion then turned to what exactly a museum leader was.

The group started off down the 'function' route. It was suggested that the museum leader was a 'captain of the ship'. This analogy worked quite well, up to the point where they began considering the relationship of the ship to other ships. The problem here is that we all tend to think of leaders of an organization being the person 'in charge' and with whom lies some ultimate authority. In reality, in few cases – if indeed any – leaders actually have full control of 'their' organizations. Things tend to be much more complicated, with many 'stakeholders' having a say or influencing (directly or indirectly) what happens within and to an organization. Furthermore, what is the relationship between the captain and the ship's culture? Is one determined by the other? And if so, which is which?

Undeterred, the group identified a number of leadership functions in museums and galleries:

- Responsibility
- Takes informed decisions
- Allocates resources
- Motivates
- Negotiates
- Instigates
- Represents
- Delegates
- Obtains resources
- Unifies
- Is accountable

But it was quickly observed that these functions may not necessarily be attributed to only *one* person in the organization ('the person at the top'). Some or many of them may be functions exercised by other people within (or even possibly outside?) the organization. This led to discussion about what may be the difference between 'the person at the top' and other leaders. How many 'other leaders' an organization may have is usually determined by each organization's unique circumstances: size, structure, objectives, the existence of clearly defined special projects and so on.

This led naturally to some discussion about how these 'leaders' related to each other and particularly what role this left for 'the person at the top' – the traditional leader. It was rapidly realized that having many leaders could be beneficial in terms of organizational dynamics and the achieving of objectives; but, equally, many leaders operating with little reference to each other – or even as rival loci of power within the organization – could be disastrous. At this point the group set aside this knotty problem and addressed the issue of leadership attributes.

In discussion the group were cautious about the personal qualities required of a leader. They were not convinced that 'personality' was necessarily especially important. To them 'personality' was too closely associated in popular thinking with someone who is believed to have 'charisma' or is 'a character' or is 'bubbly'. To them it was much more important that the leader had the ability to 'make things happen' and that they had a 'management style' appropriate to the organization. As one member of the group said: 'The leader doesn't have to "speak" but somebody does!' The most important leadership skills may be in recognizing this and facilitating it. The leader had a very important 'overview' role: identifying what were the KEY SUCCESS FACTORS for the organization and ensuring that they were addressed, deploying the appropriate resources (including people) to achieve it.

This inevitably led the group back to the question of what distinguishes 'the leader' from other leaders within the organization. To facilitate discussion, the session leader offered ten possible roles for a museum leader and some functions or activities which might be associated with them (Table 16.1). The group used these as a basis for trying to identify those leadership role/functions which were uniquely those of the head of the organization. This exercise, it was suggested, is essential to ensuring that the leader is effective. The leader needs to be focused or he or she may not only be personally ineffective but will also undermine the effectiveness of others (i.e. the boundaries of the leader's role need to be defined, communicated and accepted by everyone in the organization).

Table 16.1   Roles of the museum leader

- An individual
- Visionary
- Advocate and Ambassador
- Professional
- Mentor
- Empowerer
- Communicator
- Manager of Learning
- Strategic Manager
- Executive

The group's discussions led to the identification of a number of specific (and possibly generic) roles for the museum leader:

1.   *Consideration of the long-term future of the museum/gallery organization*
     This should include attention to:

     (a)   vision/mission
     (b)   strategies (related to market/stakeholder changes)
     (c)   structures

2.   *Systems and framework*
     The leader must ensure that the museum 'works', including ensuring the appropriate deployment of resources, the existence of efficient work systems and the existence of clear communication channels.

3.   *Stakeholder management*
     Many – perhaps all – members of the museum will have contact with external stakeholders. But it is the leader's particular role to ensure their aspirations are satisfied (as far as possible) and that the museum benefits from its stakeholders rather than is endangered by them.

4.   *Exemplar*
     The leader has to 'set the tone' for the museum; his or her example is an important influence on both its external image and its internal motivation. To do this effectively the leader has to be equally respected by peers, less experienced colleagues and stakeholders alike.

5.   *Ultimate arbitration*
     'The buck stops here'. Notwithstanding our earlier conclusion that no leader is in sole command of an organization, the museum will need someone to arbitrate on difficult issues, situations etc. Only the leader can – or should – have this role.

6.   *Recruitment*
     This was added to the group's list on the insistence of a very experienced observer and led to a discussion about how influential the leader could be – or indeed should be – in recruitment matters. One thing was clear, however: the leader has a crucial role in changing the culture of the museum – whether by judicious recruitment or by releasing existing staff.

This concluded the session. The group had successfully identified the key areas where they – as museum leaders – should be focusing their thinking and action. They could then identify any shortcomings in their own skills or attributes and remedy them as part of the process of becoming outstanding museum leaders.

The second research exercise was questionnaire based. Before attending the focus group, each of the 12 members had been asked to circulate a questionnaire to five colleagues at their institution. Of the 60 distributed, 39 complete questionnaires were returned directly to the author, a return of 65 per cent.

The questionnaire explored just three issues in museum leadership but required quite considerable thought from the person completing it.

The four key questions were:

A.   Leaders may have many *functions* in an organization. Please list FIVE, in priority order, which you would expect a good leader of a museum/art gallery to carry out.

B.   Leaders may require many *personal qualities*. Please list FIVE in priority order, which you would hope that a good leader of a museum/art gallery should have.

C.   Leaders may require *specific qualifications or attributes* to be effective. Please list FIVE in priority order, which you would expect a good leader of a museum/art gallery to have.

D.   Of all the functions, qualities and qualification/attributes you have listed, which FIVE in priority order, do you regard as the most important?

Attached to the first three questions were prompt lists of possible answers to help respondents marshal their thoughts.

Since it was known where each questionnaire was returned from it could have been possible to cross-tabulate the replies according to type of institution but the sample was too small to make such an exercise statistically valid.

The free-form nature of the responses – which extended well beyond the prompts offered – meant that there were a large number of different specific responses. Many of these could, however, quite legitimately be grouped together.

To achieve a balanced picture of respondents' intentions, three different measures of importance were used in analysing the responses to each question. First of all the number of times that a type of response appeared anywhere in the list of five responses was counted up. These 'appearances' were then expressed as a percentage of the total possible. So, in Table 16.2, for example, the function 'Produces a clear vision and focuses activities on achieving it' is mentioned by 33 out of the 39 respondents, scoring 85 per cent. Secondly, the numbers of times a type of response was ranked first as top priority is also noted in the 'First Choices' column. So, in our example 'Produces a clear vision . . .' was first choice for 24 of the respondents. Finally, the five responses are attributed a score, 1 for first,

Table 16.2   Leadership in museums: functions of a leader (n = 39; functions appearing less than 10 times not included)

Function	Appearances	%	First choices	Ranked score
Produces a clear vision and focuses activities on achieving it	33	85	24	1.36
Ensures adequate funding	23	59	0	3.22
Unifies team and maintains morale	21	54	1	3.71
Establishes policies, goals and strategies	19	49	8	2.11
Monitors performance	15	38	0	4.27
Sets clear objectives for individuals/team	14	36	0	2.64
Ensures service is understood/respected	13	33	2	3.08
Represents the institution externally	10	27	0	3.90

Table 16.3   Leadership in museums: personal qualities in leaders (n = 39; qualities appearing less than 10 times not included)

Personal quality	Appearances	%	First choices	Ranked score
Is able to communicate	29	75	9	2.45
Can develop an effective team	22	56	5	2.82
Is able to delegate tasks	18	46	0	3.78
Is able to motivate	14	36	3	2.71
Gains respect and sets example	14	36	5	2.86
Has energy, enthusiasm, activism	13	33	2	2.69
Supports and shows loyalty	12	31	0	4.33
Is both fair and firm	10	27	0	3.30
Has persistence and toughness	10	27	0	3.50

2 for second etc. and the total for each is presented as a Ranked Score, 1.36 in the case of our example.

The findings presented in Table 16.2 show that respondents indicated on all measures that the single most important function of a museum leader is to pro- duce a clear vision and focus activities on achieving it. Two other functions achieved a ranking of less than 3.00 and both of these are clearly closely linked to the most important function: these are establishing policies, goals and strategies and setting clear objectives for individuals of the team. Taken together all three indicate that respondents see the overall function or role of the museum leader as being its strategist.

The other two important functions – ensuring adequate funding and ensuring that the service is understood/respected – relate to the leader's stakeholder manager role. Responsibility for the museum's relationship with key stakeholders – and particularly those relating to funding and governance – is a crucial role and respondents clearly feel that this should be vested in the leader.

Table 16.3 reveals a rather more normal set of results for what museum respon- dents consider to be the important personal qualities in their leaders. Top ranked here is the ability to communicate. Does this reflect a perception (perhaps based on experience) that museum leaders are not always good communicators? If that is so then this has to be rather an ironic finding given that a significant function of museums per se is to communicate.

Two qualifications for museum leadership are pre-eminent according to Table 16.4. Supporting what we have already found, respondents stress that the museum leader needs to understand strategic issues. Perhaps this is assumed to include a knowledge of political and legislature issues and an understanding of the sector, accounting for their lower ranking. However, top position goes to the belief that museum leaders must have professional credibility. This does not necessarily mean they are professionally qualified and have had their career in museums, but it is safe to assume that this is what many respondents would expect. Regardless of what skills 'outsiders' may bring in – or indeed how valued they may be at some other

Table 16.4 Leadership in museums: qualifications of leaders (n = 39; qualifications appearing less than 10 times not included)

Qualification	Appearances	%	First choices	Ranked score
Must have professional credibility	31	79	13	2.42
Understands strategic issues	26	67	8	2.23
Knowledge of political and legislative issues	23	59	0	3.43
Understands sector and opportunities	22	57	0	3.18
Experience in maintaining professional standards	12	31	5	2.58

Table 16.5 Leadership in museums: overall leadership characteristics (n = 39; characteristics appearing less than 10 times not included)

Overall characteristic	Appearances	%	First choices	Ranked score
Produces a clear vision and focuses activities on achieving it	29	74	19	1.76
Ensures adequate funding	14	36	0	3.79
Is able to communicate	13	33	4	2.15
Must have professional credibility	12	31	2	3.42
Establishes policies, goals and strategies	11	28	2	2.54
Understands strategic issues	10	27	0	3.50

level in the organization – leadership is seen as the domain of someone who must be professionally credible to museum professionals.

Finally, Table 16.5 attempts to bring together all the findings and indicate the key factors in museum leadership. The clear first choice is that the museum leader produces a clear vision and focuses activities on achieving it. Two others in the list – 'establishes policies, goals and strategies' and 'understands strategic issues' – are obviously linked to this function. From this it is evident that, referring back to our earlier discussion about types of leadership, *strategic leadership* is what museum professionals want most for their organizations. After that – and allied to it – the leader must be able to secure funding. And what type of person should this leader be? He or she must have professional credibility and be able to communicate.

Taking the two sets of research findings and trying to reconcile them is an interesting exercise. The focus group – made up of individuals whose thoughts might be focusing on how they would operate as leaders in the not too distant future – tended to be a little introspective and concentrated much of their efforts on *what* a leader might do, and, to a lesser extent, *how* it might be done. Their colleagues, however, were much clearer in their assessment of what was required: strategic leadership. The inference is that this may be lacking in many museums – perhaps because of the uncertainties indicated by the focus group debate or more generally because museum managers may be poor strategic thinkers. To explore this a little further this researcher decided to test the degree of strategic thinking in museums by examining a large number of mission statements, in the expectation that they ought to indicate the strategic position of the museum and encapsulate the broad views of the leader.

Mission statements: the management research evidence

As with leadership, there has never been a universally accepted definition of a mission statement. Out of the many definitions on offer this paper has adopted Fred David's 1989 suggestion:

> An enduring statement of purpose that distinguishes one organisation from other similar enterprises . . . a declaration of our organisation's 'reason for being' . . . reveals the long-term vision of our organisation in terms of what it wants to be and who it wants to service.

Most definitions refer to vision or long-term purposes (e.g. Matejka *et al.* 1993 and Klemm *et al.* 1991). But there is little in the way of agreed terminology – 'mission statement', 'corporate statement', 'aims and values', 'purpose', 'principles', 'objectives', 'goals' and 'responsibilities' and 'obligations' all having been used to describe missions (Klemm *et al.* 1991). Nor can one expect to find much consistency in the form or context of mission statements. They can be as short as a simple sentence or run to many pages. They can be a single statement of a hierarchical series of statements. Sometimes they refer to 'aims', 'objectives' or 'targets' and appear in effect to be statements of business strategy. In others there may be a greater focus on values, beliefs, ethics and philosophy. They may refer to internal or external stakeholders; they may be vague or very specific: they can be unrealistically aspirational or a dull functional definition (Davies and Glaister 1996).

Some researchers have tried to link mission statements with successful business performers and then to prescribe appropriate frameworks for creating a 'good' mission statement (e.g. McGinnis 1981; David 1989). Inevitably these have not been complementary, although they were generally in some way customer-orientated and attempted to embody attitudes rather than specific programmes of action. The most innovative approach in recent years has been the creation of the 'Ashbridge mission model' which endeavours to reconcile conflicting views about mission statements in one model.

This model links purpose (why the company exists), strategy (the competitive position and distinctive competence), values (what the company believes in) and behaviour standards (the policies and behaviour patterns then underpin the distinctive competence and the value system). Taken together these can create a sense of mission which gives a meaningful focus to the organization's activities (Campbell and Tawadey 1990; Campbell and Yeung 1991). However, the universality of this model has been challenged (Piercy and Morgan 1994), it being suggested that different needs may require different types of mission statements.

If there is not yet complete agreement on what constitutes a good mission statement there is at least broad agreement that they are necessary, or at least useful. The concept of 'mission' being a key element in any organization has been around for over twenty years:

> A business is not defined by its name, statutes or articles of incorporation. It is defined by the business mission. Only a clear definition of the mission and purpose of an organisation makes possible clear and realistic business objectives. (Drucker 1973)

Most of the reasons for producing and using mission statements fall within one or more of four basic areas: (1) to give a clear definition of the business; (2) to explain the business to external stakeholders; (3) to establish a starting point for the strategy process; and (4) to motivate and inspire employees within the business, including instilling appropriate values among them (Davies and Glaister 1996).

When transferred from the business sector to the public and not-for-profit sectors, it can be seen that the key importance of the mission statement probably lies in its role of stating quite clearly the purpose of the organization in such a way that that purpose can be clearly communicated to internal and external stakeholders. In a sector where organizations have multiple goals and multiple stakeholders (sometimes conflicting with each other), this can make mission statements an important tool in facilitating consistent decision-making and empowerment of managers.

Mission statements: the evidence from museums and galleries

A full research study of how museum mission statements are formulated, by whom and why, has not yet been undertaken. Nor has an assessment been made of how they are used and if they have any apparent impact on individual museums or the sector in general. Structured interviews with a pilot sample of 15 museum managers strongly suggested that the conclusions of such a study would be little different from a recent detailed assessment of mission statements in institutions of higher education. 'Very mixed in context, they appear to be poor on the degree of participation during formulation and weak in their application' (Davies and Glaister 1996: 291).

Nevertheless, a contents analysis of 270 museum and gallery mission statements has been undertaken to provide an overview of to what extent they reflect the acknowledged leadership role of providing strategic direction for the organization. That the two are always linked cannot be proven but, as has been suggested, one common criticism of mission statements is that they are too often the result of the leader's view rather than being the outcome of a major consultative exercise with all stakeholders.

In this contents analysis six key questions were asked of each mission statement:

1.   Does the statement appear to be 'official' or just made up in response to this study?

2.   Does the statement convey a sense of the museum's values?
3.   Is the statement purely functional or does it convey a sense of the museum's aims?
4.   Does the statement emphasize the museum's collections, visitors or both?
5.   Does the statement refer to stakeholders?
6.   Does the statement follow the MA or ICOM definition of a museum?

These are not generally the 'classic' type of analytical questions asked of business mission statements, usually designed to test the existence or absence of pre-determined mission statement features such as strategy, behaviour standards, ethical references and so on (see e.g. David 1989). However, in this case a pre-liminary examination of the mission statements suggested that such an approach might be at least premature and possibly even misleading.

Official mission statements

The statements were assessed to gauge whether they have the impression of being 'official' validated documents, carefully conceived and probably formally adopted by the museum. Strong indicators of 'unofficial' statements were those not copied from an official document, grammatically poor or evidently incomplete. As a result no less than 37 per cent of the 270 mission statements were declared 'unofficial' and invalid.

Values

The values of the museums were identified using a key word approach. The three main values were concerned with education (in its broadest sense), access and enjoy-ment. Of the 171 valid questionnaires, 61 referred to education.

> The advancement of the education of the public in the maritime archae-ology and heritage of the local areas. (Yarmouth Maritime Heritage Centre, Isle of Wight)

A further 31 made reference to understanding (14), knowledge (6), inform (6), learn (4) and enlighten (1).

> To promote the appreciation and understanding of the men and women who have made and are making British history and culture through the medium of portraits. (National Portrait Gallery)

Access was also an important value, mentioned 26 times.

> Promoting creativity, artistic excellence, and accessibility through a pro-gramme of stimulating exhibition, interpretative work and activities. (Wolverhampton Arts and Museum Service)

Even more popular, however, were references to enjoyment, which occur in 35 of the statements.

> To enable and enhance public enjoyment and appreciation of the natural, artistic and cultural heritage of the District of Woodspring. (Woodspring Museum)

Other values referred to were indicated by the word 'interest' (15), 'quality' (11) and 'stimulate' (7).

> To collect, preserve and interpret items which excite curiosity and interest in the history of Tamworth and its people. (Tamworth Castle Museum)

> The museum and heritage service will provide high quality services for the Royal Borough of Kingston. (Kingston-Upon-Thames Museum and Heritage Centre)

> To communicate and stimulate curiosity and fascination in the cultural and industrial heritage of inland waterways. (The Boat Museum, Ellesmere Port)

In total, 132 of the 171 valid questionnaires made some reference to values (77 per cent).

Stakeholders

There were many references to some of the broader stakeholder constituencies associated with museums, public (52), all (15), visitors (12), nation (2) and customers (2) all received mentions.

> The museum exists to promote the public's understanding of the history and contemporary practice of science, medicine, technology, and industry. (The Science Museum)

> To promote the services of Bolton museums and art gallery through the care, interpretation and development of the collections for the enjoyment and education of all. (Bolton Museums and Art Gallery)

In addition to this 41 statements made reference to more specific sets of stakeholders, such as 'residents' or 'community'.

> The museum service aims to provide a high quality service to Newham residents that is educational, accessible, relevant and popular. (Newham Museum Service)

> To provide a museum service to all people living in or visiting Wakefield Metropolitan District. (Wakefield Museums Service)

This type of statement is of course most common among local authority museum services. Specialist museum services such as company or regimental museums, frequently make reference to specialist stakeholder groups.

Functional or strategic?

Two-thirds of the mission statements analysed may be described as functional. Only 33 per cent of them made any reference to aims and none contained any statements which could be interpreted as being an indication of the museum's strategy. A typical example of a functional mission statement is:

> To collect, document, preserve, exhibit and interpret material evidence
> and associated information concerning the human and natural history of
> the Stewartry for the public benefit. (The Stewartry Museum)

The conservative nature of the mission statements is emphasized by the fact that 66 per cent of them focused on collections and visitors and all, of course, made reference to collections.

This emphasis on the function of museums is reinforced by the heavy reliance of many statements on the Museums Association (MA) or The International Council of Museums (ICOM) definition of a museum, although few were quite as blatant as the respondent for Egham Museum, who stated that their mission statement was 'as per ICOM definition for the local area of Egham, Eaglefield Green, Virginia Water and Thorpe'. Our analysis found that 70 per cent of statements contained at least three out of the six elements in the MA definition. Some statements almost replicated word for word the MA definition.

> To collect, preserve, document, exhibit and interpret material evidence
> of Hereford and Worcester's history for the public benefit.

Others simply utilized the key words or adapted the basic definition to their local needs.

Conclusions

We have agreed that the literature on leadership and mission statements indicates that there is a very wide range of views about the empirical evidence available to us. The studies (largely carried out in the for-profit business sector) suggest that there is little consensus about the most appropriate approaches to leadership and that even the most recent mission statement models are contentious.

However, our study of what managers expect of a leader in museums gives a much less equivocal picture. The importance attached to the leader engaging in strategic leadership is quite clear. This may well reflect a considerable degree of concern and uncertainty, related to the weak position museums tend to hold in their operating environment. But it is a positive pointer to what leaders need to be doing.

One opportunity available to leaders is to use mission statements to clearly communicate the strategic direction of the museum for the benefit of all stakeholders but, perhaps particularly, their operational managers. The basic contents analysis which we have carried out suggests that this opportunity is not yet being fully realized, but the importance of communicating to stakeholders – highlighted by the focus group – is at least recognized.

Mission statements' potential as a leadership tool is probably not well understood. Most managers (in interviews) indicate that they are sceptical of their value and see them as something which they feel they ought to provide to satisfy an external stakeholder – usually a funding body – as part of the strategic planning process. This negative image of the mission statement is further reflected in the type of statement produced – functional rather than strategic. Certainly a link between mission and leadership is rarely made by museum leaders or managers themselves.

Our findings require further investigation but there is a strong suggestion that the requirements of museum leadership are readily recognizable. Furthermore, while the usual concerns about style and method cannot be set aside, the museum leader could considerably enhance his or her effectiveness by making more strategic use of the mission statement. As a whole, this piece of research emphasizes the importance of the leader's role as strategist and stakeholder manager while not denying that other roles may also be significant, depending upon the museum's particular circumstances. The museum leader emerges as a strategy, stakeholder and contingency manager.

Note

Stuart W. Davies, formerly Director of Strategy and Planning at the Museums, Libraries and Archives Council in the UK, has written extensively on issues of museum management. This chapter first appeared in Kevin Moore's edited volume, *Management in Museums* (1999).

References

Bennis, W. and Nanus, B. (1985) *Leaders: The strategies for taking charge* (New York: Harper and Row).

Campbell, A. and Tawadey, K. (eds) (1990) *Mission and Business Philosophy* (London: Butterworth-Heinemann).

Campbell, A. and Yeung, S. (1991) 'Brief Case: Mission, Vision and Strategic Intent', *Long Range Planning* 24 (4): 10–20.

David, F. (1989) 'How Companies Define their Museum', *Long Range Planning* 22 (1): 90–7.

Davies, S.W. and Glaister, K.W. (1996) 'Spurs to Higher Things? Mission Statements of UK universities', *Higher Education Quarterly* 50 (4): 261–94.

Drucker, P.F. (1973) *Management: Tasks, Responsibilities and Practices* (New York: Harper and Row).

Klemm, M., Sanderson, S. and Luffman, G. (1991) 'Mission Statements: Selling Corporate Values to Employees', *Long Range Planning* 24 (3): 73–8.

Kotter, J.P. (1990) *The Leadership Factor* (London: Collier Macmillan).

McGinnis, V. (1981) 'The Mission Statement: A Key Step in Strategic Planning', *Business* November/December: 39–43.

Matejka, K., Kurke, B. and Gregory, B. (1993) 'Mission Impossible? Designing a Great Mission Statement to Ignite Your Plans', *Management Decision* 31 (4): 37–47.

Piercy, N.F. and Morgan, N.A. (1994) 'Mission Analysis: An Operational Approach', *Journal of General Management* 19 (3): 1–19.

Shackleton, V. (1995) *Business Leadership* (London: Routledge).

Chapter 17

Interim Directorships in Museums

Their impact on individuals and significance to institutions

Robert I. Goler

Introduction

CHANGE IN ORGANIZATIONAL leadership is generally seen as a period of stress, from the board member who is asked to take a more active administrative role, to the staff who can feel that their institution is 'rudderless.' Throughout the nonprofit sector such transitions are being recognized increasingly as an important and potentially beneficial time in the life of a cultural organization. Museums wishing to foster staff loyalty and to maintain programmatic continuity should adopt this perspective when planning the search for a new director.

Several factors are contributing to this realization. First, the average tenure of museum directors is becoming shorter. In the late 1980s, Douglas Noble determined that executive directors in museums remained at their posts for an average of 7.3 years, a figure that he found comparable to other nonprofit organizations at the time. That figure now appears to be shortening. A 1999 survey by Compass Point found that the average tenure of nonprofit leaders had dropped to 5.9 years, with a median tenure of just 4.25 years.[1]

This situation is compounded by leadership burnout in the museum profession. The challenges of arts leadership are not new, but they do appear to be on the rise. A quarter century ago, Toole (1974) lamented the museum director as a 'sandwich man,' charged to move the institution forward with dynamic exhibitions and competent management, while perilously balancing his personal scholarship with the ever-pressing needs of the museum's competing constituencies. In the 1990s, the imperative of a director to be a skilled fundraiser, as well as a scholar, connoisseur, and administrator was reiterated by Riley and Urich (1996). In an article published more recently, Schwarzer (2001) noted that the increasing financial

Source: *Museum Management and Curatorship*, vol. 19, no. 4 (2004): 385–402.

complexity of museums, coupled with changes toward more inclusive management styles and the need to balance audience and curatorial goals, have further increased the tensions on museum leaders. The stress once associated with the largest and most prominent of museum directorships now appears to have spread deep into the museum community. Combined with the increasing frequency of executive turnover, this change suggests that new attitudes on transitions are required.

New literature on cultural organizations argues that museums would benefit from using executive transitions as a period of strategic assessment. Research conducted by Ferrin (2002) on museums, and Thibodeau (2002) on nonprofit performing arts groups, points to the benefits of hiring an independent professional as an interim director. These 'deliberate' interims, as they are called in this paper, are sometimes able to offer independent thinking and decisive actions. Similar approaches have long been used in religious organizations and institutions of higher learning.[2] Ferrin and Thibodeau acknowledge that most cultural organizations shy away from this approach, primarily because of the higher costs associated with hiring an interim while simultaneously conducting an executive search. A secondary concern is that an outsider often requires time to learn enough about the organization in order to make effective leadership decisions, at which time the post would be assumed by the new appointee. On the other hand, having an independent assessment of the organization's strengths and weaknesses can identify issues that would impede the search for a new director. In time, as more museums turn to outside professionals for executive transition services, it would be useful to revisit this approach.

There is much to be gained from greater use of deliberate interims, but meanwhile most cultural organizations continue to appoint an interim director from within the ranks. This situation is unlikely to change in the near term, and it is important for the museum community to better understand the significance of this pattern. Part of the challenge facing decision-makers in the museum community is the relative paucity of detailed information on personnel decisions and the social ecology of museums. Museum professionals and scholars have underscored the importance of better understanding the implications of staffing decisions in museums. In the preface to a volume of case studies on museums undergoing change, Elaine Heumann Gurian noted that 'management has a responsibility to pay attention to the psychological and emotional well-being of their staff and themselves.' The goal, she argues, is to 'allow workers to concentrate better on quality performance' (Gurian 1995). Similarly, Schwarzer (2001: 67) has called for more attention to the human resources of museums, with specific attention to the needs of staff members during transitions to help 'create a bright future for all our talent.' A survey of interim museum directors that I conducted sheds some light on the impact of these experiences upon the individuals who serve as interims.

Between 1993 and 1996, museum professionals were invited to participate in a survey of interim leadership. This survey, the first on this topic conducted in the museum field, solicited information from those who had served as interim directors. Among the data requested were the type of institution served, the duration of the interim directorship, demographic and professional information on the interim leader, as well as on the outgoing and incoming leaders. A total of 52 interim experiences reflecting the direct involvement of 48 different individuals were ultimately selected for inclusion in this study. (The survey methodology is described in Appendix A.) Their responses suggest that interim directorships constitute a pivotal moment in the careers of museum professionals.

The individuals who participated in the survey worked in a range of institutions closely mirroring the diversity of America's museums. To gauge the range of survey participants, a comparison was made between the museums they represented and the advertised positions for museum directors during a 12-month period, within the period of the internship directorship survey (Table 17.1).

Using the categories established by the American Association of Museums for the Museum Universe Survey illustrates that there are no significant variations between the survey participants and those museums seeking directors in the survey period.[3] In both groups, art museums are most numerous, followed closely by history museums and historic sites. There were slightly fewer specialized museums in the survey pool (9.8% compared to 16.7%, Table 17.1a), but this category was third in each group.

Table 17.1   Disciplinary distribution of institutions

(A) Comparison of all categories

Discipline	% in survey (N = 52)	% advertised (N = 221)[a]
Aquarium/arboretum	0	0.9
Art	33.3	36.7
Children's	3.9	3.2
General	5.9	4.1
History/historic site	33.3	29.4
Natural history	9.8	5.0
Nature center/planetarium	0	0
Science/technology	3.9	4.1
Specialized	9.8	16.7
Zoo	0	0
Total	**99.9**	**100.1**

(B) Comparison of largest categories

Ranking	Survey	AVISO
1st	Art[b]	Art
2nd	History/historic site[b]	History/historic site
3rd	Specialized[c]	Specialized
4th	Natural history[c]	Natural history

Notes:
[a] These figures were compiled from the monthly personnel listings in the 1995 issues of *AVISO*, the American Association of Museum's newsletter and the leading recruitment organ for the museum profession. Variance of totals from 100% reflect fractional calculations.
[b] Tied with 2nd place.
[c] Tied with 4th place.

The survey data also point to some general characteristics of interim directorships. Specifically, it is possible to identify the average duration of an interim directorship, to judge how frequently interim directors assume the permanent directorships, and to reflect upon the subsequent career directions of those who served as interims.

Interim appointments

In most cases, boards appoint a senior staff member who is generally a deputy director, curator or development officer. Amidst the flurry of activity surrounding the departure of a leader, a great deal of effort goes into strategies to maintain forward momentum and organizational continuity. Appointing an internal individual is seen as a means of advancing the organization's current agenda. Rarely does anyone stop to consider the impact of an internal appointment on both the candidate and the museum. This survey helps to delineate this impact.

Trustees tend to select an individual in whom they have observed signs of maturity and who has been active in fulfilling the institution's mission. Evidence of service with the organization appears to be generally sought after, with an emphasis on providing continuity and stability. The typical profile of an interim is a female in her early 40s, who has served as a senior manager at the organization for seven years (Table 17.2). The ages of the interims ranged from 21 to 73 years, with an average of 42.9 years (Table 17.2b). The average length of service with the museum prior to appointment was 6.7 years (Table 17.2c), although this factor varied widely. In one case, a professor with 34 years of affiliation with a university museum was selected with the knowledge that he would then retire from the university. At the other end of the spectrum, it is interesting to note that half (50.0%) of those chosen to be interim directors had been at the museum for less than five years, and that nearly one out of seven (14.3%) had been with the organization for less than one year. It was not unusual for an individual to join the staff only to find that s/he was interim director a few months later! Precisely why these newly hired staff members were chosen is a topic for further investigation.

Duration

The average duration of interim directorships was 10.7 months (Table 17.3a). The experiences documented in the survey ranged from three weeks to 41 months, with the largest percentage (21.2%) lasting 12 months. This is consistent with Ferrin's (2002: 11) conclusion that 'the typical museum can expect a period of up to nine months to elapse' between permanent directors.

Supplemental pay

Most interim directors saw increases in their paychecks. Seven out of ten interims received a pay increase for the duration of the interim period ranging from 'a

Table 17.2   Interim candidate characteristics[a]

(A) Gender (N = 48)	
Female	74%
Male	26%

(B) Age in years (N = 48)	
20–29	10.6%
30–39	25.5%
40–49	42.6%
50–59	17.0%
60+	4.3%
	100%
Average	42.9 years

(C) Years of service (prior to appointment, N = 42)	
0–1	14.3%
1–5	35.7%
6–10	28.6%
10+	21.4%
Average	6.7 years

NB: The reasons for the change in N values are because (a) one interim director began a second interim within a single year; and (b) several interim directors had non-employee relationships with the Museum prior to appointment that rendered their 'years of service' ambiguous.
Note:
[a] Data for deliberate interims not included.

pittance' to 'a permanent adjustment to my salary' (Table 17.3b). In addition, a significant proportion of those who did not assume the permanent directorship obtained salary increases in the positions to which they returned following the transition. For those who left the museum for new posts, it can be safely assumed that a substantial number received pay increases, particularly those who went onto museum directorships elsewhere.

There appeared to be no causal correspondence between the receipt of supplemental pay and subsequent appointment to directorships. However, as all of the men and all but two of the women who were ultimately offered the directorship had received bonus pay, the receipt of additional pay did seem to be a significant indicator in advancement. Does paying an interim director increase the chances for the interim to assert authority? Or does it make the board more cognizant of that individual's leadership abilities? Further investigation is needed to determine if this is indeed a true indicator, and how it functions.

Table 17.3   Characteristics of interim situations

(A) Duration in months, reported in quarters ($N = 52$)

1–3	13.5%
4–6	17.6%
7–9	15.3%
10–12	34.6%
13–15	7.6%
16–23	0.0%
24+	11.5%
	100.1%
Average	10.7 months
Shortest	3 weeks
Longest	41 months

(B) Supplemental pay ($N = 52$)

Yes	69.2%
No	30.7%
	99.9%

Background experience

Those selected as interim directors did not come from any particular programmatic area or department of the museum. Interims came from administrative (deputy or assistant director, vice president of finance), curatorial (curator, director of collections), and education departments. While one would expect that there would be a correlation between the size of an institution and the designation of an interim director from the administrative ranks (reflecting the inherent hierarchy of a larger bureaucracy), this was not always the case. For example, in the case of one college-run institution, the administrative assistant was designated. A noteworthy exception, however, was for individuals who had previous experience as interims. These individuals were more likely to be tapped for the interim directorship than were their colleagues, a circumstance that prompted one individual who had served three times as an interim to describe himself as being 'type cast as an Acting Director.' None of the institutions represented had a dual leadership structure, and it would be worth further investigation to explore the dynamics of the interim experience in such situations.

Leadership effect

The transition to the interim directorship can be a traumatic, and intense, form of role initiation for the incumbent. The individual moves overnight from a staff position with internal collegial relationships and external professional goals, into a managerial role where her/his performance is being judged externally by a new set of professionals (including major funders and other critical organizational stake-holders), as well as internally by both the staff s/he supervises (including former colleagues) and the trustees to whom s/he reports.[4] As one former interim director explained: 'The experience made me aware of the difficulties of being promoted from a pool of peers, dealing with a group of older male trustees and having little credibility with both.' Nevertheless, the interim directorship appears to be a for-mative period in the careers of museum professionals.

A significant proportion of interim directors went on to become directors. Overall, one out of every three interims went on to lead either the institution at which they served as interim (Table 17.4a), or another institution later in their career (Table 17.4d). At the same time, fully one-quarter of the unsuccessful candidates soon left the museum. In short, life after an interim directorship was rarely the same as before.

Serving in an interim position stimulated leadership interest in some indi-viduals and gave them enhanced confidence and credibility as managers. As one respondent noted, 'I established a new network of personal contacts.' 'The interim directorship was great to have on my resume as an experience when starting my career,' commented another, 'and became a launching pad from grad school to the directorship path.' In this sense, appointment to an interim directorship provides a significant opportunity to test and develop the skills for managerial responsibilit-ies. 'During my tenure as interim director,' another respondent recalled, 'I "learned the ropes" intensively. The experience helped to offset my lack of formal museum training.'

Compared with the overall pool of interim directors, those who applied for the permanent position were more than twice as likely to receive the appointment (45.5% over 19.1%, Table 17.4a). The evidence in this survey suggests that a slightly higher percentage of female interim directors were subsequently appointed to the institution's directorship (21.6% as compared with 19.1% for the overall pool). Survey participants were asked to track the course of their career subsequent to the interim experience. Numerous individuals (both male and female) remarked on the fact that the interim experience gave them the confidence and experience to assume directorships at other museums later in their careers. In addition, for those who were appointed director at the institutions where they had served as interim director, one out of seven interim directors who were unsuccessful can-didates subsequently went on to become directors at other institutions. Together 60% of the interim directors went on to permanent directorships at some point in their careers. Interim directorships appear to be a strong indicator of future executive leadership appointments.

As would be expected, those individuals who applied unsuccessfully for the permanent directorship were more likely to leave the museum than those interims who had not applied (25% as opposed to 18.9%, Table 17.4c). One respondent, who left the institution shortly after the new director's appointment (and became a director elsewhere after four months' unemployment), summarized his reaction in blunt terms: 'I was deemed to be unqualified.' The fact that this individual was subsequently appointed director at another institution, following four months of

Table 17.4 Career impact of interim directorships

(A) Rate of director appointment (for interim directors)

All interims	19.1%
Interims who were candidates	45.5%

(B) Post-interim retention rates (for all non-directors)

Remained at museum	81.1%
Former job	(70.0% of above)
New position	(30.0% of above)
Left institution[a]	18.9%
Interims who later became directors	14.6%
	100.0%[b]

(C) Post-interim retention rates (for unsuccessful director applicants)

Returned to former duties	33.3%
Assumed new duties	41.7%
Departed institution[c]	25.0%
	100.0%

(D) Post-interim directorship appointments (for all non-directors)

Interims who later became directors[d]	14.6%

Notes:

[a] Individuals who indicated that they departed as a result of the interim directorship (e.g., clashes with new director, personal dissatisfaction). Period prior to departure ranged from one week to 20 months.

[b] Total includes respondents who served as interims more than once at the same institution; two became candidates during their second interim experience at the same institution, and another during a third interim experience.

[c] Individuals who indicated that they departed as a result of the interim directorship (e.g., clashes with new director, personal dissatisfaction). Period prior to departure ranged from one week to 20 months.

[d] Those who accepted directorships later in their career (after the interim appointment).

unemployment, only underscores the critical role that organizational culture plays in museums and the leadership appointments of trustees.

The fact that up to one-quarter of all interim directors left their museums upon the conclusion of their assignments appears noteworthy. The vacancies they left behind constituted a 'second wave' of departures, the first being that of the former director. These 'second wave' departures seem to be an unexpected consequence of the boards' intentions to select individuals who would provide long-term continuity to the museum (Table 17.4b).

The high rate of 'second wave' departures is not unique to the museum community. Investigations by Farquhar indicate that this is a common phenomenon in both the public and nonprofit sectors. Her study of 43 public administration executives found that 'almost half of the interim directors who did not get the [director] job were gone within a couple of years' (Farquhar 1991).

There may be a number of reasons for the high rate of 'second wave' departures, in addition to the disappointment of not getting the directorship. The stress of developing new relationships with a range of individuals (especially the director–board dynamics unique to the executive position), representing the museum to multiple stakeholders, and simultaneously developing effective leadership skills, pose special challenges to the interim director. When one considers that one out of seven interim directors were designated within less than one year's service at the organization, and that virtually all found themselves reporting to a board of trustees rather than to a single supervisor, perhaps it is less surprising that so many interims left the institution following their temporary appointments. Some respondents indicated that they had difficulty returning to their former posts after exercising executive authority. Others remarked on stressful relationships with the new director, including the belief that they were perceived as a threat to that individual's authority.

Post-interim experience

Of those who remain at the museum after the selection of a new director, 30% received new positions that also included a permanent salary adjustment (Table 17.4b). The most prevalent titles used for these positions were 'associate' or 'deputy' directorships and, in most cases, represented a new managerial level for the organization. In some cases, these arrangements were made explicitly to retain individuals who were seen to be valuable employees. One interim who received a new position after completing her second interim directorship in five years commented: 'Since I had successfully been Acting Director for so long, I would not have planned to stay if the current arrangement had not been made.' Reflecting on the newly created position he received after an interim appointment, another proclaimed: 'I now have a greater commitment to the institution than prior to the search.' Those who were unsuccessful candidates for the directorship were more likely (41.7% as compared with 30%) to secure these new positions within their museums than were those interims who chose not to be candidates (Table 17.4c).

Multiple interim experiences

A small cohort of respondents reflected alternative approaches to the most common interim experience. The first of these were individuals who had served as interims more than once. Most of these served twice, and two had been interim directors on three different occasions. Among those who had served two interim periods, half were promoted to the permanent directorship after their second interim directorship, reporting that they had been asked to assume the helm of their organization following the short and unsuccessful tenures of individuals who had been appointed directors in the first search. 'I was given opportunities to make leadership decisions,' remarked one individual about her first interim experience. 'I then had to learn how to gracefully pick up strings left untied by an unethical director.'[5]

Deliberate interims

The second group within the survey comprised six 'deliberate' interim appointments. These individuals were hired specifically to serve as interim directors and were not candidates for the permanent position. They included an artist (for an art museum), an independent curator, and a trustee. While too small a pool from which to draw general demographic characteristics, these individuals appear to fit the general criteria of maturity and commitment to mission. A small number of organizations turned to trustees for interim leadership. The current emphasis of increasing board diversity, including efforts to recruit active business and corporate leaders, makes it doubtful that this option will become widespread. The trustees' desire for the organization to maintain a stable position within the community also may have influenced this selection.

These deliberate interims provided a special style of leadership to the organization. Since they were not interested in a regular position at the museum and would never work as a peer with those they supervised, they were able to assert an authority comparable to that of a permanent director. These individuals were also able to make independent assessments about the organization, identifying strengths and weaknesses among the programs, staff, and structure that could be brought to the attention of the trustees and that would help orient the new director. One individual noted that 'not being a regular staff person put me in a different relationship with the board,' and enabled her to implement a progressive personnel policy and win increased authority for the directorship, a change that simplified her successor's job. Finally, in some cases, deliberate interims were able to develop skills uniquely suited to transitional situations. Two respondents to the survey had been recruited to interim positions at museums specifically because of their experience as deliberate interims elsewhere. One individual jokingly commented that, having served at two museums in his community, he was wondering whether the third museum in town was waiting for him to conclude his current assignment before it fired its director!

When properly handled, interim directorships can identify previously unknown, or under-developed, skills among those on staff. Farquhar (1991: 201; 1994: 53) describes the interim period as 'a strategic window' that can bridge the difficulties of the past with the plans for the future into 'an active and challenging time for employees and a watershed organization transition'. It also is a period that provides the opportunity for the interim to acquire the skills of executive leadership, while refining an understanding of the obligations of facilitating organizational goals over professional plans (Chapman et al. 1988: 85–87). In this manner, an individual who has professional or charismatic abilities may become accustomed to the responsibilities of organizational authority. As one interim noted: 'I had not been perceived as having ability to run anything. The board was surprised and pleased with my performance.' This individual used her professional knowledge to develop executive authority. The ability to exploit the dynamic qualities of this period, however, demands a clear vision of what can be accomplished and how to motivate the staff, trustees, and stakeholders. This vision needs to be articulated.

Further investigations

Significant questions about interim director appointments remain open for further investigation. Additional research on the dynamics of how interim leadership operates within the museum community would be helpful, particularly in the form of a comparative study of institutions representing different disciplines and scales of operation. Most important is the need to understand how the selection of an internal interim director alters the social ecology within the museum. What dynamics take place when an interim director returns to his or her former post? Are there ripple effects on staff, trustees, and volunteers when an internal interim director leaves the museum? What about external stakeholders? Does the departure of a long-standing development director or influential curator impact the museum's relationship with its funders and donors beyond what would normally be expected when a director leaves? How does the decision to select an internal candidate affect future transition procedures at the museum?

It seems clear that interim directorships have significant influence on individual career paths and upon the attainment of institutional goals. The reality that an employee could be appointed, often without prior consultation, to a position that invariably alters his or her career path also raises significant ethical questions. Since it appears that serving as an interim has serious implications for the post-interim employment pattern of an individual, boards need to consciously weigh the prospect of losing their second most significant staff member. In addition, there may be concern that asking a staff member to assume the duties of the interim directorship will interrupt that individual's ability to serve the organization in an area where s/he has proven competence. Is that a responsible action for the organization to take?

Ethical considerations

The interim directorship also prompts important ethical considerations. No figures have been compiled on those who have declined the opportunity to serve as an interim director, but the power differential between a board member and a second-level staff member may make it extremely difficult for the latter to reject an interim post. After all, s/he is committed to the institution and its goals, wants to see those activities continue, and may be concerned that declining the offer could damage his or her standing within the organization. Not to mention the honor of being asked to assume a position of greater responsibility. Yet, for some, there must be reticence about leaving one's 'career' to fill in as an interim director. Will relationships with colleagues be altered? What about the stress associated with management responsibilities? At what point does the prospect of a higher income become a factor?

Further investigation needs to be conducted to confirm the degree to which the selection of newly hired staff members for interim posts is primarily a phenomenon of small institutions. Given the surprisingly high percentage of interims drawn

from among newly employed individuals, coupled with the enormous responsibilities and career implications of being chosen to serve as an interim director, museum
associations may wish to provide specialized support and training to interim directors.
Some nonprofit organizations have begun to offer executive transition services to
the sector as a whole to help support such efforts.[6] In recent years, sessions on
interim directorships have appeared on the annual meeting programs of some museum
associations. Case studies about interim directorships may also prove beneficial to
those attending graduate and mid-career training programs.[7]

Raising awareness of the myriad issues associated with interim periods for trustees
is another important effort to undertake. The abilities of boards to respond to transitional and traumatic episodes varied dramatically, and the newly issued templates
for executive transition from the Museum Trustee Association are an encouraging
sign that professional standards of care can be established for these situations.[8] While
I am unaware of any legal issues that have arisen specifically related to interim directorships, it is not difficult to imagine a scenario where claims of negligence (or
at least poor judgment) in the selection of an unqualified individual might surface.

In addition to the effects of the interim directorship on individuals, it is important to understand how interim directorships alter organizations. Ten months can
be a long time in the life cycle of a nonprofit, and the increased uncertainties associated with transitions can generate anxiety among staff and funders. One investigation of interim nonprofit sector presidents concluded that 'the acting or interim
condition is not a healthy condition, either for the individual occupying the position
or for the institution itself' (Chapman *et al.* 1988: 88). Ferrin has suggested that
interim leadership can adversely affect fundraising. He reported decreased levels
of contributed income for many museums, particularly those with annual operating budgets over US$2 million. In those where a trustee or deliberate interim
was appointed, however, giving increased (Ferrin 2002: 12–13). This is borne out
anecdotally in my research. For example, an independent curator who was offered
an interim directorship at a second-tier institution in the midst of substantial capital
campaign, noted that board members had expressed anxiety about the museum's
substantial capital campaign and wanted assurances that they would be able to tap
her extensive professional and social networks.

Second wave departures

The limited evidence that exists suggests that interim directorships do not play a
significant role in staff turnover. The surprisingly high percentage of 'second wave'
departures of interim directors is, however, a noteworthy exception. Losing the
second most senior professional at a time when the newly appointed director is
just getting acquainted with the organization can only exacerbate the difficulties of
executive transition. Precisely because of these factors, museums should approach
interim periods as a normal part of organizational life. This means putting greater
emphasis on succession planning and on the long-term career development of the
entire staff, with particular attention to senior and mid-level personnel.[9]

Interim directorships are too common and too important to be treated with
stopgap measures, or to be perceived as 'holding periods.' Indeed, it may be that

greater knowledge of interim directorship characteristics will help organizations respond to the increasing rates of executive turnover. As one sociologist noted after completing service as an interim dean, 'all leadership is temporary' (Hall 1995). While this may be true, the process by which succession occurs is important. In his study of newly appointed CEOs, Gifford (1997) noted that outside appointees were more likely to improve organizational performance than were internal candidates, primarily because the outsider was seen by employees as being above internal politics and having the capacity to introduce new ideas from outside the organization. If the museum field continues to turn primarily to insiders for interim appointments, it is important to develop strategies that increase the effectiveness of future interim appointments.

The remarkable nature of 'second wave' interim director departures is that they contradict the fundamental assumptions that guided the selection of the interim director in the first place. By appointing an individual who was mature and had a record of significant service with the museum, one can adduce that the trustees were attempting to maintain continuity and stability within the organization. Who better to select than the second-most prominent professional on staff? Retention of interim directors after the appointment of a new director would seem to be important, yet fully one-quarter of the interims in the study subsequently leave the institution after the designation of the permanent director. As a result, the organization loses both the first- and second-most prominent staff members in succession, not to mention any other staff members who may depart during the interim period, and the new director is left to recruit a new senior staff member. The desire of the newly appointed director to establish a firm power base may also play a role, as several respondents noted that they were perceived as a threat to the new director once they returned to the staff ranks. The opportunity for the new director to undertake this recruitment may represent a positive sign of change for the organization, but it would be important to closely examine the specific circumstances in order to weigh the need for 'cleaning house' against the value of organizational continuity. How can boards provide additional recognition to these individuals? To what extent do incoming directors want to rely on the insights of interim leaders?

Further study should explore the reasons for 'second wave' departures. To what degree, or at what point, do individuals realize that leadership positions are not for them? As one interim reflected: 'The experience made me committed to the idea that I *never* want to be a director.' How many are burned out and frustrated from the pressured dynamics of holding a position of limited authority and/or reduced staffing? Are they forced out by the incoming director? Do they wish to apply the managerial skills they acquired? What steps might institutions take to retain this group of experienced and valuable managers?

If transitional situations are to be addressed as a normal phase of organizational life, it is critical that realistic assessments of the duration, limits of authority, compensation, and post-interim possibilities be recognized. Museums that encourage ethical and organizationally sound decision-making, support mutual respect between staff and trustees, and watch for innovation in diverse professional arenas will have a greater chance of effectively using the remarkable opportunities offered by interim directorships.

Appendix A
Survey methodology

The survey was a two-page questionnaire and was completed voluntarily. Most of those who participated in the survey were self-selecting. However, when I learned of an interim situation that fit the criteria of the survey, I did solicit participation from the incumbents. Copies were distributed at two successive annual meetings of the American Association of Museums, and at the annual meetings of several regional museum associations. In addition, notices soliciting participation appeared in several museum newsletters (e.g., Southeast Museums Conference Newsletter). Participants were asked to submit completed forms by mail or fax.

A total of 64 questionnaires were returned. Of these, 25% were excluded from consideration because critical information was not provided or available, leaving a total pool of 48 participants documenting 52 interim directorships. (Four individuals reported two interim experiences and two more had served three times! Note, however, that not all of these multiple experiences have been included in the tabulations.) It also should be noted that six respondents, whom I have called 'deliberate interims,' had been hired specifically for the interim period and are included in the survey results where appropriate. However, in those instances where their responses do not fit the groups of the traditional interim directors (e.g., length of service prior to appointment), they have not been included in the calculations. Seventeen respondents in the resulting pool (35.4%) were interviewed by phone to review the accuracy of the information and to solicit additional anecdotal comments. Information provided by the participants was not verified by other sources.

The majority of the forms were completed within a reasonable time from the interim experience, increasing the prospect that the information is reliable. While the responses were received at varying lengths of time from the interim experience, 59% were completed within three years of the experience. Approximately 20% of the participants submitted survey forms while still serving as interim directors (and their experiences were tracked until their interim service was completed). In some cases, the participants were contacted to confirm specific points and to track changes in their impressions of the impact that the experience had made upon their careers.

Governance of the institutions in which the interim directorship occurred was also examined. The categories for these groupings were: Private, an independent 501-c-3; Subsidiary, an organization that was governed by a private nonprofit organization (e.g., university or college gallery); and Government. Comparison with the most recent national figures, drawn from the *Data Report from the 1989 National Museum Survey* (1992), indicates consistency with the broadest characteristics of the museum profession (Table 17.1). Information was not collected on the specifics of board structure or on the involvement of the board (or search committee) in the interim period.

It was not feasible to determine and analyze the budget sizes of the museums represented in the interim directorship survey or in the *AVISO* advertisements from available records. Further research should be conducted into the possible relationships between budget size and the strategies for interim directorships.

Notes

Robert I. Goler is a Professor in the Arts Management Program at the American University (Washington DC). This paper was first published in 2004 in *Museum Management and Curatorship*, vol. 19, no. 4.

1   Noble (1988) and Wolford *et al.* (1999). Museum leaders use a range of titles including chief executive officer, director, executive director, and president. For the purpose of this article, the title 'director' refers to the staff member with primary responsibility for the overall operation of the museum. In some cases, these individuals also hold board positions.

2   For discussions of interim directorships in these contexts, see Porcher (1980) and Fretwell (1995).

3   For a description of these categories, see *Museums Count* (1994: 27–30).

4   Toole (1974). For a study of the emotional and political challenges faced by newly appointed managers, see Hill (1992).

5   Paradoxically, in such circumstances, the short term 'permanent' director becomes the de facto interim director. For an insightful analysis of the scenarios caused by 'broken' leadership, see Farquhar (1994: 45).

6   See, for example, the services of CompassPoint to the Bay Area in California (www.compasspoint.org) and those of Transition Guides to nonprofits within Maryland (www.transitionguides.com). In both cases, services are offered to organizations on a fee-for-service basis with substantial subventions made possible through private foundation subventions.

7   A discussion of various pedagogical strategies to improve interim directorships appears in Goler (2003). Sessions were held at the 2003 annual meetings of the American Association for State and Local History and of the Western Museums Conference. By contrast, the sector-wide Alliance for Nonprofit Management has hosted workshops on interim directorships at each of its past four annual meetings.

8   Fisher and Boland, *Executive Transitions* (2003). This volume, combining a narrative and computer-based templates, offers a flexible work plan for boards.

9   For a discussion of the need to give emerging leaders in arts organizations greater managerial training, see *Succession: Arts Leadership for the 21st Century* (2003).

References

Chapman, John E., Chapman, Judy P., and Lobstetter, John O. (1988). The acting or interim leadership position: expectations, perceptions, realities. *Health Care Management Review*, 13(4).

Farquhar, Katherine (1991). Leadership in limbo: organizational dynamics during interim administrations. *Public Administration Review*, 51(3).

——— (1994). The myth of the forever leader. *Human Resource Management*, 34(1).

Ferrin, Richard W. (2002). *The Time Between*. Wakefield Connection, Knoxville, TN.

Fisher, Daryl, and Boland, Colleen (2003). *Executive Transitions*. Museum Trustee Association, Washington, DC.

Fretwell Jr., E.K. (1995). *The Interim Presidency: Guidelines for University and College Boards*. Association of Governing Boards of Universities and Colleges, Washington, DC.

Gifford Jr., Dan (1997). CEO turnover: the importance of symbolism. *Harvard Business Review*, 75(1), 9–10.

Goler, Robert I. (2003). Developing pedagogical tools for more effective interim museum directorships. A paper presented at the Annual Research Conference of the Smithsonian Center for Education and Museum Studies, December 4, 2003 (Available online at <museumstudies.si.edu/goler.pdf>).

Gurian, Elaine Heumann (1995). Preface. In Elaine Heumann Gurian (ed.), *Institutional Trauma: Major Change in Museums and its Effect on Staff* (p. 20). American Association of Museums, Washington, DC.

Hall, Douglas T. (1995). Unplanned executive transitions and the dance of the subidentities. *Human Resource Management*, 34(1), 91.

Hill, Linda A. (1992). *Becoming a Manager: How New Managers Manage the Challenges of Leadership*. Penguin Books, New York.

Museums Count (1994). American Association of Museums, Washington, DC.

National Museum Survey (1992). *Data Report from the 1989 National Museum Survey*. American Association of Museums, Washington, DC.

Noble, Douglas (1988). Turnover among museum directors. *Museum Management and Curatorship*, 7, 25–32.

Porcher, Philip (1980). *What You Can Expect from an Interim Pastor and Interim Consultant*. Alban Institute, Washington.

Riley, Gresham, and Urich, Stephen (1996). Art museum directors: a shrinking pool?. *Museum News*, 75(1), 48–49.

Schwarzer, Marjorie (2001). Turnover at the top: are directors burning out?. *Museum News*, 81(3), 43–49.

Succession: Arts Leadership for the 21st Century (2003). Illinois Arts Alliance Foundation, Chicago, pp. 34–38, 88–92.

Thibodeau, Bruce (2002). *The Performing Arts in Transition*. Arts Consulting Group, Los Angeles.

Toole, K. Ross (1974). The sandwich man: a hard role. *Museum News*, 52(9), 41–42.

Wolford, Timothy, Allison, Mike, and Masaoka, Jan (1999). *Leadership Lost: A Study on Executive Director Tenure and Experience* (p. 8). Compass Point, San Francisco.

Marketing the Museum

Introduction to Part Three

Richard Sandell and Robert R. Janes

Marketing. Three syllables that conjure up images of used-car salesmen, seedy advertising ploys, and continued inducements to conspicuous consumption.

C.L. Fronville, 'Marketing for Museums', p. 169

THE ADOPTION AND APPLICATION of marketing theory and practice in museums have been the subject of fierce and impassioned debate among professionals since the early 1980s (McLean 1997). While some have argued that marketing offers a powerful means through which museums can achieve their missions, others have viewed it with suspicion and have remained sceptical of its appropriateness or fearful of its influence. Although, in recent years this polarized thinking has lessened as museum marketing has become both increasingly widespread and more sophisticated in its application, the extent to which it has been embraced nevertheless remains uneven, and considerable confusion and misunderstanding still surround its purpose and potential.

As a number of commentators have observed (Kawashima 1997; Lewis 1992), there are two distinctive approaches to conceptualizing the role of marketing within the museum literature. The first views it rather narrowly as a set of techniques or tools designed to bring about increased public interest in, and take up of, the museum's (existing and predetermined) offerings. Here, marketing is frequently conflated with sales and publicity practices that are bolted onto existing museum functions in an attempt to address the problems of declining attendances and diminishing funding. Marketing staff and departments operate in a relatively compartmentalized fashion, deploying advertising, public relations and promotional tools in an attempt to attract audiences whose needs and interests have rarely been identified and remain poorly understood.

The second, very different, conceptualization of marketing sees it as an overarching philosophy or orientation: one which places the public at the centre of the museum's operations and which, to a greater or lesser extent, influences all its functions and activities. Here, the museum is attuned to the needs of its visitors and the communities it seeks to serve. Its varied offerings are informed by an awareness and understanding of the interests, perceptions, expectations, needs and preferences of both existing and potential audiences. Marketing is seen as an approach that permeates and helps to guide the entire organization – it is both a function of senior management and a way of working in which all museum personnel are enlisted. In this context, marketing is not concerned solely with communication and promotion, but also plays a part in shaping the museum's strategies and approaches to forward planning.

It is this broader conception of marketing, as both an orientation and a set of specialized practices which, we would argue, is the most useful way to understand its purpose and to realize its value. To view marketing in this way is not, however, to imply that a museum's priorities and overall direction should be wholly determined by the needs of visitors and the forces of the marketplace. As many commentators have observed, such an approach could potentially lead to a compromising of the organization's mission and the distortion of its activities (Lewis 1992). Rather, marketing should be viewed as a process which enables museums to achieve their objectives by building and sustaining relationships with a range of audiences (McLean 1997). Traditionally associated with efforts to increase audiences and maximize income, there is also growing recognition of the part that marketing can play in helping museums to achieve their socially oriented goals, to broaden access and engage groups that have traditionally been underrepresented in their audience profiles.

The articles included in this section of the reader offer diverse perspectives on the subject. While some provide an overview of the key issues that have featured in ongoing debates about the use of marketing within the museum context, others discuss the findings of empirical research into specific aspects of practice or present specific case studies and examples which demonstrate the impact of marketing on museum thinking and operations.

The opportunities and benefits, as well as the challenges and risks associated with museum marketing, are addressed in the articles by Jean-Michel Tobelem and Neil and Philip Kotler. Tobelem's perceptive analysis makes a powerful case for the value of marketing while drawing attention to the need to bend its application to the specificities of the museum. Marketing philosophy and practice, he argues, cannot be transplanted without modification from the for-profit environment in which they originated and have been most fully developed. Rather, they must be adapted to suit the requirements of the museum context. Neil and Philip Kotler draw on wide-ranging research and a rich array of examples to examine the application of specific marketing strategies, tools and techniques to the challenge of equipping museums to thrive in an increasingly competitive environment.

The articles by Zahava Doering, Ruth Rentschler, Carol Komatsuka and Alix Slater appropriately turn our attention specifically to museum audiences. Doering's categorization of the different ways museums view their publics helps to show how the changing environments within which organizations are operating can shape the nature of their relationships with audiences and, more particularly, the ways in which visitor experiences are conceived and evaluated. Rentschler highlights the impact of the fragmentary and partial understanding of audiences with which many museums operate, and proposes the greater use of segmentation as a means to understand the diverse needs and expectations of different user groups. She also introduces the concept of relationship marketing as a process by which museums can attempt to build long-term, sustainable relationships with their visitors, while acknowledging that little formal research has been conducted to explore the potential usefulness of this approach. Alix Slater's comprehensive analysis of museum membership schemes makes an important contribution towards addressing this gap in knowledge through in-depth empirical investigation of organizations in the UK. Komatsuka's account of the ways in which the Japanese American National Museum sought to gain a better understanding of its visitors provides a powerful illustration of the value of audience research as a tool for achieving broader organizational objectives. The museum's use of innovative approaches to researching visitor experiences also illustrates the trend towards collaborative, partnership-based museum practices.

The final two contributions, by Victoria Alexander and Andy Martin, consider the wide-reaching effects on museum operations of shifting economic circumstances and, in particular, diminishing public funding. Alexander's research highlights the growing influence of market forces and the impact on museum activities and goals of an increasing reliance on income generated through private sector support and commercial activities. Martin focuses on the thorny issue of admission charges and examines the effects of their removal on the visitorships of British museums. While free admission has often been viewed as a means by which access to museums can be increased, the findings of the study he describes highlight the importance of understanding the multiple barriers which continue to deter some groups from visiting.

References

Fronville, C.L. (1985) 'Marketing for museums: for-profit techniques in a non-profit world', *Curator*, 28(3): 169–182.

Kawashima, N. (1997) *Museum Management in a Time of Change*, Centre for the Study of Cultural Policy, Warwick: University of Warwick.

Lewis, P. (1992) 'Museums and marketing', in J.M.A Thompson *et al.* (ed) *Manual of Curatorship: a guide to museum practice*, London: Museums Association/ Butterworth.

McLean, F. (1997) *Marketing the Museum*, London and New York: Routledge.

Chapter 18

The Marketing Approach in Museums

Jean-Michel Tobelem

Introduction

MUSEUMS AND MONUMENTS have been propelled into a world of economics which is fundamentally foreign to them. They are not only subjected
to the rigours of theoretical economic analysis but may also thereby come to be
seen in narrowly financial terms: operating budget, manpower requirements, commercial returns, visitor numbers, value of acquisitions . . . Indeed, today we talk
of the museum industry and the institutions as 'cultural enterprises', seeing curators in the same light as company managers (Musées et économie 1992a, b). One
observes concurrently the increasing involvement of museums in all forms of market mechanisms accompanied by the new techniques of management demanded by
the changed environment and increasing complexity of the issues to be addressed
(exhibition planning, fund raising, budget control, computerization, etc.). Museums,
in the company of the entire cultural sector, have therefore become progressively
preoccupied with business concerns about costs, financing, evaluation, development,
and profitability. Economics, of which the discipline is overwhelmingly theoretical,
and management, with its more practical aims, have thus increasingly acquired legit-
imacy in a domain from which they had previously been excluded, that of culture
(Côté 1991). These ways of thinking have brought with them their traditional tools
of analysis and particularly the use of statistical methods and economic modelling.
  Likewise, perceptions of 'cultural heritage' have changed. This is demonstrated
by the growing importance accorded to the economic spin-off to be derived from
the cultural heritage by state bodies and local administrations on the one hand,
and the emergence of a thriving private commercial sector exploiting the resources
of the cultural heritage on the other. Be it driven by local or national economic

Source: *Museum Management and Curatorship*, vol. 16, no. 4 (1998): 337–354.

development, the need to establish tourism policies, or general urban renewal, the potential economic impact of monuments and museums today lies at the centre of the problematical issues posed by the cultural heritage. Meanwhile the projects designed to develop monuments and sites proliferate, including in France, for example, the Pont du Gard, Carnac, the Palace of the Popes at Avignon, Vézelay, Provins, the Pointe du Raz, Conques and the châteaux of the Valley of the Loire, even though each of these sites has different characteristics and, consequently, presents different problems. Presentation, management, marketing, and commercial exploitation are terms in the new vocabulary which flourishes with reference to both museums and monuments.

The causes of this phenomenon appear to be of several types: the penetration of economic theory into the non-commercial sector, the increase in the revenues to be generated by cultural tourism, and the growing power of local politicians in the cultural domain. It is in this context that marketing, a concept until recently all but unknown to museums, tends to put in its appearance, even though considerable confusion still reigns as to its precise objectives and methods. It therefore seems necessary to define marketing more precisely, to establish the reasons for its appearance, to see how it may be applied within the world of museums, to note its specific characteristics in this particular context, and to examine those risks which may be incurred through its uncontrolled use by those in charge of such institutions.

Based on a programme of research work on the subject, the approach adopted here consists of demonstrating, with particular reference to French experience, the evolution of the marketing approach in museums, and seeking to illustrate the relevance of this discipline as compared with other methods of analysis; while at the same time stressing that it is not the only answer to all the questions museums ask themselves and that the conditions appropriate for its application demand a certain number of precautions.

What is marketing?

For many people marketing is traditionally seen as the technique which a business employs to sell its products (cars, detergent) or services (banking, data management) to consumers, mainly by means of advertising. This initial response is notwithstanding the fact that marketing itself has experienced a twofold transformation of which the people who use the technical vocabulary are not always fully aware. On the one hand, the consumer has progressively been moved into the centre of the marketing operation, and on the other hand, the concept has been extended into the world of public service and non-profit institutions (Tobelem 1997).

The first phenomenon to be addressed is the evolution of marketing from product-centred to consumer-centred, since in the begining it was the product intended for the market place which was the focus for those in business responsible for marketing. Above all, the product had to be improved in order to sell it to a maximum number of consumers. In a second phase, emphasis was placed on the rationalization of the production process. Thanks to a parallel improvement of distribution systems, the economically more advanced societies entered the era of mass consumption marked by the diffusion of Henry Ford's production techniques.

The period which followed, overshadowed by the recession of the 1930s, made the necessity of selling the first priority of businesses, using all the panoply of advertising devices in the attempt to influence the act of purchasing by the consumer. Today's marketing situation is characterized by the importance accorded to the individual consumer – to the analysis of his needs, characteristics, perceptions, and aspirations – thus differing quite profoundly from its original conception (Kotler and Andreasen 1987).

Here we find a complete reversal of perspective which necessitates a painstaking analysis of preferences and preoccupations of the most knowledgeable and sophisticated consumers since this change passes from a marketing based on supply to a marketing centred on demand. Studies and research therefore must guide organizations to make available products ever better adapted to consumer needs. One can try to transpose this schema of analysis to the world of museums. In the first stage, which reflects a situation on its way out, the attention of those responsible is focused on the collections, ignoring the wishes of the public. Generally satisfied with what he presents and how he presents it, the curator tends to blame the ignorance or indifference of visitors for low attendance figures. In the second stage, he is forced to improve the effectiveness of the museum by improving the quality of the individual visit and thereby increasing attendance figures. The museum will present more temporary exhibitions, create new programmes and offer new services, without necessarily defining precisely the requirements of the visitors (and the wishes of non-visitors) and without being able to evaluate precisely the degree of satisfaction achieved. Nonetheless, these last years have shown an increase in published museum visitor studies, providing an indication that many museums want to know more about the expectations of different types of public.

The third stage would be for a museum to use communications and public relations in order to raise its profile. The crude assimilation of marketing into publicity is a sign that this policy has come to be seen as an end in itself. This state of affairs is actually based on the supposition that all that is required is to provide better information for potential visitors for them to frequent the museum. Once again, many museums are grappling with the necessity to communicate more effectively with the public and have established policies in that direction. In the last case, the entire institution is alert to listen to the visitor. The degree of consistency in this listening process allows us to class the organizations according to how they respond to complaints, undertake studies on consumer satisfaction, find out about the needs and preferences of the visitors, choose and train their personnel to meet these criteria, and, in the final analysis, whether or not they really try to improve the services they offer. To do this the institution must be ready to adapt while continuing to respect professional, scientific, and artistic standards. Though often in a fragmented manner, elements of this policy can be found, to differing extents, in museums which, it must be underlined, cannot all be brought together in the same table of analysis because of their extreme diversity.

This summary schema seems to indicate that many museums, and in particular those which ignore marketing or have a false concept of it, are to be found at one of the first three stages and consequently are not in a position to use marketing for what it is today: a tool for analysis and a means for action which allow an organization, commercial or non-commercial, to achieve its objectives fully. Whereas for a private enterprise this would mean achieving the highest possible profit, a museum could instead choose as its goal the education of the visitor, or the stimulation of his awareness of specific facets of history, science, or art, and not merely his commercial exploitation (Kotler and Andreasen 1987).

Seen from this angle, museums must make every effort to imbue their personnel with the notion that they are there to serve the public and that they must continuously improve the quality of the services offered. Unfortunately, people working in museums, as well as those in public relations departments, are sometimes ill-placed to appreciate public perceptions of their establishments. Thus, for example, those in charge of a large museum in Virginia, United States of America, were most surprised to learn that many non-visitors thought that the museum charged an entry fee when entry to the museum was completely free of charge, and imagined the museum to be a cold place, closed in on itself, and where nothing much happened although every week, if not every day, a new programme was offered, and in addition a new wing had just been inaugurated . . . This public perception is fundamental since it will determine the way in which an individual visit develops, notwithstanding the reality of the perceived phenomena (Fronville 1985).

The second phenomenon to be addressed is the extension of marketing outside the commercial sphere. Over the last thirty years, the extension of marketing to non-profit organizations has been witnessed by those serving social needs, universities and also cultural institutions (Mokwa et al. 1984; Mayaux 1987). In order to transpose the marketing concepts from the world of profit-making organizations, the notion of EXCHANGE was used to characterize the nature of the relationship which is established between the consumer and the institution. In the process thus defined the first gives up something he values (time, money, energy, values, habits) in exchange for a beneficial element (economic, social, or psychological) offered by the institution. In this way, the visitors to the museum pay an entrance fee or sacrifice part of their free time to gain access to the collections, to partake in an educational activity, or to attend a lecture. In spite of some theoretical opposition, a consensus appears to have been reached accepting the validity of this extension of the marketing concept to outside the commercial sphere (Bigley 1987).

However, the difficult task for those responsible for marketing lies in combining two elements: on the one hand the objectives to be attained and on the other consumer satisfaction, and this through acting on the level, pace, and nature of the demand of the target population in a way which allows the institution to fulfil its mission. Kotler and Andreasen distinguish six principal types of demand:

- Absence of a demand: the consumers are not interested in or indifferent towards the product; for example a certain number of people declare that they are not interested in Modern Art and do not go to museums of that type.
- A latent demand: the consumers feel a need which is not met by any of the existing products; the role of marketing is to measure the size of this potential market and to develop those products and services which would satisfy that demand. For example, many people are interested in archaeology but are not satisfied by the way in which this discipline is presented in museums. And yet, it must be remembered that the exhibition with the highest visitor attendance in France remains that of Tutankhamen in 1961.

- A flexible demand: the institution is faced with a drop in demand for one or several of its products on a cyclical basis. Those responsible for marketing must analyse the reasons for this decline and attempt a remedy through modifying what is on offer, through searching for new markets or by improving communications. With regard to museums, the planning of temporary exhibition programmes, a new wing, the presentation of new collections, or the search for a new public, may be the answer to that concern and tend to foster the success of one establishment in contrast to another which remains set in its ways.

- An irregular demand: most institutions experience variations in demand according to seasons, days or hours of the day. For example, museums in tourist areas face an increased demand over the weekends and during the holiday season, and by contrast they are less visited during the week and out of season. Changes which attempt to spread out the visits better could be envisaged.

- A satisfactory demand: the institution is satisfied with the level of demand for its products. Those responsible for marketing must endeavour to maintain this level in anticipation of changes in demand or indeed the arrival of intensified competition. Furthermore, they could also regularly verify customer satisfaction. The emergence of numerous new museums forces the older institutions to improve the quality of their services in order to maintain their 'market share', a factor which takes precedence over collaboration between museums.

- An excessive demand: some organizations are faced with a demand higher than they can cope with under acceptable conditions. In museums, prestigious and popular temporary exhibitions may lead to overcrowding which will spoil the quality of the visit. The marketing services must attempt to reduce demand temporarily or permanently, or spread it, in a selective or non-selective fashion. The introduction of compulsory timed tickets in France from the Toulouse-Lautrec exhibition in Paris in 1992 has tried to forestall the problems of queuing and excessive crowding.

Why introduce marketing into museums?

The intoduction of marketing into museums can be attributed to four factors whose relative importance depends on the country and the nature of each institution.

First factor, the growth of museums

Museums today are complex organizations with a diversified range of activities (temporary exhibitions, research, educational programmes, fund raising, publications, cultural services, commercial activities) involving sizeable budgets and numerous staff (Peterson 1986; Ballé 1987; Labouret and de Narp 1990). In France, the modernization of museums is usually accompanied by a considerable rise in the number of employees and services on offer. Similarly, in the United States of America, museums and historical societies have seen a considerable increase in their budgets,

staff numbers, and programmes over the last decades, although traditional financial resources could not keep up with these new needs (Bryan 1989). However,
some museums still contain unexploited resources, be it due to the feebleness of
the visitor services, insufficient effort devoted to publicity, or an under-exploitation
of economic and tourist 'spin-offs' (Greffe 1990). Inversely, the example provided
by certain museums shows that the establishment of a development policy can have
positive results, as will be shown below.

The spin-offs expected by local authorities from highlighting the cultural
heritage are generally the creation of an enhanced tourist flow, greater expenditure on accommodation, and improved product sales and catering, as well as benefit
to planning and development, job creation, and the establishment of new channels
for economic development (see, for example, silk in the Cévennes, shipbuilding at
Douarnenez, or the cutlery industry at Thiers . . .) leading to the establishment
of a clearly identifiable brand image on which to base advertising.

As the report of the Délégation à l'Aménagement du Territoire et à l'Action
Régionale (DATAR), which is dedicated to national cultural development, indicates,
'until recently, immovable cultural property has been perceived by the majority of
those responsible in local communities as a burden. Today it is instead considered
to be an essential part of a national or regional/strategic cultural plan and an opportunity for development' (Latarget 1992). Besides, the strategies of the French cities
and regions currently operate through communication channels based on the active
promotion of cultural activities and publicizing their rich cultural heritage.

On this subject many observers tend to contrast management in the public
and private sectors, the latter being considered to be more dynamic. Actually, even
if the state and the local communities appear to demonstrate great efficiency in the
conservation and restoration, their success in the management of monuments generally seems to be less assured. The inadequate staffing of the organizations charged
with their administration and promotion, a certain weakening of their responsibility, and the burden of the complex regulations of public accountability constitute
serious handicaps and do not exactly encourage commercial and touristic dynamism.
One might, for example, point out that certain museums which are publicly
administered do not benefit financially from the development of the revenue they
generate (museum shop sales, entrance charges, restaurant receipts). As the curator
of the Domain of Versailles once said, 'the park has thousands of resources to be
exploited. But why make the effort if we don't benefit from the money earned?'
(Quoted by Saffar 1992.)

Second factor, the question of financing

The weight of ever greater financial constraints following a reduction in state funding, and/or the need to find new financial resources in order to allow museums to
expand, forces them to find ways to generate supplementary funds and to establish
the means for better communications directed towards various target groups.

The advent of particular attention to marketing generally coincides with financial difficulties being encountered by museums: for example, the recession and
budgetary restrictions at the beginning of the 1980s in the United States of America,

Thatcherism in Great Britain, and the new financial needs of Canadian museums arising from their modernization. In reverse, the probability of particular attention being given to marketing is usually less the closer one comes to a financial system which is entirely funded by the public sector (Pommerehne and Frey 1980; Rosenthal 1982; Mercillon 1977). Nonetheless, this has not deterred the directors of French public museums from concerning themselves with analyses of visitors, as one can see from the considerable number of published studies carried out on the subject worldwide.

As far as the United States of America are concerned, under the impact of reduced public subsidies, a slowing down of the economy, less favourable fiscal advantages than were previously available, and a rise in overheads, the museum directors introduced new techniques of management in the fields of marketing, fund raising, and commercial activities. Because of this, market forces have exercised a more visible influence on American museums during recent years, which has been translated into increased publicity budgets, greater interest in visitor studies, more general drive to increase visitor numbers by means of blockbuster exhibitions, and the expansion of sponsorship (Tobelem 1990).

At the same time, these museums were faced with the need to increase their own resources such as the income derived from their capital investments (endowment funds), as well as from entry charges and subscriptions, both of which can sustain intensive programme activities (at the time of writing the Metropolitan Museum in New York and the Art Institute of Chicago each boasted more than 90,000 members). Finally, the revenue from developing museum shops has vastly expanded. For example, at the time of writing, the commercial income of the Metropolitan Museum amounted to about 50 million dollars a year (including a huge mail order business) and that of the Smithsonian Institution was about 40 million dollars (here we are talking about turnover and not profit). For these reasons a number of museum directors today have benefitted from being trained in two areas, scholarly studies (art, history, science, or education) and business administration. In fact, the former Director of the National Gallery in Washington was nominated one of the best administrators of a non-profit organization by the magazine *Business Week*, and as far as his successor was concerned, his well-known management skills were a deciding factor in his selection (cf. *Newsweek*, 11 May 1992).

Third factor, the competitive environment

This revolves around the competitive environment into which the proliferation of cultural institutions and the increased range of leisure time activities has propelled the museums and monuments. Thus the fact that the museums themselves are not commercial institutions does not mean that they are not operating within a market (DiMaggio 1985; Bayart and Benghozi 1993). However, museum curators are not always fully aware of the competitive situation in which their institution finds themselves; the 'products' of cultural institutions are considered as being completely different from each other. A science museum does not see an art museum or a children's museum as a direct competitor. Reality is often different since the time available to individuals is by definition limited and a great number of temptations are on offer to them: going to see a play, visiting an exhibition, going out to a restaurant, watching a sports event . . . (Kotler and Andreasen 1987).

Similarly, a city of a certain size offers a great variety of museum experiences and, consciously or not, each one of them will try very hard to attract a maximum number of visitors. This does not take into account the emergence of numerous other cultural institutions and that museums are in direct competition with each other to receive – severely limited – financial resources, whether they come from public sources or from private donors. This vision of the role of competition is enriched by recognition of the fact that, for an establishment, the competition is that which is perceived as such by the visitor, and does not restrict itself to institutions of the same kind. If the individual consumer thinks that a visit to the museum competes with gardening or arranging a party for friends, then, according to Kotler, those activities enter into direct competition with the museum.

Finally, the last factor in the appearance of marketing in museums is the need to know the visitors better

This means helping the museum to fulfil its mission through adjusting its message, indeed to seek to understand better the perceptions and expectations of non-visitors in order to catch the interest of particular groups (Braverman 1988; Fronville 1985). As a matter of fact, in many museums, what is presented is directed to a theoretical visitor and in the final analysis is addressed to an educated public without sufficiently investigating the means needed in order to adapt the message to the expectations, motivations, and respective habits of different visitor groups (or segments) (Beaulac et al. 1991). Among the panoply of studies and research tools of qualitative or quantitative inspiration which have been developed in the museum sector, market analysis aims in particular 'to define the client groups susceptible to museum visiting, to evaluate the impact of these visits on the stated objectives and the available resources, and to determine the groups to be taken into account in the preparation of programmes' (Trottier 1987).

In those institutions where marketing is marginalized, consumer research is neglected. According to Kotler, 'on the basis of various studies it can be suggested that the difficulties some organisations encounter are not always caused by ignorance or lack of motivation on the part of the consumer'. On the other hand, in museums which have adopted a marketing approach, marketing services do not only strive to react to changes in the needs, wishes, and perceptions of the consumer, but even try to anticipate them. Research with regard to an institution's 'market' allows the comprehensive assessment of consumers and a means to test decisions on a sample target group in order to ensure that they are efficacious (Kotler and Andreasen 1987).

The application of marketing in museums

If marketing is seen in a restrictive way, as only the introduction of a sales technique used by private enterprise, its introduction into museums inevitably meets with legitimate resistance, particularly from the scholarly staff. The principal restraint stems from a vision of marketing as essentially a technique aimed at augmenting commercial receipts and visitor numbers without regard for the scholarly and educational mission of the museum. To introduce such a marketing philosophy into a museum would then be equivalent to administering a museum solely in accord with visitor demands and to abandon the objectives of research, conservation, and curatorship (Curry 1982; Bigley 1987).

In fact, most museums do not have a department or even an individual with special responsibility for marketing, or else their activity is essentially limited to issuing press releases and public relations exercises if one sets aside the commercial activities (it is, however, true that the staffing of museums is all too often very limited). Otherwise it is the financial motivation which is the driving force for the use of marketing, more than the study of the public and taking into account its wishes, expectations, motivations, and needs. However, the lack of sufficient resources often in itself hampers the development of a marketing policy, particularly in the area of segmenting communications and services which requires considerable resources (Beaulac et al. 1991).

In a number of countries (France, England, the United States of America) governments have encouraged museums to develop their own resources and, with sometimes rather exaggerated expectations, to attract sponsors. If it is true that in France the most important part of financing museums continues to come from public sources (sensibly it is fairly divided between the State and local communities) it cannot be denied that the tendency is nonetheless an evolution towards an increasing proportion of private funding. Under the influence of Italian and American companies, exhibition sponsorship in France made its appearance about fifteen years ago (ICI, relatively recently, participated in the restoration of the famous painting by Veronese *The Wedding at Cana* in the Louvre and was the sponsor of the exhibition *The Century of Titian* in the Grand Palais, Paris).

According to ADMICAL, the French association dedicated to the development of patronage by businesses, museums 'have for ten years appeared to be the outstanding places for the cultural expression of the economic world'. Thus nearly half of all museum curators in France would have experienced this patronage. One can mention the examples established by the Fondation Paribas in the area of publishing catalogues of museum collections, by the Fondation du Crédit Coopératif, which chose to help the Federation of Ecomuseums, or by the Casino group of companies in associating itself with the Museum of Contemporary Art in Saint-Etienne (ADMICAL 1990). As far as UAP is concerned, it has gone into partnership with the new Galerie du Jeu de Paume in Paris, which at the time of writing allowed the latter to receive 5 million francs a year, excluding assistance in the field of communications. The Chairman of the company is the President of the Administrative Council of the Jeu de Paume, a visible sign of the involvement of this company and one which reflects the concern of companies to anchor their activities advantagously in the long term and to concentrate their sponsorship resources within a relatively small number of operations.

However, French museums still do not pursue systematically an active policy of private fund raising and only rarely have a skilled spokesperson to publicize such patronage. With regard to the French national museums, the patronage of about thirty companies has nonetheless made contributions of many tens of millions of francs since 1985. Thus the participation of private enterprise in museum activities should develop in the future. The existence of the procedure of co-financing established by the Conseil Supérieur du Mécénat (High Council of Patronage), inspired by the American system of 'matching grants', should be emphasized here. Bringing together private funds and public resources, the Conseil can provide additional support for cultural operations which have received contributions of patronage.

The Cité des Sciences et de l'Industrie de La Villete in Paris has fully developed its partnership with business in ways which cannot merely be called sponsorship. There are several types of collaboration: co-productions in the permanent collections and for temporary exhibitions (Philips, UTA, Elf-Aquitaine, Hermès, Matra, Renault, Rhône-Poulenc, Bull, Hewlett-Packard, CGE, Gaz de France, Michelin, Institut Mérieux); exhibitions mounted by the companies themselves to present their products and research activities (SNECMA, National Office of Studies and Research of Aerospace . . .); sponsorship actions for big projects of the Cité, such as the Cité des Enfants; the participation within projects under *Youth and Training* designed for students and teachers (*Classes Villette* welcomed at different companies, conferences arranged at the same time as the *Villette Discussion Forums*); cooperation on the international level (Rhône Poulenc has thus presented a travelling exhibition in the United States of America); special operations such as an 'Open Day' thanks to the national gas company of France in 1990 for instance; the renting of the *Géode* and the conference rooms of the congress centre for general assemblies, conventions, etc.

With reference to the cultural heritage, the activities in 1990 permitted the renovation of the Arc de Triomphe (Aerospatiale, Rhône Poulenc), the dredging of sand at the Mont Saint-Michel (American Express), and restoration of the gardens of the Château of Versailles (Ciba Geigy). Besides, one can cite the restoration of the priory of Ganagobie in the Alpes de Haute Provence, particularly thanks to the participation of the groups Bouygues, Ciments Lafarge, and Crédit Lyonnais (furthermore it is planned that the priory will in due course host seminars of private enterprises). Also in 1990, the Fondation du Crédit Agricole contributed the sum of 5 million francs to different associations furthering the promotion of rural culture (restoration of the birth place of Bernard Palissy, rehabilitation of Alphonse Daudet's mill, etc.). Moreover, the renovation of the Old Stock Exchange in Lille brought together twenty-four enterprises from the region in an action of cultural sponsorship (ADMICAL 1991). In Reims, the interprofessional committee of Champagne wines decided to co-finance with 4 million francs the restoration of the Reims Cathedral (the contribution being made by the State amounting to 50 million francs . . .). The cultural heritage then has become the preferred carrier for a company's message, relying on the strong social and cultural anchorage of monuments within their environment which assures a high-profile 'visibility' for the operation in the eyes of the public.

As far as foundations are concerned, the Fondation EDF has sponsored several projects featuring the flood-lighting of historical monuments (Château of Haut-Koenigsbourg, Mont Saint-Michel, etc.), while financial support of the Fondation Paribas aims at increased publicity for the heritage of the National Library (a three-year partnership on the theme of *The Memory of the Future*). Where the John Paul

Getty Trust (Getty Conservation Institute) is concerned, it carries out important actions in the area of protection and conservation of the World Heritage: to cite the Roman mosaics of Paphos (Cyprus), the mural paintings of Nefertari's tomb at Thebes (Egypt), the Buddhist caves of Datong (China), the manuscripts of the library in St. Petersburg (Russia), and also the historic centre of Quito (Equador). Finally, the activities of several thousand smaller associations in all areas of the cultural heritage must not be forgotten, nor those of some tens of thousands of volunteers working on archaeological digs and historic sites.

French museums have in addition been urged to maximize the returns on their resources through the operation of shops, restaurants, and paying programmes, and by hiring out parts of their premises. Encouraged by public demand, itself engendered by the increased display of professionalism in the services offered and rendered, they are providing themselves with more and more of the services they had previously lacked and consequently with the means for limited self-financing. The creation of welcoming reception areas, the organization of special events, and the development of a marketing approach are, by their nature, able to diversify the financial resources of museums which, however, have to be careful to preserve the integrity of their original missions – that is, the curating and conservation of the collections, their study, and the education of the public.

One may cite, as an example, the printed textiles museum in Mulhouse, which possesses several million swatches and some 50,000 larger examples. Its specialized documentation facility (SUD) allows it to provide essential specialist services to the textile industry both in France and abroad, thus generating an income for its operations. One hundred and fifty companies can be considered regular clients of which half are foreign firms, particularly English and American. Follow-up for clients is assured by means of the computerized databases. This museum is also developing commercial activities by means of a specialized boutique, mail order services, and sales outlets located in retail shops, all of which project the image of the museum outside Mulhouse and raise its profile. Finally, the museum creates new products based on the samples which are in its collections. The SUD and the commercial activities provide each about a third of the museum's overall budget.

The example of social history museums in France also demonstrates that a museum can cover fifty percent or more of its operating costs through self-financing, as is achieved by the ecomuseums of Haute Alsace, Chazelle-sur-Lyon, and Quercy. Besides, new systems of administration are being established to replace management by direct municipal control, which is now considered too restrictive. These take the form of formally constituted associations, 'mixed economy' companies or limited companies (for commercial activities) in order to achieve greater autonomy in the running of museums. Indeed, organizational and administrative restrictions often hamper the development of innovative policies in museums, while the burden of administrative procedures does not exactly encourage the search for more subtle management styles, although the big national museums in France already benefit from a greater autonomy through the decentralization of certain funding and the Louvre has acquired the semi-autonomous status of an *établissement public*.

However, those in charge of institutions do not always realize the importance of adopting a commercial policy which their museum can develop, though it will be necessary, like in other areas, to take into account the museum's size and the number of its staff. A certain number of big museums still lack an attractive museum shop capable of generating a meaningful revenue. Moreover, the inadequate range of products offered and the absence of a coherent commercial strategy displayed by many French museums leads one to conclude that their commercial potential is today still under-exploited. Conversely, the Réunion des Musées Nationaux – the organization administering the commercial activities of (French) national museums – has considerably increased its turnover which exceeds 250 million francs (primarily realized in the Louvre, the Musée d'Orsay, and Versailles) and has launched a successful mail order operation. As for the Centre Pompidou, it sold 75,000 copies of the catalogue produced for the exhibition on *Vienna* (1986) following on 80,000 copies of the *Salvador Dali* catalogue (1979).

In some museums the operation of shops has become an efficient business whose primary objective is financial profitability. Moreover, their physical location within the museum now depends less on whim and more on the careful analysis of visitor movements. On the other hand, sales are also dependent on trends in fashion or critical opinion which those responsible for the museum must follow, or even anticipate, as well as the phenomenon of those vast temporary exhibitions which are accompanied more and more systematically by the 'merchandising' of goods exploiting the content of the exhibition (Morin 1987; Rudman 1989; Tobelem 1990). For the majority of museums, however, any income gained from trading is primarily a means of creating a modest revenue which will allow the institution to fulfil its educational function and to organize programmes for its public. The difference from private enterprise remains in the use of commercial benefits which are not distributed among directors or shareholders but are fed back into the museum's budget, at least in those cases where the museum is financially autonomous.

In order to increase visitor numbers, certain museums are increasingly being led into adopting a perspective coloured by the specific requirements of cultural tourism which will require a revolutionary change in mentalities, involving a new policy for welcoming visitors, better media relations, and the development of additional programmes. This factor is particularly significant when one is aware that foreign tourists often make up a crucial proportion of visitor numbers. Museums capable of collecting this 'manna' in a professional way are well on the way to being able to generate significant revenues of their own, and in proving that they may constitute a force for local development they may even be able to attract new partners. In this way, the Dutch national tourist organizations 'would like to see more tourist events of a quality like the *Van Gogh* and *Rembrandt* exhibitions which are easy to sell to an international public. With 90,000 visitors (of which 55% were foreign tourists) and a revenue for the tourist industry of 525 million Dutch Guilders (1.6 billion French Francs), the *Van Gogh* exhibition in 1990 whetted the appetite of every professional' (Vels Heijn 1992).

In France, at the time of writing, an overall figure for visitors of monuments was estimated at 15 million a year. Moreover, according to the Ministry of Culture, the open day event of historic monuments has attracted 4 million visitors in 1991. By comparison, figures for museums (including Versailles, Fontainebleau, etc.) showed between 60 and 70 million visitors a year (also counting free entries). The increase in visits of tourists during these last years has considerably strengthened the importance of cultural tourism. 'By comparison, visitor behaviour has evolved, methods of publicity have been modernised and administrative structures diversified, the spin-off in terms of financial flow and employment increased' (Patin 1989). In particular, the rise in visitor numbers, the demands of the public (among them many foreign visitors) and the hopes of the tourism industry impose new practices in the area of visitor reception, be it accompanying services, signposting and labelling, visitor comfort, or the educational content of the visit.

In museums, marketing can then be used to rationalize the total process of developing their own resources, going through the creation or speeding up of commercial programmes (shops, restaurants, hiring out of premises), intensifying efforts to raise funds from individuals and companies, as well as the launching of subscription programmes, but also in order to allow the museum to gain its cultural objectives more efficiently. This management tool effectively offers museums a framework for analysis and intervention in a variety of domains (Fronville 1985):

- for educational programmes: market analysis will facilitate the establishment of a range of the activities the museum proposes for different, previously identified, publics (school visits, conferences, guided tours, films, books . . .);
- for membership and fund raising programmes: the marketing approach will be used to increase the number of museum members and propose partnership programmes with private enterprise;
- in order to raise own income: be it from museum shops, commercial programmes associated with temporary exhibitions, rental of premises, licences or concessions;
- in the field of public relations: their purpose will be the consistent exploitation of every past programme by various media, publicity, and the communication techniques of sponsors.

These different aspects of marketing policy may be found in museums but are rarely linked up with each other in a coherent, rigorous, and coordinated manner which would allow the definition of a marketing stategy in accordance with the aims of the institution. Generally speaking, 'the marketing approach is not integrated within a general managerial process based on carrying out the mission of the institution' (Beaulac et al. 1991). Efectively, few institutions have at their disposal a true marketing plan.

The specificity of marketing in museums

A study by Allen and Schewe (cited by Kotler and Andreasen 1987) examining the way in which museum directors think of marketing shows that museum professionals, if compared to commercial marketing practitioners, are less inclined to seek data on what visitors would like to find in museums. They freely admit that their 'product' must satisfy everyone rather than being geared towards particular discriminating consumers; but they are less interested in adjusting their prices and usually do not wish to change their distribution strategy. Finally they are less likely to want to modify in future the nature of the products and services offered to consumers.

Does this mean that those responsible for cultural institutions must yield to the exigencies of the taste of the public and conceive their programmes solely according to its wishes? This would reveal a poor understanding of marketing; when in reality one must START with the concerns felt by the visitor, his or her needs and wishes, and then interpret them. Thus, in the case where studies underlined that the public imagined museums to be the reserve of an intellectual and social elite, a museum might endeavour to set up programmes directed towards a public unfamiliar with the museum environment, to create a relaxed and informal atmosphere, and to programme events likely to bring in non-visitors to discover what a museum really is. One result of such a philosophy is the high degree of satisfaction manifested by visitors who then become the best advocates for the institution, spreading its reputation through word of mouth information. To the contrary, some people in responsible positions do not care sufficiently to make the museum an interesting place for visitors or to respond to their requirements in the exhibition areas, even if everything indicates that they are not satisfied with what is on offer for them, and when this is not simply due to a lack of human or financial resources (Helleu 1991).

In France, such a shift inevitably gives rise to difficulties because, unlike in the Anglo-Saxon countries, little account has been taken of the economic dimension until recently: 'in their turn, monuments and the historic heritage have acquired a double status. Works conveying knowledge and pleasure are made available to all, together with cultural products, manufactured, packaged and distributed for consumption. The metamorphosis of their original functional value into economic value is being realized thanks to "cultural engineering", a vast network of public and private enterprise for which an army of organizers, communicators, development facilitators, engineers and cultural mediators are working' (Choay 1992).

Considering that certain organizations genuinely believe that they are in touch with the consumer or, at least, would like to become so, Kotler and Andreasen have defined a number of criteria which allow us to determine whether or not they really are:

- The type of product offered leads those responsible for museums to estimate it very highly, and this does not accord easily with the phenomena of straight refusal or indifference. Thus some curators are genuinely perplexed when confronted with a public disinterested in an exhibition although it shows high-quality objects.
- Ignorance or lack of motivation on the part of the consumer are held responsible for the lack of success of an institution. A museum director may think it will be enough to intensify publicity or to find new attractions to draw visitors into his museum, in this way breaking their 'natural' inertia.
- Marketing is likened to promotion: the questions of image, communications material, press releases, publicity . . . will attract the attention of those responsible to the detriment of other elements of marketing such as the fixing of prices, the selection of products, and their distribution.
- Rather than employing a marketing specialist, it is more likely that someone with a knowledge of the world of museums will be chosen or perhaps a former employee of the institution; though it also could be someone with a

special knowledge of media relations. In this case the standing of the person will be not so much increased by the mastery of a technique, i.e. marketing, but rather through the knowledge of a particular product or a talent for communications which is to be brought into play in fighting ignorance and lack of interest in potential visitors.

• Ignorance concerning the market encourages a simplistic view which in turn leads to a search for one or two strategies destined for the most obvious sectors and to a distrust of innovation and risk taking. Thus the public of the museum is likened to a monolithic group which does not leave room for alternative and complementary strategies.

Marketing practitioners, in fact, emphasize segmentation following from the fact that the market resembles a combination of numerous sub-segments which are objectives for separate marketing programmes. Segmentation is defined as 'the action of regrouping the units making up a market of sub-groups in such a way that each group is characterised by homogenous needs and that the different groups are separated from each other by virtue of their differing requirements' (Beaulac et al. 1991). Consequently, museum visitors are made up of a local public, professionals, school groups, French tourists, foreign tourists, et al. Similarly, educational programmes can be directed towards a public of school or university students, adults, the aged, the disabled . . . This more sophisticated approach leads to the establishment of differentiated strategies (positioning) using distinct communication channels and addressing different target groups (targeting). In the opposite case, effective strategies for one population segment can very well be rejected by another consumer group whose motivations are contrary to those of the first group.

To illustrate this, let us single out a segment of well-informed art lovers who wish to see a sophisticated exhibition drawing on the work of advanced artists. A communication strategy which merely consists of publicizing the exhibition programme and the prospect of the discovery of new talents risks rejection by a clientele more interested in a visit to a museum as an informal family outing, and who might feel intimidated by being unfamiliar with the world of art. This schema indicates that there exist two distinct communication strategies which need to be elaborated while trying to avoid an overlap of the campaigns (Kotler and Andreasen 1987). On the other hand the primary objective of those responsible for the museum ought to be the definition of a global project derived from the mission of the institution, expressed through a strong concept and taking into account the aspirations of visitors (see below).

Nonetheless, the application of marketing in museums, as well as for any non-profit institution in general, comes up against one particular difficulty, that is, 'performance' measurements of the institution which may result in the overestimation of the significance of the quantitative criteria since they lend themselves more easily to such evaluation. How then to measure if the content of a museum visit has become more educational or the museum has increased the quality of life? The temptation to prioritize areas where achievement can be readily quantified is an inherent danger: for example, over attention to the size of the budget, visitor numbers, commercial benefits, etc. (Ames 1989).

The risks of uncontrolled application

The central question which all museum directors worrying about the perspectives offered by marketing ask themselves is the following: would the introduction of the technique place at a risk their professional standards, the integrity of the institution, and its scientific, historic, or artistic programmes? Would it not, after all, by trying to please the greatest number, lower the quality of the institution?

To this the theoreticians of marketing reply that marketing is not an end in itself; it can only be a means at the service of the organization, intended to allow it to attain its defined objectives efficiently. Marketing then is one branch of administration among others and it is the responsibility of the leaders of the institution to determine in which area or areas it is to be applied. Equally, management may thus decide to ignore the concerns of marketing in favour of other criteria considered more important (Kotler and Andreasen 1987).

The temporary exhibition programme of a museum could resort to marketing considerations either fully, or in part, or not at all. One notes that some museums in their temporary exhibition programmes attempt to balance 'popular' exhibitions with those of more limited appeal which cater better for higher artistic aspirations. Nonetheless, once that programme has been established, it is the marketing service which will have to contribute to its success within the given limits, and by starting with a clear understanding of local visitor characteristics. Similarly, those responsible for marketing must establish the description, the presentation, price, and distribution of museum programmes according to the criteria established through visitor research, without however modifying their content.

The only guideline available to ensure that the marketing policy of the museum will be implemented in order to achieve its objectives resides in the establishment of the museum's MISSION and constant awareness of it. Indeed, if this mission is not clearly defined and has not been assimilated by all staff members and the governing body, a strong marketing management would have no difficulty in imposing its own criteria of judgement and appraisal. The risks of deviation are important and widely underlined by the most critical observers: the temporary exhibition programme will tend to follow the most conservative tastes of the public to the detriment of exhibitions which are more ambitious but less assured of popular success; requirements for research and conservation of collections will take second place; and, finally, the educational objectives of the museum will be considered to be less important than the financial outcome (Ames 1989; Bryan 1989; Tobelem 1990).

Among these risks of deviation one ought to underline those which relate to temporary exhibition programming and actions of sponsorship. Those responsible for museums have been progressively led to conclude that big temporary exhibitions are beneficial for their operating budgets and to measure their impact on sponsorship and other financial resources, be it a spectacular rise in entrance receipts, a remarkable augmentation in the number of members, an increment in commercial revenue, or an enhanced reputation for the museum. The Director of the Metropolitan Museum in New York, Philippe de Montebello, has long ago admitted to being worried about the increasing dependence of big museums on temporary exhibitions which, according to him, have had an undeniable influence on the functioning of these institutions. Indeed, these big exhibitions (the so called 'block-busters') have become powerful instruments for development and a means to balance the museum's deficit. Since then the temporary exhibition programme of the museum tends to be considered by museum managers to be at the service of the museum's budget and not the other way round . . . (Montebello 1984).

With regard to patronage, it is well known that it is difficult to rouse the interest of commerce or industry for some temporary exhibitions, whatever the quality and ambitiousness of the project. Those responsible in the museum must therefore be careful not to be carried away towards a programming policy influenced unduly by the search for financial partners. Besides, one notes an increase of temporary exhibitions whose originality and scholarly content is not always evident, but whose assured popularity offers all guarantees of positive responses for the sponsor in the media. Museums must also determine the type of relationship which can possibly be entered into with commerce or industry so as not to yield to excessive demands by them.

Yesterday, marketing was still associated with the world of private enterprise and the quest for profit, and then extended to the sector of non-profit organizations before being applied to the world of culture; today it has widened its field of operations to museums. The admission of this management technique is justified in the current financial situation of museums (commercial revenue, patronage, fund raising) as well as in the requirements of contemporary communications (publicity, public relations, direct marketing, mounting of events).

But beyond this approach, whose guiding consideration is more efficient management, marketing also provides the theoretical and practical tools for an analysis of the public (and the non-public) of museums which proceed from a crucial determination to realize the institution's objectives and accomplish its mission. However, only precise knowledge of the expectations and perceptions of visitors will allow museums to achieve this effectively (Garfield 1992), as the numerous initiatives undertaken in the field confirm (debates, research, studies and reflections on different visitor categories, expectations of the public, museum education, evaluation of exhibitions, etc.).

To reconcile these two orientations (efficient management and fulfilling the objectives of the institution) in a practical way, museum management must shoulder the responsibility to establish a coherent model and set out an unequivocal strategy based on the formal educational, scientific, and cultural mission of the museum in the service of which any marketing policy will be implemented. If this mission is precisely defined, and if priorities are clearly stated, any risk of deviation which may arise from the application of uncontrolled marketing techniques can probably be forestalled and marketing will remain a valuable tool serving the museum.

Editorial note

This article, originally appearing in the journal *Publics et Musées*, 2, Presses Universitaires de Lyon, 1993, has been reprinted verbatim from the translated form subsequently published in 1998 in *Museum Management and Curatorship*, vol. 16, no. 4, pp. 337–354.

Note

Jean-Michel Tobelem has written extensively on museums, management and marketing. This paper was first published in 1998 in *Museum Management and Curatorship*, vol. 16, no. 4.

References

ADMICAL (1990) *Répertoire 1989–1990 du Mécénat cultural*. Association pour le Développment du Mécénat industriel et commercial, Paris.

—— (1991) *Répertoire 1990–1991 du Mécénat cultural*. Association pour le Développment du Mécénat industriel et commercial, Paris.

Ames, P. (1989) Marketing in museums: means or master of the mission? *Curator*, 32.

Ballé, C. (1987) Les nouveaux musées, une incidence institutionnelle de l'evolution culturelle. *Brises*, 2.

Bayart, D. and Benghozi, P.-J. (1993) *Le tournant commercial des musées en France et à l'étranger*. La Documentation Française, Paris.

Beaulac, M., Colbert, F., and Duhaime, C. (1991) *Le marketing en milieu muséal: une recherche exploratoire. Groupe de recherche et de formation en gestion des arts*. Ecole des Hautes Etudes Commerciales de Montréal.

Bigley, J.D. (1987) Marketing in museums: background and theoretical foundations. *Museum Studies Journal*, 3(1), fall–winter.

Braverman, B.E. (1988) Empowering visitors: focus group interviews for art museums. *Curator*, 31/1.

Bryan, C.F. Jr. (1989) How far have we come, how far do we go? *History News*, July–August.

Choay, F. (1992) *L'allégorie du patrimoine*. Editions du Seuil, Paris.

Curry, D.J. (1982) Marketing research and management descisions. *The Journal of Arts Management and Law*, spring, 12(1).

DiMaggio, P. (1985) When the profit is quality: cultural institutions in the market place. *Museum News*, June, 28–35.

Fronville, C.L. (1985) Marketing for museums: for-profit techniques in the non-profit world. *Curator*, 28/3.

Garfield, D. (1992) Frances Hesselbein: Managing for the mission. *Museum News*, March–April, 66–67.

Greffe, X. (1990) *La valeur économique du patrimoine*. Anthropos-Economica.

Helleu, E. (1991) Musées: le 'livre noir' des visiteurs. *L'Evénement du Jeudi*, 18–24 July, 98–101.

Kotler, P. and Andreasen, A.R. (1987) *Strategic marketing for non-profit organizations*. Prentice-Hall, Englewood Cliffs.

Labouret, C. and de Narp, O. (1990) *Le nouveau visage des musées: la vocation culturelle et le service du public*. Institut La Boétie, Paris.

Latarget, B. (1992) *L'aménagement culturel du territoire*. La documentation française.

Mayaux, F. (1987) Le marketing au service de la culture. *Revue française du marketing*, 113.

Mercillon, H. (1977) Les musées institutions à but non lucratif clans l'économie marchande. *Revue d'économie polilique*, 4, T, LXXXVII.

Mokwa, M.P., Dawson, W.M., and Prieve, E.A. (1984) *Marketing the Arts*. Praeger, New York.

Montebello, P. de (1984) The high cost of quality. *Museum News*, August, 46–49.

Morin, F. (1987) Un musée peut-il être rentable? *Science and Vie Economie*, 25, February.

Musées et économie (1992a) *Actes des troisièmes rencontres nationales des musées*, Musée Guimet, 13 et 14 juin 1991. Direction des Musées de France, Paris.

—— (1992b) *Musées et collections publiques de France*, 197, 4, Paris.

Musées et gestion (dir. Michel Côté) (1991) *Musée de la Civilisation*. Université Laval, Québec.

Musées et marketing (dir. Jean-Michel Tobelem) (1997) *Publics et Musées*, 11–12, January–June, July–December 1997. Presses Universitaires de Lyon.

Patin, V. (1989) *La valorisation touristque du patrimoine culturel*. Développement culturel 83, Département des Etudes et de la Prospective, December.

Peterson, R.A. (1986) De l'imprésario à l'administrateur, le rôle du contrôle de gestion dans l'évolution de l'administration des arts. *Colloque international de Marseille*, sous la direction de Raymonde Moulin, La Documentation française.

Pommerehne, W.W. and Frey, B.S. (1980) Les musées clans une perspective économique. *Revue internationale des Sciences sociales*, XXXII(2), 325–362.

Rosenthal, A. (1982) Museums jump into the marketing game. *Advertising Age*, September, 27.

Rudman, A. (1989) Les musées ouvrent boutique. *Le Monde Affaires*, 1, April.

Saffar, Y. (1992) Les déficits du 'monument business'. *Capital*, September.

Tobelem, J.-M. (1990) *Musées et culture, le financement à l'américaine*. Ed. W/MNES, Mâcon.

Trottier, L. (1987) *Les études de marché dans quelques établissements muséologiques du Canada*. In Presse de l'Université du Québec, 10(1), 103–119.

Vels Heijn, A.-M. (1992) L'art au service du tourisme? *La lettre des musées et des expositions*, 42, February.

Chapter 19

Can Museums be All Things to All People?

Missions, goals, and marketing's role

Neil Kotler and Philip Kotler

Introduction

MUSEUM MANAGERS STRUGGLE WITH the issues of maintaining their museum's integrity as a distinctive collecting, conserving, research, exhibiting, and educational institution, and, at the same time, making their museum more popular and competitive. The traditional standard for collections based museums has been well articulated by a former Director of London's British Museum, Sir David M. Wilson: 'Museums are about the material they contain. The first duty of the museum curator is to look after that material. . . . His second duty is to make that material available to whoever wants to see it.'[1] Yet, as museum activist Kenneth Hudson has pointed out, the shift in museum focus to serving audiences has been developing over nearly a half-century. Hudson writes: '. . . [O]ne can assert with confidence that the most fundamental change that has affected museums . . . is the now almost universal conviction that they exist in order to serve the public. The old-style museum felt itself to be under no such obligation . . . The museum's prime responsibility was to its collections, not to its visitors.'[2]

Whatever the reason for the focus on audience (e.g., public subsidy and accountability, need to generate revenue, pressure to include under-served groups), museums are seeking ways to reach a broader public, forge community ties, and compete effectively with alternative providers of leisure and educational activities. Museums, decades ago, were content to reach a small, narrow and self-selected audience. Their narrow programmatic focus in the past (i.e., the focus on collections and scholarly and professional activities) reflected their small, relatively homogeneous constituency base. Today, museums are not only reaching out to larger audiences and building demand among new groups, they are designing proactively

Source: *Museum Management and Curatorship*, vol. 18, no. 3 (2000): 271–287.

the arrangements, services, and offerings which will generate satisfaction and positive outcomes for their visitors. In the process, museum managers and staff are discovering assets and resources which museums possess and were in the past often overlooked.

Change is pervasive in today's museums, and the boundaries which once separated museums from other recreational and educational organizations are blurring or breaking down altogether. A growing number of museum leaders are concerned about competition from the entertainment and cultural districts in central cities, cyberspace, restaurants, sports arenas, and those shopping malls which also present collections and exhibitions, as well as from the growing number of new museums proper, and history and science centers. Sony built the $160 million, 350,000 square-foot Metreon in downtown San Francisco as the urban equivalent of a Disney theme park combined with a suburban shopping mall. Four floors contain shops, restaurants, a movie theater, and a 3-D IMAX screen, along with a fantasy land inspired by the Maurice Sendak children's books, a video game arcade, and an interactive computer gallery which explores how technology works. In Chicago, Disney opened Disney Quest, a theme park and play space fitted into a department store. Virtually every entertainment conglomerate is building its own variation. At other museums which occupy grand, imposing buildings and generate popular perceptions of inaccessibility and elitism, managers are seeking ways to make their facilities more congenial, comfortable, and even mundane. The Cleveland Museum of Art, with one of the loveliest classical buildings in the museum world, convenes each year a colored chalk competition on the sidewalks surrounding the Museum building. Children and families are encouraged to express their creativity by chalking up the sidewalks and, in the process, they feel more at home at the Museum. Other museums are focusing their energies on building bridges to their neighbors and making themselves increasingly a vital part of community life.

If the public today stands at the center of museum thinking, how do visitors view the museums they visit? Casual visitors, according to audience research, enjoy their visits, but want more information and orientation, a higher level of comforts and services, and more human contact in museums. Increasingly, museum constituencies are asserting their claims for programs and services. Claims on resources are multiplying, as are the constituencies which are demanding more services. The result is that museum managers are working double-time, to raise the comfort level for visitors, provide a range of programs, and, in addition, expand their overall audience. Not surprisingly, museum managers, laboring under tight budgets, are hiring marketers and business experts to help them identify tradeoffs, make choices, and keep costs down. The challenge in running museums, then, is to determine, in the midst of competing claims for resources, a realistic set of goals and the strategies and tools which can accomplish the desired changes.

Museums engage in goal-setting and strategic planning and marketing to achieve greater visibility, enlarge their offerings, develop a broader audience, and raise income. At the core of the challenge is making the right choices of goals and strategies and allocating adequate resources. Museum managers are homing in on several questions to guide the choices. What goals fit with the museum's strengths and best promote its core mission? Who are the museum's main constituencies and what is the relative level of attention to pay to each constituency? What goals and strategies

should be set for each constituency? What is the optimal program mix, including exhibits, interactive elements, and other interpretative methods, which can
promote a diversified offering for visitors and satisfy their varying needs? What
indicators can be used to measure goal achievement?

A related challenge to goal-setting and strategy implementation is the challenge
of defining the outcomes and results which managers seek to achieve from their
programs and operations and their audiences. As Peter Drucker has observed about
all organizations, whether for-profit or non-profit: 'Marketing is so basic that it cannot be considered a separate function. It is the whole business seen from the point
of view of its final result, that is, from the customer's point of view.'[3] This article
examines three museum strategies for building audience, support, and income
(common goals on today's museum agendas), explores the interrelationships of
missions, goals, and strategies, brings to bear research on visitor and staff perspectives, and delineates the role of strategy and marketing in museums.

Setting goals

Setting goals and monitoring progress in achieving them form a critical part of the
strategic marketing process in which many museums are engaged. A museum, for
example, may enjoy support from members and important constituencies, yet it
has to expand and diversify its audience in order to achieve broader community
support as well as increased income. In this case, the museum has to frame a goal
of attracting under-served groups, among others. In other cases, a museum can enjoy
a relatively stable visitorship, including a flow of tourists, but lack connections with
and loyalty from important constituency groups. Or, a museum may find it necessary to position itself differently, forging a new image and identity, as a means to
attract new segments such as young people, families with young children, and young
professionals.

Goal-setting has to reflect a sense of mission and knowledge of a museum's
strengths and weaknesses, as well as research regarding the visitors the museum
seeks to serve and the competitive environment in which the museum exists.
The latter is a significant factor. Museums which seek to expand their audience or
bolster their community ties have, first, to identify the competition they face and
then determine the distinctive niche they can occupy in relation to the segments
of the public they want to serve and their audience needs. In other words, goals
ultimately have to reflect the interests and needs of consumers (the museum audience, members, and supporters). And the relation of a museum to its audience is
an exchange relationship: visitors derive benefits from museums and at the same
time incur certain costs (in time, convenience, and expenses) in participating in
museums; and museums derive benefits from the public such as revenue, donations,
and political support.

Goals are interrelated, forming part of a larger pattern of activity, and, therefore, have to be determined as part of a broader strategic framework. For example,
a museum may seek to build a larger audience. Yet the goal of audience development can depend on another goal: raising public awareness and visibility. The latter
goal, in turn, may depend on achieving yet a third goal: redefining the museum

image and identity and, in particular, correcting negative information and image. Goals have to be viewed as instrumental in nature, contributing to or detracting from yet other goals and the enterprise as a whole. Goals in the museum world, in addition, can be differentiated, for analytical purposes, as audience goals – offering or product goals – and organizational and competitive goals, although each set is interrelated and interdependent. Once goals are set, a strategic plan can be established for ordering them as a set of priorities, sequencing them over time, and finally accomplishing the goals. Lastly, goals have to be specific, measurable, and achievable. Table 19.1 lists ten major museum goals in relation to three strategies. Goals are sorted into three groups. Audience growth, membership growth, donor growth (the latter, in particular, deal with business and organizational support), and community service constitute the audience goals. Improving offerings and programs, and improvement of the museum's services, including exterior and interior design, constitute product or offering goals. Four goals comprise the organizational and competitive category: redefining a museum's image and raising public visibility; expanding earned income; building a more customer-centered organization (in which staff training forms a major element); and building collaborations and partnerships with other museums and organizations in the community, which can include co-marketing, cost-sharing, and other functions.

The three sets of goals are interrelated. For example, audience goals and product goals have to interpenetrate one another for either set to be successful. From a marketing perspective, successful organizations, including museums, have to reflect their audiences and, specifically, the needs of different groups and segments and the benefits they seek as consumers. Yet, as an analytical tool, it is useful to differentiate museum goals into three sets. Traditional-minded museums, while never static or oblivious of their audience, tend to focus on their collections and other resources and, typically, they generate organizational change from the inside outward. Art museums and natural history museums tend to focus more on their collections and internal resources than science centers and museums. The latter, typically, have smaller collections and are more focused on developing programs for particular audience segments, especially children and their families.

Three strategies for building audiences and improving the museum-going experience

Now let us turn to the three strategies outlined in Table 19.1. Strategies are game plans which occur in a given period of time and reveal how an organization can reach its goals. The first strategy, improving the museum-going experience, will have a large impact on the museum's audience and offering goals. The second strategy, community service, will raise the museum's image and local impact. The third strategy, market repositioning toward entertainment, aims to increase the museum's attractiveness and competitiveness in relation to alternative leisure activities. These strategies are not mutually exclusive. Indeed, elements of each can be combined, depending on the end-goals involved. Each strategy, however, represents a different direction and emphasis, roughly corresponding to the distinction among 'audience goals,' 'product goals,' and 'organizational/competitive goals,'

Table 19.1 Museum goals and strategies

Strategies	Audience Goals			Product Goals		Organizational/Competitive Goals		
	Audience Growth	Membership Growth	Donor Growth	Community Service	Improving Offerings & Programs	Improving Design & Services	Image-building	Building a Consumer-centered Organization	Increasing Income	Generating Collaborations & Partnerships
Strategy # 1 Improving museum-going experience										
Strategy # 2 Community service										
Strategy # 3 Market repositioning toward entertainment										

as outlined in Table 19.1. As models, these strategies represent different tradeoffs, divergent agendas, and they generate varying degrees of tension and conflict with core museum missions. For example, the first strategy of improving the overall museum-going experience of visitors corresponds closely to the emphasis implicit in achieving audience and offering goals. The third strategy, 'market repositioning,' is most closely related to achieving organizational change and competitive goals. Each strategy, in addition, involves different choices in allocating a museum's resources.

Strategy # 1: Improving the museum-going experience

The first strategy aims to improve the museum-going experience for visitors by providing richer exhibits and programs, better services and design elements, and more accessible and comfortable facilities. Strong exhibitions and programming, as well as good design and services, are major ingredients, but form only part of the experience. Casual visitors to large museums, typically, spend an hour or so in a museum and divide their time between exhibits, the restaurant, and the gift shop. Audience research reveals that, for the majority of visitors, social and recreational experiences are as important or more important than educational and intellectual ones. Exhibitions, with their limited texts, selective objects and compressed narratives, are often less efficient means of gathering information than books, magazines, newspapers, and the Internet. Research on European museum audiences indicates further that diversion, curiosity, and spontaneity are more characteristic of visitor intentions than structured learning.[4] For this reason, museum managers, aiming to improve visit quality, have to consider the range of visitor expectations and experiences, as well as the range of the museum's offerings and services, as integral parts of a total visitor experience.

Improving the museum-going experience involves going beyond the traditional emphasis on objects and collections and even the emphasis in recent years on information and education. Generating experiences involves activities in which visitors can directly participate, intensive sensory perception combining sight, sound, and motion, environments in which visitors can immerse themselves rather than behave merely as spectators, and out-of-the-ordinary stimuli and effects that make museum visits unique and memorable. Not all museum offerings have to be intense and immersion-like; what is needed is variety and balance in offerings along with scope and range. Research into visitors' expectations, needs, and behaviors should guide the design of museum-going experiences. Museum managers, years ago, were content with counting visitors and, later on, sought to identify types and backgrounds of those visitors. In recent years, audience research has been providing data which illuminates visitor perceptions and attitudes, thus enabling managers to respond proactively to the visitor needs and design environments and experiences those visitors can enjoy.

To improve offerings and services, museum staff have to go beyond imagining what they think visitors want. They have to question visitors directly, and a good deal of relevant audience research already exists. For example, pioneering studies by Marilyn Hood in the 1980s described visitor attitudes and behaviors in all types of recreational arenas, including museums. Hood found that consumers sought six types of benefits and values in their recreational activity: 1) being with people and enjoying social interaction; 2) doing something worthwhile; 3) feeling comfortable with the surroundings; 4) enjoying the challenge of a new or unusual experience; 5) having a learning opportunity; and 6) participating actively. In the museum setting Hood found that active museum-goers looked for a set of benefits different from casual, occasional visitors. The former sought the benefit of learning, coupled with the challenge of novel experiences and doing something worthwhile, to a greater degree than the latter.[5]

Audience research further reveals that the majority of visitors are part of social groups (family or friends) and that their behavior is influenced by the interests and attitudes of the group. John Falk points out that museum visitors vary in their backgrounds and interests and that, while some are focused on ideas, information, and cognitive learning, others favor emotional, sensory, and kinesthetic modalities. Furthermore, visitors expect recreational and social experiences and perceive museum visits as an interconnected mosaic which begins with the outing and incorporates all aspects of the visit, including the departure. The availability of convenient parking, ease of physical access to the museum building, cleanliness of the facilities, and friendliness of staff, all rank high in importance alongside quality exhibitions and programs.[6]

Museum visitors seek variety in the offerings. Many feel a reverence toward the objects and collections in museums. Visitors seek after celebrative experiences in which they connect with the past, encounter inspiring examples, express pride in their heritage, honor important events, and bask in great achievements in art and culture, science, and governance. Regular visitors to art museums, in particular, embody a keenness for aesthetic experiences and things of beauty which can sweep them away in experiences of awe and enchantment. Visitors expect learning and cognitive experiences as well, and to encounter things in museums which contrast with the routines of work and everyday life.[7]

Zahava Doering, Director of the Institutional Studies Office at the Smithsonian Institution, has studied visitors' expectations, attitudes, and behaviors over a number of years. Her studies shed light on predispositions and assumptions which visitors bring to their museum visits. Doering's studies indicate that visitors arrive in museums with 'their own visit agendas and sense of time,' frequent those exhibits and programs 'with whose point of view they expect to agree,' and they respond best to museum activities 'that are personally relevant and with which they can easily connect.' The great majority of visitors are involved in four types of museum-going experience: social experiences; cognitive (information-gathering, meaning-making) experiences; object experiences (viewing beautiful, rare, or valuable things, such as the Hope Diamond at the Smithsonian's Natural History Museum); and introspective experiences, in which objects and settings trigger memories and associations, feelings of spiritual connection, and a sense of connectedness to a culture and community.[8]

In making improvements in exhibits and programs, managers have choices in terms of exhibit designs which offer different levels of information, reach different groups, and employ different formats such as interpretative text, story-telling, interactive elements, and simulation of an environment, mood or historical situation. Creating a variety of exhibits and programs has the advantage of appealing to several different audience segments. An example is the First Division Museum at the Cantigny Estate in Wheaton, Illinois, built by Col. Robert McCormick, publisher of *The Chicago Tribune* newspaper, to honor the fighting men of this army division and their wartime experiences. Vintage tanks and other military equipment from two World Wars stand in a park outside the museum, not unlike pieces of sculpture a visitor can find in a sculpture garden, while inside the Museum, war-related events and military achievements are richly interpreted in a series of galleries. In the newest section, visitors can walk through a World War I battlefield trench, listen to the sounds of war, and experience the travail and suffering. They also walk through a French village as it stood just after being shelled and can imagine the civilian calamity which has been inflicted.

Large museums organize 'blockbuster' exhibitions which offer visitors one-of-a-kind experiences, and years afterwards visitors can recall these exhibitions vividly because of their intensity and scale. Smaller museums, lacking the resources to organize such large-scale exhibitions, have to find ways to change and renew their displays from time to time and exploit creatively their collections and presentational designs. More and more museums are utilizing media and interactive elements to expand the visitor's sense of immediacy and participation. One element in the museum-going experience can usually be improved: the extent of visitor contact with staff. The majority of visitors arrive with friends or family, yet they express a desire for added contact with staff. Exhibition programs and behind-the-scenes tours with docents and staff offer opportunities for visitors to ask questions, offer comments, and share their experiences. Museums are experimenting with programs which allow visitors at designated times to come together in a museum space, along with staff, to reflect together on their museum experiences. The latter activities enrich museum visits and humanize what can be intimidating objects and settings. Services form a significant part of museum offerings and include: convenient parking and access to mass transit; outdoor lighting and security; ample seating, dining, and shopping facilities; trained staff who are responsive and friendly to visitors; wayfinding and user-friendly gallery design that make it easier for visitors to move around the museum; and furnishing richer information and context regarding objects, collections, and exhibits, such as narratives, historical analysis, databases, biography, and a variety of interpretative tools.

Finding one's way around museums with large, complex buildings, for example, can be a stumbling block for first-time visitors. Large museums typically provide visitors with maps of galleries, exhibitions, and other physical facilities within the museum. The National Gallery of Art in Washington, D.C. has taken this one step further in its electronic Micro-Gallery. Visitors to the Micro-Gallery, situated at one of the major entrances, can sample the Gallery's collection and temporary exhibitions on a computer screen; absorb all kinds of contextual information such as biographies, time-lines, historical information, and art criticism; locate the specific works and treasures they want to view; and design their own personal tours with instructions printed out for finding their way. The Hirshhorn Museum and Sculpture Garden, part of the Smithsonian Institution in Washington, D.C., moved its gift shop from an out-of-the-way basement area to the main entrance area and combined it with a visitor information desk operated by volunteers. Prior to the change, visitors entered the Museum with little opportunity to obtain information and orientation. Information desks and gift shops at entrances work well in acclimating visitors.

The Museum of Science in Boston has invested in recent years considerable resources in way-finding improvements. Today, visitors move about the Museum, using color-coded signage and directions as well as computer-generated and brochure maps. The Baltimore Museum of Art provides, on request, lightweight folding chairs for visitors who like to sit down in the galleries. It is a flexible arrangement which encourages visitors to spend more time viewing the art works. The Oregon Museum of Science and Industry has created a family room with board games and abundant seating so that large or extended families can move about at different paces, allowing, for example, grandparents to relax and play the board games while the grandchildren are running off in multiple directions. Museums contain a great deal of sensory stimuli and visitors can easily feel overwhelmed and exhausted by the experience. Improved services such as seating, activity rooms, gift shops, and restaurants not only satisfy a visitor's need for comfort and diversion, but also encourage visitors to spend more time in museums.

Augmented services such as social events and continuing education are yet another form of service museums are increasingly offering. Museum visits usually are sociable experiences and managers are organizing a rich array of events which deepen a visitor's or member's relationship with the museum: e.g., opening night events for new exhibitions; holiday, seasonal, and commemorative events; special programs for targeted groups, such as art workshops for families with young children, and young professionals' socials.

Museum staff have choices regarding the extent to which they can influence and manage the museum-going experiences of their visitors. Years ago, museum audiences were smaller, more homogeneous, and more self-selective. Today, museum audiences are wide-ranging and more diverse and, therefore, are seeking after a variety of experiences, benefits, and satisfactions. Museums are better-equipped today as a result of both visitor research and technological means to provide differing levels of information, narrative, and cognitive experience as part of their displays. The issue is the extent to which managers want to influence proactively or design the elements of visitors' experiences, as against the degree to which they want to leave their visitors alone. For art museums, particularly, the matter of designing the visitor experience is a complicated one. On the one hand, art museums seek to safeguard the visitor's direct encounter with works of art, minimizing distractions in the form of noise, congestion, and a deluge of media and printed material. On the other hand, art museums recognize that many visitors need information and interpretative tools in order to appreciate the artworks they are encountering.

There is no single formula which museums can employ for shaping visitors' museum experiences. Different types of museums will strike different balances. Yet from a consumer point of view, managers should look upon their museum, in varying degrees, as a designed environment and arrangement of activities, services, and experiences which will have value for their visitors. Managing services and orchestrating experiences is a direction managers are taking to transform museums from being simply places to visit on the occasion of a special event or 'blockbuster exhibition' to being places to visit regularly because they offer exceptional services, settings, and ambiences in every season.

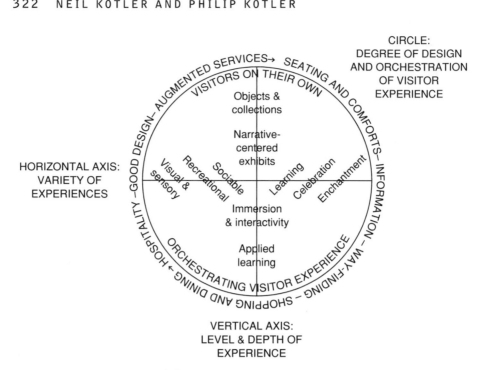

Figure 19.1   Dimensions of the museum-going experience

Figure 19.1 outlines three dimensions of a designed museum-going experience. The horizontal axis indicates a range of visitor experiences, which includes visual, sensory, and aesthetic experience; recreational, sociable, and learning experiences; and the experiences of celebration and enchantment. The vertical axis identifies levels of intensity in museum-going experience, from relatively passive viewing of collections to active immersion experience and applied learning. The circle indicates the degree of services, including interior and architectural design, augmented services, information, hospitality, dining, and shopping. In this first strategy, objects, exhibitions, and interpretative programs continue to be the focal points of the museum-going experience, while improvements in facilities, services, and programs serve to facilitate and reinforce the museum-going experience for a broader audience. An emphasis on improving services, to be sure, may divert resources from collections care and exhibition development, but overall, this strategy, of the three, is that most closely linked to the traditional core activities of museums.

Strategy # 2: Community service

The second strategy places its emphasis on expanding community service. Many American museums developed out of a sense of place and community. Local historical societies organized museums in the 19th century to celebrate heritage and community history. Historic houses have commemorated great figures, families, and historic periods, while historic sites captured the drama of great events. Art museums presented regional art, and natural history museums illustrated regional flora and fauna and their natural development. At a later time, 'halls of fame' arose, celebrating great achievements in sports, invention, industry, and technology, while their sponsors, followers, and enthusiasts represented extended communities of memory, spirit, and ideas.

In the early decades of the 20th century, John Cotton Dana at the Newark Museum in New Jersey was a pioneer in developing the educational role of museums and links to schools, a major expression of community service. Dana conceived a museum 'to be of immediate, practical aid to all of the community that supports it.' Museum collections were seen as educational tools which could be useful to young people; collections of industrial tools, of design elements, and of art and crafts were made available to help young people appreciate the practical arts and train some to become tradesmen, craftsmen, and artists. Special collections were used in schools and students became apprentices in the museum.[9] Adult education was a goal of several prominent Chicago museums, such as the Field Museum of Natural History and the Museum of Science and Industry. Set in public parks and nature preserves, these museums were designed to inspire an appreciation of nature and educate adults who lacked formal education or who were recent immigrants. Today, museums are building partnerships with schools. The Smithsonian Institution, for example, provides technical training and support, along with instruction and curriculum materials, for museum-oriented model schools in Washington, D.C.

Community service in recent years has assumed a broader meaning than education. Some museums have made themselves a vital part of community life and instruments in fostering a community's sense of identity and solidarity. Local historical museums have played significant roles in deepening the sense of communal identity, celebrating heritage and interpreting community traditions and mores. Regional museums, such as the Genesee Country Village and Museum in upstate New York, organize a variety of holiday, commemorative, and seasonal events to strengthen community ties, reinforce the sense of belonging, and, additionally, augment their audiences. The Missouri Historical Society in St. Louis has evolved into a leading forum for discussion of neighborhood and community issues and of efforts to generate policy to solve those problems. The Johnson County Museum in Shawnee, Kansas, in the early 1990s, forged a new identity as a community-centered museum emphasizing the cultural practice and heritage of different ethnic and cultural groups in the region. The Museum invited residents to help the Museum build its collections by donating objects which illustrate local history and culture. It reoriented its displays to focus on different groups, generating a far higher level of participation among community members than had occurred in the past. Museums function as community meeting places, and children's and youth museums, especially, have developed important roles as educational centers, meeting places, and community development arms.

Museums in the late 20th century have evolved yet another community function, as economic development engines in the form of attractions and tourist destinations which can contribute to a community's growth in jobs and income. Downtown developers and city governments view museums, cultural and entertainment districts, as projects to stimulate economic revitalization. An example is the Davenport (Iowa) Art Museum which is situated in a hard-to-reach, outlying neighborhood. With support from the municipal government, as well as private donors, the museum board will build a new $15 million downtown museum which is expected to infuse new life in the downtown area and serve to attract other cultural and entertainment organizations. In the summer of 1999, a British architect was hired to design the new museum. Museum architecture as well as exhibitions and public programs are tourist attractions. An example is the Guggenheim Museum in Bilbao, Spain. Public authorities in Bilbao, in the depressed Basque region of Spain, invested $100 million to build the extraordinary Frank Gehry-designed museum in Bilbao, which has overnight become one of Europe's greatest tourist destinations.

Community service embraces services which are useful in fulfilling the common needs of a community as a whole, yet it also includes initiatives which reach specific groups, such as under-served ethnic groups, families with children, and young professionals, whose participation can be vital. The Memorial Art Gallery in Rochester, New York, in the late 1980s and early 1990s, became aware of its aging membership and declining support groups. As a means to attract younger visitors and members, the Gallery created a monthly event for young professionals known as 'First Friday,' offering a variety of activities, including drinks, light meals, lectures, gallery tours, and jazz performances which has become a leading social event for younger members of the community. The monthly events average more than 1,000 participants and a growing number are recruited as members and patrons. The Field Museum in Chicago has reached out to new segments, such as under-served ethnic and cultural groups, by organizing outdoor summer ethnic arts and cultural festivals. Community service also has manifested itself in recent years in the form of museum collaborations and partnerships to promote art and culture and raise the visibility of museum offerings and services. A group of museums in Providence, Rhode Island, for example, has joined together in leasing a downtown building to generate a cultural district of greater visibility, appeal, and service. Groups of local museums have formed marketing partnerships to generate joint advertising, collaborate on admissions fees and offer common tickets, and to build purchasing co-operatives to reduce operating costs.

The second strategy, it can be argued, gives the most emphasis to identifying, segmenting, and targeting the public, the consumers, and the members of a given community and region. Community participation and support, after all, is accomplished by the involvement of the various segments of the community and new museum offerings and programs have to be tailored to meet the needs of different segments. The community service strategy, thus, can be viewed as a change strategy which moves from the outside (the audience, the public) inward into the museum organization (the offerings and services). Embracing community service also is a means to build audience and support over the long run. Thus the community service direction has evolved from a focus on education based on collections and exhibitions to a focus on community needs in a broader sense. In the process, what were once known as 'ancillary' services have become major elements of museum operations alongside core functions. A focus on community service does not necessarily involve sacrificing the core mission of a museum, and in the best of worlds the former will bring in more visitors and active participants. However, greater interaction with and dependence on the community can lead museums to rethink their collections, displays, and programs, and move in the direction of diversifying their collections and programs, and, perhaps, replacing some parts with others.

Strategy # 3: Market repositioning toward entertainment

The third strategy can involve far-reaching change. It occurs when a museum redesigns its facilities and offerings in a sweeping rather than incremental manner in order to attract an entirely new audience to make itself competitive with other leisure activity organizations, or to become a place which is popular and entertaining with a broad and diverse audience. Market repositioning means, in some cases, a substantial move away from a museum's traditional audience and thus the need to build entirely new constituencies. Although this third strategy involves potentially the most drastic transformation of the core activities of collecting, conserving, exhibiting, and educating, it is not always easy to judge when a museum's range of offerings, overall, reinforce its educational mission and when new offerings change the balance and tip the museum instead in the direction of an entertainment center. The very definition of 'entertainment' has changed during the past century and more. The American museum pioneer, Charles Willson Peale, opened a museum in Philadelphia in the 1780s and promoted it as a place of 'rational entertainment,' by which he meant a combination of designed settings and experiences for recreation along with educational offerings. Although a museum director, Peale was also a showman who understood that visitors had to perceive an attraction to exist before they would be available for learning. The contemporary concept, 'edutainment,' sets out to capture the same idea: attractive and entertaining presentation and design can facilitate educational goals.

From early times, museums have presented themselves, in part, as akin to performances, happenings, and theatrical experiences. These sometimes functioned as interpretative devices for collections and at other times as atmospherics and extra attractions. Dioramas built in natural history museums from the the late 19th century, for example, sought to provide visitors with richer interpretative contexts for stuffed animals and birds. Historical museums and historic homes have featured displays of costumes, story-telling, and quasi-theatrical performances as means of helping visitors to understand better different historical situations. Many museums are hybrids composed of collecting institutions with story-driven and interactive learning and entertainment centers. A growing number of them call themselves history and science centers precisely as a means to build an identity as broader-based learning centers rather than simply organizations devoted purely to objects and material culture. What basically differentiate museums from non-museums are the collections of authentic objects and materials, assembled and conserved in accordance with the core purposes of preservation, enlightenment, edification, and education, which museum staff are expected to accomplish.

Museums seek to fulfill their educational missions in varied and innovative ways. Objects and collections alone may not be the most effective means to cover a particular topic or tell a particular story, and museums may offer displays with hands-on and interactive elements, immersive environments, multiple media, and narratives. The Exploratorium in San Francisco, one of the most celebrated science

NEIL KOTLER AND PHILIP KOTLER

326   NEIL KOTLER AND PHILIP KOTLER

centers in the world, has an overriding goal of teaching science and inspiring young people to engage in scientific experiments. To accomplish that mission, it offers visitors hundreds of scientific experiments and demonstrations as well as themed displays which tell the story of science. Yet very few of the Exploratorium's offerings contain original scientific instruments, artifacts, or archival material. The Smithsonian Institution installed in the summer of 1999 an interactive display entitled *Microbes: Invisible Invaders . . . Amazing Allies*. Designed primarily for children and their parents, this display generated large, enthusiastic audiences, although it was a departure from traditional Smithsonian exhibitions. *Microbes* offered an exuberant educational experience without including treasured objects of medical history, even though great treasures of the history of medicine reside in Smithsonian collections, such as the original vial of Salk polio vaccine. Many museums are experimenting with different combinations of collections, themed displays, and interactive offerings. Indeed, the Minnesota History Center, in Minneapolis, has redesigned its offerings and galleries to engage visitors in the process of reliving history. A series of small theaters offer visitors emotional, even cathartic, experiences revolving around the sense of family and the sense of place. Visitors can manipulate cubes with layered information in the exhibit halls which offer different types of visitors varying levels of information and engagement.

Transformation can take other forms too. Changes at the Smithsonian's National Museum of Natural History in Washington, D.C., exemplify a movement toward greater entertainment-oriented experience, while the museum works to maintain a balance between museum purposes and marketing requirements. The museum opened its Discovery Center in 1998–1999, consisting of three facilities which set out to serve the needs of a large audience: a significantly enlarged and redesigned gift shop with better-quality merchandise; an expanded restaurant with a greater variety of cuisines; and a new 3-D IMAX theater. Although the new center has generated increased visitors and revenue, some argue the museum should have invested the funds in refurbishing its 50-year-old displays rather than investing in a new entertainment facility within the museum. Another example of repositioning is the Guggenheim's summer 1998 exhibition 'The Art of the Motorcycle.' The Guggenheim often has exhibitions dealing with design. The motorcycle exhibition aimed, in addition, to reach into popular culture and segments of the public that rarely if ever visited art museums. The exhibition was one of the most popular ever held at the Museum.

Market repositioning can also involve examining a museum's community, finding out what needs are not being addressed, and repositioning the museum to serve the community better. The last example is the most transforming. The Strong Museum in Rochester, New York, was a traditional museum known for having one of the world's most distinguished doll collections, along with regional historical artifacts. Visitor numbers had declined precipitously by the early 1990s and museum leaders decided to strike out in new directions. They commissioned substantial market research and launched a strategic planning process, in which members of the community were asked to recommend alternative museum concepts. This resulted in transforming the Strong into a family- and children-centered museum, for which there was an unmet need in the community. Today collections co-exist with hands-on, interactive programs, narrative-driven displays, performances, and family activities, and this has generated significant additional community involvement and has expanded both audience and income. These examples illustrate the range of market repositioning strategies available: innovation in offerings; innovation in community service; and innovation in competing in recreational and tourist markets.

Criticism of market repositioning strategy

What are the objections to the market repositioning strategy? The first objection is that the strategy can diminish scholarship, authenticity of the collections, and staff professionalism, which lie at the core of the museum mission. Museums are standard bearers in which the public should place its trust, while converting museums into mere entertainment centers renders them no different from ordinary entertainment media and robs them of their primary educational purpose. Once museums lose their distinctive core mission, they will have to compete in the marketplace with the entertainment industry, whose resources are far more substantial. Competing as entertainment arenas will not provide museums with a level playing field; on the contrary, museums will have to compete with real entertainment products and they are likely to be perceived as second-rate in comparison.

A second objection is that museums are distinctive institutions which focus on the role of objects and material culture in understanding history, science, art, and culture. Few other institutions can play this role and any movement of museums toward non-collection-based displays and programs denies society alternative approaches to knowledge. A third and related objection is that in giving emphasis to entertainment, museums remove from society the few remaining varieties of recreational activity. Popular tastes run to thrills, adventure, and emotional stimulation and these are readily available in existing mass media. What is needed are counterpoints – influences which will elevate public taste – for which museums are uniquely suited. Furthermore, audience research shows that museum visitors appreciate the extraordinary range of collections presented that allow them to step outside of the routines of work and everyday life. The ideal situation in a museum, as veteran managers have observed, is to nurture staff devotion to collections and their interpretation and at the same time motivate staff commitment to helping visitors fully enjoy what a museum has to offer. The passion which curatorial staff have toward collections and encouraging the public to be equally passionate about them lies at the heart of the museum mission. This is what generates care and quality. The manager's role is to encourage staff, mollify their fears, and demonstrate that opening up the museum to new and broader audiences will not jeopardize integrity and standards.

Marketing's role in museum goal-setting and strategy

A growing number of museums are hiring marketing experts to help them accomplish their goals. Goals which relate to external factors, audiences, and the environment (e.g., building audiences, improving the museum-going experience, increasing sales, developing competitive programs) are particularly well-suited to

Table 19.2   Marketing tools and techniques for museums

Research and analysis	Researching the environment, including market opportunities and competitive threats, organizational assessment, including strengths and weaknesses, market and visitor analysis
STP:	
Segmentation	Identifying different segments of museum audiences, consumers of other recreational activities, and non-visitor groups, and their differing needs and expectations
Targeting	Selecting segments to target for the museum audience (e.g., families with young children, educated adults, senior citizens, young professionals, tourists)
Positioning	Defining an image identity that will differentiate a museum from other comparable organizations and satisfy needs of target segments
Marketing mix:	
Product	Managing and renewing exhibits, collections, programs; creating new offerings and services
Place	Designing a comfortable museum facility as well as distributing museum offerings to schools, traveling exhibits, and websites and other electronic media
Promotion	Advertising public relations, directing marketing, sales promotion, and integrated communications to audiences, collaborators, and competitors
Price	Pricing admissions, memberships, gift shop merchandise, special events, donor acknowledgment, discounts, to attract visitors in all seasons, including off-season, and to attract under-served constituencies

marketing. Table 19.2 identifies a series of marketing tools and techniques which can help museums achieve their goals, and these include the so-called marketing mix, the basic factors which affect consumer behavior. The list is as follows: 1) research, including environmental and competitive analysis, organizational assessment, audience and market research; 2) techniques of segmenting different audiences, targeting the groups the museum seeks to attract, and positioning the museum as delivering the benefits sought by the target groups; 3) product development, including management of existing products as well as generating new ones; 4) distribution, ways a museum can distribute its offerings widely, beyond the museum walls; 5) promotion, consisting of tools of advertising, public relations, direct marketing, which communicate offerings to different target groups; 6) pricing, or the determination of what to charge for different museum offerings which will increase audience and income; 7) service and relationship marketing, which aims to create close bonds with target groups (in the case of museums, repeat visitors); and 8) strategic planning, the long-range activity by which the museum visualizes and plans its future and sets its priorities. These represent the tool box which museum managers can apply to their particular challenges and problem-solving. Basic to each of the tools and techniques, and a basic assumption behind marketing, is that a transaction and a relationship with museum visitors, members, and supporters has to reflect an exchange of benefits and costs, both for the public and for the museum.

Marketing's ability to assist museums flows both from the tools and techniques it offers and from the ability of marketing staff to influence constructively the museum organization in all its operations. Some museums have hired marketing staff but have relegated them to one corner of the museum operation, typically promotional activity. Marketing, however, is broader than simply promotion. Marketing is best able to facilitate a museum's goals and strategy when marketing staff can participate in and lend their expertise to all museum tasks, including programs and education, facility and interior design, as well as membership and development. Marketing professionals, under the best circumstances, will have relationships with all other museum staff and offices and a marketing director's advice will be sought in all roles, especially those affecting audiences, supporters, and other parts of the external environment.

Can museums be all things to all people?

The challenge for museum managers is to safeguard the museum mission while reaching out to a larger public and offering a richer museum-going experience for visitors. The risks in diluting the core activities of collections, scholarship, and education cannot be minimized. Yet, without an audience and community support, even the greatest exhibition and collection will fail to generate response. While museums cannot respond to every demand put forward by a constituency group, they can make sound choices. Managers have alternatives in designing and orchestrating visitors' experiences. They can leave visitors alone, to fend for themselves, or else they can provide ample orientation and information, welcoming behavior by staff, and design satisfying experiences for their visitors.

Can a museum be all things to all people? Not easily or productively, simply because most museums are strapped for funds, especially the program funds needed to satisfy diverse constituency demands. Experience has shown that museums, like other organizations, are best able to play to their strengths and are foolish to offer things of indifferent quality at which other competitors excel. From a marketing point of view, museums have to address their audience needs while cultivating new groups of visitors and leading their audience to even greater experiences and benefits. If museums cannot serve everybody in a uniform way, they can set priorities for the target groups they can best serve and fit programs and staff to meet their needs. And museums can develop a fuller relationship with their constituencies, converting one-time transactions involving a single visit or occasional visits into relationships involving regular, active participation.

In setting goals and strategies, museums develop a clear view of their strengths and weaknesses and a vision of the kind of internal culture and structure which is most likely to generate desired outcomes. Having ambitious though realistic goals, relating these to the mission and the desired audience mix, knowing the audience and how to lead it, and finding the strategies and tools most effective in reaching the goals, is the best recipe to put forward for museums grappling with issues of change, innovation, and preserving integrity.

Notes

In *Museum Strategy and Marketing: Designing Missions, Building Audiences, Generating Revenue and Resources* (1998) **Neil Kotler and Philip Kotler** combined their extensive experience (of both museums and marketing theory and practice) to produce a comprehensive analysis of museum marketing. This paper was first published in 2000 in *Museum Management and Curatorship*, vol.18, No.3.

1   David M. Wilson, 'What Do We Need Money For?' in T. Ambrose (ed.), *Money, Money, Money, and Museums*, Edinburgh (Scottish Museums Council) 1991, p. 11.
2   Kenneth Hudson, 'The Museum Refuses to Stand Still,' *Museum International*, No. 197, January–March, 1998, p. 43.
3   Neil Kotler and Philip Kotler, *Museum Strategy and Marketing: Designing Missions, Building Audiences, Generating Revenue and Resources*, San Francisco (Jossey-Bass) 1998, p. 348.
4   Zahava D. Doering, 'Strangers, Guests or Clients? Visitor Experiences in Museums,' paper presented at a Weimar, Germany, conference, *Managing the Arts*, 17–19 March 1999, Washington, D.C. (Institutional Studies Office, Smithsonian Institution) 1999, p. 4; see, also, Nobuko Kawashima, 'Knowing the Public: A Review of Museum Marketing Literature and Research,' *Museum Management and Curatorship*, vol. 17, no. 1, 1998, p. 32.
5   Marilyn G. Hood, 'Staying Away: Why People Choose Not to Visit Museums,' *Museum News*, April 1983, pp. 50–57.
6   John H. Falk and Lynn D. Dierking, *The Museum Experience*, Washington, D.C. (Whalesback Books) 1992, pp. 25–37; 129–133.
7   Kotler and Kotler, op. cit., pp. 34–36.
8   Doering, op. cit., pp. 7–13.
9   John Cotton Dana, *The New Museum*, Woodstock, VT (Elm Tree Press) 1917.

Chapter 20

Strangers, Guests, or Clients?
Visitor experiences in museums

Zahava D. Doering

Overview

> Museums, like many other heritage attractions, are essentially experiential products, quite literally *constructions to facilitate experience*. In this sense, museums are about facilitating feelings and knowledge based upon personal observation or contact by their visitors.
>
> (Prentice, 'Managing Implosion,' p. 169)

DEPENDING ON TIME, PLACE, and history, museums have displayed many attitudes toward visitors, some explicitly and some implicitly. Over the 12 years that my colleagues and I have been working to provide Smithsonian museum staff with information about their visitors, I have encountered a number of these viewpoints. As I reflected on the often striking differences between these perspectives, I concluded that these many stances could be grouped under three major models of how museums see visitors: viewing visitors as strangers, viewing them as guests, and viewing them as clients. I found that this framework gave us a new perspective on our past work and provided a direction for our future applied research. In this article, in part a description of our research and in part a personal reflection, I discuss these three types of attitudes toward visitors, some of their implications, and where these ideas have led the Institutional Studies Office.

Three types of attitudes toward visitors

The history of museums might appear to suggest a sequential development from stranger to guest to client. But even a cursory examination of current museum styles

Source: *Curator*, vol. 42, no. 2 (1999): 74–87.

suggests that all three still exist across our institutions and even coexist (sometimes harmoniously and sometimes not) within single museums. These attitudes, styles, and approaches to visitors are the products of historical situations, collections, and individuals.

Strangers.   In this mode the museum maintains that its primary responsibility is to the *collection* or to some other aspect of the work and not to the public. Many curators understandably take this posture, as do institutions primarily devoted to research. Such museums emphasize 'object accountability.' The public, while admitted, is viewed as strangers (at best) and intruders (at worst). The public is expected to acknowledge that by virtue of being admitted, it has been granted a special privilege.[1]

Guests.   In this posture, perhaps most common in our museums today, the museum assumes responsibility for visitors. The museum wants to 'do good' for visitors out of a sense of mission. This 'doing good' is usually expressed as 'educational' activities and institutionally defined objectives. The visitor-guests are assumed to be eager for this assistance and receptive to this approach.

Clients.   In this attitude the museum believes that its primary responsibility is to be *accountable* to the visitor. The visitor is no longer subordinate to the museum. The museum no longer seeks to impose the visit experience that it deems most appropriate. Rather, the institution acknowledges that visitors, like clients, have needs and expectations that the museum is obligated to understand and meet.[2]

How did these attitudes or styles evolve and how do they inform the present?

Visitors as strangers

Solinger (1990) reminds us that the ancient Greeks referred to a museum (Gr. *mouseion*) as a center of learning. She goes on to note that 'the most renowned early museum was housed under the auspices of the library of Alexandria, founded in the third century B.C.' and then describes how the museum's resident scholars took part in scholarly discussion, research, and teaching. This museum also contained 'statues, scientific instruments, zoological specimens and a botanical and zoological park' (ibid.: 1). In the description, we recognize the precursor of present-day universities, museums, and libraries. Universities, she notes, have become 'formal sources and prime purveyors of higher education, while libraries have evolved into resource centers' (ibid.: 2).

In their historic transformation, many museums maintained scholarly or teaching roles, but this specialization of functions between universities and museums led to particular emphases. Thus, the museum's traditional focus on collecting, preserving, and exhibiting objects has redefined the scholarly function as research related to objects and the education function as teaching the public about objects in the collection.

Given their object-based orientation, it is not at all surprising that museums expended considerable resources on maintaining their collections and took 'accountability for objects' as a paramount responsibility. Conservation and preservation, security, and safety are givens in the museum environment, and collections management systems have kept pace with technological development.

The rationale for making some collections available for public viewing, especially in the late eighteenth and early nineteenth centuries, relied on ideas such as moral uplift, character development, skill training, education for the masses, and acculturation. At the same time, as reflected overtly in very restricted visitation hours, dress codes, and regulations governing visits, the orientation was to the 'stranger' in the title. Most museums existed to collect, preserve, and study their collections – whether or not they were visited. Historical forces have compelled cultural institutions to retreat from this position, at least publicly, but it is still part of the culture of many institutions and the more traditional departments within them.

While maintaining distance from the public, nineteenth-century museums saw themselves as having an educational role, both in Europe and the United States. In summarizing the history of education in museums, Hein (1998) notes that in the latter half of the nineteenth century, governments increasingly assumed responsibility for social services and education and viewed museums as one of the institutions that 'could provide education for the masses.' At the same time, however, schools supported by public funds were developing as social institutions. Of special importance for our later discussion of measurement is Hein's observation that schools 'measured and tested' while museums did not.

> But, unlike museums, they [schools] quickly developed an accountability system – inspectors, tests, and standard curriculum as well as public discussion of what schools were for, how they should be run, and whether they were doing their intended job. . . . Museums, although equally public institutions in most countries, did not establish similar approaches to assessing impact on their clients. It was assumed that people would learn, be enlightened, and be entertained by their visits to museums without any reference to the study of visitors' experiences. (Hein 1998: 5)

Visitors as guests

In the United States, the number of museums has grown fourfold in the last 25 years. The most recent estimates (1992) count 8,200 independent museums.[3] During the same 25 years, the profession as a whole has put increasing emphasis on the educational role of museums. Between 1969 and 1992, the American Association of Museums considered the overall mission of museums in three publications: *The Belmont Report* (AAM 1969), *Museums for a New Century* (AAM 1984), and *Excellence and Equity: Education and the Public Dimension of Museums* (AAM 1992). All three reports stressed the responsibility that museums have, together with other social institutions, to educate. The latest report did so forcibly, stating the museums should:

enrich learning opportunities for all individuals and to nurture an enlight-
ened, human citizenry that appreciates the value of knowing about its
past, is resourcefully and sensitively engaged in the present and is determined to shape a future in which many experiences and many points of
view are given voice. (AAM 1992: 25)

An educational mission implies a relationship with visitors akin to that of 'hosts'
and 'guests,' in which museums not only are more accommodating to visitors but
also take some responsibility for what happens to them.

When museums see visitors as guests, they pay considerable attention to
hosting functions. Advertising, outreach programs, and affordable membership programs, among other methods, are used to invite the public to museums. Restaurants,
shops, and theaters have been added as amenities appropriate to hosting behavior.
In some cases, museums have been totally rebuilt in order to provide more of these
amenities.

Having welcomed an ever-increasing public into their buildings, what do
museums offer these guests? They offer them the knowledge and perspectives of
their professional staff. In my experience this usually means that the staff aims to
provide visitors with motivation, attitudes, and ideas that mirror their own development and thinking. They seem to assume that visitors share the overall concerns
and values of curators and educators and have come to the museum looking for
guidance and instruction. Consequently, most exhibition aims are stated as some
kind of change that the museum wishes to induce in the visitor as it brings those
individuals closer to the state of mind of the museum's professionals.

Visitors as clients

Today, increasingly, there is pressure on American social institutions to be accountable for 'products,' to demonstrate effectiveness and social worth – to show that
they are 'successful.' Social institutions are being called on to justify both public
and private support in an increasingly competitive environment.[4] These pressures
are pushing museums more toward viewing their visitors as clients.

In fact, Weil (1997) has suggested that the museum's role toward the public
will change radically and

> will have been transformed from one of mastery to one of service.
> Toward what ends that service is to be performed, for whom it is to
> be rendered, and how, and when – those are all determinations that
> will be made by the museum's newly ascendant master, the public.
> (ibid.: 257)

The idea that a museum could be accountable to a visitor in the way that a
professional is accountable to a client probably originates in the corporate world.
Corporate management principles and approaches, especially from the service
sector, are being applied to museums with increasing frequency.

In the museum field itself, there seems to be a general and growing sense that the familiar paradigms of both the institutions and their visitors are inadequate. Perry *et al.* (1997) recently wrote,

> Once defined primarily in terms of their collections, museums are now collections-based only as far as their collections serve people – through research, education, stewardship, and more. This shift means that the institution's role must be defined as much by how it serves people as by how it preserves objects. (ibid.: 26)

In response to this situation they propose,

> First, the museum field needs a clear articulation of what it means to be a museum today. . . . For only when museums have a clear notion of who and what they are and should be, especially in relation to their communities and society, will they be able to assess the many different ways they are and are not effective. (ibid.: 27)

Do we need to redefine museums? I am not sure. Instead, museums may need to more clearly and accurately recognize their present roles within a larger society and take advantage of its implications. In other words, I believe that museums *do* need to rethink their relationship with visitors.

Museums need to acknowledge the implications of museum-going as a *leisure-time activity*. As such, museum-going is one of many activities that serves our need for 'personal self-definitions and agendas for development,' in the words of Kelly and Godbey (1992: 449). In *The Sociology of Leisure*, they write,

> However, leisure is not just a social phenomenon that reflects the institutional structure of the society. It is also a realm of openness in which individuals take action that has consequences for who they are and who they are becoming. There is a developmental dimension to leisure that runs through the entire life course. Children learn and develop in play. In fact, most critical early socialization occurs in play. Throughout the life course, individuals inaugurate and revise lines of action that are intended to enable them to become the kind of persons they want to be and to have some sort of ongoing community with others with whom they want to share some significant part of their lives. Leisure, then, is closely connected with personal self-definitions and agendas for development. Its meaning is more than momentary, however much it may be focused on the quality of the experience. (ibid.: 25–26)

If, then, museums were to acknowledge their leisure activity role, it follows directly that they would also be admitting their role as 'service' institutions, perhaps more akin to libraries than to universities. They would see themselves as a resource for personal development, places in which the needs of users (like those of readers in libraries) are *primary* and respected as such.

What might all this mean for museums? What could it mean for their relationship with visitors? What could it mean for 'performance measurement,' or for assessing the effectiveness of exhibitions and museums more generally?

Generally, programmatic performance has been measured from an *institutional* perspective, by asking whether or not the exhibition or program meets the needs of the institution at this particular point in its cycle of growth and change. Those institutional needs may focus on visitors, staff, donors, or on nonvisitors, but they are still seen from the point of view of the museum.

Exhibitions for visitors, for example, have had goals such as involvement, learning, attitudinal or behavioral change, increased income, or expanded donations. Exhibitions for staff have aimed for the recognition of peers or advancement of knowledge. Exhibitions for nonvisitors have sought publicity, notice, recognition, favorable opinion, or an expanded audience. *Whatever goal was chosen, it was typically chosen on the basis of professional opinion as to what accomplishment would best serve the museum at that moment.*

Whether relying on expert opinion, or peer review, or scientific studies of visitors, the underlying assumption has usually been that 'we,' the museum staff, know what it is we need to accomplish and the yardstick of 'success' is the extent to which 'they,' the visitors, respond to our offerings in the ways that we intend. As I noted above, this is the classic 'host and guest' relationship.

But accelerating change in our environment suggests that we start to consider some alternative scenarios. As a colleague phrased it, 'What might we learn if studies were owned by the visitor rather than by the institution?' What if we began to seriously think of visitors as 'clients' with needs that museums were responsible for meeting? For one thing, the success of an exhibition, a public program, or a museum visit might have a very different meaning for visitors or potential visitors than it does for an institution.

What do visitors want?

Shortly after the Institutional Studies Office was established at the Smithsonian, we were asked to conduct studies aimed at assessing how successful exhibitions and programs were in achieving the goals of the planning staff. Our paradigm was the guest model, and our work was generally directed to informing the hosts of the extent to which they had succeeded in effectively communicating to their guests. We started, in every case, by working closely with the exhibition team to make sure we understood their goals and objectives for visitors. Although we asked visitors why they came in a general way, we never explored in depth what they wanted or expected from the visit or an exhibition.

Several years ago, upon reviewing the studies our office had conducted, we found that exhibitions and programs designed to be communication media rarely conveyed the desired messages to even half of their visitors. Can this be called success?[5] What does it mean that 20%, 50%, or 65% of visitors understood the basic themes and messages? If we assume that everyone who came to the exhibition wanted or expected to get a message and, hence, was available to receive it, then 50% or less seems to be a rather low level of accomplishment. But what if all visitors were *not* willing to receive messages in the exhibition? Perhaps, we reasoned, those individuals who got the message were the *only* ones who came to the exhibition or program seeking that type of experience or information. Perhaps the other 80%, 50%, or 35% had equally legitimate needs that were not even considered by the museum and not met. Or, if they were being met, we did not know it.

We stepped back, reviewed our work and summarized our conclusion in two short sentences: 'Visitors make use of museums for their own purposes, and from varying perspectives. The museum can influence these outcomes but cannot control them.'

This position shifted the emphasis away from the museum's aims and toward the visitor's desires. It became our framework for thinking about past work and for organizing future research.

Once we assumed that visitors use museums as leisure-time activities, we saw in our own work evidence that visitors arrive with their own visit agendas and sense of time. As leisure-time participants, people come *without* sharply defined 'learning goals.' Surely there are better, faster, more comfortable, and more efficient ways to gather factual information. Books, magazines, newspapers, and, more recently, the expanding electronic media, are widely available to most of these visitors.

Our studies also showed that people tend to frequent the museums and exhibitions that they think will be congruent with their own attitudes, with whose point of view they expect to agree. They respond best to exhibitions and themes that are personally relevant and with which they can easily connect. Consequently, we found that most museum visitors acquire little new factual knowledge.

Some of the exhibitions we studied aimed to change attitudes and alter individual behavior, but we found that visitors were unlikely to fundamentally alter their view about a subject as a result of visiting a museum. While we concluded that exhibitions were both inefficient and ineffective methods for communicating new information or changing attitudes, we also concluded, however, that they can be powerful tools for *confirming, reinforcing*, and *extending* existing beliefs.[6]

We acknowledged that individuals come to museums with different *entrance narratives*, or internal storylines, and different perspectives and expectations toward the experience of visiting a museum.[7] These concepts – the entrance narrative and the experiences that visitors find satisfying in museums – merit additional discussion.

The entrance narrative

The *entrance narrative* may have three distinct components:

- A basic framework, that is, the fundamental way that individuals construe and contemplate the world.
- Information about a subject matter or topic, organized according to that basic framework.
- Personal experiences, emotions, and memories that verify and support this understanding.

We hypothesize that the museums or exhibitions visitors find most satisfying are those that resonate with their entrance narrative and confirm and enrich their existing view of the world.

Some researchers have focused on the context and texture of this experience of 'finding resonance' or 'enriching existing views.' Silverman (1993, 1995), for example, describes it as 'interpretation' or 'meaning making,' of the kind identified in studies of history. From this point of view the museum visitor engages in active, creative, intellectual, and emotional processes that include remembering, imagining or revering objects, taking objects as symbols, and using objects to tell stories to others. When visitors are viewed as 'meaning makers' the museum's educational role shifts from providing authoritative interpretation to facilitating the varied interpretive activities of visitors and encouraging dialogue and negotiation among those different views.

Carr (1993) has written of this meaning making as an act of personal transformation:

> To see the museum as an open work is to recognize that it is always discovered by its users in an unfinished state, not unlike seeing it as a laboratory, or a workshop for cognitive change. It is a setting where the museum offers tools, materials and processes for systematic exploratory approaches to experience and purposive thought that leads one further toward insight – and toward the occasional, exquisite transforming surprise. The great museum allows its users an opportunity to understand the transformations of others. The great museum assists its users to ask – and to answer – the question, *What transformation is possible for* me *here?* (ibid.: 17)

Hein (1998) is one of the leading proponents for a 'constructivist museum,' that is, a museum that organizes itself around the principle that visitors construct their own knowledge in the museum. He stresses the need for museums to help the visitor connect with what is familiar and to offer a range of 'learning modalities' that reflect the learning styles and individual needs of visitors.

Our thinking has also benefited from the increasing consideration of museum issues by the individuals based in academic nonprofit consumer research. Prentice (1996), for example, affirms that the emphasis in evaluating the success of museums and exhibitions should be on the experience of visitors, rather than on the goals of the museum staff. Prentice accepts that much of the museum experience is provided by visitors as a result of prior (or subsequent) ideas, and he emphasizes the relationships between museum consumption and all other acts of cultural consumption. He writes, 'through what they seek and do visitors to museums contribute to the production of their own museum "product" (namely, their experience) and the settings formally used . . . are only part of the "production" process' (ibid.: 170).

More specifically, Prentice draws attention to visitors' 'demand for insight,' and links this to a typology of experience that is based on the distinction between 'insiders' and 'outsiders.'

Consequently, we have begun to devote some of our effort toward empirical research based on understanding the visitor's point of view, rather than the institution's. We are concerned with how visitors approach museums and what types of 'museum experiences' they want.

There are at least two, somewhat overlapping, traditional objections raised by some museum professionals to judging performance or assessing needs primarily from the visitor's viewpoint. The first is that it might influence museums to 'pander' to visitors, thus damaging the present mission and destroying the value of cultural institutions. These critics assume that visitors really want amusement, entertainment, simplicity, and a watered-down experience. The second objection is that visitor-centered research is inherently offensive because it resembles marketing research in the profit-making sector.

In both cases the underlying assumption seems to be that *the values and desires of the visitors are inherently inferior to those of the museum professional*, and consequently suspect. But existing museum visitors are relatively well-educated and obviously go to museums in order to have the kinds of experiences that they cannot easily obtain elsewhere. Would they be satisfied with an intellectual Disneyland or cultural McDonald's?

Visitor experiences in museums

Our recent research is based on the assumption that, out of a range of other leisure activities, some individuals select museum-going because they want to do something *in particular* in museums. They want to engage in activities that are especially well-suited to the museum environment. Many Americans seem to want these experiences.[8]

What are the experiences that visitors come to museums to get? Through in-depth interviews, sample surveys, and analyses of visitor comments, our office has constructed a working list of types of museum experiences.[9] The experiences visitors find most satisfying in museums form four categories, which we have named object experiences, cognitive experiences, introspective experiences, and social experiences.

We have incorporated the complete list of 14 experiences into survey questionnaires. Whether visitors are asked what they are looking forward to, or what they have found satisfying, they are generally able to identify their valued experiences on this list without difficulty, and to select the one they value most.

This list of satisfying experiences has evolved in the course of our work. We may yet change or add to it as we pursue the research. Studies in nine Smithsonian museums[10] support the four experience types as distinct.[11]

Visitors are diverse in their interests and are looking for these different types of experiences in museums. If museums want to be accountable to their visitors, they should at least respect and consider as valid each of these four types of museum experiences.[12] Museums should contain different kinds of spaces explicitly designed to enhance these experiences – places that foster the direct experience of objects; those that present learning as a first-rate experience; those that encourage private imagination; and those that enhance interactions among visitors.

FOUR TYPES OF SATISFYING EXPERIENCES

Object experiences
   Being moved by beauty
   Seeing rare/uncommon/valuable
   things
   Seeing 'the real thing'
   Thinking what it would be like to
   own such things
   Continuing my professional
   development

Cognitive experiences
   Enriching my understanding
   Gaining information or knowledge

Introspective experiences
   Reflecting on the meaning
   of what I was looking at
   Imagining other times or places
   Recalling my travels/childhood
   experiences/other memories
   Feeling a spiritual connection
   Feeling a sense of belonging or
   connectedness

Social experiences
   Spending time with friends/
   family/other people
   Seeing my children learning
   new things

The setting: access to experiences

A museum that is accountable to visitors for certain kinds of experiences will pro-vide settings that support and enhance those experiences and will remove barriers or constraints that interfere with or detract from them. Although experiences are closely intertwined with the places where they occur, people are capable of making distinctions between the characteristics of an experience and the attributes of its context.

'Servicescape' is a term used to describe all aspects of the environment in which a transaction takes place, exclusive of the product (Bitner 1992). Thus, for example, the location of a central bank, its imposing columnar façade and grand staircase, uniformed doorman, polished stone floors, hushed voices, neatly arranged brochures, complementary coffee, and trimly dressed cashiers can be the servicescape for a banking transaction. In this example, the servicescape communicates a dis-tinct message of grandeur and tradition, imposes specific behavior patterns on the clients, and invokes definite feelings.

The servicescape concept has been extended to leisure services where, it is asserted, both functional and hedonic (emotional) motives drive consumption (or use). Put another way, the utilization of leisure services is also driven by non-utilitarian motives. Research that examines the impact of servicescapes (or service environments) shows that clients' perceptions of service quality and their result-ing satisfaction with the primary service rendered is related to decisions to return (Wakefield and Blodgett 1994). In Bitner's definition, (1) spatial layout and func-tionality, and (2) elements related to aesthetic appeal, are two critical aspects of the servicescape. The former affects the comfort of the individual directly. The latter affects the ambience of the place.

Kurtz and Clow (1998) suggest four dimensions of servicescapes:

- Physical facility (exterior and interior)
- Location
- Ambient conditions (temperature, noise, odor)
- Interpersonal conditions (between clients and staff)

In museums, what aspects of the servicescape should be considered and monitored? Stokes (1995) stressed the importance of the arrival experience (setting the tone for the experience), the physical setting (layout and wayfinding), the type and quality of communication between museum personnel and guests (communication strategies), and theming and entertainment. Rand (1997) also suggests comfort, orientation, and welcome. Looking specifically at museums, Kirchberg (1998)[13] focused on three clusters of setting attributes:

- Arrival experience and welcoming (e.g., hours, signs, initial personnel attitudes)
- Orientation and peripheral service in the museum (e.g., museum guides, amenities)
- Personal communication (e.g., manner and responsiveness of interactions)

In the future we hope to investigate alternative measures of the museum servicescape in order to obtain a complete picture of the quality of the visitor experience in the museum.

Concluding comments

My bias favors listening to visitors and responding to their needs and interests, and so I encourage museums to treat visitors as clients, to respect and provide the kinds of experiences they report as most satisfying, and to ensure a setting in which such experiences are facilitated. This approach does not diminish the professional role of museum staff or the recognition of their expertise in any way. Change, for museums, can be difficult and slow, as Conforti (1995) noted specifically with regard to art museums:

> Programmatic change in museums is also limited by the rather simple reality that these institutions are less than perfectly flexible social entities, constricted as they are by their own history and past programmatic assumptions. Museums are shaped by the structures and narratives, the aesthetic values and critical perspectives of art histories past, as well as by the pedagogical and political goals of societies and regimes which have now evolved further. And in museums, the values and assumptions of the past have been structured into stabilizing mechanisms that ultimately constrict change. (ibid.: 340)

Conforti argues that among the impediments to change, forces that are simultaneously stabilizing and constricting include museum founding charters and mission statements, governance and professional structures, permanent collections, and architecture. I believe that we have a responsibility to adjust our approaches to visitors before change is imposed from the outside. The move toward a client model, to me, seems to be inevitable and unavoidable, and I do not think this should be viewed negatively. Change also offers the promise of renewal and revitalization. The more we respect and understand the needs of diverse audiences, the closer we come to them, and the more we merit their trust.

Notes

Zahava D. Doering is Editor of *Curator: The Museum Journal* and Senior Social Science Analyst, Office of Policy and Analysis, at the Smithsonian Institution. This paper was first published in 1999 in *Curator*, vol. 42, no. 2.

1   Hudson (1975) provides some vivid descriptions of 'strangers' in museums.
2   Tobelem (1997) uses the term *exchange* to characterize the relationship between visitor and museum. He contends that most museum professionals have misperceptions of marketing and do not realize that (1) the consumer has been moved increasingly to the center of the marketing operation, i.e., there has been a shift from product-centered to consumer-centered marketing; and (2) it has been extended into the world of public service and nonprofit institutions.
3   The National Research Center of the Arts, Inc. (1975) estimated 1,821 museums in 1971–1972.
4   For example, the federal government has also been emphasizing its role as a 'service' institution. The public sector is under intense scrutiny to improve its operations so that it can deliver products and services efficiently and at reduced costs to the taxpayer. Program effectiveness considerations have led many agencies to ask what the public sees as the mission. This review, in turn, has led to the reshaping of missions and performance measurements.

   In 1993, Public Law 103–62, the Government Performance and Results Act (GPRA) was passed. It represents a federal commitment to strategic planning and performance measurement. Under GPRA, beginning with the fiscal 1999 budget cycle, all federal agencies will be required to have performance measurements in place and report annually on their progress. This shift to outcomes, rather than inputs and outputs, represents a paradigm shift. For a discussion of the possible effect of GPRA on museums, see Timberlake (1999).
5   The question of what constitutes 'success' in museum exhibitions is unresolved. Serrell (1998) claims that it can be calculated mathematically on the basis of observed behaviors.
6   In this respect, as Treinen (1993) points out, museum-going resembles mass-media consumption (ibid.: 90).
7   Aside from our work, we find evidence to the entrance narrative in various visitor studies. A good example is found in Macdonald (1992). The study underscores the entrance narrative of visitors, both specific content and cultural dimensions. It shows that exhibitions have 'implicit messages' that exist in the minds of visitors even before they visit them and that the museum may unintentionally reinforce these messages.

8   In the United States, at least, two out of three American adults visit at least one
     museum, zoo, aquarium, or historical site each year. Many visit multiple venues
     many times (Doering 1995).
9   For more about satisfying experiences in museums, see Pekarik *et al.* (1999).
10   Freer Gallery of Art, Arthur M. Sackler Gallery, Hirshhorn Museum and
     Sculpture Garden, National Museum of American Art, National Portrait
     Gallery, Renwick Gallery, National Museum of Natural History, National
     Zoological Park, National Air and Space Museum, and National Museum of
     American History.
11   For more on this research, see Pekarik *et al.* (1999).
12   'Equal' respect is not to be misunderstood as 'equal proportions' or 'equal floor
     space'; we support balance (i.e., not strict equality, but representation).
13   The research was conducted under the auspices of the Bertelsmann Foundation.

References

American Association of Museums (1969). *America's museums: The Belmont Report.*
    Washington, DC: Author.
—— (1984). *Museums for a new century: A report of the Commission on Museums for a New
    Century.* Washington, DC: Author.
—— (1992). *Excellence and equity: Education and the public dimension of museums.*
    Washington, DC: Author.
Bitner, M.J. (1992). Servicescapes: The impact of physical surroundings on customers
    and employees. *Journal of Marketing*, 5(2), 57–71.
Carr, D. (1993, November). *A museum is an open work.* Paper presented at the meet-
    ing of the American Society for Cybernetics, Philadelphia, PA.
Conforti, M. (1995). Museums past and museums present: Some thoughts on institu-
    tional survival. *Museum Management and Curatorship*, 14(4), 339–355.
Doering, Z.D. (1995). *Who attends our cultural institutions? A progress report* (RN 95–5).
    Washington, DC: Smithsonian Institution.
Hein, G.E. (1998). *Learning in the museum.* London: Routledge.
Hudson, K. (1975). *A social history of museums: What visitors thought.* Atlantic Highlands,
    NJ: Humanities Press.
Kelly, J.R., and Godbey, G. (1992). *The sociology of leisure.* State College, PA: Venture
    Publishing, Inc.
Kirchberg, V. (1998, August). *Visitor service evaluation by mystery visitors: Results of an
    application in museums.* Paper presented at the Eleventh Annual Visitor Studies
    Association Conference, Washington, DC.
Kurtz, D.L., and Clow, K.E. (1998). *Services marketing.* New York: John Wiley & Sons.
Macdonald, S. (1992). Cultural imagining among museum visitors. *Museum Manage-
    ment and Curatorship*, 11(1), 401–409.
National Research Center of the Arts, Inc. (1975). *Museums USA: A survey report.*
    Washington, DC: The National Endowment for the Arts.
Pekarik, A.J., Doering, Z.D., and Karns, D.A. (1999). Exploring satisfying experi-
    ences in museums. *Curator: The Museum Journal*, 42(2), 152–173.
Perry, D., Roberts, L., Morrissey, K., and Silverman, L. (1997). Listening outside
    and within. *Journal of Museum Education*, 21(3), 26–27.

Prentice, R. (1996). Managing implosion: The facilitation of insight through the provision of context. *Museum Management and Curatorship*, 15(2), 169–185.

Rand, J. (1997). The 227-mile museum, or, Why we need a visitor's bill of rights. *Visitor Studies: Theory, Research and Practice*, 9, 8–26.

Serrell, B. (1998). *Paying attention: Visitors and museum exhibitions*. Washington, DC: American Association of Museums.

Silverman, L.H. (1993). Making meaning together: Lessons from the field of American history. *Journal of Museum Education*, 18(3), 7–10.

—— (1995). Visitor meaning-making in museums for a new age. *Curator: The Museum Journal*, 38(3), 161–170.

Solinger, J.W. (Ed.). (1990). *Museums and universities*. New York: Macmillan.

Stokes, E. (1995). Through the eyes of the guest: How guest services can influence the visitor studies agenda. *Visitor Studies: Theory, Research and Practice*, 7, 3–6.

Timberlake, S.A. (1999). The effect of the Government Performance and Results Act on museums. *Visitor Studies Today*, 2(2), 8–10.

Tobelem, J. (1997). The marketing approach in museums. *Museum Management and Curatorship*, 16(4), 337–354.

Treinen, H. (1993). What does the visitor want from a museum? Mass-media aspects of museology. In S. Bicknell and G. Farmelo (Eds.), *Museum visitor studies in the 90s* (pp. 86–93). London: Science Museum.

Wakefield, K.L., and Blodgett, J.G. (1994). The importance of servicescapes in leisure service settings. *Journal of Services Marketing*, 8(3), 66–76.

Weil, S.E. (1997). The museum and the public. *Museum Management and Curatorship*, 16(3), 257–271.

Chapter 21

Museum Marketing
Understanding different types of audiences

Ruth Rentschler

Introduction

THIS CHAPTER EXAMINES THE relationship that museums have developed
with their audiences, and undertakes a brief history of the development of that
role. It draws examples from museum marketing in four Commonwealth countries: the UK, Australia, New Zealand and Canada, which have a similar history
and funding approach. One of the most serious issues facing museum marketers
today is the erosion in the proportion of revenue provided by government, which
needs to be supplemented by audience revenue and giving from individuals and trusts.
This tripartite funding model – government, audience and 'sponsor' income – is
essential to museum sustainability. The erosion of government income gives marketing a boost, as it becomes an important tool for helping to fill the funding gap
left by declining government revenue. This chapter contributes to understanding
the relative value of different types of audiences to museums. Audiences are important, especially when government support is reduced and the arts are both pressured to be more business-like and more attuned to the needs of diverse audiences.

The last two decades have seen considerable debate and significant change
in museums. First, there is a shift in government attitudes to funding, access and
diversity or distinctiveness, which led to a need for increased marketing in museums.
Second, there is a shift in interest from the individual artist to the industry, which
in the mid-1990s led to recognition of the importance of new marketing approaches
for the development of museums (McLean 1995). Government initiatives have encouraged creative industries development, with a shift in focus to the importance of
marketing for artistic success and sustainability (Johanson and Rentschler 2002).

Source: pp. 139–158 in F. Kerrigan, P. Fraser and M. Ozbilgin (eds) (2004) *Arts
Marketing*, Oxford: Elsevier.

Creative industries demonstrate a move away from 'art for art's sake' and towards an acceptance of the economic, social and aesthetic value of culture, where the arts are treated 'as ingredients in a new cultural mix' (Volkerling 2001). While specific categories vary slightly from country to country, creative industries embrace activities which have individual creativity, skill and talent as their origin as well as the potential for job and wealth creation through the generation and exploitation of intellectual property (Volkerling 2001). In general, creative industries incorporate categories that embrace literature, multimedia, music, broadcasting, films, computer games, and even extend to craft, fashion and town planning, as well as including the traditional performing arts and museums. Museums are placed as part of this larger industry mix, which has been controversial. Some see the new industries model as giving museums more political clout in the wider framework. Others see the model as a betrayal of the hegemony museums held in the high arts, where economic values are seen to outweigh intrinsic cultural value.

Despite these initiatives, evidence shows that audience numbers are declining in some museums (Museum of Victoria annual reports 1999–2002). With the threat of Disney-style theme shows and blockbusters, the need to review museum approaches to marketing is urgent (McLean 1995). Museums are exhorted to adopt audience techniques that are related to the accountability factor. The key is striking the right balance between finding new audiences and nurturing existing ones. This chapter offers three perspectives on marketing for museums that present a solution to these issues. The first perspective is evident in the arts marketing literature, where it was demonstrated that marketing as a concept has only been considered in the last 20 years maximum and has undergone a change in orientation from a product focus to an audience focus in that time. Scant attention has been paid to segmenting audiences beyond 'goers' and 'non-goers' in the literature examined. The second perspective links museum viability to government policy: that less money is available in government coffers for each museum and that commercial approaches to generating income need to be undertaken. Despite this economic pressure, museums also recognise the social requirement to ensure access to audiences across the community. This third perspective is of crucial concern to museums. Traditionally they have focused energy and effort on development of their product to the exclusion of development of their customer base and audience activities. This approach is rapidly changing. Improved audience research is seen as an opportunity to increase long-term museum viability, and to enable them to meet social and economic obligations.

Museums need to rely more heavily on marketing in this climate. Understanding audiences is an important part of museum marketing. Audiences are analysed using audience studies. DiMaggio *et al.* (1978), Thomas and Cutler (1993), Kawashima (1998) and Rentschler (1998, 2002) have all reviewed audience studies in museums. Their work showed overwhelmingly that audiences were well-educated, professional and predominantly white. While these studies were conducted over several decades, during which significant demographic shifts have occurred in the population, there has been no change in the profile of museum audiences. This fact has led those interested in audience research in museums to conclude that there is one audience for museums. These reviews indicate that audience studies have rarely segmented audiences. Most audience studies compare users and non-users, with a small number of studies more recently researching audience diversity (Bennett and Frow 1991; Robertson and Miglorino 1996). Because of the demographic homogeneity of museum audiences, it has become politically necessary for governments to insist that non-profit organisations which receive at least part of their income from government, try to broaden their audiences. However, the relational marketing needs of the organisation may not align with this social and economic imperative. How can non-profit museums both meet their social and economic marketing needs? If most studies treat audiences as one audience, despite the plethora of audience studies, what knowledge of audiences are museum marketers lacking?

Museums defined

This chapter discusses museums and argues that they have changed. 'Museum' derives from the classical Greek word 'museion', a place of contemplation, a philosophical institution or a temple of the muses (Committee of Inquiry on Museums and National Collections 1975; Lewis 1992; Murphy 1993). The first recorded instance of the use of the word 'museum' to describe a collection relates to the de Medici material at the time of Lorenzo il Magnifico (1449–92) (Lewis 1992).

The word 'museum' is chosen in this chapter in preference to the word 'gallery'. This choice is in accord with the international preferred usage of the word and a sense of change (Murphy 1993). Non-profit museums can no longer remain static places of contemplation, tied to attitudes opposed to a general diffusion of knowledge. In considering the change in meaning of 'museum', it is contended that it applies equally to 'art museum' and that the term 'museum' refers to those organisations which operate *both* as a museum and art museum (Australia Council 1990, 1991, 1992, 1993, 1994, 1995; Hancocks 1987; Hendon 1979). Museums hold art works in their collections. Museums and art museums combined hold art works and other objects in their collections. The approach taken in this chapter is supported by the Piggott Report (Committee of Inquiry on Museums and National Collections 1975: 16) which states:

> the border between the themes of an art museum and a general museum is often blurred . . . [which] encourages us to see these institutions as variations of the one species.

Museums have traditionally been defined by function rather than by purpose (Thompson 1998; Weil 1990). Functional definitions relate to activities performed in the museum and are object-based: to collect, preserve and display objects. More recently, there has been a shift in definitions. Purposive definitions now relate to the intent, vision or mission of the museum where the focus is on leadership and visitor services: to serve society and its development by means of study, education and enjoyment (Besterman 1998). These definitions are illustrated in Figure 21.1.

As museums themselves are changing to meet the needs of a changing world, so too important concepts change. Change has led to an increased interest in researching museums and to a reappraisal of their purpose, evident in the changing

Functional	Museums acquire, conserve, communicate and exhibit art for study and education	Object-based
Purposive	Museums are for people to enjoy and to learn from collections which are held in trust for society	People-based

Figure 21.1   Shift in museum definitions

definition of the word 'museum'. The change in definition has been gradual and has been influenced by prevailing social and philosophical attitudes.

Noble's (1970) five basic responsibilities of a museum represent a ground-breaking definition that has proved enormously useful as an evaluative tool for judging a museum's functions (Weil 1990). The functions (acquisition, conservation, study, interpretation and exhibition) form an entity. Noble stated:

> they are like the five fingers of a hand, each independent but united for common purpose. If a museum omits or slights any of these five responsibilities, it has handicapped itself immeasurably. (1970: 20)

More recently, Noble's definition has been organised around three principles:

> to preserve (to collect is viewed as simply an early step in that process), to study (a function that remains unchanged) and to communicate (this third function being a combination of Noble's final two, i.e. to interpret and to exhibit). (Weil 1990: 58)

The American Association of Museums' definition is in similar vein:

> . . . [a museum is] an organised and permanent nonprofit institution, essentially educational or aesthetic in purpose, with professional staff which owns and utilises tangible objects, cares for them and exhibits them to the public on some regular schedule. (Weil 1990: 45)

In the 1990s the discussion of definitions introduces a new point of emphasis. The emphasis shifts from objects to leadership and visitor services (in the service of society and of its development) which has particular relevance to this chapter. The International Council of Museums (1995) definition establishes the pattern:

> A museum is a nonprofit making, permanent institution in the service of society and of its development, and open to the public, which acquires, conserves, researches, communicates and exhibits, for purposes of study, education and enjoyment, material evidence of people and their environment. (International Council of Museums 1995: 3)

Besterman (1998) develops the pattern, clearly putting people first in the *draft* definition of museums for the Museums Association in the UK:

> Museums are for people to explore and learn from collections for understanding and inspiration. To do this, a museum collects, safeguards, researches, develops, makes accessible and interprets collections and associated information, which it holds in trust for society. (Besterman 1998: 37)

More recently, the Museums Association (UK) definition of museums enhances the point about the transformation of museum definitions from functional to purposive: 'museums enable people to explore collections for inspiration, learning and enjoyment' (2002).

The increasing recognition in this definition of people, society and the contextual pressures impacting on museums raises important questions concerning the museum's audiences. The order in which attributes appear in museum definitions reflects the development of the museum's role from an inwardly focused concentration of resources, to an outwardly focused distribution and dispersal of resources to the community, to audiences and to the wider public (Besterman 1998; Murphy 1993). The common ground of all definitions is that they consider the collection central to the museum's function. However, more recent definitions focus increasingly on museum leadership and the importance of visitor services. Further, they focus on the non-profit nature of the organisation.

Museum marketing then and now

It was not so long ago that Alan Andreasen in the *Journal of Arts Management and Law* wrote about the confusion in arts organisations between marketing and selling (Andreasen 1985). In this first special issue on consumer behaviour and the arts, a lead was taken by an academic journal as to the importance of marketing for the arts. In Australia, museum marketing, particularly increased audience participation, has been the primary objective of arts organisations since the 1994 release of the cultural policy statement *Creative Nation* (Commonwealth of Australia), where a shift in emphasis from supply to demand was highlighted. Attendance levels, venue occupancy rates, subscription purchases and the number of members have become important performance measures for arts organisations (Kotler and Kotler 1998; Kotler and Scheff 1997; Radbourne 1998). Marketing research, marketing strategies and marketing plans have become commonplace management activity. However, studies in 1998 (Radbourne) and 2001 (Rentschler) show that the costly marketing effort for current patrons is not increasing frequency or attracting new patrons sufficient for organisations to develop without ongoing high levels of subsidy and corporate and private philanthropy. Research shows that museums in Commonwealth countries rely on three sources of income: government income, audience income and sponsorship/philanthropy. For example, in Australia, longitudinal analysis of museum income streams shows their dependence on a balance of income sources for survival. In this environment, museums are at risk (Rentschler

2001). This highlights the need for greater emphasis on finding out more about attracting new and retaining existing audiences.

The adoption of marketing methods by museums, then, is of recent origin and their applicability to museums is still debated. For example, in 1979–80 a 'broad marketing plan' was drawn up by the National Gallery of Victoria in Australia and specific tasks relating to the marketing of the museum undertaken. Increased attention was being given to activities that not only attract visitors to the museum but also encourage them to return on a regular basis. This seems to be a shift into viewing the museum more as a commodity or product in the marketplace, not as something existing outside the needs or wants of the public. This is very early to consider marketing matters in museums. Similarly, in the UK, arts marketing awareness has increased from the 1980s. According to the International Council of Museums, it is now accepted that 'political, social and economic development cannot be divorced from the human and cultural context of any society' (1997). Therefore, while transformations in museums aim to realise equity in access to resources and opportunities, the fundamental objective is to attain higher levels of excellence in all areas of life by involving the entire population and drawing on the broad diversity of local culture, heritage, experience and knowledge. The Australia Council's recent discussion paper, *Planning for the Future: Issues, Trends and Opportunities for the Arts in Australia*, highlights an awareness of this international development, arguing that 'advocating for the arts in the public policy arena is not inimical with the notion of an intrinsic value for the arts. On the contrary, it reflects the diversity of values within the arts sector and beyond' (Australia Council 2001: 4).

Reflecting the stated concerns of arts representatives, this chapter acknowledges the dependence of the maintenance and growth of the nation's artistic resources upon marketing. Marketing requires innovation and renewal and that:

> innovation [is] dependent on diversity, creativity and the interaction between the two, and the connection of new products with new markets. (Australia Council 2001: 14)

Concern about government funding for innovation and diversity is at the forefront of the report. Community ownership and fostering a connection with local communities is a challenge for Australian arts organisations, which see the strengthening of community support for the arts to be a key factor in increasing box office income, corporate and philanthropic support and political will (Australia Council 2001). Although there is no central body responsible for cultural policy at the federal level in Australia, established statutory authorities operate as agencies responsible for cultural affairs in different cultural areas. Arts organisations report that increased leadership is required in order for them to enter more fully into the nation's political debates and to counter anxiety that:

> Art . . . is being seen as increasingly redundant in a materialistic society. Artists are part of the culture but artists and scientists do not lead the culture. (Australia Council 2001: 17)

According to arts leaders involved in the Australia Council report, in this country the arts have not yet succeeded in seizing the agenda outside the arts policy area (Australia Council 2001).

New Zealand sentiments mirror those expressed in Australia:

> How can the true extent and value of creative activity be determined? Not all cultural activity can be measured through the production and consumption of goods and services, and not all cultural output has a dollar value. However, quantifying the economic features of cultural activity through a statistical model may help provide an insight into the larger reality that is 'culture'. The ability of statistics to 'quantify' is their greatest strength. (Statistics New Zealand 1995: 15)

This approach has been extended and confirmed in more recent reports on government intentions to back a strong creative industry sector (Heart of the Nation Project Team 2000), although the thorny issue of indicators for both economic and social value of arts and culture remains to be resolved. In the UK, Australia and New Zealand, creativity is prized, but within an industry framework, which focuses on access to economic resources through a diverse funding base.

In Canada, contemporary questions regarding museum policy centre upon access and participation, particularly how to encompass all ethno-cultural groups (Weppler and Silvers 2001). Museums are looking to define their wider sense of purpose, making museums an integral part of their communities in the new pluralist society (Goa 2001). During the last decade, Canadian arts organisations have relied increasingly on private support. Corporate sponsorship of the arts in Canada has increased dramatically during the last two decades, and the demand for support continues to grow. The interest of the Canadian private sector in the arts is primarily associated with the sponsorship of productions of performances, the purchase of visual arts and the provision of operating or acquisition funds for public art galleries and museums. Canada still has relatively few foundations with extensive programmes to support and develop the arts and the humanities. Corporate awareness and its potential role in this area is also relatively recent, although it has been greatly increased by the efforts of the Council for Business and the Arts in Canada (Culturelink 2001).

The rhetoric associated with marketing sees the arts as industries, which can be classified and outputs measured. In Canada (Standing Committee on Canadian Heritage 1999), the notion of creative industries is seen as interdependent with the arts. The same emphasis is seen in New Zealand cultural reports (Heart of the Nation Project Team 2000), as well as UK and Australian cultural policy development (Kawashima 1998). Museums, where they are specifically mentioned, help define national identity, are examples of innovative practice and must increase access, diversity and distinctiveness, while diversifying their funding sources. Striving for national symbols and linking culture with industry resonates with politicians who have to divert funds to non-profit organisations and justify the expense.

The increasing globalisation and internationalisation of cultural activities has had an isomorphic effect on museum marketing in developed nations. Most prominent has been a shift in emphasis from development of the artistic product to a focus on organisational marketing culture and visitors that comes from intellectual enquiry into the nature of cultural production that has been emerging for two decades or more. Overall, there has been an increasing emphasis on audiences as a means of achieving both greater museum development and greater income security. Increasingly, it is impossible to rely on government income alone in a changing environment. Certainly, the reality is that museums operate within a tripartite income structure, seeing income being derived from government, audience activities and individual or group giving. Museums from the four countries discussed in this chapter have characteristics in common due to their shared cultural heritage. Here the philanthropic role is one for government, as well as for sponsors and individuals. Previous research has shown a gradual scaling back of government activity in many areas of public life, with a new focus on cultural policies and a changing financial environment, which affects museums (Rentschler 2002). Ideologically, there is a move away from elitism and connoisseurship to community access and audience development, with an increasing focus on diversity of income but maintenance of the income mix. The most significant problem in museums has been income uncertainty and the increased complexity in the context, which has been volatility in funding over time.

This shows a strategic response to change in museum marketing (see Table 21.1). Marketing is approached positively, even in an environment of change and resource-scarcity, as marketing initiatives are often funded from grants. This is a sign that museums are undergoing a paradigm shift towards a stronger organisational marketing culture and focus on the audience. Considering the often-limited resources for marketing that restrain possibilities, it is even more remarkable that museum marketing has changed so much in a short timeframe.

Table 21.1 shows the evolutionary stages of museum marketing, culminating with a postmodern focus on audience deepening and diversification as part of

Table 21.1   Museum marketing then and now

Evolution of museum marketing	Product focus	Selling focus	Marketing science focus	Postmodern marketing focus
Product	Object-centred	Need effort to sell	Enhance with services	Differentiate audience segments
Marketing function	Data gathering	Sell benefits; build brand identity	Promote as means of communication	Shared service philosophy across the museum and with its people
Marketing position	Low resources; low status	Increased resources	Management status	Strategic integration
Market knowledge	Irrelevant	Need to locate	Profile	Needs; wants; attitudes and behaviours
Segmentation	General, socio-demographic	Visitor studies	Geo-demographic	Attitudinal and behavioural change

Source: cf. Morris Hargreaves McIntyre (2002)

organisational philosophy. Inspiration for a museum marketing approach is found in sources which extend beyond traditional marketing theory. It has already been mentioned that non-profit museums lack marketing capabilities. As a consequence, very little of the marketing literature is directed to them. Instead, a new literature is developing led by theorists in entrepreneurship and post-modernism, but with an appreciation of marketing and its shortcomings for museums (Brown 1993; Fillis 2002). What such authors recognise is the need to base the marketing concept both on satisfaction of wants and the process of economic change that better fits with the idea of entrepreneurship and the small organisation. This is leading to a reorientation of the marketing concept, so that it adjusts to the needs of the smaller organisation (Blenker 2001). The current author has developed this process further by linking these new concepts to the non-profit museum (Rentschler 2001).

Marketing and the non-profit museum

In the new century of competitiveness and globalisation, non-profit museums are as concerned with marketing as are their for-profit cousins. However, marketing is complicated for the following reasons: the non-profit nature of the 'business'; its non-financial objectives; the necessity to cater to multiple publics some of whom pay and others who do not; the necessity for collaboration as well as competition with competitors; and the need to foster identity as well as education, research and entertainment for visitors. Further, in the recent past museums regarded marketing with suspicion. Not any more.

Marketing is defined as a social and managerial process by which individual paying and non-paying visitors obtain what they need through creating, offering and exchanging with others' products and services of value. As far back as 1969, Kotler and Levy identified marketing as concerned with how transactions are created, stimulated, facilitated and valued, the main purpose of marketing being to create and distribute values among the market parties through transactions and market relationships. Carson (1985) has pointed out the characteristics of small-firm marketing, such as limited resources, lack of specialist expertise and limited impact. These characteristics manifest themselves in non-profit museums, as they are mostly small to medium-sized organisations. Further, museums are resource-scarce, impacting their ability to hire specialist marketers of the highest quality and expertise and hence limiting their ability to make an impression in a competitive and crowded marketplace. This view is consistent with studies of small entrepreneurial firms (Blenker 2001).

Marketing in small firms needs to be relevant, appropriate and relative to the position of the firm in its life cycle. As many museums are older organisations, with limited resources and marketing expertise, marketing in these organisations needs to be change-focused, opportunistic in nature and innovative in approach. This approach aligns with Carson's (1985) view as to the central focus of marketing in small firms. Accordingly, marketing in museums exists between the museum and external social entities. The notion of museums as social entities is not a new one (see, e.g. Bhattacharya et al. 1995; McLean and Cooke 1999). It sees museums as consisting of salient group classifications, which may be based on categories such as demographics, gender or race as well as membership or values. These categories create social identification such as the perception of belonging to a group. It is a concept which helps to make sense of change in our social, cultural, economic and political context, which has either a fixed notion of identity or a fluid and contingency-based notion. Thus, identity can change as circumstances change. The latter view sees identity as a social concept which forms links with society. It is therefore important to manage the marketing and social interface by overcoming some of the barriers mentioned above and including the identity factors important to museums' social role.

The museum experience

Museums offer a diverse range of experiences to the people who visit them. Museums deal in ideas, objects and satisfactions not found elsewhere. Ideas and experience derive from natural and human-made objects and sensory experiences. The presentation of these ideas, objects and satisfactions is founded on research, scholarship and interpretation. Museums are engaging in wider self-assessment of their programmes and projects, due to changing contextual circumstances. In Australia, *A Study into Key Needs of Collecting Institutions in the Heritage Sector* (Deakin University 2002) identified the transformation which has occurred in collecting institutions in the last decade in terms of access and preservation, but that this 'needs to be coupled with the need for quality visitor experiences' (ibid.: 9). This has led to a reassessment of the importance of marketing to museums.

Over the last 20 years, marketing has become one of the most important and exciting components of management strategy. Marketing was once considered a 'dirty word' in the arts, seemingly incorporating all that was 'commercial'. Now, however, marketing is recognised as a legitimate tool for enhancing the visitor experience, the product portfolio and assessing the organisational marketing culture. This tripartite relationship is illustrated in Figure 21.2.

From research conducted in museums (Deakin University 2002; Rentschler and Gilmore 2002), it is clear that they are developed in two of the three elements illustrated in Figure 21.2. The attitude towards visitors (and indeed non-visitors) has developed over the last century until now people who work in museums understand the importance of visitors from a marketing perspective. Traditionally, museum people have focused on the product portfolio, such as collections, research display and objects. Indeed, museums are institutions which collect, research, display and interpret objects. It has been argued cogently that their very existence depends on the possession of a collection (McLean 1994). While collection care and interpretation are acknowledged as basic museum functions, declining public funding and accountability pressure have led to the discovery of museum marketing as an important contribution to museums' viability (Rentschler 1998). This discovery has led to changing behaviours in museum personnel, so that the beginnings of an organisational marketing culture are created. The total reinvention of Museum of New Zealand Te Papa Tongarewa (Te Papa) in Wellington, New Zealand is a case in point. Its transition moved from being part of the national museum and art gallery, as two separate institutions, to flagship national museum. Te Papa expresses New Zealanders' national identity, biculturalism,[1] customer orientation and positive

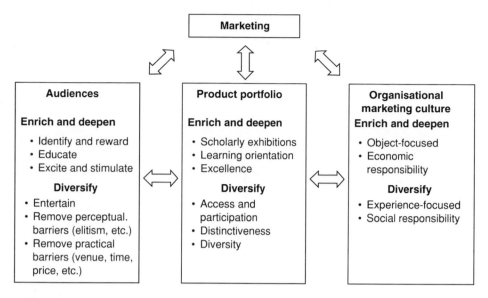

Figure 21.2   Tripartite audience, product and organisational marketing model

commercial focus in a time of economic restructuring. Total reinvention occurred in the 1990s. Its success is a result of breaking with tradition and taking risks: its popularity – more than 2 million visitors in the first year of operation – is a consequence of the fact that, while serving visitors' needs, it is also something new for New Zealanders. Positioning the museum within an organisational marketing culture has been central to its outlook.

It has been argued that museums need marketing, and especially so when understanding their audiences, in order to be competitive in the future and achieve their mission. Countering this is an environment poorly suited to the introduction of marketing initiatives. Apart from the small-firm capabilities mentioned earlier in this chapter, there is the traditional curatorial focus of key staff in museums, which by training and preference focuses on the object. However, marketing is increasingly being seen as an essential museum activity by museums themselves (Kelly and Sas 1998). Hence, marketing serves the museum's mission rather than compromises it (Reussner 2002). Part of this change is reflected in a better understanding of what marketing is and what it can achieve. Marketing provides opportunities for creativity and imagination in expanding the visitor experience through a wide range of activities, with the foundation of that expansion based firmly on an understanding of visitors and the organisational marketing culture.

Post-modern museum marketing: an argument for segmentation

The conventional view of museum marketing is that it should be formalised, comprehensive and linear. This approach is epitomised by the textbook approach to marketing. Here the argument is that this is an inappropriate model for museum marketing. In fact, a more informal, creative and flexible approach could be adopted

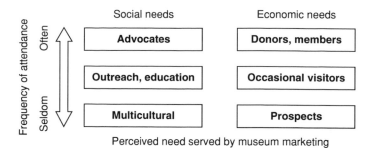

Figure 21.3   Types of audiences by needs served and frequency of attendance

which suits the service environment of museums and the policy framework (cf. Brown 1993). This approach makes considerable demands on the museum organisation in time, commitment and focus. The model illustrated in Figure 21.3 suggests that museum marketing can be introduced sympathetically without destroying the cultural values which represent its strength. It allows for sectional implementation of marketing, so that success in achievement of results is demonstrated progressively.

A purposive museum meets the audiences' social needs through the type of exhibitions they put on, programmes and activities they offer, ancillary programmes and events, and relationships they build with potential or traditional audiences. On the other hand, the economic needs come from the museum, so audiences (including donors and sponsors) can be seen to meet the museum's needs. Within those categories, there are the subcategories of prospects, occasional visitors, members, donors, educational visitors, multicultural visitors and advocates – akin to O'Riordan's (2002) 'mosaic of minorities'. The recent census in Australia mirrors a country in which we are moving towards a more multicultural society (Cleary and Murphy 2002). The results make it difficult to describe what is typical in Australia, as increasing diversity is driven by immigration. It is clear to most organisations that quality and sustainability are best achieved by focusing on what matters most to the audience. Understanding attitudes and characteristics of the potential and actual audience through audience research is the most important precondition for being responsive to their needs. This has become more urgent in the latest snapshot of the Australian population that identifies consumer trends and provides a window on the consumer mind (O'Riordan 2002). However, the recent National Museum of Australia Review (DCITA 2003) highlights the political climate in which museums operate, which may constrain them in fulfilling such a mission.

Audience research that looks at the specific profiles and needs of the subcategories within an existing audience body is scant (Johnson and Garbarino 1999). Urgent economic and social questions for museums and for the society whose needs they meet can be answered by appropriately understanding audiences. As audience research requires an investment of time, money and staff, it is important that audience studies are conducted effectively, understanding whether they are conducted for social and/or economic purposes. Nonetheless, the lines between the two types of marketing research are blurring as population shifts occur. Traditionally, for example, the function of multicultural audience research has been perceived as meeting *social* needs. However, considering the multicultural nature of western democracies, it can be argued to be of *economic* benefit as well. An effective use of audience research is strategically important to museums in this changing marketplace.

The goals of inclusiveness, accessibility and use by a broad range of people are acknowledged as primary public duties of museums. The emphasis on accessibility implies a change of attitude towards the museum audience. Only by understanding how to offer a valuable, enjoyable experience to a greater diversity of audiences and thus gain their support can any museum increase its accessibility and audience base.

Customer orientation does not necessarily force museums to meet demands of a prospective audience that compromises their mission and their integrity. On the contrary, museums are balancing their aims and duties on the one hand and the preconditions and needs on the part of the audience on the other (Rentschler and Gilmore 2002).

To combine the organisational and creative aims of museums with the expectations of customers, museums may develop in two directions simultaneously:

(a) Invest in audience research to crystallise the important attitudes and characteristics of their members, non-member visitors and non-visitors; and, on this base

(b) develop the attracting power to retain and build on the current audience base by providing a service that satisfies a multiplicity of audiences and potential audience needs.

Understanding diverse audiences

Recently, articles on the arts have appeared on diverse audiences and relationship marketing (Bhattacharya *et al.* 1995; Johnson and Garbarino 1999; Rentschler *et al.* 2002). An underlying theme in these publications is that such programmes enable consumers to identify with the corresponding organisations: in the case of museums, drawing infrequent visitors inside their doors and making them regular visitors, members and donors. Research shows that different audience segments visit for different reasons (Wiggins 2003). This is often discussed in conventional marketing but less often in museum marketing. It also relates to the drivers of visitation, what causes repeat visits and how to understand visitors.

The notion of a ladder of customer relationships, ranging from transactional at the bottom to relational at the top, is a formative concept in marketing. It is argued that organisations can analyse customers on a continuum of exchanges, pursuing both transactional and relational marketing simultaneously as not all customers want the same relationship. In museums, it is possible to segment the visitor base into groups that vary in their responsiveness to transactional or relational marketing (cf. Johnson and Garbarino 1999 in performing arts organisations). Not only can different types of visitors be separately identified but they also interact differently and can be treated differently. Hence, Melbourne Museum greatly increased its youth audience when it exhibited 'body art', an exhibition on tattooing and body piercing, just as the Powerhouse Museum in Sydney, Australia, increased its youth audience when it held an exhibition on the history of contraception. Both exhibitions generated much publicity in the media and drew large crowds from niche target groups. However, an exhibition at the Art Gallery of New South Wales on Indigenous art drew the young professionals as well as the traditional 40+ audience. Lumping audiences together as 'goers' is of limited use. Segmenting them on a ladder of opportunity makes more sense.

The problem in museums is that publications on relationship marketing often are based on anecdotal evidence rather than on research. Surveys in performing arts organisations suggest that major audience groups have relational differences (Johnson and Garbarino 1999). Similar findings are known in museums (Falk and Dierking 1992). For example, low relational visitors are driven by overall satisfaction, and can be irritated or dissuaded from repeat visits by poor facilities, displays or services such as in restaurants. However, committed visitors, such as members, have a relationship with the museum and seek something different from their visits. They seek trust and commitment rather than satisfaction, suggest Johnson and Garbarino. These implied differences suggest that transactional marketing programmes focused on managing satisfaction are more successful with low relational visitors, while relationship marketing programmes focused on trust and commitment are more successful for high relational visitors.

Museums routinely incorporate visitors as members; however, they often know little about them and create even less leverage from that membership. In academic terms, there is little literature on museum membership. In practical terms, understanding museum members helps managers and curators develop ideas about how identification can be used for visitor retention (Bhattacharya *et al.* 1995). While other work has focused on alumni and identification, there has been less analysis done on museum members and identification.

Why has there not been more interest in the relational marketing opportunities of museum members? A review of visitor and non-visitor studies suggests they rarely look at member differences. If researchers focus on demographic or lifestyle factors, members appear not to differ from occasional visitors. Because of the demographic homogeneity of high culture, marketing managers have tended to see them as one audience (Johnson and Garbarino 1999). Based on theories of relationship marketing, members are more relational than occasional visitors, but even within the member grouping there are differences between members. Members often provide volunteers to the museum as well as patrons, donors and advocates, who provide their time, talents and money to sustain it. A member base is also an indication of community support that is vital when arguing for government funding.

Research shows that the identification of members leads to increased loyalty to the organisation. In the case of visitors, this has the desirable consequences of high brand loyalty and positive word of mouth, an aspect of museum marketing that has constantly been identified as a means of spreading the word about product efficacy. The benefits of increased loyalty and positive word of mouth are well known (Bhattacharya *et al.* 1995). For cash-strapped museums, understanding the benefits of identification can lead to sustainable competitive advantage and improved financial results. Identification is defined as creating an interface with the causes or goals that the museum embodies and espouses. Thus, when a museum stands for specific causes, visitors are loyal because they identify with the museum mission.

Museums often have categories of membership, ranging from individual to family and higher contributing levels of membership or patrons. All membership categories offer benefits such as special viewings of exhibitions, guided tours, monthly newsletters and a calendar of activities, plus discounts of purchases in museum shops. Higher level members such as patrons are given additional benefits such as free guest admission to receptions and recognition in the museum annual report.

At the top of the ladder are patrons. Patrons are motivated by the social relationship and the satisfaction it engenders. The donor receives an intangible satisfaction that relates to their personal motivations: an enhanced degree of self-esteem; a feeling of achievement; a new status or a sense of belonging (Mixer 1993). The social exchange relationship contains some expectation of continuity.

Businesses and foundations interact with museums as patrons too. They provide services, personnel and gifts-in-kind, as well as money. For example, the National Gallery of Victoria has a successful partnership with the Ian Potter Foundation, which invested $15 million in the new art museum on Federation Square, Melbourne. In other cases technology has been provided to museums by computer companies. However, different motives drive the exchange processes of businesses and foundations. Many large foundations fund innovative projects that individual patrons shy away from. However, their interest in innovation is generally confined to fields linked to company strategic direction. In other words, businesses have health, education and cultural needs to satisfy their employees. Museums, as non-profit organisations, have financial, personnel and management needs that corporations can provide. Thus the two types of organisations enter into exchanges in order to ensure both organisations' functional success. Social exchange is more open, less contractual and less bounded by time commitments than commercial exchange, but there is an implicit assumption that benefits will accrue to each organisation. In fact, one of the areas researchers grapple with is how to evaluate social exchange transactions, so that returns and benefits can be quantified.

Marketing can be considered as those museum activities that pay tribute to museums' social *or* economic mandate and responsibility by broadening access, not only through increasing visitor numbers, but also by increasing the variety of audiences reached. Bennett (1994) picks up these arguments in his study of non-goers to South Australian history museums and art galleries. He argues that for a mixture of economic and political reasons, museums and art galleries are increasingly dependent on the number of visitors they attract, either directly (through entrance fees) or indirectly (through diverse public use) which ensures continued public funding. To quote Bennett:

> the dynamics of access policies and the requirements of effective marketing are really the recto and verso of the same set of issues. (Bennett 1994: 6)

Museums need to find a balance between their object-based focus and market awareness, brought forward by visitor orientation.

Cause related marketing (CRM) picks up this notion. It is generally defined as joining a non-profit and commercial organisation in order to raise funds and awareness for a cause while building sales, awareness and corporate image (Rentschler and Wood 2001). Hence, museums can benefit from liaisons with commercial interests. The customer can purchase at their discretion and they may, by their continued use of a product, donate on more than one occasion. Thus, museums can get more hits per visitor for a limited ongoing work input and limited intrusion into the lives of the audience.

CRM enables consumers to identify with the museum. By aligning themselves with worthy causes or implementing policies that are radically different from standard practice, museums enable visitors to identify with what the organisation represents (Bhattacharya et al. 1995). For example, the new-age cosmetic companies support natural ingredients which shy away from animal testing, while universities have alumni to encourage a sense of belonging to the organisation. Museums use these strategies to ensure identification on the part of visitors by linking exhibitions and research to social issues and by drawing visitors 'inside' the organisation by making them members, volunteers and patrons. Research has consistently shown that members identify with the organisation. This leads to increased loyalty to the organisation, high brand loyalty and positive word of mouth (Bhattacharya et al. 1995). Increased loyalty provides benefits. For example, some studies show that retaining existing customers is up to six times less expensive than luring new ones (Rentschler et al. 2002). High brand loyalty is seen as different from identification: loyalty is necessarily tied to causes or goals an organisation embodies. In other words, a museum can foster visitor identification with its social mission by linking with other social causes. Brand loyalty is a deliberate choice to purchase a brand stemming from past positive experience with its use. Positive word of mouth is most important to museums: it builds visitor numbers, visitor retention and social identity for visitor identification.

Conclusion

This chapter investigated the consequences of museums becoming more oriented to their audiences, while at the same time recognising the importance of their product portfolio and organisational marketing culture. Over the last quarter century, museums have recognised the need for changes in marketing to be met by moves towards greater management and financial autonomy (Rentschler and Gilmore 2002). In the past, being successful in a museum meant focusing on cultural heritage collection, preservation and research. For a long time this focus went unchallenged. Although marketing has become more important to museums, there is still only fragmentary knowledge on visitors and non-visitors. A better understanding of audience profiles is still needed, particularly concerning segmentation, so that targeting of visitors can achieve greater benefits for museums.

The need for decreasing reliance upon government income has seen each museum move from an attitude of dependence – bemoaning the government's abandonment of the organisation – to an increasingly positive attitude in which innovative post-modern marketing has become central to museum operations. This needs to be achieved in unique ways, according to each museum's individual strengths and means – the Art Gallery of New South Wales in Sydney, Australia, never wavers from its central focus upon diverse and engaging public programming, maintaining effective publicity and harnessing its popular profile to attract sponsor-ship; while Canterbury Museum in Christchurch, New Zealand, has recently adopted the notion of 'total visitor experience', reshaping its operations to embrace a whole new vision. In these ways, museums are recognising audience differences, encour-aging governments to recognise the range and diversity of their product portfolio and developing their organisational marketing culture to reflect them.

Where should museum marketing go from here? There are three implications that emerge from this chapter. First, alternative segmentation approaches need development via psychographic and attitudinal measures, as they promise a more accurate picture of audiences and provide information that is of more practical use than mere demographics (cf. Schulze 1992). There is also an opportunity to fur-ther segment the audience into occasional visitors, regular visitors and types of mem-bers, as performing arts research suggests that there is more variability in these groups than there is in visitors and non-visitors (Johnson and Garbarino 1999). There is a danger in drawing too strong conclusions from performing arts research and its applicability to museums, due to differences in entry fee policies – no entry fee means audience is a drain on resources, whereas entry fee means it is 'box office' – unless museums also develop products and services within the museum for which audiences pay.

Apart from expanding their view beyond visitors and non-visitors, museums can consider a much larger group of *stakeholders* as communication partners and thus, as a subject matter for audience research, such as members and patrons. Second, the fear that a greater orientation on visitors will lead to a decreased concentra-tion on the product portfolio is not necessarily the case. As Gainer and Padanyi (2002) found in a study on non-profit arts organisations, an increased marketing focus and greater popularity does not necessarily lead to decreased artistic reputation. In fact, growth in artistic reputation and audience satisfaction lead to increased resources, both at the box office and through higher artistic reputation. Gainer and Padanyi state that this is presumably due to the funding provided by public agencies and by donors, who want to support excellence. Finally, as Kotler and Scheff (1997) state, there is danger of competitive myopia where museums view their competitors as only museums: a segment that has too narrow a focus for instigating effective competitive marketing strategies. While there is verbal recog-nition of broader competition, an adequate strategic approach – entailing its closer examination and developing targeted strategies – is still in its infancy, even though, for example, it had been stated as important by the McKinley Douglas (1995a, b) report on the New Zealand museums sector. Conventional marketing concepts are often seen to fall short of museum marketing needs, most of which are small, non-profit organisations. But if museums can adapt and adopt the innovative, flexible principles which are applicable to them in a post-modern age, they stand to gain the opportunity of understanding the values of different types of audiences.

Notes

Ruth Rentschler is Executive Director of the Centre for Leisure Management Research and Program Director of the Arts and Entertainment Management Program at Deakin

University and has published extensively on museum marketing and related topics. This chapter first appeared in *Arts Marketing*, edited by Kerrigan, Fraser and Ozbilgin (2004).

1   Biculturalism is policy recognition of the two peoples of New Zealand, European settlers and the indigenous Maori inhabitants of New Zealand, who signed a treaty with the settlers.

References

Andreasen, A.R. (1985). Marketing or selling the arts: an organisational dilemma. *Journal of Arts Management and Law*, 15 (1), 9–20.

Australia Council (1990). Museums, Art Museums and Public Galleries: Report of a Survey, 1988–89, *Research paper No. 3*, May, Australia Council, Redfern.

—— (1991). Museums 1990: Art Museums, Museums and Public Galleries in Australia and New Zealand. *Research paper No. 6*, May, Australia Council, Redfern.

—— (1992). Museums 1991: Art Museums, Museums and Public Galleries in Australia and New Zealand. *Research Paper No. 7*, July, Australia Council, Redfern.

—— (1993). Museums 1992: Art Museums, Museums and Public Galleries in Australia and New Zealand. *Research Paper No. 9*, June, Australia Council, Redfern.

—— (1994). Museums 1993: Art Museums, Museums and Public Galleries in Australia. *Research Paper No. 12*, May, Australia Council, Redfern.

—— (1995). Museums 1994: Art Museums, Museums and Public Galleries in Australia. *Research Paper No. 14*, June, Australia Council, Redfern.

—— (2001). Planning for the Future: Issues, Trends and Opportunities for the Arts in Australia, Discussion Paper – February 2001. www.ozco.gov.au.

Bennett, T. (1994). *The Reluctant Museum Visitor: A Study of Non-goers to History Museums and Art Galleries*. Sydney: Australia Council.

Bennett, T. and Frow. J. (1991). *Art Galleries: Who Goes?* Sydney: Australia Council.

Besterman, T. (1998). Saying what museums are for – and why it matters. *Museums Journal*, April, 37.

Bhattacharya, C.B., Rao, H. and Glynn, M.A. (1995). Understanding the bond of identification: an investigation of its correlates among art museum members. *Journal of Marketing*, 59, October, 46–57.

Blenker, P. (2001). In search of an adequate marketing approach for small entrepreneurial firms. In *Research at the Marketing/Entrepreneurship Interface* (Hills, G.E., Hansen, D.J. and Merrilees, B., eds.), pp. 70–85. Chicago: University of Illinois.

Brown, S. (1993). Postmodern marketing? *European Journal of Marketing*, 27 (4).

Carson, D.J. (1985). The evolution of marketing in small firms, in marketing and small business (special issue). *European Journal of Marketing*, 19 (5), 7–9.

Cleary, P. and Murphy, C. (2002). Census mirrors real Australia. *The Australian Financial Review*, 18 June, 1–8.

Committee of Inquiry on Museums and National Collections (1975). *Museums in Australia 1975*/The Piggott Report. Canberra: AGPS.

Commonwealth of Australia (1994). *Creative Nation*. Canberra: Australian Government Printing Service.

Culturelink (2001). www.culturelink.org.

DCITA (2003). *Review of the National Museum of Australia, its Exhibitions and Public Programs* (a report to the Council of the National Museum of Australia. AGPS, Canberra). www.nma.gov.au/aboutus/council_and_committees/review.

Deakin University (2002). *A Study into the Key Needs of Collecting Institutions in the Heritage Sector*. Final Report, Deakin University, Faculty of Arts, Cultural Heritage Centre for Asia and the Pacific, Melbourne.

DiMaggio, P., Useem, M. and Brown, P. (1978). *Audience Studies of the Performing Arts and Museums: A Critical Review*. Washington, DC: National Endowment for the Arts.

Falk, J.H. and Dierking, L.D. (1992). *The Museum Experience*. Washington, DC: Whalesback Books.

Fillis, I. (2002). Creativity, marketing and the arts organisation: what can the artist offer? *International Journal of Nonprofit and Voluntary Sector Marketing*, 7 (2), 131–45.

Gainer, B. and Padanyi, P. (2002). Applying the marketing concept to cultural organisations: an empirical study of the relationship between market orientation and performance. *International Journal of Nonprofit and Voluntary Sector Marketing*, 7 (2), 182–94.

Goa, D. (2001). Communities and Museums: Building Lasting Relationships. Canadian Museums Association. www.museums.ca/diversity/pubrelationships.htm.

Hancocks, A. (1987). Museum exhibition as a tool for social awareness. *Curator: The Museums Journal*, 30 (3), 181–92.

Heart of the Nation Project Team (2000). *Heart of the Nation: A Cultural Strategy for Aotearoa New Zealand*. Wellington: McDermott Miller.

Hendon, W.S. (1979). *Analysing an Art Museum*. New York: Praeger.

International Council of Museums (1995). *Statutes: Code of Professional Ethics*. Paris: ICOM.

Johanson, K. and Rentschler, R. (2002). The new arts leader: Australia Council and cultural policy change. *International Journal of Cultural Policy*, 8 (2), 167–80.

Johnson, M.S. and Garbarino, E. (1999). Customers of performing arts organisations: are subscribers different from nonsubscribers? *International Journal of Nonprofit and Voluntary Sector Marketing*, 6 (1), 61–77.

Kawashima, N. (1998). Knowing the public: a review of museum marketing literature and research. *Museum Management and Curatorship*, 17 (1), 17–40.

Kelly, L. and Sas, J. (1998). Separate or inseparable? Marketing and visitor studies. Paper presented at ICOM *Conference Marketing and Public Relations*. Melbourne, Australia: 12–14 October.

Kotler, N. and Kotler, P. (1998) *Museum Strategy and Marketing: Designing Missions. Building Audiences and Generating Revenue and Resources*. San Francisco: Jossey-Bass.

Kotler, P. and Levy, S.J. (1969). Broadening the concept of marketing. *Journal of Marketing*, 33, January, 10–15.

Kotler, P. and Scheff, J. (1997). *Standing Room Only: Strategies for Marketing the Performing Arts*. Boston, MA: Harvard Business School Press.

Lewis, G. (1992). Museums and their precursors: a brief world survey. In *Manual of Curatorship: A Guide to Museum Practice* (Thompson, J.M.A., ed.), 2nd edn., pp. 5–21. Oxford: Butterworth-Heinemann.

McKinley Douglas Ltd. (1995a). *A Framework for Funding and Performing Measurement of Museums in New Zealand*. Wellington, New Zealand: Museum Directors Federation.

—— (1995b). *Resource Guide Developing Performance Indicators in New Zealand Musuems*. A resource guide for museums, their boards, funders and stakeholders developed by Peter Ames and participants during four one day workshops. Wellington, New Zealand: Museum Directors Federation.

McLean, F. (1994). Services marketing: The case of museums. *The Service Industries Journal*, 14 (2), April, 190–99.

—— (1995). Future directions for marketing in museums. *European Journal of Cultural Policy*, 1 (2), 355–68.

McLean, F. and Cooke, S. (1999). Museums and cultural identity: shaping the image of nations. In *Heritage and Museums: Shaping National Identity* (Fladmark, M. ed.), pp. 147–60. Shaftesbury: Donhead.

Mixer, J.R. (1993). *Principles of Professional Fundraising: Useful Foundations for Successful Practice*. San Francisco: Jossey-Bass.

Morris Hargreaves McIntyre (2002). Unpublished document.

Murphy, B. (1993). *Museum of Contemporary Art: Vision and Context*. Sydney: Museum of Contemporary Art.

Museum or Victoria Annual Reports (1999–2002). www.museum.vic.gov.au/about/annreport.asp.

Noble, J.V. (1970). Museum manifesto. *Museum News*, April, 17–20.

O'Riordan, B. (2002). Advertisers home in on their targets. *The Australian Financial Review*, 18 June, 8.

Radbourne, J. (1998). The role of government in marketing the arts. *Journal of Arts Management, Law and Society*, 28 (1), spring, 67–82.

Rentschler, R. (1998). Museum and performing arts marketing: a climate of change. *Journal of Arts Management, Law and Society*, 28 (1), 83–96.

—— (2001). Entrepreneurship: from denial to discovery in non profit art museums? *Research at the Marketing/Entrepreneurship Interface* (Hills, G.E. Hansen, D.J. and Merrilees, B. eds.), pp. 582–94. Chicago: University of Illinois.

—— (2002). Arts marketing: the age of discovery. *Journal of Arts Management, Law and Society*, 32 (1), 7–14.

Rentschler, R. and Gilmore, A. (2002). Services marketing in museums. *International Journal of Arts Management*, 5 (1), 62–73.

Rentschler, R. and Wood, G. (2001). Cause related marketing: can the arts afford not to participate? *Services Marketing Quarterly*, 22 (1), 57–69.

Rentschler, R., Radbourne, J., Carr, R. and Rickard, J. (2002). Relationship marketing, audience retention and performing arts organization viability. *International Journal of Nonprofit and Voluntary Sector Marketing*, 7 (2), 118–30.

Reussner, E. (2002). Strategic management for visitor-oriented museums: a change of focus. *International Journal of Cultural Policy*, 9 (1).

Robertson, H. and Miglorino, P. (1996). *Open Up! Guidelines for Cultural Diversity*. Sydney: Visitor Studies Australia Council.

Schulze, G. (1992). *Die Erlebnis-Gesellschaft. Kultursoziologie der Gegenwart*. Frankfurt, New York: Campus Verlag GmbH.

Standing Committee on Canadian Heritage (1999). *A Sense of Place, a Sense of Being: The Evolving Role of the Federal Government in the Support of Culture in Canada*. Ninth Report of the Standing Committee on Canadian Heritage, Ottawa. www.pch.gc.ca (no page numbers).

Statistics New Zealand (1995). *New Zealand Cultural Statistics*. Wellington: Ministry of Cultural Affairs.

Thomas, E.G. and Cutler, B.D. (1993). Marketing the fine and performing arts: What has marketing done for the arts lately? *Journal of Professional Services Marketing*, 10, 181–99.

Thompson, G.D. (1998). Performance measurement in museums and New Zealand's service performance reporting model. Paper presented at the *Accounting Association of Australia and New Zealand Conference*, Adelaide, 6–8 July.

Volkerling, M. (2001). From cool Britannia to hot nation: creative industries policies in Europe, Canada and New Zealand. *International Journal of Cultural Policy*, 7 (3), 437–55.

Weil, S.E. (1990). Rethinking the museum: an emerging new paradigm. *In Rethinking the Museum and Other Meditations*, pp. 57–65. Washington, DC: Smithsonian Institution Press.

Weppler, N.R. and Silvers, R. (2001). A museum vision. Canadian Museums Association. www.museums.ca/diversity/pubrelationships.htm.

Wiggins, J. (2003). Motivation, ability and opportunity to participate: a reconceptualization of the RAND model of audience development. *Proceedings of the 7th International Conference on Arts and Culture*, Milan, Italy, 29 June–2 July.

Chapter 22

Expanding the Museum Audience through Visitor Research

Carol M. Komatsuka

I F LISTENING IS ONE OF THE KEYS to a successful relationship, the practice of companies listening to their customers and museums listening to their members, donors, and visitors is the first step toward a healthy and mutually beneficial relationship.

Before joining the staff of the Japanese American National Museum (National Museum), I had a long career at a national financial institution that spent hundreds of thousands of dollars annually on consumer research. Focus groups, customer satisfaction surveys, and closed account telephone studies were just some of the methods used to provide insight for new product development, brand advertising, and sales training. In addition, there were studies that measured awareness of the company before and after a major advertising campaign ran. Some of these studies were also conducted in Spanish, Mandarin, and Cantonese to better understand the increasingly diverse customer base. The research provided a direct link to, and a voice for, the customer and the public and generated solid directional information that shaped the institution's business plans and marketing strategies.

In the early 1980s a group of Little Tokyo businesspeople and World War II veterans joined forces to create what would become the Japanese American National Museum. This group had no previous experience founding a museum; none of them sat on the board of any other museum and, if asked, would probably admit that museum going was not a frequent leisure time activity. In fact, at that time few arts and cultural institutions could serve as models for an institution that aspired to become a national museum. Without a research budget, a staff formally trained in the research discipline, or consultants to provide expertise, the early founders and staff of the National Museum forged a community-based,

Source: In A. Kikumura-Yano, L. Ryo Hirabayashi and J.A. Hirabayashi (eds) (2005) *Common Ground*, Boulder: University Press of Colorado.

collaborative approach to gather the information and support needed to establish, grow, and sustain the first museum in the nation to share the story of Japanese Americans.

The National Museum's approach was actually quite simple in concept: it created direct linkages among museums, museum professionals, cultural and historical institutions, and the local communities they serve. The collaboration centered on a committee structure that included local representatives who, for the museum's staff, became an informal, ongoing, and dynamic sounding board and partner for the issues, concerns, and opinions of the local constituency. To call this 'consumer research' in the traditional sense would be impossible. The National Museum had never referred to the information gleaned, the trends recognized, or the changes observed as 'research.' However, in retrospect, the institution's unwavering commitment to community engagement has provided the direction and focus for its programs and its ability to connect with its many diverse audiences.

This three-way collaboration among the National Museum, local institutions, and the 'community' – the people whose family stories and experiences embody the local history – was formally named the National Partnership Program (NPP) and helped establish the institution's national presence. The NPP produced three exhibitions from 1993 to 1998: In *This Great Land of Freedom: Japanese Pioneers of Oregon*, *The Kona Coffee Story: Along the Hawai'i Belt Road*, and *From Bentō to Mixed Plate: Americans of Japanese Ancestry in Multicultural Hawai'i*.

As the National Museum matured, the institution's research methodologies evolved to include traditional research vehicles such as one-on-one interviews, small group discussions, and telephone and mail surveys. The institution's expansion into more formal research studies, however, has not diminished the importance of or distracted from its first commitment: to listen to the community.

Three examples illustrate the evolution of research in the more than twenty-year history of the Japanese American National Museum.

Research through collaboration

The exhibition *From Bentō to Mixed Plate: Americans of Japanese Ancestry in Multicultural Hawai'i* is the National Museum's most traveled exhibition and is the result of the NPP's Hawai'i Project. The exhibition debuted at the Bishop Museum in Honolulu in 1998 and has since been displayed at the Japanese American National Museum in Los Angeles, the Arts and Industries Building of the Smithsonian Institution, and the Lyman House Memorial Museum in Hilo. In 2000 it made its international debut at the Okinawa Prefectural Museum in the capital city of Naha, the National Museum of Ethnology in Osaka in 2001, and the Hiroshima Prefectural Art Museum and the Niigata Prefectural Museum of History, both in 2002.

The Hawai'i Project was launched three years before Bentō opened at the Bishop. The project was led by Dr. Akemi Kikumura, project director, and Dr. Margaret Oda, then vice chair of the National Museum's Board of Trustees and chair of the project. To engage the community, a number of committees were formed: the Scholars Committee, the Research and Collections Committee, the Education Committee, and the Campaign and Development Committee. Partnerships were established with local institutions such as the Japanese Cultural Center of Hawaii, the Japan-America Society of Hawai'i, the Hawaii Okinawa Center, the Hawaii United Okinawa Association, and the Kona Japanese Civic Association. Finally, local professionals were selected to curate, design, and coordinate all aspects of the project and exhibition.

The benefits of the NPP are numerous. The dialogue, the give-and-take, and the learning that results are critical to the process. Both the National Museum and the local community benefit from this interaction. For example, the Hawai'i educators who sat on the Education Committee provided direction to ensure that educational components in the Bentō exhibition, including the media arts presentations and teacher training materials, were linked appropriately with the Hawai'i Department of Education curriculum. Meanwhile, the National Museum organized a Multicultural Institute, held concurrently in Hawai'i and California, and linked Hawaiian educators with their counterparts from the mainland United States, Japan, Brazil, and Canada – providing a forum for dialogue on critical issues related to cultural identity and values faced by ethnic groups and nations around the world.

The three-way collaborative approach pioneered by the NPP has been refined and expanded by the National Museum beyond the Japanese American community. Finding Family Stories was the National Museum's first partnership project that focused on the arts. Finding Family Stories was first launched in 1994 with the Korean American Museum in Los Angeles, then expanded to four additional partners, and from 2000 to 2003 involved the California African American Museum, the Chinese American Museum, and Self Help Graphics & Art, a community-based Latino arts organization. The Boyle Heights Project was the institution's first partnership to focus on the multicultural and multifaceted history of one neighborhood in Los Angeles. The project culminated with an exhibition that opened in fall 2002.

Research for exhibition projects

By the mid-1990s the National Museum had created and opened twelve exhibitions in Los Angeles and had increasing inquiries from a number of museums interested in having these exhibitions on loan. Among the first requests was one from the Ellis Island Immigration Museum in New York for America's Concentration Camps: Remembering the Japanese American Experience, which had debuted at the National Museum in Los Angeles in 1994.

The incarceration of Japanese Americans during World War II was an unprecedented event and a traumatic one for individuals, families, and the community. The Japanese American National Museum's commitment to research and collect first-person stories was for many the first time they had discussed the experience that had occurred more than fifty years before. As a result, the exhibition, although based on historical facts and figures, was organized from a personal – and emotional – point of view. It was an opportunity to tell the story and hear the voices of those who had lived – and survived – the camp experience.

Knowing that the visitor audience on Ellis Island would be different in composition – with far fewer Japanese Americans – from the audience that attended the exhibition in Los Angeles and also knowing that the exhibition would travel to other venues nationally, the institution engaged People, Places & Design Research, Northampton, Massachusetts, to conduct a visitor study in the closing months of the run. The study was conducted as an exit interview to assess visitors' experiences, including their prior knowledge about the camps and responses to the exhibition and its content. A total of 214 visitors comprised the study sample, and prior to that, fifty visitors participated in the pretest of the questionnaire. Analysis of the results focused on understanding the visitors' perceptions and attitudes about the exhibition and the events portrayed.

As expected, visitors to the Ellis Island museum were very diverse: 69 percent European American/white, 6 percent Japanese American, 6 percent Latino, 3 percent Japanese national, 3 percent other Asian American, 2 percent African American, and 11 percent other. Most visitors – 62 percent – were aware of the evacuation of Japanese Americans. Not surprisingly, slightly over 40 percent of the visitors were foreign tourists, and of these, 73 percent were not aware of the incarceration of Japanese Americans.

Key findings from the visitor research

Generally, people revealed an understanding of the exhibition's communication goals, recognizing that the incarceration took place within a context of limited acceptance of Japanese American people in the United States. Of those surveyed, 73 percent believed the camps were established because Japanese Americans were not fully accepted prior to World War II, and 12 percent thought establishing the camps was 'normal' wartime behavior.

Prior to the opening of the exhibition at Ellis Island, some segments of the Jewish community were concerned about the use of the term *concentration camp* in the exhibition title. During the pretest of the questionnaire, there was some indication that visitors felt the title was inappropriate. In the survey, visitors were given the opportunity to comment on the title, and although some were shocked at the use of the words *concentration camp*, over 95 percent recognized the title as accurate and appropriate.

Although the majority of the questions focused on people's perceptions and opinions, one factual question that could influence attitudes and perceptions was asked: 'What percentage of those incarcerated were American citizens of Japanese ancestry?' The issue of citizenship is critical to understanding the climate and political action during World War II, so it was important that exhibition visitors understood that two-thirds of those incarcerated were American citizens. This fact was repeated a number of times in the exhibition. The survey revealed that 59 percent of respondents answered incorrectly, with 35 percent of those having no response. To place more emphasis on the citizenship issue, a number of recommendations were made to include incorporating graphic elements such as a bar chart, graph, or something similar showing the percentage of American citizens who were incarcerated.

Between 1999 and 2000, America's Concentration Camps traveled to the William Breman Jewish Heritage Museum in Atlanta, Georgia, and the California Historical Society in San Francisco. Because of limited budget and human resources – and while the National Museum's *From Bentō to Mixed Plate: Americans of Japanese Ancestry in Multicultural Hawai'i* continued its national and international travel schedule — the decision was made to forgo making changes or additions to the exhibition. With the understanding, however, that the citizenship issue was paramount, steps were taken to ensure that this and other critical facts were emphasized in docent training, teacher training materials, and school tour preview packages that supported the exhibition in future locations.

Research to reach audiences

The opening of the new 85,000-square-foot Pavilion in January 1999 provided the opportunity to quickly expand and increase the on-site visitor audience and make the Japanese American story more accessible to a wide range of visitors. Prior to the opening, the James Irvine Foundation provided the National Museum with a generous grant to conduct a series of visitor and member research studies. The foundation felt studies of this nature would be invaluable in the first years of the Pavilion's operations as the institution determined how best to serve its visitors and expand its audiences. The first study occurred during the summer of 1999, the second during the spring and summer of 2001, and the third during winter 2002–2003.

The National Museum once again commissioned research to provide information about the characteristics and perceptions of the visitor audience. It also sought to explore in-depth reactions to the exhibitions and to solicit visitors' interests and opinions as a way to inform future plans. In addition, the research provided a start in developing a profile of visitor characteristics and a better understanding of who visits and why.

To gather this information, an interview survey was developed to allow interviewers to speak directly with visitors who had seen the exhibitions. A conscious decision was made to recruit and train interviewers from among the volunteers and staff rather than contracting with an outside consultant or firm. This decision was motivated by the recognition that regular visitor surveys are vital to the successful growth of the National Museum. This process would allow for the development of valuable new skills under the guidance of People, Places & Design. In addition, exposing volunteers and staff directly to visitors and providing a means for them to listen directly to visitor comments were other desired outcomes of the project.

The first survey was conducted in the period July–September 1999, shortly after the opening of the Pavilion. In addition to visiting the new Pavilion, visitors were able to view Common Ground: The Heart of Community, an exhibition that explores more than 130 years of Japanese American history including the World War II experience, as well as the art exhibitions Bruce and Norman Yonemoto: Memory, Matter, and Modern Romance and A Process of Reflection: Paintings by Hisako Hibi. The final sample was composed of 377 interviews with randomly selected visitors. This research does not include school or group tour visitors, which represent a significant and diverse visitor segment.

The survey provided a wide range of informative data and confirmed the fact that Japanese Americans were the core audience – comprising 55 percent of the total. This chapter, however, will focus on one new audience that held significant potential: art museum visitors. In light of the National Museum's commitment to the arts and its pioneering work in the area of Japanese American art history, this was welcome news. Although the art museum-going audience was diverse and included a segment of the Japanese American visitors, the survey also indicated that nearly a fifth of the Japanese American visitors had not visited any museum in the past two years. Results showed that whereas 33 percent of the European American/white visitor audience had visited 11+ museums in the past two years and 3 percent had visited no museum, for the Japanese American audience these figures were 5 percent and 19 percent, respectively.

The National Museum viewed these findings as significant opportunities. The museum could introduce the arts and make them more accessible to Japanese Americans through programs that spoke personally to their experience. Additionally, the European American visitors' increased experience with museums in general – and with art museums in particular – was encouraging in light of the National Museum's exhibition schedule, which included plans for five art exhibitions over the next two years. In the survey, the regular museum visitors responded positively to virtually any topic about art or the performing arts, yet they were also interested in cultural issues. This audience also expressed higher-than-average interest in repeat visits.

Using the information from the research, the National Museum sought to provide a stronger bridge between the institution's programs and its audiences through the art exhibition Henry Sugimoto: Painting an American Experience. Sugimoto was a promising young artist who had studied in Paris and was beginning to establish himself in the San Francisco Bay area before the start of World War II. The war and his incarceration transformed his life and his art, and the retrospective included a significant number of the works he produced in the Jerome and Rohwer, Arkansas, concentration camps. A number of new initiatives and enhancements targeted at both the art museum visitors and Japanese American visitors were initiated. Some of the key components include:

- *Public relations* – The National Museum retained the public relations firm Ruder Finn Arts and Communications Counselors, a company the institution had worked with successfully on the opening of the Pavilion and one previous exhibition.
- *Documentary video* – To provide an additional channel for access, a documentary on the life and art of Henry Sugimoto was produced by the National Museum's Media Arts Center.
- *Interactive education stations* – The education unit developed two interactive activities within the Sugimoto exhibition.
- *Directional assistance for visitors* – To provide visitors with guidance for viewing the exhibition (located in two buildings), the marketing and curatorial units created a ticketing system and increased directional signage; the Visitor Services staff encouraged visitors to visit both exhibition galleries.

- *Art museum partnerships* – Two partnership programs were initiated with the Museum of Contemporary Art (its Geffen Contemporary Building is adjacent to the National Museum); the partnerships consisted of an upper-level members' exchange and a reciprocal admissions program.
- *Member/donor targeted plan* – To make the Sugimoto exhibition more accessible to members, donors, and volunteers, a number of activities, field trips, classes, hands-on art workshops, and increased promotion in the member calendar and magazine were initiated in preparation for the exhibition.

The second round of research began with the opening of the Sugimoto exhibition in March 2001, with the majority of the surveys completed from April to June 2001. Here are significant findings.

Ethnicity

There was a shift to a more diverse audience: a 14 percent decrease in the percentage of Japanese Americans and a corresponding increase in other groups. The report from People, Places & Design indicates that there is no reason to believe these shifts are a result of seasonality but that they should be considered indicative of expanding awareness of the museum among those without a personal connection. The exhibition was covered extensively in major media, including the *New York Times*, the *Los Angeles Times*, and local television. The proportion of European American visitors was highest (53 percent) during the first two weeks after Sugimoto opened.

Reason for visit

Findings indicate a shift from 1999, as more visitors cited that they were coming for specific exhibitions and programs, now the top reason for visiting. The Sugimoto exhibition was the primary destination (12 percent) among all visitors, and repeat visitors were even more likely to come to see something specific than were first-time visitors (31 percent versus 10 percent). Visitors in the 1999 study who cited 'personal involvement'[1] as the reason for their visit may have been coming back for new exhibitions. Also affecting visitation was an increase in school-related projects, most likely related to seasonality, and the member newsletter – which appears to have been playing a more significant role, indicating that members who visited utilized museum publications for information.

To analyze the role of temporary exhibitions in a museum's attendance figures, it is important to find out the proportion of visitors who say they are aware of a specific exhibition and the proportion who say it was a primary factor in their decision to visit. For Sugimoto, 33 percent were aware of the exhibition, and 12 percent came specifically to see it. Both figures are above average for temporary exhibitions (not including major blockbuster shows at art museums). Awareness of this exhibition and of Henry Sugimoto was higher among Japanese Americans than among European Americans.

Exhibitions seen today

Art museum visitors of all ethnic groups spent more time than non-art museum visitors in the Sugimoto exhibition, and they watched more of the video. Ethnicity was unrelated to the amount of time spent viewing the exhibition or the video. Because the exhibition was in two parts – Part I in the Historic Building and Part II in the Pavilion – steps were taken to better ensure visitors were aware of the dual locations, as mentioned previously. It appears that more people went to the Historic Building first to see Part I of the Sugimoto exhibition in spring 2001 (37 percent) than had been the case with the Heart Mountain exhibition in 1999 (20 percent). Overall, visitors spent an average of 36 minutes viewing the Sugimoto art exhibitions versus fewer than 20 minutes for both the Yonemoto and the Hibi exhibitions.

Most memorable

Visitors were asked about the most memorable image from their visit. Although Common Ground: The Heart of Community was the most salient and memorable feature of their visit for two-thirds of the visitors, People, Places & Design stated in its final report that the fact that one-third mentioned Sugimoto is 'impressive considering that Common Ground is a large, engaging, and immersive exhibition that is intellectually accessible to all visitors.' The Sugimoto video was rated positively in the context of overall enjoyment of the visit. Those who enjoyed it most were repeat visitors, art museum visitors, and people over age sixty-five. Key messages visitors took from the video were perseverance despite hardships (17 percent), overview of his life as an artist (14 percent), and his love of art, or following your dreams, doing what you love (12 percent).

The findings from the Sugimoto research indicated that the enhancements and new activities implemented to provide greater visitor access to the arts were having an impact. The decision was made to expand and tailor these activities to the Boyle Heights project. The Boyle Heights team worked to engage new partners and a multicultural community composed of past and current neighborhood residents, using the National Partnership Program's approach of working in collaboration to research, develop, and share a window into a part of Los Angeles' diverse history. The project also provided the opportunity to expand targeted marketing and public relations plans specifically directed at key audiences (Latino and Jewish American communities that have strong connections to Boyle Heights), as well as the member/donor strategies launched during the Sugimoto exhibition.

Initial findings from the on-site research study conducted during the exhibition's closing months, January–February 2003, indicate that the exhibition made an impact on several fronts.

Audience shifts

The study indicates shifts in the visitor profile. As expected, the ethnic composition of the audience continued to change, with a significant decrease in the percentage of Japanese Americans – 27 percent of attendees during Boyle Heights versus 41 percent during Sugimoto – and an increase in Latino visitors, from 7 percent to 17 percent, and European American visitors, from 30 percent to 38 percent. Whereas the ethnic composition shifted during the survey period, general admission during the run of the show increased by 46 percent. The survey was an opportunity to learn more about seasonal factors that impact attendance. The 'winter' audience was primarily local (84 percent lived in the Los Angeles and surrounding areas versus 65 percent in spring and 56 percent in summer, when tourism increases). The exhibition also appears to have had a positive impact in providing access to new audiences; the survey found that the percentage of first-time visitors remained high (60 percent), which is not typical of winter/local audiences, and the proportion of member visitors was lower than seen in previous surveys.

Perceptions of the Boyle Heights exhibition

Because Boyle Heights was the institution's first exhibition on the multifaceted history and diversity of one neighborhood, it was vital to understand if visitors believed this exhibition 'fitted in' with the other exhibitions and if visitors understood its theme. The study found that most visitors recognized and could articulate the fact that Boyle Heights was a multicultural exhibition, with one-third mentioning the aspect of different ethnic groups living together and getting along. A total of 72 percent of the visitors (63 percent of whites, 84 percent of Japanese Americans, and 71 percent of Latinos) indicated that the Boyle Heights exhibition fitted in with the others. This finding is significant and heartening because the National Museum is dedicated to finding new programs and approaches to link diverse communities and their experiences.

National Museum as a 'destination'

The National Museum actively partners with city, county, and regional organizations to market the greater Los Angeles area as a growing arts and culture destination. Since the on-site research studies were initiated in 1999, results show that the National Museum is increasingly becoming a specific 'destination' for visitors. The survey found that 50 percent of visitors came to 'see something specific' (44 percent came for Boyle Heights) versus 19 percent in 2001 and 10 percent in 1999. Repeat visitors are increasingly motivated to visit when they see press coverage of exhibitions and programs.

Although it would be premature to claim a trend based on three research studies conducted at different times of the year, it appears that the National Museum's schedule of arts, history, and cultural programming that shares the Japanese American experience and its commitment to initiate a range of activities that provide more access is helping to achieve the museum's two goals; to make the arts and museum going more accessible to Japanese Americans and to diversify and increase the museum's audience. Comparisons of visitors' perceptions in the 1999,

2001, and 2003 studies suggest that people appreciate the variety of exhibitions and programs and are moving toward a greater understanding of the National Museum's mission. The studies indicate that the National Museum is developing into a cultural institution that blends history and art in an engaging way.

Summary

In *Museum Strategy and Marketing: Designing Missions, Building Audiences, and Generating Revenue and Resources* by Neil Kotler and Philip Kotler, the authors devote a chapter to marketing research and information-gathering tools. They assess the role of marketing research in museums by observing that as museums fight for the consumer's attention, the need for market information is more critical than ever. They also acknowledge that marketing research is often resisted for three reasons: high cost, lack of technical knowledge among the staff, and the fear that applying such research will compromise the museum's mission and integrity.[2]

Although the Japanese American National Museum has made significant strides in incorporating the visitor's voice in its planning, the barriers cited by the Kotlers are real. On site visitor studies and mail surveys conducted by a research firm can cost $20,000 or more. Supporting the commitment to research by hiring staff with the experience to manage and implement a comprehensive research plan is likely to be inefficient and cost-prohibitive. In addition, establishing the disciplined practice of applying the findings from studies to future program development is an ongoing challenge.

As museums and other history/culture/arts institutions strive to expand their role as providers of a unique form of education and experience, and they compete for the little leisure time available to most people, the need to consider the value of visitor research and the appropriate role it can play in shaping the institution's programs, communications, and development plans is critical. As the Japanese American National Museum celebrates the tenth anniversary of its opening to the public, it reconfirms its commitment to listen – to the voices of the community, to the experiences of partner organizations, and to the hopes of its leadership, staff, and volunteers. In this way, may the National Museum remain '[a] place that reminds you of what it means to be a citizen . . . in all senses of the word; a place of courage, grace, and conviction,' in the words of one visitor to the Common Ground exhibition.

Notes

Carol M. Komatsuka is Vice-President of External Affairs at the Japanese American National Museum, Los Angeles. This chapter was first published in 2005 in *Common Ground: The Japanese American National Museum and the Culture of Collaborations* edited by Akemi Kikumura-Yano, Lane Ryo Hirabayashi and James A. Hirabayashi.

1   In the survey, 'personal involvement' was selected by those whose visit was motivated by a personal connection to Japanese American experiences, such as 'My

parents were in camp,' 'My uncle fought in the 422,' or 'I had a friend who was put into a camp.' The primary reason for their visits was not to see a specific exhibition or participate in a public program.

2   Neil Kotler and Philip Kotler, *Museum Strategy and Marketing: Designing Missions, Building Audiences, and Generating Revenue and Resources* (San Francisco: Jossey-Bass, 1998).

Chapter 23

Revisiting Membership Scheme Typologies in Museums and Galleries

Alix Slater

Introduction

THE FIRST RECORDED BRITISH museum Friends' group dates from 1909 at the Fitzwilliam Museum, Cambridge.[1] There has been a sustained and incremental growth in membership organisations since the 1970s, and there are approximately 3.5 million memberships held in the UK.[2] There is relatively little published about membership schemes in either the UK or USA; only a handful of academic studies, practitioner guides and reports for policy makers exists. Friends' schemes, however, can be a source of loyal supporters who often volunteer, make donations and act as advocates for museums and galleries.

The aim of this paper is to refine an existing set of characteristics and criteria that can be used by Friends' managers to identify the position of their own membership scheme in relation to others; map the organisational performance of 90 membership schemes affiliated to museums and galleries, of varying sizes from across the UK; and to use this information to extend and enhance a typology of membership schemes developed by Hayes and Slater[3] (see Appendix). This study is therefore important to the museum sector as a whole as this process of classification is an important part of developing theory.

Membership organisations

There is no agreed definition of a Friends' scheme; they are described as membership schemes, societies and associations; however, they share a common purpose

Source: *International Journal of Nonprofit and Voluntary Sector Marketing*, vol. 9, no. 3 (2004): 238–260.

of supporting the host organisation.[4] In this paper the term 'membership scheme' will be used. Slater's recent audit of membership schemes at UK heritage sites[2] updated Heaton's[1] earlier estimates of the numbers of membership organisations and concluded that there are probably some 3.5 million memberships in the UK. In 2002, 300 membership groups subscribed to the umbrella organisation, the British Association of Friends of Museums (BAFM). Within these 300 organisations are, cumulatively, 230,000 memberships.[2] National Museums have at least another 150,000 members,[2] English Heritage 470,000[5] and the National Trust more than 3 million.[6] Slater's research[2] also suggests that there has been a sustained and incremental growth in membership groups in the UK since 1970.

The main sources of information for membership managers in the UK are both more than a decade old: 'Members Matter', a practitioner manual on how to set up a membership organisation;[7] and Burns Sadek Research Ltd's study published by the Arts Council of Great Britain of member motivations across the museum and arts sectors.[8] In the museum sector reports on the role of membership organisations have been commissioned; for example, Boyden Southwood's research into Friends' and Members' schemes for the Arts Council of Great Britain in 1990,[9] Heaton's[1] report on the state of membership organisations for the Museums and Galleries Commission, and more recently a consortium of organisations commissioned a project to examine the contribution of friends and support organisations to Yorkshire's museums, archives and libraries.[10] Cordrey's article on the role of members[11] has also been well cited and in the last two years, articles on setting up branches of Friends in the USA[12] and the impact of free admission on memberships[13] have also been published in the sector's professional magazine, *The Museums Journal*. A recent report on income generated by museums and galleries sponsored by the Department of Culture Media and Sport also commented on the financial contributions membership schemes have made, and their management.[14] Evaluations of membership schemes do exist, but are not in the public sphere.

The academic literature on memberships in the cultural sector is equally sparse and fragmented across international sociology, museology and business journals. There are two key areas of research: members' behaviour, and the nature of membership organisations. Knoke[15] studied commitment and detachment in voluntary associations, Cress et al.[16] length of membership and participation, and Bhattacharya[17] how members' characteristics relate to lapsing behaviour in paid membership contexts based on a study of art gallery members. With Glynn et al.[18] the same author examined members' perceptions of museum membership, usage of benefits and their identification with the membership organisation.[19] Slater has taken this research further, examining motivations and behaviour of members of a Friends' organisation at a national museum in the UK.[20]

There appears to be only one study of a membership organisation in the cultural sector although broader research on membership organisations in the wider voluntary sector often encompasses a sample of cultural organisations. Lansley[21] presented a case study of the National Trust from a sociological perspective and concludes that the size, complexity, centralisation, extent of ideological commitment and constitutional and structural factors will influence a membership organisation.

American sociologist Horton Smith[22,23] studied two types of member benefit organisations in the wider not-for-profit sector: those set up to serve members for mutual benefit (intra-beneficial), and those set up to serve the public (extra-beneficial). He found that the latter operated with paid staff, while the former relied more on volunteers and fees and made the observation that 'volume of members is important to member benefit groups and that some corners are cut on quality in attracting the numbers desired'.[23] More recently Hayes and Slater[3] have attempted to address this dearth of literature on memberships in the cultural sector by developing a typology of membership schemes.

Typologies

Hambrick[24] argues 'classification is a fundamental cognitive aid. To classify things is to know one or two key attributes about an object and then infer (sometimes reliably, sometimes not so reliably) other attributes of the object.' As Rich argues 'it provides a means for ordering and comparing organisations and clustering them into categorical types without losing sight of the underlying richness and diversity that exist within the type'.[25] It is 'both process and end result';[26] a method of bringing order to a complex world.

There are two approaches to classification: typologies and taxonomies. Sometimes the terms are used interchangeably; however, taxonomies are derived from empiricism, based on numerical methods and hierarchal with each vertical level of abstraction encompassing all the levels below it.[27,28] Typologies are more common in the social sciences and tend to be conceptually driven.[24-26] A useful definition is, 'A purposive, planned selection, abstraction, combination and (sometimes) accentuation of a set of criteria with empirical referents that serves as a basis for comparison of empirical cases'.[29] At one end of the spectrum there are typologies that have grown out of personal insight and/or on a limited number of dimensions; they are heuristic and based on *a priori* theory often resulting in superficial and oversimplified views of organisations.[25] They may be useful to describe a group of similar organisations, but will probably have limited explanatory or predictive power.[24] Carper and Snizek[30] argue that such classifications 'fail to pass even the most elementary tests of logic and are little more than tautologies'. At the other end of the spectrum are effective multidimensional typologies that Rich[25] states should be judged not by how 'neat' they are, but by their 'ability to replicate reality'. These may have taken an *a posteriori* approach that uses empirical observations to inform them. It has been argued that typologies can be evaluated on their consistency, or alternatively the discovery of inconsistencies and their versatility.[31] Bailey[26] agrees and suggests that success is the ability to identify the fundamental characteristics on which to base classification. Typologies are an important part of formulating theory and testing hypotheses as they allow the researcher to form opinions and theorise without having to find 'a one model fit alls'. Rich[25] also argues that typologies allow knowledge to be transferred to related areas and enables the management of types, while Bailey[26] suggests that they can be used as criteria for measurement.

Typologies of membership schemes

Hayes and Slater's[3] original typology of membership schemes took the approach described by Rich. It evolved from the literature and the findings of a postal questionnaire that was sent to membership managers of large London museums and galleries (those with more than 100,000 visitors per annum at the time of the study).[4] The typologies were organised around seven areas: the nature of the membership base; the purpose of the scheme; the types of benefits that were being offered; 'openness' of recruitment; governance; approaches to fundraising and marketing; and evaluation.

In order to evaluate the organisational performance of the membership schemes and benchmark them against the typologies, 11 characteristics were identified against which each membership scheme was scored. The 11 characteristics were:

—   degree of autonomy/integration
—   number and stratification of membership categories
—   extent of differentiated brand identities and values attached to stratified categories
—   channels of entry to membership
—   fundraising approaches
—   focus on longitudinal relationship
—   extent of professionalism
—   an organisation's strategic dependence on a membership scheme
—   level of business planning underpinning membership schemes
—   promotional methods
—   application of audience research and evaluation.

Each characteristic had criteria that were positioned in relation to each other and scoring was based on a three-point Likert scale. For example, against the characteristic 'the number and stratification of membership categories' a membership scheme with one membership category would have scored 1 (low); a scheme with stratified categories based on demographic criteria and patterns of behaviour would have scored 2 (medium); and a scheme with stratified categories that enabled members to personalise their membership package would have scored 3 (high). Within the scoring there was flexibility to score 1.5 or 2.5 if a scheme was deemed to 'sit' between two criteria. The 11 characteristics were equally weighted. The minimum score that could be achieved was 11 (if an organisation was rated 1 against all 11 characteristics), and the maximum 33 (if an organisation scored 3 on each). The author divided the range so that scores of 11 to 18 represented the 'Social Club Group'; 19 to 26 the 'Public Members' Scheme'; and 27 and above the 'Integrated Membership Scheme'. Each membership scheme was plotted on axes representing the number of members and their cumulative score. The authors recognised that this segmentation was to some extent arbitrary; however, it was presented as a spectrum reflecting a range of schemes relative to each other.

The 'Social Club Group' was at one end consisting of a handful of devoted individuals who ran a small social club with no formal constitution. At the other end of the continuum was an 'Integrated Membership Scheme' managed by the core management team, and operated to fulfil the museum's strategic objectives. Between these two bi-polars was a 'Public Members' Scheme', a semi-professional organisation, that may be managed by a separate body, or be part of the host organisation.

The benefit of this typology of membership schemes is that it is multi-dimensional and reflects reality. The characteristics that have been developed to complement it also allow membership managers to benchmark their scheme against it. Retrospectively, it is clear that some refinements were needed both to the characteristics and to the criteria to reflect no, or limited activity at the lower end of the scale, the nature of a broader range of organisations and to improve clarity in some instances as some organisations were receiving a score of 1, rather than 0. A classic example was that there was 'no application of audience research and evaluation' or 'business planning'. The result was that in absolute terms some schemes received artificially high scores and would have been positioned further down the scale although their relative positions would not have altered. Even in the original sample, there was a diverse range of organisations, and at times, the criteria were not subtle enough to recognise relatively large differences between their operations. The purpose of this research is to address these issues, first by refining the characteristics and criteria, by plotting the findings of a postal questionnaire to a large and diverse group of membership schemes across the UK and enhancing and extending the original typologies.

Methodology

To test the typologies on a large sample of heritage sites across the UK of differing natures, sizes and geographical locations, a questionnaire was sent to 260 members of the British Association of Friends of Museums (BAFM) in March 2002. BAFM is an umbrella organisation that exists on subscriptions from Friends' schemes and offers advice and support in return. This was 87 per cent of their membership base and included all their members who were willing to receive information from a third party. One hundred and thirty-two questionnaires were returned, of which 127 were usable. Non-responses were not followed up due to the high initial response rate within the sample: 49 per cent ($n = 127$) of those who received questionnaires and 42 per cent of the complete membership base. This paper focuses on the organisations that described themselves as museums and/or galleries and provided information about their membership base ($n = 90$). Nine museums were not included in the sample because of missing data. Other sites in the sample included historic houses, gardens, a ship and railway; they are to be considered in a separate paper due to their diversity.

As discussed earlier, this study provided the opportunity to revisit the characteristics and criteria and to refine rather than redefine them; for example, fundraising and marketing have been brought together. The left-hand column in Table 23.1 shows the characteristics used in the first study and the right-hand column how the remaining ten characteristics have been regrouped under five sub-headings; in some instances new characteristics were added, which have been grouped under five sub-headings. For example, 'Degree of autonomy/integration' was originally measured

Table 23.1   Comparison of characteristics and refined characteristics used to score membership schemes

Characteristics in original study	Refined set of characteristics
Degree of autonomy/integration (1) Organisation's strategic dependence on membership scheme (8)	*Degree of autonomy/integration and strategic value of the membership scheme* Degree of integration into the organisation Organisation's strategic dependence on membership scheme Relationship between membership and organisational objectives (new) Relationship between membership activities and organisational objectives (new) Cooperation with the organisation (new)
Number and stratification of membership organisations (2) Focus on longitudinal relationship (6)	*Number and stratification of membership categories* Number of membership categories Focus on longitudinal relationship Status of membership base (new)
Extent of differentiated brand identities and values attached to stratified categories (3) (deleted) Channels of entry to membership (4) Fundraising approaches (5) Promotional methods (10)	*Fundraising and marketing approaches* Channels of entry to membership Fundraising approaches Marketing communications
Extent of professionalism (7) Level of business planning underpinning membership organisations (9)	*Extent of professionalism* Degree of volunteerism, honorary and paid posts Level of business planning underpinning membership organisation Charitable status of the organisation (new)
Application of audience research and evaluation (11)	*Application of audience research and evaluation* Frequency of evaluation Extent of evaluation (new)

by one criterion, but now encompasses characteristics 1 and 8 from the original study, as well as three new statements with which respondents were asked to agree or disagree. They have been weighted so that the three combined equal a score of 1. Number 3, 'extent of differentiated brand identities and values attached to stratified categories', was problematic due to the subjective method of measurement and has now been omitted. See Table 23.1.

The criteria were refined using an iterative process. As the author's knowledge of smaller membership schemes has broadened, particularly those that fit the 'Social Club Group' typology, subtle refinements have been made to the criteria. The benefits of this approach are that the characteristics and criteria more clearly reflect the reality of membership schemes in the 21st century, and within a study of some 90 different schemes, it allows membership managers to map their position more easily on the axes and against the typologies. Table 23.2 illustrates the new characteristics with the criteria that were used in this study. Readers are referred to Hayes and Slater's original paper[3] to compare the two sets of criteria.

A postal questionnaire was sent to the sample. It had a three-fold purpose: to elicit information about the nature of membership organisations to enable the author to undertake an audit of the size and scope;[2] to elicit information about each membership scheme so that it could be scored against the new criteria and plotted on two axes; and to extend and enhance the original typologies. Respondents were asked: when the scheme and organisation were founded; the nature of their site; if they had any other membership schemes besides the Friends; the purpose of their scheme; if the Friends is incorporated into a formal department, or not; whether it had charitable status; the number of members; segmentation of membership categories; benefits offered; approaches to fundraising and marketing; recent tactics to retain, or recruit new members; the importance of a range of benefits; about their evaluation; formal planning; relationship with the organisation. All these are reflected in the criteria in Table 23.2.

Using the same approach as in the earlier study, the information collected from the questionnaires enabled the author to score each membership scheme against the new criteria. This was done using an Excel spreadsheet and totals calculated for each. Where necessary, scores of 0.5, 1.5 and 2.5 were used. As the new approach to scoring allowed scores of 0 to be awarded, the scoring now starts at 0 rather than 11. Zero to 14 represents the 'Social Club Group', 15 to 28 the 'Public Members' Scheme' and 29 to 42 the 'Integrated Membership Scheme'. The scores of the 90 museums and galleries have been plotted on Figure 23.1 against the size of the

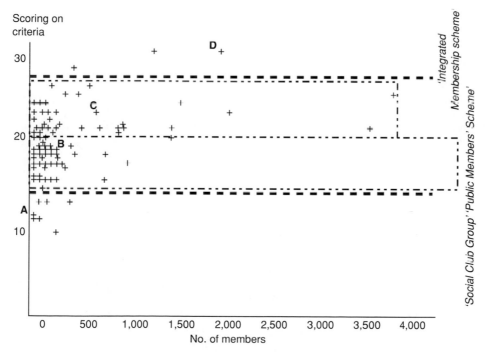

Figure 23.1   Scores of organisational performance of museums across the UK
(n = 90)

Table 23.2 Refined characteristics and criteria for scoring organisational performance of membership schemes

Characteristics	Criteria and scoring		
	1	2	3
Degree of autonomy/integration and strategic value of membership scheme			
Degree of integration into the organisation	Autonomous (external) e.g. completely separate organisation	Semi-autonomous (intermediate) e.g. separate organisation, outside of the formal management of the organisation but perhaps housed in museum offices and with representation on museum committees/boards	Fully integrated (internal) e.g. in the development or marketing department
Organisation's strategic dependence on membership scheme	May rely on members for fundraising and as a source of volunteers but not recognised as having strategic value	Has a recognisable strategic value but only partly harnessed by the organisation e.g. may be part of fundraising and marketing goals	High dependence with explicit and quantifiable objectives and strategies e.g. part of three or more areas e.g. fundraising, marketing and audience development goals
Relationship between membership and organisational objectives*	We operate as an independent entity and fulfil our own objectives that may be different from the host organisation – strongly agree	We operate as an independent entity and fulfil our own objectives that may be different from the host organisation – agree	We operate as an independent entity and fulfil our own objectives that may be different from the host organisation – strongly disagree
Relationship between membership activities and organisational objectives*	Our membership activities are fully integrated with organisational objectives – strongly disagree	Our membership activities are fully integrated with organisational objectives – agree	Our membership activities are fully integrated with organisational objectives – strongly agree
Cooperation with the organisation*	We cooperate with the organisation but have our own aims and objectives – strongly agree	We cooperate with the organisation but have our own aims and objectives – agree	We cooperate with the organisation but have our own aims and objectives – strongly disagree

Number and stratification of membership categories			
Number of membership categories	One generic membership category	Two or more categories based on demographic criteria	Flexible pick and mix approach to enable members to personalise behaviour and giving
Status of membership base	Declined in the last five years	Stayed the same	Increased over the last five years
Focus on longitudinal relationship	Relationships are socially driven	Focus on acquisition of members with occasional attempts to reactivate those who have lapsed and/or some evidence of encouraging a relationship e.g. legacies	Focus on retention, calculating total lifetime value (TLV) and historical records. Database management is used to inform strategies for maximising a member's potential
Fundraising and marketing approaches			
Fundraising approaches	Limited fundraising e.g. Gift Aid and occasional donations.	Ongoing approach to fundraising driven by flagship projects. Diverse methods selected on their fitness for purpose e.g. fundraising for acquisitions, education and capital projects	Strategic fundraising approach integral to achieving organisational objectives. Multiple tools employed and routes for developing members 'giving habits', e.g. legacies, Gift Aid, monthly giving, higher level membership categories
Marketing communications	Very limited marketing communication tools e.g. mainly word of mouth, possibly Friends' desk/sales desk and leaflets	Wide range of marketing communication tools used e.g. Friends' desk, sales/ticket desk, special events, website, printed materials	Extensive range of integrated marketing communication tools to achieve strategic communication objectives e.g. Friends' desk, sales/ticket desk, special events, website, printed materials, member-get-member campaigns, joint promotions, purchase of mailing lists, telephone and mailing campaigns
Channels of entry to membership	Closed by invitation through social network	Open membership, multiple channels promoted through the host organisation	Open membership, multiple channels including hosts, affiliates and mass marketing campaigns

Table 23.2 (*cont'd*)

Characteristics	Criteria and scoring		
	1	2	3
Extent of professionalism			
Degree of volunteerism, honorary and paid posts	Amateur – run by volunteers with honorary posts	Increasing formalisation of structures, possible paid employees to administer the scheme	Paid internal staff with relevant expertise e.g. marketing, relationship management, fundraising, able to draw on IT and marketing communication resources
Charitable status of the organisation	Some form of constitution	Independent organisation without charitable status	Independent organisation with charitable status
Level of business planning underpinning membership organisation	Limited business planning e.g. a business or fundraising plan	Tactical rather than strategic planning undertaken with short- to medium-term emphasis in two or more areas	Strategic planning, collaboration between departments and long-term emphasis across a number of areas e.g. fundraising, business, audience development, marketing
Application of audience research and evaluation			
Frequency of evaluation	*Ad hoc* evaluation	Evaluation every 3–5 years	Systematic research and evaluation to inform strategic planning e.g. on an annual or bi-annual basis
Extent of evaluation	Number of members	Number of members and motivations for joining	Number of members, motivations, and behaviour

Note: All of the characteristics were equally weighted with the exception of those marked *, where the three statements combined had the same weighting as one of the other characteristics membership base. The author also used the information from the questionnaires to develop three case studies in order to test this system of scoring against the original typologies. Did a score of 12 or 18 using the new criteria really reflect a 'Social Club Group' model or a 'Public Members' Scheme' respectively? See Table 23.3.

Findings

Seven membership schemes fit the classic 'Social Club Group' typology. Three were groups of enthusiasts working towards opening a museum; the other four were affiliated to small museums with low visitor numbers. The membership bases were small, less than 76 for those scoring 12 or under, and between 130 and 500 for the three schemes that were on the cusp of this typology scoring 14. Typically they had one membership category and were established groups, pre-dating 1992. The key benefits for members were intrinsic, such as events, previews, information and publications. A key characteristic of this typology is limited access; this was evident with word of mouth and recruitment in the museum (if there was a site) being the primary tools, and visitor figures, where known, were less than 20,000. Two of the three organisations that scored 12 did not have sites and the situation of the third was unknown. Four schemes undertook no fundraising and the other three were tactical, for example, encouraging occasional donations. Not surprisingly, those that scored highest had charitable status, but none demonstrated business planning and only one organisation undertook any type of evaluation.

As in the original study[3] there was a cluster of diverse organisations in the 'Public Members' Scheme' typology ($n = 80$) operating both on the periphery of the 'Social Club Group' and on the cusp of the 'Integrated Membership Scheme' typologies. This group included independent and publicly run museums and encompassed town, city, county, regional and themed museums, some of which had collections of regional and national significance. Forty per cent had fewer than 20,000 visitors and two-thirds fewer than 40,000 visitors. Sixteen per cent had 100,000 visitors or more. Membership bases ranged from 40 to 4,159.

There appear to be four sub-groups within the 'Public Members' Scheme' typology. In the bottom left-hand quartile there is the greatest concentration ($n = 41$); these are small local authority or independent museums, for example, situated in a regional town. Scoring between 15 and approximately 21, most had membership bases of less than 200. Those that were on the cusp of the typology had been categorised as 'Public Members' Schemes' largely due to their outlook, which was outward, rather than purely for member benefit as was the norm for those in the 'Social Club Group'. They have been classified as a new sub-group, 'Emerging Public Members' Schemes'. This reflects their approach, but recognises they are only just moving into the second typology and still have many of the characteristics of the 'Social Club Group' typology in terms of their management.

In the top left-hand quartile there are 20 schemes. These also had relatively small membership bases of up to 500 members and were a blend of local authority district, large town, city or regional museums and independent museums, some of which have significant collections. Their higher scores were a result of better management across the board; for example, by having more stratified membership

Table 23.3 Case studies

Characteristics	'Classic Social Club Group' (A)	'Emerging Public Members' Scheme' (B)	'Aspirant Integrated Membership Scheme' (C)	'Emerging Integrated Membership Scheme' (D)
	Founded in 1992 35 members Benefits: regular meetings to update position on the museum No physical museum	Founded in 1835, established in its current form in 1991 350 members Benefits: free admission to special exhibitions; Friends' private views; information mailings 40–59,999 visits pa	Founded in 1966 750 members Benefits: free admission; information mailings; Friends' events 20–39,999 visits pa	Founded in November 2000 2,183 members Benefits: free admission to special exhibitions; private views; discounts in shop; information mailings; priority booking; and Friends' events No. of visitors not known More than one site
Degree of autonomy/integration and strategic value of membership schemes				
Degree of integration into the organisation	Originally formed as a group of interested people to find a site for a museum in the area	A separate organisation outside the formal management of the organisation	A separate organisation outside the formal management of the organisation	Part of the development department. Has an advisory council with staff sitting on it
Organisation's strategic dependence on membership scheme	Members are recognised as being important for fundraising, as a source of volunteers, advocates and audience development; however, they are not part of organisational goals or plan	Recognised as a fundraising tool and as a source of volunteers, and to a lesser extent as an audience development tool; however, it is not part of organisational goals or plans	Recognised as a fundraising tool, audience development tool and as a source of advocates; however, it is not part of organisational goals or plans. There are member volunteers, but their recruitment is not seen as a primary function of the Friends	Recognised as having strategic value. This is partly harnessed by being part of the organisation's fundraising goals

Relationship between membership and organisational objectives*	Although they operate as a separate entity their objectives are congruent with the host organisation	Members do not operate as a separate entity and have congruent objectives with the host organisation	Members do not operate as a separate entity and have congruent objectives with the host organisation	Part of the organisation and therefore not a separate entity with independent objectives
Relationship between membership activities and organisational objectives*	Activities are not fully integrated with organisational objectives	Activities are partly integrated with organisational objectives	Activities are fully integrated with organisational objectives	Membership activities are fully integrated with organisational objectives
Cooperation with the organisation*	They partly cooperate with the organisation, but also have their own aims and objectives	They cooperate with the organisation, but also have their own aims and objectives	Aims and objectives are congruent with the host organisation	As part of the development department, aims and objectives are congruent with the organisation
Number and stratification of membership categories				
Number of membership categories	One generic category of membership scheme and also a subscription scheme that runs alongside it. No charge for membership	One generic category of membership scheme with a low membership fee	Four membership categories based on demographic criteria i.e. single, joint, junior, family membership categories	Flexible pick and mix approach to enable members to personalise behaviour e.g. friend, family friend, guest friend, guest family friend, student friend
Status of membership base	Stagnant	Declined in the last five years	Expanded in the last five years. The museum was in trouble and membership increased from a stagnant 200–375 members to 750 today and is being retained	Expanded in the last two years as it was a new membership scheme
Focus on longitudinal relationship	Relationships are socially driven	Encourage giving from members, just starting to be more proactive and to retain and reactivate members, and to evaluate the scheme	Encourage giving from members and evaluate their behaviour	Focused on recruitment Using evaluation to explore members' attendance and giving behaviour

Table 23.3 *(cont'd)*

Characteristics	'Classic Social Club Group' (A)	'Emerging Public Members' Scheme' (B)	'Aspirant Integrated Membership Scheme' (C)	'Emerging Integrated Membership Scheme' (D)
Fundraising and marketing approaches				
Fundraising approaches	No evidence of fundraising. Donations are not encouraged beyond the membership fee; nor is there a charge for membership	Ongoing fundraising, including occasional donations, legacies and Gift Aid	Ongoing fundraising, including donations with membership fee, occasional donations and Gift Aid	Strategic fundraising approach integral to achieving organisational objectives. Emerging tools for developing members 'giving habits' e.g. donations with membership fee and Gift Aid, and a higher level membership category
Marketing communications	Word of mouth and press releases about their activities	Limited range of marketing communication tools: general leaflets, sales/ticket desk, word of mouth special events and joint promotions	Limited range of marketing communication tools: general leaflets, word of mouth and special events	Wide range of marketing communication tools: general leaflets, website, word of mouth, member-get-member, joint promotions and purchase of mailing lists
Channels of entry to membership	Word of mouth	Open membership promoted through the host organisation and also marketing campaigns	Open membership promoted through the host organisation	Open membership, multiple channels promoted through the host organisation and also marketing campaigns

Extent of professionalism			
Degree of volunteerism, honorary and paid posts	Amateur – run by volunteers with honorary posts	Amateur – run by volunteers with honorary posts	Amateur – run by volunteers with honorary posts	Paid coordinator, supported by voluntary chairman and a committee
Charitable status of the organisation	Independent organisation without charitable status	Independent organisation with charitable status	Independent organisation with charitable status	Managed by the Development Department but has charitable status
Level of business planning underpinning membership organisation	None	None	None	Some strategic planning within the department e.g. fundraising and business plans
Application of audience research and evaluation			
Frequency of evaluation	None	In the process of evaluation	Evaluate every 3–5 years	Systematic research and evaluation to inform strategic planning on an annual basis
Extent of evaluation	None	Not available	Number of members, motivations for joining and their giving behaviour	Number of members, motivations, attendance and giving behaviour
Total score	12	18	23	31

Note: All of the characteristics were equally weighted with the exception of those marked *, where the three statements combined had the same weighting as one of the other characteristics categories, making attempts to recruit and retain members, more sophisticated fundraising and more frequent and in-depth evaluation. Their success may also be partly attributed to their collections, giving them greater market attractiveness, and subsequently a greater pool from which to attract members. Despite many of them having relatively small membership bases due to the nature of the organisation, they are typical of public members' schemes and have been classified as 'Established Public Members' Schemes'.

In the bottom right-hand quadrant were a handful ($n = 5$) of underperforming schemes. They received similar scores to the first group but potentially had a much greater sphere of influence and market demonstrated by the size of their membership base, location, resources, infra-structure and visitor numbers. They have been classified as 'Stagnating Public Membership Schemes' rather than 'Emerging' as they have been in this typology for some time but have not progressed to an 'Established Public Members' Scheme'. This sub-group and its nomenclature are designed to warn membership managers that this is a dangerous position to be in.

In the top right-hand quartile were fewer but larger museums ($n = 14$). Many were located in cities, with membership bases of 500 to 2,000 members reflecting the significance of their collections, size of the museums and larger potential market. What differentiates them from the organisations in the quadrant below is their 'outward' focus, either their purpose to support the organisation in terms of recruiting volunteers, fundraising, audience development, or as a source of visitors, their marketing and management. The surprising finding of this group was the number of schemes with 500 or more members that were being entirely administered by volunteers. Those that employed staff were either on the cusp of the 'Integrated Membership Scheme' typology or the membership scheme was one of the responsibilities of the curator or another paid member of staff. This group has been given the label 'Aspirant Integrated Membership Schemes' as their approach suggests active organisations that are aspiring to become larger, more inclusive organisations that are working with the organisation. They may or may not stay in this group depending on wider organisational issues, such as integration into the museum. Resources could ultimately hinder their movement into the final typology.

Three membership organisations scored 29–31, at the lowest end of the 'Integrated Membership Scheme' typology; they have some, but not all of the characteristics of this typology and have been termed 'Emerging Integrated Membership Schemes'. They have scored higher than other schemes because they are either integrated into a museum department and have paid staff, or are working very closely with museum departments and are recognised as having strategic value. In the original typologies it had been assumed that physical integration into a museum department was a prerequisite for inclusion in this category. This research suggests that this is not necessarily true, although it will be essential to become a truly integrated scheme.

Table 23.3 presents four case studies from the sample to illustrate typical membership organisations from the three typologies. The first case study is a classic 'Social Club Group'. A museum trust, it scored 12 on Table 23.2 and is one of the three organisations clustered towards the vertical axis. Two examples of 'Public Members' Schemes' are included to reflect the heterogeneity and new sub-groups in this typology. The first illustrates an 'Emerging Public Members'

Scheme' that still has a number of traits of a 'Social Club Group'. It scored 18, and is mapped in the lower, left-hand quartile of this typology. A local authority museum, it had fewer members than some schemes in this sub-group, but a relatively high number of visitors. The 'Aspirant Integrated Membership Scheme' scored 23, and is plotted in the top right-hand quadrant of this typology, reflecting its outward approach. It was chosen as the membership base is relatively large, but not at one of the polars; it scored midway up this typology and is a regional museum. Finally, a case study of an 'Emerging Integrated Membership Scheme' was chosen; an umbrella organisation for a number of galleries to contrast with the other case studies. See Tables 23.2 and 23.3.

Conclusions

This study suggests that the 'Social Club Group' typology is present in both national and small private and public museums and galleries. Organisations scoring 12 in this study can be described as 'Classic Social Club Groups' comprised of enthusiasts. Membership normally expands through word of mouth and they have characteristics of the organisations that Horton Smith called intra-beneficial.[23] The organisations that scored slightly higher have more open access, and while they are still focused on member benefit, they are moving towards the next typology. A larger sample could identify a new sub-typology, 'Aspirant Public Membership Schemes'.

In the original study by Hayes and Slater[3] it was suggested that sub-groups may exist in the 'Public Members' Scheme'. Three groups were suggested: 'emerging', 'developing' and 'established' schemes reflecting their role and position within the organisation, autonomy from the host organisation, external marketing and level of business planning. This research has enabled the author to look at 80 organisations that had characteristics of this typology and as a result four groups have been identified with nomenclature that reflects their current outward focus, management and potential movement. The four sub-groups are:

- 'Emerging Public Members' Schemes'
- 'Established Public Members' Schemes'
- 'Stagnated Public Members' Schemes'
- 'Aspirant Integrated Membership Schemes'.

'Emerging' schemes, as the name suggests, have just moved into the typology. They are amateur organisations, run by volunteers with limited market potential, and are unlikely to move beyond an 'Established' scheme, but within their resources could increase their professionalism, become more open in terms of membership and strategic in the way they operate. The 'Established' schemes, with 500 or fewer members, but scoring at least 21 are 'outward' looking and professionally managed; this is what makes them distinct. While some are likely to be limited by their potential influence, within this group there were local authority, large town, city, regional and independent museums; those with collections that have wider appeal and influence may eventually become 'Emerging Integrated Membership Schemes'. As Horton Smith identified,[22] volume of members is perceived as a sign of success, but as this study shows, this is not necessarily the case and some of the larger schemes are underperforming due to poor management, rather than the limited appeal of their collections and potential market. The 'Stagnant Public Members' Schemes' and 'Aspirant Integrated Membership Schemes' are in fact affiliated to similar organisations in terms of their goverance, potential market and the significance and broad appeal of their collection. What distinguishes the latter group is their approach and professionalism; for example, their approach to fundraising, marketing, management and focus on audience development. There is obvious movement upwards from the former to the latter.

It would appear that the market potential dictated by location and nature of the collection may be two critical factors mediating the size of membership bases. Movement is therefore more likely to be vertical than horizontal on Figure 23.1, due to management and an 'outward' focus rather than a significant increase in the size of the membership base. Schemes that have small numbers may do better to balance their efforts on retaining and developing a relationship with existing members and encouraging new members, rather than just recruiting extra numbers through unplanned promotions, the worth of which have not been evaluated.

In Hayes and Slater's earlier study[3] the 'Public Members' Scheme' was described as 'semi-professional' and it was suggested that there may be paid staff such as an administrator, or in some cases, a director. The second scenario that was described was integration into the host organisation, with designated staff, or where administration of the scheme was a responsibility of the marketing or development departments. This typology also placed greater emphasis on fundraising which could be separate or additional to the host's fundraising department. These are luxuries not afforded by most organisations in this study and reflect the difference between the structure and resources of national and other museums and would appear to be a characteristic of an organisation that has just emerged into the 'Integrated Membership Scheme' rather than a 'Public Members' Scheme'. The typologies have been changed to reflect this.

The advantage of the nomenclature that has been used to describe the new subtypologies is that it can also be adapted for the 'Social Club Group' and 'Integrated Membership Schemes'; for example, 'Aspirant Public Membership Scheme' or 'Emerging Integrated Membership Scheme'. In this study, the three membership organisations that scored above 29 were most definitely 'Emerging Integrated Membership Schemes', rather than established schemes. They scored highly on some criteria, but showed weaknesses in other areas such as developing longitudinal relationships with members and strategic planning. See Table 23.3.

This paper contributes to the literature in this field and the wider museum sector for two reasons: it has refined characteristics and criteria for identifying typologies of membership schemes and by refining and developing further subtypologies it has contributed to the development of theory in this area. Additional benefits for membership schemes are that the new criteria reflect the homogeneity of membership schemes in the UK, they can plot their position in relation to other organisations in Figure 23.1, and evaluate their position in relation to other typologies using the case studies in Table 23.3 and the Appendix. Membership managers are advised to consider whether any mediating factors such as their location, influence of their collection and governance will influence their organisation and whether they should strive to move to a new sub-group or typology. The strategic focus and functional responses that Hayes and Slater[3] outlined in their first paper, alignment, convergence and unification, remain useful contributions to practitioners. This study has reinforced the recommendations that are outlined in this earlier paper and readers are referred to this if they wish to reconsider the strategic direction of their organisation.

Further research

There is an obvious need for further research on memberships in the wider heritage sector. The next step is to use the new characteristics and criteria to plot the heritage organisations in the sample to test, and if applicable, expand the typologies. Further studies that encompass membership schemes that were not in this sample could also contribute to the theory in this area. It would also be interesting to compare and contrast membership schemes more generally, rather than focusing on Friends' schemes as this study did.

Appendix: Revised typologies of membership schemes

Social Club Group: emergent, voluntary and informal	Public Members' Scheme: established, semi-professional organisation	Integrated Membership Scheme: reinvented, professional function/department
Membership		
Active belongers and enthusiasts	Diverse membership base e.g. motivations, demographic profile and behaviour	Growth and consolidation of membership base
Local membership		Recognition of diverse motivations, demographic profiles and behaviour
Small membership base, possibly declining	Wider geographic spread, possibly with overseas members	
One membership category	A focus on increasing membership base	Increasing stratification of membership categories or discrete brands to match market segments
Narrow range of motivations, typically intrinsically driven	Stratified membership categories	Wide geographical extent, possibly with an active overseas branch
Affluent members with wide sphere of influence		Corporate members will be recognised and developed linking to other fundraising activities such as sponsorship
Recognition of members' professional expertise		Sense of community/belonging fostered though programming and communications
Individual members value opportunity to influence the organisation		Emphasis is on longitudinal management and maximisation of relationships

Social Club Group: emergent, voluntary and informal	Public Members' Scheme: established, semi-professional organisation	Integrated Membership Scheme: reinvented, professional function/ department
Purpose/mission		
Originally adopted an advocacy role

Formalisation of social network further to own social interests together with altruistic motivations towards the host organisation

Driven by core of members with personal agendas

Key milestones in the development of the organisation e.g. acquisitions and funding of specific projects | The mission has diversified to include fundraising and income generation

Organised volunteerism among members and identification of opportunities for involvement

While the membership base will have grown, advocacy will remain the provenance of key stakeholders and small sub-groups

Social networking confined to specific sub-groups

Mission formalised and reflected in constitution

Not an audience development tool | Focus has shifted away from volunteerism and advocacy towards fundraising and development potential

Relationship focused

Audience development function emerging and strategies developed to exploit this potential |
| *Benefits* | | |
| Intrinsic motivations important

'Soft' rather than 'hard' benefits accrue to members | 'Hard' tangible membership benefits will have been introduced

Sub-groups will be motivated by a range of intrinsic and fiscal factors

Greater balance of 'hard' and 'soft' benefits offered

Reciprocal relationships with other organisations | Membership brands established with different values and personalities attached e.g. membership costs, benefits, nomenclature will be tailored

'Hard' and 'soft' benefits in equilibrium but tailored to specific sub-sectors

Higher value members recognised, added value offered and personalisation or relationship encouraged

Social networking encouraged among sub-groups |
| *Recruitment* | | |
| Selective recruitment policy

Membership likely to be expanded through social network or invitation

Self-perpetuating/ snowball approach

Recruitment is not a priority as it would detract from social club experience | Multiple routes to membership

'Open invitation' to prospective members in organisational literature

Membership is 'marketed' and hard-sell strategies employed to increase volume | Multiple and new routes to membership through affiliations

Profiling of high value members to identify acquisition targets and successful approaches

Strong emphasis on retention |

Social Club Group: emergent, voluntary and informal	Public Members' Scheme: established, semi-professional organisation	Integrated Membership Scheme: reinvented, professional function/department
Structure/Governance		
Ownership and autonomy of organisation a key characteristic	Autonomous management	Integration gives host a high degree of control and involvement
Charitable status possible	Democratic processes introduced	Possible integration into one of the organisation's departments e.g. marketing, development, communications or public affairs but this is not a prerequisite as the scheme may be a separate charity from the host
Formal mechanisms of governance and voluntary roles develop quickly e.g. secretary, treasurer, chairman	Increasing formalisation of structures and possibly paid employees to undertake administration and management	
	Host organisation seeking opportunity to have greater control of activities	Part of the organisation's strategic planning and policies
	Likely to have charitable status	Formalised planning
	May have representative on the organisation's board	Professional management. Will have paid staff that could still be assisted by volunteers
		May have board representation or be included in the senior management team
Fundraising		
Ad hoc, driven by members for projects they deem to be of value	Greater emphasis on flagship fundraising projects	Increasingly sophisticated techniques and more ambitious targets employed
Unsophisticated methods, particularly those with a social dimension e.g. galas	Fundraising becomes an ongoing activity	Emphasis on encouraging regular giving, and ongoing commitment
Likely that key individuals will make large donations and receive recognition, e.g. influence, position, status	Wider range of methods employed	The value of scheme and database is recognised and 'sold on' to third parties
	Methods selected for their fitness for purpose rather than social benefits	
Promotion		
Membership organisation is not formally promoted	Scheme actively promoted to prospective members	Website presence
Word of mouth dominates	Likely to produce own literature	Professional management adopting proved marketing and fundraising strategic approaches using a diverse range of marketing communications tools
Organisational literature may acknowledge the contribution of the group and key individuals	The scheme may have a clearly defined identity	Proved relationship marketing techniques employed
	Website presence	Brand positioning and differentiation communicated through strategic marketing communications
		Literature uses organisational house style

Social Club Group: emergent, voluntary and informal	Public Members' Scheme: established, semi-professional organisation	Integrated Membership Scheme: reinvented, professional function/ department
	Evaluation	
No formal evaluation of scheme is undertaken	Some *ad hoc*, summative evaluation	Evaluation, audience and market research undertaken and used to inform planning on an holistic basis
High degree of self-congratulation occurs	Simple criteria e.g. profiling are used for evaluation and unlikely to be comparable or integrated with research undertaken by the host	Lifetime values of members calculated
Members may have an inflated sense of worth to the organisation	May or may not be shared with host	Cost of servicing members calculated and 'expensive' members discouraged

Note

Alix Slater is Senior Lecturer in Heritage & Museum Management at the University of Greenwich. This paper was first published in 2004 in the *International Journal of Nonprofit and Voluntary Sector Marketing*, vol. 9, no. 3.

References

(1) Heaton, D. (1992) 'Museums amongst friends: the wider museum community', Museum and Galleries Commission, HMSO, London.
(2) Slater, A. (2003a) 'An audit of friend's schemes at UK heritage sites', *International Journal of Heritage Studies*, Vol. 9, No. 4, pp. 357–373.
(3) Hayes, D. and Slater, A. (2003) 'From social club to integrated membership scheme: Developing membership schemes strategically', *International Journal of Nonprofit and Voluntary Sector Marketing*, Vol. 8, No. 1, pp. 59–75.
(4) Slater, A. (1999) 'Relationship marketing as a strategic tool for managing museum and gallery membership schemes and enriching relationships with members'. Unpublished dissertation for the MA in Museum Management, University of Greenwich Business School.
(5) Brabbs, C. (2001) 'Open to all', *Marketing*, April, pp. 12–21.
(6) National Trust (2003) '3 Millionth Membership Milestone for National Trust', www.nationaltrust.org.uk. Accessed 25th February 2003.
(7) Raymond, C. (1992) 'Members Matter, making the most of membership schemes in the arts', Arts Council of Great Britain, London.
(8) Burns Sadek Research Limited (1992) 'Qualitative research conducted to examine the motivations for membership of friends' schemes', The Arts Council of England, London.
(9) Boyden Southwood (1990) 'Research into friends and members schemes', Arts Council of Great Britain, London.

(10) Edwards, C. (2002) 'Friends like these . . . A study of the contribution of friends and support organisations to Yorkshire's museums, archives, and libraries', Community Heritage Partners, Resource, Yorkshire Museums Council, British Association of Friends of Museums.

(11) Cordrey, T. (1995) 'What are friends for?' *Museums Journal*, Vol. 95, No. 10, pp. 19–20.

(12) Murray, S. (2002) 'Friends like these', *Museums Journal*, Vol. 102, No. 11, pp. 24–25.

(13) Nightingale, J. (2003) 'Members only', *Museums Journal*, Vol. 103, No. 4, pp. 30–31.

(14) National Audit Office (2004) 'Income generated by the museums and galleries', TSO, London.

(15) Knoke, D. (1981) 'Commitment and detachment in voluntary associations', *American Sociological Review*, Vol. 46, April, pp. 141–158.

(16) Cress, D.M., McPherson, J.M. and Rotolo, T. (1997) 'Competition and commitment in voluntary memberships: The paradox of persistence and participation', *Sociological perspectives*, Vol. 40, No. 1, pp. 61–79.

(17) Bhattacharya, C.B. (1998) 'When customers are members: Customer retention in paid membership contexts', *Journal of the Academy of Marketing Science*, Vol. 26, No. 1, pp. 31–44.

(18) Glynn, M.A., Bhattacharya, C.B. and Rao, H. (1996) 'Art museum membership and cultural distinction: Relating members' perceptions of prestige to benefit usage', *Poetics*, Vol. 24, pp. 259–274.

(19) Bhattacharya, C.B. (1995) 'Understanding the bond of identification: An investigation of its correlates among art museum members', *Journal of Marketing*, Vol. 59, October, pp. 46–57.

(20) Slater, A. (2003b) 'Users or supporters? Understanding motivations and behaviours of museum members', *Curator*, Vol. 46, No. 2, pp. 182–207.

(21) Lansley, J. (1996) 'Membership participation and ideology in voluntary organisations: The case of the National Trust', *Voluntas*, Vol. 7, No. 3, pp. 221–240.

(22) Horton Smith, D. (1991) 'Four sectors or five? Retaining the member-benefit sector', *Nonprofit and Voluntary Sector Quarterly*, Vol. 20, No. 2, pp. 137–150.

(23) Horton Smith, D. (1993) 'Public benefit and member benefit non-profit, voluntary groups', *Nonprofit and Voluntary Sector Quarterly*, Vol. 22, No. 1, pp. 53–68.

(24) Hambrick, D.C. (1984) 'Taxonomic approaches to studying strategy: Some conceptual and methodological issues', *Journal of Management*, Vol. 10, No. 1, pp. 27–41.

(25) Rich, P. (1992) 'The organisational taxonomy: Definition and design', *Academy of Management Review*, Vol. 17, No. 4, pp. 758–781.

(26) Bailey, K. (1994) in Greig, I.D. (2003) 'Towards a typology of consumer survey research', *European Journal of Marketing*, Vol. 37, No. 10, pp. 1,314–1,331.

(27) McKelvey, B. (1982). See Ref. (24).

(28) Rosch, E. (1978) in Greig, I.D. (2003) 'Towards a typology of consumer survey research', *European Journal of Marketing*, Vol. 37, No. 10, pp. 1,314–1,331.

(29) McKinney, J. (1967) in Greig, I.D. (2003) 'Towards a typology of consumer survey research', *European Journal of Marketing*, Vol. 37, No. 10, pp. 1,314–1,331.

(30) Carper, W.B. and Snizek, W.E. (1980). See Ref. (25).

(31) Greig, I.D. (2003) 'Towards a typology of consumer survey research', *European Journal of Marketing*, Vol. 37, No. 10, pp. 1,314–1,331.

Chapter 24

A Delicate Balance
Museums and the marketplace

Victoria D. Alexander

A S WE APPROACH THE MILLENNIUM, museums across the globe are taking stock and looking toward the future. Museum managers face challenges in a variety of areas, not the least of which is securing a stable funding base. As governments curtail spending on cultural activities, museums increasingly look to other avenues, especially donations from the private sector.

Much can be learned from the experience of American art museums in soliciting corporate and individual resources. Currently financed by a mix of government, corporate, foundation, and individual grants, American museums have a funding history quite different from that of most European museums in that they have traditionally been philanthropic endeavours supported by élite individuals, sometimes aided by the local municipal government. Not until the mid-1960s did the Federal Government start to fund museums in a meaningful way. State governments also began to participate, mostly in the late 1960s, and largely in response to moneys available from the Federal Government to encourage state involvement in the arts. Most government funds, whether at the state or federal level, are given through an 'arms length' system (an independent intermediary agency is allocated funds directly from the government budget and then passes these on to the arts organizations), and are usually not available for operating expenses. Most of the support comes in the form of grants for specific projects. Charitable foundations became important for museums from the 1950s and corporations began to fund them in meaningful numbers in the late 1960s. Although individual contributors remained important, museums came to rely on a broad range of financial aid and as a result they have had a few decades of experience in cobbling together support from a variety of sources.

What are the effects of this funding situation on museums in the United States? I looked at this question in a detailed study in which I examined annual reports of

Source: *Museum International*, vol. 51, no. 2 (1999): 29–34.

thirty art museums, interviewed a number of staff (curators, directors, and educators), and statistically analysed over 4,000 exhibitions. I would like to describe some of my findings, especially the impact of this experience on exhibitions and on the museum as a whole. I will then draw attention to the situation in the United Kingdom, which is a good example of a country moving from a largely government-based funding system to one that is more market based.

How do sponsors affect exhibitions? The answer is, more indirectly than directly. Although funding itself often makes an exhibition possible, which would not have been so otherwise – clearly a direct effect – backers rarely meddle with the contents or format. Critics assert that business firms distort exhibitions by requiring museums to include pieces of questionable merit or to exclude works that might be controversial or place the sponsor in a bad light. Interestingly, I found no examples of this type of intervention in exhibitions by corporate funders. Indeed, the only interventions I was able to learn about were cases where a museum's board members had pressed for an exhibition of objects they owned! Museum personnel work rather hard to find funding for exhibitions that they themselves wish to mount. The exhibition plan usually comes first and the resources second. Indeed, curators and directors are careful to avoid grants that might come with strings attached.

This does not mean that financial aid comes free, so to speak. Indeed, I found that funders had a profound impact on exhibitions, stemming from the simple fact that they pay for what they like and decline to support what they do not like. Institutional contributors, new to the museum world in the 1950s and 1960s, have preferences distinct from those of the previously dominant individual funders. For instance, both government and corporate sponsors prefer exhibitions that draw large audiences, although for different reasons: government wishes to bring a social good to the many (and reach taxpayers and voters), while business firms hope to increase the advertising potential of the philanthropic dollar. Put together, this means that popular exhibitions are easier to finance and their number thus increases as a proportion of the total. Blockbuster shows, displays of Impressionist art, travelling exhibitions and those based on a theme (e.g. the window in art), to mention several popular types, become more common.

Government funders, especially those giving grants through a peer-review system (as is the case for the National Endowment for the Arts), also favour exhibitions with art-historical merit, a goal shared by museum curators but not for the main part by corporate backers. It is therefore not surprising that government agencies support a significant number of scholarly exhibitions. Corporations do not actively shun such shows, but it is clear from the statistics that they do not seek them out.

During most of the late 1960s up to the early 1980s, the amount of money available to art museums in the United States rose dramatically and with it the number of exhibitions. And although popular shows were the principal beneficiaries, a fact commented upon by many observers, scholarly exhibitions also increased. (The 'losing' types of exhibition were those focusing on local artists, the community or children.) But the urgent question these days is: 'What happens when the funding pie shrinks?' This is a matter I shall return to.

Another more subtle and troublesome way in which funding might affect exhibitions is that museum people must keep potential sponsors in mind from the earliest stages of the planning process. As a consequence, it is possible that museums constrain themselves in order to win support. As Philippe de Montebello, Director of the Metropolitan Museum, has stated: corporate funding is 'an inherent, insidious, hidden form of censorship . . . but corporations aren't censoring us – we're censoring ourselves'. Let me be clear, however. Most curators and directors say that, to the best of their ability, they do what they want and refuse to bend to the wills of funders. I found that American curators were proud of their exhibitions and the most successful museum managers were ingeniously creative in matching exhibitions to backers, thereby reaching their own goals.

A change of mission

The growth of popular exhibitions underscores an important change in the mission of art museums during the last few decades. In the United States, they have moved from an élitist conception of their duties toward a more populist view due to a number of different factors. First, the general ethos of the late 1960s led to attacks on many types of institution thought to be too exclusive. Second, as museums became more reliant on external resources, they needed to attend to their sponsors' interests, notably the desire to attract a broader audience. Third, as American museums successfully courted a variety of funding sources, they began to hire new kinds of staff – fundraisers, accountants, and others with specialities outside of art history. These people changed the balance of power, bringing in a more businesslike approach to running museums.

One perennial difficulty is finding adequate funding for operating budgets. Capital expenditure and special projects lend prestige to donors; paying the guards' salaries and fixing leaky roofs do not. American museums generate income from the commercial potential of their collections and buildings. They have opened restaurants, cafés, and bookshops, and offer programmes, lectures, special events, fundraising activities, and even art classes and packaged art tours abroad. More recently, museums have moved beyond mere postcards, posters, T-shirts, and books to such endeavours as selling by mail order, setting up satellite shops in distant cities, and licensing designs and images for upscale clothing, jewellery, wallpaper, and fabrics. These ventures can be quite lucrative. The Metropolitan Museum, perhaps the world's most successful in commercial terms, earned nearly $9 million through its auxiliary activities in 1997. Commercial ventures are also enjoyed by museum visitors who appreciate being able to stop for a snack, take home a souvenir and borrow a touch of class for decorating their bodies and homes.

Needless to say, these changes in mission have exacerbated tensions in museums – notably between the business and the curatorial sides. Has the shift in mission hurt scholarship and conservation? I don't believe it has. The actual number of these activities has most certainly increased in American museums since the 1950s, and curators have indeed been able to use sponsors' money in very clever, creative ways to see works conserved, researched, and published, display cases built, and galleries refurbished.

Nevertheless, as a proportion of the total number of activities found in museums, conservation and scholarship take a smaller part than before. This is a key source of conflict. Curators have, in fact, lost power and autonomy and this is very difficult for them, as it would be for any professional in similar circumstances. Pointing to the sums of money spent to set up and run the commercial services and to the projects cancelled for lack of funds, they argue that art history and preservation are suffering. The issues are far from straightforward and rest on fundamental questions. What exactly should a museum do? How can museums meet rising public expectations? Should they try to earn money when external funds are in short supply? If external money is considered 'tainted', should museums scale back their activities rather than accept such money? And who determines what kinds of money are 'tainted'? These issues are hotly debated and compromise is often difficult.

The story of American art museums in the last few decades can be briefly summarized: less élitism, more populism; more attention to development, fundraising and revenue generation; more vibrant exhibitions and programmes; more scholarship and conservation (but not as a proportion of the whole range of museum activities); and more internal conflict. This tale will sound familiar to managers in all types of American museums, not just art museums. And increasingly, this story will become familiar to museums worldwide, as the more market-driven approach to museum management – sometimes called the American model – spreads across the globe.

The 'American model' in the United Kingdom

In the United Kingdom, policy changes by the Thatcher government thrust British museums into a more market-driven system. Though they have met this challenge with some success, museums struggle to find funding. They must rely on a wide variety of sources, from project grants and private sponsors to admission fees, collection boxes, shops, and cafés. But they face a number of problems in winning this support.

Many grants by national or local government for projects must be matched by external partners. But there are too many museums (not to mention other cultural, educational, and charitable organizations) seeking out too few potential sponsors. The same large corporations, known to be active in cultural philanthropy, are approached by numerous worthy organizations. Some of these corporations are based outside the United Kingdom, so museums from several countries compete for their largesse. It is clear that matching grants work best when a pool of partners exists, but in the United Kingdom the pool is only half full. One innovative scheme seems to help with matching grants: a museum's auxiliary activities are incorporated into a separate organization which can then provide funds as an external partner.

The American experience shows that tax policies make a difference in giving: donations to museums fall when tax laws become less favourable. The British tax policies for corporate donations help fundraising, as they permit corporations to deduct gifts to museums under advertising expenses; however, they are not as conducive to individual donations as those of the United States. Furthermore, the philanthropic tradition in the United States is well established for the arts. This is rarely the case in the United Kingdom, especially for small contributions; consequently, British individuals are much less likely to sponsor their national or local museums.

Museums in the United Kingdom face an additional difficulty that those in the United States do not. For the most part, American museums charge admission fees and Americans, in general, expect to pay them. These fees can be steep, for instance $10 per adult for the Museum of Fine Arts in Boston. American museums have also been more active in selling annual memberships to individuals and families which entitle them to avoid the admission charge. Together, memberships and admissions can generate a sizeable income, often up to 10 per cent of the annual budget. Moreover, many American museums are able to rely on income from their endowments, a source that does not exist to any significant degree in the United Kingdom.

Charging for admission or establishing 'voluntary contributions' collected at the door (by an employee who is trained to stare gorgon-like when wallets do not open) is a contentious issue in the United Kingdom. Most British citizens feel that as taxpayers they have already given to their local and national museums and that an admission fee is asking them to pay twice. In lieu of the charges, however, many museums have set up collection boxes to tap the visitor's generosity. The trick is to educate the public as to the high costs of running museums and the great importance of contributing a few pounds. Many British museums have succeeded with a strategy of charging for entrance to special exhibitions which are separated from the permanent collections. (Likewise, American museums often charge a distinct admission fee for their most popular special shows.)

In the United Kingdom, museums can apply for lottery money (on a matching basis), which can be used for capital expenditures only. This is a useful source of funding that is not available in the United States. However, such recourse brings its own complications. More than one museum has been known to be building on a new site while vital repairs at the home site must be neglected for lack of funds. Ironically, lottery money was limited to capital expenses in an attempt to ensure that the government would not divert budget money away from museums on the excuse that operating funds could be found in lottery profits. But the government has slashed the culture budget anyway.

To the casual observer, in sum, British museums these days look very much like their American counterparts. By necessity, they are involved in numerous fundraising and commercial ventures, and have stepped up activities, such as special exhibitions, to attract audiences. As in the United States, the larger, better-established museums have been more successful in generating income. But British museums exist in an environment that is, in many respects, less conducive to a market model than in the United States. And even American museums do not find it easy to break even.

Management challenges

It is a shame that governments must cut subsidies to museums, for a nation's heritage is its treasure. Although museums would do well to band together to lobby their governments to continue funding, such cuts are nevertheless inevitable to some extent. Current political climates, as well as demands from more needy sectors such as education and health care, will make it difficult to resist the move toward less government support. It is imperative that museums be creative about financing and do it in a way that maintains their core functions — scholarship, conservation, curatorship, and education. The challenge to management is to keep in view the importance of the traditional roles of museums while at the same time taking on newer ones such as attracting audiences and selling products.

I believe that developing commercial activities, along with project funding, is imperative for museum survival in the next century. Nevertheless, the danger exists that if museums are squeezed too tightly, all the revenue-generating effort of their best people will not suffice to preserve core functions. The threat lies in not having enough money. Commercial activities are not the problem, but because they are especially needed when more traditional sources of funding are insufficient, they may symbolize it.

Some critics have argued that museums have come to resemble shopping malls, but this comparison is neither accurate nor helpful. Museum managers must, against the protest of critics and purists, avail themselves of a wide variety of fundraising and revenue-enhancing efforts. But museums must also preserve culture and heritage and cannot be diverted too much in the direction of entertainment. At the same time as they learn to use sophisticated financial tools, managers must resist the efforts of government bureaucrats and the economically mindful who wish to measure museums with financial yardsticks and quantify the arts in terms of their value to consumers. The arts, heritage, and knowledge must be valued as ends in themselves, not as numbers on an accountant's computer. Museums must succumb to the inevitable, in moving toward a more businesslike model for their operations and revenue, without losing sight of conservation and connoisseurship. Keeping this difficult balance, even more than securing funding itself, will be the real challenge for museum managers in the next millennium.

Note

Victoria D. Alexander is the author of *Museums and Money: The Impact of Funding on Exhibitions, Scholarship and Management* (1997). This article was first published in 1999 in *Museum International*, vol. 51, no. 2.

Chapter 25
_____

The Impact of Free Entry to Museums

Andy Martin

Background

IN RECENT YEARS, MUCH HAS BEEN written about the topic of social inclusion in the museum and gallery sector. Of course it is important that the national museums and galleries, set up over a period of many years, should be perceived to be welcoming by all sectors of society. After all, their purpose is not merely to exist, or even to conserve objects for future generations, they are here for everybody's benefit. Since the early 1990s, when the majority of the national museums and galleries started charging for entry, there has been a sea change in attitudes in the sector. More and more marketers and managers are ensuring that these institutions have become outward-facing and driven by public demand, rather than inward-looking and conservation focused. To some, this has represented the 'dumbing down' of museums and galleries, but for many people this process has dragged these institutions into the twentieth, if not yet the twenty-first, century.

It is within this context that the Secretary of State for Culture, Media and Sport committed to ensuring free entry for all visitors to national museums and galleries; and, by December 2001, all those national museums and galleries which had been charging for admission had returned to a free entry basis.

Market and Opinion Research International (MORI) has been working for many years with a number of national institutions, conducting surveys among visitors, potential visitors, Friends and other stakeholder audiences. At the end of 2001, MORI found that many of its clients were decidedly uncertain about the future. What impact would 'going free' have? Would those who might be described as 'socially excluded' (on whom museums' funding agreements were often based) be encouraged through the doors? Would the money visitors saved on entrance fees be spent in the shops and restaurants? Only time would tell.

Source: *Cultural Trends*, vol. 12, no. 47 (2002): 3–12.

In early summer 2002, one of the questions was well and truly answered – the Department of Culture, Media and Sport (DCMS) announced a 62 per cent increase in visitor numbers in the seven months since entry charges were scrapped. The Victoria and Albert Museum (V&A) led the way with a staggering 157 per cent increase (helped, presumably, by the relatively recent opening of the much admired British Galleries). It was reported that a total of 7,031,722 visitors had been to the national museums and galleries between December 2001 and June 2002 – an increase of 2.7 million people year on year. While it is known that DCMS tends to use the terms 'visitors', 'people' and 'visitor numbers' to refer to visits per se, as a researcher two questions sprang to mind:

- Did these figures mean there were actually a lot more people visiting museums and galleries, or were the same people visiting more frequently?
- Was the boost in visiting restricted to the national museums and galleries, or were more people visiting museums and galleries generally?

MORI decided to see what more could be discovered about these extra visits. Four questions were placed on the MORI GB Omnibus study between 8–13 August 2002,[1] asking a representative cross section of the British public about their museum-going habits in general. It should be stressed here that the statistics in this paper refer solely to British people: MORI's visitor surveys tend to find that roughly two-thirds of visitors to the major museums and galleries are British, with North Americans and Europeans making up the majority of the remainder. Clearly, the last two years have been extremely difficult for the British tourism industry, with the foot and mouth outbreak being followed swiftly by the September 11 attacks in the US and war in Afghanistan. Visit numbers to the UK have tumbled (whilst, for a period at least, a proportion of the British population became less confident about travelling to the major cities), so this research is set against a rapidly moving backdrop.

Leisure visits

MORI's research discovered a significant increase in the proportion of the British public who had visited at least one museum or gallery in the preceding months. When asked about a variety of leisure attractions, 37 per cent said that they had been to a museum and 31 per cent had visited an art gallery. Taking into account the crossover of attraction visiting, 45 per cent of the public had been to at least one or the other. This represents one of the most popular leisure pastimes, as Figure 25.1 demonstrates.

MORI has been asking about leisure habits (using slightly different comparator activities) over a number of years. Since the late 1980s, for example, it has recorded a steady rise in the proportion of the public who visit the cinema every year – from 32 per cent to the 59 per cent in Figure 25.2. By contrast, museum and gallery visiting has been in the doldrums during this period.

The previous peak, at 44 per cent, was in 1991, tailing off to a low of 33 per cent in 2000. In the last two years, therefore, there has been a rise of around one-third in the proportion of the public visiting a museum or gallery.

'Which, if any, of these have you done in the past 12 months?'

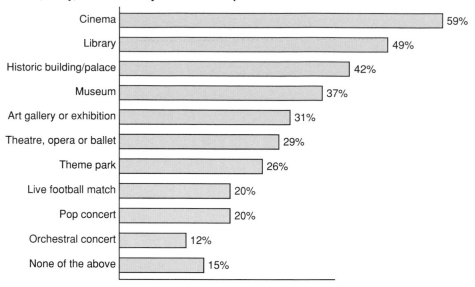

Figure 25.1   Leisure habits, 2002
Note: Base – all British adults aged 15+ (2,095), August 2002
Source: MORI

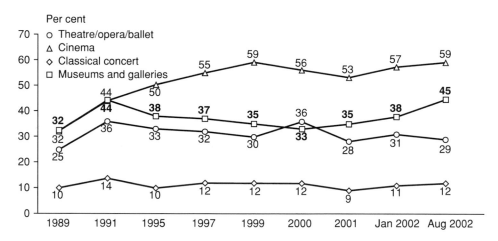

Figure 25.2   Leisure activities enjoyed in the past 12 months, 1989–2002
Note: Base – *c.* 2,000 each time
Source: MORI Omnibus Surveys, 1989–2002

The impact of new attractions, such as Tate Modern, cannot solely account for this increase; the proportion who had visited a museum or gallery in 2001 rose only slightly to 35 per cent. The only real change in the sector over this period was the abolition of entry charges. As Figure 25.2 shows, the increase started immediately – 38 per cent had visited a museum or gallery when this was measured in January 2002. Meanwhile, other popular activities have continued on a fairly even keel.

Who is visiting?

The abolition of entry charges was designed, above all else, to tempt those who were not in the habit of museum-going to give it a try. In particular, non-traditional museum-going groups – such as social classes D and E, those without higher educational qualifications and older people – were supposed to be encouraged to visit.

These groups have traditionally always been less inclined to visit museums, whether through lack of interest, lack of awareness or other mental or physical barriers. In a report for Resource (MORI 2001), MORI found that: 'social class is one of the key indicators as to whether people do or do not visit museums and galleries – with higher social classes far more likely to visit. ABC1s account for 70 per cent of museum and gallery visitors but only around half of the British population (49 per cent).'

In some ways, it has to be said that the DCMS's policy has been a staggering success. Visiting has increased across all age groups, for example. In 2000, 28 per cent of all those aged 55 and over said that they had visited a museum or gallery in the previous 12 months, but by 2002, this figure had risen to 43 per cent. There has also been a rise in museum visiting among those in the DE social classes (those where the head of household is an unskilled manual worker) – from 20 per cent in 2001 to 25 per cent in 2002. The increase is even more pronounced among C2s (skilled manual workers), rising from 28 per cent to 39 per cent.

These increases, though, are not solely responsible for the huge growth in museum visiting. As Table 25.1 shows, there have been significant increases among all groups, including those who have always tended to be well-represented in museums and galleries.

Put another way, whilst the number of people coming through the door might have dramatically increased, the profile of a typical 'population' of museum or gallery visitors has remained relatively stable – and firmly biased in favour of the 'traditional' visitor groups.

Table 25.1   Proportion of the British public that visited a museum or gallery, 1999 and 2002

	1999 %	2002 %
All groups	35	45
15–34	33	43
35–54	42	48
55+	24	43
AB	56	62
C1	39	53
C2	29	39
DE	23	25

Note: Base – around 2,000 adults aged 15+
Source: MORI Omnibus surveys, 1999 and 2002

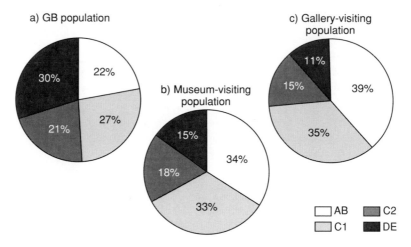

a) GB population

b) Museum-visiting population

c) Gallery-visiting population

AB   C2
C1   DE

Figure 25.3   Population profiles, August 2002
Note: Base – all respondents (2,095)
Source: MORI Omnibus, 8–13 August 2002

Figure 25.3a shows the profile of the British population, set alongside the profile of visitors to museums (Figure 25.3b), and galleries (Figure 25.3c). It is easy to see, for example, that whilst just under half of the British population is currently classified as being in the ABC1 social groups, around two-thirds of those who visit museums and three-quarters of all those who go to art galleries fit into this category.

Looking at this issue from another angle, 18 per cent of the British population now have a first degree, a Masters degree, or a PhD. Among museum visitors, this rises to 30 per cent. In galleries, this rises even further to 36 per cent. Conversely, whilst 26 per cent of the population have no formal qualifications, in museums and galleries this proportion is just 12 per cent.

Geography also plays a part, as might be expected. The south of England accounts for 31 per cent of the British population, but 40 per cent of museum visitors and 43 per cent of those who visit galleries. The further away people live from London – the location of the majority of the national museums and galleries – the less likely they are to visit.

In other ways, though, the profile of visitors does match the population fairly well. Men and women are split fairly equally (49 per cent and 51 per cent respectively in the population at large, compared with 52 per cent and 48 per cent in museums). Those aged 15–34 are just a little less likely than average to visit museums and galleries, whilst the 35–54 age group tends to be marginally over-represented.

It is interesting to note that museum- and gallery-goers are generally 'culturally active'. It might be expected that the sorts of people who visit museums or galleries may also be more likely than average to go to orchestral concerts, the ballet or the theatre.

What is, perhaps, more surprising – as Figure 25.4 shows – is that they are also more likely than average to go to the cinema, pop concerts and even theme parks.

'Which, if any, of these have you done in the past 12 months?'

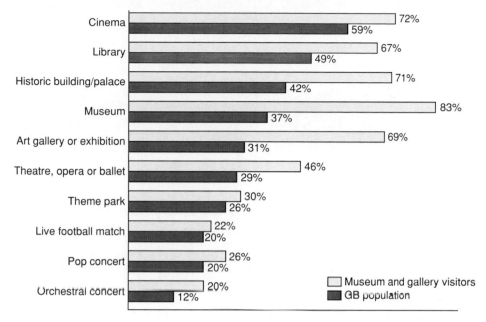

Figure 25.4   The leisure habits of museum and gallery visitors, 2002
Note: Base – all GB population (2,095), August 2002
Source: MORI

The impact of free entry

It is now known that visitor numbers have risen significantly, and that there has been an increase of ten percentage points in the proportion of members of the public saying that they had visited a museum or gallery in the preceding 12 months. When asked more directly about their behaviour, it seems that even more claim to have reacted to the reintroduction of free entry. A total of 7 per cent say that 'I know that admission charges have been scrapped and have been on a lot more museum and gallery visits this year than I did last year'. Another 8 per cent say they have been on one or two more visits this year than last.

On the other hand, as Figure 25.5 demonstrates, it is not particularly encouraging to note that two in five members of the public were not even aware of free entry. (This could, however, be interpreted as representing a further 18.4 million potential visitors.)

Unfortunately for those claiming that free entry has acted significantly to improve social inclusion, the proportions of certain sub-groups within the population who claim to have made more museum and gallery visits as a result of free entry make depressing reading. While 15 per cent of the British public say they have made more visits, this rises to 20 per cent among ABC1s, 21 per cent among people living in the south and 29 per cent among people with a degree. Conversely, it falls to 11 per cent for both C2DEs and those with a top educational qualification of O Levels/GCSEs or their equivalent.

'As you may or may not be aware, the admission charges at most of Britain's national museums and galleries were scrapped last December. Please tell me which of these statements best describes your behaviour since then.'

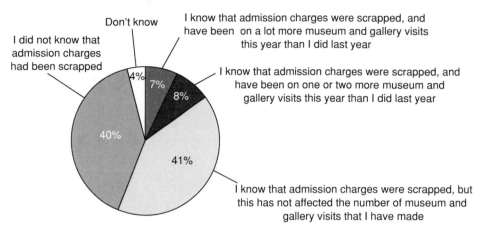

Figure 25.5   The impact of free entry to museums and galleries, August 2002
Note: Base – all GB population (2,095), August 2002
Source: MORI

Barriers to entry

In addition to the 40 per cent of the public who are not even aware that entrance charges have been scrapped, a similar proportion knows that the national museums and galleries are free to enter, but have not made any more visits. Among this group, the most common reason given is a lack of time – cited by 43 per cent. It is interesting to speculate, though, on the extent to which this 'lack of time' translates to a lack of interest; after all, if someone cannot make some time over a seven-month period to visit a museum or gallery, then it can probably be assumed that there are simply a lot of other things that they would rather do with their time. A further 23 per cent of this group (or around one in ten of the general public) say that, despite knowing about free entry, they simply have not thought about making a museum or gallery trip.

Transport and money issues do still prevent some people from visiting (predominantly DEs, those without formal qualifications and people living in the north of England), but, as Figure 25.6 shows, the implication would appear to be that for the majority of non-attendees, museums and galleries simply do not appeal all that much.

Whether this means that museums and galleries should stop trying to convert those who have so far shown no interest, or whether they need to completely revamp their outlook in order to gain wider appeal, is a moot point. It is worth looking further afield to set this in some sort of context. One of the most inclusive leisure time activities in the UK today is cinema. It's relatively cheap, there's a wide range of films available, to suit all types, and there's plenty of enticing (if not exactly healthy) food and drink available. Yet regular MORI research shows (as demonstrated by Figure 25.4), that in a typical year around three in five of the British

'Which, if any, of these reasons describes why you have not made any more museum or gallery visits, despite admission charges being scrapped?'

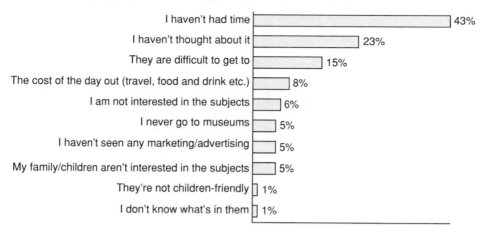

Figure 25.6   Reasons for not visiting museums or galleries, 2002
Note: Base – all aware of free entry, but who have not made more visits (830)
Source: MORI

public go to the cinema one or more times. So four in ten people don't even get out to the cinema in a 12-month period. Three in four don't go to theme parks. Four in five don't go out to watch live sports events. At the end of the day, people are all different, and it should not be expected that everyone will be interested in the same things.

Impacts on behaviour

So what about the group who do go to museums and galleries? What are they doing differently now to this time last year? Encouragingly for those attractions charging for entrance to special exhibitions, one in four (26 per cent) say that they are now more likely to pay to go into an exhibition. One in five (21 per cent) will donate more and one in seven (15 per cent) are more likely to buy a guidebook or hire an audio guide. In fact, 47 per cent say that they will spend more on different aspects of their trip to a museum or gallery than they would have done when they had to pay for entry. This is higher among:

- ABs (57 per cent)
- people living in the south of England (58 per cent)
- women (60 per cent)
- 15–34 year olds (60 per cent)
- people with degrees (60 per cent).

Turning these figures on their heads, of course, it is perhaps a little dispiriting to learn that more than half of visitors are not spending any more money in museums

'Which, if any, of the following statements descibe how your behaviour has changed regarding museum and gallery visits since admission charges were scrapped hast December?'

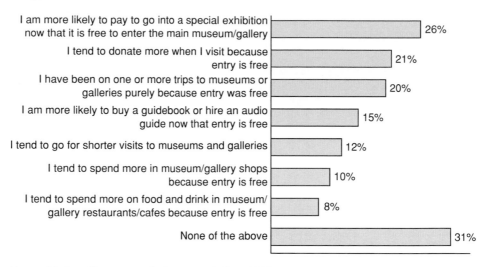

Figure 25.7   Changes in behaviour, 2001–2002
Note: Base – all aware of free entry and have visited at least one museum or gallery in the past 12 months (684)
Source: MORI

and galleries even when they get in for free – for many people it seems that perhaps 'free entry' equates to a 'free trip' altogether.

Figure 25.7 shows general behavioural changes. It is interesting to note that just one in five of those who know about free entry, and who have been to a museum or gallery recently, say that this was purely because they knew that entrance was free. Perhaps the simple act of removing the entry charges to museums and galleries has made people start to consider visits when previously they would have done something else?

Implications

So what can be concluded from these statistics?

Clearly the number of people coming through the doors of Britain's national museums and galleries has increased significantly since 2001. Whilst this vindicates the removal of entry charges, in that the institutions have been 'opened up' to a larger proportion of the British general public, two distinct concerns remain.

First, although there has been an increase in visiting among those who might be described as being 'socially excluded', the most significant impact on visiting appears to have been among those groups who traditionally have always gone to museums and galleries. People with a degree are almost four times as likely as those with no formal qualifications to say that they know charges have been scrapped and to have made more visits as a result.

Faced with subsidies which have, in real terms, fallen steadily over the years, most museums, if left to their own devices, would as every private sector business does, target the 'low hanging fruit' – put on exhibitions and market their wares to the sorts of people who have proved over the years that they appreciate what museums and galleries offer. The government continues, though, to press museums and galleries to become more inclusive. Successive culture ministers have stressed the need to attract more of those who traditionally have not been regular attendees, and what is more, they have the financial clout to ensure that valuable time and energy is spent in attempting to persuade the remaining 'absentees' to come through the door.

Second, as the Director of the Natural History Museum pointed out at the Museums Association Conference in 2002, the increase in visitor numbers brings its own pressures. A large proportion of visitors are not spending any more money inside museums and galleries than they did when they had to pay to get in. Funding agreements need to be put in place which will not, therefore, penalise those institutions which are successful in attracting more visitors, as they have been encouraged to do. The only viable alternative, it seems, would be an early return of entrance charges.

One thing is sure: whilst visiting museums and galleries remains one of the most popular leisure activities in this country, the debate about the way ahead will go on for the foreseeable future.

Notes

Andy Martin is Head of Leisure Research at MORI (Market and Opinion Research International). This article was first published in 2002 in *Cultural Trends*, vol. 12, no. 47.

1   The MORI Omnibus is conducted every week and consists of circa 2,000 face-to-face interviews with the general public aged 15 and over. It offers a unique sample based on census enumeration districts with 210 sampling points across Great Britain. For more details about the survey itself, visit: http://www.mori.com/omnibus/index.shtml.

References

MORI (2001) *Visitors to Museums & Art Galleries in the UK*. London: Resource.

Index

The Engaging Museum
Developing Museums for Visitor Involvement
Graham Black

'*The Engaging Museum* charts a logical path from audience development to interpretation in the gallery, synthesising much thinking of the last 20 years into a textbook of practical value to the student and museum professional.'

Simon Knell, *University of Leicester*

'As an academic textbook it serves us well, fully developing each topic, and is replete with supporting information and quotes by reputable sources recognized as being on the cutting edge of visitor studies and museum educational curriculum and evaluation.'

David K. Dean, *Museum of Texas Tech University*

'Graham Black gets to the core of what a museum might aspire to in visitor-centred experience, including interpretive planning based on research, a defined audience and multi-layered opportunities for visitors. He has put into print our goals and aspirations – a truly inspirational read.'

Adera Causey, *Hunter Museum of American Art, Chattanooga*

This very practical book guides museums on how to create the highest quality experience possible for their visitors. Creating an environment that supports visitor engagement with collections means examining every stage of the visit, from the initial impetus to go to a particular institution, to front-of-house management, interpretive approach and qualitative analysis afterwards.

This holistic approach will be immensely helpful to museums in meeting the needs and expectations of visitors and building their audience base and includes:

- chapter introductions and discussion sections
- supporting case studies to show how ideas are put into practice
- a lavish selection of tables, figures and plates to support and illustrate the discussion
- boxes showing ideas, models and planning suggestions to guide development
- an up-to-date bibliography of landmark research.

The Engaging Museum offers a set of principles that can be adapted to any museum in any location and will be a valuable resource for institutions of every shape and size, as well as a vital addition to the reading lists of museum studies students.

ISBN10: 0–415–34556–1 (hbk)
ISBN10: 0–415–34557–X (pbk)

ISBN13: 978–0–415–34556–9 (hbk)
ISBN13: 978–0–415–34557–6 (pbk)

Related titles from Routledge

Reshaping Museum Space

Edited by Suzanne Macleod

At no other point in their modern history have museums undergone such radical reshaping as in recent years. Challenges to create inclusive and accessible spaces open to appropriation and responsive to contemporary agendas have resulted in new architectural forms for museums, inside and out.

Reshaping Museum Space pulls together the views of an international group of museum professionals, architects, designers and academics highlighting the complexity, significance and malleability of museum space and provides reflections upon recent developments in museum architecture and exhibition design. The problems of navigating the often contradictory agendas and aspirations of the broad range of professionals and stakeholders involved in any new project are discussed in various chapters that concentrate on the process of architectural and spatial reshaping.

Contributors review recent new build, expansion and exhibition projects questioning the types of museum space required at the beginning of the twenty-first century and highlighting a range of possibilities for creative museum design.

ISBN10: 0–415–34344–5 (hbk)
ISBN10: 0–415–34345–3 (pbk)

ISBN13: 978–0–415–34344–2 (hbk)
ISBN13: 978–0–415–34345–9 (pbk)

Available at all good bookshops
For ordering and further information please visit:
www.routledge.com